CANADIAN MEDICAL LAW

An Introduction for Physicians, Nurses
and other Health Care Professionals

THIRD EDITION

BARNEY SNEIDERMAN,
B.A., LL.B., LL.M.

JOHN C. IRVINE,
M.A. (Juris.), B.C.L.

PHILIP H. OSBORNE,
LL.B. (Hons.), LL.M.

THOMSON
™
CARSWELL

National Library of Canada Cataloguing in Publication

Sneiderman, Barney, 1938-
 Canadian medical law : an introduction for physicians, nurses and other health care professionals / Barney Sneiderman, John C. Irvine, Philip H. Osborne.—3rd ed.

Includes bibliographical references and index.
ISBN 0-459-24074-9

 1. Medical laws and legislation—Canada. I. Irvine, John C., 1946-
II. Osborne, Philip H. III. Title.

KE3646.S63 2003   344.71'041'02461   C2003-901926-8
KF3821.S63 2003

The acid-free paper in this publication meets the minimum requirements of Amercian National Standard for Information Sciences - Permanence of Paper for Printed Library Materials, ANSI Z39.48-1984.

One Corporate Plaza
2075 Kennedy Road
Scarborough, Ontario
M1T 3V4

Customer Care:
Toronto 1-416-609-3800
Elsewhere in Canada/U.S. 1-800-387-5164
Fax 1-416-298-5094
World Wide Web: http://www.carswell.com
E-mail: orders@carswell.com

Preface

The second edition of this text appeared in 1995, and the flood of legal developments since that time warrants a new edition. The feedback that we received after the first and second editions reassures us that we have produced a user-friendly test for health care professionals, and we trust that readers of the third edition will feel the same. We have stated the law as of March 2003. We must, however, caution the reader that no textbook can substitute for legal advice if one is considering the implications of a course of action. We certainly stand by what we have written. But if you have personal legal concerns relating to issues that we have covered, please consult a lawyer.

One of the authors (B.S.) would like to thank the following for critiquing chapters from Part 2: our colleague Professor Lorna Turnbull for critiquing Chapter 15; Karen McEwen, Research Associate, Health Law Institute, Dalhousie University, for critiquing Chapters 19, 20, and 22; Dr. Peter Markesteyn for critiquing Chapter 25; and Larry Fishman MD, who read the entire Part 2 and offered innumerable suggestions and comments to ensure its readability for health professionals. We also thank the following for permission to reprint excerpts from their health care directives in Chapter 24: Drs. Ezekiel and Linda Emmanuel, Dr. Peter Singer, and Dr. William Molloy. And special thanks to our research librarian, Muriel St. John, who patiently and efficiently dealt with the all too many demands placed upon her by one of us (B.S.). Also, thanks to two law students for assisting with research: Sharon Reid and Jennifer Kubas. And lastly, our deepest appreciation to our Carswell editor, Patti Bayley-Thompson.

Addendum

Professor Barney Sneiderman (author of chapters 14-26), Faculty of Law, University of Manitoba.

Professor John Irvine (author of chapters 5-9 and 11), Faculty of Law, University of Manitoba.

Professor Phil Osborne (author of chapters 1-4 and 10), Faculty of Law, University of Manitoba.

Professor Peter Carver (author of chapter 13), is Assistant Professor, Faculty of Law and Faculty of Rehabilitative Medicine, University of Alberta.

Jennifer Shulz (author of chapter 12), Faculty of Law, University of Toronto.

TABLE OF CONTENTS

PART II
SPECIAL ISSUES

All of Part II was written by Professor Sneiderman, with the exception of Chapter 25, section 4, "The Euthanasia Policy of the Netherlands", which was co-authored by Professor Maria Vernhoef.

Chapter 15 **Issues In Reproductive Choice: Part 2**

TABLE OF CASES

References are to chapter number and subsections within each chapter.

1

INTRODUCTION TO THE LEGAL PROCESS: A CASE OF MEDICAL MALPRACTICE

SUMMARY

This chapter describes and explains the nature of the civil litigation process against the background of *Mac-Donald v. York County Hospital*, a reported case of medical negligence brought by a young man against his attending physicians and the York County Hospital. Relevant factors relating to the decision to commence litigation are surveyed and the litigation process is discussed in chronological sequence. The first step, *pleadings*, involves the technical documentation used by the patient to assert a legal claim and by the defendant to resist that claim: the statements of claim and defence. This is followed by *procedures of discovery* which permit each side to gather legally relevant information from the other before trial. The power to gather information is provided to facilitate a settlement of the claim and thereby avoid a trial. This is followed by a consideration of the preparation for trial, the conduct of a trial, and both fact-finding and the finding and application of relevant legal principles by the judge. Finally the appeal process is considered. The composition and role of the provincial courts of appeal and the Supreme Court of Canada is explained. Each step in the litigation process is illustrated by reference to the *MacDonald* case.

CASE STUDY: *MACDONALD v. YORK COUNTY HOSPITAL* (Ontario, 1976)[1]

On the evening of March 19, 1969, David MacDonald, 18, was admitted to the emergency department of the York County Hospital. He had suffered a fracture dislocation of his left ankle in a motorcycle accident. A cursory examination was conducted by Dr. Fearon, a general practitioner, who noted the serious displacement of the ankle. However, within ten minutes MacDonald was turned over to the care of Dr. Vail, a well qualified general surgeon.

Dr. Vail ordered x-rays of MacDonald's ankle. He then manipulated the patient's leg and applied a thin plaster cast from the base of the toes to the groin. The reason that a thick cast was not applied was that Dr. Vail intended, at a later time, to perform an open reduction of the ankle because it was not perfectly aligned when the cast was applied.

Unfortunately, vascular insufficiency caused gangrene in the toes of MacDonald's foot and three successive amputations were required. On April 16 MacDonald's toes were amputated by Dr. Vail and another physician. On April 24 his foot was amputated above the ankle. A third amputation about eight to ten inches below his knee was performed on July 27 at another hospital. The last procedure was required so that a prosthetic device could be properly fitted to his leg.

1. INTRODUCTION

Our purpose in this chapter is to describe the legal process of *civil litigation* as it unfolded in the course of the law suit that David MacDonald brought against Dr. Fearon, Dr. Vail and the York County Hospital. Much of the story is found in the written judgments of the judges who heard the case. Where the judgments are silent we must assume that the usual procedures and practices were followed. The civil procedure of each province has its own idiosyncracies and peculiarities: The fundamental nature of the process, however, is uniform and it is that process which will be explained.

2. PRELIMINARY CONSIDERATIONS

In Canada there is a rising tide of litigation against physicians. Medical errors and mistakes are more likely to result in legal proceedings than in the past. The rise in liability insurance premiums reflects the increase in claims. Medical professionals seem to have a sense of vulnerability to dissatisfied patients with unrealistic expectations and to aggressive and avaricious lawyers willing to sue at the drop of a hat. The increase in claims cannot be denied but from the viewpoint of the patient's lawyer any fear of a flood of unwarranted and baseless claims is quite unfounded. The lawyer acting for a patient in a medical malpractice claim is very much aware of the complexity, the delay, the expense and the risk of litigation. Successfully suing a physician is a difficult task and a variety of factors must be carefully weighed before he advises his client to file suit.

Initially it was necessary to explain to David MacDonald that physicians and other medical professionals are not liable merely because some error or mistake has been made, or because the medical treatment has failed to achieve the desired result. The plaintiff must prove that his injury was caused by the physician's failure to take care: that the physician was *negligent*. Judges weigh the evidence with great care. They are reluctant to find a physician liable for an injury unless clear and cogent evidence proves his negligence. At this early stage a lack of relevant information may have made it difficult for the plaintiff's lawyer to advise MacDonald about his chances of success. He would have had his client's account of what happened but the really critical evidence, such as the hospital records, the defendant-physicians' records, the nurses' notes, reliable opinions of medical experts, and the explanation of the defendants would not be available until much later in the litigation process.* Even then the plaintiff's lawyer would need the assistance of a medically qualified person to explain and interpret the evidence as it is acquired. Furthermore a plaintiff's lawyer knows that in most medical malpractice cases, he faces a formidable opponent. Most physicians are members of the Canadian Medical Protective Association (C.M.P.A.). The C.M.P.A. is a mutual defence organization which defends its members against legal claims and pays the damage award when the defence is unsuccessful. The C.M.P.A. retains highly skilled and experienced counsel who defend with substantial skill, determination and vigour those cases which go to trial. The C.M.P.A. also has the advantage of greater resources and often has immediate access to all pertinent information. Finally, for all plaintiffs in medical malpractice cases there is the haunting spectre of failure. The consequences of an unsuccessful law suit are that after years of expense, anxiety, and frustration, the plaintiff receives no monetary compensation and is liable, not only for his own lawyer's fees,

---

* Today, the plaintiff's position is much improved in this respect. In *McInerney v. MacDonald*[2] the Supreme Court held that patients have a full and immediate right of access to all information in the physician's and hospital's notes, records and files.

but also for any legal costs awarded to the successful defendants.* Medical malpractice litigation is not commenced lightly or frivolously. Lawyers advise their clients to sue only after careful consideration persuades them that there is, in spite of the difficulties involved, a reasonable likelihood of success.

3. PLEADINGS

In most provinces, the first stage of the civil litigation process entails the drafting of a *statement of claim*. This document must be served on the defendant and a copy must be filed in Court. Although the form and language of a statement of claim is highly legalistic, its purpose is clear and understandable. It is designed to inform the *defendant* that an action is being brought against her and also to advise her of the nature of the claim. The defendant is then in a position to defend against the claim. The statement of claim issued in the *MacDonald* case included: the identities of the plaintiff and defendants (the *parties to the action*); a brief description of the facts from which the claim arose; the allegations of the defendants' negligence which formed the legal basis of the claims and a demand for *damages* to compensate for the injury. The statement of claim was served on all three defendants, Dr. Vail, Dr. Fearon and the York County Hospital. The claim against the hospital was based on the principle of *vicarious liability*: All employers are responsible for the negligence of their employees if the negligence is committed in the course of their employment. In the *MacDonald* case, the plaintiff sought to hold the hospital liable for the alleged negligence of the nurses who had attended him.

One feature of statements of claim should be noted. On occasion, individuals who appear to have little apparent involvement with the injury are included as defendants, and it is not unusual for the statement of claim to include a number of allegations of negligence which, at the end of the day, are clearly unfounded. One may wonder why lawyers appear to be so indiscriminate in naming defendants and so unfocussed in respect of the pertinent issues of negligence. This "shotgun" approach is largely explained by the fact that the plaintiff's lawyer lacks legally relevant information when the statement of claim is drafted and served on the defendants. The plaintiff will not succeed at the trial unless she is able to establish an alleged act of negligence against at least one of the defendants named in the statement of claim. It is for this reason that a prudent lawyer prepares a statement of claim which includes allegations of all conceivable acts of

---

* Contingency fee arrangements whereby the plaintiff's counsel agrees to be paid solely from a percentage of the settlement or judgment award can reduce the cost of losing.

negligence which may have caused the accident against all persons who may have been negligent. The situation is sometimes exacerbated by the plaintiff's delay in seeking legal advice. Legislation in all provinces requires that medical malpractice litigation be commenced within a certain period of time. If a lawyer is only consulted at the eleventh hour, a hastily prepared and broadly drafted statement of claim is unavoidable. The lawyer must act to protect his client's rights before the limitation period (normally one or two years after the negligent act) has expired.*

By the time of trial, the focus will probably have substantially narrowed to a few key allegations of negligence against one or two defendants. In the *MacDonald* case, the primary allegations of negligence were that Dr. Vail put the cast on too tightly, that he failed to provide sufficient padding between the plaster and the leg, that he failed to respond appropriately to signs of circulatory impairment, and that he failed to visit his patient with sufficient frequency. The claim against the hospital was that the nurses had charted the symptoms of circulatory impairment in MacDonald's toes over a 19-hour period but had not alerted Dr. Vail or any other physician to the situation. At trial the claim against Dr. Fearon was not pressed. It is not clear why he was named as a defendant. The action was probably brought against him out of an abundance of caution and for the purposes of *discovery* (which will be explained shortly) rather than from any belief that he was to blame for the tragedy. When a defendant receives a statement of claim it is forwarded to the C.M.P.A. or her liability insurer who will conduct the litigation on her behalf. The defendant's insurer may at this point accept liability and pay damages negotiated by the plaintiff's lawyer and the insurer. The more common step, however, is for the defendant to file a *statement of defence.*

Although a statement of defence may concede some non-contentious factual claims made in the statement of claim, it usually contains a categorical denial of the allegations of negligence and indicates an intention to defend against the claim. Statements of claim and defence are known as the pleadings. Both sides are now formally joined in an adversarial relationship.

4.   DISCOVERY

In the *MacDonald* case, three years elapsed from the time of the injury to the date of trial. Part of that time was consumed by the *procedures of discovery,* which usually lead to a settlement between the parties. The settlement process is one of negotiation between opposing lawyers. The

---

* A fuller account of limitations of actions is found in Chapter 7.

expectation is that an agreement can be reached whereby the plaintiff will waive his right of action in return for a sum of money. Since the efficient functioning of the administration of justice requires that most cases be settled before trial, there are a series of discovery procedures that can be set in motion to facilitate the chance of settlement. These procedures are designed to maximize the information that each side has about the claim. Chances of settlement are enhanced because each party is in a position to evaluate the strength of the claim and its likelihood of success. Overall, fewer than 10 per cent of claims go to trial. In medical malpractice cases, the plaintiff's counsel is more likely to resort to discovery procedures because he usually feels the want of information more keenly than the other side. There are four such procedures: (1) *examination for discovery*; (2) *discovery of documents*; (3) *independent medical examination of the plaintiff;* and (4) *discovery by interrogatories.*

The *examination for discovery* permitted MacDonald's counsel to question each defendant. The questioning takes place under oath, before a court reporter, who records all questions and answers. Portions of the discovery transcript (the verbatim record of the testimony) may be introduced as evidence at trial and may be used in cross-examining defendants in order to highlight inconsistencies between the defendant's testimony in court and his testimony at the examination for discovery. In the *MacDonald* case, Dr. Vail was examined for discovery. Dr. Fearon may also have been examined. This may, in part, explain why he was sued: had he not been a party to the action, the plaintiff's counsel would not have been able to examine him for discovery. Both physicians would have been questioned with great care about their respective roles in the medical treatment of David MacDonald. A recent trend in some provinces is to broaden the scope of examination for discovery by including not only the parties to the action but also witnesses. This approach naturally increases the amount of information available before trial.

The second form of discovery is *discovery of documents.* Each side can be forced to produce all documents relevant to the litigation. At the time of the *MacDonald* case, this was a procedure of great importance since it allowed access to medical and hospital records and notes. The nurses' notes are often of particular value in determining the patients condition and treatment. Indeed, they were critically important in the *MacDonald* case. Today however, thanks to the Supreme Court decision in *McInerney v. MacDonald* (mentioned earlier), the plaintiff has immediate access to all information pertaining to his/her medical treatment. In some provinces legilsation facilitates access to such information (e.g. Manitoba's *Personal Health Information Act*). Nevertheless, there may be other pertinent documents relating to the litigation and they will be secured by each side through the discovery process. Some documents are, however, privileged and disclosure is not required. Solicitor-client privilege extends to correspondence, conversations and statements between physicians and their lawyers and between the plaintiff and his lawyer. Information obtained from witnesses in contemplation of the trial is also privileged.

Thirdly, the defendant may request an independent medical examination of the plaintiff to determine the extent of the plaintiff's injuries.

Finally, there is the much less common discovery procedure known as *discovery by interrogatories*. Its purpose is similar to the examination for discovery but it involves a series of written questions asked of the parties to an action.

In Ontario, a choice must be made between examination for discovery and interrogatories. Consequently, interrogations were not used in the *MacDonald* case. Some provinces allow both procedures.

Once the procedures of discovery have taken place, the parties are more evenly matched in terms of knowledge and information and the issues will probably have been narrowed. The lawyers are positioned to make an informed evaluation of the strength of the plaintiff's claim and the defence to it. Settlement discussions are likely at this stage. At this point, a plaintiff may unilaterally abandon her claim because new information has rendered it clearly unsustainable. Or, a defendant may feel so confident that no offer of settlement is forthcoming. However, most litigation results in a settlement. An offer to settle is made *without prejudice*, which means that it cannot be used by the plaintiff as evidence of wrongdoing if the case goes to trial. A plaintiff is generally under substantial pressure to accept a reasonable offer of settlement. She may get more at trial, but then again, she may lose and get nothing. The plaintiff must balance the certainty of the lower sum against the chance of a higher sum. There may also be pressure on the defendant to settle. A refusal of a plaintiff's reasonable offer to settle may lead to a higher award and costs being payable by the unsuccessful defendant. In recent years the prospect of settlement has been enhanced by the introduction in several provinces of compulsory or voluntary mediation between the parties. If a settlement acceptable to the parties cannot be reached, they must prepare for a trial.

5. PRE-TRIAL MOTIONS

A complicating and delaying factor is that there may be procedural or technical disputes between the parties which sometimes can be settled only by collateral court actions. Such disputes are resolved by *pre-trial motions* brought before the Court. The conflict may range from an assertion that a statement of claim is vexatious and frivolous and ought to be quashed summarily, to a motion to strike out a particular defendant *(e.g.,* Dr. Fearon) on the grounds that there is no basis on which he can possibly be found liable, to the claim that certain documentary evidence, such as lawyer-client communications, is privileged and thus not subject to discovery procedures. Pre-trial motions are time consuming, and judicial rulings are subject to appeals which compound the delay.

6. PREPARATION FOR TRIAL

The lawyers must decide what evidence to introduce at trial. Plaintiff's counsel will determine which witnesses to call and what written records or notes to use in order to prove the negligence of the defendants. The defendants are not required to prove an absence of negligence. The *burden of proof* is on the plaintiff. She must show on the *balance of probabilities* that the physician was negligent. This standard of proof may be contrasted with the criminal law requirement of proof "beyond a reasonable doubt." The less onerous civil standard requires that the judge be persuaded the injury was more likely caused by negligence than by non-culpable causes. Nevertheless, defendants will normally testify to their side of the story and provide an explanation of the plaintiff's injuries which is consistent with due care. Each witness is subject to *direct examination* by the lawyer who calls him, and opposing counsel is then permitted to *cross-examine* the witness. The purpose of cross-examination by counsel is to elicit facts favorable to her client which may have been neglected or passed over summarily and to seek inconsistencies in the witness's testimony in order to reduce that witness's credibility. Its purpose is to enhance the cross-examiner's case and to undermine the opponent's case. A *re-examination,* by the lawyer who called the witness, is then permitted to clarify matters raised for the first time in cross-examination that could not reasonably be expected to have been raised in her direct examination. In the *MacDonald* case, written notes and records were admitted in evidence and the trial judge heard the testimony of Dr. Vail, Dr. Fearon, the plaintiff and members of the hospital staff.

It is remarkable that neither side in the *MacDonald* case called *expert witnesses*. In theory, an expert medical witness is a highly qualified, experienced and respected member of the medical community who practices, teaches, or does research in the branch of medicine at issue in the particular case. Each side usually retains the services of a medical expert at an early stage of the case. The expert helps explain and interpret the medical evidence as it emerges during the discovery process. Experts may also provide written reports on the plaintiff's medical condition and on the medical treatment delivered by the defendant. If these reports are going to be used at the trial, they must be made available to the other side before trial. However, these tasks are subsidiary to the major role of a medical expert, which is to testify at the trial. The expert will inform the Court of current medical knowledge and approved practice and will give his opinion on the propriety of the defendant's actions and whether they comply with current and approved medical practice. The role of the expert is not to act as an advocate for one side. His role is to assist the Court in putting a proper interpretation on the evidence. Professional detachment and objectivity must be maintained.

Nevertheless, the plaintiff's lawyer will attempt to find an expert witness who is prepared to testify to the defendant's lack of care, skill or knowledge. The expert witness will ordinarily explain the medical procedure at issue and the manner whereby the defendant failed to achieve the standard of competence demanded of physicians. That a case is not settled before trial usually indicates that there are issues of fact and/or law that are highly contentious. It is therefore to be expected that the defendant will call experts to vindicate his conduct and to affirm his skill and competence. One may wonder if a judge (or jury) is assisted in the determining of negligence when there is a clash of opinions of equally qualified experts. However, the process of examination and cross-examination not only educates the judge, but also helps her to clarify the issues and determine whose opinion more correctly expresses the appropriate standard of care. Physicians are sometimes reluctant to testify as expert witnesses against colleagues. This is not surprising. No professional relishes the task of publicly criticizing a colleague's conduct. The adage, "there, but for the grace of God, go I", may well run through his mind. It is also fair to note that physicians are often uncomfortable with the adversarial process. Collegiality, teamwork, and cooperation are valued in the practice of medicine but are largely incompatible with the conduct of a civil trial in an adversarial system. Nevertheless, few plaintiffs proceed to a medical negligence trial without the support of expert witnesses. It is not clear why no expert witnesses were called in the *MacDonald* case. It may have been decided that the issues were simple enough to fall within the understanding of the lay mind (the trial judge). In any event, the only physicians to testify were the two defendants, Dr. Vail and Dr. Fearon.

7. PRE-TRIAL CONFERENCE

There has been a trend in recent years toward the use of pre-trial conferences. When the parties are ready for trial, a conference is held by opposing lawyers and the judge. The factual situation and the legal arguments are discussed. The purpose of the pre-trial conference is to identify points of contention, narrow the issues, and encourage settlement. It is a last-ditch effort to avoid a trial.

8. THE TRIAL

Most medical negligence trials are heard and decided by judge alone, in which case the judge determines the facts and applies the law to the facts. In some provinces, medical negligence cases may be tried by judge and jury.* When that happens, the judge determines the legal issues and the jury determines the factual issues. In trials by judge alone, the judgment of the Court is not always given at the end of the trial. The judge may wish to take time to decide the case and may wish to provide written reasons for her decision. The *MacDonald* case was tried by judge alone in the Ontario High Court. The trial took seven days and judgment was delivered on May 3, 1972 by Mr. Justice Addy.

(a) Facts

Fact finding is one of the judiciary's most important and difficult tasks. The *MacDonald* case came to trial three years after the event, and considerable skill and judgment were required to determine what actually happened when the plaintiff was in hospital. Since judges frequently hear conflicting accounts from witnesses, they must make findings of fact based upon their evaluation of the credibility of witnesses. In *MacDonald* the trial judge was forced to make a finding of credibility because he was faced with two conflicting accounts of the plaintiff's medical care: one by Dr. Vail and the other by MacDonald, Dr. Fearon and the nurses. On almost all points of conflict, the trial judge rejected the testimony of Dr. Vail.

The facts as found by the trial judge were as follows. In the late evening of March 19, Dr. Vail placed the plaintiff's leg in a cast. It was too tight, and insufficient padding was placed between the cast and MacDonald's foot. This was particularly serious because it was likely that such a serious fracture would give rise to further swelling. Dr. Vail gave no special instructions to the nursing staff although he did prescribe painkillers. During the late morning of March 20 the patient's toes became swollen and he said there was no feeling in them. His complaint was charted by the nurses and drawn to Dr. Vail's attention when he visited his patient at 2:00 p.m. The nurses expressed their concern to Dr. Vail and pointed out that in addition to the other symptoms, the patient could not move his toes. Dr.

---

* The use of a civil jury in a medical case is in practice a rarity, except in British Columbia and Ontario.

Vail conducted a cursory examination of the patient but left no further instructions. Nor did he seek a consultation. From 2:00 p.m. on March 20th to 8:45 a.m. on March 21 (almost 19 hours), the nurses charted the continuing deterioration of the patient's foot.

By the morning of the 21st, the patient's toes were cold and blue. He could neither feel nor move them. At 8:45 a.m. on the 21st, Dr. Vail bi-valved the cast which led to some improvement in the colour of the foot. At 1:00 p.m. the cast was spread open further, and again the colour of the leg improved. For the remainder of that day and into the next his toes were mottled, blue and swollen. Although Dr. Vail was aware of the patient's condition, his only response (other than to administer painkillers) was to perform a fasciotomy on the afternoon of March 22. The cast was completely removed and a vertical incision was made in the mid-calf area to determine the source of the trouble. Dr. Vail did not discover the cause of the circulatory impairment and he was unable to find a pulse below the ankle. The trial judge concluded that most of the damage had occurred by the morning of March 21. He found that it was caused by excessive compression of the leg in the cast, which stopped either venous circulation or both venous and arterial circulation to the foot.

The trial judge rejected Dr. Vail's explanation of the cause of the damage. Dr. Vail's opinion was that the circulatory problem resulted from a blockage, laceration, or spasm in the arteries of the foot, and that the damage had been caused by the initial motorcycle accident and not by the ankle swelling in the cast. In his view, his inaction was defensible because there was no medical procedure that could remedy the circulatory impairment. He claimed that it was unnecessary to consult with a specialist, to give special instructions to the nurses, or to prescribe a different course of treatment. All that could be done was to wait and determine the extent of the irreparable damage to the foot.

The trial judge treated Dr. Vail very harshly. He stated that his "theory of the severed artery" was "concocted" in an attempt to justify his handling of the case. The judge supported his view by noting that Dr. Vail had failed to take steps that would have been appropriate if he had suspected an arterial problem. He did not order an arteriogram. He did not consult with a vascular surgeon. He made no mention of the severed artery theory in his operative report after the amputation surgery on April 16. Nor did he request the pathologist to examine the foot for arterial damage after the second operation. He did not refer to the severed artery theory until the examination for discovery. In sum, the trial judge did not regard Dr. Vail as a credible witness.

The admissibility in evidence of the nurses' notes enabled the trial judge to evaluate their conduct more easily. He found that the nurses had failed to alert Dr. Vail or any other physician to the dramatically worsening condition of the patient's foot over the 19-hour period from the afternoon of March 20 to the morning of March 21.

(b) The Law

The application of legal rules to the facts as found by the trial judge (or jury) dictates the outcome of a case. Law in Canada is both *statutory* and *common law* (judge-made law). Statutory law results when Parliament and the provincial legislatures enact legislation within their respective jurisdictions. Legislation which is contrary to or inconsistent with the *Canadian Charter of Rights and Freedoms* is unconstitutional. The nullification of an unconstitutional statutory provision is illustrated by the 1988 *Morgentaler* case[3] in which the Supreme Court struck down the abortion provisions of the *Criminal Code*. Most of our law is found in legislation. That was, however, not always so. The English legal system, to which all provinces except Quebec are heir, was created in large part by judge-made law (the common law). The dominance of legislation as the primary source of law is a phenomenon dating from the mid-19th century. The common law which began to emerge in the 11th century has produced our basic legal principles and concepts, legal language, modes of legal reasoning, and divisions of law into separate categories (for example, torts, contracts and property). The foundation and structure of English law are judge-made.

The details of the historical process are beyond the scope of this text, but broad generalizations may be useful. The seeds of the common law were planted when judges were appointed by the strong centralized government that followed the Norman conquest of England (1066 A.D.). The fundamental role of a judge is to settle disputes. Since the judges had no law to guide them, decisions were made on the basis of custom, tradition, societal norms, and common sense. In so doing, the judge would make a ruling on the dispute before him. The decision, however, was not relevant only to the litigants. It soon became apparent that justice required that the decision in a particular case should be followed and applied in similar future cases. The judgments were recorded to provide precedents for later disputes of a similar kind. The accumulation of cases over the course of centuries has produced a large and sophisticated body of law. Consistency and predictability are achieved by the *doctrine of precedent,* which declares that courts of lesser status *must* follow the rulings of higher courts. Thus, once the Supreme Court decided that physicians owe a duty of reasonable care to their patients, all lower courts were obliged to accept and apply that ruling. Flexibility, dynamism, and growth are achieved by the notion that the doctrine of precedent applies only when there is a basic similarity between the facts of the case at hand and the earlier case. Considerable legal energy is expended on the question whether earlier cases *apply* or may be *distinguished* on factual grounds. If the facts in the case before the Court are different from the facts of the earlier (precedent) case, the Court is not bound to decide in accordance with the precedent. It may do so, but it is not required to. In many areas of law, the common law process continues as Canadian judges build on the English foundation by establishing new rules. Democratic values are protected by recognition that both federal and provincial legislation take precedence over inconsistent or contradictory common law.

This brief description of the common law process is essential because most of the law relating to the rights and duties of physicians is found in the branch of judge-made law called *tort law*. The *law of torts* deals with situations where one person has injured or damaged another. The law of torts determines whether the injurer must pay compensation to the injured. When a physician has caused harm to a patient, the judges will turn to earlier medical cases for guidance.

A significant feature of the common law process is that lawyers are unable to give definite and dogmatic answers to a particular question or issue until it is judicially resolved. There are numerous medical issues that have yet to be addressed by the judiciary. The breakneck speed of biomedical progress raises novel legal issues that sooner or later must be addressed. Until an issue is definitively resolved by an authoritative court, lawyers can only speculate on the likely outcome. Predicting such legal trends is an art and not a science. Consideration must be given to basic legal concepts, to legal solutions adopted elsewhere and to the outcome that seems best for society (public policy). But until an actual case arises and is authoritatively decided, there is an inevitable period of legal uncertainty.

In *MacDonald,* the applicable common law principles were not in dispute. The courts have consistently held that physicians and nurses owe a duty to their patients to exercise that degree of skill, knowledge, and care that a reasonably competent member of their profession would display in the same circumstances. The plaintiff must also prove that the defendant's negligence *caused* her injury. If the physician is a specialist, the standard of care is raised to that of the reasonably competent member of that specialty. In *MacDonald,* the judge ruled that the appropriate standard of care applicable to Dr. Vail was that of the reasonably careful general practitioner. Although Dr. Vail was an experienced general surgeon, the lower standard of care was chosen because no surgery was involved during the critical period before the fasciotomy.

In applying the law (that is, the standard of care of the reasonably careful general practitioner) to the facts, the trial judge made the following findings of negligence against Dr. Vail. He applied an insufficiently padded cast when there was a substantial risk of the ankle swelling; he failed to supervise the condition of the patient or to give special instructions to the nursing staff; he failed to take appropriate steps when the symptoms of circulatory impairment became obvious by the afternoon of March 20; he failed to consult or obtain the assistance of a specialist; he failed to remove the cast to alleviate the patient's circulatory problems at his 2:00 p.m. visit; and, during the 19-hour period when the permanent damage occurred, he failed to check on his patient or to arrange that he be seen by another qualified physician.

The hospital was also held liable for the negligence of its nursing staff. The trial judge found negligence in the failure to alert either Dr. Vail or another physician to the rapidly deteriorating condition of the patient's foot between 2:00 p.m. on March 20 and 8:45 a.m. the following day. The action against Dr. Fearon was not seriously pressed and was dismissed by the Court.

The trial judge awarded $42,000 in damages against Dr. Vail and the hospital. Although each was responsible for payment of the full amount of $42,000, in practice each would pay one half of the award. The judge also awarded costs to the plaintiff. Legal costs are a standardized amount of money tied to the legal procedures and the time and effort of the lawyer. These costs would cover some part of MacDonald's legal fees.

Most litigation does not go further than the decision of the trial judge. However there is always the possibility of an appeal to the provincial Court of Appeal.

9. COURT OF APPEAL

If the losing party at trial believes that the trial judge decided the case wrongly because of some error of fact or law, he may appeal and seek to convince the Court of Appeal that the trial judgment ought to be reversed. The litigant seeking to reverse the judgment is called the *appellant,* and the other party, the successful party at the trial level, is called the *respondent.* In *MacDonald,* both Dr. Vail and the hospital appealed to the Ontario Court of Appeal, and MacDonald cross-appealed on the ground that the award of damages was inadequate. Normally three judges hear the appeal and the decision is by majority.

The basis of an appeal is either factual or legal error. There are, however, limits to the ability and desire of appellate courts to resolve factual questions. Appellate courts rarely reverse findings of fact because their knowledge of the trial is limited to the written transcript (the verbatim record of the trial testimony). The Appeal Court is not, therefore, in a position to judge the credibility of witnesses. The trial judge is better equipped to evaluate credibility because he sees and hears the witness. The result is that appellate courts are primarily concerned with issues of *law*. The Court decides if the appropriate legal rules have been properly applied to the factual situation. When an appellant convinces the Court to reverse the trial decision, the Court will normally enter judgment in his favour. It may order a new trial. This occurs most often when there has been an error in the admissibility of evidence. Evidentiary rules seek to ensure that only reliable and relevant evidence is placed before the Court. Admissible evidence may be wrongfully excluded at trial and/or inadmissible evidence such as hearsay may be included. When that happens, the appellate court may decide that the case was not properly heard and that a new trial is in order.

A panel of three Ontario Court of Appeal judges heard the appeal in the *MacDonald* case. The arguments of counsel lasted five days and the Court's written decision was handed down on October 2, 1973. There were two written judgments; by Mr. Justice Brooke and Mr. Justice Dubin. Since Mr. Justice Kelly agreed with the judgment of Mr. justice Dubin, the latter's judgment is the majority opinion. That of Mr. Justice Brooke was a concurring opinion. If he had disagreed with the majority it would have been a dissenting opinion.

Dr. Vail's principal argument on appeal related to the manner in which the trial judge had dealt with his testimony. He took issue with the trial judge's decision to prefer the opinion of Dr. Fearon, a general practitioner, over his opinion as an experienced general surgeon. Mr. Justice Dubin conceded that Dr. Vail may have been treated too harshly by the trial judge but he concluded that even accepting Dr. Vail's explanation there was still evidence of negligence. Even if the cause of the injury was arterial, Dr. Vail ought to have sought the advice of a specialist and prescribed anti-coagulant drugs. In addition, the charts disclosed that Dr. Vail had paid inadequate attention to his patient, thereby exhibiting a lack of concern for his welfare.

Mr. Justice Brooke was also critical of the trial judge's treatment of Dr. Vail's testimony. He indicated that he accepted Dr. Vail's theory of the severed artery. Notwithstanding that concession, his view was that the tightness of the cast was a contributing cause to the injury and that failure to ease pressure on the leg by removing or cutting the cast was negligent. He added that when the symptoms of circulatory impairment arose, Dr. Vail ought to have sought advice from a specialist and administered anti-coagulants. Although all three judges were uncomfortable with the trial judge's finding of fact, they concluded that even if Dr. Vail's explanation was true he was still negligent. Dr. Vail's appeal was therefore dismissed.

The hospital appealed against the finding that the nurses were negligent. The Court focussed on the issue of causation because the plaintiff must prove that the negligence caused or contributed to the injury. The Court agreed with the trial judge that the nurses' failure to alert Dr. Vail to the deteriorating state of the patient's foot during the critical 19-hour period amounted to a failure to take care. However, Dr. Vail had testified at the trial that if he had been contacted, he would not have issued any additional instructions nor would he have prescribed any treatment. His testimony was consistent with his view that MacDonald had by that time suffered irreversible damage to his foot. The Court found that the failure to call Dr. Vail was of no consequence because he would not, in any event, have done anything for his patient. The appeal of the hospital was granted since the negligence of the nurses did not cause or contribute to the plaintiff's injury. Since Dr. Vail was the only defendant found liable, he had to pay the entire sum awarded as damages. MacDonald's appeal that the damage award was inadequate was dismissed as being without merit.

10. SUPREME COURT OF CANADA

Dr. Vail appealed to Canada's court of last resort: the Supreme Court of Canada. One must seek permission of the Court to bring an appeal in a civil case and that permission is usually reserved for cases which raise serious legal issues. At the time of the *MacDonald* appeal, a party could appeal as of right if the sum contested was in excess of $10,000.

The Court is comprised of nine judges who sit in an odd number — three, five, seven or nine — to prevent evenly split decisions. The number of judges hearing a particular case depends upon its significance. The appeal in the *MacDonald* case was heard by five judges of the Supreme Court in October 1975. The Court reserved its decision. One can imagine David MacDonald's anxiety as he waited for the Court's decision. One defendant had been exonerated by the provincial Court of Appeal. If the Supreme Court allowed Dr. Vail's appeal, MacDonald would receive no damages. He would have to pay his own legal expenses, and he might have to pay legal costs to the successful defendant. In all likelihood, this would be financially devastating. Four months after the hearing, on February 25, 1976, the Court gave its judgment. It was delivered by Mr. Justice Ritchie, who spoke for the whole Court. He dismissed the appeal. He concluded that there was sufficient evidence of negligence. He agreed with the Court of Appeal that Dr. Vail was negligent in that he neglected the patient, failed to consult with a vascular specialist and failed to order anti-coagulant drugs. After seven years the litigation ended. David MacDonald had won.

11. CONCLUSION

It is important to put this case in perspective as it is but one of a handful of cases that reach the Supreme Court of Canada. Most cases are settled, few go to trial, fewer go to the Court of Appeal and fewer still go to the Supreme Court. Nevertheless the *MacDonald* case does illustrate the complete process of civil litigation. It also underscores the nature of a medical negligence action. It is time consuming, expensive, difficult and inherently unpredictable and risky.

NOTES

1. [1972] 3 O.R. 469, 28 D.L.R. (3d) 521 (H.C.), affirmed in part (1973), 1 O.R. (2d) 653, 41 D.L.R. (3d) 321 (C.A.), which was affirmed (sub nom. *Vail v. MacDonald*) [1976] 2 S.C.R. 825, 66 D.L.R. (3d) 530, 8 N.R. 155.
2. [1992] 2 S.C.R. 138, 12 C.C.L.T. (3d) 255, 137 N.R. 35, 7 C.P.C. (2d) 269, 93 D.L.R. (4th) 415.
3. *R. v. Morgentaler*, [1988] 1 S.C.R. 30, 63 O.R. (2d) 281n, 62 C.R. (3d) 1, 44 D.L.R. (4th) 385, 37 C.C.C. (3d) 449, 31 C.R.R. 1, 26 O.A.C. 1, 82 N.R. 1.

2

CONSENT TO TREATMENT

SUMMARY

This chapter deals with the application to medical care of the fundamental right of persons to be free from unwanted physical interference. Medical care is wrongful and a *battery* unless the patient has given consent to it. This is not a mere formality. It is an essential pre-requisite to the provision of medical services. The difference between express and implied consent is explored and issues of proof of consent and written consent forms are considered. Consideration is given to the right to treat patients who are unable to consent if medical treatment is necessary to save life or health. The patient's right to revoke and refuse consent is explained and the power to provide a conditional consent is examined. Finally the importance of a patient's mental capacity is explained, and some legislative initiatives are canvassed.

CASE STUDY: *ALLAN v. NEW MOUNT SINAI HOSPITAL* (Ontario, 1980)[1]

On November 1st, 1972, Jane Allan, 35, was admitted to the New Mount Sinai Hospital in Toronto for a dilatation and curettage. On the evening before surgery, she was visited by an anaesthesia resident. She told him that she wished to speak with the attending anaesthetist before the operation. This was arranged and the attending anaesthetist, Dr. Hellman, met with Mrs. Allan the next morning. The conversation, which took place after Mrs. Allan had received 10 milligrams of valium, was held in the hall outside the operating room. Mrs. Allan said to Dr. Hellman, "Please do not touch my left arm. You'll have nothing but trouble there." Her concern was prompted by the fact that on an earlier occasion there had been some difficulty in finding a vein in her left arm. Dr. Hellman replied, "We know what we are doing." Mrs. Allan was then wheeled into the operating room.

Contrary to her instructions, Dr. Hellman administered sodium pentothal through a vein in her left arm, as was his custom. Shortly after the operation began it became apparent that more anaesthetic was required and Dr. Hellman injected additional sodium pentothal. When the patient did not respond he noticed that the needle had slipped out of the vein and that some of the anaesthetic had entered the surrounding tissue. The needle was reinserted and the surgery was completed uneventfully.

Unfortunately, Mrs. Allan suffered a rare, severe and unexpected reaction to the anaesthetic solution in her arm. This required her to remain in hospital for one month rather than the anticipated three days, and she was absent from work for eight months. She suffered considerable pain during the course of her recovery and she was told to expect some minor permanent discomfort. She sued Dr. Hellman for damages and won. Mr. Justice Linden of the High Court of Ontario held that although Dr. Hellman was not negligent in the administration of the anaesthetic, he was liable in *battery* for adopting a procedure to which the patient had not consented. Although the Ontario Court of Appeal later ordered a new trial on a technical point of pleading, it did not fault the reasoning of the trial judge.

1. INTRODUCTION

Most physicians are keenly aware of the need for the patient's consent to the proposed treatment, yet many are unfamiliar both with the role of consent in the legal analysis of the physician/patient relationship, and with the variety of difficult consent-related issues. A number of these issues have yet to be authoritatively addressed by Canadian courts. Some will be considered in this chapter, with occasional reference to *Allan v. New Mount Sinai Hospital.*

2. BATTERY: A GENERAL DEFINITION

The tort* of battery plays an important role in protecting persons from unwanted physical interference. Any direct and intentional interference with a person which is either harmful or offensive to a reasonable sense of dignity is unlawful. There is no need to prove that the interference caused harm. Battery provides a wide protection of one's physical integrity. It is

---

*   A brief definition of "tort law" can be found in Chapter 1.

as much a battery to push a person rudely out of the way as it is to stab or shoot her.*

It is well established that the right to personal security may be waived. A person has the power to *consent* to physical interference that she deems desirable or beneficial. The public is no doubt most familiar with and appreciative of the necessity for consent in respect of intimate sexual relationships but there are a wide range of circumstances where physical interference or contact is commonly permitted. Examples include the necessary physical contact between players of a contact sport such as football, ice hockey or wrestling; an embrace or social kiss between friends; and a handshake of introduction. In such circumstances, the physical contact is excused on the grounds of consent. Legal theory views consent as a defence to an action of battery. The plaintiff has only to prove the harmful or offensive interference in order to establish a case of battery. The defendant is then required to prove, on the balance of probabilities, that the plaintiff consented to the interference.

3. BATTERY AND MEDICAL TREATMENT

Surgery and medical procedures usually amount to a battery unless the patient has consented to the treatment. This legal framework, which underscores the right of an individual to control his medical treatment, is reflected in the well-known words of an American judge that, "Every human being of adult years and sound mind has a right to determine what shall be done with his body."[2] The concept of consent in recent years has received increasing attention from the courts. This is partly a reflection of a gradual change in the physician/patient relationship from a paternalistic model to a participatory model. Generalizations are dangerous, but there are indications that the physician/patient relationship is in a period of evolution. Under the paternalistic or traditional model, the physician holds the stronger position. He has a monopoly of power and knowledge and there is an expectation that an acquiescent patient will normally agree without question to the proposed treatment. The underlying assumption is that since the physician knows best, he will determine what course of treatment is in the best interests of the patient. In recent years there has been a greater concern for patients' rights, which has resulted in a greater emphasis on the patient's active involvement in the decision-making process. The relationship is becoming more egalitarian and participatory. A number of factors explain this shift in emphasis. People are better educated

---

* A battery may also amount to a crime under the *Criminal Code*. A prosecution may be warranted where there is a clear intention to cause personal injury.

and are more interested in medical matters than in the past. The print and television media inform the public of current medical issues and treatment. The consumer movement, which has raised the consciousness of the consumer in the marketplace, has had an impact on the consumer of medical services. The feminist movement has made the public more aware of and more sensitive to unequal relationships. The current discussion of rights occasioned by the *Canadian Charter of Rights and Freedoms* may also be playing a role in the focus on patients' rights.

The result is that patients are becoming more assertive, more knowledgeable and more willing to take control of matters involving their health care. Courts are sensitive to these changes and the "doctor knows best" attitude has become increasingly unacceptable. The trial judge in *Allan v. New Mount Sinai Hospital* commented in this regard. The crucial question in the case was whether the plaintiff had consented to the use of her left arm for the administration of the anaesthetic. She testified that she had not consented and the judge accepted her evidence:

> [T]he plaintiff's version of the conversation deserves credence, because of Dr. Hellman's attitude toward the discussion with the patient before surgery. He described it as a mere formality to put the patient at ease. If he felt this way, it is unlikely that he would view seriously any instructions from his patients about which arm he should use. He thought he knew what was best for the patient and that her wishes were unimportant.[3]

The judge then issued a timely warning, not only to Dr. Hellman but also to all physicians.

> [O]ur law is clear that the consent of the patient must be obtained before any surgical procedure can be conducted. Without a consent, either written or oral, no surgery may be performed. This is not a mere formality; it is an important individual right to have control over one's own body, even where medical treatment is involved. It is the patient, not the doctor, who decides whether surgery will be performed, where it will be done, and by whom it will be done.[4]

As the judge explained, the law relating to battery protects the patient's autonomy by recognising her right to determine her own medical treatment. It also reflects a desire to foster meaningful communication between physician and patient and to encourage a more participatory and egalitarian physician/patient relationship.

4. BATTERY AND NEGLIGENCE: A LAWYER'S PERSPECTIVE

In the normal course of events, the patient consents to treatment and then the medical procedure is accordingly carried out. Battery is the appropriate remedy for unauthorized treatment. An action in negligence is appropriate if damage is suffered in the course of the authorized treatment. In almost all cases, however, the lawyer will consider the possibility of a claim in battery. The reason is that it is more advantageous to sue in battery than in negligence. In a battery action, the plaintiff has to prove only that the medical treatment or surgery took place. The defendant-physician must then prove that the patient consented to the procedure. If consent can not be proved, the entire procedure is unauthorized and wrongful. It is no excuse that the physician acted in the best interests and for the benefit of the patient.

In a negligence action, the plaintiff must prove the negligent act, causation and damage. Negligence can often not be proved without the assistance of expert witnesses. The *Allan* case provides a useful illustration. In that case, the plaintiff tried to establish that Dr. Hellman had been negligent, but failed. The judge held that Dr. Hellman had used the appropriate degree of care and the fact that the needle had slipped out of the vein was not indicative of negligence. But, the judge held that Dr. Hellman failed to prove that Mrs. Allan had consented to the use of her left arm for administering the anaesthetic. Liability was, therefore, imposed in battery. Although the plaintiff suffered a rare and unforeseeable reaction to the anaesthetic, the defendant in a battery action is responsible for all the consequences of his wrongful act. The end result may seem harsh, given that a competent and prudent anaesthetist was held legally responsible for an extremely rare reaction which would likely have occurred even if he had used the patient's right arm. The result underlines the importance of consent and the value that the law attributes to the patient's right of self-determination.

5. EXPRESS AND IMPLIED CONSENT

The patient's consent need not take any particular form. The consent may be oral, written or implied from the conduct of the patient. It is common to differentiate between express and implied consent. *Express consent* is found when the patient has explicitly authorised the medical examination, treatment or surgery. The patient may expressly ask his physician for a physical examination or may request that he remove a wart or treat a laceration. Or, the patient may expressly agree to a course of action proposed by the physician. An affirmative response to a suggestion that a gastroscopy is in order is an express consent to the procedure. Another form of express consent lies in the completion of a written consent form. When a patient reads, *understands* and signs a written consent to treatment or surgery there is express consent. By way of summary, an express consent is established when a patient declares his willingness to submit to medical treatment.

In the day-to-day practice of medicine, physicians continually rely on implied consent. *Implied consent* is found where a patient's conduct indicates a willingness to submit to medical treatment. Consent will be found if it is reasonable to assume that consent was given. For example, there is implied consent when the patient presents his arm for an injection, opens his mouth for a throat examination or presents himself at a medical laboratory with a physician's requisition for a blood test and x-ray. Actions sometimes are equivocal. In those situations the Court must do its best to determine, on the basis of common sense and the assumptions of reasonable people, whether the patient's conduct may fairly be regarded as indicating consent.

An interesting aspect of the *Allan* case is the relationship between the plaintiff's express prohibition against use of her left arm to anaesthetise her and her subsequent conduct. Since Mrs. Allan was conscious when the anaesthetic was administered, one may conclude that she consented to the use of her left arm. It could have been argued that although she asked that her left arm not be used, her subsequent conduct *implied* that they were only words of caution and that at the critical moment she *was* willing to allow the anaesthetist to inject her in that arm. The judge refused to draw that inference on the grounds that her later conduct could not reverse a clear prohibition expressed only moments earlier. This is understandable in the particular circumstances. Mrs. Allan was in the operating room facing imminent surgery. One should not expect a patient to argue for her right of self-determination in such intimidating surroundings.

6. PROOF OF CONSENT

The consent of the patient must be proved by the defendant-physician. This is sometimes difficult to do. The trial may be years after the event and memories are often unreliable. Particular difficulties arise when there is contradictory evidence of an oral consent. The only evidence may be the conflicting testimony of physician and patient. In those circumstances, the judge will have to make a finding of credibility between the physician and the patient. The patient may be in an advantageous position. It is more likely that a patient can recall the specifics of a conversation about surgery or treatment which was of great concern to her. The physician, on the other hand, is often unable to recall the precise nature of a conversation with one of many patients. The problem is illustrated by the *Allan* case. Mrs. Allan was quite definite and dogmatic about the words exchanged between her and the anaesthetist. On the other hand, Dr. Hellman honestly and understandably testified that he could not remember exactly what he said to the patient. He could only speculate as to what he probably said to her. It is not surprising that the trial judge accepted the plaintiff's evidence.

Implied consent may also present problems. The passage of time may make it difficult to determine not only the patient's conduct, but also what reasonable assumptions might be drawn from that conduct. This explains why hospitals, in particular, resort to written consent forms. A consent form is *not*, however, conclusive proof of a patient's consent. It is evidence of consent, but that evidence must be weighed against any conflicting evidence in order to determine if the patient truly consented to the procedure in question. It might be shown, for example, that the patient failed to understand the language in which the consent form was written, or that she did not understand the form because she was sedated when she signed it or that the patient clearly did not read the form before signing. The courts are concerned with the reality of consent, not with the illusion of consent created by a signed document. Nevertheless, the consent form does play a valuable role. It provides sufficient evidence of consent to require the patient to explain the discrepancy between the document and her state of mind when it was signed.

The obligation to secure the patient's consent clearly lies with the physician. The duty is non-delegable. Although it is not illegal, the physican should not rely upon a nurse or other member of the hospital staff to secure the patient's consent. The attending physician is personally responsible and will be liable if others fail to secure his patient's valid consent.

It is not common practice to use written consent forms for treatment outside hospitals. Physicians tend to rely on the patient's express verbal consent or implied consent. There is little danger in this practice. Yet there are occasions when it is prudent to make a note of the consent on the patient's record: when the procedure carries a high risk of injury or when injury is inevitable, when the patient has exhibited vacillation or difficulty in determining the appropriate treatment and, when there is any friction or problem in the physician/patient relationship. The physician's best guide is probably common sense.

7. EMERGENCY TREATMENT

There are circumstances in which a patient is unable to consent to treatment. He may be rendered unconscious by an accident or by illness, as in the case of a heart attack. He may be severely intoxicated or under the influence of an illicit drug. It would, of course, be inappropriate to refuse therapeutic treatment on the ground that the patient could not consent. The law has for a long time contained rules which provide a privilege to interfere with the interests of another on the ground of necessity. Consequently, when a patient is unable to consent, the physician has the right to provide treatment which is urgent and necessary to preserve his life and health. This legal privilege is referred to as the *emergency doctrine*. A physician may consult with the members of the patient's family and may seek their guidance and approval. This is a useful practice which can minimize the risks of dispute and controversy, but it is more of a courtesy extended to the family than a legal requirement.

8. EXTENDED PROCEDURES

It may happen that during the course of surgery to which a patient has expressly consented, an additional and unforeseen ailment is discovered. The surgeon may be tempted to remedy the additional problem by extending the surgery beyond that to which consent has been given. The critical question is whether there is consent to the additional procedures. The courts have resolved the issue by resort to the emergency doctrine. The surgeon is legally protected if the extended procedure is urgently required to preserve the life and health of the patient. In *Marshall v. Curry* (Nova Scotia, 1933),[5] the surgeon removed one of the plaintiff's testicles in the course of an operation to repair a hernia. No liability was imposed because the testicle was grossly diseased and postponing remedial surgery would have endangered the plaintiff's life and health. But if the extended procedure is merely convenient, desirable or expedient, it will amount to a battery. The appropriate course of action is to complete the surgery originally intended and in due course discuss the matter with the patient and seek consent for a second operation. The case of *Murray v. McMurchy* (British Columbia, 1949)[6] is illustrative. During a Caesarian section, the surgeon sterilised the patient by tying her fallopian tubes. He sought to justify the procedure by claiming that he had discovered tumours in the wall of the patient's uterus, which, in his view, made a second pregnancy inadvisable. The Court imposed liability in battery. The Court stated that even if the surgeon's view was correct, there was no need for urgent action to preserve the life or health of the patient.

Some written consent forms seek to overcome this distinction by stating that the surgeon, in addition to the stipulated procedure, "shall have the right to carry out any further procedure that may be deemed *advisable, desirable, beneficial* or *convenient* and in the patient's best interests." It would be unwise for physicians to rely on words such as these because, in most cases, judges will refuse to uphold them. The reasons are clear. When the consent form is signed the patient's attention is focussed upon the primary ailment and, if the consent form is read at all, it is read quickly and without reflection. There is no true consent to a term which purports to give a "carte blanche" to the surgeon. The term may be effective, however, if the extended procedure is both curative and minor. In *Pridham v. Nash Estate* (Ontario, 1986),[7] the patient consented to a laparoscopy to discover the source of pain in her pelvic area. The surgeon discovered an adhesive band from her pelvis to the anterior abdominal wall. He concluded that this condition resulted from prior surgery and may well have been the reason for the pain. He lysed the adhesions and the surgery was completed uneventfully. Unfortunately, in the course of lysing the adhesions he perforated the ileum. The judge held that the term of the written consent form approving "additional procedures as may be advisable" protected the surgeon from the patient's claim in battery. In his view it was not reasonable to require a second operation to remedy such a minor problem. A surgeon can, however, only be sure of legal protection under this kind of clause when, being unsure of the precise malady, he directly asks the patient for a blanket consent to exploratory and remedial surgery. Again, it is the reality of the blanket consent rather than any vague and general words on a consent form that is legally effective.

There may be uncertainty about the scope of the patient's initial consent such that an issue arises as to whether that consent covers an extended procedure. In *Brushett v. Cowan* (Newfoundland, 1990)[8], the plaintiff-patient had suffered persistent problems with her leg. The defendant-physician wondered whether a lump in her leg was malignant. He accordingly recommended a muscle biopsy for which the plaintiff provided a written consent. However, the physician extended the procedure to include a bone biopsy because the adjacent bone tissue appeared abnormal. Some days later the patient broke her leg at the site of the bone biopsy and consequently sued the physician for battery. The trial judge ruled in her favour on the grounds that she had consented only to a muscle biopsy and that the extended procedure was not justified as an emergency procedure to preserve her life and health. However, the Newfoundland Court of Appeal reversed. The Court focused upon the language in the consent form that authorized "further and alternative measures", and it went on to determine that the background circumstances indicated consent to an ongoing and comprehensive diagnostic process to determine the cause of her complaint. It concluded that the physician had not committed a battery because the consent was sufficiently broad to encompass the bone biopsy.

9. CONDITIONAL CONSENT

The patient's right to determine his own medical treatment means that he can give a conditional consent. An Alberta decision illustrates the point. In *Mulloy v. Sang* (Alberta, 1935),[9] the plaintiff, who had badly damaged his hand in a farming accident, sought medical treatment from the defendant-physician. The patient consented to examination and treatment of the hand, but stated very clearly that under no circumstances was it to be amputated. The reason for his limited and conditional consent was that the patient wished to consult his personal physician before any irreversible steps were taken. The defendant replied that he would be guided by the condition of the hand when he examined it under general anaesthetic. The patient made no reply. On examination, the defendant concluded that the hand could not be saved and he performed an amputation with all due care and skill. On purely medical grounds the decision was unimpeachable. Nevertheless, liability was imposed in battery. The plaintiff had given a conditional consent which the physician had not honoured. Evidence establishing the inevitability of the amputation, and that the physician had acted in the best interests of the patient, afforded no defence.

The *Allan* case can also be viewed as a case which involved a conditional consent. Mrs. Allan consented to the surgery on the condition that the anaesthetic not be injected in her left arm. The anaesthetist failed to honour the condition and was accordingly found liable for battery. A patient's consent may be conditional upon a variety of circumstances. Consent to surgery is usually given on the basis that a particular surgeon will operate. It may be given on condition that interns play no part in the surgery, that a certain kind of anaesthetic be used, or that an incision be made in a particular place. Any departure from the terms of the consent will amount to battery.

There are cases in which it is difficult to determine the scope of the consent and to decide on the proper interpretation of words or actions. Since physicians and patients are not generally aware of the legal framework of the battery action, their actions and words are often not tailored to, and do not reflect, the subtleties of legal analysis. This is illustrated by the *Allan* and *Mulloy* cases. The words in the *Allan* case were, "Please don't touch my left arm. You will have nothing but trouble there." Mrs. Allan then watched the anaesthetist inject her left arm. The judge interpreted the language as a clear prohibition against using her left arm. An alternative interpretation is that Mrs. Allan was merely alerting the anaesthetist to a previous problem. It was an expression of concern, not a prohibition. Support for that interpretation may be found in her failure to protest when her left arm was used. The Court preferred the former interpretation.

The same issue arose in the *Mulloy* case. After the patient indicated that he did not want his hand amputated, the physician replied that he would be guided by its condition. The patient made no further comment. One can interpret that silence as acquiescence to the physician's remark or one can take the view that once the patient has made his position clear there was no need to press the point. The judge preferred the latter interpretation.

A judge will interpret such ambiguities as best she can, seeking the most reasonable interpretation. As the cases illustrate, ambiguity may well be resolved against the physician because the burden of proving consent rests on his shoulders. Many of these difficulties can be avoided by improved communication between physician and patient. The physician must ensure that he and the patient are in clear agreement on the type of surgery or treatment. If the patient is making unwise or unreasonable demands, the physician must discuss the situation and seek to persuade her to change her mind. If the patient's demands are impractical or unsafe, the physician can and should refuse to perform the procedure.

10. REVOCATION AND REFUSAL OF CONSENT

The patient also has a right to modify or withdraw consent in the course of treatment. The right of a patient to stop a procedure was recognized by the Supreme Court in *Ciarlariello v. Schacter* (1993),[10] where a patient withdrew her consent to a cerebral angiogram when difficulties were encountered. The only exceptions to the power to withdraw consent are when the patient is so affected by medication that an effective withdrawal is beyond the patient's capacity or when immediate termination would be life-threatening or pose immediate and serious problems. In some cases, defendant-physicians have claimed that calls to "stop" a procedure were in fact cries of pain rather than a withdrawal of consent. However, continuing in the face of any indication of reluctance, objection or refusal is inadvisable. The physician should immediately investigate the patient's concerns and determine her wishes.

A patient may also modify her consent. This is illustrated by the *Allan* case. It may be assumed that Mrs. Allan had signed a normal consent to surgery which would have included a consent to anaesthetic procedures. In her conversation with Dr. Hellman outside the operating room, she modified her consent by asking that her left arm not be used to administer the anaesthetic. When the physician ignored her instructions, he thereby committed a battery.

A patient clearly has the right to refuse a proposed treatment, and, indeed, has the right to refuse all treatment. Physicians often exhibit discomfort with a refusal to consent to therapeutic life-saving treatment. A physician's commitment to treat and heal may clash with a patient's desire to be left alone. But there is no doubt that an adult of sound mind has the right to refuse treatment. This rule is applicable to the terminal cancer patient who refuses life-prolonging measures and to persons refusing life-saving measures on religious or other grounds.* A physician may seek to persuade her patient to change his mind, but she commits a battery if she is unsuccessful and nonetheless proceeds to treat. If the physician's conduct is particularly high-handed and exhibits contempt of the plaintiff's rights, a sum of money called punitive damages may be awarded in addition to compensatory damages. Its purpose is to punish the defendant for disregarding the patient's right to refuse treatment.

A related issue is the validity of a signed card that prohibits, in advance, the performance of specified medical procedures. This issue arose in *Malette v. Schulman* (Ontario, 1990).[11] The plaintiff was seriously injured and rendered unconscious in an automobile accident. The treating physician decided on reasonable grounds that a blood transfusion was indicated. Before blood was administered, a nurse drew his attention to a signed card found in the plaintiff's purse. The card stated that the patient was a Jehovah's Witness and that blood should not be administered under any circumstances. The physician ignored the instructions on the card and administered the blood. The plaintiff sued the physician in battery. The defendant marshalled an array of arguments why a physician had no duty to follow the instructions of an unwitnessed, undated card. The plaintiff may have changed her religious beliefs before the accident and neglected to destroy the card. The card may have been signed because of family or religious peer pressure. If conscious, she might well have changed her mind in the face of imminent and avoidable death. There was no evidence of the cardholder's state of mind when she signed the card. The Ontario Court of Appeal was not persuaded and ruled that the blood transfusion amounted to a battery. Its position was that the card contained an unqualified prohibition against the administration of blood based on religious conviction. There was no evidence to suggest that the card did not reflect her current intentions. It was designed to express the plaintiff's wishes in circumstances in which she would be unable to speak for herself. That was precisely the situation that arose. The Court confirmed the award of $20,000 in damages.

---

* See Chapter 13 for the distinction between life-prolonging and life-saving measures.

A number of provinces have recently regularized procedures that enable health care consumers to make health care decisions to cover future contingencies. Health care directives may be used to control the nature, extent, and duration of medical treatment when and if one becomes mentally incompetent to decide for herself because of age, illness, or accident.*

11. VOLUNTARY CONSENT

Consent must be given freely, voluntarily and without undue pressure or influence. One situation where this issue can arise is in connection with decisions made by patients who are under the influence of pre-surgical tranquilizing medications. In one case an anaesthetist successfully persuaded a sedated patient to change her mind about the method of anaesthetization. The judge imposed liability because the patient's decision was not given freely and voluntarily. Each case, however, will depend on its own facts. The judge must determine the degree of pressure brought to bear upon the patient and whether it was sufficient to affect the decision-making process. The physician must bear in mind that the patient has the full right to control his medical treatment. The physician may advise and persuade but further pressure risks the validity of the consent.

12. CONSENT TO STERILIZATION

Some hospitals have adopted the practice of obtaining the consent of both spouses to sterilization procedures. The practice stems more from a desire to foster good public relations and spousal harmony than from legal obligation. There is no legal requirement that a physician secure a spousal consent. The position is the same in respect of abortion. Since a variety of medical procedures affect the family unit, there is no reason to isolate sterilization or abortion for special treatment.

13. CAPACITY TO CONSENT

The power to exercise autonomous decision-making is based upon the patient's mental competence, and there are circumstances in which a patient may lack the mental capacity to decide. A patient may be in the advanced stages of Alzheimer's disease or some other condition that diminishes one's mental faculties, or the patient may be severely intoxicated or otherwise impaired by drugs, or the patient may be mentally retarded or have suffered brain damage. In each such case, the caregiver must determine whether the

---

* Such legislation is canvassed in Chapter 23.

patient is competent to make treatment decisions. The primary test of competency is whether the patient can understand the information relating to her condition and the foreseeable risks and consequences of the proposed treatment. Clearly each decision is fact-specific and requires a scrupulous assessment of the patient's intellectual capacity. A finding of incapacity means that the patient's "consent" is a legal nullity.

There are, however, various options open to a caregiver when a patient who needs treatment lacks the capacity to consent. Firstly, if the patient needs urgent and immediate treatment to preserve life or health, treatment may be administered in accordance with the *emergency* doctrine. Secondly, formal steps may have been taken to appoint a substitute decision-maker in cases in which the patient's incompetence flows from a pre-existing condition such as mental retardation. In fact, all provinces have enacted legislation authorizing the appointment of such substitute decision-makers. Thirdly, as noted earlier the patient may have signed a health care directive, either giving future treatment instructions or else appointing a proxy to make such decisions. (As illustrated by the case of *Malette v. Shulman,* the "directive" need not assume the form of a formal document.) Fourthly, provinces such as Ontario and British Columbia have recently enacted statutes that enable the next of kin of mentally incompetent patients to provide substituted consent to treatment.

Regrettably, cases will arise in which none of these alternatives is available to deal with an incompetent patient. In that event, the concept of in-family substituted consent may be used. It is based upon the notion that the incompetent patient's loved ones are best positioned either to know her treatment wishes or — when such wishes are unknown — to know what decision serves her best interests. Canadian courts have yet to consider the legal status of an in-family substituted consent for an incompetent patient. However, it is likely that such consent would meet with approval, given that the principle has found endorsement in provincial legislation such as the *Health Care Consent Act* (Ontario).* In any event, it is sound practice to seek a treatment consensus amongst the next of kin of incompetent patients, if only to obviate a law suit by a disgruntled family member. It is of course axiomatic that the physician ensure that the next of kin are seeking to protect the patient's interests because not all families are willing or able to do so.

---

* Discussed later in this chapter.

14. LEGISLATIVE INITIATIVES IN ONTARIO AND BRITISH COLUMBIA

We have thus far considered the common law principles relating to consent to treatment. Two provinces, Ontario and British Columbia, have chosen to clarify and codify the law in the area of consent and capacity. The Ontario *Health Care Consent Act*, 1996[12] and the British Columbia *Health Care (Consent) and Care Facility (Admission) Act*[13] balance fundamental common law principles of self-determination and the protection of the rights of persons deprived of the mental capacity to makes health care decisions.

The Ontario *Health Care Consent Act*, 1996 is a complex Act dealing with consent to medical treatment, admission to care facilities and personal assistance services. A brief sketch of the provisions of the Act relating to treatment decisions must suffice here. The Act reiterates the common law principles that there must be consent to treatment and the consent must relate to the treatment proposed, be informed, be given voluntarily and must be obtained without misrepresentation or fraud. The patient must have the mental capacity to give consent. Capacity is defined as the ability to understand information about the proposed treatment and to appreciate the reasonably foreseeable consequences of giving and withholding consent. While the Act creates a presumption of capacity it is the treating physician's responsibility to assess her patients' capacity. A finding of incapacity must be communicated to the patient. A central feature of the Act is the right of the patient to appeal to the Consent and Capacity Review Board to review that finding or to have the Board appoint a representative to act on behalf of the patient. An application may also be made to the Board by another person to act as the patient's representative. Unless there is an emergency, the treatment must be withheld to permit the review process and any appeal to take place. The Act also provides a list of substitute decision makes who may act on behalf of the incapacitated patient. The Act directs substitute decision makes either to follow the wishes of the patient if made known before the advent of incapacity or if it is not possible to determine such wishes to act in the best interests of the patient.*

The British Columbia *Health Care (Consent) and Care Facility (Admission) Act*, not all of which is in force, has the same public policy grounding. It likewise declares that the patient must be mentally competent to consent to treatment and that the consent must be treatment-specific, informed and voluntary. The legislation also lists in order of priority sub-

---

* See the discussion on surrogate decision-making in Chapter 21.

stitute decision makers who may act on behalf of the incapacitated person. A review and appeal process is also contemplated.

The significant contribution of the Ontario and British Columbia statutes lies in the provision of review procedures and a clear and organized system of substitute decision making.

15. CONCLUSION

Consent is an essential prerequisite to medical treatment and must not be underestimated or viewed as a mere formality by physicians. Medical treatment, particularly in hospitals, is provided by a wide range of professionals, including physicians, consultants, house physicians, registered nurses, licensed practical nurses, diagnostic technicians, orderlies and many others. The provision of medical services inevitably becomes less personal as each individual in the hospital bureaucracy carries out his appointed tasks. It is at times overlooked that this orchestration of health care providers is directed not by hospitals or physicians but by individual patients exercising their right of self-determination; a right that will continue to receive the fullest protection of the law.

NOTES

1. (1980), 28 O.R. (2d) 356, 11 C.C.L.T. 299, 109 D.L.R. (3d) 634, 4 L. Med. Q. 146 (H.C.), reversed on other grounds (1981), 33 O.R. (2d) 603, 19 C.C.L.T. 76, 125 D.L.R. (3d) 276 (C.A.).
2. Mr. Justice Cardozo, in *Schloendorft v. Society of New York Hospital*, 105 N.E. 92 (U.S. N.Y., 1914), at p. 93.
3. Mr. Justice Linden (1980), 28 O.R. (2d) 356 (H.C.), at p. 364.
4. *Ibid.*
5. [1933] 3 D.L.R. 260, 60 C.C.C. 136 (N.S. T.D.).
6. [1949] 1 W.W.R. 989, [1949] 2 D.L.R. 442 (B.C. S.C.).
7. (1986), 57 O.R. (2d) 347, 33 D.L.R. (4th) 304 (H.C.).
8. (1987), 42 C.C.L.T. 64, 40 D.L.R. (4th) 488, 64 Nfld. & P.E.I.R. 262, 197 A.P.R. 262 (Nfld. T.D.), reversed (1990), 3 C.C.L.T. (2d) 195 (Nfld. C.A.).
9. [1935] I W.W.R. 714 (Alta. C.A.).
10. [1993] 2 S.C.R. 119, 15 C.C.L.T. (2d) 209, 100 D.L.R. (4th) 609, 151 N.R. 133, 62 O.A.C. 161.
11. (1990), 2 C.C.L.T. (2d) 1 (Ont. C.A.).
12. S.O. 1996, c. 2, Schedule A.
13. R.S.B.C. 1996, c. 181, as amended by *Health Care (Consent) and Care Facility Act*, S.B.C. 2000, c. 46.

3

THE CONSENT OF MINORS

SUMMARY

This chapter deals with the power to authorize the medical treatment of persons under the age of majority (18 or 19 years). The law reflects the gradual development of children from total dependence upon their parents to the attainment of full capacity to control and direct their own lives at the age of majority. The chapter discusses three categories of minors: *infants, immature minors,* and *mature minors,* and the common law rules relative to them. Medical treatment of infants (children up to approximately 6 years) without parental consent is a battery. Parents have the right to authorize not only necessary and beneficial treatment but also non-therapeutic treatment which does not cause or risk permanent harm to the child. Parents have no power to authorize non-therapeutic treatment which is harmful to the child. The rules relating to immature minors differ only to the extent that an immature minor may have a power to veto reversible and irreversible non-therapeutic procedures which are not harmful to the child, for example, ear piercing. A mature minor is one with the capacity to understand the nature and consequences of medical treatment. Such a person has the power to consent to medical treatment and parental consent is not necessary. The extent of a mature minor's power is discussed. Finally a survey is made of the legislation passed in some provinces to clarify the issue of consent of minors.

CASE STUDY: *JOHNSTON v. WELLESLEY HOSPITAL* (Ontario, 1970)[1]

The plaintiff, a 20-year-old male, sought treatment to remove facial scars, marks and pitting caused by acne. The procedure proposed by the physician and agreed to by the plaintiff was known as the "slush" treatment. Frozen carbon dioxide and acetone were applied to parts of his face. It was intended that the slush would cause frostbite, which would destroy the surface of the epidermis. Scabs would form which, in due course, would fall off. This treatment usually reduced scarring and pitting. The treatment was not successful and Johnston suffered additional scarring as well as considerable pain and suffering. The age of majority in Ontario was 21 years at the time of his treatment. Johnston sued the physician in battery, arguing that the procedure was wrongful because parental consent had not been given before the physician treated the plaintiff. The trial judge dismissed the action, ruling that in the circumstances the plaintiff was a mature minor and parental consent was unnecessary.

CASE STUDY: *C. (J.S.) v. WREN* (Alberta, 1986)[2]

A 16-year-old girl who was living at home became pregnant by her boyfriend. Several weeks later the girl moved out of her parents' home and did not return. In due course she went to the defendant-physician for an abortion. The physician was willing to perform the abortion and approval was granted by a therapeutic abortion committee as then required by the *Criminal Code*. The parents sought a judicial order to prevent the abortion on the grounds that a minor could not be given an abortion without parental consent. At this time the age of majority in Alberta was 18. The judge refused to make the order and his decision was upheld on appeal. She was a mature minor and parental consent was not required.

1. INTRODUCTION

At the age of majority, which is 18 in some provinces and 19 in others, a person becomes an adult and has full capacity to consent to medical treatment or to decline it. Persons under the age of majority are classified as *minors*. In Canada there is considerable uncertainty about when parental consent is necessary before minors can receive medical treatment. This is a matter of some concern because, unless the emergency doctrine applies, the medical treatment of a minor without the requisite parental consent may amount to a battery.*

Parental consent to medical treatment of minor children is one of a variety of legal issues arising in the context of the development of children from total dependence on their parents to the attainment of full capacity to

---

* The tort of battery is discussed in Chapter 2.

control and direct their own lives at the age of majority. Parents are legally obliged to provide care and support for their minor children, including the provision of necessary and beneficial medical care. Clearly, parents cannot discharge these responsibilities without the right to control, direct, and supervise their minor children. Consequently, they have the legal right to secure and direct medical treatment that serves the best interests of their minor child. During the course of the child's minority, the legal rights and obligations of parents gradually diminish and the rights and responsibilities of children correspondingly increase.

The general concept that children gradually attain legal capacity as they mature is widely accepted. However, because there are few reported cases, the common law has yet to develop a clear and consistent framework of legal rules to guide the resolution of individual cases. This lack of case law is indicative of the fact that most disputes in this area are resolved by parents, physicians and hospital administrators without resort to litigation. There is a substantial body of legal literature containing useful analyses of the various issues, but this is legal opinion rather than judicial authority. The most prudent and reliable course is to develop a legal framework which is consistent with the reported cases and reflects the concept of gradual evolution from full parental control to complete extinguishment of parental rights.

For the purpose of analysis, three categories of minors will be discussed: *infants, immature minors* and *mature minors*. Only the concept of a *mature minor* has received clear judicial recognition. *Infants* are minors up to the age of approximately six. This stage is marked by the total dependence of the child on her parents, an inability to understand the concepts of and the relationship between illness and treatment and, hence, a total incapacity to have any input in the decision-making process.

Immature minors are children older than approximately six, who have some understanding of illness and treatment but do not satisfy the judicially recognized mature minor test. The age of six is chosen because that is the approximate age when judges are prepared to impose legal liability in the tort of negligence. At that age a child is deemed to understand the notion of risk of injury and the need for care. It is, therefore, likely that a court would accept that age as indicative of a capacity to understand the basic notions of illness and medical treatment. It would not seem unreasonable that some consideration be given to the wishes of an immature minor.

A *mature minor* is one who has the capacity to fully appreciate the nature and consequences of medical treatment and thus has the maturity to make his own decision. In most circumstances, a mature minor has the capacity to give a valid consent to treatment.

A discussion of each category of minors will clarify the common law position on the medical treatment of minors.

2. COMMON LAW

(a) Infants (Children up to the Age of Approximately Six)

The primary obligation of parents is to act in the best interests of their children. Consequently, parents clearly have the power to authorize beneficial and therapeutic medical treatment for their infant children. It is equally clear that in the absence of an emergency, or judicial or legislative authority, medical treatment of an infant without parental consent constitutes battery. The parental power to consent overrides any refusal of treatment by the child. One would hope that parents and physicians would attempt to mollify an infant's concern and allay fears, but the legal position would appear to be that parents have the ultimate authority to consent to therapeutic treatment. The reason is that an infant is not considered to have the understanding or knowledge to play a meaningful role in the decision-making process. The law's position is consistent with the conduct of reasonable and responsible parents. Most parents will authorize vaccinations and medical examinations and treatment in spite of the vigorous objections of an infant. Indeed, the parental power of consent extends beyond purely therapeutic treatment to encompass reversible and irreversible non-therapeutic treatment so long as there is no permanent deleterious effect on a child. This is reflected in the generally accepted power of a parent to authorize circumcision and ear piercing. It would also include giving blood donations, the extraction of teeth in the course of purely cosmetic orthodonture to enhance the likelihood of evenly spaced and straight permanent teeth and, possibly, transplants of regenerative tissue such as skin or bone marrow.*

Parental authority over infants is not absolute. At common law, parents lack the power to authorize non-therapeutic treatment which either harms the infant or which risks a detrimental result. Parents have no power to authorize non-therapeutic sterilization, or the donation of a kidney.** The extent of parental power to consent to enrolling an infant in medical research is less clear. It would be necessary to consider such questions as the need to use infants, the potential benefit to society, possible benefit to the infant and the degree of risk to the infant's health.

---

*   See Chapter 17 on Organ and Tissue Donation.
** Tissue and organ donation by minors is discussed in Chapter 17.

It is also clear that parents lack authority to withhold beneficial and therapeutic treatment necessary for the life or health of their infant, whether on religious or other grounds. The provision of such medical treatment is a parental obligation and the law can override parental refusal to consent. The appropriate course of action is outlined in provincial child welfare legislation. If necessary and beneficial medical treatment is denied to a child, he is regarded as a child "in need of protection." The legislation normally permits a child welfare official to give the necessary consent.

This power is commonly exercised when parents who are members of the Jehovah Witness faith refuse to authorize necessary blood transfusions. It is clear that the protection of parental religious beliefs does not outweigh the mutual interest of the child and the public in the protection of human life and health. A useful example of the exercise of these statutory powers is *D., Re* (Alberta, 1982).[3] In that case, a child was born after a 38-week gestation period and immediately developed a severe respiratory illness, an infection known as Group B streptococcal septicemia. The family physician and consulting specialists all agreed that the child's life was in danger and that a blood transfusion was immediately required. The parents, on religious grounds, refused to consent to a blood transfusion. The Director of Child Welfare applied to have the child declared in need of protection under the Alberta *Child Welfare Act*.[4] The Court held that the child was in need of protection and that apprehension and medical treatment were necessary and proper. The Court refused to strike down the legislation as contravening the protection of religious freedom under the *Charter of Rights and Freedoms*. The judge stated:

> As between the state's right to safeguard the health and welfare of children and the rights of parents to freely practice their religion, the former must prevail. If a responsible adult refuses to accept a blood transfusion for himself or herself on religious grounds, the state should not and will not intervene, but when medical treatment, that is, a blood transfusion, is withheld from the offspring of the adult, the state must and has valid legislation to intervene.[5]

This view was affirmed by the Supreme Court in *B. (R.) v. Children's Aid Society of Metropolitan Toronto* (1994),[6] which dealt with the administration of blood to a newborn over the objection of her Jehovah's Witness parents. The child was made a ward of the Children's Aid Society under the provisions of the Ontario *Child Welfare Act*. The Society authorized a blood transfusion in respect of exploratory surgery, to confirm a diagnosis of infantile glaucoma. The Court held that the legislation did not infringe the parents' right to liberty or their right to religious freedom. One judge commented that "the right to liberty (under ss. 7 and 2(a) of the *Charter of*

Rights and Freedoms) does not include a parent's right to deny a child medical treatment that has been adjudged necessary by a medical professional."[7]

A parental decision against treatment does not, however, necessarily trigger legal intervention even if the consequence of the decision is that the child will die. The critical issue is whether the child is "in need of protection." A court would, for example, refuse to intervene when parents consent to the withdrawal of artificial life support during the final stages of a terminal illness.*

(b) Immature Minors

Immature minority is distinguished from infancy by the child's increased knowledge and understanding of illness and treatment. The capacity of understanding may be quite sophisticated in a child approaching the age of maturity. The immature minor is, nonetheless, deemed to lack the maturity for independent decision-making. The law accordingly provides that an immature minor cannot be treated without parental consent. The emergency doctrine aside, there is no doubt that it is the parents' right and obligation to authorize all necessary and beneficial care. It is likely that in most cases parents have the authority to override an immature minor's refusal of therapeutic treatment. In other words, an immature minor's refusal to consent to necessary medical treatment is probably inoperative.

Whether an immature minor can reject a parental decision to provide reversible and irreversible non-therapeutic treatment which is not permanently detrimental to the child is unclear. It is submitted that the minor *ought* to have a right to veto parental consent authorizing such treatment. By definition, these procedures are elective and are not required for the maintenance of life and health. The law will probably recognize an immature minor's refusal to consent to such procedures as blood donation, cosmetic surgery, ear piercing, the donation of regenerative tissue or cosmetic orthodonture. Such a veto power would recognize the gradual increase in a child's powers towards self-determination and reflect the gradual diminution in the parents' right to control medical treatment. Parental rights are also qualified by an incapacity to authorize non-therapeutic treatment which harms the child or risks harm without compensating advantage. More doubt surrounds the issue of medical research. Much will depend upon the need to use immature minors and the overall risks and benefits of the research. The joint consent of both parents and the immature minor may be necessary.

---

* Further discussion of this issue can be found in Chapter 17.

Intervention under child welfare legislation may have to be resorted to if, on religious or other grounds, a parent refuses to authorize necessary medical treatment or surgery.

(c) Mature Minors

Minors in this category have the capacity to consent to most forms of medical treatment. There is some uncertainty, however, as to precisely when the minor acquires this power. This uncertainty only compounds problems such as teenage alcoholism, drug abuse, pregnancy, abortion, sexually transmitted diseases, and contraception. Minors are confronting these issues at a progressively younger age and strongly held and competing views must be reconciled. The minor may wish to exclude parents from all aspects of the medical problem and may make confidentiality a condition of treatment. She may wish to assert her growing sense of autonomy and individual responsibility. Parents are naturally reluctant to relinquish control over the provision of medical treatment to their minor children. A child may be in the full bloom of adolescent rebellion, and the parents may regard it as imperative that the law preserve parental involvement until the child is quite close to the age of majority. There is also a public interest dimension to consider. The societal impact of alcohol and drug abuse, adolescent pregnancy, and sexually transmitted disease is unavoidable. The public interest is served by ensuring that minors have unimpeded access to appropriate and prompt medical care. It would not be well served by rules creating impediments to such care. To some extent, the physician gets caught in the cross fire. His first priority is to provide necessary medical services to his patient. Whether a parent himself or not, the physician may also, however, be sensitive to the concerns of his patients' parents and their desire for involvement in the medical care of their minor children. The clash of interests is well illustrated by the case of *C. (J.S.) v. Wren,* in which the issue of abortion caused a bitter dispute between parents and child. One can sympathize with each side, as did the Alberta Court of Appeal which expressed sympathy to both parents and child for the "unfortunate confrontation."

There is some case law as to when parental consent is no longer necessary. In the High Court of Ontario case of *Johnston v. Wellesley Hospital,* the trial judge held that a 20-year-old minor was able to give a valid consent to medical treatment. In the trial judge's view, a minor capable of fully appreciating the nature and consequences of medical treatment can give a legally effective consent. This principle is known as the *mature minor rule.*

For some years after the *Johnston* case was decided, the scope of this rule was uncertain. The patient in *Johnston* was twenty years old and an adult person in every respect other than age. Furthermore, the treatment was of a relatively minor nature. *Johnston* was an easy case which, therefore, provided little guidance for cases involving minors some years under the current age of majority. In this regard, the 1986 decision of the Alberta Court of Appeal in *C. (J.S.) v. Wren* is more helpful. The patient was 16, the medical procedure was more serious, and the decision involved difficult moral considerations which were not an issue in the *Johnston* case. The Alberta court nevertheless reaffirmed the *mature minor rule*. The Court recognized that parental rights do exist and do not wholly disappear before the age of majority. As the child matures, however, the degree of parental control must decrease correspondingly. Parental consent is not necessary when the child has sufficient intelligence to enable her to understand fully the proposed treatment. The minor was a "normal, intelligent sixteen-year-old" and the Court decided that, at her age and level of understanding, she had the legal capacity to make up her own mind.

The advantage of the mature minor rule is that it permits an individualized determination of the capacity to consent. This flexibility, however, may be outweighed by the disadvantage of uncertainty. It may be difficult for the physician to determine the maturity of her minor patient and she may be misled by falsehood. Furthermore, the courts have not yet given guidance as to the age below which parental consent is normally required. A presumption of incapacity below a certain age would provide some needed guidance to physicians without sacrificing an individualized approach to the issue of capacity. Although there is no legal authority on point, a presumption of incapacity to consent to medical treatment under the age of 13 would not be unreasonable.

Another approach which has secured some judicial support is the *emancipated minor rule*. It provides that a minor can validly consent to medical treatment when she is married, living on her own, or has shown in some other way independence from her parents. Such a minor is considered to be emancipated from parental control and able to make her own decisions. The emancipated minor rule is easier to apply in practice than the mature minor rule since a minor's marital status and living arrangements can be established by objective evidence. The Court in *C. (J.S) v. Wren*, for example, may have found the case easier to decide under the *emancipated minor rule*. The minor had left the family home and had been making her own decisions.

In many cases, the emancipated minor rule will produce the same result as the mature minor rule. However, the weight of authority clearly favours the mature minor rule because it addresses the minor's maturity directly. Undoubtedly, this is the better overall approach. For educational or financial reasons, many minors live at home through the full course of their minority. The law should reflect these social realities, and a minor's intelligence and understanding should be the touchstone of capacity to consent to medical treatment.

One of the more contentious and difficult areas in the application of the mature minor rule is the provision of oral contraceptives to teenagers. There is the potential for sharp conflict between health care providers, parents and teenagers. One view is that oral contraception should be available to all sexually active females at any age, as a young woman who is sexually active and seeks contraceptives independently of parental involvement satisfies the conventional notion of maturity as defined as a knowledge and understanding of the nature of the sought for health care. On the other hand, there is the view that cognitive maturity precedes the emotional and moral maturity which may be seen as important precursors to sexual activity. It is unlikely, however, that any special rule will be developed to deal with this issue, particularly given the application of the conventional concept of maturity to termination of pregnancy in *Wren*. The question came before the highest court in England in *Gillick v. West Norfolk & Wisbech Area Health Authority*.[8] In England, legislation declares that persons over 16 have the same power of consent to medical treatment as adults. The issue in *Gillick* was whether a physician could prescribe oral contraceptives to a female under 16 without parental consent. In affirming the mature minor rule, the Court held that it must be decided in each case whether the adolescent has sufficient understanding of the nature and risks of contraception to make up her own mind. There was some difference in emphasis among members of the Court. One placed emphasis on maturity alone; another cautioned that the physician should be satisfied that the treatment serves the best interests of the patient. Overall, however, the rule drawn from the case is one of maturity or, as it is known in England, "*Gillick* competence."

There are other dimensions to the contraception issue. Proof of maturity will establish the legality of the treatment, but as with all medical treatment, there are professional and ethical standards which guide physicians. The failure to comply with these standards exposes physicians to allegations of unprofessional conduct, which may result in disciplinary proceedings by professional licensing bodies. The outcome of the proceedings will depend upon the current ethical and professional standards of the profession. Bear in mind that the physician is not obliged to provide contraceptives to mature minors. In that regard, a variety of matters should be addressed. The physician should explore the nature of the parent-child relationship, the possibility of parental involvement, and should refrain from promoting or encouraging early sexual relationships. The physician should advise and inform the patient of the risks of sexual activity and of the means of protection from disease. Careful evaluation should be made of the patient's medical and physical condition. Appropriate emphasis must be given to the self-determination of mature persons and the need for strict confidentiality. The physician will be well served by such a holistic approach to care, counselling, advice and information.

There continues to be some debate about the scope of a mature minor's power of consent, which may well be narrower than that of an adult. The common law concepts of maturity and emancipation were developed to enable persons under the age of majority to secure necessary and beneficial medical care without parental consent. There is, therefore, logic to the view that the power of consent must be related to the purpose of the rule, and that a mature minor has the power to consent only to beneficial and therapeutic treatment. There is scant legal authority on point. Although the *Wren* and *Johnston* decisions did not expressly limit the consenting power of mature minors, the treatment in the former was by definition therapeutic because it had been sanctioned by a therapeutic abortion committee, and the cosmetic procedure in the latter was expected to provide emotional and psychological benefits.

The alternative view is that maturity brings a more complete autonomy, and that the mature minor has as full a right to self-determination as an adult. It is likely that the former view would be regarded as too narrow. There is little doubt that a mature minor has the power to consent to reversible and irreversible non-therapeutic treatment which has no permanent deleterious effect. Consequently, a mature minor has the power to consent to termination of pregnancy for non-therapeutic reasons, blood donation, cosmetic surgery, cosmetic orthodontia, and possibly very low risk research and experimentation. It is also likely that the power to consent extends to refusal of treatment, including a power to refuse life-prolonging treatment. The extent of the judiciary's commitment to the autonomy of a mature minor will be tested in situations where she refuses life prolonging treatment which holds a reasonable prospect of benefit.* Courts have indirectly recognized the right of a mature minor to refuse chemotherapy offering a slight prospect of success by refusing to view such a minor as "in need of protection" under child welfare legislation. However, the situation is more difficult when treatment offering a good prognosis is refused. This can arise in respect of cancer treatment or advanced eating disorders. Some English courts have suggested that there is a continuing judicial and parental power to override a refusal which is viewed as not in the best

---

* This issue is discussed in Chapter 20.

interests of the minor patient. The alternative view is that the decision is ultimately for the mature minor alone. After all true autonomy empowers one to make decisions for oneself that others might view as ill advised and contrary to conventional wisdom. Similar questions arise in respect of a mature minor's power to consent to irreversible non-therapeutic treatment which has a permanent and damaging effect. A mature minor might not have the power to consent to a non-therapeutic sterilization and the power to consent to high risk non-therapeutic research and experimentation is unclear. Consequently, it may well be that a person only acquires a full, unrestricted right of self-determination on majority.

3. LEGISLATIVE INTERVENTION

In some provinces, the uncertainty and unpredictability created by the mature minor rule has prompted legislation specifying the circumstances in which a minor has the capacity to consent to medical treatment. Of particular note is the Medical Consent of Minors Act, which was adopted as a legislative model by the Uniform Law Conference of Canada in 1975. In that Act, the age of consent to medical treatment without parental consent is set at 16. At that age a minor acquires the full capacity of an adult. The sole consent of a minor under the age of 16 is valid if the physician believes that the minor is capable of understanding the nature and consequences of the treatment and the treatment is in the best interests of the minor. The opinion of the treating physician that a minor under 16 has the capacity to consent must be supported in writing by a colleague. This draft Act, which is intended to supplant the common law, has been adopted only in New Brunswick. The New Brunswick *Medical Consent of Minors Act*,[9] excludes contraceptive procedures from its broad definition of medical treatment. Presumably the common law will control the necessity of parental consent on the question of contraceptive measures for minors.

In British Columbia, s. 17 of the *Infants Act*[10] deals with the consent of minors. In large part, it merely codifies the common law. A minor's consent is sufficient if the health care provider is satisfied that she understands the nature, consequences, and reasonably foreseeable benefits and risks of the proposed health care. However, the mature minor's right of self-determination is limited by the requirement that the health care provider make reasonable efforts to ensure that the treatment serves the minor's best interests. This limitation may undermine a mature minor's right to autonomy and confidentiality. In an unsuccessful constitutional challenge of the legislation in *Ney v. Canada (Attorney General)* (British Columbia, 1993),[11] the judge observed that a consideration of all relevant factors, including moral and family issues, may be necessary to determine the minor's best interests and that circumstances may require consultation with parents.

The power of minors to consent to treatment in Ontario is controlled by the *Health Care Consent Act*, 1996.[12] A minor may consent to or refuse treatment when she has an understanding of the information relevant to the treatment and an ability to understand its reasonably foreseeable consequences. No liability attaches to a health care provider who gives treatment in good faith and who reasonably believes that the minor had the requisite capacity to consent. Findings of incapacity may be appealed to the Consent and Capacity Review Board.

In Quebec, the principles relating to the consent of minors are found in Articles 14-18 of the *Civil Code*.[13] The *Code* draws a distinction between medical treatment which is "required by the state of health" of the minor and that which is not required by her state of health. Article 14 states that a minor over 14 may consent to required treatment. If, however, the minor is confined to a health or social services establishment for more than 12 hours, her parents or tutor must be informed. A refusal by a minor over 14 to consent to required treatment may be overridden by judicial order or, when there is an emergency and the minor's life is in danger or his or her integrity is threatened, the consent of a parent or tutor is sufficient. Patients over the age of 14 may give consent to non-required health care unless it entails a serious risk to health and may cause grave and serious effects, in which case parental consent is required. Parental consent is necessary in respect of all minors under the age of 14.

Some provinces have regulations under provincial hospital management legislation which deal with the age of consent. In Saskatchewan[14] and Prince Edward Island,[15] parental consent is required for non-emergency surgery on all patients under the age of 18 unless the minor is married. Ontario has a similar regulation setting the age at 16.[16] In the Northwest Territories,[17] there is a special regulation on the discharge of patients contrary to medical advice, which declares that an in-patient may only be discharged under the authority of a written order signed by the patient, the attending medical practitioner, the hospital, the board or if the patient is under 19 by the parent or guardian — provided that the parent or guardian also signs an accompanying statement releasing the hospital from responsibility for the discharge. It should be noted that there is some doubt about the legality of such regulations. It has been argued that regulations made under hospital management legislation can not affect the age of consent since the patient's autonomy is not a question of hospital management.

This pot-pourri of legislative action shows that our law makers are beginning to grapple with the hard questions as to when and in what circumstances minors should be permitted to consent to medical treatment.

Despite the difficulties, it is likely that legislation will increasingly be utilized to clarify issues relating to the medical treatment of minors.

4. DEFENSIVE PRACTICE

Lawyers are often called upon to advise clients how best to minimize the risk of disputes and thereby prevent potential litigation. In areas of legal uncertainty, preventative legal advice dictates a prudent course of action which is unquestionably within the law. There can then be no chance of legal liability. From this standpoint, a careful and protective lawyer who wishes to shield a physician from all risk of being sued in battery, might advise that no medical treatment of any kind be given to *any* person under the age of majority without parental consent. This advice may not reflect the state of the law, however, and significant problems could arise if this approach were adopted by the medical profession generally. But it is a course of action that would completely protect a physician from the risk of being sued for treating a minor without parental consent. Hospital consent forms requiring parental consent for treatment of all patients under the age of majority reflect this ultra-conservative approach. Hospital consent forms requiring spousal consent to sterilization or abortion also reflect defensive legal practice. Although it is very unlikely that spousal consent is a legal requirement, until an authoritative court has ruled on the question, the risk, albeit slight, that a court might take a different view, remains. This kind of legal advice has the advantage of administrative efficiency and certainty; its disadvantage is that it is out of touch with current medical practice. Physicians routinely treat patients under the age of majority and, within the current legal boundaries, have every right to do so.

5. CONCLUSION

Although there is uncertainty and unpredictability on issues involving the medical treatment of minors, the general trend is apparent. Both the common law and legislation are lowering the age at which minors have the capacity to consent to medical treatment. This trend is very much in line with broad social patterns. Children mature earlier, physically, socially and intellectually and are confronted at an earlier age with significant medical problems about which they are better educated and better informed than has been true in the past. Family units are often no longer the idealized close-knit, supportive and protective institutions of an earlier age. The law must reflect and embody this reality.

NOTES

1. (1970), [1971] 2 O.R. 103, 17 D.L.R. (3d) 139 (H.C.).
2. (1986), [1987] 2 W.W.R. 669, 49 Alta. L.R. (2d) 289, 35 D.L.R. (4th) 419, 76 A.R. 115 (C.A.).
3. (1982), 22 Alta. L.R. (2d) 228, 30 R.F.L. (2d) 277, 2 C.R.R. 329 (Prov. Ct.).
4. R.S.A. 1980, c. C-8, s. 6 [now am. 1988, c. 15, s. 6].
5. Mr. Justice Catonio, in *D., Re* (1982), 30 R.F.L. (2d) 277 (Prov. Ct.), at p. 281.
6. [1995] 1 S.C.R. 315.
7. *Ibid.,* at 430, *per* Major J.
8. (1985), [1986] 1 A.C. 112, [1985] 3 W.L.R. 830, [1985] 3 All E.R. 402 (H.L.).
9. S.N.B. 1976, c. M-6.1.
10. R.S.B.C. 1996, c. 223.
11. (1993), 79 B.C.L.R. (2d) 47 (S.C.).
12. S.O. 1996, c. 2, Schedule A.
13. *Civil Code* of the Province of Quebec.
14. *Hospitals Standards Regulations*, R.R.S. 1979, Reg. 3231, s. 55 made pursuant to *Hospital Standards Act*, R.S.S. 1978, c. H-10.
15. *Hospital Management Regulation*, R.R.P.E.I. 1981, c. H-11, s. 48 made pursuant to the *Hospital Act*, R.S.P.E.I. 1988, c. H-10.
16. *Hospital Management Regulation*, Ont. Reg. 518/88, s. 25 [now am. R.R.O. 1990, Reg. 965] made pursuant to the *Public Hospitals Act*, R.S.O. 1980, c. 410 [now am. R.S.O. 1990, c. P.40].
17. *Hospital Standards Regulations*, R.R.N.W.T. 1980, Reg. 274, s. 88 [now am. 1990, c. T-6], made pursuant to the *Territorial Hospital Insurance Services Act*, R.S.N.W.T. 1974, c. T-4 [now am. *Hosptial Insurance and Health and Social Services Act*, R.S.N.W.T. 1988, c. T-3].

4

INFORMED CONSENT

SUMMARY

This chapter explains the nature and extent of a physician's obligation to provide relevant medical information to her patient so that the patient's consent to treatment is an informed consent. The duty of a physician to secure an informed consent was explained in the landmark 1980 decision of the Supreme Court, *Reibl v. Hughes.* The Court declared that the legal obligation to give information was part of the physician's obligation of care to her patient. Liability is based on a breach of the physician's duty to give information and a causal link between the breach of this duty and the injury. This duty includes both answering a patient's questions and volunteering information of the nature, material risks and alternatives of the proposed treatment and of the consequences of inaction. In determining whether the disclosure has been sufficient the Court considers what a reasonable person in the patient's circumstances needs to know in order to make an informed and sensible decision. Causation is established by proof that a reasonable patient in similar circumstances, if the requisite information had been given, would have refused consent. Subsequent judicial refinement of these principles and the attitude of the courts in special circumstances such as cosmetic surgery, the inquisitive patient, waiver of the right to know, therapeutic privilege, medical research and innovative procedures are considered. Finally, the impact of the informed consent doctrine on the role of physicians is considered.

CASE STUDY: *REIBL v. HUGHES* (Ontario, 1980)[1]

The plaintiff, Reibl, 44, sought medical treatment for persistent headaches and hypertension. When the defendant, Dr. Hughes, examined him, he discovered that the plaintiff had a major occlusion of the left carotid artery. The occlusion created the risk of a stroke. The physician persuaded the patient to undergo an internal carotid endarterectomy to remove the blockage. The patient was not informed that the proposed surgery entailed an inherent, unavoidable and significant risk of a stroke which could prove fatal. The patient, a native Hungarian whose English was poor, was also under the erroneous impression that the surgery would alleviate his headaches and hypertension. During or immediately after the surgery he suffered a massive stroke which left him paralysed on the right side of his body and impotent.

The Supreme Court of Canada imposed liability on the basis of the physician's negligence. The defendant was not negligent in the performance of the surgery. He was held liable for his failure to provide sufficient information about the nature of the surgery and its attendant risks to enable the patient to give an informed and rational consent. The Court held that if Mr. Reibl had been given the requisite information, he would not have consented to the surgery and, consequently, would not have suffered the disability caused by the stroke. Personal considerations would have led him to postpone the surgery for many months, if not to forego it completely.

CASE STUDY: *FERGUSON v. HAMILTON CIVIC HOSPITALS* (Ontario, 1983)[2]

The plaintiff, Ferguson, aged 58, underwent bilateral carotid arteriography to determine if his eye trouble (amaurosis fugax) was an early sign of carotid artery stenosis. He was informed of some of the risks inherent in a carotid arteriography but was not told about the risk of stroke. The procedure, which was performed carefully and uneventfully, indicated no carotid artery stenosis. While the plaintiff was in the recovery room, he complained of symptoms which later developed into incomplete quadriplegia. The plaintiff was left with some limited sensation and mobility in his arms but none in his legs. He lost all sexual function and was rendered incontinent. His condition was permanent and irreversible.

The trial judge refused to impose liability. He ruled that the physician ought to have told the patient that the procedure entailed an inherent risk of stroke. However, even if the requisite information had been given, a reasonable person in the position of the patient would still have consented to the procedure. No liability was imposed because the failure to disclose the risk of stroke did not *cause* the plaintiff's injury.

CASE STUDY: *HAUGHIAN v. PAINE* (Saskatchewan, 1987)[3]

The plaintiff, Haughian, 55, complained of paresthesia, pain and disability in his right arm. The defendant-neurosurgeon diagnosed a cervical-disc herniation and recommended a laminectomy and discotomy. After the surgery the plaintiff developed paralysis in his legs and in parts of his arms. The defendant operated a second time and removed a piece of Oxycel, a surgical gauze, from inside the dura. The patient recovered from the paralysis but suffered a severe and adverse personality change.

The Saskatchewan Court of Appeal held that the physician had failed to inform the patient that the laminectomy and discotomy involved a small risk of death and total paralysis, and that "conservative management" was an alternative to immediate surgery. The Court held that in the circumstances this was negligent. Furthermore, if the physician had supplied the requisite information the plaintiff would not have suffered the temporary paralysis and the dramatic personality change because a reasonable person in his position would not have consented to the surgery.

1. INTRODUCTION

In Chapter 2, it was noted that the physician/patient relationship is in a state of evolution. Two models of that relationship were compared. One is the *traditional* model, in which a paternalistic and authoritarian physician, acting in what she perceives to be the best interests of the patient, dictates the appropriate treatment to an unknowledgeable and acquiescent patient. The second is the participatory model, in which the physician/patient relationship is more egalitarian because the patient plays an active role in decision-making. It was noted that the courts appear sympathetic to and supportive of this change from a traditional to a more participatory relationship. The attitude of the courts is indicated by their emphasis on the patient's consent and reminders that it is the patient and not the physician who must determine the course of medical treatment. The courts have realized that the key to a more egalitarian and participatory physician/patient relationship is knowledge and information. A patient's right of self-determination cannot be exercised sensibly unless the patient has enough relevant information to make an intelligent and rational decision. At the outset the physician has a monopoly of relevant information and a participatory relationship cannot arise until the physician shares knowledge about the nature of the illness, the options available, the consequences of inaction, and any significant and material risks of alternative courses of action. Furthermore, that information must be delivered in a manner that can be readily understood by the patient.

Over the past twenty years, the courts have spent considerable time and energy reshaping the law to impose *legal* obligations on physicians to disclose relevant medical information to patients. As in many areas of the law, the judicial task has been to balance competing interests. The courts clearly support the right of patients to receive sufficient information to enable an informed and rational consent and they wish to encourage physicians to treat patients as mature, intelligent partners in deciding the course of medical treatment. At the same time the courts are mindful of the reality of medical practice. Physicians do not have the time to provide each patient with a lengthy and discursive "seminar" on the particular ailment. Moreover, care must be taken not to require the disclosure of each and every possible risk of medical treatment. Frightening a patient about extremely remote risks may not be in the patient's best interests.

Until 1980, the extent to which a physician owed a duty of disclosure and the nature of the legal wrong committed by the physician who failed to discharge that duty, were both unclear. The Supreme Court provided guidance on both questions in its landmark 1980 decision, *Reibl v. Hughes.*

2. BATTERY OR NEGLIGENCE?

The Court in *Reibl v. Hughes* recognized that there are two distinct legal approaches to informed consent cases: battery and negligence. A battery analysis focusses on the validity of the patient's consent. As discussed in Chapter 2, medical treatment amounts to a battery unless it is authorised by a valid consent. It is arguable that if the patient has not received relevant information about the medical treatment, the consent is uninformed and consequently invalid. If such a consent is invalid, it follows that the medical procedure constitutes a battery for which the doctor is legally liable. This method of legal analysis is particularly advantageous to the patient. Although the patient must prove the battery (the physical interference with his body), the burden then falls upon the physician to prove that an *informed* consent was given by the patient.

The alternative theory, which is based upon negligence, focusses on the physician's obligation of care. Its premise is that a physician's obligation of care extends beyond a duty to treat with reasonable care and skill, to include an obligation to provide sufficient information to enable a patient to make an informed and intelligent decision as to what shall be done with his body. This approach is favourable to physicians because the patient must prove not only that the physician was negligent but also that the negligence caused the plaintiff to suffer loss.

In *Reibl v. Hughes,* the Supreme Court held that a physician's failure to disclose inherent risks of medical procedures falls within the scope of *negligence* doctrine. The Court ruled that battery involved a deliberate invasion of one's bodily security which was without privilege or consent. It was restricted, therefore, to cases in which no consent at all had been given to the medical procedure or in which the treatment was clearly beyond the consent that had been given. This narrow conception of battery would include those cases in which the very nature of the proposed surgery and treatment was misrepresented and a different procedure was carried out. It would not include, however, those cases in which the substance of the patient's complaint is not that there was no consent to the proposed treatment, but that there was insufficient disclosure of attendant risks. The Court appears to have preferred the negligence approach over battery in these cases because it allows for a more sensitive balance to be drawn between the interests of patients and physicians.

3. THE NEGLIGENCE MODEL: *REIBL v. HUGHES*

In *Reibl v. Hughes,* the Supreme Court carefully discussed the essential components of the negligence action: (1) the duty of disclosure; (2) the determination of negligence and (3) the requirements of causation and damage.

The Court ruled that a physician is under a clear legal obligation to provide information to her patient. In general, the physician discharges this obligation by answering fully and frankly all questions asked by the patient and, in addition, by volunteering information about the nature and gravity of the proposed treatment, any material risks attendant upon the procedure, alternative procedures and their risks, and the likely consequences of inaction. The Court went on to formulate a more particular definition of the appropriate standard of care to apply on a case by case basis and considered two different formulations: the *professional disclosure standard* and the *full disclosure standard.*

The *professional* disclosure standard requires the Court to determine what the reasonable physician mindful of her duty of disclosure would have told her patient in circumstances similar to those of the patient in the actual case before the Court. The Court then determines whether the defendant-physician has met that standard. So long as she has told her patient what the *reasonable physician* would tell her patient in the same circumstances, there is little likelihood of liability. This standard works to the physician's advantage because it permits her to avoid liability by complying with standard medical practice and professional norms.

The *full* disclosure standard is somewhat of a misnomer. It does not mean that physicians must disclose every risk of a procedure without reference to degree or seriousness. It does, however, focus upon the plaintiff-patient. It seeks to determine whether the physician has provided, in the light of what she knows or ought to know about her patient's personal circumstances, sufficient information to allow a *reasonable patient* in those circumstances to give an informed consent. This approach is more advantageous to patients since the degree of disclosure must be tailored to the individual circumstances of the patient. While expert witnesses are necessary to establish the nature and degree of risk of the medical treatment, evidence from the patient and her family is also required to identify the individual circumstances and concerns of the patient. Ultimately, whether the physician has provided sufficient information to the patient is fully decided by the courts, and not by the current standards of medical practice.

The Supreme Court adopted the full disclosure standard and found Dr. Hughes liable for failing to give sufficient information to his patient. The Court based its decision on a number of grounds: (1) the surgery involved a significant risk of stroke and death; (2) there was no emergency; (3) there was no neurological deficit; (4) the consequence of refusing surgery was the risk of stroke in four or five years; and (5) although the patient had some difficulty with the English language, he was emotionally stable and able to make a rational decision if he had been given the appropriate information. In light of these factors the Court concluded that the defendant was negligent in failing to inform his patient about the material risks of the surgery, the consequences of inaction, and that his hypertension and headaches were unrelated to the arterial blockage. In particular, Mr. Reibl ought to have been told that there was a risk of a stroke both during and shortly after surgery.

One continuing problem with the *full disclosure requirement* is the degree of inquiry that the physician must make in respect of a patient's personal circumstances. The Court stated that the physician must take into account what she knows or *ought to know* about the patient. The emphasized phrase indicates that the physician is obliged to make sufficient inquiry to ensure that the relevant considerations and circumstances are addressed. The extent of this inquiry is discussed later in the chapter.

Another equally vital element of the negligence model that must be addressed is *causation*. Negligence theory demands proof of a causal link between the negligent act and the patient's injury. The patient must prove that if the requisite information had been given, she would have refused to consent to the medical treatment and, thus, would have avoided the injury.

There were two different approaches to causation open to the Supreme Court: the *subjective test* and the *objective test*. The former attempts to determine what the plaintiff-patient herself would have decided if there had been a proper disclosure of information. The latter seeks to determine the decision that a reasonable patient would have made and ignores the personal idiosyncracies and circumstances of the particular patient.

Both tests are subject to criticism. The *subjective test* is criticized for placing undue emphasis upon the plaintiff's evidence that if she had been properly informed of the risks she would *not* have gone ahead with the procedure that caused her harm. Arguably, the test places a premium on the bitterness and hindsight of the patient to the disadvantage of the physician, resulting in the causation issue invariably being resolved in the patient's favour. The strict *objective test* is equally disadvantageous, however, because it places a premium on the medical evidence relating to the advisability of the treatment in the light of inherent risks and anticipated benefits. If the information provided by the physician was medically justifiable and in the interests of the plaintiff, the likelihood of the patient proving causation is slim. The reasonable patient would usually follow the advice of her physician whether or not the requisite disclosure of information was made. Satisfying the Court that the reasonable patient would have withheld consent becomes an onerous burden.

The Supreme Court sought to escape the dilemma by adopting a *modified objective test*. The test requires the judge to determine what a reasonable person *in the patient's particular position* would have done. Account must be taken of special considerations affecting the particular patient, so long as they are reasonably based and relate to the risks of the treatment or surgery. In *Reibl v. Hughes,* the Court took into account the elective nature of the surgery, the degree of risk involved, and that its purpose was to reduce the risk of stroke. Balanced against these factors was the evidence of a significant risk of stroke or death during or immediately after surgery. While a strictly objective test would seek to determine what the reasonable patient would decide to do in that situation, the Court also took into account that Mr. Reibl would have qualified for a retirement pension if he had continued in his employment for 18 months. The Court held that this was a personal consideration that was relevant to the causation issue. The Court concluded that a reasonable person *in similar circumstances* would, at the very least, have postponed the surgery until after the pension had vested.

Since all essential elements of negligence liability were established, Dr. Hughes was found liable for the damage suffered by Mr. Reibl.

4. DISCLOSURE REQUIREMENTS SINCE *REIBL v. HUGHES*

A survey of the reported cases since *Reibl v. Hughes* indicates that the courts are not placing an intolerable burden on physicians. Most cases concern medical treatment which has resulted in serious harm to the patient. The courts have ruled that a risk of serious consequences must be disclosed even if the chance of its occurrence is slight. Thus they have required disclosure where there is a relatively small risk of death, stroke, paralysis, impotence, sterility, incontinence, vision or hearing loss, serious voice impairment and serious nerve damage. The cases that introduce this chapter — *Reibl v. Hughes* (stroke and death), *Ferguson v. Hamilton Civic Hospitals* (stroke and death), and *Haughian v. Paine* (death and paralysis) — typify cases involving a low risk of grave consequences. Special note should be taken of the risks arising from the use of prednisone. There are a number of cases that have held that the side effect of avascular necrosis in hip and shoulder joints is a material risk which must be disclosed.

It has also been ruled that disclosure of the most serious risk does not free the physician from the obligation to disclose additional serious risks. In the *Ferguson* case, the defendant-physician told the patient about the risk of death but not about the risk of stroke. It was argued that the physician was not bound to disclose the risk of stroke since he had mentioned the most serious risk (that is, death). Since the patient knew that death was a risk and still consented to the procedure, it was argued that a disclosure of lesser risks would not have led him to refuse the procedure. The Court rejected the argument, stating that a reasonable person might be prepared to run the risk of death but not the risk of a stroke.

It is clear that risks that are commonly known or relatively minor need not be disclosed. There is ordinarily no duty to explain that surgery involves scarring, bleeding, pain and risk of infection. There is no need to explain that a scalpel blade might break or that an intravenous needle might sometimes slip out of a vein. There is no duty to discuss all the risks involved in general anaesthesia. There may of course be exceptions to the general rule. For example, the risks of general anaesthesia must be disclosed if there is a choice between a general, local or spinal anaesthetic.

Predicting the judicial reaction to a case involving a significant risk of relatively moderate loss is more difficult. An example is nerve damage resulting from oral surgery for the removal of third molars (wisdom teeth). There is a 5 per cent risk of some temporary nerve involvement, and a less than 1 per cent risk of permanent nerve damage. Some cases have held that such risks are not material and need not be disclosed. However, the weight of recent authority is to the contrary. This conflict of judicial opinion illustrates that the standard of disclosure must be tailored to the particular patient and that no general rule can be established. Clearly, however, the courts are not requiring a lengthy discussion of all possible risks, but rather are concentrating upon *material* risks; those risks that the patient needs to know in order to give an informed consent. Although most cases have focussed upon the degree and seriousness of the risk, the courts have also deemed it necessary for the physician to provide information about alternative treatments, particularly if one alternative involves significantly greater risk than another. The patient must also be advised of the consequences of inaction so that she can weigh the risk of foregoing the procedure against the risk and likelihood of success of remedial treatment. *Haughian v. Paine* provides a useful illustration. The defendant-physician failed to inform the patient that there was a choice between conservative treatment and surgery. Conservative treatment included supervised rest, traction, a course of muscle relaxants and physical therapy with analgesic medication. The patient was also not told that conservative treatment would not foreclose future surgical intervention if his condition failed to improve. The Court held that such information was clearly material, and that the patient ought to have been given a chance to evaluate each alternative and to make an informed choice.

In 1993 the Supreme Court had another opportunity to discuss the issue of disclosure. In *Ciarlariello v. Schacter* (1993)[4] the Court considered a case in which the plaintiff-patient had undergone two cerebral angiograms in order to detect the location of a subarachnoid haemorrhage. The Court found that the patient was fully informed of all material risks, including that of death. During the course of the second procedure, she experienced discomfort and withdrew her consent. When she calmed down she agreed to the completion of the procedure. Shortly after the resumption of the angiogram, she suffered an allergic reaction to the dye and was rendered a quadriplegic. It was argued that a further explanation of risks should have been given to the patient before the resumption of the test. In reaffirming its commitment to the principles outlined in *Reibl v. Hughes*, the Court nonetheless held that there was no need to have outlined the risks again. The interruption of the test had introduced no new circumstances. There was no change in the risks involved nor in the cost/benefit ratio of the procedure. The patient was sufficiently informed to make an informed decision to continue the test. In any event, no reasonable person in her position would have refused continuance of the angiogram.

Overall, the courts have been quite liberal in interpreting the disclosure requirement. Courts are not reluctant to characterize risks as material. It is not possible to construct an infallible test to determine the extent of information required in a particular case. As a rule of thumb, a physician would be well advised to pose and answer the following question: If I were this patient, what would I want to know before deciding whether to agree to the proposed surgery or treatment? If there is any doubt about the answer disclosure should be made.

5. CAUSATION SINCE *REIBL v. HUGHES*

The modified objective test of causation in *Reibl v. Hughes* proved to be difficult both for plaintiffs to satisfy and for the courts to apply. Many plaintiffs were unable to convince the Court that a reasonable person in her position, given the requisite information, would have refused to consent to the procedure. This is not surprising because physicians as a general rule do not recommend a course of action unless it is therapeutic and in the patient's best interests. *Ferguson v. Hamilton Civic Hospitals* is illustrative. (The facts are set out at the beginning of this chapter and are not significantly different from those in *Reibl v. Hughes.*

The judicial difficulties in applying the test flowed from the uncertainties inherent in the modified objective test. It required the court to consider the decision-making of a reasonable person in the plaintiff's particular circumstances or position. It did not describe or catalogue the range or kind of personal factors that should be attributed to the reasonable person. There was initially a great deal of unevenness on this issue. In some cases, causation was determined on little more than an assessment of the ailment, the proposed treatment, the inherent risk of the treatment and the consequences of inaction (similar to a strict objective test). In other cases, the court took into account such a wide range of personal considerations and personality traits that the test was almost indistinguishable from a subjective test. The matter remained unresolved until the Supreme Court revisited the issue in *Arndt v. Smith* (1997).[5] In that case, the plaintiff contracted chickenpox in the course of her pregnancy. The defendant physician chose not to tell her patient that this posed a small risk of serious birth defects to her child. The child was born with serious disabilities and the plaintiff argued that if she had been told of this risk, she would have terminated her pregnancy. The trial judge applied the modified objective approach, and, after noting that the plaintiff had a particular desire for children and a suspicion of mainstream medicine, he concluded that a reasonable person in her particular circumstances would not have terminated her pregnancy. The British Columbia Court of Appeal ordered a new trial ruling that the modified objective test had not been applied correctly. A majority of the Supreme Court affirmed the modified objective test and held that the trial judge had applied it properly. The Court indicated that a wide range of personal factors may be included to modify the reasonable person test. A court may take into account all the objectively ascertainable circumstances of the patient such as her age, income, marital status, any special considerations affecting the patient, including those that she raised with her physician, and all the patient's reasonable beliefs, fears, desires, expectations and concerns. The modified objective test eliminates consideration only of the patient's idiosyncratic, unreasonable and irrational beliefs and subjective fears that are unrelated to the material risks of the medical treatment. In the opinion of the majority, therefore, it was appropriate to ask what the reasonable pregnant woman, who had a particular desire for children, who was sceptical of mainstream medicine, and who had expressed no particular fears of having a disabled child, would have done had she been told of the small risk of birth defect. That is what the trial judge had done and his conclusion that the reasonable woman in these circumstances would not have terminated her pregnancy was upheld.

Although the Court re-affirmed the modified objective test, it has approved the use of so many personal factors that it may not, in practice, be significantly different from the subjective test favoured by the minority of the Court. This has been confirmed by the judicial decision making since *Arndt v. Smith*. The cases indicate that the judges are making generous use of personal factors and circumstances in applying the modified objective approach. Nevertheless plaintiffs continue to have difficulty in satisfying the test. Furthermore *Arndt* creates new challenges. In an ethnically and religiously diverse society, it is difficult to draw a line between beliefs and concerns that are reasonable and those that are not.

6. SPECIAL SITUATIONS

(a) Cosmetic Surgery and Procedures

Courts impose onerous obligations to inform when the procedure is of a cosmetic nature. When procedures are elective and non-therapeutic, the physician must give a more ample account of the nature and risks of the procedure, the nature and risks of alternative methods or procedures and the risk of failure of the proposed treatment. It is true that some cosmetic surgery does promise emotional and psychological benefits, but this does not diminish the necessity of complete disclosure if the *primary* purpose is cosmetic. This stringent disclosure standard also recognizes that the patient seeking cosmetic surgery may be hyper-sensitive to her physical appearance. Surgical failure or additional disfigurement may be devastating. It is essential that the patient clearly understand the risks involved.

White v. Turner (Ontario, 1981)[6] and *Sinclaire v. Boulton* (British Columbia, 1985)[7] are two illustrative cases in which the plaintiff has succeeded under the informed consent doctrine. In *White v. Turner*, the defendant-plastic surgeon performed an unsuccessful mammoplasty. The scarring of the breasts was more extensive than the plaintiff had expected, the nipples were misplaced, and the breasts were box-like in appearance. The trial judge stated the obligation of the cosmetic surgeon:

> Where an operation is elective, as this one was, even minimal risks must be disclosed to patients, since "the frequency of the risk becomes much less material when the operation is unnecessary for his medical welfare.".. A *fortiori*, in a case where the predominant aim is a cosmetic one, possible risks affecting the appearance of the breasts such as undue scarring, the box-like appearance and the poor position of the nipples, must be classified as material.[8]

The defendant had failed to discuss material risks and was liable to the plaintiff since a reasonable person in her particular circumstances would not have consented to the surgery had she known of the risks.

In *Sinclaire v. Boulton*, the defendant-surgeon performed breast augmentation surgery on the plaintiff. The prosthesis was inserted behind the breasts rather than behind the muscle, resulting in hypersensitivity of her right breast and permanent numbness in her left breast. In response to the plaintiff's inquiry, the surgeon had assured her that she would experience no loss of feeling or sensation in her breasts. The Court found that the defendant was negligent because there was a known risk of an impairment in sensitivity. The Court applied a causation test that recognized a number of personal considerations: the defendant's assurance that the plaintiff would lose no sensation in her breasts; the importance of the sensitivity of her breasts in her marital relationship; and evidence that her husband had not pressured her to undergo this surgery. The Court deemed it appropriate to place heavy emphasis upon personal considerations when surgery is elective and cosmetic.

More recent cases have further emphasized the importance of giving full information about anticipated scarring in cosmetic surgery. Not only must the position, extent and nature of the scarring be disclosed but also, in appropriate circumstances, the risk of keloid and hypertrophic scarring must be discussed. While scarring may not always be a material risk in therapeutic surgery, it is otherwise in the case of cosmetic surgery.

(b) The Inquisitive Patient

A physician not only has an obligation to volunteer information relating to medical procedures, but she must also answer the patient's questions fully and honestly. A patient may want more information than a physician would normally give her. The physician must be sure to answer all questions carefully and correctly. She must not brush them aside or otherwise treat them as insignificant. This reflects the full disclosure standard which is tailored to the individual patient. When a patient asks a question, she is indicating that the information sought is material to her decision-making. This is illustrated by *Sinclaire v. Boulton.* The plaintiff asked about the risk of any change in the sensitivity in her breasts. The Court showed little hesitation in finding liability when the answer was incorrect. A physician ignores special concerns and inquiries at her peril.

(c) Waiver of the Right to Know

A full disclosure standard must recognize that some patients prefer to have little or no information about medical procedures. A patient may have total confidence and faith in his physician and may wish to forego all discussion of risks, complications, or alternatives. A person may wish to discuss the general nature of the proposed treatment but prefer that the physician not tell him what could go wrong. Again, the physician must be guided by the patient. Although the patient has the right to waive the right to be informed, the physician must proceed with caution. There should be disclosure unless the patient waives that right in the clearest possible terms. For the physician's protection, the patient's decision should also be properly documented.

(d) Therapeutic Privilege

On occasion, a physician may feel that disclosure of material risks is not in the best interests of a particular patient because of the risk of psychological or physical harm. In *Reibl v. Hughes,* the Supreme Court did recognize such a so-called "therapeutic privilege." The Court stated that emotional factors could render a patient unable to cope with all the facts relevant to the recommended treatment. In such circumstances, the physician would be justified in withholding or generalizing information which otherwise would require more specificity. It is likely, however, that the scope of therapeutic privilege is very narrow. A broad discretion to dispense with the normal disclosure requirements would threaten the patient's right to fully informed self-determination. In the one case on this issue since *Reibl v. Hughes,* a trial judge, after recognizing the tentative opinion of the Supreme Court and the threat to patient autonomy, concluded that therapeutic privilege is not a part of Canadian law at all. In *Meyer Estate v. Rogers,*[9] the defendant-radiologist failed to disclose a 1/40,000 risk of death arising from an intravenous pyelogram. The Court held that it was a material risk and that the failure to disclose could not be justified on the basis of a therapeutic privilege. The radiologist had claimed that such information would needlessly increase the anxiety of the patient which would in turn increase the chance of an allergic reaction to the hypaque dye. Until this matter is firmly resolved by a more authoritative court, physicians should proceed with the upmost caution on the matter of therapeutic privilege.

(e) Medical Research

The common law doctrine of informed consent to medical treatment is an important protection of those persons who agree to be the subject of medical research. Although there is some narrowly targeted legislation, a great deal of research is self-regulated. Institutions in which research is undertaken, such as hospitals, universities and government funded research bodies, normally have research ethics boards or committees which review research protocols to ensure that they meet national and international codes of ethical conduct in medical research involving persons. The subjects of research must, however, rely on the common law to provide remedies when they are harmed by inherent risks of the research procedures of which they have not been told.

As early as 1965, the Saskatchewan Court of Appeal had the opportunity to consider the duty of a physician conducting medical research. In *Halushka v. University of Saskatchewan,*[10] the plaintiff, a 21-year-old university student, consented to serve as a subject for medical research. He was offered $50 to test a new drug. He was informed by the two defendant medical researchers that the test entailed minimal risk. He was told that a small incision would be made in his arm, that a catheter would be inserted in a vein, and that "there was nothing to worry about." The drug tested was a new anaesthetic agent, "Fluoromar", and the test required a catheter to be passed through the chambers of his heart. The only benefit to the plaintiff was the $50 payment. During the procedure, the plaintiff suffered a cardiac arrest. The defendants took immediate steps to resuscitate the plaintiff by manual massage. An incision was made from the breastbone to his armpit to allow the defendants to reach the heart. The plaintiff's heart began beating again after one minute and 30 seconds. The plaintiff was unconscious for four days and remained in hospital for 10 days. The Saskatchewan Court of Appeal held that there was no negligence in the manner in which the test had been performed. Nevertheless, liability was imposed on the physicians, and it was made clear that the fullest possible disclosure applies to medical research. Where no therapeutic advantage to the subject is anticipated, the nature of the research and all risks, possibilities and opinions must be described in a forthright, open and honest manner. Therapeutic privilege has no application and in all probability the subject's right to disclosure cannot be waived. There is nothing in *Reibl v. Hughes* to suggest that the Supreme Court would quarrel with the *Halushka* decision.

(f) Innovative Procedures

The courts have been careful to distinguish innovative procedures from research. Innovative procedures are medical advances directed toward therapeutic ends, whereas research is one aspect of scientific investigation that is designed to enhance the field of human knowledge. This distinction was drawn by the Alberta Court of Appeal in 1981 in *Zimmer v. Ringrose*.[11] The Court stated that to "hold that every new development in medical methodology was 'experimental' in the sense outlined in *Halushka . . .* would be to discourage advances in the field of medicine."[12] The standard of disclosure in respect of innovative procedures is therefore not quite as stringent as in research. This may be more of a theoretical than a practical distinction. It is still necessary to inform the patient that the procedure is innovative and to provide a full account of the degree of risk, the chance of success, the nature of the procedure and the advantages and disadvantages of more conservative or traditional treatment.

Courts also distinguish between different kinds of innovative procedures. There is a significant difference between an innovative procedure supported by clinical studies and experience and approved by a significant body of medical opinion, and an innovative procedure unique to one physician, unsupported by clinical studies and frowned upon by the College of Physicians and Surgeons. In respect of the latter, the courts are considerably more demanding. The cases of *Zimmer v. Ringrose* and *Coughlin v. Kuntz* (British Columbia, 1987)[13] fall into and illustrate the second category.

In *Zimmer v. Ringrose*, the plaintiff had told the defendant-gynaecologist that she wished to undergo sterilization. After mentioning various methods of sterilization, he informed the plaintiff of a new technique utilizing silver nitrate paste as a means of blocking the fallopian tubes. The plaintiff consented to the new treatment, which, unfortunately, failed. The Court ruled that the physician was under a duty to disclose the relative novelty of the procedure and of its failure to gain general medical acceptance.

In *Coughlin v. Kuntz,* the physician performed an anterior cervical discectomy which involved the use of a methyl methacrylate spacer. Its purpose was to relieve shoulder pain. It was held that the plaintiff had been inadequately informed about the proposed surgery. He had not been told that the procedure was novel and unique to the defendant and that it was under investigation by the College of Physicians and Surgeons which had recommended a moratorium on the procedure. The defendant had said nothing about the risks entailed in the use of the artificial spacers, alternative courses of treatment or that other physicians had recommended that the plaintiff-patient not undergo neck surgery. The Court held that the defendant was liable for omitting to inform the patient on all these matters. It also held that the performance of the operation was itself negligent because it was experimental and unsupported by clinical study. In addition to the compensatory award, the defendant was assessed $25,000 in punitive damages. It is clear that innovative treatment will range from the untried experimental treatment (as in *Coughlin*) to responsible advances in medical science which are supported by both clinical studies and a significant section of the medical community. Judges will adjust the disclosure standard accordingly.

(g) Reproductive Choice

Physicians must exercise particular care and caution when procedures affect reproductive capacity. Sterilization and abortion are procedures in respect of which the courts will impose a high standard of disclosure. Since they are often not necessary for the preservation of life and limb, there is no excuse for neglecting to make a full disclosure of information and risks. Therapeutic privilege is irrelevant and the validity of waiver is doubtful. Prior to securing a consent for sterilization, it is essential to discuss the advantages and risks of alternative techniques, the reliability of each procedure and whether or not the sterilization is reversible. When the patient seeks an abortion, the physician must discuss the various techniques and the risks associated with each. The physician should advise the patient of the relative merits of having the abortion in hospital or at a free standing clinic. A very full disclosure is also necessary regarding methods of contraception. Alternative methods and the risks and reliability of each must be disclosed fully and frankly.

7. THE IMPACT OF THE DOCTRINE OF INFORMED CONSENT ON THE ROLE OF PHYSICIANS

(a) The Physician as Teacher

The decision in *Reibl v. Hughes* recognizes that the role of the physician extends beyond that of healer to that of teacher. The physician has an obligation to teach the patient about her ailment, the benefits and risks of alternative treatment and the consequences of inaction. Current trends indicate that this responsibility is likely to become more extensive in the future. Even now sound medical practice may require that more information be given to a patient than is currently required under the informed consent doctrine.

Physicians sometimes express concern about this emerging role as teacher. In a busy medical practice, there is little time to share information about illness and the choice of treatment. It is clear that the Supreme Court did assume that it would be the physician who, in the course of conversation with the patient, would provide the requisite information. There is no reason, however, why the physician may not arrange for an appropriately trained nurse, assistant or receptionist to provide information. Use may also be made of brochures, pamphlets or standard form letters containing the requisite information. Some hospitals have begun to use video cassettes to explain the nature of treatment or surgery. It is important, however, that the physician carefully review information prepared by others to ensure that it is not a slick public relations exercise designed to reassure and encourage patients by unduly minimizing material risks or ignoring real perils. The information must contain the kind of balanced account of the procedure and its risks as is required by the Supreme Court. There is a further important caveat. The *full disclosure standard* requires that information be tailored to the particular patient and her circumstances. This precludes total reliance on standardized informational material. There must be some direct input from the physician herself. In most cases it will be sufficient for the physician to assure herself that the information has been understood by providing an opportunity for questions and by providing additional information required by the patient's personal circumstances. It must also be remembered that the duty to inform the patient is the physician's personal responsibility and that she is ultimately responsible for ensuring that the patient has the requisite information. Nevertheless, planning, flexibility and innovation can prevent the role of teacher from becoming unacceptably burdensome and impractical.

(b) The Physician's Duty to Know the Patient

One aspect of the decision in *Reibl v. Hughes* that has attracted little comment is the physician's duty to know the personal circumstances of her patient and to tailor the disclosure of information accordingly. The Court stated that the physician must take into account what he knows or *ought to know* about the patient and her personal circumstances. The emphasized words indicate an obligation to inquire about the patient's personal circumstances if they are not known. This requirement does not seem unreasonable where a physician in family practice has a longstanding professional relationship with her patients. The physician may know a great deal about her patient's personal concerns, aspirations and circumstances. It is, therefore, not unreasonable in the context of family practice to require that the physician be acquainted with the broader context of a patient's life. She ought to be treating her patients, not merely their current ailment.

In other areas of medical practice, the duty to be familiar with the patient's personal concerns may be burdensome. Consulting specialists, emergency room physicians, surgeons, and physicians practising in 'walk in' clinics and abortion clinics may know little about the patient's life situation. It is unreasonable to expect the physician in these circumstances to conduct a broad inquiry to elicit the patient's lifestyle. Such an inquiry, if made, may be resented by the patient. In these situations it is probably sufficient for the physician to ask very general questions. The patient may be asked if there are personal, family or occupational relationships or concerns that are particularly affected by her illness or treatment. The patient may be asked how the illness or treatment is affecting her life. Or, the patient may be asked if the illness and treatment will create particular problems or difficulties that the physician should know about. It is unlikely that a court would require a physician in these circumstances to do more.

(c) The Physician as Adviser

An issue that has been resolved since *Reibl v. Hughes* is that of the responsibility of the physician as adviser. The courts have carefully distinguished between a physician's duty to provide sufficient information to ground an informed consent and the physician's role in advising her patient. Although there is a legal obligation to inform, there is no legal obligation to recommend a particular course of action. In *Zamparo v. Brisson* (Ontario, 1981),[14] the plaintiff suffered from a partial hearing loss in her left ear. It was caused by unilateral otosclerosis. The defendant-physician informed her that a stapedectomy might correct the hearing loss. He explained the risks involved in the surgery and the plaintiff gave her consent. In the course of the surgery, the physician palpated what appeared to be a membrane with a hook instrument. Unfortunately, the "membrane" was a portion of the facial nerve, and the plaintiff suffered a paralysis on the left side of her face. The plaintiff argued that the physician ought to have done more than explain the pros and cons of the surgery. He ought to have considered that for many years, the plaintiff coped well with her impaired hearing and that he should have advised her not to undergo the surgery. In essence, it was argued that the physician ought to have volunteered his own assessment of whether the potential risks outweighed the potential benefits.

The Ontario Court of Appeal rejected that position, holding that a physician owes no duty to advise a patient. The decision is consistent with the underlying rationale of the doctrine of informed consent which is rooted in the concept of individual decision-making on the basis of all relevant information. The doctrine is designed to assist the patient to exercise her right of self-determination. An obligation on the physician to tell the patient what to do would contradict that policy.

(d) The Physician and Errors, Blunders and Misadventures in the Course of Treatment

A 1986 decision of the New Brunswick Court of Appeal illustrates the expansive nature of the informed consent doctrine. In *Kueper v. McMullin*,[15] the defendant-dentist performed a root canal on the plaintiff. In the course of the procedure, a drill bit broke off and became tightly lodged in one of the canals. The defendant was unable to remove it but chose not to tell the plaintiff. He continued the procedure and filled the cavity, treating the drill bit as part of the filling. The plaintiff did not learn what had happened until months later when she consulted another dentist in respect of pain in that tooth. Subsequently the drill bit was removed and the plaintiff suffered no further pain.

The Court ruled that the case was distinguishable from recent informed consent cases, since the risk of a drill breaking was not a material risk that ought to have been disclosed before the root canal procedure took place. Nevertheless, the Court ruled that the dentist was obliged to tell the patient that something had gone wrong in the course of treatment and to discuss alternative remedial measures. The patient was conscious, alert and capable of making a choice of treatment. However, the action failed on the grounds of causation since a reasonable person in the plaintiff's position would have agreed to the remedial procedure that the defendant had followed. The decision is significant because it indicates that the physician's duty of disclosure does not terminate when the patient consents to treatment. The duty continues during both the course of the procedure and post-operative care. It is the physician/patient relationship which gives rise to the duty to inform and that duty does not cease until the relationship terminates. This view is consistent with the underlying purpose of the informed consent doctrine. It is to foster a more participatory relationship in which the patient is able to exercise her right to self-determination in a meaningful way.

(e) The Physician's Professional and Personal Attributes

The primary purpose of the informed consent doctrine is to provide a patient with information about the nature of her malady, treatment options and the associated risks and benefits of those treatment options. This will assist the patient to make an informed decision about what is in her best interests. There is, however, other information which a patient may deem pertinent such as the professional qualifications, experience and reputation of a surgeon and her relevant personal traits such as alcoholism, HIV positive status and emotional instability.

There is no case law in Canada dealing with disclosure of professional information about a physician or surgeon. It is likely that Courts will be hesitant in extending the current law to require disclosure of factors such as the physician's inexperience, high infection rates, failure rates or a history of patient complaints to professional regulatory bodies. These matters have generally been dealt with by peer review, by determining the extent of hospital privileges, by professional regulatory associations and by inquiries of the physician by the patient. Nevertheless, the matter is not free of doubt. In the *Report of the Manitoba Pediatric Cardiac Surgery Inquest*.[16] Associate Chief Judge Murray Sinclair stated that the lack of experience of the surgeon, and the state of experience and level of functioning of the surgical team ought to have been disclosed to the parents of the patients.

The disclosure of information on personal traits such as the physician's health, emotional stability, substance abuse or personality is even more controversial because it threatens the privacy interests of health care professionals. There has only been one Canadian decision that has touched on the issue. In *Halkyard v. Matthews*,[17] the plaintiff argued that he should have been told by the defendant surgeon that he suffered from epilepsy. The Alberta Court of Appeal held that disclosure was not required. The epilepsy was well controlled by medications and the plaintiff's loss was unrelated to the physician's medical condition. More difficult questions will no doubt arise, such as the need to disclose conditions such as HIV positive status or alcoholism which may endanger the health of a patient. The court will then have to evaluate and balance the patient's interest in personal safety and the physician's interest in privacy.

8. CONCLUSION

In 1980, the Supreme Court applied a broad brush to paint a legal framework for the development of the informed consent doctrine. The Court sought to ensure rational and informed decision-making by encouraging improved communication between physician and patient and by recognizing the patient's right to control her own destiny. In essence, the Court sought to encourage a more equal and participatory physician/patient relationship. In doing so the Court was careful to refrain from telling physicians how to practice medicine and from imposing upon them onerous and impractical requirements. The requirements of the informed consent doctrine do not unduly restrict or inconvenience physicians in the practice of their profession. The disclosure standard is in truth a fair reflection of good medical practice. The Court has declared that the authoritarian and paternalistic aspects of the traditional physician/patient relationship are no longer acceptable. Patients must be treated as autonomous and equal partners in the process leading to the patient's choice of medical treatment.

NOTES

1. [1980] 2 S.C.R, 880, 14 C.C.L.T. 1, 114 D.L.R. (3d) 1, 4 L. Med. Q. 209, 33 N.R. 361.
2. (1983), 40 O.R. (2d) 577, 23 C.C.L.T. 254, 144 D.L.R. (3d) 214 (H.C.), affirmed (1985), 50 O.R. (2d) 754, 33 C.C.L.T. 56, 18 D.L.R. (4th) 638 (C.A.).
3. [1987] 4 W.W.R. 97, 40 C.C.L.T. 13, 37 D.L.R. (4th) 624, 55 Sask. R. 99 (C.A.), leave to appeal to S.C.C. refused [1987] 6 W.W.R. lix (S.C.C.).
4. [1993] 2 S.C.R. 119, 15 C.C.L.T. (2d) 209, 100 D.L.R. (4th) 609, 151 N.R. 133, 62 O.A.C. 161.
5. [1997] 2 S.C.R. 539.
6. (1981), 31 O.R. (2d) 773, 15 C.C.L.T. 81, 120 D.L.R. (3d) 269, 5 L. Med. Q. 119 (H.C.), affirmed (1982), 47 O.R. (2d) 764, 12 D.L.R. (4th) 319 (C.A.).
7. (1985), 33 C.C.L.T. 125 (B.C. S.C.).
8. Mr. Justice Linden, in *White v. Turner* (1981), 31 O.R. (2d) 773 (H.C.), at p. 793, citing Mr. Justice Grange in *Videto v. Kennedy* (1980), 27 O.R. (2d) 747, 107 D.L.R. (3d) 612, 4 L. Med. Q. 44 (H.C.), reversed on other grounds (1981), 33 O.R. (2d) 497, 17 C.C.L.T. 307, 125 D.L.R. (3d) 127 (C.A.), at p. 758 [27 O.R.] and p. 622 [107 D.L.R.].
9. (1991), 6 C.C.L.T. (2d) 102 (Ont. Gen. Div.).
10. (1965), 52 W.W.R. 608, 53 D.L.R. (2d) 436 (Sask. C.A.).
11. (1981), 16 C.C.L.T. 51, 124 D.L.R. (3d) 215, 28 A.R. 69 (C.A.), leave to appeal to S.C.C. dismissed (1981) 28 A.R. 92, 37 N.R. 289 (S.C.C.).
12. *Ibid.*, p. 60.
13. (1987), 17 B.C.L.R. (2d) 365, 42 C.C.L.T. 142 (S.C.), affirmed (1989), 42 B.C.L.R. (2d) 108, 2 C.C.L.T. (2d) 42 (C.A.).
14. (1981), 32 O.R. (2d) 75, 16 C.C.L.T. 66, 120 D.LR. (3d) 545 (C.A.).
15. (1986), 37 C.C.L.T. 318, 30 D.L.R. (4th) 408, 73 N.B.R. (2d) 288, 184 A.P.R. 288 (C.A.).
16. Sinclair M., Report of the Manitoba Pediatric Cardiac Surgery Inquest: An inquiry into twelve deaths at the Winnipeg Health Sciences Centre, www. pediatriccardiacinquest.mb.ca/ch10/informedconsent.html.
17. (1998), 43 C.C.L.T. (2d) 171 (Alta. Q.B.), affirmed (2001), 4 C.C.L.T. (3d) 271 (Alta. C.A.).

5

MEDICAL NEGLIGENCE: AN OVERVIEW

SUMMARY

In this chapter, we look first of all at some illustrative cases; cases which afford typical illustrations of the way in which the *tort* or civil wrong of negligence is applied in lawsuits against physicians. Then, turning to analyze the concept of negligence, we find that this term, used as a legal term of art, means rather more than mere carelessness. It is a tripartite concept, connoting the existence of a duty of care owed by one person to another; the breach of that duty of care by substandard conduct; and resultant damage of a legally compensable kind. For physicians, as for other professional people, the critical question is usually the question of breach of duty — in other words, what standard of care and skill does the law require? The tenor of the chapter is a reassuring one, for it emerges that the standard of care and competence required, if a physician is to escape liability, is not some exalted standard presumptuously imposed by the judges, but is ordinarily the standard prevailing within the medical profession iself. It is gauged by the practices and standards ordinarily observed and reasonably to be expected among the defendant-physician's own professional peers. The concept of negligence emerges as essentially a straightforward one, relatively free of technical language or esoteric ideas. Its aim is to afford reasonable levels of protection or compensation to patients, without demanding from physicians the attainment of unreasonably perfect standards of performance.

CASE STUDY: *CHUBEY v. AHSAN* (Manitoba, 1976)[1]

Mrs. Annie Olson, 49, was married with four children. She had a painful back condition, and was referred by her family doctor to the defendant Dr. Ahsan for examination. Dr. Ahsan, a specialist in orthopaedic surgery, determined after taking her history and examining a series of x-rays that one of her lumbar discs must be removed. The procedure was properly explained to Mrs. Olson, her consent was duly obtained, and the operation proceeded. During surgery, considerable blood loss was noted — some 1,500 to 2,000 cc. — and replaced with 1,000 cc. of blood by transfusion, sufficient to keep the patient's pulse at a normal level. After the surgery, the wound was closed in the usual manner, but without a drain because it was free of blood at the time of closing.

Initially, Mrs. Olson appeared to be recuperating normally, and Dr. Ahsan left to attend to other patients. But, after half an hour in the recovery room, the patient's condition began to deteriorate rapidly. It was obvious that she was haemorrhaging internally. She was swiftly opened up, to reveal a ruptured abdominal aorta, and a bruise on the vena cava; both lesions being located directly beneath the area of the disc surgery. Prompt and diligent repair procedures were carried out, but to no avail. The following morning, Mrs. Olson died from irreversible shock, brought on by the massive aortic haemorrhage. On behalf of her estate and her dependents, Mr. Chubey, her executor, brought an action in negligence against Dr. Ahsan.

At trial, it appeared that the operation here undertaken by Dr. Ahsan, though prudently undertaken and performed with perfectly orthodox technique, was of a kind described as "a nightmare to orthopaedic surgeons" because of the proximity of the aorta to the disc. The thorough removal of degenerated disc material would inevitably require complete exploration of an area invisible to the surgeon, who must be guided entirely by "his sense and precision of feel" and his knowledge of anatomical detail. Expert evidence was divided as to whether scientific measurement of the vertebrae would assist in this precarious enterprise, or merely generate a false sense of security in the surgeon; but all agreed — indeed Dr. Ahsan himself did not dispute this — that the aorta and vena cava must have been damaged during the surgery by either the pituitary rongeur or curette. The statistical evidence showed that this was a recognized risk of such an operation, though one which materialized only once in every 7,000 disc operations, and even then only proved fatal in 50 per cent of these exceptional cases.

The trial judge dismissed the action, holding that no negligence could be imputed to Dr. Ahsan upon the evidence. The blood loss during the operation was high, but not so alarming that it should have alerted Dr. Ahsan to the fact that he had inadvertently damaged these major blood-vessels. The damage to those vessels did not in itself bespeak negligence, but rather misfortune — the incidence of a peril inseparably connected with this very delicate and dangerous surgical procedure, where only an "onion-skin thickness of ligament" separated the field of surgery from the important, vulnerable and largely hidden blood vessels pulsing beneath. The Manitoba Court of Appeal, though divided in opinion, affirmed the dismissal of the action, holding that Dr. Ahsan had shown the appropriate standard of care and skill. He should not be held liable for what was in truth not negligence, but misadventure or misfortune.

CASE STUDY: *REYNARD v. CARR* (British Columbia, 1983)[2]

Mr. Reynard, 29, the plaintiff in this case, was an active sportsman and a partner in an auto parts company. He was a married man with a young child. Complaining of a chronic bowel disorder, he visited his general practitioner, the defendant Dr. W, who referred him to Dr. S, a gastroenterologist. Dr. S's diagnosis was guarded, but he prescribed a course of prednisone, informing Dr. W that the dosage should presently be reduced. Later, Dr. S prescribed more prednisone, and also imuran, a drug known to carry the risk of toxicity to the bone marrow. All these prescriptions proved useless and were discontinued, while Mr. Reynard's condition deteriorated still further. He asked Dr. W to find him another specialist and was referred to the defendant, Dr. Carr. Dr. Carr diagnosed ulcerative colitis and prescribed (among other things), a further course of prednisone. For a while, the doses of this steroid were reduced, but when no improvement was noted, their strength was increased, and "bumped" still further whenever flare-ups occurred.

As time went by, Mr. Reynard noticed severe pains in his shoulders, but his prednisone medication was continued. When his hips also began to give trouble, Dr. W ordered x-rays which disclosed serious bone degeneration in the hip and shoulder joints. Dr. W did not immediately disclose this, but eventually referred his patient to Dr. F, a rheumatologist who promptly and correctly diagnosed avascular necrosis. The prednisone treatment was stopped immediately, and the unfortunate Mr. Reynard underwent first a proctocolectomy, then a series of five more operations to replace his hip and shoulder joints with synthetic implants. More surgery seemed inevitable, in the fullness of time, to renew the artificial joints. Equally foreseeable was a gradual increase in his general level of debility. Faced with this discouraging prospect, Mr. Reynard had suffered depression, resorted to alcohol abuse, and undergone temporary marital disjunctions. He now sued both Dr. W and Dr. Carr in negligence, arguing that they had failed in their respective duties of care and skill towards him. In particular, they had prescribed prednisone for far too long, at too high a dosage and with inadequate monitoring procedures. Moreover, they had failed to advise him of the very real risk of avascular necrosis, which any competent gastroenterologist should have known to be associated with the protracted use of prednisone.

Both defendants were held liable, for a sum initially assessed at $775,000, but reduced on appeal to $451,000. Both physicians had failed in their duty to communicate diligently with each other, so as to monitor the course of the prednisone treatment and its effects. Both had been at fault, too, in failing to disclose to their patient either the alternative of surgical treatment, or the very real risk of avascular necrosis attendant upon prednisone use. Both of these failures had contributed causally to the sad plight in which Mr. Reynard now found himself, and both constituted actionable negligence.

CASE STUDY: *CABRAL v. GUPTA* (Manitoba, 1992)[3]

Mr. Cabral, an autobody repairman, was hammering a steel door when he felt something enter his eye. He consulted Dr. Gupta, an ophthalmologist, who examined the eye and conducted tests, but could find nothing wrong, and prescribed eye drops. A second visit and examination again disclosed no injury. No screening X-ray was conducted on either visit.

Two years later, Mr. Cabral suffered a sudden and serious deterioration of vision in that eye. His family physician referred him to another ophthalmologist, who by means of an X-ray determined that there was indeed a metal particle in that eye, a particle which over time had caused serious reactive conditions. The prognosis was poor, but Mr. Cabral was referred for retinal surgery. The surgery disclosed a seriously torn retina, and the metal particle still could not be located. Shortly after the surgery, a retinal detachment occurred, and Mr. Cabral became blind in the right eye. The damaged eye had to be removed to avert the danger of sympathetic ophthalmia developing in the left eye.

In an action against Dr. Gupta, the defendant conceded that his failure to conduct an X-ray at the outset had been a breach of his duty of care to Mr. Cabral. However, his counsel argued that in all probability Mr. Cabral would have suffered severe visual impairment anyway, even if Dr. Gupta had detected the metal particle at the first opportunity. On the preponderance of expert medical evidence, the trial judge concluded that more probably than not, perhaps a 70 per cent likelihood, a timely diagnosis would have made possible surgical interventions which would have saved the useful sight of the injured eye. Accordingly, he entered judgment in favour of Mr. Cabral while reducing the measure of damages by 30 per cent to reflect the possibility that remedial surgery might have failed anyway.

On appeal, this deduction from the award was held to have been in error. Once Mr. Cabral had shown that it was more likely than not that Dr. Gupta's negligence had caused his loss of sight, he was entitled to an award representing the full monetary value of his loss, and the possibility that even timely surgery might have failed could not in point of law justify any reduction from that figure.

1. THE CONCEPT OF ACTIONABLE NEGLIGENCE

Much is heard these days about *medical malpractice actions* and *malpractice liability.* Indeed, we have already made free use of such expressions several times in this book. But it should be explained at this juncture that "malpractice" is not a term of art in legal contexts. Rather it is a generic expression apt to cover a variety of professional wrongdoings and liabilities. Negligence and wilful wrongdoing by a physician are certainly within its scope. And there is case law which suggests, not very surprisingly, that "malpractice" is an expression broad enough to cover the tort of battery, which we have already encountered.

Whether "malpractice" embraces claims for breach of contract against a culpably inept physician, in appropriate circumstances, seems still to be a disturbingly open question. The vagueness of the malpractice notion is in truth harmless enough, except perhaps when it is used (as sometimes happens) in liability insurance policies, where absolute clarity should always be the goal. But one thing can be said with complete confidence: 95 per cent or more of those actions brought against medical professionals, and colloquially labelled "malpractice suits," are, in strict analysis, actions in the tort of negligence.

This rampant and ubiquitous civil wrong of negligence dominates the modern law of torts and covers virtually every area of social behaviour, from the manufacturing of goods to the driving of vehicles; from the maintenance of road signs to the giving of professional advice; from the supervision of delinquents to the performance of brain surgery. Negligence represents by far the most likely type of civil action with which a physician may expect to be confronted. We have already encountered it in connection with the physician's duty to inform a patient of the nature of the proposed therapy and its more important attendant risks. In this chapter, and those that follow, we must take time to anatomize this most important area of tort law.

First, a number of preliminary observations must be made. It is inevitable that a cause of action so often advanced against physicians by disgruntled patients will be seen by the medical profession as having a threatening aspect. But quite apart from the fact that the threat is not very formidable in practice and that the number of successful lawsuits is quite modest, it should be emphasized at the outset that neither its conceptual framework nor its terminology are calculated to add any new terrors to the tort of negligence. While legal historians can trace the liability of physicians back into the darkest periods of the early Middle Ages, such investigations add nothing to our understanding of the modern law of negligence in general or of medical negligence in particular. The truth is that the conceptual skeleton of the modern law of negligence was not fully evolved until well into the present century. Many scholars point to the year 1932 as the crucial date; the year which produced the famous Scottish case of *McAlister (Donoghue) v. Stevenson*.[4] That case involved (oddly enough) a plaintiff who claimed to have been made ill because she drank from an opaque ginger beer bottle which proved to contain the decomposing cadaver of a snail. It prompted a famous judgment by Lord Atkin, a great British jurist, in which scholars can discern all the essential elements of the modern law of negligence.

Those elements, despite the indefatigable efforts of legal scholars to make them sound complex and imposing, remain conspicuously and commendably simple in all their essentials. They reflect the adoption of common sense ideas and realistic standards, and are expressed in straightforward language. Consider, if you will, the case studies with which this chapter begins. As summaries, they reflect quite faithfully the type of terminology to be found in the arguments and judgments in those cases. The lawyers bring into play such expressions as "duty of care and skill", and "standards of care and skill." They contrast "negligence" with "misadventure", or "mere errors of judgement." Any technical and imposing language to be found in the judgments is the contribution, and no doubt the necessary contribution, of the medical profession.

Another circumstance which may seem reassuring is the great caution and, strange to relate, the humility with which Canadian judges have approached the task of evaluating the standards and practices of professions other than their own. There has always been a wise reluctance to say to a surgeon (or, for that matter, an architect or an accountant) "We know your profession ordinarily adopts such-and-such a technique, but we judges of course know much more about your profession than you do, and consider that technique to be actionably negligent!" While in very rare and extreme cases[5] the courts will castigate as negligent a usage widely observed in another learned profession, such cases are conspicuous by their very rarity. Ordinarily, as we shall see, the courts are content to allow each profession, to a very large extent, to set its own standards of acceptable practice and its own required level of care and skill. So, when a doctor is held liable in negligence, it will not usually be because he has failed to attain some exalted standard of competence prescribed by lawyers, on or off the bench. It will be because the defendant-physician has failed, on this occasion, to meet the standards of care and skill prevailing in his own profession, and established by his professional peers.

A constant danger — and the courts continually warn themselves against it — is the trap of "wisdom by hindsight", of concluding after the unhappy outcome of an operation, for instance, that any reasonable surgeon should have foreseen the unlucky complication which arose, and should have guarded against it. This danger is often compounded by the bitterness of the stricken patient, who may be more readily forgiven for being wise after the event. As we have seen in Chapter 4, this problem has in recent years necessitated the changing of the causation rules in negligence cases relating to informed consent, and the adoption of the modified objective causation test in such cases. The temptations of hindsight are a leading theme in the case of *Roe v. Ministry of Health; Woolley v. Ministry of Health,*[6] a 1954 decision of the English Court of Appeal which is so often referred to, both in Canadian and English courts, that we may pause to consider it at this juncture.

Mr. Roe and Mr. Woolley, the plaintiffs in this case, went into hospital for minor surgery on the same day in 1947, and each was given spinal anaesthesia, nupercaine being injected intrathecally between the lumbar vertebrae. The glass ampoules containing the nupercaine, as they came from the makers, were not sterilized on the outside, and to guard against possible contamination from the exterior and the label, it was common practice to immerse the ampoules in a solution of phenol for some considerable time prior to their use. On this occasion, the operations proceeded without apparent mishap, but it was discovered afterwards that both patients were afflicted with severe spastic paraplegia — paralyzed, indeed, from the waist down. It was determined that microscopic cracks or fissures in the glass ampoules, quite invisible to the naked eye, had allowed the infiltration of phenol into the nupercaine. The phenol, injected with the anaesthetic, had been sufficient to corrode the nerves of the spinal cord. In 1947, the risk of such contamination was generally unknown; indeed, it was tragic cases like Mr. Roe's which first brought the danger to prominent notice in the medical literature. Had Dr. Graham, the anaesthetist, been negligent? The trial judge, and a very strong appeal court, all said no. The words of Lord Denning's judgment, so often quoted in subsequent cases, seem to be worth quoting again:

> If the anaesthetists had foreseen that the ampoules might get cracked with cracks that could not be detected on inspection they would, no doubt, have dyed the phenol a deep blue; and this would have exposed the contamination. But I do not think their failure to foresee this was negligence. It is so easy to be wise after the event and to condemn as negligence that which was only a misadventure. We ought always to be on our guard against it, especially in cases against hospitals and doctors. Medical science has conferred great benefits on mankind, but these benefits are attended by considerable risks. Every surgical operation is attended by risks. We cannot take the benefits without taking the risks. Every advance in technique is also attended by risks. Doctors, like the rest of us, have to learn by experience; and experience often teaches in a hard way. Something goes wrong and shows up a weakness, and then it is put right. That is just what happened here. Dr. Graham sought to escape the danger of infection by disinfecting the ampoule. In escaping that known danger he, unfortunately, ran into another danger. He did not know that there could be undetectable cracks, but it was not negligent for him not to know it at that time. We must not look at the 1947 accident with 1954 spectacles. The judge acquitted Dr. Graham of negligence and we should uphold his decision.[7]

It will be obvious by now that an unfortunate or even catastrophic result does not, in point of law, invariably (or even usually) denote negligence, in and of itself. On rare occasions, the circumstances of a medical mishap will be so strongly suggestive of blameworthy carelessness and point so strongly to the defendant professional as the person responsible for it, that it will be hard indeed for him or her to escape liability in negligence. We consider such cases in Chapter 7, later on. But they are in truth exceptional cases. If we ponder the *Roe* case for a moment, or the case study, *Chubey v. Ahsan,* with which this chapter began, we see cases of tragic medical error — or cases which with the benefit of hindsight can be seen as such. In both, our sympathy, and that of the Court, is naturally accorded to the unlucky patient. Yet liability is in both instances very properly denied by the Court. Time and time again we see the courts stressing that to be wrong is not in itself to be negligent; and that human errors of judgment, whether in a physician's cognitive processes or her physical dexterity as a surgeon, are not themselves indicative of negligence — unless such errors were of a kind that a normally competent and careful physician would not have made.

Lawyers are fond of saying that "negligence" as a legal term means something much narrower and more complex than when the word is used in everyday speech. So it does, but there is in essence nothing very mysterious about it. An acceptable definition of legal negligence might be attempted in a single sentence: Negligence consists in a breach of a duty of care or skill, antecedently owed by one person to another; a breach which results in foreseeable and compensable harm to that other person or some interest of his. To be sure, such a definition begs almost as many questions as it answers. Most, it is hoped, will be answered in this chapter and the next. But from this rough analysis, three indispensable elements of a negligence action can be distilled: (1) The plaintiff must show that the defendant owed to him a duty of care or skill; (2) The plaintiff must show that that duty was broken by the defendant, in that the requisite standard of care and skill demanded by the duty was not met; and (3) The plaintiff must show that he suffered damage of a legally compensable kind, caused, and foreseeably caused, by the breach of duty.

Each of these ingredients may generate its share of complexities and puzzles. The general law of negligence is replete with them. But in the specific context of medical negligence, remarkably few of these controversial issues arise in practice. In an action in negligence against a physician, there is ordinarily no room for any argument about the duty of care: for where a doctor/patient relationship exists, so, with absolute certainty, does a duty of care and skill (and other legal duties too) owed by the doctor to the patient. So element (1) is ordinarily quickly satisfied. Element (3) — the complex of issues relating to damages — is more intricate these days than it used to be, due to developments in the law of *causation-in-fact* which will be discussed in due course. But these problems, difficult when they arise, are relatively uncommon. The damage, in most medical negligence cases, is of a very obvious and tangible kind (physical injury) which the law readily compensates; has plainly been caused by the course of treatment complained of; and is just the sort of thing which the reasonable physician would foresee as the probable result of ineptitude on his part. So that element (3), insofar as it generates any difficulty at all, usually does so at the very basic level of *computing quantum* — that is, in arriving at the right figure, in dollars and cents, that is needed to compensate the injured patient.

It is in the consideration of element (2) — interchangeably referred to as the *breach of duty* or *standard of care* issue — that the major battles over liability are usually fought in medical negligence cases. Expert evidence is adduced by both sides to determine what is the standard of practice, the accepted technique, and the prevailing level of competence and skill current in the profession when treating like cases. This enables the Court to gauge the standard against which the defendant physician's performance must be judged. Then, the Court must evaluate the evidence and determine as best it can what the defendant did or did not do, and so decide whether the standard was met or not; whether the duty was discharged or broken. So it is that many contested medical negligence cases are not in the last analysis truly legal disputes at all; it is in conflicts of fact, disputes over evidence, that battle is truly joined. Because of this, the precedents afforded by previous judgments offer less reliable guidance in medical negligence cases than in other legal contexts and are treated accordingly with rather less deference. Each new case tends to devolve in large measure upon its own detailed facts and, within the very broad and generalized conceptual framework imposed by the law of negligence, is decided simply upon those facts without any real dispute as to the applicable legal rules or doctrines.

In the following chapter, the three essential members of the conceptual framework, *duty, breach* and *damage*, will be examined, and it will sometimes become apparent that this neat tripartite classification breaks down, in practice, rather frequently. In particular, the distinction between the ambit of the duty of care, and the kind of conduct involved in its breach, is often exposed by the caselaw as rather an artificial piece of line-drawing. The truth seems to be that negligence is a single concept, and the trichotomy of duty, breach and damage a construct which legal scholars superimpose upon it for didactic purposes. Since, however, it does enable us to maintain some sense of direction as we enter the dense forest of caselaw on this subject, we will stick with the traditional three-part conceptual framework, and approach the whole topic by dealing sequentially with the three essential ingredients of negligence.

NOTES

1. [1975] 1 W.W.R. 120, 56 D.L.R. (3d) 231 (Man. Q.B.), affirmed [1976] 3 W.W.R. 367, 71 D.L.R. (3d) 550 (Man. C.A.).
2. (1983), 50 B.C.L.R. 166, 30 C.C.L.T. 42 (S.C.), reversed in part (1986), 10 B.C.L.R. (2d) 121, 38 C.C.L.T. 217 (C.A.).
3. (1992), 83 Man. R. (2d) 2, 13 C.C.L.T. (2d) 323 (C.A.).
4. [1932] A.C. 562 (U.K. H.L.).
5. See, *e.g., Anderson v. Chasney,* 57 Man. R. 343, [1949] 2 W.W.R. 337, [1949] 4 D.L.R. 71 (C.A.), affirmed [1950] 4 D.L.R. 223 (S.C.C.). This case is discussed in Chapters 7 and 9.
6. [1954] 2 Q.B. 66, [1954] 2 W.L.R. 915, [1954] 2 All E.R. 131 (C.A.).
7. *Ibid.,* at p. 137.

6

MEDICAL NEGLIGENCE: THE ESSENTIAL ELEMENTS

SUMMARY

This chapter examines in some detail the three essential elements in any claim for professional negligence — the showing of a duty of care; the issue of breach of duty (often termed the standard of care issue); and the proof of compensable damage flowing from the breach.

In considering the duty of care, we note that this usually arises as an inseparable incident of the physician/patient relationship. But questions may arise, firstly as to whether such a relationship truly exists upon the facts in evidence; and secondly, where it is clear that no such relationship came into being, as to whether the doctor broke a duty of care in the very evasion of such a relationship.

The duty of care, once formed, is seen to be a multi-faceted bundle of obligations (which will be considered separately in Chapter 8). Cautionary mention is made of the law of contract and its dangers for the physician who promises too much; and of the possibility that even under ordinary negligence principles, a doctor may find herself exposed to duties and liabilities towards persons other than her patient.

The breach of duty or *standard of care* question is addressed with reference to the general practitioner, the specialist, and (most difficult of all) the novice professional. It is seen that the law seeks in every instance to demand an objective standard of reasonable care and skill, determined by the standards ordinarily observed by the defendant physician's own professional peers. No allowance is made for inexperience or other such subjective or personal factors, but the law accepts that mistakes do not in themselves indicate negligence, and that infallibility cannot be demanded. Those factors which influence the mental processes of the hypothetical "reasonable physician" in governing her conduct are scrutinized in the light of decided cases, and particular consideration is given to the situation in which a physician allows non-clinical factors to influence her professional judgment while treating a patient.

The final ingredient, the requirement that damage be proved, is shown to be in truth a complex of issues, all potentially difficult. There is the issue of *causation-in-fact*, usually straightforward but capable of generating puzzling dilemmas, potentially threatening to the medical practitioner. There is the quite different question of remoteness of damage, a crucial issue which vests great discretionary power in the judge, and is sometimes enlivened by curious variations, especially when a plaintiff's injury can be seen to have multiple causes. Finally there is the matter of quantum, the complex of rules (recently overhauled) whereby courts determine exactly how much money a defendant must actually pay to the victim of his negligence.

The chapter closes with an excursus on the phenomenon of vicarious liability, whereby an employer, innocent of any fault, may be found legally responsible for the negligence or otherwise wrongful acts of an employee, committed in the course of employment; and whereby partners may find themselves sharing legal responsibility for each others' errors.

1. THE DUTY OF CARE

When does a physician come under a legal duty of care and skill in the provision of medical treatment? The simple answer to that question is that the law imposes such a duty whenever a physician/patient relationship exists between a doctor and another person. That facile answer — for facile it is — is sufficient to dispose of this issue in the great majority of cases. Whatever should be the nature of the physician/patient relationship in an ideal world, the reality is ordinarily a relationship of great dependence and reliance. The patient may fairly be expected to co-operate, but it is the physician who has the power to guide and direct, while the vulnerable patient lacks the knowledge to contradict and (with some obstreperous exceptions) can be seen to be reposing confidence in and reliance upon the physician's skill and judgment. It is ultimately from this relationship that the legally imposed duty of care and skill arises.

Of course, it is not always as simple as that. Doubts may arise as to whether a true physician/patient relationship has arisen, generating a duty of care to the patient. Such doubts arose in the case of *Leonard v. Knott* (British Columbia, 1980).[1] Mr. Leonard's employer arranged with Dr. Knott to provide a "package executive health programme" for its fifteen senior executives. Among them was Mr. Leonard, 45, a married man. His participation was voluntary, but he submitted himself to the annual medical check-up comprised in the "package", and Dr. Knott (who adamantly refused throughout the trial to refer to such examinees as "patients", reserving even the term "client" for their corporate employer) sent him for a radiological examination of the kidneys and urinary tract, to be done by means of an intravenous pyelography. He did so before taking Mr. Leonard's medical history, seeking such a history from his family doctor, or doing any routine office testing. The pyelography was performed by the second defendant, Dr. Dundee, a radiologist, after only a short interview. Sadly, Mr. Leonard suffered an allergic reaction to the contrast medium used in the pyelography; and despite strenuous efforts to save him, died a few hours later. Sued by the widow, Dr. Knott contended in vain that Mr. Leonard had not been his patient, and that accordingly his only duty was to Mr. Leonard's employer, not to the unlucky victim himself. Both the trial judge and appeal court found Dr. Knott liable and the appeal judges felt that Dr. Dundee too must bear some of the blame. The trial judge, who alone addressed the issue, gave very short shrift to the defence contention that no physician/patient relationship existed, stating that he had "no doubt whatever that from a legal if not a medical point of view there existed between him and each such examinee a physician-patient relationship", calling into play the appropriate duties of care and skill, owed to such patient. This, of course, is a case of harm actually inflicted by the physician upon the examinee. It is as yet an unresolved question in Canadian law whether a doctor conducting such an examination upon a person at the instigation of that person's employer or insurer is similarly exposed to liability to such persons if, through carelessness, a serious and obvious condition is not diagnosed and disclosed to that person. Certainly a powerful argument might be made for the imposition of liability in such a case.In most cases, the incidence of the physician's legal duty of care is addressed simply by considering whether a physician/patient relationship was truly in existence. Exceptional cases do arise, however, where it is acknowledged that no such relationship came into being, but where the very substance of the plaintiff's complaint is that the physician broke a moral and indeed a legal duty by her forbearance from entering into such

a relationship with one who desperately needed her help. This problem —
an age-old subject of legal debate — is called the problem of the "Good
Samaritan." Is a doctor who witnesses an accident on the way home from
hospital under any duty to stop her car and lend assistance to the injured?
The traditional response of the common law to this question has been a
consistent and callous "no." Neither a doctor nor anyone else is obliged,
so far as the general law is concerned (that is, apart from any more humane
directions in professional codes of ethics) to lend assistance to a stranger,
however grave that person's plight may be. So, if our doctor ignores the
accident victim, neither criminal nor civil liability can be imposed upon
her. If, however, she does stop and lend assistance, she should be aware
that if she contrives, perhaps under very difficult circumstances, actually
to make the injured person's condition worse by clumsy ministrations, she
will to that extent be exposed to negligence liability at the suit of her
ungrateful patient.* Moreover, even if her treatment saves the accident
victim's life, she will not ordinarily be able to secure any fee for her services
unless the patient expressly or impliedly solicited them; though it is to be
noted that Canadian courts have on occasion demonstrated a remarkable
gift for divining "implied requests" even from unconscious and suicidal
patients! All in all, the law has not encouraged the Good Samaritan. The
physician has no duty to act as such, but if she assumes that role, she
assumes with it the concomitant duty of care and skill which goes with any
physician/patient relationship.

A cautionary note should be sounded at this point. While the basic
rule remains clear that a doctor is not obliged to intervene, even in emergencies, to aid those who are not her patients, and while, indeed, a doctor
may decline to accept any person as a patient for any reason (or for none
at all),** there is reason to suppose that there may be exceptions to both
those propositions. If, for example, the doctor is the only doctor serving a
remote or isolated community, a court might well declare that the extreme
degree of exclusive dependence reposed by local residents in that lone
practitioner generated a duty of care which would preclude her from turning
away a patient — at least where the condition of the patient was serious

---

* In some provinces, this situation has been corrected by statute. By the Emergency Medical Aid Act
of Alberta, enacted in 1969, a doctor, medical assistant or nurse, gratuitously rendering assistance
in any medical emergency outside a hospital or clinic, is protected from any liability unless *gross*
negligence is shown. Similar protection, remarkably enough, is afforded even to lay people who try
to give first aid at the accident scene. In the same year, Nova Scotia enacted similar provisions, but
chose only to protect physicians. Newfoundland copied the Alberta Act in 1971, Saskatchewan in
1976.

** The issue of when a doctor, for whatever reason, can unilaterally divest himself of a patient, is
considered in Chapter 8, under "The Duty to Attend the Patient".

and time-sensitive and the patient's opportunities to travel in search of alternative care unrealistic. An analogy, albeit somewhat imperfect, might be drawn with the case of a ship's captain, whose exclusive control over the fate of his passengers has been held to engender an actionable duty of care, when a passenger falls overboard, at least to make reasonable efforts to rescue him.[2] In a remote wilderness scenario, the dependence and vulnerability of the sick or injured person, seeking the attention of the only available physician, is surely no less. Another difficult question relates to the potential liability of emergency departments (and their personnel) who incautiously turn patients away. In the English case of *Barnett v. Chelsea & Kensington Hospital Management Committee* (1968),[3] three night watchmen drank tea which had been murderously laced with arsenic. All became violently ill, and presented themselves at the emergency department. A doctor was telephoned, but directed the nurse on duty to send the men home. One of the men died. His widow lost her action against the hospital — but only because it would have been too late anyway to save this man's life. There had, said the judge, been a duty of care, owed by the hospital and its staff to this man, and it had been broken. The action failed simply upon the issue of *causation-in-fact*, addressed later in this chapter.

Obviously, once it is assumed by a physician, the duty of care and skill has many different facets. Every aspect of the physician's conduct, from his availability to the patient to his care in diagnosis and treatment, from his diligence in explaining that treatment to his prudence in making referrals or seeking second opinions, are all facets of the comprehensive duty of care and skill, implicit in the physician/patient relationship.

At risk of stating the obvious, we should perhaps note here that not every aspect of a physician's obligation of care and skill flows strictly from the physician/patient relationship. It is self-evident that in driving his or her car to or from the clinic or hospital each day, a physician owes to other road-users the same duties of care and skill, actionable in negligence, as are owed by any other driver. So too regarding the safety of his premises (his clinic, for example) — a doctor owes duties of care to all manner of visitors, not just patients, to ensure that those premises are reasonably safe, just as he owes such duties as a householder to his domestic guests and visitors. Such duties, interesting though they may be, are outside the scope of this book, since they are part of the general law and not peculiar to a doctor's activities in his professional capacity.

What we shall do in this book is attempt an overview of those duties which arise out of the physician/patient relationship, and which may collectively be regarded as aspects of the physician's duty of care and skill towards the patient. One of these duties — the duty to inform the patient of the nature of proposed treatment and the more significant risks attending it — is a duty governed by principles so recently received into Canadian law, so intricate and so frequently invoked (often alongside other alleged breaches of duty), as to warrant a separate chapter in this book (Chapter 4). The other duties commonly recognized as part and parcel of the general duty of care might be catalogued as follows:

(1)   The duty to attend the patient;

(2)   The duty of due care and skill in diagnosis;

(3)   The duty to maintain adequate and accurate patient records;

(4)   The duty to refer patients in appropriate cases to other physicians, or otherwise seek out specialist advice;

(5)   The duty of due care and skill in treatment, surgical or otherwise: including the duty to provide adequate after-care to patients;

(6)   The duty to communicate diligently with other professionals involved in the patient's case; and

(7)   The duty to supervise, when appropriate, one's junior colleagues or other professionals subject to one's direction.

It would be rash to pretend — and there is no warrant for claiming — that this list is complete; but it is hard to imagine a negligence action against a physician which could not be reduced to one or more of these headings. In Chapter 8, after we have perused in outline the whole structure of a negligence action, we will return to consider each of these duties or topics in turn.

Before we move on to look at the standard of care issue, however, it is important to note a few further points about the duty of care itself. Firstly, physicians often operate as a team, or otherwise in conjunction with other health care professionals. Such people — nurses, radiographers and fellow physicians of varying specialties — will themselves owe to the patient duties of care and skill complementary to that of the physician principally responsible for the patient at any given time. These complementary duties may arise either out of the positions occupied by these other professionals within the organizational structure of the hospital, out of the pattern of treatment (successive referrals to specialists, therapists or technicians of varying function), or out of specific delegations of responsibility expressly made by the treating physician. While the treating physician is ordinarily entitled to rely upon his professional colleagues to do their particular jobs with due care and skill, this does not mean that his own duty is significantly diminished. Rather, the multiplicity of potential defendants (or duty-breakers) generates new responsibilities for the treating physician: responsibilities to monitor or "keep tabs" on those procedures entrusted to the other professionals; to communicate sufficiently with them and with the patient to ensure that nothing is overlooked, inappropriately duplicated, unduly delayed, or "skimped"; and to ensure that the patient is at all times receiving that information to which the newly-refurbished law of informed consent entitles him. Some of these responsibilities we shall encounter in Chapter 8 when considering in detail the physician's duty to communicate with fellow professionals, and to select or supervise employees or subordinates with due care.

A further point concerning the duty of care must now be made, a point which may sound arid and technical, but which has important practical implications. It sometimes happens — very rarely these days — that a doctor's duty of care and skill is held to arise not just as a legally imposed duty ordained by the tort principle of negligence, but as well (or instead), out of a *contract*. Much sophistry and technicality used to surround this issue, but now, for practical purposes, all a doctor needs to know is that if he "contracts" — that is agrees, clearly and for reward or the prospect of some reward — to do a certain thing or achieve a particular result, failure to achieve it may well result in an action for damages for breach of contract in circumstances where the tort of negligence would have no application. If a plastic surgeon says to his patient, "Mr. Bloggs, I believe that surgery might make that scar on your forehead less noticeable", he promises no more than that he will use reasonable care and skill to achieve that happy result. If he fails to show due care and skill, of course, he can be sued for negligence, and quite possibly for breach of contract too. It does not matter much, for in both contexts the surgeon's obligation — to show proper care and skill — is precisely the same, and the disappointed patient, who can only recover his damages "once over", will find little or nothing to choose between the "tortious negligence" and "breach of contract" avenues of litigation. Suppose, however, our plastic surgeon rashly promises something more, and says, "I will so re-model your nose that it will look exactly like this (indicating a picture), without scar or blemish of any kind." If he then fails to fulfil this promise, the disgruntled patient may sue him for breach of contract, even though the hapless surgeon can show that he used heroic diligence and extraordinary skill in performing the surgery. For contractual liability is "strict"; that is, it does not devolve upon fault in any way, as does negligence. If you promise contractually to achieve something and do not achieve it, you are liable for breach of contract. The moral surely needs no pointing: never, however sincere the physician's desire to encourage a patient, should a result be *guaranteed*. Only due care and proper skill should be promised, perhaps with some prediction* of the likelihood of success.

---

* See Chapter 4.

We have discussed the duty of care in this section as if it affected only the physician's obligations to her patient. Ordinarily, that will be so. But it should be recognized that there will be times when a physician will be deemed to owe a legal duty of care to persons who are not her patients at all; so that the finding of a physician/patient relationship is not the sole and exclusive source or touchstone of a legal duty of care. Indeed, duties may be owed by physicians to members of the public at large, to people as yet unknown to them. Suppose, for example, that our physician administers to her patient a drug capable of sudden or insidious soporific effect, then sends him away without inquiring of him whether he came by car and is thinking of driving home. If some member of the public is killed or injured when such a patient falls asleep at the wheel, the physician will certainly be liable to this victim or his bereaved family. Because injury to the public at large was foreseeable to any reasonable person in the doctor's position, she was under a duty of care, owed to all members of the community, to take reasonable steps to protect them from such an occurrence, which duty was conspicuously broken in the example given. Likewise, in *MacPhail v. Desrosiers* (Nova Scotia, 1998),[4] a woman was allowed to drive home only a few hours after undergoing an abortion procedure. She lost control of her vehicle, struck an oncoming vehicle, and sustained serious injuries, as did the occupants of the other car. They too were successful in their negligence action against the clinic staff. An analogous example would be the liability of a psychiatric hospital whose staff neglects to control an obviously dangerous patient. The hospital may be liable in negligence to anyone whom that patient may injure; as was held in the Ontario case of *Lawson v. Wellesley Hospital* (1978).[5]

In the United States, there is a considerable body of case law which imposes negligence liability upon physicians who omit to warn relatives, or other persons foreseeably at risk, when patients present themselves with symptoms of highly contagious diseases, or when mentally ill patients indicate their intentions of harming third parties. Obviously, such situations create a legal and ethical dilemma, since imposing a duty to warn potential victims will inevitably clash with the physician's obligation of confidentiality. Accordingly, we shall defer discussion of such matters until Chapter 11, where the obligation of confidentiality and its proper limits are discussed.

There are other situations, too, where a physician's carelessness may render him liable to someone other than his patient. If the patient is killed by the physician's negligence, the dependants of the patient (and sometimes other family members) will have a statutory right of action, discussed later in this chapter. If the patient is merely injured, claims may be advanced in some provinces by spouses (for deprivation of *consortium,* or marital companionship in all its aspects), by other family members (for lost "guidance, care and companionship") and even by employers (for deprivation of their employee's valuable services). However, the most striking example of a duty owed to a non-patient is surely the case of *Urbanski v. Patel* (Manitoba, 1978),[6] where a physician, performing a tubal ligation and expecting to find an ovarian cyst, found what he thought was precisely that. He removed it, only to realize afterwards that it was an ectopic kidney, and, by reason of a congenital anomaly, the only kidney his patient had possessed. Hoping to spare his daughter a lifetime on dialysis, the patient's father donated a kidney, but the transplant was a failure and the organ was rejected. The *father* successfully sued the surgeon. Apparently then, the surgeon owed a duty of care not only to his patient, but to any close family member who would foreseeably and voluntarily submit to harm in a reasonable attempt to "rescue" the patient, should she be imperilled by the surgeon's negligence.

The *Urbanski* case is regarded by some as going too far, and certainly represents the uttermost limit to which the law will extend physicians' duties of care towards non-patients. Nonetheless, it memorably illustrates the truth, easily overlooked, that a physician's duties may be owed to persons other than his patients, persons indeed whom he may never have met; but who should have been within his contemplation, however anonymously, while the patient was treated.

It should be noted, as a qualification to the foregoing, that the courts will not recognize a duty owed by a health-care professional to a non-patient third party, where such a duty might potentially conflict with the duty owed to his or her patient. Consider, for example, the strange case of *Freeman v. Sutter* (Manitoba, 1996).[7] A young woman sought an abortion, at the persuasion of Freeman, the biological father of the foetus, from Dr. Sutter. The procedure was not successful, the mother elected to bear the child, and when it was safely born, obtained a court order requiring the father to pay maintenance for the support of the child throughout its minority. When the father sued Dr. Sutter in professional negligence for causing him financial loss in this way, the Manitoba Court of Appeal gave him short shrift, saying that as he was not a patient of the defendant physician, no duty of care was owed to him, but only to his patient, the mother, who had not complained of the treatment she received.

Putting such complexities aside, we may reflect that the vast preponderance of the case law dealing with medical negligence deals with liability within the doctor/patient relationship. To that we must now return, to deal with the second element or ingredient in any negligence case.

2.   BREACH OF THE DUTY OF CARE: THE "STANDARD OF CARE" QUESTION

Let us suppose that the first element of a negligence action (the showing of a duty of care owed by the defendant to the plaintiff) has been established. In our context, the mere showing of a true doctor/patient relationship will do the job. Next, the plaintiff-patient must show that that duty of care or of skill was broken in some material aspect. In other words (for it is the same proposition) the patient must show that the standard of care and skill, prescribed by the law, was not attained by the defendant physician.

We have already seen that on this issue, the law is wisely reluctant to tell professionals in other disciplines how to conduct themselves. As one British Columbia judge crisply put it, the "less courts try to tell doctors how to practice medicine, the better." Only in the realm of informed consent, and then only to a limited degree, have the judges methodically declined to treat the collective judgment of the medical profession as a virtually irrefutable yardstick of sufficiency as to both care and competence. Quite simply, and subject only to exceptions of the utmost rarity, a physician need only fear negligence liability when he has fallen short of the standards of skill or care prevailing among his professional peers.

The leading case on this issue is still that of *Crits v. Sylvester* (Ontario, 1956).[8] The defendant in that case was a specialist in anaesthesiology. The plaintiff, a 4-year-old boy, needed a tonsillectomy. In the operating room, Dr. Sylvester injected sodium pentothal which quickly rendered the small patient insensible, enabling Dr. Sylvester to insert a vinyl tube into the child's trachea between the vocal chords, through which the principle anaesthetic, an ether-oxygen mixture, would be administered. After only 30 seconds of subjection to this gaseous mixture, the child was noted to be developing cyanosis. Dr. Sylvester reached swiftly for the "oxygen bag", and so manipulated it that oxygen was forced into the patient's lungs. As soon as the boy's colour improved, Dr. Sylvester began to disconnect the oxygen tube at a point about four inches from the ether can and eight inches from the patient's face. As he did so, he noticed a blue flame between his hand and the ether can, and a violent explosion occurred, causing extensive second and third degree burns to most of the child's head and face. The evidence clearly suggested that this explosion had been caused by static electricity. It was argued that this was a peril which Dr. Sylvester should have foreseen and guarded against, by employing widely recognized precautionary techniques or by turning the flow of oxygen to the ether can off, rather than merely down, while the boy was being "oxygen bagged." Dr. Sylvester was ultimately held liable in negligence for failing to take such measures, but the Ontario Court of Appeal made it clear that such a conclusion was never to be reached lightly. As the Court said, in words which have been frequently quoted in later years:

> The legal principles involved are plain enough but it is not always easy to apply them to particular circumstances. Every medical practitioner must bring to his task a reasonable degree of skill and knowledge and must exercise a reasonable degree of care. He is bound to exercise *that degree of care and skill which could reasonably be expected of a normal, prudent practitioner of the same experience and standing,* and if he holds himself out as a specialist, a higher degree of skill is required of him than of one who does not profess to be so qualified by special training and ability. [Emphasis added.][9]

Later cases have lent a sharper focus to these words, and have corrected in particular some misapprehensions which the phrase "same experience and standing" might conceivably generate. Every physician who holds himself out as qualified to practice medicine will be required at all times to show to each patient not only the same diligence, but also the same competence and skill as would reasonably be expected of the average, reasonably proficient "run-of-the-mill" member of the medical profession. No more. No less — on pain of liability for negligence. This approach seeks to set an objective test, against which the treatment provided at the material time by any defendant physician may be evaluated. The defendant physician need not show that he demonstrated the ultimate in state-of-the-art professional excellence at the crucial period; nor will it necessarily be enough to show that he earnestly "did his best", if his best was not good enough to meet the objective standard of what the average fellow professional would have done in like circumstances. No doctor or surgeon is required by law to meet, at all times or at any, the standards set by those in the vanguard of the profession. At the same time, lapses of care and skill which momentarily depress the standard of performance below the norm set by the generality of the profession, will create the danger of negligence liability. While no physician is required to show megalomaniac fixation with every new development in his area of expertise, a slack and unreflective adherence to old and tried procedures, or a below average measure of inquisitiveness about developments in one's field, may raise this spectre of negligence.

Inexperience, too, can be perilous. It is implicit in the very nature of an objective standard of care and skill that it cannot be qualified to accommodate the subjective circumstances of any individual defendant, and inexperience is just such a subjective or personal circumstance. By way of example, consider Dr. Backstrom, who found himself performing surgery, for the first time, to correct a diagnosed case of de Quervain's disease. In doing so, he severed a nerve in Mrs. McKeachie's wrist, leading to a painful neuroma, partial paralysis of the patient's arm, and development of Sudeck's osteodystrophy. In the litigation which followed *(McKeachie v. Alvarez* [British Columbia, 1970]),[10] he was held negligent, absolutely no allowance being made for his inexperience. A similar fate befell young Dr. Munthali, who, in *Dale v. Munthali* (Ontario, 1977),[11] vainly pleaded his inexperience when sued in negligence for failing, with fatal consequences, to diagnose pneumococcal meningitis. In these and many other cases, the courts have applied the full "average practitioner" standard with undiminished rigour in the interest of protecting patients. Inexperience is treated as a misfortune and a temporary peril, not a privilege or excuse, and the neophyte's best defence is an alert readiness to accept his limitations, and to seek advice and make referrals with due alacrity when challenged with cases to which his powers are not yet equal.

What, it may be asked, of the budding professional who is not even fully qualified yet to practice medicine, but is at a sufficiently advanced stage in his education to be given responsibility for patients? What, in particular, of the liability of interns? It is a curious and perhaps discreditable phenomenon in our law that the standard of care required of interns — or for that matter of those residents who lack a general licence to practice medicine — is still an issue clothed in some doubt. Such professionals-in-training ordinarily and quite legitimately bear the appellation "Doctor" and their conduct and bearing, and the deference accorded to them by other hospital personnel, may afford no clue to the hapless patient that he is being treated by anyone less than a fully qualified physician or specialist.

These considerations were determinative in the leading case of *Fraser v. Vancouver General Hospital* (British Columbia, 1952).[12] Mr. Fraser, a robust man of 31, sustained multiple injuries in a motor vehicle accident, and was duly brought into the defendant hospital's emergency ward. He complained, among other things, of pain and stiffness in his neck. He was examined by the two interns in charge of the ward that night, and x-rays were duly taken and examined by the interns. What they failed to notice, as they sent Mr. Fraser home in the small hours of the morning, was that he had sustained a dislocated fracture of the neck, which had been plainly visible upon the x-ray. A few days later he was dead, the immediate cause of death being a paralysis of the small bowel. Evidently the sympathetic and parasympathetic nerves had been interfered with by the progressive displacement of the dislocated second cervical vertebra. As a result, Mr. Fraser had suffered an adynamic ileus, and the resultant paralysis of the bowel killed him. A jury found the interns negligent for failing to diagnose the cervical fracture and so initiate its prompt stabilization, or, in the alternative, for failing to recognize their own inability to read the x-rays properly. The hospital was "vicariously liable" — a phenomenon we shall look at later — for that negligence. In due course, the Supreme Court of Canada affirmed this entire judgment. Mr. Justice Rand stressed that much more was required of an intern than to be "a mere untutored communicant between [the family physician] and the patient", where he was exercising functions dressed in "all the ritual and paraphernalia of medical service." The judge said further:

> . . . he must use the undertaken degree of skill, and that cannot be less than the ordinary skill of a junior doctor in appreciation of the indications and symptoms of injury before him, as well as an appreciation of his own limitations and of the necessity for caution in everything he does."[13]

That standard — the standard of a "junior" doctor duly aware of his own limitations — had not been met in this case. As we have seen, the standard required of a "junior" physician is precisely the same as that of a more experienced one; a standard which may well be beyond the young professional's capacity, unless, mindful of his inexperience, it is discharged obliquely by promptly invoking the assistance of more senior colleagues.

What remains uncertain is the standard of care the law demands of a student, an intern, or any other incompletely qualified professional who identifies himself as such to the patient. Upon general doctrinal grounds, such a disclosure might be thought to lower the standard of skill demanded by the law towards the intrepid patient who allowed such a novice to practice upon him. But there is no doubt that the law would nonetheless stress the novice's obligation to show extreme caution, and to refer the case to more experienced professionals as soon as a reasonable person in his position of inexperience would feel himself approaching the bounds of his own competence. At the same time, those fully qualified professionals working with a student, an intern or a novice physician may well find that their own legal responsibilities are augmented, and that their duty of care to the patient involves on such occasions the obligation to keep an eye upon, if not actively to supervise, their junior brethren.

Happily, the law is in a more settled state where the liability of specialists is concerned. A quick glance back to *Crits v. Sylvester*[14] will remind us that when a professional person holds himself out to the public in general, or a patient in particular, as being a specialist in some sub-discipline of the profession, a higher standard of skill (that of the fellow specialist of average competence in that area) is automatically required by the law. That is by no means a standard of infallibility, however. In *Johnston v. Wellesley Hospital* (Ontario, 1970),[15] the "slush treatment", used by the defendant, a specialist in dermatology, to remove the acne scarring from the plaintiff's face, was an extremely painful failure. Yet the treatment given had been in accordance with the orthodoxy favoured by other dermatologists, and Dr. Williams was accordingly exonerated of any actionable negligence. The worst that could be said — and that, only in retrospect — was that he had committed an error of judgment in allowing the carbon dioxide slush to be in contact with the patient's skin for so long. He had nonetheless met the required standard, that of his fellow specialists.

It was not so in the older case of *McCaffrey v. Hague* (Manitoba, 1949),[16] where Mr. McCaffrey, an elderly farmer afflicted with eczema on his legs, was referred by his rural general practitioner to the defendant, a radiologist in Winnipeg. When Mr. McCaffrey showed up for his 23rd and final x-ray treatment, it was administered using a contact and cavity therapy apparatus, apt for the treatment of deep-seated cancers but hardly so for skin problems. Not surprisingly, Mr. McCaffrey's legs were very badly burned. The judge stated emphatically that "A higher degree of skill is required from one who holds himself out to be a specialist, as the defendant did."[17] The standard was that of fellow specialists in the relevant sub-discipline. The defendant, who somewhat ingenuously testified that he had used this machine because it was the only one he happened to have in the office on that particular day, had signally failed to meet that enhanced requirement of skill which the law demanded of him as a "specialist."

In the ordinary medical negligence case application of the "average fellow professional" standard of care and skill presents little or no doctrinal difficulty. Such problems as do arise tend to be practical ones; for example, the problem of ascertaining just what the prevailing standards and practices of the profession are. Sometimes, the expert witnesses called by each side will differ fundamentally in opinion as to what the reasonable physician would have done in the circumstances, forcing the Court to choose between their conflicting perceptions. Sometimes, it will be apparent that upon a particular point of medical theory, the medical profession is itself starkly divided. Such problems will be addressed in Chapter 7 when considering how negligence is proved.

For the time being, it can be said that in applying the "reasonable fellow practitioner" standard of care and skill, the courts typically take into account certain rather obvious factors. Where a patient's condition is known to the physician (or ought to be known to a reasonably alert and competent physician in her position) to be fraught with peril, the degree of care required will be proportionately greater; for the reasonable doctor (like any other reasonable person in any walk of life) will govern her conduct according to the measure of risk which the situation seems to engender.

Consider, for example, the Alberta case of *Edmison v. Boyd* (1987).[18] Mrs. Edmison was overweight and suffering from renal rickets, a heart murmur and dwarfism. She was pregnant, and the defendant obstetrician noted that she was "high risk", and would probably have to undergo Caesarean delivery. But as the pregnancy progressed, he offered only routine care, taking no special steps to monitor developments by ultrasound or biophysical tests. When he eventually realized that the baby was smaller than normal, and almost static in growth, he ordered tests for a week hence. But by that stage — the 37th week — it was too late. Before the test could be run, the plaintiff went into labour. Hospital staff alerted the defendant obstetrician to developments, yet it took him three quarters of an hour to arrive from his office, some five minutes distant. By the time he arrived, fetal heartbeat had ceased, and the baby had been delivered with her umbilical chord wrapped around her neck. She was resuscitated, but was left a spastic quadriplegic. Both the trial judge and the Alberta Court of Appeal found the defendant negligent. Given his perception that mother and child were in a high risk category, extraordinary care would have been shown by the reasonable, average obstetrician, and was accordingly required of this defendant. "Something more than ordinary care should have been apparent", as the trial judge put it. Timely tests should have been conducted, and the pregnancy monitored with particular watchfulness. Consultations with other physicians who had been involved in her case should have been more assiduously conducted, and discussions with the mother herself should have been more frequent and more thorough. Even on the day of the birth, the defendant had shown an inadequate measure of urgency, both in giving instructions to the hospital staff, and in speedily attending at the delivery himself. Had he been there with proper swiftness, he could have performed a forceps delivery and spared the baby some ten minutes of "strangulation." While the defendant had not known precisely why the baby was in jeopardy, he had perceived the risk. He should have "expected the unexpected", and paid special consideration accordingly.

Not only the special vulnerability of the particular patient, but any other factor augmenting the perceivable risk, will be regarded by the law as enhancing the degree of care to be taken by a physician, both in monitoring the patient's condition and in taking such precautionary measures as any sensible professional would show in the circumstances. Sometimes, for example, a physician using a new or experimental treatment must recognize the need for special care and attention in doing so — quite apart from the greater obligation (discussed in Chapter 4) to explain to the patient the attendant risks of such new therapy. In *Neufeld v. McQuitty* (Alberta, 1979),[19] for example, Mrs. Neufeld, having already undergone a mastectomy, a bilateral ovariectomy, and various forms of radiotherapy and chemotherapy, was found still to be suffering from cancer, and it was decided to treat her with two drugs, adriamycin and vincristine. The former, described professionally as a "nasty" drug because of its extreme toxicity, was, as the judge put it, "a novel, if not experimental" form of treatment. It was known that any extravasation would cause severe burning. This risk, it was held, carried with it an increased obligation on the part of the physician administering the drug to show special care in the use of the intravenous equipment. The adriamycin did cause severe damage by extravasation into the plaintiff's hand, but while stressing that the standard of care must always be commensurate with the perceived risk, the Court held that the defendant physician had not been negligent. Like Dr. Ahsan in the case of *Chubey v. Ahsan*,[20] Dr. McQuitty had been reasonably engaged in a very perilous method of therapy. Like Dr. Ahsan too, he had by misfortune visited harm upon the patient; but like Dr. Ahsan, he was shown to have used that measure of care and skill appropriate for confronting the perceived peril. In such circumstances, the misfortune which befalls a patient cannot be ascribed to negligence. At worst it is categorized as a non-culpable and non-compensable "error of judgment." More often, as in Dr. McQuitty's case, it may more properly be termed sheer misfortune.

In short, then, the reasonable physician will show a degree of care and skill, in every case, commensurate with the risks reasonably to be perceived. The likelihood of a risk's occurrence and the gravity of the consequences should it transpire, are factors which the hypothetical "reasonable physician" will weigh in the balance when governing his actions. Other such factors include the relative ease or difficulty of prudential or precautionary techniques and the availability or relative effectiveness of alternative therapies with lesser or different attendant risks. If this seems rather obvious, so it should. The law, once again, is trying to set and maintain reasonable, comprehensible and attainable standards of professional performance. It does not demand infallibility.

At this juncture, it is unfortunately necessary that we consider, if only to dismiss it, the heretical doctrine known as "the locality rule." For many years, there has been a sporadic tendency for Canadian judges to express themselves in such terms as: "The medical man must possess and use, that reasonable degree of learning and skill possessed by practitioners in *similar communities* in similar cases."[21] Such language seems to say that the law will demand a lower standard of care or skill from a rural practitioner than from his urban counterpart. It should be emphatically stated here that this is not the law, but an impolitic fallacy born (as all respectable authorities, judicial and academic, acknowledge) of the loose use of language. It is true, and perhaps inevitable, that a medical practitioner far from any major urban centre will have many disadvantages which may diminish his success rate or efficacy of performance compared with those of his urban colleagues. Hospitals with their sophisticated facilities and ample specialized staff may be too distant for convenient or timely use and second opinions from specialist colleagues may be more difficult to obtain when needed, as may access to all the current literature. Even so, it is hard to see why a rural practitioner should be held to a lower standard of care or skill, when working within the limitations and exigencies of his geographical situation, than would be expected of his colleagues in the city. Allowances should, and will, be made for the difficulties placed upon rural practitioners by their physical circumstances and excusably limited resources; just as the law makes allowances for an urban practitioner performing an emergency operation at a roadside accident. But with the medical profession seeking to ensure a high and consistent minimum standard of proficiency upon all its members, there seems no excuse for the law to stipulate disparate standards of care or skill depending upon the character of the neighbourhood in which a physician practices. Despite the occasional recrudescence of loose judicial remarks which appear to lend support to such a discriminatory approach, it is certainly not sound or respectable legal doctrine.

Readers may have noticed that whenever the foregoing text speaks of "reasonable care and skill", or the care and skill to be expected of the "reasonable practitioner", the standard of "reasonableness" seems always to be assessed by reference to purely medical, or clinical criteria. The same has been uniformly true of the case law, both in Canada and other common law jurisdictions. In recent years, however, a new and troubling "standard of care" issue has begun to present itself, even if so far it has received more overt attention and discussion from those learned in medicine than from legal scholars. The issue is quite simply this. To what extent is a physician entitled, when treating a patient, to temper or qualify his or her clinical judgment by reference to economic considerations, and provide a less than optimal standard of treatment in deference to "cost-containment" considerations? The pressures exerted upon physicians, by governments and by hospital administrators, to keep down costs are both real and understandable. Are physicians at liberty to yield to such pressures even if it means some displacement of medical judgment and the provision of inferior treatments? Or is such a stance a breach of the standard of care required by law?[22]

As yet, there is very little guidance in the case law on the subject, which may seem strange but is readily explicable by reference to the relative novelty of the issue, and by reasons founded upon doctrines of causation-in-fact, discussed later in this chapter.[23] Such authority as there is, however, suggests that the physician who allows his or her clinical judgment to be influenced by cost-saving considerations does so at the risk of liability, for the "reasonable standard of care" demanded by the law seems to accommodate only judgments based upon purely medical or scientific considerations. Furthermore, the developing law as to a physician's "fiduciary" responsibilities, discussed in Chapter 11, tends to the same conclusion by stressing the doctor's duty of undivided loyalty to the patient, undeflected by competing loyalties to the hospital, say, or to those governmental agencies which may be financing the provision of care.

The leading American authority, *Wickline v. State of California*,[24] was decided in 1986, and centred upon the responsibilities of a physician who had failed to insist upon extended post-operative hospitalization for his patient, allowing his clinical judgment to be overcome, he confessed, by his concern for the cost-containment agenda of Medi-Cal, the "health care payors" involved in the case. The California Court of Appeal was uncompromising in its condemnation of this approach, observing that "The physician who complies without protest with the limitations imposed by a third party payor, when his medical judgment dictates otherwise, cannot avoid his ultimate responsibility for the patient's care" – insisting that "While we recognize, realistically, that cost consciousness has become a permanent feature of the health care system, it is essential that cost limitation programs *not be permitted to corrupt medical judgment.*" [Emphasis supplied]

It is noticeable that more recently, without being referred to the *Wickline* case, a judge in British Columbia has reached exactly the same conclusion. In *Law Estate v. Simice* (British Columbia, 1994),[25] Mr. Law, a very unhealthy man of 51, had died of an intercranial aneurism while under the care of the defendant physicians, who (it was held) had failed in various respects to show reasonable care and skill in interpreting their patient's symptoms. They were duly held liable for his death; but what is interesting for present purposes are the following observations of Mr. Justice Spencer, which though not forming a binding part of the reasons for his decision, are unequivocal and forceful statements of a clear position:

> I must observe that throughout this case there were a number of times when doctors testified that they feel constrained by the British Columbia Medical Insurance Plan and by the British Columbia Medical Association standards to restrict their requests for CT scans as diagnostic tools. No doubt such sophisticated equipment is limited and costly to use. No doubt there are budgetary restraints on them. But this is a case where, in my opinion, those constraints worked against the patient's interest by inhibiting the doctors in their judgment of what should be done for him. That is to be deplored. I understand that there are budgetary problems confronting the health care system. I raise it in passing only to point out that there were a number of references to the effect of financial restraint on the treatment of this patient.

I respectfully say it is something to be carefully considered by those who are responsible for the provision of medical care and those who are responsible for financing it. I also say that if it comes to a choice between a physician's responsibility to his or her individual patient and his or her responsibility to the medicare system overall, the former must take precedence in a case such as this. The severity of the harm that may occur to the patient who is permitted to go undiagnosed is far greater than the financial harm that will occur to the medicare system if one more CT scan procedure only shows the patient is not suffering from a serious medical condition.[26]

It is important to note that these strictures are confined to a particular context, that of a physician in his or her dealing with a particular patient. They do not address the question of the potential liability (if any) of hospitals and those who administer them, when the standards of care provided fall due to financial constraints. Nor do they purport to deal with the dilemma of the physician who finds herself serving on those very hospital committees whose task it is to allocate and priorize the expenditure of diminishing resources. In the vital context of the doctor-patient relationship, however, the apparent refusal of the Courts to dilute the physician's required standard of care by admitting economic considerations ensures the preservation within the system of a healthy tension: for as one American scholar has observed, "Cost containment has advocates aplenty; if the patient cannot count on the support of his own physician, he may have no-one to protect his interests."[27]

3. DAMAGES

Let us suppose that a physician, owing a duty of care to her patient, has broken her duty of care to that patient by failing, perhaps very conspicuously, to live up to the required standard of care. Let us suppose too that the plaintiff has been able to convince the Court of this by incontrovertible evidence. It by no means follows that the plaintiff will win his action, for it is an indispensable ingredient of any cause of action in negligence that the plaintiff show he has suffered damage. Damage, that is, of a legally compensable kind, caused by the defendant's breach of duty. The breach of duty, in other words, is not a tort or legally compensable wrong in and of itself. Carelessness or ineptitude, even in flagrant breach of duty, is not actionable "in a vacuum." It is damage, the last essential element in the conceptual framework of negligence, which is necessary and sufficient to complete a potentially successful cause of action against the physician.

Several quite distinct issues arise here, all of great importance. They can conveniently be categorized as follows:

(1) The issue of causation-in-fact;

(2) The doctrine of remoteness of damage; and

(3) The evaluation of legally protected interests; the question of "quantum."

Each of these headings presents its own difficulties. Let us briefly look at them in turn.

(a) The Issue of Causation-in-fact

This issue boils down to a self-evident proposition. A patient who wishes to sue his doctor for negligence must show a duty of care owed to him, a breach of that duty, and damage. But not "any old damage" will do. It must be damage which as a factual matter of cause-and-effect results from the breach of duty. The classic legal approach to this essentially common sense factual question has been the so-called "but for" test. The Court asks itself, "Would the plaintiff have suffered this item of harm (or suffered it so extensively or so early in life) but for the breach of duty committed by the defendant physician?" If the answer is "Yes, he would have suffered it anyway", then that damage was not caused, in fact, by the negligent breach of duty. But if the answer is negative, the breach of duty is deemed to be the cause-in-fact of that harm, and the Court proceeds to the further questions of remoteness and, if necessary, of quantum.

The case of *Mang v. Moscovitz* (Alberta, 1982)[28] will serve to illustrate the point. Mrs. Amy Mang, 31, the mother of two small children, went into hospital for a routine therapeutic abortion by dilatation and suction curettage, followed by an abdominal tubal ligation. She came out a severely spastic quadriplegic, incapable of speech and requiring constant nursing care. She had suffered, it appeared, hypoxic encephalopathy during the course of the operation, a condition evidently caused by an air embolism. At trial there was evidence of carelessness during the operation by an intern, E, who initially failed in his efforts to intubate Mrs. Mang prior to the abortion, and subsequently contrived to pierce her bladder with a surgical knife at the commencement of the tubal ligation. Both of these blunders, however, had been promptly and efficiently corrected by more senior personnel. Neither had caused real damage, and neither — and this was the crucial point — had in any way contributed causally to Mrs. Mang's ultimate plight. "But for" these negligent blunders, events would have unfolded just as they did. The intern's negligence was not the cause-in-fact of any of the damage now complained of, and the plaintiff accordingly lost her case.

There are times when a plaintiff will find it very hard to prove causation-in-fact — the nexus between the defendant's breach of duty and the plaintiff's sufferings — upon the balance of probabilities, as the law requires.* This may be particularly so in the context of medical negligence, where the causal sources of particular symptoms or sufferings may be highly speculative, exceedingly diverse or completely unknown to science. In such circumstances, the courts have sometimes been persuaded to soften the rigours of the "but for" test, so as to relieve the injured patient who has proved a negligent breach of duty by his physician from the need to go further and "prove the unprovable" by establishing that such breach of duty actually caused his present sufferings. In other words, when faced with insuperable obscurities of fact upon the issue of causation, the courts, rather than apply the "but for" test to the undoing of a plaintiff, have sometimes "cut the Gordian knot", and resolved the issue, as between the innocent patient and the duty-breaking doctor, in favour of the former. This has happened in two types of situation.

The first is where more than one doctor has broken his or her duty to the same patient. Each was working upon him simultaneously and one of them, in breach of his duty of care and skill, inflicted harm on the patient; but it cannot later be determined which of them did so. To apply the "but for" test here, requiring the plaintiff to show on a balance of probabilities that the one or the other doctor caused him hurt, would enable both doctors — both, remember, shown to be in breach of duty — to escape liability completely, sheltering behind the impenetrable obscurity of the facts. It is clear, though, that that is not what happens. Rather, the law in such circumstances shifts the burden of proof to the duty-breaking physicians, and requires that each show it was not his negligence which caused the harm. Failing that, they will be required to share the blame and foot the bill in equal shares.

It is important to notice the limitations of this principle, a principle commonly known as the Rule in *Cook v. Lewis*.[29] It applies only where multiple defendants have all been in breach of their duties of care to a plaintiff in circumstances where the evidence is utterly obscure as to which of their respective acts of negligence actually caused the plaintiff's loss. It will accordingly never operate to impose liability upon someone who is wholly blameless. In particular, it does not apply to the scenario in which just one member of a surgical team has evidently been negligent, but where it is impossible in the aftermath to say which of those various persons committed the blunder. The Rule in *Cook v. Lewis* will not, in such a situation, lump the innocent together with the guilty and require each to

---

* The nature of a plaintiff's burden of proof is explained in Chapter 1.

prove his innocence, much less compel them all to share the legal responsibility. In a 1976 decision of the Supreme Court of Canada,[30] it was made quite clear that in such cases, the plaintiff must still bear the burden, presumptively an impossible one, of bringing home the charge of negligence to one or other of the defendants. *Cook v. Lewis* can be used to infer causal responsibility on the part of duty-breakers, but never as a means of inferring the breach of duty itself.

If such evidentiary niceties of "burden-shifting" and the like seem obscure and abstruse, it should be remembered that in practice, such technicalities may be decisive of difficult cases. The same can be said of another supposed burden-shifting rule relating to cause-in-fact, which in recent years was a source of heated controversy in Canada, and anxiety too, to those who represented health-care professionals. The rule in question is known as the rule in *McGhee v. National Coal Board*,[31] after a decision of the House of Lords, the ultimate court of appeal in the United Kingdom. McGhee's work involved prolonged exposure to abrasive brick dust. His employer, the defendant Board, provided no washing facilities at the workplace, so that poor McGhee had to cycle home each day caked in an abrasive patina of perspiration and brick dust. He contracted dermatitis and sued his employer, but was quickly met by the "but for" test of causation-in-fact. To be sure, the employers had owed McGhee a duty of care, and had broken it; but McGhee could not positively show that the resultant delays in removing the daily accumulations of brick dust each day were what had caused his dermatitis. The House of Lords, reversing the lower courts, said that it did not matter. They said that where a plaintiff could show that by a negligent breach of duty, a defendant had created a risk or materially increased (perhaps only slightly) an existing risk of a particular kind of harm; and where harm of that very kind had subsequently materialized; the law would infer, in the absence of evidence to the contrary, that it was the breach of duty which caused the harm. In other words — and one very distinguished judge in *McGhee* made this quite explicit — the burden of proof would be upon the defendant duty-breaker to show that his negligence did *not* cause the plaintiff's harm.

Such a principle is particularly powerful in medical contexts, where the precise sequence of cause and effect in the development of a patient's symptoms is often cloaked in complete scientific obscurity, and where, as a result, it may be impossible to say which of several causes (including, it may be, a doctor's careless blunder) actually caused a particular item of harm. In such cases, relieving the patient of the burden of proving the unprovable cause, and shifting it onto the shoulders of the errant doctor, dramatically "changes the rules of the game" so far as litigation against physicians is concerned.

Until quite recently, the *McGhee* doctrine seemed to be taking firm root here, being adopted by no less than six appellate Courts in this country.* In some instances, this was done in medical cases. However, in 1988, the House of Lords returned to the issue, and in an abrupt turnabout, declared that their judgments in *McGhee* had been misinterpreted, and that the case had effected no such radical change in the law as had been widely supposed. There was no basis in legal principle, they said, for "shifting" the burden of proof from where it ordinarily lay, on the shoulders of the plaintiff, however obscure and impervious to scientific analysis might be the sequence of cause and effect leading up to the plaintiff's injury. This turnabout occurred in *Wilsher v. Essex Area Health Authority*,[32] to which we must now turn.

The infant plaintiff in *Wilsher* was born nearly three months premature, and immediate measures were taken to monitor the partial pressure of oxygen in his arterial blood. A sensor, mounted on a catheter, was passed through the umbilical artery into the aorta. By mistake, and in breach of the duty of due care and skill, the catheter was inserted into a vein instead, resulting in false PO_2 readings, taken from the heart instead of the aorta. The physicians on duty saw the X-ray but failed to notice the mistake, which remained undetected for several hours. During that period, excessive levels of oxygen were administered in reliance on the false readings. It had since been learned that the baby was suffering from retrolental fibroplasia, resulting in partial blindness. Voluminous expert evidence adduced at trial established that there was an irreconcilable conflict of opinion as to the cause of this affliction, some experts regarding it as a sad but familiar complication of the very fact of premature birth; others inclining to the view that it had been caused by the negligent conduct of the PO_2 monitoring procedures. Since there seemed little doubt that over-administration of oxygen might in some measure increase the risk of this symptom, the plaintiffs urged the Courts, in these circumstances, to apply *McGhee* and resolve the causation-in-fact issue in their favour. The lower Courts did so; but the House of Lords rejecting the so-called *McGhee* doctrine as we have seen, ordered a new trial. The burden of proof as to causation-in-fact would not, they said, shift to the defendants whenever their negligence could be shown to have created or augmented a risk. The question would always remain whether the plaintiff had produced enough evidence to warrant the inference that, on a balance of probabilities, the breach of duty had caused the damage.

---

* The Federal Court of Appeal, and those of British Columbia, Manitoba, New Brunswick, Nova Scotia and Saskatchewan.

As this sentence suggests, plaintiffs would be assisted in this context by two considerations. First, said the House of Lords, it must be remembered that "scientific proof", proof beyond a peradventure or even beyond reasonable doubt, has never been required of plaintiffs in civil proceedings — in contrast with the criminal law, where proof beyond a reasonable doubt is of course the norm. All a plaintiff need do is persuade the Court that on a balance of probabilities — that is, more likely than not — the physician's breach of duty caused the patient's injury. Secondly, it was observed that in reaching such a conclusion, a court was entitled to have resort to "a robust and pragmatic approach to the facts", meaning, it seems, that commonsense principles of reasonable inference may be employed to supply gaps in the chain of cause-and-effect as supported by hard evidence.

Canadian authority, swift to follow the authority of *McGhee* just a few years previously, was equally quick in abandoning it, and adopting the analysis in *Wilsher*. The crucial Canadian case was *Snell v. Farrell*,[33] an appeal from New Brunswick which was decided by the Supreme Court of Canada in 1990. Mrs. Snell, aged 70, was advised by Dr. Farrell, an ophthalmologist, to undergo cataract surgery, to be performed under local anaesthetic. In accordance with standard practice, a needle was inserted into the retrobulbar muscles behind the eyeball. As he performed this task, Dr. Farrell noted a slight discolouration below the eye, suggestive of a small retrobulbar bleed. Expert evidence was uniform in insisting that the proper course, when this fairly common contingency occurs, is to discontinue the operation. But Dr. Farrell, convinced that the haemorrhage was very small in this instance, proceeded to complete the surgery. After the operation it became clear that the bleeding had intensified, and when after some months the vitreous chamber cleared itself of blood, it was obvious that the optic nerve had atrophied, with resultant loss of sight in that eye. On behalf of Dr. Farrell, it was argued that the optic nerve atrophy might have resulted from a stroke in the back of the eye — an eventuality not uncommon among patients who, like Mrs. Snell, suffered from high blood pressure and diabetes. It was argued that Mrs. Snell had failed to prove that it was Dr. Farrell's ill-advised proceedings which had caused Mrs. Snell to lose the sight of her eye. But the New Brunswick Courts entered judgment for Mrs. Snell, and the Supreme Court of Canada, explicitly adopting the analysis in the *Wilsher* case and rejecting the *McGhee* doctrine, affirmed that Dr. Farrell should be held liable. To adopt this stance is not to indulge in mere speculation, as the Court stressed: rather, it allows commonsense inferences of what is probable and what is not, to be used to eke out the affirmative evidence provided by a plaintiff. Otherwise, the physician who has broken his duty of care and skill might be allowed to shelter behind the aetiological uncertainties of medicine, in defiance of justice and good sense.

We cannot unfortunately leave the issue of causation-in-fact without addressing a couple of other vexed issues. The former of these is one which our courts are addressing more consistently than in the past, though the approach they are taking is not self-evidently a just one. The problem is sometimes called the "loss of a chance" problem, and is well illustrated by the leading English authority, *Hotson v. East Berkshire Area Health Authority*,[34] decided by the House of Lords in 1987. Young Hotson, aged 13, fell out of a tree he was climbing, and sustained an acute traumatic fracture separation of the left femoral epiphysis. The defendant physicians failed to diagnose or treat his injury for five days. In the event, the boy suffered avascular necrosis of the epiphysis of the hip joint, resulting in a permanent deformity of the left hip, wasting of the left leg, and severely impaired mobility. The trial judge, reviewing the scientific evidence before him, concluded that even if there had been timely diagnosis and treatment, there was a 75 per cent chance that avascular necrosis would have developed anyway, in the wake of this injury. Both the trial judge and the Court of Appeal awarded the young plaintiff a sum representing the value of the 25 per cent. chance that he would have been cured. But the House of Lords said that all these judges were wrong. A plaintiff, said their Lordships, must always prove on a balance of probabilities that any item of harm, for which he seeks compensation, was in fact caused by the defendant's breach of duty. That means the plaintiff must show a "50 per cent plus" probability that his loss or injury was so caused. If he can only show a 49 per cent probability, or less (as in the *Hotson* case) he should recover nothing. Compensation should not be given for the statistical chance (less than a preponderant probability) that the injury might have materialized. Conversely, if a plaintiff *can* surmount this hurdle and convince the Court that upon, say, a 51 per cent probability his injuries were caused by the defendant's breach of duty, (his failure, perhaps to diagnose or treat his condition appropriately) that plaintiff will be entitled to damages reflecting the entire loss, without any "discount" to reflect the chance that even appropriate treatment might have failed.

This remarkably inflexible "all or nothing" approach, which far from being logically inevitable, contrasts strongly with the methods adopted in European legal systems, seems for the time being to be firmly entrenched in Canadian case law, having recently been reaffirmed by the Supreme Court of Canada in *Laferrière c. Lawson* (Quebec, 1991).[35] It explains the result reached in another recent Canadian case, *Cabral v. Gupta*,[36] which we used as our third case study at the start of Chapter 5, and will repay further reflection in light of the foregoing analysis.

Finally, there is a complexity which has only surfaced relatively recently, only in medical negligence cases and so far, it would seem, only in Ontario. In the case of *Meringolo v. Oshawa General Hospital* (Ontario 1991),[37] a patient sustained brain-damage during a bronchoscopy, leaving him in a permanent vegetative coma. The trial judge, in what most would have considered an entirely orthodox approach, reviewed all the evidence, expert and otherwise, and concluded that the defendant doctors had not broken their duty of care and skill. In doing so, he expressed a preference for the opinions of the doctors' medical experts, over those called by the defendants. He then declared that in these circumstances he need express no firm conclusion as to what did in truth cause the patient's brain damage. The Court of Appeal reversed that judgment, saying that it had taken an erroneous approach to the issues. All questions of breach of duty and whether any such breach caused the harm should have been deferred until a wholly antecedent question of fact — a far more fundamental issue of causation — had been decided; namely, just how did the plaintiff come to sustain brain-damage that day? Whenever such issues are a matter of debate or contestation, it is only after deciding that fundamental question that the legal questions of duty, breach of duty, and causation-in-fact should be addressed. The Court's concern here seems to be with the dangers of "tunnel vision", since once a finding of breach of duty is made, or, as in *Meringolo* itself, a finding that none was committed, a court may all too easily be drawn into a facile conclusion as to causation-in-fact, or decide that no such finding need even be made. The *Meringolo* doctrine, adding a new preliminary question to the reasoning in medical negligence cases, has taken firm root in Ontario law. It remains to be seen whether judges in other provinces will feel persuaded to follow it.

(b) Remoteness of Damage: The Issue of "Proximate Cause"

A quite different issue attending the "damage" component of negligence concerns the above-noted two phrases, which are used interchangeably to refer to the same idea. This is not a simple commonsense, factual idea, like causation-in-fact, but rather is a separate and logically subsequent idea, born of law and public policy. The law recognizes that any human action may have many consequences, some immediate, some long-term, some obvious and expected, others farfetched and beyond the scope of ordinary human prevision. To hold a person liable for all the consequences of his negligent actions would be impractical and unfair. At some point, litigation must end, and accounts be closed. For this reason the law has devised rules of *remoteness of damage,* which declare that some consequences of a negligent act are too "remote" or too tenuously consequential to form the subject-matter of an action for damages. In such cases, it may well be beyond doubt that as a factual matter of cause-and-effect, on any application of the "but for" test considered above, the particular item of damage was caused by the defendant's breach of duty. But the law, applying its remoteness of damage rules, may say that nonetheless the defendant need not pay damages in respect of that item. It is just "too remote" or "insufficiently proximate" to be recoverable.

What, then, is the applicable criterion governing remoteness of damage in Canadian law? The answer to this question was laid down in a series of cases in the 1960s, the two landmark decisions being known, oddly, as the *Wagon Mound Cases, No. 1 and No. 2.*[38] These two cases were decided in 1961 and 1966 respectively by the Judicial Committee of the Privy Council, then as now the final court of appeal from many Commonwealth jurisdictions. Between them, these two cases, both dealing with the consequences of a fuel-oil spillage and resultant fire in Sydney harbour, laid down the following test. A consequence of a breach of duty will be considered sufficiently proximate (that is, not too remote) to be compensable in damages if it is of a general type or kind which *ought to have been foreseen* as a reasonable possibility (though not necessarily as very probable) by a reasonable person in the defendant's position, giving consideration, just before the breach of duty occurred, to the likely consequences of any such breach on his or her part. This "reasonable foreseeability" test may sound vague, and it is — but its very vagueness allows the courts a good measure of "flexibility" in order to do justice between the parties. A court can give free rein to its sense of fairness in drawing the line, in any given case, between those results of a negligent act for which the defendant should be made to pay, and those which should remain uncompensated.

We have already seen cases in which the remoteness of damage issue was hotly debated. In *Leonard v. Knott,*[39] for example, it was unsuccessfully argued that the risk of a patient's death from a severe reaction to the intravenous pyelography was so slight and unforeseeable that it should be regarded as too remote to be recoverable. The Court considered that the risk, though statistically small, was foreseeable, and foreseeable as a possibility so grave that a reasonable doctor would not disregard it. Damages were recoverable accordingly for the patient's death. Contrast this with the case of *Worth v. Royal Jubilee Hospital* (British Columbia, 1980),[40] in which the same court held that a psychiatric patient and placidyl addict could not recover for the paraplegia she sustained when, taking advantage of a lapse in custodial care or supervision, she scaled a wall and fell thirty feet. It was adjudged that nothing in her conduct would have alerted reasonable hospital personnel to foresee an attempt at "elopement", least of all by such a perilous route.

Simple, vague and inherently flexible, the foreseeability test of remoteness is sometimes criticized for introducing an element of unpredictability into the case law. But its status as sound law is not in doubt. Sometimes, however, complicating factors enter the scene. An example of this is the famous *thin skull rule*. A plaintiff will sometimes recover full compensation for injuries sustained due to the negligence of another, even though those injuries greatly exceed in magnitude anything which a reasonable person in the defendant's position might reasonably have foreseen. This happens when a plaintiff proves to have been suffering from some latent frailty — haemophilia, perhaps, or some condition rendering the bones unusually brittle — so that the defendant's negligence, which would foreseeably only slightly injure a "normal" person, catastrophically harms the plaintiff. In such cases, the "thin skull rule" provides that the plaintiff shall recover not only for that measure of harm which might reasonably have been expected, but for the full measure of harm actually sustained. At first sight, this might seem to contravene the foreseeability test of remoteness, since it involves compensating the plaintiff for damages much greater in magnitude than might have been expected. But this apparent disparity is rationalized by stressing that the foreseeability test only relates to the general type or kind of harm suffered. If the harm actually incurred was of such a foreseeable kind (so the argument goes) the fact that the *extent* of such harm, within the foreseeable category, was beyond the limits of reasonable prevision, is treated as an irrelevance.

Cases in which the thin skull rule has been explicitly used in the medical negligence context are exceedingly rare. Probably this is because a doctor by the very nature of her calling is trained to anticipate and to take timely precautionary measures to test or allow for the peculiar frailties and idiosyncracies, physical and mental, of individual patients. There can be no doubt, however, that a physician who negligently inflicted harm upon a patient who, by virtue of some truly latent vulnerability, suffered more extravagantly as a result than would a "normal" person, would be responsible to the full extent of the harm actually done. More frequent are those somewhat different cases — commonly called *crumbling skull* cases — in which a defendant physician has not by his negligence triggered a latent or clandestine predisposition to harm, but rather has exacerbated or accelerated the deterioration of a previously manifest or discoverable malady. In such a case, the Court will face the difficult task of deciding whether, and to what extent, the physician hastened or augmented sufferings which had already been in some measure inevitable, even before his intervention. In such a case, the physician will be liable only for that superadded dimension of suffering which was his contribution to the patient's plight.

It is not uncommon for the negligent behaviour of more than one person to be visited cumulatively or successively upon a plaintiff. Such cases are the stuff of interminable debate in the legal textbooks. Usually, courts tend to hold all the negligent parties responsible for the harm they collectively cause — holding them, as we say, "jointly and severally liable", while proclaiming and apportioning the respective degrees of responsibility, in percentage terms, amongst them. Such a course is provided for by statute in every province. When this happens, the injured party can enforce his judgment for the full amount of his loss against any one of those found responsible: and that luckless one, having paid, must then "seek contribution or indemnity" from his fellow defendants, in proportion to the measure of responsibility judicially allotted to them.

From time to time, though, one physician's negligence towards, say, a patient, will be followed by another act of negligence by another person, so extreme, so unexpectable or otherwise so manifestly overwhelming in its significance as to make the initial act of negligence seem insignificant as a source of the ultimate catastrophe. These cases exemplify the legal phenomenon of *novus actus interveniens,* a drastic "all-or-nothing" doctrine which is spurned by the judges in all but the clearest cases in favour of *joint and several liability,* with its flexible regime of apportionment, outlined above.

A good example of *novus actus interveniens* occurred in the important Ontario case of *Yepremian v. Scarborough General Hospital* (1978).[41] Tony Yepremian, 19, had felt ill for days, with extreme thirst and frequency of urination, as well as nausea. A general practitioner, Dr. G, diagnosed tonsillitis and pharyngitis, and sent him home with medication, advising him that he might quench his thirst with soft drinks. His condition worsened that evening, with the onset of hyperventilation, vomiting, and continued frequency of urination. His brothers took him to Scarborough General Hospital, where he was examined in the Emergency Department by Dr. C, the doctor on duty. By this time, the patient was semicomatose, but Dr. C, while making no diagnosis, prescribed phenobarbital and valium, and telephoned Dr. R, the internist on call. Dr. R directed Tony's admission to the ICU where a urinalysis was ordered (on a "routine", not a "stat" basis). The following morning, Dr. R saw his patient, but still failed to spot the real problem. It was at noon that day that a nurse detected on the patient's breath the "fruity" odour which betrayed at last the fact that Tony Yepremian was suffering from acute diabetes, and lapsing progressively into a diabetic coma. Dr. R (who was also, incidentally, a specialist in endocrinology) promptly administered insulin, but too late to prevent a cardiac arrest which left this young man with permanent brain damage. It was held by the Ontario courts that both Dr. G and Dr. C, general practitioners, had been negligent; but that the supervening negligence of the specialist Dr. R — who by exercising reasonable care and skill could still have averted any significant harm — was so overwhelmingly significant in causing the ultimate calamity that it should be deemed entirely to "insulate" the prior wrongdoers, Dr. G and Dr. C, from liability. It was, in short and technical language, a *novus actus interveniens;* a finding which spelled total ruin for the plaintiff's case, since for reasons unknown he had sued the hospital and all the physicians *except* Dr. R! There is much more to be learned from this case. We shall return to it presently.

It will have occurred to readers that the person whose negligence or misconduct is most frequently superadded to that of a defendant physician is not some other doctor or some official third party, but the patient himself. The patient fails to take his medication as directed, or to keep appointments for post-operative assessment or therapy, or to undergo simple remedial surgery to correct the physician's confessed errors. Such cases are not dealt with by the all-or-nothing doctrine of *novus actus interveniens,* but by the application of two much more flexible concepts — the ideas of *contributory negligence* and *mitigation of loss*, respectively. Where a patient shows a lack of ordinary, reasonable regard for his own health or safety, and thereby increases the risk or the measure of harm caused by his doctor's concurrent negligence, that is "contributory negligence", and is governed in every province by statutory rules of apportionment. Under such contributory negligence legislation, varying in name and terminology though much the same in substance throughout Canada, the injured patient will not recover an award of damages commensurate with the full extent of his suffering. The award will be proportionately reduced, to reflect the extent to which he himself, by his own fault, was the author of his misfortune. When the doctor's negligent acts are at an end and the harm inflicted has manifested itself, but the patient-victim wilfully and unreasonably declines treatment which could easily reduce his sufferings (or perversely embarks upon conduct which will maximize them), that is regarded as a failure in the patient's own duty to "mitigate his loss", and again — this time by an ordinary, judge-made common law rule — the plaintiff will be denied recovery to the extent that he has brought his own sufferings upon himself. The conceptual distinction between contributory negligence and the doctrine of mitigation of damages is in truth a difficult and elusive one, but in the end it all comes to much the same thing — a patient who has himself to blame for some portion of his misery will to that extent find his remedy in damages reduced.

Let us suppose that (as usually happens in real life) a patient, injured by his physician's negligent breach of duty, has successfully negotiated the hurdles of causation-in-fact and remoteness of damage. The only question remaining is the stark one of how much money he will be awarded by way of damages.

(c) The Evaluation of Legally Protected Interests: The Question of Quantum

Ignoring esoteric possibilities which lie outside the scope of this small book, we can confidently say that a doctor is only likely to be sued in negligence for inflicting one of two kinds of harm on a patient: namely, personal injury (with all the ancillary losses, pecuniary and otherwise, which flow from it); and death. The rules governing the assessment or quantification of damage awards in both these contexts were revolutionized in Canada by a series of judgments handed down by the Supreme Court of Canada on January 19, 1978. Three of those cases[42] dealt with the proper approach and technique to be used when computing damage awards in personal injury cases. These are known to lawyers as "the trilogy" and, as developed in subsequent cases, have formed the primary point of reference in all personal injury suits (against physicians or anyone else) ever since. The fourth case[43] similarly revolutionized the law of damages where a defendant's negligence has killed the victim. While the outcome is far from perfect, the result has been a Canadian law of damages which is acceptably uniform across the country and which far surpasses in its sophistication, rationality and humaneness anything to be found upon the subject elsewhere in the English-speaking world.

When the new rules were introduced in 1978, the level of personal injury awards, whether against physicians or any other class of defendants, certainly rose abruptly. One may doubt, though, whether the average level of awards has done anything more than keep pace with inflation since that date. Yet strident efforts, which might most charitably be described as ill-informed, have been made to blame the soaring cost of Canadian liability insurance premiums largely upon the modest and reasonable reforms of 1978. It is perfectly true that the volume of claims with regard to personal injuries, whether in medical or other contexts, has risen very significantly since that date. But as stated before, the real value of awards is not continuing to increase. We cannot here pursue any lengthy debate about the supposedly looming liability insurance crisis, but one may doubt whether the rising cost of policies can justly be ascribed in any significant measure to the modest and reasonable reform of the law of damages. That law we shall now briefly examine.

When death has been caused by a negligent act, whether of a physician or not, any negligence action brought against the person responsible must be founded upon a provincial statute, for it is a curious fact that originally, our law did not allow tort claims in respect of fatalities. If one's victim died, his cause of action died with him! That was changed long ago by statute, and every province of Canada now has (under one name or another) fatal accidents legislation. These statutes, though they vary a good deal, have as their common objective the provision of a remedy to the *dependents* of a person wrongfully killed, to compensate them for their monetary losses arising out of the death. In several provinces, too, damages may be awarded to compensate the family of the deceased for the lost "guidance, care and companionship" of the deceased person, though in some jurisdictions such claims can be made only when the loss is reducible to money, and not as a compassionate allowance irreducible to pecuniary measurement. Damages for grief or bereavement as such are clearly not recoverable, with the exception of Alberta, where a monetary "cap" is put on such claims, the precise figure varying according to the relationship that each respective claimant bore to the deceased.[44]

Quite apart from these fatal accident claims by bereaved dependents, a negligent doctor might in some provinces face another action, known to lawyers as a "survival action." Again wholly a creature of provincial statutes, such an action is brought by the *estate* of the dead person himself, and tends to be limited in its function to the recovery of funeral and testamentary expenses, plus any pecuniary losses sustained by the stricken victim prior to his death.

Personal injury claims may sometimes be rather more elaborate. When the injury caused by a doctor is relatively slight and specific — for example, the unnecessary and avoidable amputation of a big toe — the courts will look at the range of other awards made by courts in comparable cases, and will use those readily available figures as a rough guide in assessing the appropriate sum to be given as general damages to the particular plaintiff. The facts of the individual case will still be determinative, however. The loss of that big toe will obviously produce a larger award for a ballerina than for a bricklayer. But such cases will rarely necessitate any elaborate exercise in employing the rules laid down in the trilogy. To see those in their full complexity, we must suppose a more extreme case, a case of general disability.

Suppose that by the rushed and clumsy performance of a carotid endarterectomy, a surgeon has rendered a young and intelligent patient irreversibly quadriplegic. The patient is fully alert to his condition and now facing, with undiminished mental acuity, the prospect of a lifetime trapped in an inert body. Even in such situations of long-term ongoing disability, the courts in most provinces have only one type of remedy at their disposal. That remedy is a once-and-for-all lump sum award of damages against the surgeon; a sum sufficient to compensate the patient, so far as money can do it, for the sufferings he must face, and the material needs which must be met, during the rest of his life. The courts are painfully aware that this crucially important task of assessment is fraught with all sorts of uncertainties, irreducibly speculative in character. With the help of actuaries and their tables — extrapolations of collective human experience, nothing more — the Court can make an educated guess about the prospective pre-accident and post-accident life expectancies of the individual, and about his pre-accident working-life expectancy too. With some help from economists, testifying as expert witnesses, the Court can estimate the likely long-term interest rates which will tend to augment, over time, the value of the lump sum award when invested by the plaintiff. At the same time, though, helped by the same expert witnesses, the Court must estimate the likely impact, over the same period, of inflation eroding the real value of the award and its investment proceeds. The medical uncertainties and therapeutic needs of the plaintiff, as the years go by, must also be considered, as must all the contingencies of life which might conceivably increase or diminish the plaintiff's need for money, to make his life bearable in the future. While the courts remain tied to a non-reviewable system of one time lump sum awards, they must continue these unnervingly speculative exercises in educated clairvoyance. Governments and law reform agencies are actively examining the feasibility of schemes of periodic payments or other alternatives to the lump sum system, which may eliminate some of the unpredictable variables involved in damage assessment; but, for the time being, Canadian courts do their earnest best to resolve their doubts as rationally as they can, and arrive at a lump sum fairly reflecting the plaintiff's perceived need for compensation.

There is one situation in which these problems can be avoided. That is where the parties "settle out of court", and the defendant agrees to "pay by instalments", so to speak, for the rest of the plaintiff's life. In such cases, the lawyers on both sides can arrange what is known as a "structured settlement", a mutually advantageous device whereby the defendant, instead of paying a large lump sum to the plaintiff, purchases for him (often for a considerably smaller outlay) an annuity, inflation-indexed and payable monthly for as long as the plaintiff shall live. Such an arrangement, while eliminating many of the built-in uncertainties attending lump sum awards, may offer greater security to the plaintiff and less cost to the defendant (or his liability insurer). Its most attractive feature, as matters stand at the present, is that the annuity payments received by the plaintiff are not regarded by the authorities as income, and are accordingly tax-free in his hands, which would emphatically not be true of the interest accruing upon a lump sum award. One of the most prominent cases ultimately resolved by the arrangement of a very sensible structured settlement was, as it happens, the otherwise unhappy case of *Yepremian v. Scarborough General Hospital.* * Having lost his action against the hospital by the narrowest of margins in the Ontario Court of Appeal, the plaintiff was offered a settlement of this kind, and so spared the necessity, expense and uncertainty of a further appeal to the Supreme Court of Canada.

Such solutions are often eminently more sensible from every point of view than any lump sum payment. Yet most Canadian courts presently lack power to *order* such a structured settlement,[45] which can only be arrived at consensually, by agreement between the parties.

In reality, where an agreed settlement is possible in medical cases, the agreement will be between the plaintiff and the defendant's liability insurer or medical protective association. Statistics issued by C.M.P.A. consistently show a rate of settlement which far outstrips the number of court-ordered damage awards. Up-to-date statistical information giving emphatic proof of this phenomenon is provided in Chapter 10, *post.*

Suppose that no settlement can be reached. The judge must then use the trilogy cases and the guidelines they contain to work out a carefully itemized calculation of lump sum damages. The aim is to compute a capitalized sum which, together with the income it can be expected to generate, will provide sufficient money during the plaintiff's period of disability to recompense all his compensable losses and provide all his reasonable and compensable needs. In cases of long-term disability, this must be done on an "exhausting fund principle", so devised that in theory the money will be sufficient to meet these needs for exactly as long as required, exhausting itself finally on the day when, by death or otherwise, the need is extinguished. The law does not want, after all, to provide windfalls for the estates of accident victims at the defendant's expense.

Enough has been said to show the relative sophistication of Canada's law of personal injury damages, and the anxious care with which the courts approach the task of computation. Every component in the award is itemized, explained and justified: global awards of random sums, snatched capriciously out of thin air, will not be countenanced. It is this need for our judges to show the detailed workings of their minds which protects Canadian defendants, not least medical professionals, from the extravagant, irrational and ruinous awards which have triggered massive liability insurance costs and a socially damaging "malpractice crisis" in less happy jurisdictions.

---

* See page 113-4, *supra.*

(d) The Concept of Vicarious Liability

All the component elements in a negligence action have now been looked at in some detail. Before turning to consider the practical problems of proving negligence, a few miscellaneous points must be disposed of.

Readers will have noticed that in several cases already examined, the lawsuit has been filed not only against the supposedly negligent doctor who has been sued, but also against the hospital, or the clinic in which that doctor was operating at the fateful moment. That was so, for example, in *Fraser v. Vancouver General Hospital;* in *Johnston v. Wellesley Hospital;* in *Worth v. Royal Jubilee Hospital* and in *Yepremian v. Scarborough General Hospital,* all considered earlier in this chapter. This is done because of the well-established legal doctrine of *vicarious liability,* which holds certain persons or entities liable for the wrongdoing of others, not because they themselves are in any sense at fault, but simply by virtue of their status *vis-à-vis* the actual wrongdoer. The most important rule here is that an employer (or "master" in the law's antique terminology) is deemed vicariously responsible for any negligence committed by an employee (or "servant"), "in the course of his or her employment." Accordingly, if a member of a hospital's house staff negligently injures a patient, that patient may sue *not only* the culpable staff member, but the hospital as well; and if the cause of action is made out upon the evidence, both these defendants will be held jointly and severally liable for the full amount of damages due.

Of course, not every physician with hospital privileges is thereby considered an "employee" of the hospital, so as to attract this doctrine. On the contrary, most physicians enjoying hospital privileges are considered to be "independent contractors," to whom the rules of vicarious liability will not attach, and whose blunders cannot be laid to the hospital's account. Let us briefly consider again the *Yepremian* case.[46]

The first physician in that case, who failed to diagnose Tony Yepremian's diabetes, was a general practitioner not employed by the hospital. The second was a general practitioner on duty in emergency; again, an independent contractor. Dr. R, the internist who negligently missed the third and critical opportunity to diagnose the rapidly deteriorating diabetic condition, was not sued at all. Even if he had been, the hospital would not have been exposed to vicarious liability, for once again, Dr. R, though a member of the attending specialist staff, was not an employee of the hospital. All those involved in the case who were hospital employees — the nurses and laboratory technicians — had performed admirably in accordance with approved practice and all instructions forwarded to them by the doctors. The plaintiff's only hope of fixing the hospital with legal responsibility lay not in the doctrine of vicarious liability, but in the contention that the hospital itself owed a non-delegable duty to provide reasonable care and skill to each patient admitted. That suggestion was rejected by a majority of the Ontario Court of Appeal, which explained the limited nature of the hospital's own duty. The Court held that the hospital was obliged to take reasonable care in the selection of personnel and the provision of appropriate facilities and equipment; but that did not make it liable every time physicians chosen with such due care, operating within the organization of the hospital but not "employed" by it, made a mistake injurious to a patient. The hospital had not undertaken, still less broken, any special duty to supervise those physicians treating Tony Yepremian, nor had it contracted to provide error-free treatment. Though in the end, as we have seen, the hospital chose to make an agreed settlement with this young man, there was in the opinion of the majority of appeal judges no ground for imposing on the hospital an obligation to compensate him.[47]

The concept of vicarious liability may affect a physician in two other ways. The first should be obvious. If a doctor's own employee — her office staff or nurse — behaves negligently towards a patient, the doctor may herself be held vicariously liable for that negligence. The other matter is far less obvious: vicarious liability applies not only to fix an employer with liability for an employee's wrongs; it also applies as between partners. A physician who practices in partnership with others will find herself exposed to joint and several liability along with all the other partners for the negligent acts of any one of them done in the course of the partnership and, for that matter, for the negligent acts of the servants of any of those partners. That liability is unlimited, and the injured patient, once he receives judgment, can enforce it against the partnership assets, if necessary to the point of exhaustion; and then proceed against the personal assets of any partner or partners.* Consider for a moment the 1974 Alberta case of *Dowey v. Rothwell*.[48] Mrs. Dowey had for years been a patient of Dr. M, a member of the defendant partnership, who treated her with phenobarbital to control the frequency and severity of her *grand mal* epileptic seizures. One day, feeling a seizure to be imminent, she came to the clinic, described her symptoms to the attending nurse (no doctor being present) and was told to lie down on the examining table. The nurse then left her for about one minute — just long enough for Mrs. Dowey to suffer a seizure and fall to the tiled floor of the examining room, sustaining a severely comminuted fracture of an arm. The Court held that the nurse (who was not sued) had

---

* Every doctor contemplating practice in tandem with others should for this and other reasons seek legal advice as to whether partnership, incorporation or some other model of mutual organization best serves his or her needs.

been negligent in leaving the patient alone in those circumstances, and for that negligence the partnership as a whole was held vicariously liable.

In leaving this topic of vicarious liability, it should be noted that quite often, where an employee (for example, an intern or resident) has been negligent, only the employer (for example, the hospital) is actually sued, the plaintiff doubtless considering the hapless employee "not worth suing." In such cases, the hospital's liability will be discharged by its liability insurer. But that should afford cold comfort to the negligent intern, for the insurance company can thereupon sue him, under what is termed a "subrogated right of action", to recoup the outlay which it has incurred as a result of his careless breach of duty to his employer. It behoves every such employee, then, to make sure that he or she is explicitly specified as one of the "insured parties" under the employer's liability policy, or to seek individual protection through membership in the C.M.P.A. or the purchase of personal liability insurance.

NOTES

1. [1980] 1 W.W.R. 673 (B.C. C.A.).
2. See *Horsley v. MacLaren* (1971), [1972] S.C.R. 441, 22 D.L.R. (3d) 545 [Ont.]. Astonishingly, but in accordance with what we have seen of the "Good Samaritan" issue, earlier cases had steadfastly maintained that no such duty existed at all.
3. [1969] 1 Q.B. 428, [1968] 2 W.L.R. 422, [1968] 1 All E.R. 1068.
4. (1998), 170 N.S.R. (2d) 145 (C.A.), additional reasons at (1998), 173 N.S.R. (2d) 273 (C.A.)
5. (1977), [1978] 1 S.C.R. 893, 76 D.L.R. (3d) 688, 15 N.R. 271.
6. (1978), 84 D.L.R. (3d) 650, 2 L.M.Q. 54 (Man. Q.B.).
7. [1996] 4 W.W.R. 748, 29 C.C.L.T. (2d) 215 (Man. C.A.): The case, though peculiar, is not unique: see the almost simultaneous decision of the English Court of Appeal in *Goodwill v. British Pregnancy Advisory Service*, [1996] 2 All E.R. 161.
8. [1956] O.R. 132, 1 D.L.R. (2d) 502 (C.A.), affirmed [1956] S.C.R. 991, 5 D.L.R. (2d) 601.
9. *Ibid.*, p. 143.
10. (1970), 17 D.L.R. (3d) 87 (B.C. S.C.).
11. (1977), 16 O.R. (2d) 532, 78 D.L.R. (3d) 588, 1 L. Med. Q. 234 (H.C.), affirmed (1978), 21 O.R. (2d) 554, 90 D.L.R. (3d) 763, 2 L. Med. Q. 231 (C.A.).
12. [1952] 2 S.C.R. 36, [1952] 3 D.L.R. 785.
13. *Ibid.*, p. 46.
14. *Supra*, note 8.
15. [1971] 2 O.R. 103, 17 D.L.R. (3d) 139 (H.C.); see also Chapter 3.
16. [1949] 2 W.W.R. 539, [1949] 4 D.L.R. 291 (Man. K.B.).
17. *Ibid.*, p. 542, Mr. Justice Campbell citing Charlesworth's Law of Negligence, 2nd ed., p. 401.
18. (1985), 62 A.R. 118 (Q.B.), affirmed (1987), 51 Alta. L.R. (2d) 43, 77 A.R. 321 (C.A.), leave to appeal to S.C.C. refused 51 Alta. L.R. (2d) xli (note), 80 A.R. 320 (note), 79 N.R. 396 (note) (S.C.C.).
19. (1979), 18 A.R. 271 (T.D.).
20. [1975] 1 W.W.R. 120, 56 D.L.R. (3d) 231 (Man. Q.B.), affirmed [1976] 3 W.W.R. 367, 71 D.L.R. (3d) 550 (Man. C.A.); see also Chapter 5.
21. Mr. Justice Abbott, in *McCormick v. Marcotte* (1971), [1972] S.C.R. 18, 20 D.L.R. (3d) 345 at 21 [S.C.R.] (emphasis added).
22. A full discussion of the issue may be found in Irvine, "The Physician's Duty in the Age of Cost-Containment", (1994) 22 **Manitoba Law Journal** 345, updated in Irvine, Case Comment: *Law Estate v. Simice*, (1995) 21 C.C.L.T. (2d) 259.

23. *Post*, p. 104.
24. 228 Cal. Rptr. 661 (Cal. Ct. App., 1986).
25. (1994), 21 C.C.L.T. (2d) 228 (B.S. S.C.), affirmed (1995), 27 C.C.L.T. (2d) 127 (B.C. C.A.).
26. *Ibid.*, at p. 240, per Mr. Justice Spencer.
27. Morreim, E.H., "Cost Containment and the Standard of Medical Care", (1987) 75 **Cal. Law Review**, 1719 at 1746.
28. (1982), 37 A.R. 221 (Q.B.).
29. (1951), [1951] S.C.R. 830, [1952] 1 D.L.R. 1.
30. *Kolesar v. Jeffries* (1977), (sub nom. *Joseph Brant Memorial Hospital v. Koziol*) [1978] 1 S.C.R. 491, 2 C.C.L.T. 170, 77 D.L.R. (3d) 161, (sub nom. *Kolesar v. Joseph Brant Memorial Hospital*) 15 N.R. 302.
31. (1972), [1973] 1 W.L.R. 1, [1972] 3 All ER. 1008 (H.L.).
32. [1988] 1 All E.R. 871 (H.L.).
33. [1990] 2 S.C.R. 311, 4 C.C.L.T. (2d) 229.
34. [1987] A.C. 750, [1987] 2 All E.R. 909 (H.L.).
35. [1991] 1 S.C.R. 541, 6 C.C.LT. (2d) 119.
36. (1992), 13 C.C.L.T. (2d) 323 (Man. C.A.).
37. (1991), 46 O.A.C. 260 (C.A.), leave to appeal refused (1991), 50 O.A.C. 159 (note) (S.C.C.): followed and explained in *Grass (Litigation Guardian of) v. Women's College Hospital* (2001), 5 C.C.L.T. (3d) 180 (C.A.), leave to appeal refused (2002), 293 N.R. 194 (note) (S.C.C.). And in *Liuni (Litigation Guardian of) v. Peters* (2001), 8 C.C.L.T. (3d) 207 (C.A.), leave to appeal refused (2002), 2002 CarswellOnt 1103, 2002 CarswellOnt 1104 (S.C.C.).
38. *Overseas Tankship (U.K.) Ltd. v. Morts Dock & Engineering Co.*, [1961] A.C. 388, [1961] 2 W.L.R. 126, [1961] 1 All ER. 404 (New South Wales P.C.); *Overseas Tankship (U.K.) Ltd. v. Miller Steamship Propriety Ltd.* (1966), [1967] 1 A.C. 617, [1966] 3 W.L.R. 498, (sub nom. *Wagon Mound (No. 2.)*) [1966] 2 All ER. 709 (New South Wales P.C.).
39. (1979), [1980] 1 W.W.R. 673 (B.C. C.A.); see note 1, *supra*.
40. (1980), 4 L. Med. Q. 59 (B.C. C.A.).
41. (1978), 20 O.R. (2d) 510, 6 C.C.L.T. 81, 88 D.L.R. (3d) 161, 2 L. Med. Q. 216 (H.C.), reversed (1980), 28 O.R. (2d) 494, 13 C.C.L.T. 105, 110 D.L.R. (3d) 513, 3 L. Med. Q. 278 (C.A.), leave to appeal allowed (1980), 120 D.L.R. (3d) 337n (Ont. C.A.).
42. *Andrews v. Grand & Toy Alberta Ltd.*, [1978] 2 S.C.R. 229, [1978] 1 W.W.R. 577, 3 C.C.L.T. 225, 83 D.L.R. (3d) 452, 8 A.R. 182, 19 N.R. 50; *Thornton v. Prince George Board of Education*, [1978] 2 S.C.R. 267, [1978] 1 W.W.R. 607, 3 C.C.L.T. 257, 83 D.L.R. (3d) 480, 19 N.R. 552; and *Teno v. Arnold*, [1978] 2 S.C.R. 287, 3 C.C.L.T. 272 , 83 D.L.R. (3d) 609, 19 N.R. 1.
43. *Keizer v. Hanna*, [1978] 2 S.C.R. 342, 3 C.C.L.T. 316, 82 D.L.R. (3d) 449, 19 N.R. 209.

44. See *Fatal Accidents Act*, R.S.A. 1980 c. F5, s. 8, as amended in 1994 and R.S.A. 2000, c. F-8, to increase the "cap" figures.

45. This was reluctantly but emphatically asserted by the Supreme Court of Canada in *Watkins v. Olafson* (1989), 50 C.C.L.T. 101 (S.C.C.). In Manitoba, the province from which the *Watkins* case emanated, the picture has since been altered by statute. Manitoba's Queen's Bench Act, C.C.S.M. c. C280, s. 88.2 enables a Manitoba court to award damages by way of periodic payments, on an application to that effect by either party. So far, Manitoba is seemingly alone in this respect though both Ontario and British Columbia may in limited circumstances allow such measures.

46. *Supra,* note 41.

47. This aspect of the *Yepremian* case, dealing with the legal duties of public hospitals as such, is further explained in the New Brunswick case of *Bateman v. Doiron* (1992), 8 C.C.L.T. (2d) 284 (N.B. Q.B.), affirmed (1994), 18 C.C.L.T. (2d) 1 (C.A.), leave to appeal refused (1994), 150 N.B.R. (2d) 80 (S.C.C.): where the important point is made that what is a reasonable standard of staffing or of facilities may vary according to what is reasonably to be expected in a particular size or type of community. As we go to press, some doubt has been cast upon the universal validity of the *Yepremian* doctrine, and the limited nature of a hospital's non-delegable duties: see *Jaman Estate v. Hussain*, [2002] 11 W.W.R. 241 (Man. C.A.).

48. [1974] 5 W.W.R. 311, 49 D.L.R. (3d) 82 (Alta. T.D.): a case discussed further in Chapter 9, *post*.

7

MEDICAL NEGLIGENCE: DEFENCES AND PROBLEMS OF PROOF

SUMMARY

At the risk of stating the obvious, the best defence to an action of negligence is to show that no negligence was committed, or that any failure on the physician's part did no harm to the patient. If negligence causing harm be shown, the defences recognized by law are few indeed. There is the partial defence of contributory negligence, considered already. Then there are various statutes of limitation, which declare that after an allotted period of time, no lawsuit can be commenced. The difficulties generated by such "statutes of repose", as they are sometimes called, are examined here.

A number of issues introduced in Chapter 1 are then re-examined more fully. The methods used by a disgruntled patient to establish negligence against his physician are looked at. Attention is then given to the critical issue of whether and to what extent the observance of practices ordinarily used by the profession as a whole (or by a considerable segment of the profession) will be regarded as dispositive of the critical issue of whether the physician's duty of care and skill has been properly discharged.

1. DEFENCES

Much heavy weather is made in the legal textbooks about "defences to the action for negligence"; but in truth these are of very limited scope. At the risk of stating the obvious, a doctor's best "defence" is to show that he did not commit any actionable negligence in the first place. This can be done (albeit rarely) by showing that no relationship arose creating any duty of care to the plaintiff. More commonly, the physician may be able to demonstrate that no breach of the duty occurred — either by showing that the mishap complained of was a mere error of judgement[1] or that the treatment conformed to the practice approved by the medical profession as a whole, or a considerable segment of it. Sometimes, too, as we have seen, the doctor can nip any negligence action in the bud by showing that the damage complained of was not caused by his error, or at least not "proximately" so. All these matters have been examined in the previous chapter. A physician who can avail himself of any of these arguments has no need of "defences" in the technical sense of that word, for there is simply no valid cause of action in negligence against which he has to defend himself.

Yet true "defences" do exist. One, the flexible and usually only partial defence of *contributory negligence,* was considered in the previous chapter. Another defence, far more drastic because it totally debars any remedy for the plaintiff, is the statutory phenomenon of *limitation of actions,* embodied in a miscellany of provincial statutes. These statutory provisions, sometimes aptly termed statutes of repose, are designed to lay disputes to rest by ordaining that after a specified period of time, the cause of action will be deemed *statute-barred* if an injured party has not taken the first step towards seeking a remedy and filed his *statement of claim* by the allotted date. This extinguishment of legal rights of action by the effluxion of time gives rise to numerous complexities which fall outside the scope of this book. It is based on public policy, which requires that legal disputes be resolved with due despatch; and also upon the common sense reflection that after a time, memories become stale or distorted, and witnesses harder to find and less reliable in their recollections.

Most plaintiffs in negligence actions for personal injury are given two years in which to commence proceedings either under the general provincial limitation legislation, or under other statutes governing the particular kind of negligence situation in issue. The "clock begins to tick" at the moment when a cause of action "arises." That was traditionally construed as being the moment harm was inflicted, and in former times it was accordingly possible for a plaintiff to have lost his cause of action by the passage of time before he had even had a chance to become aware of the harm negligently done to him. Such an unfair result was especially conceivable in cases of medical negligence, where the results of a physician's ineptitude might remain latent until the limitation period had safely elapsed. This is one reason why special limitation periods for actions against physicians and hospitals have been created by statute in all Canadian jurisdictions, displacing the "general" limitation period formerly applicable.

In many provinces, while the actual period allowed is either kept at two years (as in Manitoba, Newfoundland, the Northwest Territories and Nova Scotia) or even reduced to just one (as in Alberta, Prince Edward

Island and Saskatchewan), the "starting-point" is altered, and the limitation clock only starts to run at that (admittedly rather elusive) point in time when the professional services, provided by the defendant physician, ceased. That may be considerably later than the date when the harm was done, so giving the patient more time to become aware of his plight, and commence proceedings accordingly. But the spectre does still arise of a grievously-harmed patient losing his right to sue before he is even aware he has one. This is particularly anomalous now that Canadian courts applying the *general* limitation statutes have made it clear, in very recent years, that they will not regard the clock as starting until that time when a reasonably alert plaintiff would *become aware* of the harm done to him. In view of this approach, the special "medical" limitation periods may look suspiciously like legislation mollycoddling the medical practitioner. Accordingly, in three provinces (British Columbia, New Brunswick and Ontario), the legislation has been altered to specify that even in actions against physicians, time shall not start to "run" until the patient has had a reasonable chance to become aware of his situation.[2] As will be apparent, the issue of limitations is one blessed with very little uniformity, and one with such potential for injustice, to either physician or patient, that it must be continually monitored and "fine-tuned" by law reform agencies.

2. HOW NEGLIGENCE IS PROVED

Attention has already been given, in Chapter 1, to the rules and practices of civil procedure and litigation which give shape to actions against physicians. But more must be said about what might be termed the techniques of proof.

First of all, it should be noted that jury trials in civil actions against medical practitioners, though theoretically possible in every province, are in reality something of a rarity in Canada. Their degree of rarity ranges from extreme infrequency (in, for example, Ontario) to virtual inconceivability (as in Manitoba). In practice then, by reason sometimes of procedural rules, sometimes of local convention and sometimes of judicial discretion (especially if the case is expected to involve complex scientific evidence), the case will be heard by a judge sitting alone. He or she will decide all issues which arise in the case, whether on legal or factual questions. The plaintiff, in an action of medical negligence, bears the legal burden of proof in the case. This means he must convince the judge, on a balance of probabilities,* that the facts in the case, properly understood, bespeak a duty of care, breach of this duty, and proximate damage resulting from that

---

* Not, it should be noted, "beyond reasonable doubt"; see Chapter 1.

breach. This is done by the calling of witnesses and sometimes by the introduction into evidence of various documents (including hospital records) and exhibits.

A critical role is often played by the expert witnesses. These are professional persons who are not called to testify because of what they know of the particular events which gave rise to the action, but rather because their qualifications enable them to speak authoritatively about the technical or scientific issues in the case, about their perceptions and opinions as to what the defendant actually did and about whether in so doing he acted in accordance with, or in defiance of, the approved practice current in the medical profession.

If by adducing evidence of this kind the plaintiff fails to raise even a fair inference of negligence, or any sort of case to be answered, the action may be dismissed there and then. Otherwise, while the plaintiff still carries the overall burden of proof, it will be prudent for the defendant physician to produce his evidence and call his expert witnesses, in an attempt to neutralize or negate the plaintiff's case. Under procedural rules in all provinces, each side is allowed only so many expert witnesses (the number varies from three to five) and, for reasons which need not be debated here, plaintiffs may sometimes find it hard to find persons of the requisite stature to perform this thankless task. The task, as we have seen, is not to act as a supernumerary advocate for "one's own side", but to assist the Court in placing the proper interpretation on the evidence; a role which cannot properly or convincingly be discharged if scientific objectivity is abandoned, or if any suggestion of partisanship can be discerned.

It is on the issue of standard of care and the subsequent issues of causation that the expert testimony is likely to be of most significance. Assuming, as is usually the case, that a plaintiff can initially establish the doctor/patient relationship and so its concomitant duty of care and skill, battle will usually be joined in earnest on the question of whether the defendant doctor breached that duty by failing to meet the required standards. Here, the plaintiff must try to elicit from his expert witnesses testimony which may persuade the Court that the defendant physician departed culpably from the normal standards of skill, judgment or behaviour prevailing in the profession. The defendant will seek by his witnesses to place a diametrically opposite complexion upon the evidence. Finally, the Court will decide.

Sometimes, it will happen that the mere proof by the plaintiff of the events which unfolded, and the results which ensured, will be so eloquent of negligence on the defendant physician's part that the introduction of expert evidence may be superfluous. When ordinary common sense, applied to the circumstances of the case, suggests unequivocally that such things could not have occurred without negligence on somebody's part; and suggests with equal stridency that that "someone" must surely have been the physician treating the plaintiff; then it will be prudent, as a matter of tactics, for that physician to come up with cogent evidence to dispel the strong inference that he was negligent. Such a use of circumstantial evidence may be determinative even though the plaintiff can produce no evidence (or not enough evidence) to show how in truth the accident occurred. And the defendant physician, or other health-care professional, will then face the prospect of persuading the court that the mishap could plausibly have resulted from other causes, not attributable to any want of care or skill on his part. If the defendant fails to do this, the court will be entitled to draw the inference of negligence, and hold him liable without further ado.

By way of example, swabs and instruments left inside surgical patients have on occasion been held to raise this kind of commonsense inference. But the judges have never been comfortable in drawing conclusions of this kind in a medical context. Conscious of a lack of relevant professional experience, they tend to do so only after hearing enough medical evidence to convince them that the accident under consideration is truly one that would not ordinarily have occurred without medical negligence. So it is that in several cases already referred to, the courts declined to find liability simply upon circumstantial evidence.

That was so in *Johnston v. Wellesley Hospital,** because in that case there was in fact considerable evidence of a non-circumstantial nature upon which to determine how the injury happened, and whether anyone was to blame. Nor was the mere recital of events allowed to be sufficient to fix the unlucky surgeon with liabiltiy in the cases of *Chubey v. Ahsan*** and *Powell v. Guttman (No. 2);*† and there are legions of other cases where accidental medical or surgical mishaps have been held to be precisely that, and not in and of themselves sufficiently suggestive of negligence to support a finding of liability without the need for further evidence and inquiry.

Until very recently, the use of circumstantial evidence, by itself, to justify a finding of liability was referred to by lawyers as if it represented an actual principle of law, expressed in the Latin maxim 'Res ipsa loquitur' ("the matter speaks for itself").

Some explanations of this supposed legal principle tended to refer to it as "shifting the burden of proof" in civil cases onto the shoulders of

---

* See note 1; see also Chapter 3, Case Study.
** (1974), [1975] 1 W.W.R. 120, 56 D.L.R. (3d) 231 (Man. Q.B.), affirmed [1976] 3 W.W.R. 367, 71 D.L.R. (3d) 550 (Man. C.A.); see also Chapter 5, Case Study.
† [1978] 5 W.W.R. 228, 6 C.C.L.T. 183, 89 D.L.R. (3d) 180, 2 L. Med. Q. 279 at 291 (Man. C.A.).

defendants, and became quite mysterious in distinguishing between "legal" and "evidentiary or tactical" burdens of proof. But in 1998, the Supreme Court of Canada decided that the time had come to sweep all this sophistry away. In a non-medical case, *Fontaine v. British Columbia (Official Administrator)*,[3] they declared that the Latin maxim was no longer to be used in our courts, nor regarded as expressing any legal principle, still less "shifting" any burden of proof. All it had really ever been, said the Supreme Court, was an acknowledgment that circumstantial evidence may be so overwhelming in its inference of responsibility and culpability as to place on a defendant a formidable task of explanation if he is to exonerate himself from the inferences which are apparent to the eye of commonsense. We may doubt whether the rejection of the old maxim, or the "doctrine" which it was supposed to embody, will make any real difference to the way cases are decided, in medical contexts or otherwise. Nor is there any reason to suppose that the older cases, applying the maxim (or declining to do so) would yield different results nowadays. Cases in which a Court will feel justified in making a finding of liability against a medical professional simply upon the basis of circumstantial evidence — that is, just because it is hard to see any other explanation for the way events unfolded as they did — will continue to be rare, and confined to the most extreme and glaring of cases.

Usually, then, the plaintiff's efforts at trial will be directed to producing as much cogent and persuasive evidence as possible of a want of due care and skill — a breach of the duty of care — and harm resulting from that breach. The defendant-physician's usual response to this, and his most potent riposte if he can achieve it, is to show that in everything he did, he adhered to the practices usual among his fellow physicians when dealing with like cases, and showed in doing so the care and skill normally to be expected of average members of that peer group. That is what Dr. Ahsan achieved in *Chubey v. Ahsan*, and scores of other examples might be cited in which doctors have been exonerated by reason of their proven adherence to professional orthodoxy.

One frequently cited case on point is the 1959 Alberta case of *Challand v. Bell*.[4] Mr. Challand fell while working in his cattle barn, and broke both the radial and ulnar bones at the mid-third of the forearm. One of these bones punctured the flesh, causing an open wound, and Mr. Challand lost no time in visiting his local general practitioner Dr. Bell. Dr. Bell x-rayed the arm and spread the wound with forceps. Then, forming the impression that no foreign bodies were present and that the wound was clean, he applied gauze soaked in merthiolate, set the fracture and applied a cast, before sending Mr. Challand home with a prescription for penicillin and streptomycin. Over the next 36 hours, a deterioration of circulation and excessive swelling were noted, and a rather alarmed Dr. Bell sent his patient to the University Hospital in Edmonton. There, acute fulminating gas gangrene was swiftly diagnosed, and Mr. Challand's arm amputated just below the elbow. He sued Dr. Bell, his principal contention being that Dr. Bell had been negligent in failing to perform an initial debridement of the wound. But the evidence showed that gas gangrene was relatively rare and difficult to diagnose in its early stages, while debridement was a meddlesome technique, not lightly to be undertaken by a physician confronted with a seemingly clean wound. Further — and this was crucial — the evidence showed that nine doctors out of ten would have given precisely the same treatment, no less and no more, that Dr. Bell gave. The action was dismissed.

For the most part, then, evidence of adherence to universally observed procedures and standards will be conclusive in favour of the defence; but not always. The courts have jealously maintained an ultimate discretion, exercised only in the very rarest of cases, to castigate as negligent a practice universally observed by another profession. This will happen when no professional or technical expertise is required to evaluate the wisdom or imprudence of the practice in question; that is, when ordinary common sense would condemn such a practice as unacceptably hazardous. Not surprisingly, such cases are rare in medical contexts, but they are not unknown. One such case is the widely cited *Anderson v. Chasney* (Manitoba, 1949).[5] Little Anderson, aged five, entered a Winnipeg hospital in 1947 for a tonsilloadenoidectomy, to be performed by Dr. Chasney. The surgery was uneventful, but a sponge was left at the base of the child's nostrils, and he fatally asphyxiated on it later that day. The evidence showed that while taped sponges were available at the time, and while Dr. Chasney might have called upon a nurse to keep count of the sponges as they were inserted and removed, his failure to take either of these precautionary measures was entirely consonant with normal practice in many, perhaps most, other Canadian hospitals at that date. That evidence did not protect Dr. Chasney from liability. The practice he observed might have been almost universal within the profession, but was so obviously fraught with quite unnecessary peril that it was held to constitute actionable negligence.

That said, conformity to universal professional practice generally affords a safe refuge. Conversely, the use of novel, experimental or idiosyncratic techniques puts a physician in a precarious legal position where negligence suits by disappointed patients are concerned; for however well-principled the physician may be, his deviation from ordinary practice may well be considered as no less than unprivileged experimentation at the patient's expense, and, as such, plainly negligence. A more common dilemma arises where the expert evidence discloses the absence of any real consensus — where, in other words, there is more than one body of respectable medical opinion upon a particular point. A recent English case of the highest authority[6] declared that in such a situation, the proof by a defendant-physician of his adherence to one or other of the rival schools of thought should ordinarily be considered to dispel any suggestion of negligence, even if the Court should itself find the other body of opinion more convincing. In *Brain v. Mador* (Ontario, 1985),[7] Mr. Brain was treated for epididymitis, and scarcely a month after its symptoms subsided, sought a vasectomy. The operation was performed uneventfully, but triggered a recrudescence of the epididymitis, and prostatitis too. Despite treatment, one of the patient's testicles atrophied. At trial, the expert evidence disclosed considerable division of opinion as to the wisdom of performing a vasectomy upon someone known to have suffered epididymitis so very recently. All agreed that caution and watchful hesitancy were required, but they differed greatly as to how much temporization was appropriate. The Ontario Court of Appeal quoted and approved the *Maynard* case, no doubt conscious of the absurdity of a panel of lawyers purporting to act as final arbiters in a dispute between doctors. Yet they held the defendant doctor liable. While this may seem to conflict with *Maynard,* it does not, really, for the judges in the *Brain* case discerned only one respectable body of medical opinion; the rather elastic opinion that vasectomies should be undertaken circumspectly and without undue haste in the aftermath of genital infections. On the evidence, the defendant had not shown the required measure of caution, and could not point to, or shelter behind, any opposing body of academic or professional opinion, urging doctors to be "bloody, bold and resolute" in such situations.

All the essential elements of a negligence action against a physician have now been examined, as have the defences which may be called upon, and many of the practical problems of proof which commonly arise. In the next chapter, no new doctrinal issues need be broached. Instead, the specific duties encompassed by a physician's general duty of care and skill will be examined, and the way in which Canadian courts have given substance and detail to these various obligations in familiar medical contexts will be illustrated.

NOTES

1. See, e.g., *Johnston v. Wellesley Hospital* (1970), [1971] 2 OR. 103, 17 D.L.R. (3d) 139 (H.C.).
2. While in some other provinces, such as Manitoba, a plaintiff who is apparently "out of time" may apply to have the statutory bar lifted in such circumstances: *Limitation of Actions Act*, C.C.S.M. c. L150, s. 14(1); and see *Fehr v. Jacob,* [1993] 5 W.W.R. 1 (Man. C.A.), additional reasons at (1993), 16 C.P.C. (3d) 382 (Man. C.A.).
3. (1997), [1998] 1 S.C.R. 424.
4. (1959), 27 WWR. 182, 18 D.L.R. (2d) 150 (Alta. S.C.).
5. 57 Man. R. 343, [1949] 2 W.W.R. 337, [1949] 4 D.L.R. 71 (C.A.), affirmed [1950] 4 D.L.R. 223 (S.C.C.).
6. *Maynard v. West Midland Regional Health Authority* (1983), [1984] 1 W.L.R. 634, [1985] 1 All E.R. 635 (H.L.).
7. (1985), 32 C.C.L.T. 157, 9 O.A.C. 87 (C.A.), leave to appeal to S.C.C. refused (1985), 13 O.A.C. 79 (note), 64 N.R. 240 (note) (S.C.C.). See also *Belknap v. Greater Victoria Hospital Society* (1990), 1 C.C.L.T. (2d) 192 (B.C. C.A.).

8

MEDICAL NEGLIGENCE IN SPECIFIC CONTEXTS

SUMMARY

All the essential elements of an action in negligence have now been addressed. This chapter turns to examine the working of those principles from a variety of different perspectives germane to the daily work of the physician. This is done by dissecting the physician's all-important duty of care and skill into its component strands — each of which may be considered as a duty in its own right, as well as an element in the overall duty. There is no definitive or sacrosanct catalogue of these duties, but the breakdown here adopted seems comprehensive; embracing the duty to attend the patient; the duty to diagnose; the duty to refer; the duty to treat and to provide appropriate aftercare; the duty to communicate with fellow-professionals; the duty to keep full and accurate records; and the duty to supervise junior colleagues. Only the duty to communicate with the patient and provide him with sufficient information is omitted, simply because it has been discussed at length in earlier chapters.

The chapter concludes with some reflections upon the limited utility and fairness of tort law, and anticipates the fuller discussion of such issues, and of possible alternative schemes of compensation, to be found in Chapter 10.

1. INTRODUCTION

The foregoing chapters examined all the essential features of negligence doctrine. It only remains to illustrate the way these rules work by giving further examples, which cover the more usual contexts in which complaints of medical negligence arise. There is nothing, then, that is doctrinally new in this chapter. The case law to be examined is approached under discrete headings — "The duty to attend", "The duty to diagnose" and so on. The full list of such "duties" has already been set out in Chapter 6, at p. 90. But it bears repetition to stress that these so-called duties are really just facets of the compendious overall duty of care owed by a physician to a patient. Consistently with everything we have seen in the preceding chapters, the duty of care will in every instance be fulfilled, and the standard of care and skill required of the physician duly met, if regard is had to the dictates of commonsense, and to the practices and norms ordinarily observed by the medical profession.

One of the most important and frequently litigated aspects of a physician's duty — the *duty to disclose* to the patient the essential *nature* of the proposed treatment, and certain of the *risks* which may attend it — has already been examined in detail. Accordingly, only a reminder need be given that this "informed consent" issue is nowadays more than ever a very common basis for lawsuits. Disgruntled patients often tack on a claim based on "breach of the duty to inform", to allegations that the physician committed breaches of other duties or facets of professional responsibility. The other duties imposed by the law upon physicians will now be considered.

2. THE MULTIPLE ASPECTS OF THE DUTY OF CARE AND SKILL

(a) The Duty to Attend the Patient

All the textbooks assure us that a doctor has no duty to attend or pay any attention to a person who is not yet a "patient" of that doctor. In this connection, physicians should be aware that it does not take much evidence to persuade a Court that a doctor/patient relationship indeed came into being, with all its attendant responsibilities. Yet the general proposition of law still holds good, that a physician may refuse to accept anyone as a new patient. We have already suggested however (Chapter 6, pp. 88-9), that recent developments in the law of negligence may demand some measure of qualification to this sweeping and potentially inhumane rule, especially since it relates so awkwardly to the dictates of the Canadian Medical Association's Code of Ethics. It can still be stated with some confidence that whenever a physician would foresee that a sick or injured person would realistically have timely access to the help of another physician, no legal liability will result from turning that person away, and refusing to add him to one's list of patients. But where such alternative treatment is not likely to be available, at least in time to avert significant deterioration in the patient's condition, it may well be that Canadian courts will discern a duty to render professional assistance. That would not drive one to the conclusion that doctors must, as a matter of law, stop their cars and attend at every traffic accident they happen to encounter. But it would preclude the sole practitioner in a remote community from turning away with impunity a seriously injured or sick person who sought his professional assistance for the first time.

More problematical is the position of the doctor who finds herself the only physician on a crowded aeroplane, and has to decide in midflight whether to declare her professional identity, and go to the aid of a fellow-passenger who has been taken ill. If she does not, and her inaction subsequently comes to light, will she be liable to the stricken passenger for any resulting harm he may have suffered? In truth, it is hard to distinguish this case from that of the lone backwoods practitioner, just considered. And it is not inconceivable that a bold Canadian court might impose liability. It seems more likely, however, that a court would stop short of doing so, fearful of opening the door to liability in the roadside-accident scenario, where the physician's immunity from suit, however callous his non-intervention may seem, has so long been one of the commonplaces of the law. If pressed to make the distinction between the case of the sole practitioner in a remote outpost, and the physician on the plane, the Court would probably stress that the former "holds himself out" as being available to help the sick; whereas the latter is at pains to preserve her anonymity. Thus (it might be argued) the rural practitioner induces reliance by potential patients, and so assumes a duty of care; while his colleague on the aeroplane does not. This line of reasoning is of course specious. For it seems quite probable that the emergency patient arriving at the remote clinic on the tundra may not have "relied" upon any "holding-out" by the physician stationed there, and may indeed only have learned of his existence after illness or accident struck. Yet it is submitted that he might still sue the doctor who turned him away, if harm resulted. If the courts stop short of imposing liability upon the physician in the aircraft, or him who passes by the roadside accident, the line will be drawn as dictated by expediency, rather than remorseless logic. While case law is scanty, it can confidently be predicted that the courts will move slowly, step by cautious step, in extending the physician's obligations to emulate the Good Samaritan.

Related difficulties arise when a physician wishes to terminate the doctor/patient relationship. The physician should ordinarily give timely notice of his intent to do so, since an abrupt severance of the relationship — if it causes damage to the patient — may well prove actionable. The "if" in the foregoing sentence, though, is a very big "if." For example, a physician, who from reasons of fear refused to give further assistance to a patient who announced he had AIDS, would not necessarily face legal liability for negligence or anything else. If there are other and more intrepid physicians by whom that patient will foreseeably be accepted and treated, our more faint-hearted doctor may discharge his legal responsibilities by referring the unwanted patient (save in situations of life-threatening emergency) to such a courageous colleague. It is only in the rare instance where no such alternative assistance is available, or where the loss of time involved in a referral may imperil the patient's safety, that the law may impose liability. For otherwise, the law might well say that there was a breach of duty; but none of that resultant damage, necessary to found a cause of action in negligence.

Let us suppose that a doctor/patient relationship has unquestionably come into being, but that the patient now complains, in an action for negligence, that he was harmed by the physician's blameworthy inattention to his case. That is the sort of case we are talking of when we speak of the duty to attend. It means the duty to make oneself, as a professional person, physically available to treat one's patient, and to *pay due attention* to that patient's case for so long as the malady lasts and the doctor/patient relationship subsists. As always in negligence cases, the law's demands in this context will vary greatly according to the facts of the particular case. The physician who shows less urgency or compunction in visiting or checking on his patients than would be shown by most of his fellow-professionals in like circumstances may well be found liable if damage to the patient results from his laxity. As Madame Justice Picard has noted in her valuable text on medical jurisprudence, a physician "may be infamous among his colleagues for his lack of diligence in attending on his patients in hospital, or among his patients for his failure to keep office appointments or return calls, yet there will be no liability if this unprofessional and substandard conduct falls short of causing foreseeable injury to the patient."[1]

In assessing what degree of diligence or promptitude is required to discharge this duty, regard may be had not only to the plight of the patient, as perceived by the doctor, but also to the weight and urgency of that doctor's other responsibilities at the crucial time. The old Ontario case of *Smith v. Rae,* in 1919,[2] is still sound law on this point. An "expectant father" telephoned Dr. Rae, advising him that the mother-to-be was in labour, the baby being some two weeks overdue. He urged Dr. Rae to come "right away", but Dr. Rae was in the midst of his evening surgery, and replied that with four or five other patients yet to see, he could not conveniently attend for another hour. A nurse, in attendance on the mother, had told the father that the baby would probably not arrive for another three hours or more, so the father made no further steps to urge haste. In the event, the child was delivered very precipitately only minutes after the telephone conversation. It was a breech presentation, and the child died. The Ontario Court of Appeal, overturning a jury ruling, absolved the doctor of any negligence. His duty, they said, had been to "act reasonably, having regard to all the circumstances"; that did not entail the obligation to "drop everything", in the absence of any indication that a critical situation, one of real emergency, was unfolding.

Of course, the degree of urgency reasonably to be required of a physician will depend upon the information available. It will be incumbent upon the physician to show an appropriate degree of inquisitiveness, and to ask any questions which may be necessary, in order that he may sensibly assess the seriousness of the patient's position. If the asking of the appropriate questions fails to dispel the vagueness of the symptoms, and those symptoms (e.g., abdominal pain) might conceivably suggest something more than a trivial and transient disorder, the prudent course would be to direct the patient promptly to the doctor's office, or to the emergency department of a local hospital. Incautious and uninquisitive dismissal of vague symptoms may well invite liability, as illustrated by the case of *Dale v. Munthali* (discussed later in this chapter).

Obviously, in cases of this kind, the duty to attend merges inextricably into the duty to diagnose. Such overlaps between the "duty to attend" and other sub-categories of the general duty of skill and care are very common. In *Considine v. Camp Hill Hospital* (Nova Scotia, 1982),[3] for example, the plaintiff suffered impotence and urinary incontinence after undergoing a transurethral resection of the prostate. Loose practice, in breach of the duty of care and skill, was clearly shown. For one thing, the patient had not been properly informed of the risk of these unfortunate results. It was surmised, moreover, that this lapse might have been due to the failure by the very senior urologist in charge of the case to speak to his patient at all until after the surgery. He had delegated such matters entirely to a senior resident in urology. In the event, the action was dismissed for want of any evidence of negligence in the treatment provided, and because a reasonable patient in Mr. Considine's position, properly informed of the risks, would have consented anyway to run those risks. But the judge described the failure of the senior surgeon to meet personally with his patient, and talk with him about the impending surgery, as "somewhat incredible" — conduct which might well have attracted legal liability, had any harm to the patient been shown to have resulted from it.

Here then, the duty to inform and the duty to attend were inseparably connected. In *MacDonald v. York County Hospital*,[4] the famous case with which this book began, the defendant Dr. V was held liable for the amputation of his patient's gangrenous leg. The defendant was faulted on two grounds: his tardiness in attending his patient after putting his severely fractured leg in a temporary cast, and his failure to respond with due urgency to warning signs brought to his attention by nurses. It is immaterial whether we ascribe such failures to the physician's breach of his duty to attend, or to his duty to provide appropriate aftercare. The reason is that these headings do not represent discrete and watertight compartments, but are merely facets of the overall duty to show due care and skill to the patient.

In 1981, the Ontario courts were called upon to decide *White v. Turner,*[5] an action brought against a plastic surgeon for alleged negligence in the performance of a mammoplasty which produced distressing results. While the defendant was adjudged to have performed the surgery with undue haste, and to have failed also in his duty to inform his patient of material risks, he was absolved from the additional claim of negligence in failing to attend upon his patient after the surgery. After looking in on his patient, Dr. Turner had informed her that he would be out of town for a week, but was leaving her in the capable hands of Dr. H. This was not negligence, said the judge:

> There was some evidence that Mrs. White was upset by Dr. Turner's absence during part of her convalescence. Although it is certainly disconcerting for a patient to learn that her doctor will not be personally available during her entire convalescence, this is not negligence as long as adequate alternative arrangements are made, as was done here. Doctors are human, too, and they are entitled to attend conferences and take vacations, as long as appropriate steps are taken to see that a competent substitute is available to their patients during their absence. It may have been unwise for Dr. Turner to leave Mrs. White following her surgery in the light of subsequent developments, but it was definitely not negligence to do so.[6]

Very different was the case of *Videto v. Kennedy,*[7] decided in the Ontario Courts in that same year. Mrs. Videto suffered an accidental perforation of the bowel while undergoing a tubal ligation. She was discharged from hospital before this mishap, and the severe peritonitis which resulted, came to light. It was a Friday night, and the doctor's office number was unattended at weekends. His home telephone was unlisted. Another telephone number, suggested by the hospital, was tried in vain. As the judge observed "I find the arrangements made by the defendant doctor for post-operative care in the event of complications just about non-existent, and I find it difficult to condone the omission . . . . It seems to me that in the circumstances the duty lay upon the defendant to ensure that the patient would get attention in an emergency situation, and if he did not make those arrangements, to himself communicate with the plaintiff or her relatives as to her condition .... Perhaps I cannot describe his conduct as callous, but I can and do describe it as casual."[8] The damages awarded for this negligent behaviour were relatively modest, since it had only resulted in some delay in performing a life-saving laparotomy, a procedure which would anyway have been necessary, once the peritonitis manifested itself. The patient was entitled to damages only for the extra discomfort sustained while fruitless efforts were made to contact the surgeon: and for any protraction of her convalescence which might be shown to be due to the resultant unnecessary delay in performing the laparotomy.

(b) The Duty to Diagnose

This duty, again arising out of the doctor/patient relationship as a facet of the general duty of care and skill, is of course not an obligation of infallibility. The physician's duty is to make a reasonably careful and reasonably knowledgeable assessment of the patient's condition. He must bring to the task of diagnosis that measure of professional judgement and skill, and that measure of attention and concern, which is reasonably to be expected from a fellow-practitioner of ordinary competence. That standard acknowledges that erroneous diagnoses may be made without anyone being at fault. But it does require reasonable effort, a healthy measure of attention and inquisitiveness, an open mind, and a willingness by the physician to make use of any appropriate diagnostic resources which may be reasonably available.

We have already seen cases in which negligence was discerned in the realm of diagnosis. In *Fraser v. Vancouver General Hospital,* (British Columbia, 1952),[9] for example, the failure of the two interns to detect a dislocated fracture of the neck, plainly visible upon the patient's x-rays, was held to be actionable negligence. So too was the failure of all three physicians involved in *Yepremian v. Scarborough General Hospital*[10] (*supra*, Chapter 6, p. 113) to make a timely diagnosis of diabetes in that case — a diagnosis ultimately made by a nurse. The failure of diagnostic care and skill here had several aspects. A clinical history of the patient, the first necessity of any sufficient diagnosis, had been taken, but inferences which should have been suggested by the exercise of reasonable professional judgement had not been drawn. Urinalysis, when finally ordered, was not directed with appropriate urgency, nor was a blood test done until an unduly late stage. All these failures amounted to negligence in diagnosis.

The case of *Dale v. Munthali*[11] (Ontario, 1977), already touched upon, may seem rather more severe. Mr. Dale, a middle-aged man, asplenic but otherwise normal, suddenly complained of an elevated temperature and severe and generalized bodily pain, trembling, vomiting, hearing impairment and diarrhea. His wife called Dr. Munthali, who made a house call as soon as he could. He examined Mr. Dale's ears, nose and throat, his neck and his head; listened to his chest with a stethoscope, percussed his back, took his blood pressure . . . and without further ado, diagnosed influenza.

Mr. Dale did not have the "flu." He was in fact suffering from meningitis and was in desperate need of antibiotics. Without them, his condition went from bad to worse, and, just two days after Dr. Munthali's visit, he died in hospital. The defendant physician was held liable — but not, be it noted, because he was negligent in failing to detect meningitis. Some symptoms of that disease had been present at the time of the examination, some (e.g. a stiff neck) had not. And some of Mr. Dale's sufferings (e.g. diarrhea) were not of a kind usually associated with meningitis. Yet Dr. Munthali's diagnosis was deemed negligent. Why? Because the symptoms evident upon examination were so severe as to indicate something far worse than gastro-intestinal "flu", something perhaps not yet readily identifiable, but stridently suggesting the need for immediate hospitalization and the running of urgent diagnostic tests. Such a course might have saved the patient's life. The failure to do so rendered the defendant physician liable for the patient's death.

The moral appears to be that while an inability to diagnose accurately may be entirely excusable, a glib or incurious response, or the neglect of any obvious diagnostic procedure* which might clarify the picture, will be treated as negligence if the Court feels that a physician of reasonable competence or diligence would have done more. In *Wade v. Nayernouri*,[12] for example, an Ontario case decided in 1978, a young man complained of severe headaches, dizziness and photophobia, with some nausea. The doctor who examined him for some fifteen or twenty minutes in the hospital emergency department diagnosed "migrainous headache plus nervous overtone", and prescribed "292" tablets and valium. In fact, the patient was in the early throes of a subarachnoid haemorrhage. Two weeks later, having tried to resume his ordinary activities, he collapsed and died before surgical intervention could be attempted to save him. The Court held that there had been negligence in diagnosis. In the absence of any history of migraine, a diagnosis of that complaint was simply too facile. More care should have been taken and more time expended in taking the patient's history. Equipped with the resultant information, the defendant should then either have ordered careful neurological tests and other diagnostic procedures (e.g., lumbar puncture); or should have referred the patient promptly to a specialist colleague, in this instance the neurologist on call. At the very least, a second opinion should have been sought. As the judge put it:

> In my opinion the cases have established that an erroneous diagnosis does not alone determine the physician's liability. But if the physician, as an

---

* As discussed in Chapter 6, it would be no excuse for the physician to plead that he omitted such a procedure for reasons of cost containment, if sound medical judgment would have dictated that it be performed.

aid to diagnosis, does not avail himself of the scientific means and facilities open to him for the collection of the best factual data upon which to arrive at his diagnosis, does not accurately obtain the patient's history, does not avail himself in this particular case of the need for referral to a neurologist, does not perform the stiff neck tests and the lumbar puncture tests, the net result is not an error in judgment but constitutes negligence. Of course, the doctor was acting in good faith but he failed in the ways in which I have indicated in not being more conscious of the grave symptoms that stood out before him and which were urged upon him by the patient's condition and by the information conveyed to him by his wife. I do not consider that his duty was performed by allowing Wade to leave in the condition in which he was.[13]

Once again, this does not mean that the physician must in every case canvass exhaustively every conceivable diagnostic possibility, however remote; still less, that she must employ every available diagnostic tool or technique to that end. There comes a point in the diagnostic process when the good sense, the clinical judgment and experience of the physician — used with proper commitment and concern for the wellbeing of the patient — will suggest a particular diagnosis as the correct one, and dictate action appropriate to that diagnosis. If that exercise is performed with the skill and care to be expected of a reasonably competent physician, the law will be satisfied. And in that event, the omission of elaborate or extravagant tests to rule out fanciful diagnostic possibilities will not be castigated as negligence.

In *Wipfli v. Britten* (British Columbia, 1984),[14] the defendant, a family doctor, was found liable for failure to diagnose a multiple gestation in his patient. Only after the first child (a brow presentation) had been delivered by caesarian section, and oxytocin had been applied to stop uterine haemorrhaging, was the second baby discovered, as a second doctor sought to remove the placenta. Almost smothered in meconium, this second baby survived, but in a state of permanent and severe debility, both physical and mental. It was held that the defendant had been negligent in diagnosis. His procedures for the completion of pre-natal charts had been lax, and his appointments with Mrs. Wipfli in the latter stages of her pregnancy had been too few, especially after delivery became overdue. Estriol and B-scan ultrasound tests, appropriate in her case, had not been performed. And neither Mrs. Wipfli's weight-gain nor the measurements of her fundal height had alerted the physician, as they should have done, to the likelihood of multiple gestation. All this amounted to negligence; and by the application of the now-discarded *McGhee* doctrine (see Chapter 6), the Court had no difficulty in surmounting the final hurdle of causation, and finding the defendant liable to the unfortunate infant.

We have seen that a physician may be wrong in her diagnosis, and still escape liability if that diagnosis was reached by the exercise of due care and skill. But that does not mean that a wrong diagnosis can be unreflectively and stubbornly adhered to, once commonsense and professional judgement proclaim its error. Two Alberta cases, decided in 1984, illustrate the need for continual re-evaluation of one's initial diagnosis. In *Layden v. Cope*[15], two general practitioners diagnosed gout in a patient, and successively prescribed Indocide suppositories, Colchicine, Zyloprim and Butazolidine, as well as a variety of pain killers. None of these gout treatments effected any improvement, while the patient's general health deteriorated, with symptoms of fever, nausea and generalized weakness. When eventually the patient was referred to a specialist, an advanced condition of cellulitis involving probable streptococcal or staphylococcal infection was diagnosed. Vigorous treatment with antibiotics proved unavailing, and debridement was undertaken, revealing a condition of necrosis so extensive as to necessitate amputation of the patient's leg just below the knee. The general practitioners were held liable for their tardiness in re-evaluating their initial diagnosis. The general deterioration in the patient's health, and his utter unresponsiveness to the treatment provided, should have prompted such a re-assessment much earlier, at a time when the leg might have been saved.

Similarly, in *Bergen* v. *Sturgeon General Hospital*,[16] a young woman was admitted to hospital complaining of acute abdominal pain. Both a general surgeon and a gynecologist who examined her made a diagnosis of pelvic inflammatory disease, and treated her with penicillin and Demerol. After several days, abdominal swelling, extreme pain and a "snapping" sensation in the abdomen were recorded, and at the urgent prompting of a charge nurse, the attending physician finally re-assessed her condition for what it really was — a ruptured appendix. Emergency surgery proved to be too late to save the patient, who died from septic shock. Negligence was found against certain of the doctors involved, not only for their culpable diagnostic oversight, in not performing a laparotomy to check for appendicitis; but also for their apparent "tunnel vision" which had for so long caused them to zero in upon one diagnosis to the exclusion of all others.

In situations of obvious emergency, the law is very hesitant to condemn as negligent the physician who makes a diagnostic error "in the agony of the moment." Thus in *Wilkinson Estate v. Shannon* (Ontario, 1986),[17] a young girl, run down by a vehicle, was admitted to a hospital's emergency department with injuries that were apparently relatively minor, and detained for observation. To the surprise of all, her condition worsened precipitately, and life-support systems were put in place. Within a week, brain death had occurred and treatment was discontinued. Her death was caused by a malignant cerebral oedema. Neither the physician in charge of the emergency room, nor the general surgeon who had treated the child, were adjudged negligent. Their initial diagnoses had very reasonably been guarded, and while prompt testing for electrolytes and neurological consultation might (with the wisdom of hindsight) have been desired, this was a counsel of perfection, not consonant with normal procedure when dealing with apparently minor injuries. Moreover, once serious neurological episodes began to manifest themselves, the omission to employ diuretic therapy and hyperventilation, before the arrival of a specialist neurologist, was a mistake — but an excusable error of judgement, not suggestive of negligence in the unhappy and rapidly deteriorating predicament which had here evolved.

It is instructive to contrast this case with *Seyfert v. Hospital Society (Burnaby)* (British Columbia, 1986),[18] in which a young man, drunk and abusive, presented himself at an emergency ward with a stab wound to his abdomen. The physician on duty cleaned and probed the wound, listened to the patients innards, ordered a chest x-ray, and concluded, erroneously, that neither the peritoneum nor the chest area was perforated. The wound was sutured and the patient released hours later. In fact, the transverse colon had been penetrated, and gross inflammation of the omentum had set in, requiring extensive corrective surgery. The defendant physician was held liable for his laxity in discharging the patient after so brief a period of observation, especially in view of this patient's inebriation. This was a case where an occult lesion was a serious possibility, and where a more cautious approach to diagnosis would have been indicated by usual emergency-ward practice.

(c) The Duty to Refer

There will be times when any physician will feel insecure in his diagnosis of a patient, or indeed admit her inability to make any diagnosis at all with reasonable confidence. In such a case, the duty of diagnosis is displaced by another responsibility — the responsibility to behave as any reasonable fellow-professional would do, either by seeking the second opinion of a respected colleague, or actually referring the patient to some other professional — someone whose qualifications of learning or experience raise the hope that he may be better equipped to unravel the case. Similarly, a physician who feels confident in her diagnosis may well feel that the indicated surgery would better be performed by someone more skilled in that particular procedure; and again, the duty of prompt referral will arise.

Both the need to make referrals (or seek consultations), and the promptitude with which this should be done, call for the exercise of ordinary professional judgement, often assisted by the existence of general understandings within the profession as to the proper limits of a general practitioner's competence, and as to the demarcations of competency as between the various professional sub-disciplines and specialties. Unfortunately, expert evidence may be needed to establish such conventions or understandings, which even then are not always as clear as might be desired. Thus in *Chipps v. Peters*[19] (Ontario, 1979) a general surgeon performed a hysterectomy and operated to improve his patient's bladder-function and stop the protrusion of her vagina. Unfortunately, he so foreshortened the vagina as to render sexual intercourse impossible. In the face of divided expert evidence as to whether all this surgery should have been referred to a gynecologist, the Court of Appeal inclined to the view that it had reasonably been performed by the defendant, who, having met the standard of performance reasonably to be expected of a general surgeon, was absolved of any liability.

Obviously, the propriety of non-referral may in any given case be judged not only with reference to the ordinary habits of the medical profession, but with due regard to the perceivable urgency (or otherwise) of the patient's condition, and the ready availability (or otherwise) of a specialist to whom he may be referred. The only general guidance which can be given is that a referral, or at least a consultation, should always be made when one feels oneself approaching the bounds of one's own competence or professional experience: see *Fraser v. Vancouver General Hospital* (Chapter 6, p. 96). A referral should always be made when a diagnosis cannot confidently be arrived at, and should seriously be considered when an initial diagnosis has been proved wrong by the unresponsiveness of the patient to treatment: as in *Layden v. Cope,* and *Bergen v. Sturgeon General Hospital,* considered earlier in this chapter. Obviously a referral must be made, as we have seen, when the physician anticipates that he will be absent (e.g. on vacation). And above all, a physician should always be sensible of her own limitations of training, and refrain from trespassing into areas of specialization for which her training has not equipped her. A timely referral is in such cases the only proper way to discharge the duty owed to the patient, except of course in cases of direst emergency where timely access to more expert assistance is for some reason not available.

(d)   The Duty to Treat and to Provide Adequate Aftercare

It might reasonably be supposed that errors in the actual treatment of patients would afford more instructive and thought-provoking examples in the case law than any of the other sub-headings in this chapter. But that is not the case. The law reports down the centuries are besprinkled with accounts of surgeons who have amputated the wrong limb, excised the wrong organ or applied casts of excruciating tightness; tales of forceps, sponges and swabs absent-mindedly left in body-cavities; and of patients given the wrong medication or vast overdoses of the right one. Besides these grosser errors, we find a legion of accidental "slips" — nerves and major blood vessels interfered with during surgery, the extravasation of injected fluids, and failures to anticipate, guard against or monitor the expectable side-effects of therapy. In such cases there may be purposeful debate as to whether the appropriate standard of care and skill was met in the particular instance. We could multiply examples of all these mishaps, but to do so would serve no instructive purpose. All such cases devolve in the last analysis upon this single question — whether the physician's error was compatible with the exercise of that level of care and skill ordinarily shown by his or her professional peers. If it was, then the error, however tragic its consequences, is not actionable in negligence. If that standard was not met, a negligence action will succeed.

Doctrinally, it is as simple as that, and any courtroom disputation will be confined to the realm of fact — to establishing what the defendant physician actually did, and to ascertaining whether a fellow-professional of ordinary competence would have done better. These days, the grosser forms of ineptitude referred to above will seldom be submitted to a court, for such is the cost, the stress and the publicity of litigation that both the physician and the insurer (or other protective entity which represents his interests) will often feel that a sensible out-of-court settlement is in the best interests of everyone.

A few other general propositions may usefully be distilled from the case-law: propositions which, like so much in the law of negligence, can claim no great profundity, but are simply precepts of commonsense. All the more interesting cases on negligence in actual treatment seem to devolve upon one or more of three variables; the peculiarities of the particular patient, the degree and predictability of inherent danger attending a particular mode of therapy, and the relative ease or difficulty of precautionary measures.

Little can be said about the first of these variables, save to stress the necessity of genuine communication with the patient, at all stages of the doctor/patient relationship. The absence of genuine dialogue between physician and patient is a conspicuous common feature in medical negligence cases of all kinds, from the "informed consent" cases (see *Allan v. New Mount Sinai Hospital,* in Chapter 2) to cases of negligent diagnosis and negligent aftercare.

More interesting for present purposes are the other two variables, identified above. Certain medical sub-disciplines are more inherently fraught with danger than others. The perils of anaesthesiology afford an obvious example, and strongly suggest the wisdom of leaving its practice to specialists in the field whenever it is feasible to do so. And even the anaesthetist must show constant and unremitting alertness, so sudden and so unpredictable are the hazards of his craft. In short, the degree of care required is commensurate with the risk to be perceived. Other sub-disciplines, too, may be attended by omnipresent danger, while in others, obviously, only certain procedures are so inherently fraught with peril as to demand redoubled attentiveness. With new forms of therapy, in particular, extra care may reasonably be expected, and little judicial sympathy will be found for the physician who injures his patient by failing to read with thoroughness the warnings on the bottles and packaging of new medication. These observations however, like all the others under this heading, seem so obvious as to be scarcely worthy of mention. That, no doubt, is as it should be in an area of law dedicated to striking a fair balance between the need to protect patients and the need to demand standards of patient care which are high but realistically attainable.

The duty to provide adequate aftercare is really just a facet of the duty to treat with due care and skill. In this chapter we have already seen, in the cases of *White v. Turner* and *Videto v. Kennedy,* that a physician must be available to his patient, or at least arrange for a competent substitute to attend the patient, during the period of convalescence. The case of *Brushett v. Cowan* (Newfoundland, 1987)[20] is also instructive. The plaintiff had suffered a leg injury, and the defendant, a specialist in orthopaedics, detected a palpable lump which he feared might be a sarcoma. He conducted a muscle biopsy and then, cutting into the periosteum, took a sample of that and of the underlying bone for analysis. The patient had not been advised that this would be done, nor had she consented to such a procedure. In the event, no malignancy was found, but when the patient was discharged with crutches, two days later, she was given no warning as to the dangers of dispensing with those crutches, or otherwise allowing her full weight to repose upon the weakened leg. She indulged in her ordinary daily activities, leaving her crutches aside, and the femur broke at the very site of the bone biopsy. The surgeon was held liable in battery (see Chapter 2) for his unprivileged performance of the bone biopsy. More importantly for present purposes, his failure to warn the patient of the dangers of dispensing with the crutches was characterized as negligence in post-operative care. However, he partially escaped liability for the resultant harm by reason of the patient's own contributory negligence in failing to enquire of the surgeon what use she should make of the crutches provided.

This latter case will be seen to raise a rather broader issue, the duty of the physician to instruct and to explain to the patient (or those responsible for his welfare, such as family members), all essential information required for the patient's own self-care, or for the self-administration of drugs or other therapy. Any such delegation must of course be shown to be reasonable both in the light of sound practice generally and the patient's own particular circumstances and perceived intelligence. The doctor must warn the patient of any "warning signs", or indicia of dangerous side-effects for which he should be alert. Even then, the physician must be mindful that his own duty to be available to the patient still persists, and that his duty to monitor the patient's condition can seldom if ever be wholly extinguished by delegation, even though the patient may be induced to share the responsibility for his own welfare.

(e) The Duty to Communicate with Other Involved Professionals

We have already noted the duty of a physician, a duty critical to the proper performance of his general duty of care, to communicate and enter into a true dialogue with the patient. Equally important may be the obligation to communicate diligently and efficiently with other health-care professionals (not just physicians, but nurses and others where appropriate) who are involved in the care of the patient. Failure to do this may result in liability. This is not just a matter of promptly forwarding to the physician in charge of a case the results of tests or procedures which one has been called upon to do, nor is it just a question of actively seeking out such results when they do not come through. It is a question of taking sensible initiatives, whenever commonsense and sound medical practice seem to dictate them, to compare notes on the patient's case. Only in this way can one make sure that no procedure or precaution has been overlooked because every physician involved has assumed that "someone else has done it."

A good example is afforded by the case of *Reynard v. Carr*[21] (British Columbia, 1983) one of the illustrative cases with which Chapter 5 began. That case was one of several which have considered the sad results of excessive prednisone use, and its facts can be quickly reiterated. Mr. Reynard, afflicted with ulcerative colitis, was referred by his family physician Dr. W first to one gastroenterologist (Dr. S) who prescribed prednisone and Imuran; and later to another (Dr. Carr), who prescribed prednisone again. At first, the use of gradually diminishing doses was planned, but later, as "flareups" of the bowel disease occurred, the dosage was occasionally "bumped." Problems which developed in Mr. Reynard's hip and shoulder joints were diagnosed by Dr. W as symptoms of bursitis, even though x-rays plainly showed serious bone degeneration in the joints. Yet Dr. W did not alert Dr. Carr to what he had seen, and only when Mr. Reynard was finally referred to a rheumatologist was the obvious diagnosis of advanced avascular necrosis, associated with prednisone use, finally made. Both Dr. W and Dr. Carr were held liable in negligence. Not only had there been a negligent failure to warn the patient of the risks associated with sustained and heavy prednisone use; there had been a sorry lack of co-ordination shown by these two physicians, and a culpable failure to establish either some clear understanding as to the demarcation of their responsibilities, or some efficient line of communication enabling them to compare notes and discuss their patient's case. As the judge put it, "Between hospital stays, Dr. W and Dr. Carr did not co-ordinate the drug therapy. Each remained largely ignorant of what the other was doing. Each treated the prescription of prednisone as a rather commonplace or mundane task, not demanding much in the way of medical skill. Mr. Reynard looked to both of them for advice and guidance." Their failure to provide it led to the liability of both.

Then there is *Bergen v. Sturgeon General Hospital, (supra,* p. 144), where the Alberta court found that one of the causes of Mrs. Bergen's death from an undiagnosed ruptured appendix was the dismal failure of communication between the physicians involved in her case. As the judge observed:

> There appears to be an accepted practice of what is referred to as "Curb-stone Consultations." This appears to happen when doctors casually meet in such places as hospital corridors and discuss a patient. In my opinion, this is bad practice and to be discouraged. It seems to me that when an attending physician calls in a specialist for a "Consultation" the least that might be expected is for those physicians to have a meaningful discussion between them, or among them, as the case may require, whereby each advises the other of what they did, when they did it and what should be done. In this way each would be fully aware of the procedure of the other, the findings of the other and the reasons for the diagnosis arrived at by the other. In this case, such a "Consultation" did not take place which, in my opinion, contributed to the bad result.[22]

(f)   The Duty to Keep Full and Accurate Records

The cases in which the inadequacy of a physician's record-keeping practices has led directly or obviously to the imposition of negligence liability are relatively few. Slackness in record-keeping was, to be sure, one among the several shortcomings adjudged to be negligent in *Bergen v.*

Sturgeon General Hospital, discussed in the foregoing section, while in *Reynard v. Carr,* also considered in that section, Dr. Carr's woefully inadequate medical history sheets concerning Mr. Reynard cast grave doubt upon the reliability of the doctor's recollections, and seriously compromised the persuasiveness of his defence.

There are in fact many cases like *Reynard v. Carr* in this respect. The fear that the inadequacy of one's records may result directly in misguided and harmful treatment, and hence in negligence liability, is not the only reason, or even the main reason, for maintaining good and full records. The first reason for so doing should of course be a sincere commitment to the wellbeing of the patient, but self-regarding considerations of a prudential nature are also at work. Quite apart from the statutory requirements that certain records be kept upon pain of prosecution (e.g. under the Narcotic Control Regulations), the records as a whole may be critical to a doctor's defence against any allegation of negligence or other misconduct, whether in the context of a negligence or battery trial, or in disciplinary hearings. In civil trials, particularly, there are often years of delay before the issues are aired in the courtroom. Memories on both sides fade or become distorted, as do the recollections of witnesses. Since 1970,* records made by a physician in the ordinary course of practice, and made at the time the recorded events occurred (or immediately thereafter) are admissible as evidence (though not of course conclusive proof) of what in fact transpired. No item of evidence is more potentially powerful as a shield against unwarranted charges. Composed contemporaneously with the treatment, recorded in ink,** properly dated and initialled, accurate and concise records can be worth their weight in gold to a defendant physician. Conversely, skimpy or otherwise inadequate record-keeping, or worst of all, records which appear to have been altered retrospectively in a self-serving way, may fatally undermine the physician's credibility.

(g) The Duty to Supervise Colleagues

It will sometimes happen that a physician will find himself obliged to take care not only in his own conduct while treating a patient, but in overseeing the performance of other professionals — typically junior colleagues involved in a surgical team. When that duty of supervision is broken, the more senior doctor may find himself liable alongside the junior

---

* The decisive case was the Supreme Court of Canada ruling in *Ares v. Venner,* [1970] S.C.R. 608, 73 W.W.R. 347, 12 C.R.N.S. 349, 14 D.L.R. (3d) 4: discussed more extensively in Chapters 9 and 11.

** Or some other relatively indelible medium not lending itself to easy and invisible correction "after the event": Note in this regard the discussion of computerized record-keeping, in Chapter 9, *post.*

colleague, since both will be deemed to share responsibility for the mishap. It should be noted that in such cases, what is at issue is something very different from the phenomenon of vicarious liability, discussed in Chapter 6. When the law imposes vicarious liability, it imposes upon a wholly blameless person or entity (the employer or master) a legal responsibility for the negligent or otherwise wrongful act of another (the servant or employee). In cases of negligent supervision, however, the supervisor is held liable for his own fault; there need be no suggestion that the junior colleague was in any sense his "servant"!

Sometimes, the junior colleague is so entirely subject to the control and direction of a senior physician in charge of a case, that the junior's acts will be deemed to be, in whole or in part, the actions of the senior professional. In the exercise of his professional judgement, the latter may delegate certain jobs or procedures to his "helper", but cannot in so doing entirely divest himself of legal responsibility for those acts or functions. Thus in *Considine v. Camp Hill Hospital*,[23] which we encountered earlier in this chapter, the patient underwent a transurethral resection of the prostate, with unhappy results. Both doctors involved in the surgery were ultimately absolved of any liability, but not without some criticism of the procedures they had followed. One of the surgeons involved was Dr. M, head of the urology department at the defendant teaching hospital and a professional of great experience. The other, Dr. A, was a young doctor in the second year of his residency in urology. Errors were undoubtedly made both in the pre-operative measures taken to secure the patient's consent, and in the performance of the surgery, during which the prostatic capsule was perforated. The Court concluded that the former errors were negligent, but not causally relevant, while the latter (surgical) errors were not shown to suggest any negligence at all. However, the judge indicated that in the circumstances, if any negligence had been shown on the part of Dr. A, Dr. M would have been made to share equally in the responsibility:

> Relating only to the particular circumstances of this case, it is my opinion that Dr. A was under the control and direction of Dr. M to such an extent and degree that for the procedures to which this decision is addressed, Dr. M is responsible for Dr. A. Dr. M accepted Dr. A as his assistant in this case. Dr. A was no stranger to Dr. M. He knew his qualifications and he accepted those qualifications as being sufficient and adequate to perform such procedures as Dr. M chose to delegate to him. Dr. M was present in the operating room. Dr. M clearly understood the male plaintiff was his patient. Dr. M clearly chose to delegate some or all of the procedures to Dr. A. In this way he adopted that which Dr. A did for and on behalf as though Dr. M was doing it himself. I do not know whether Dr. M billed full tariff for this TURP to

Medical Services Insurance. If he did, then I would find all the more reason to conclude as I do with respect to the matter of his responsibility for the acts of Dr. A. I am convinced that on the facts of this particular case Dr. M either accepted or must be deemed to have accepted, or both, the risks inherent in his permitting Dr. A to perform all or a part of the surgical procedure on the male plaintiff. If I had found Dr. A responsible in law for loss suffered by the male plaintiff arising out of the surgical procedures, then I would have had no hesitation in finding the defendant M equally responsible.[24]

3. CONCLUSION

All aspects of medical negligence law have now been examined in this and the foregoing chapters. The reader is now in a position to make a fair evaluation of that law, and to decide whether the law strikes a fair balance between the need to protect and compensate the injured patient, and the need to avoid making unfair or unreasonable demands upon the physician. Regardless of one's conclusion on that issue, however, a question remains that cannot help but inspire a deep sense of malaise. Every day, physicians meet with patients who suffer pain and debility, often devastating in extent, visited upon them by sheer misfortune, by genetic mischance or some inscrutable whim of nature. Often, too, they will encounter patients (like Mr. Ferguson*) whose medical treatment has, through no-one's fault at all, left them in a far sorrier state than when that treatment was first proposed. No-one is at fault, no-one is negligent, and there is accordingly no-one to whom these unfortunate people can look for full compensation. The availability of "someone to be sued" may thus be seen as a boon or consolation provided randomly to the "lucky" few by a very capricious providence. The incidence of professional "fault", rather than some other baneful agency equally beyond the patient's understanding or control, determines the incidence of compensation. The injustice of such a state of affairs, in a supposedly compassionate society, is being increasingly borne in upon the judges who in recent years have been increasingly vocal, along with academic writers, in calling for some new philosophy and mechanism to provide accident compensation to all accident victims. The ideas which have emerged, and the social experiments which have been attempted in various places to achieve these ends, are discussed fully in chapter 10.

---

* See *Ferguson v. Hamilton Civil Hospitals*, discussed previously in Chapter 4 and again in Chapter 10.

NOTES

1. Picard and Robertson, *Legal Liability of Doctors and Hospitals in Canada*, 3rd ed. (1996), p. 236.
2. (1919), 46 O.L.R. 518, 51 D.L.R. 323 (C.A.).
3. (1982), 20 C.C.L.T. 260, 133 D.L.R. (3d) 11, 50 N.S.R. (2d) 631, 98 A.P.R. 631 (T.D.).
4. [1972] 3 O.R. 469, 28 D.L.R. (3d) 521 (H.C.), affirmed in part (1973), O.R. (2d) 653, 41 D.L.R. 321 (C.A.), affirmed by (sub nom. *Vail v. MacDonald),* [1976] 2 S.C.R. 825 66 D.L.R. (3d) 530, 8 N.R. 155; see also Chapter 1.
5. (1981), 31 O.R. (2d) 773, 15 C.C.L.T. 81, 120 D.L.R. (3d) 269, 5 L. Med. Q. 119 (H.C.), affirmed (1982), 47 O.R. (2d) 764, 12 D.L.R. (4th) 319 (C.A.).
6. Mr. Justice Linden, (1981), 31 O.R. (2d) 773 (H.C.), at p. 795.
7. (1980), 27 O.R. (2d) 747, 107 D.L.R. (3d) 612, 4 L. Med. Q. 44 (H.C.) reversed on other grounds (1981), 33 O.R. (2d) 497, 17 C.C.L.T. 307, 125 D.L.R. (3d) 127 (C.A.).
8. Mr. Justice Grange, (1980), 27 O.R. (2d) 747 (H.C.), at pp. 752-53.
9. [1952] 2 S.C.R, 36, [1952] 3 D.L.R. 785; see also Chapter 6.
10. (1978), 20 O.R. (2d) 510, 6 C.C.L.T. 81, 88 D.L.R. (3d) 161, 2 L. Med. Q. 216 (H.C.), reversed (1980), 28 O.R. (2d) 494, 13 C.C.L.T. 105, 110 D.L.R. (3d) 513, 3 L. Med. Q. 278 (C.A.), leave to appeal allowed (1980), 120 D.L.R. (3d) 337n (Ont. C.A.).
11. (1977), 16 O.R. (2d) 532, 78 D.L.R. (3d) 588, 1 L. Med. Q. 234 (H.C.), affirmed (1978), 21 O.R. (2d) 554, 90 D.L.R. (3d) 763, 2 L. Med. Q. 231 (C.A.).
12. (1978), 2 L.M.Q. 67 (Ont. H.C.).
13. Mr. Justice Stark, *ibid.,* at p. 71.
14. (1982), 22 C.C.L.T. 104 (B.C. S.C.), additional reasons at [1983] 3 W.W.R. 424, 43 B.C.L.R. 1, 145 D.L.R. (3d) 80 (S.C.), reversed [1984] 5 W.W.R. 385, 56 B.C.L.R. 273, 29 C.C.L.T. 240, 13 D.L.R. (4th) 169 (C.A.), leave to appeal to S.C.C. granted [1985] 1 W.W.R. lviii, 58 B.C.L.R. xxxvii, 13 D.L.R. (4th) 169n.
15. (1984), 28 C.C.L.T. 140, 52 A.R. 70 (Q.B.).
16. (1984), 28 C.C.L.T. 155, 52 A.R. 161 (Q.B.), additional reasons at (1984), 63 A.R. 62 (Q.B.).
17. (1986), 37 C.C.L.T. 181 (Ont. H.C.).
18. (1986), 32 C.C.L.T. 224, 27 D.L.R. (4th) 96 (B.C.S.C.).
19. Ont. C.A., unreported, March 8, 1979.
20. (1987), 42 C.C.L.T. 64, 40 D.L.R. (4th) 488, 64 Nfld. & P.E.I.R. 262, 197 A.P.R. 262 (Nfld. T.D.), reversed (1990), 3 C.C.L.T. (2d) 195 (Nfld. C.A.); see also Chapter 2.

21. (1983), 50 B.C.L.R. 166, 30 C.C.L.T. 42 (S.C.), reversed in part (1986) 10 B.C.L.R. (2d) 121, 38 C.C.L.T. 217 (C.A.).

22. Mr. Justice Hope (1984), 28 C.C.L.T. 155 (Alta. Q.B.), at p. 175; see also note 16, *supra.*

23. (1982), 20 C.C.L.T. 260, 133 D.L.R. (3d) 11, 50 N.S.R. (2d) 631, 98 A.P.R. 631 (T.D.).

24. *Ibid.,* per Mr. Justice Clarke, (1982), 20 C.C.L.T. 260 (N.S.T.D.), at pp. 283-84.

9

NURSING LIABILITY

SUMMARY

The torts of negligence and battery, explained in the previous chapters, are not only of concern to physicians. Those torts, and the rules of informed consent which straddle them both, provide guides also to the conduct of all health-care professionals, and not least to nurses, who provide hands-on care to patients, and are nowadays engaged in increasingly sophisticated forms of therapy carrying correspondingly diverse risks of harm to patients. In this chapter, we provide a synopsis of the principles governing these areas of liability, examining them from the special perspective of the professional nurse and illustrating them with references drawn from decided cases involving allegations of nursing malpractice. The impact of liability insurance is also assessed.

Particular attention is paid to the importance of charting and record-keeping, not only because of its critical importance to patient care, but because of its evidentiary significance, and its usefulness as a protection for nurses who may unfortunately find themselves involved in litigation.

Finally, issues of patient privacy, and the nurse's obligation to preserve the secrecy of confidential patient information, are considered, as reflecting other important facets of the nurse's role.

1. THE NURSE AND LIABILITY INSURANCE

The legal principles discussed in the foregoing chapters are by no means confined in their application to the activities of physicians, but rather apply with equal force and validity to all health care professionals. The fundamental legal principles of negligence, battery, and the doctrine of

informed consent apply without significant variation in cases against den-
tists, chiropractors, physiotherapists, occupational therapists, midwives[1]
nurses and all other professionals who provide health care. Thus, the earlier
chapters of this book may profitably be studied by all such professional
and occupational groups. In addressing the liability of nurses[2] as a discrete
topic, we inevitably commit ourselves to a large measure of repetition and
cross-reference. Few of the ideas considered in this chapter will be new to
readers who have studied the preceding pages, though it is to be hoped that
the examples provided and the points chosen for particular emphasis will
give food for thought.

When one considers how much of the "hands-on" health care received
by Canadian patients is performed by nurses, one is at first sight surprised
at how few reported cases there are in which nurses have been held liable
for inadequate or inappropriate treatment of patients. One of the reasons
for this dearth of authority (always disturbing to lawyers) is undoubtedly
the ethical rigour and meticulous professionalism for which nursing has
long been famous, and which is scrupulously preserved by the disciplinary
boards and mechanisms maintained by the governing bodies of the nursing
profession. When purely ethical and humane promptings fall short, the
severity of professional disciplinary practices may well deter the nurse who
is inclined to slack or inappropriate practices, a prospect that is more
daunting than that of civil litigation.

There are other reasons, however, why nurses have so seldom been
sued. Historically, one such reason may well have been the perennially
niggardly remuneration paid to nurses, which sufficed to make them "judg-
ment-proof " (in crude terms, not worth suing). When a nurse employed
by a hospital or clinic negligently harmed a patient, the patient's attorney
would likely counsel against suing the nurse, suggesting as a more sensible
alternative an action against the employer-institution, which (as explained
in Chapter 6) would be deemed "vicariously liable" for the torts committed
by the nurse "in the course of her employment." The hospital or clinic
would offer a better prospect of compensation, having not only "deeper
pockets" but also liability insurance to cover an award of damages. Nothing
would be gained in such circumstances by suing the hapless nurse as well.

This common scenario led to some common and potentially dangerous
misconceptions. It was commonly believed by hospital employees at every
level that, not they themselves, but the hospital would "take the rap" for
any blunders that they might commit. The employer and its liability insurance policy came to be widely perceived as an umbrella against liability.
However, that perception was never a true reflection of the legal position.
Rather, there was always the possibility that the careless employee might
be sued as well as the hospital, and from time to time that in fact occurred.

Or, equally distressing to the nurse, having paid out money to defray the hospital's obligation to the stricken patient, the hospital's liability insurers might then seek to recoup the loss by a "subrogated" action against the nurse who actually did the harm.

For these reasons, it was always a good idea for nursing staff to have liability insurance coverage of their own. In recent years, such coverage has indeed become almost universal and is one of the automatic advantages normally acquired by joining the association which governs one's branch of the nursing profession. Although this is an undoubtedly sensible development, it requires one cautionary note. Liability insurance may be likened to the lightning-rod on a house. If lightning strikes the rod, the lightning conductor will carry the charge harmlessly away to earth, thereby saving the house from catastrophic harm. But its very presence, a metal spike pointing at the sky, makes such lightning strikes many times more likely. So it is with liability insurance. If a nurse does get sued, the defence costs and the damages awarded against her will be paid by the insurer up to the limits of the coverage provided, so that the nurse will not suffer crippling financial loss. However, the very existence of such coverage makes her a much more attractive quarry for the potential litigant. She is now very well worth suing, probably alongside her employer; and her court appearances will tend henceforth to be in the role of defendant or co-defendant, rather than merely as a key witness.

The ubiquity of liability insurance among modern nursing professionals, then, is one reason why we may anticipate an increased rate of lawsuits against nursing personnel. Another factor tending to the same end is of course the dramatic changes overtaking the whole character of nursing practice in recent decades. The result is that nursing has been converted from a largely menial occupation to a highly sophisticated, complex, and unquestionably more dangerous calling. The ever-expanding functions willingly assumed by nurses,[3] and their tendency to do jobs which were formerly the exclusive domain of physicians inevitably carry with them an increased exposure to potential liability.

2. THE NURSE AND THE TORT OF BATTERY

When a nurse is sued for "malpractice", this will almost invariably mean an action for battery, or for negligence, or both. Though actions for battery against health care professionals are relatively rare nowadays, we will deal with that concept first. A battery is a direct, physical interference, without lawful excuse, by one person with the body of another. Despite its violent-sounding name, a battery may be committed without great force; the gentlest of unauthorized touchings may give rise to liability in battery, and no physical harm need be shown to have resulted to the complainant. Besides providing protection from physical hurt, battery is (and for centuries has been) a tort or legal wrong which protects people's "dignitary interests", their rights to personal autonomy and to freedom from wanton, humiliating or otherwise unwelcome interference.

Nurses, of course, touch and handle patients' bodies as a routine part of their day-to-day-work: nursing is, after all, pre-eminently a "hands on" profession. Ordinarily, these touchings are not legal batteries because they are not done "without lawful excuse." The lawful excuse which makes them legal and proper is the consent of the patient, or (if the patient for whatever reason lacks capacity to consent) the consent of a surrogate decision-maker such as a parent, health-care proxy[4] or court. It should always be remembered, however, that without the valid consent of the patient or authorized consent-giver, every physical contact, however beneficent in intention or effect, will ordinarily constitute an actionable battery for which substantial damages may be awarded. The burden of proving that there was indeed a valid consent rests upon the defendant nurse — another procedural peculiarity of battery which significantly strengthens the legal position of the patient.

Physicians, at least when carrying out procedures in a hospital environment, usually protect themselves against potential battery suits by obtaining an explicit written document, signed by the patient, consenting to the particular procedures which are contemplated. As we have seen,[5] this precaution is not always sufficient to stave off an action for battery actions if the "consent" was founded upon insufficient information given to the patient. But although not always sufficient in itself, the written document is not indispensable either. In the eyes of the law, the written consent form is not in truth the consent itself; it is merely *evidence* of consent, as it is the reality of the patient's willingness to undergo the procedure which is of the first importance in point of law. An oral consent, or consent implied from conduct or body-language, is as potent a defence as any written document, provided that the Court can be persuaded that the consent was in fact freely given on the basis of a sufficiently informed understanding of the procedure in question.

The concept of implied consent is of critical importance to nurses, who typically do not receive written consents for every procedure performed. Often, it can be argued that the patient had consented to ancillary nursing procedures as part and parcel of the consent form that he signed when admitted to hospital or when consenting to prospective surgery. Still, such "blanket" consents are not in truth what protects the nurse in her daily routine. When, for example, a patient opens his mouth to receive a pill from the nurse or presents his arm for a needle, he is implicitly consenting to the procedure; for that reason the physical contact does not amount to a battery on the part of the nurse. It must be remembered, however, that just as the patient is entitled to refuse consent (however unreasonable and harmful such refusal may seem), he is likewise entitled at any time to withdraw such consent.[6] In that event, it is battery to proceed with a treatment over the objection of the patient,[7] however stubborn, foolish or self-destructive such an objection may seem to the caring nurse. Nor will "superior orders" or the instructions of the treating physician protect the nurse who ignores these rules. The mentally competent patient's rights to control what may be done to his body is an absolute one and is sternly reinforced by the tort of battery.

When the patient is not of sound mind because of disease or age, the law of battery may present particular complexities that restrict the options of nurses and other caregivers.[8] When, as will usually be the case, some identified person is endowed with the power to consent on behalf of the afflicted person, such consents will empower the nurse to perform any tasks deemed reasonably necessary for the patient's care, even over the protestations of the actual (incompetent) patient himself. But a patient who is still capable of rational decision-making, even though his decisions may sometimes seem obstinate, unreasonable and frustrating to health care providers, is still absolutely entitled to forbid any interference with his person, however beneficent. Moreover, even the patient who has lost his mental capacity can (subject to certain qualifications noted below) only be subjected to forcible treatment when such measures are consented to by a person authorized in law to give a substituted consent. Even then, only such force may be used as is absolutely necessary and only for purposes of genuine therapeutic benefit to the patient. The use of force merely for the sake of institutional convenience, or for reasons which are punitive rather than therapeutic, is not only actionable battery but also may give rise to criminal liability for assault.

Psychiatric nurses in particular may feel that the law places unreasonable restrictions on their ability to perform their already difficult tasks; and that it reflects an unrealistic approach to the sometimes dangerous environment in which they work. There are indeed circumstances in which the law will acknowledge that the use of restraints (whether physical or chemical) is both reasonable and necessary, notwithstanding the foregoing analysis, because such restraints are perceived as genuinely necessary for the protection of oneself, other staff, or other patients. The arguments of self-defence and defence of others have long been recognized as valid shields against battery liability, giving rise to a legal privilege to use such a measure of force as reasonably appears to be necessary. When the threat posed by the mentally incapable patient is a threat only to himself, the courts will likely infer the consent of the relevant person (the substitute consentgiver) to the imposition of restraints; or, to achieve the same sensible end, will press into service the so-called *emergency* doctrine.* But beyond these special situations necessitating timely and measured intervention to prevent harm, the use of force is prohibited upon pain of liability in battery: and so, no doubt, it should be.

3. THE NURSE AND THE INFORMED CONSENT DOCTRINE

No useful purpose would be served by repeating all the rules governing the issue of informed consent discussed in Chapter 4. Collectively, the rules represent the law's most eloquent and practical endorsement of the ethically-based value of patient autonomy and the unequivocal rejection of older notions of medical paternalism. The doctrine of informed consent potentially brings into play the torts of battery or negligence or both of them. It is of critical importance that nursing personnel understand that doctrine, for two quite discrete and perhaps somewhat obvious reasons.

First, in her dealings with a patient, a nurse may find it necessary to carry out procedures that are entirely conformable to orthodox nursing practice but which may be wholly mysterious to the patient, who has no idea of what is being done, or why. It is equally conceivable that a particular nursing procedure may carry the risk — statistically small, perhaps — of painful or harmful side-effects. In either case, the patient is ethically and legally entitled to a candid explanation of the nature of the proposed procedure and of any "special, material or unusual risks" that it may entail.[9] If that information is withheld, an aggrieved, hurt or disappointed patient might well sue the nurse who performed the procedure, and if the very nature of the procedure was concealed or misrepresented, the patient may sue in battery. If the attendant risks were not explained and the patient can convince the Court that such concealment induced him to submit to a procedure that he now regrets, then the patient will be advised to sue in the tort of negligence. (Either prospect is sufficiently serious to warrant a careful reading of Chapter 4.)

One must also consider the special position enjoyed by hospital nurses, whose role may provide them with opportunities, not typically shared by any other member of the health care team, to take part in serious and sustained dialogue with patients. It often happens that a patient scheduled for surgery will find himself utterly confused or lamentably ill-informed about such matters as the nature and function of the surgery, its anticipated

---

* The emergency doctrine is discussed in Chapter 2.

risks and side-effects, and available alternative therapies. This may happen due to the slackness, impatience or indifference of a physician, the shyness or diffidence of a patient who is afraid to ask questions, language difficulties, or a variety of other reasons. As time passes, patients may desperately want to give expression to their doubts and confusions, their fears and their questions, but may experience real difficulty in achieving that dialogue with the treating physician which the circumstances require. The natural response of such a patient is to unburden herself to the nurse, who will tend to be the most obviously caring, and perhaps the only person available to listen. How in these circumstances should the nurse respond?

Her initial response should be to realize that any continuing uncertainties, misconceptions, or questions troubling the patient represent an incipient system failure, still remediable but potentially serious, for which the treating physician bears primary responsibility. While the decided cases to date afford no guidance as to the nurse's proper response to such an unfortunate situation, the following propositions are suggested as a guide.

(a) For the sake of the patient, the nurse, and the treating physician, appropriate measures should be taken, either by direct notification to the treating physician or by relaying the patient's concerns along appropriate nursing channels, to ensure that the physician is made aware that her patient's "consent" still rests on an insecure informational footing.

(b) If the patient's inquiries call for a factual answer or educated opinion within the realm of the nurse's expertise, and to which a clearly "right" answer can be given, the nurse may answer the question; but having done so, she should still see to it that the treating physician is informed.

(c) Every inquiry and concern raised by the patient, and everything done or said by the nurse in response, should be promptly and fully entered in the nurse's notes, the practical and legal importance of which cannot be too firmly insisted upon (and will be more fully discussed later in this chapter).

Observance of these procedures will give realistic protection to the patient's rights of autonomy and self-determination. Furthermore, not only will they protect physicians (whether or not they are appropriately grateful) from real risks of potential litigation, but will also serve as a very practical expression of the nurse's role as patient-advocate, an important facet of modern nursing care which has been voluntarily assumed by the nursing profession even though never imposed by any rule of law.

Before we leave the topic of informed consent and the nurse's role in relation to it, two final points must be stressed. First, nurses should resist any efforts made by physicians to delegate to them the entire responsibility for securing informed consent. As stated earlier, the job of imparting the necessary information to the patient is and must remain the exclusive province of physicians, as the Royal College of Physicians and Surgeons of Canada has itself adamantly declared.[10] The fact that nurses are often handed the task of getting the consent form signed may well tend to obscure this fundamental proposition. Although the nurse might well find herself presenting the consent form to the patient for signature or otherwise serving as a witness to the consent, practices that are unlikely to cease in the foreseeable future, the nurse nonetheless should be conscious of the limited nature of her role. Moreover, she should strive to keep things that way. It is not the nurse's job to supply the gaps or deficiencies in the physician's dialogue with the patient, though as we have seen it is in everyone's interest that the nurse respond appropriately and with alacrity to ensure that when information-gaps occur, the physician is alerted in time to put things right.

Furthermore, when a nurse serves as a witness to a consent form, it should be clearly understood by all concerned that he or she is only undertaking to verify the genuineness of the patient's signature and his apparent willingness and mental capacity to sign the document. On such occasions, the nurse-witness does not assume any share of responsibility for assuring that the "consent" is based on a sufficiency of information given to the patient. That non-delegable responsibility rests of course with the treating physician.

4. THE NURSE AND THE LAW OF NEGLIGENCE

When nurses are sued, the proceedings against them are most frequently cast in the form of a tort action for negligence. This concept has been fully anatomized in previous chapters with illustrations drawn from all areas of health care field, so only a synopsis will be attempted here, enlivened by examples drawn from the reported case-law on nursing malpractice.

The tort of negligence, which governs not just medical cases but almost every imaginable sphere of human conduct, requires that the plaintiff or complainant establish three essential elements in order to recover damages from the defendant. It is not enough merely to show "in a vacuum" that the defendant behaved carelessly or ineptly towards the plaintiff. Rather, the plaintiff must show: (1) that at the material time the defendant owed him a legal duty of care and/or skill; (2) that the duty was breached by failure to achieve or maintain the requisite standard of care or skill as demanded by the duty; and (3) that resultant damage, of a kind recognized by the law as compensable, was caused by the breach of the duty.

Each of these three elements may present its own difficulties, all of which have been canvassed in previous chapters. Readers of Chapter 6 will realize that in practice the first requirement, the duty of care, will seldom if ever give rise to dispute in the nursing context. The extreme vulnerability and dependency of patients upon their nurses and the obvious capacity of nurses to cause harm to their patients by substandard care combine to create in the eyes of the law an unquestionable duty owed to each patient to provide appropriate care and professional skill.

Every nurse, then, owes a duty of care to her patient. Equally clearly, no such legal duty of care is owed to total strangers who have not entered into that nurse-patient relationship. Accordingly, there is no legal duty (and for that matter little legal encouragement or incentive) for a nurse to act as a "good Samaritan." When, for example, she encounters a stranger stricken with a heart attack or epileptic seizure in a restaurant or on a bus, or on the way home from hospital encounters a person seriously injured in a traffic accident, she has no *legal* obligation to intervene and provide appropriate care, whatever her personal or professional code of ethics may say to the contrary. Rarely, difficult situations might arise. The nurse who sees an obviously confused and distressed person in street clothes, wandering the hospital corridors in apparent need of help, should no doubt assume responsibility for seeing that someone lends prompt assistance. In the process, she should put aside nice questions (which lawyers might debate at length) as to whether she is under a legal duty to take such action.

In practice, it is the second element in a negligence action, variously known as the "breach of duty" or "standard of care" question, which tends to provide the focus of debate when a nurse is sued. What standard of care and skill is required of a nurse such that failure to attain it will be considered an actionable breach of the duty of care? As explained in Chapter 6 and elaborately illustrated in Chapter 8, the law requires of every professional person that measure of care and skill generally to be expected of the reasonable practitioner of average competence within that discipline at the material time (when the alleged act of negligence occurred). The standard against which a defendant nurse's performance will be measured, and its adequacy or inadequacy assessed, is that of her fellow-nurse (more accurately, perhaps, the fellow registered nurse, or registered psychiatric nurse, licensed practical nurse, etc., as the case may be). The measuring stick is the fellow nurse of average ability, ordinary alertness and commitment, and general "run-of-the-mill" competence with regard to current developments in her profession. It is not a standard of perfection, nor one of minimal adequacy. Having done one's best is not necessarily enough, if that "best" was inferior to the prevailing norm at the time the incident in question occurred. The Court will assess the standard as best it can, often with the help of expert witnesses called by each side to explain the prevailing standards and orthodox practices of nursing care at the material time.

The following illustrative cases will make this clear. In *Dowey v. Rothwell* (Alberta, 1974),[11] the plaintiff, who had a history of grand mal epileptic seizures and had recently discontinued her anticonvulsant prescription for phenobarbital, felt an "aura" coming on, forewarning her of a probable impending attack. Wisely, she immediately left her work place and attended at the nearby clinic of her personal physician, explaining the situation to the receptionist and asking for help. She was placed in the care of Nurse D, who had been employed by the clinic for 22 years and who had graduated as a registered nurse 40 years earlier. She escorted Ms. Dowey to an examining room, had her lie down on a narrow examining table, and stayed with her for about half an hour. When nothing happened, she left for a minute or so to look for Ms. Dowey's file. During her absence the patient experienced a severe seizure. She fell from the table onto the tile floor, sustaining a severe comminuted fracture of the arm, the broken ends protruding through the flesh.

The judge had no difficulty concluding that Nurse D's behaviour had fallen far short of the standard to be expected of a registered nurse at that time. All the nursing textbooks and the St. John's Ambulance Manual were unanimous in their insistence that the caregiver stay with the patient. Expert evidence by a highly qualified instructress in nursing was to the same effect. The judge noted as "significant" the admission by Nurse D that in her 40-year career, she had taken no refresher courses nor done anything to update her training. Her further admission that she could not remember having had training with regard to epilepsy and her (surely surprising) claim to have ever witnessed only one epileptic seizure were statements that were hardly apt to relieve her of fault. Nurse D (who was not, be it noted, actually sued) was found to be negligent, and for that negligence her employers were made vicariously liable.

Then there is the case of *Robertshaw Estate v. Grimshaw* (Manitoba, 1987).[12] In 1982, the plaintiff collapsed in his bathroom at home and was rushed by ambulance to the Grace Hospital in Winnipeg, where three physicians examined him and ran certain tests. He was discharged. But three days later, suffering violent headaches, he was taken by his wife to another major Winnipeg hospital (St. Boniface) where three more doctors examined him. Again, he was discharged. Three days later his wife found him in a coma, and he was rushed first to the Grace Hospital, and then to the Health Sciences Centre, where a CT scan showed a major intercranial haemorrhage from a saccular aneurism. By that time, it was too late to save his life. His widow sued all the numerous physicians involved in the case for negligence, but without success. She also sued the Grace and St. Boniface hospitals for the alleged negligence of their nursing staff, complaining that the charting by the nurses in both hospitals had been substandard and inadequate, thereby exacerbating the slowness of diagnosis which in turn had caused her husband's death. This claim, too, was unsuccessful.

The relevant portion of the trial judge's ruling is instructive in several respects. It depicts the standard of care required as that of the "normal prudent practitioner in the relevant field." It also stresses the Court's careful avoidance of "wisdom by hindsight", and a determination not to judge a nurse's performance by standards which at the critical time were only regarded as standards of perfection to be aspired to in the future. And finally, it provides a revealing comparison of the testimony of each side's expert witness, which points to the necessity in such a role of scrupulously maintaining an objective standpoint focused upon the realities of practice at the relevant time; in the process avoiding advocacy either for one's own side or for a practice one regards as professionally desirable. As stated by Mr. Justice Barkman of the Court of Queen's Bench:[13]

> Two expert witnesses gave evidence regarding the standard of care provided by the nurses at the Grace Hospital and the St. Boniface Hospital. It should be noted again the Court has not accepted the evidence of Mrs. Robertshaw regarding giving to the nursing staff the symptoms relating to her husband's exploding headache, sore neck and bad back. The records made by the nurses at each of the defendant hospitals must be considered in light of the facts as found by the court.
>
> The evidence of Miss R, the expert witness for the plaintiff appeared very theoretical to the court. Her criticism of the charting by the nurses in the emergency departments of both hospitals was quite extensive; and would appear to portray a standard that she personally would like to see being attained in 1982 rather than the standard that was in fact being practised in 1982.
>
> The evidence of Ms. D, the expert nurse witness for the defendant hospitals, although she had no practical experience in Manitoba hospitals, was familiar with standards in Manitoba from being chairwoman of the Standards Committee of the National Emergency Nurses Affiliation. She worked on standards for nurses across Canada in 1982. Her evidence, which I prefer to the evidence of Miss R, dealt more directly with the standards being applied in 1982 and indicated that the standards enunciated by Miss R were standards which would hopefully be attained in the future. Miss D considered the records made by the nurses in both hospitals as being up to

the standards generally being maintained in 1982, indicating, however, the standards varied from province to province. I accept her evidence in this regard and find that the services performed by the nurses in both hospitals were not below the 1982 standard.

The forms which negligence may assume in the context of nursing practice are innumerable, and no useful purpose is served by attempting an exhaustive catalogue of examples. Indeed, most of the reported cases add little or nothing to the foregoing legal analysis of nursing negligence. However, we may pause briefly to look at some typical cases, simply because they *are* typical.

A large proportion of the cases in which nurses have been held liable in negligence have involved either simple manipulative clumsiness or thoughtlessness: e.g., a hot water-bottle or heating pad left too close to the skin of an elderly or unconscious patient,[14] or, as has happened in more than one sad incident,[15] an infant scalded when a steam inhalator, new, shiny and alluring, was left within grabbing distance of the rails of his crib. We have already seen that lapses of due attention may amount to a breach of the nursing duty of care. While *Dowey v. Rothwell*,[16] *supra,* amply illustrates this proposition, the case of *Krujelis v. Esdale* (British Columbia, 1971)[17] has a special poignancy in this regard. Ten-year-old Ivars Krujelis was considered by those about him to have "over-prominent ears" and consequently underwent plastic surgery to correct this perceived imperfection. The surgery proceeded uneventfully and the patient, still unconscious, was wheeled into the post-anaesthesia recovery room. He there exhibited symptoms of cardiac arrest, but no one noticed the tell-tale respiratory distress nor the developing cyanosis, which should have signalled the need for urgent intervention. Of the five registered nurses assigned to duty in the recovery room during that critical time, three were on a coffee-break. By the time that anyone noticed that anything was amiss, the child had suffered irreversible brain damage, never recovering consciousness and remaining in a deep coma until his death three years later.

Without singling out individual nurses for blame, the judge held that their collective performance, or the system of work they had adopted, represented actionable negligence for which the hospital was held vicariously liable. Stressing that the attentiveness of monitoring by the nursing staff must be commensurate with the perceived danger inherent in each particular situation, Mr. justice Gould quoted from a judgment in another, very similar case some years previously, in which the judge had this to say on the subject of post-operative recovery rooms:[18]

> [I]t is my opinion that this is the most important room in a hospital and the one in which the patient requires the greatest attention because it is fraught

with the greatest potential dangers to the patient. This known hazard carries with it, in my opinion, a high degree of duty owed by the hospital to the patient. As the dangers or risks are ever-present there should be no relaxing of vigilance if one is to comply with the standard of care required in this room.

As commonsense would suggest, then, the standard of vigilance required to avoid imputations of negligence is not an unvarying constant. Rather, it will vary according to the function being performed, the part of the hospital in which it is being carried out, and any other factors which may bear upon the possible danger to the patient.

Cases in which the wrong drug has been given to a patient,[19] or where a medication has been given in an inappropriate manner,[20] are sadly not unknown. However, such cases so clearly indicate negligence that they add nothing of interest to our analysis. However, the allegedly inappropriate or inept administration of injections has from time to time given rise to litigation of some interest. In this connection it is instructive to compare the case of *Fiege v. Cornwall General Hospital* (Ontario, 1979)[21] with that of *Cavan v. Wilcox,*[22] a New Brunswick case finally decided by the Supreme Court of Canada in 1974.

In *Fiege,* the plaintiff was given an injection of Talwin in the left buttock by her nurse: it quickly and painfully became apparent that the sciatic nerve had been compromised. Though the matter was vigorously disputed, the judge found ample evidence that "on the balance of probabilities, the injection was made into the plaintiff's left buttock . . . not in the upper and outer quadrant, but near or over the line of the sciatic nerve." The act was found to be actionable negligence because it was an error that the reasonable average nurse would not have committed.

An injection was also at issue in the Wilcox case. Because the plaintiff had refused to present his buttock for a bicillin injection by Nurse Wilcox, she reluctantly inserted the needle in the deltoid muscle of his left arm, which was generally accepted as an alternative and suitable "second-best" site. Shortly thereafter, discolouration and swelling developed in the whole arm, and Mr. Cavan's condition declined so precipitately that his physicians could do nothing to arrest it. Gangrene developed and some three weeks later most of his left hand had to be amputated.

Unlike the plaintiff in the *Fiege* case, the plaintiff in this case was unable to present compelling evidence that the defendant nurse had done anything wrong or unorthodox. His only hope was to invoke the maxim "res ipsa loquitur",* arguing that the nature of his injury was such that it

---

* Discussed in Chapter 7 and, as there explained, no longer recognized as a valid legal doctrine.

could only be explained by some culpable ineptitude on the nurse's part. The Court disagreed and declined to apply the maxim, holding that the plaintiff's sufferings, though speculative or mysterious in origin, had not been persuasively shown to result from any negligence on Nurse Wilcox's part. Indeed, all the evidence strongly suggested that she was entirely blameless.

Other examples of nursing negligence display considerable variety. It is sometimes alleged that nursing staff, whether or not they have been sufficiently alert in monitoring the patient, were culpably slow in alerting the treating physician to disturbing changes in a patient's condition. This was the principal argument raised (successfully) against the nursing staff in *MacDonald v. York County Hospital* (Ontario, 1976)[23] the case we carefully analyzed in Chapter 1. A similar complaint was at issue in *Khan v. Salama* (Ontario, 1986).[24] The defendant physician had administered an epidural anaesthetic to his pregnant patient, and a nurse had later given a "top-up" dose of the same anaesthetic. Almost immediately, the patient experienced a dramatic drop in blood-pressure, followed by cardiac and respiratory arrest. She suffered irreversible brain damage, and went into a persistent vegetative state. Her baby died. Dr. Salama was held liable because the Court concluded that the initial catheterization had evidently penetrated the dura and entered the subarachnoid space, leading to the predictably catastrophic result. The defendant nurse was accused of negligence in failing to sound the emergency bell with due promptitude when the patient's blood pressure had plummeted. The judge exonerated her for two reasons, which are equally interesting and instructive.

(a) Any delay on her part had been due to surprise at a situation for which neither her training nor her experience had prepared her, and had led her to spend two minutes verifying her readings before sounding the bell. That, said the judge, was in retrospect an error; but not every error is to be characterised as actionable negligence. If, as here, it was the kind of error which any average, reasonable and sensible nurse might have made in a like predicament, it should be classed as a "mere error in judgement" — which is not actionable in negligence or anything else.

(b) Quite apart from that, the judge observed that: "Even if [the nurse] were held to be negligent for failing to call for help earlier, I cannot say that her negligence was causative of Mrs. Khan's present condition." As lawyers would say, "Causation-in-fact" was not proven. A plaintiff in a negligence case must always show that as a matter of cause and effect, the defendant's breach of duty was what caused the harm of which he now complains: and in this case the plaintiffs had simply failed to establish the causal connection.

A multiplicity of cases could be presented in which nurses have been deemed careless or unskilful in other ways and in other contexts, including ineptitude while assisting in surgery.[25] But enough has been said to illustrate the broad principles used by the courts to set the appropriate standards of care and skill against which a defendant nurse's performance will be measured.

Readers will by now probably have reflected that the kind of substandard professional performance which attracts liability will often have other, more immediate and more serious consequences for the nurse than the prospect of being sued. Serious lapses may well provide proper grounds for dismissal from employment, and perhaps also for disciplinary proceedings by the nurse's governing body.[26] It is important, however, to realize that despite a large measure of overlap, these various retributive consequences stand on their own. That which will justify the dismissal of a nurse from her employment will not necessarily provide grounds for professional discipline, whether for incompetence, "professional misconduct", or "conduct unbecoming a member."

Consider, for example, *Crandell v. Assn. of Registered Nurses (Manitoba)* (Manitoba, 1976).[27] In that case, the Court held that while a whole sequence of employers might have been justified in discharging Nurse Crandell from their employment (as being temperamentally ill suited to work as part of a team), that did not mean she was "incompetent" within the meaning of the statute governing professional discipline. The suspension of her practising certificate was accordingly lifted. It must also be realized that even if a nurse has demonstrated persistent incompetence or shown herself incorrigibly prone to unprofessional or "unbecoming" behaviour, that will not necessarily mean that she is open to a negligence action. It is not until the misconduct or incompetence harms a patient, causing damage of some legally recognised kind, that an action for negligence will lie against her. The infliction of damage, actually caused and foreseeably caused by the substandard conduct, is the final but entirely indispensable prerequisite of a negligence action. However, until that happens, the nurse may live in well-justified fear of dismissal or professional discipline, even if not yet at risk of a lawsuit claiming negligence.

Before we finally leave the topic of negligence, it must be pointed out that the average "reasonable practitioner" standard of care required by the law applies to a nurse from the very first day that he or she acquires full practising qualifications. As was pointed out with regard to physicians in Chapter 6, no allowance is made for inexperience.[28] Still, the inexperienced nurse may always discharge her duty of care by calling upon the assistance of more seasoned colleagues when she feels that she has reached the boundaries of her competence.

Also in line with the law governing physicians, it seems clear that the nurse who professes specialised qualifications in a particular sub-discipline of nursing will be held to the standard not of the average fellow-nurse but of the average nurse engaged in that particular specialty. This will be the case whether or not such areas of specialization are formally recognized by the professional association to which she belongs. Finally, while individual characteristics such as inexperience will afford no excuse in law for substandard nursing care, the environment in which the nurse works will be taken into account. Thus, the nurse in a remote northern nursing station will find that allowance is made for the particular difficulties of her situation and the greater range of functions which she must of necessity perform, in comparison to her counterpart in a big city hospital. While the same standard of care and skill will be required of the rural or isolated nurse who may be compelled in fact if not in form to function as a "nurse-practitioner", the courts will make due allowance for the difficulties of her position, and will not be swift to ascribe disappointing results to negligence on her part.

5. THE NURSE AND MEDICAL RECORDS[29]

Throughout their education, nurses are reminded constantly, even to the point of tedium, of the necessity for thorough and timely charting, accurately, promptly and intelligibly carried out. It may or may not, then, be comforting to hear that this advice or admonition is based upon sound legal grounds; and that as well as being indispensable to proper patient care, the medical record, and especially the nurses' notes, are very important legal documents.

In light of the legal and medical importance of such documentation, it is a curious fact that no universal standards have been promulgated for hospital records; although some provinces (e.g., Ontario and Nova Scotia) do have statutes setting particularized requirements for such records, most do not. The nurse who is uncertain as to the adequacy of her charting practices would do well to abide not only by the standards or protocols demanded by her employer but also by any standards promulgated by the governing professional association if the latter appear at any point to be more demanding than the former.

The medical importance of diligent and professional record-keeping is obvious. A complete, accurate and up-to-date chart is the primary and most fundamental means of communication among the various members of a health care team in a modern hospital. It is the only way of ensuring that everything that needs to be done is indeed done and that no task is inappropriately duplicated. Furthermore, charting alerts everyone concerned to changes or developments in the patient's condition. In short, it is an indispensable tool for good patient care.

Almost as important, though, as the protection of the patient, is the potential usefulness of the record in protecting the nurse from ill founded accusations of negligence or other improper conduct. The importance of the medical record in this regard derives largely from the landmark case of *Ares v. Venner,*[30] an Alberta case, ultimately decided by the Supreme Court of Canada in 1970. The 21-year-old plaintiff had broken his leg in a skiing accident at Jasper and was admitted to the Seton Hospital, where Dr. Venner reduced the fracture and put the leg in a cast. Over the ensuing days, nurses noticed and duly recorded disturbing signs that the circulation was impaired. Yet Dr. Venner failed to treat the case as an emergency until four days had elapsed, when he finally sent his patient to the University Hospital in Edmonton. A fasciotomy was performed, disclosing a complete block of circulation at the fracture site, resulting in ischemia and muscle necrosis so severe that an amputation was necessary. When Ares sued him in negligence, Dr. Venner objected vehemently to the admission into evidence of the nurses' notes. It is true that according to the state of the law at that time, their admissibility was debateable since the law had long rejected such documents as inferior, second-hand data, and had tended to insist upon the "live" testimony of nurses themselves, who could be cross-examined upon their testimony.

The Supreme Court nonetheless declared that the nurses' notes in the *Ares* case were admissible in evidence, and not merely admissible "for what they were worth", but as *prima facie* proof of the truth of the facts and events that they recorded. This ruling was fatal to Dr. Venner's attempts either to exonerate himself or (if this was the strategy) to deflect any share of the blame onto the shoulders of the nursing staff. What the *Ares* case means is that when a record (e.g., a chart entry by a nurse) is made contemporaneously with the events recorded, by someone (e.g., a nurse) who is under a duty to make such entries, their contents will be considered to be true unless the party challenging their accuracy can persuade the Court otherwise. The burden of proof, then, falls heavily upon the shoulders of the party who would challenge the veracity of the hospital record. The law as stated in *Ares* thus invests that document with enormous probative force. If the chart records that the nurse was doing her job in a competent, alert and efficient manner, it will be hard indeed for anyone, after the event, to convince a court that this was not in fact the case. *Ares v. Venner* can be seen as having converted the hospital record, the charts and nurses' notes, into a very potent shield for the protection of the nurse in any subsequent litigation, provided always that he or she had made the entries with due diligence.

In light of this development in the law, the nurse is well advised to observe practices which will tend to enhance the credibility of her entries upon the record.[31] Entries should be clear, factual and precise, and should be made as promptly after the occurrence or observation recorded as circumstances allow. Corrections should be made clearly and identified as such, preferably with an explanation for the change. Interlineations, or anything suggesting an alteration in the record after the event, should be scrupulously avoided in order to dispel any suggestion of self-serving tampering with the record in anticipation of litigation. All these precepts are designed to preserve the defensive value of the record as a shield to the nurse. But, human nature being what it is, all are from time to time disregarded.

Consider, for example, the sorry tale of *Kolesar v. Jeffries (J. Brant Memorial Hospital v. Koziol)* (Ontario, 1976),[32] (a case also known as *Kolesar v. Jeffries*, the title it bore in the lower courts.) Mr. Kolesar suffered serious and extensive injuries in a motor vehicle accident and was admitted to hospital, where major spinal surgery was promptly done. The patient was then put in a Stryker frame to stabilize his spinal graft and minimize bleeding. The nursing staff were well aware of their duties in caring for such a semi-conscious patient in a Stryker frame and were well aware too of the perils that he faced, one of the worst being the danger of regurgitation and of resultant asphyxiation in his own vomit. They knew the importance of constant watchfulness and the need to keep the patient awake and the air-passage clear lest he choke to death.

Yet that was the fate which befell Mr. Kolesar that night. He was found dead in the morning, the evidence suggesting that he had in fact been dead for some time before being discovered. In trying to determine what had happened, the Court was embarrassed by the meagre and inadequate nurses' notes which were put into evidence. Five nurses had served together on the relevant shift that night. But, as the trial judge remarked in reference to their notes:

> None worthy of the term were really kept. The nurses say it was their habit during the night shift to jot down on pieces of paper they were carrying, a note or two, and then at 5 or 6 a.m. they would get together, assisting each other to recall and record the events of the evening. An examination of all the records of the patients show little or nothing. I find it remarkable. Perhaps even more remarkable is what happened following Kolesar's death. On hearing of it, the assistant director of nursing, Margaret Cameron, examined the medical record and noted the absence of any entry from 10 p.m. on December

30th, until 5 a.m. on the 31st. She asked Nurse Malette to write up a record which is ex. 29. One is always suspicious of records made after the event, and if any credence is to be attached to ex. 29, it shows that at all times the patient was quite pale, very pale, and was allowed to sleep soundly to his death.[33]

The most fundamental precepts of record-keeping had been disregarded. Far from being, as they should have been, an impregnable testament to the fact that the nurses had done their duty, a very different and damning inference was drawn by the Court:

On a ward with a great many patients the medical record becomes the common source of information and direction for patient care. If kept properly it indicates on a regular basis the changes in the patient's condition and alerts staff to developing dangers. And it is perhaps trite to say that if the hospital enforced regular entries during each nursing shift, a nurse could not make the entry until she had first performed the service required of her. In Kolesar's case the absence of entries permits of the inference that nothing was charted because nothing was done.[34]

We need not be surprised that in these circumstances, one of the nurses was ultimately held liable in negligence for Mr. Kolesar's death.

Although *Kolesar is* an instructive and cautionary case, it should be read in the light of its own particular facts: where the patient was known to be at mortal risk and the nurse was duty-bound to a standard of unrelenting watchfulness. In contrast, there is the case of *Ferguson v. Hamilton Civic Hospitals* (Ontario, 1983),[35] in which the plaintiff had suffered a debilitating stroke either during or while recovering from a bilateral carotid arteriogram. While the principal thrust of his action was directed against his physicians and founded upon the informed consent doctrine, it was also argued that the nursing staff in the recovery room had been negligent. Mr. Justice Krever, who was of course well aware of the above-quoted remarks in *Kolesar,* was at pains to point out that the circumstances here were very different.[36]

While on the subject of nursing care, this is an appropriate place to say that, although invited so to find, I reject the submission that the absence of any nurse's entry in the nurses' record forming part of the hospital chart between 1:30 p.m. and 3:30 p.m. on June 17, 1973, is an indication of a failure in care on the part of the attending nurses. I infer that there was no observable change during that period that justified being recorded. With relation to nurses' notes this case is distinguishable from *Kolesar v. Jeffries* . . . in which Haines J. held that where there is a positive duty on the part of a nurse to perform a physical act, the absence in the nurses' record of any reference to the performance of the act justifies the inference that the act was not performed. In the absence of any evidence that good nursing practice requires the making of a note every time a nurse attends to observe a patient, even when there is no observable change in the patient's condition, it would be extending that principle too far to apply it to routine inspections of the patient by the nurses.

That said, it is prudent practice for the nurse to err on the side of zealousness and detail in making notations in order to dispel any possible inference of sloth or inattentiveness. Factual precision is also at a premium and so, of course, is conspicuous honesty and candour. These qualities were sadly lacking in the case of *Meyer v. Gordon* (British Columbia, 1981).[37]

The birth of her second child being imminent, Mrs. Meyer was admitted to a Vancouver hospital where the fetal heart rate was monitored and the dilation of the cervix measured. However, there was no inquiry about her obstetrical history, which if obtained would have revealed that the birth of her first child had been extremely precipitous. Some 20 minutes later, a different nurse (M.) examined the patient and gave her injections of Demerol and Gravol. The patient was then left on her own in the labour room in a wholly inappropriate supine position. Her husband's attempt to engage the attention of Nurse W. was brushed off as the idle vapouring of a nervous spouse. Half an hour later, Mr. Meyer returned to find his wife still alone and the baby's head emerging. This time, another nurse (T.) efficiently took charge. The birth was rapidly completed, but the baby was covered in meconium and in very poor condition. He was rushed to the intensive care unit of Vancouver General Hospital, where it became apparent that he had contracted cerebral palsy as a consequence of intrauterine distress and meconium aspiration.

The Court held that the nursing staff had been negligent in several respects. The failure to obtain Mrs. Meyers' obstetrical history, the failure to monitor attentively the progress of the delivery, and the general lack of engagement with the patient at the critical time had all served to dissipate any opportunity to detect and relieve the neonate's intrauterine distress. Even the resuscitation process had been marred by disorganization.

One cannot escape the conclusion that the judge's severe condemnation of the standard of nursing care given to the patient was seriously compounded by the inadequacy, and worse, of the nursing records. Nurse W. had used sloppy and imprecise language to describe her initial impressions, saying vaguely that the patient appeared to be in "good labour" and otherwise showing serious deficiencies of observation. Worse still, there were clear indications that entries had been tampered with (as evidenced by different-coloured ink) in order to alter numbers and give a false impression of the frequency and function of the nurses' visits to the patient in the labour room. To make matters worse, it transpired at trial that when the neonate was sent to Vancouver General Hospital, a photocopy of the chart had gone with her; this sketchy version of events, unaltered and undoctored by any subsequent tampering, entirely exploded any remaining credibility which the nurses might have enjoyed, when it was produced in court.

The moral is plain: accurate and full notes, honestly and diligently entered, will protect the nurse's credibility and go far to dispel any imputations of negligence. Vague and infrequent entries, punctuated by long gaps, will tend to have an opposite and very damaging effect, and efforts at clandestine or surreptitious alteration of the record will be easily detected and utterly undermine the nurse's credibility.

Before we leave this subject, a word must be said about the advent of computers as a tool for hospital record-keeping and the recording of nurses' notes. Computers have a number of obvious advantages in this regard. They save precious time both in entering and retrieving information; they avert to some degree the risk of losing data; and they may well achieve significant reductions in administrative costs. Their advantages aside, we should be aware of the more troubling aspects of the movement towards computerization. One such problem is obvious: the potential risk to the confidentiality of patient-information if strict controls over access are not in place. This is a challenge to which the manufacturers and designers of computer services are alert and which they will no doubt meet.

More troubling, however, is the effect which computerization may have upon the evidentiary potency of nursing records as a protection against negligence liability. If we recall *Ares v. Venner*, the 1970 decision which rendered nursing notes admissible into evidence and invested them with unusual probative value, these developments were justified by reference to the peculiar credibility that such notes naturally enjoyed. The focus was thus upon handwritten entries, initialled by hospital staff as events unfolded, entries recording both the times of their insertion and the identity of those making them, as well as showing (if properly done) where, when, why, and by whom any changes or additions were made.

In contrast, most computer systems have features which enable them neatly to erase, without trace and without recall, any previous entry, and to replace it with a new one. There is no personal imprint upon any entry which either points to the identity of the person who made it or informs the reader when it was made. Although a court presented with such a printout might be impressed by its neatness, it is unlikely to accord to it the same presumptive reliability as the smudgy ballpoint notes of yesteryear. Indeed, a court might well incline to regard such documents as devoid of any intrinsic credibility, for who can be sure that the entries were not put in on the eve of trial and so composed as to put a good face upon the defendants' case? In short, it is not at the present time clear that such computer-stored and computer-retrieved data would enjoy the same probative value as the handwritten notes contemplated in the "old days" by the Court in *Ares v. Venner*. It is not even certain that such print-outs would be admissible in evidence at all. If these concerns are well-founded, nurses especially will have lost the most powerful evidentiary protection they have enjoyed in the modern law. It is to be hoped that technologies will be devised which minimize the potential grounds for judicial scepticism touched upon in this chapter, so that even in the computer age the evidentiary value of nurses' notes will be preserved.

6. THE NURSE'S OTHER RESPONSIBILITIES

So far in this chapter, we have concentrated on matters relating to the torts of battery and negligence, these being by far the most likely types of lawsuit to be advanced against a nurse. While battery, as we have noted, may serve a useful purpose in protecting patients' dignitary interests, the primary and most useful function of both torts is to protect them from bodily harm. It will no doubt have occurred to readers from the nursing profession, always alert to ethical concerns and to the vital personal or "human" element in health care, that the peculiar vulnerability of the hospital patient exposes him to dignitary injuries far more subtle, but no less hurtful, than the crude phenomenon of unprivileged physical contact dealt with by the tort of battery.

The very fact of illness, compounded by the hospital patient's subjection to an institutional environment and a managed lifestyle over which he has little or no control, create a power-imbalance which may make even apparently willing compliance in nursing procedures a "voluntary" submission only in a somewhat artificial sense of that word. This is not, generally speaking, something with which the law has concerned itself when dealing with the law of battery, but it does raise ethical concerns for the professional nurse. While the analysis of nursing ethics is beyond the scope of this book,[38] there comes a point at which the realms of ethics and legal responsibility intersect and overlap: and it seems appropriate to note here that intrusions upon the dignitary interests of patients may in rare cases conceivably find legal redress through tort principles far removed from the familiar realms of negligence and battery.

One such situation is the area of invasion of privacy. In a hospital environment where patients commonly share a room with others, and where nursing care of an intimate and potentially embarrassing nature may be absolutely necessary, a huge sacrifice of personal privacy may be required of the patient. Generally, the patient will make that sacrifice in a spirit of resignation or co-operation, accepting the emotional distress or embarrassment as being a necessary evil like the pain of surgery. The same is true not only of "hands-on" procedures, but of the intrusive and highly personal questions which the nurse must often ask in order to do his or her job properly. Nurses are taught, and teach themselves, methodologies for minimizing the emotional distress and embarrassment which their patients may experience. Disregard of such concerns and techniques, whether resulting from callousness or indifference, would reflect an uncaring attitude unbecoming to a member of the nursing profession, and would be an appropriate basis for disciplinary proceedings. Whether it would also be actionable in a court of law is debateable. That is because of the strangely undeveloped state of the common law relating to invasions of privacy: several Ontario cases have indeed cast doubt upon whether any such tort is known to the common law.

Four Canadian provinces* have passed Privacy Acts, statutes which authorize courts to award damages for invasions of privacy. But, even in those provinces, it will be a rare case indeed where a patient's privacy is so grossly violated that he will think it worth the trouble of venturing upon what is still a highly speculative claim. The possibility is there, but professional disciplinary proceedings remain by far the more realistic deterrent to this variety of nursing malpractice.

That said, there is one variety of privacy-invasion which will undoubtedly give rise to a legal remedy against any nurse who commits such actions, and that is the breaching of confidentiality. As explained elaborately in Chapter 11 of this book, there is some debate among lawyers as to what *kind* of action would be the most appropriate "vehicle" for an action against a health-care professional who divulged confidential patient information. What no-one seriously doubts is that a remedy would be awarded. And in those provinces which have in recent years enacted Personal Health Information legislation — again, a matter discussed in Chapter 11 — the indiscreet nurse who improperly divulges personal health information stands exposed, in addition to any civil remedy for damages, to the very severe penalties laid out in the legislation.

Nurses by the very nature of their job learn much secret information about their patients and from their patients. They have access to intimate information gleaned from the patient's chart, from test-results, and from necessary interactions with other members of the health care team. They will often quite properly enter into conversations with their patients, and

---

* British Columbia enacted its statute in 1969, Manitoba in 1970, Saskatchewan in 1974 and Newfoundland in 1981.

further private matters will be divulged. The general rule governing such information is as clear and emphatic in the law as it is in the realm of ethics. The secrecy of such information must be scrupulously preserved, and any violation of this rule, in the absence of some lawful excuse or justification, will attract liability and as we have just seen, possible quasi-criminal sanctions as well.

The main difficulty in this area of the law is to identify when, exactly, a "lawful excuse or justification" does exist for the divulging of confidential information. In fact, the range of possible legal excuses is considerable, and is exhaustively discussed in Chapter 11, which nurses should read as being directly relevant to their situation. Where, for example, the reporting of information, received or learned in confidence, is explicitly required by a statute, this obviously overrides the patient's ordinary right to preserve the secrecy of such information. Furthermore, a nurse, like a physician, enjoys no privilege of silence in a court of law, and if asked point-blank questions, must answer them even if this will involve the breaching of what would otherwise be clear obligations of confidentiality. As readers of Chapter 11 will doubtless conclude for themselves, other exceptions to the confidentiality rule leave much to be desired in terms of specificity: the subject of imputed consent, for example, which entitles a nurse to give information (unless the patient has expressly forbidden it) to "close relatives," would seem to beg as many questions as it answers. The nurse's main consolation, in this context, is to know that courts will be slow to attach liability to judgments made in good faith by a nurse, who is accused "after the event" of revealing confidential information to a family member who should not, from the patient's point of view, have been so favoured. Another consolation is to reflect that in the entire history of the Anglo-Canadian common law, there has not been a single instance of a nurse being sued, whether successfully or otherwise, for breaking her obligation of confidentiality.

Yet the danger is there. If such a lawsuit ever does materialize, it is as likely to result from thoughtlessness, as from wilful or malevolent wrongdoing. It must be remembered that legal obligations of secrecy do not only attach to information learned "at first hand" about a patient or from that patient's own lips. Information imparted by other nurses and co-workers about their patients, whether in a formal conversational setting, or overheard in the ward, or in the cafeteria line-up for that matter, may well suggest that those colleagues are in breach of their own obligations of confidence. But it is important to realize that those who repeat and disseminate such gossip are in the eyes of the law just as liable as those who first divulged it. Whenever and however medical information about an individual is received, the test[39] is whether a reasonable person in the recipient's position would naturally appreciate its confidential character. If so, and it will almost invariably be so where medical information relating to patients or ex-patients is concerned, the information will be "impressed" with a confidential character and bind to secrecy anyone who may become privy to it. In view of the destructive power, over individuals and their families, which may be unleashed by the careless release of information, nurses will be vigilant in maintaining the discreet and humane traditions of their profession, and guarded in their release of patient information.

NOTES

1. Since the publication of our second edition in 1995, midwives have at long last joined, or perhaps more accurately re-joined, the phalanx of fully-acknowledged medical professionals in Canada, being now recognized as a discrete licensed profession by the statutes and regulations of six provinces: British Columbia, [*Midwife Regulations* B.C. Reg. 103/95, under the *Health Professions Act*, R.S.B.C. 1996, c. 183]; Saskatchewan [*Midwifery Act*, S.S. 1999 c. M-14.1; (not yet proclaimed in effect)]; Manitoba [*Midwifery Act*, S.M. 1997, c. 9]; Ontario [*Midwifery Act*, 1991, S.O. 1991 c. 31]; Newfoundland and Labrador [*Midwifery Act*, R.S.N. 1990, c. M-11]; and Quebec, *Loi sur les Sages-Femmes*, S.Q. 1999, c. 24. Nova Scotia, the Yukon and the Northwest Territories are also contemplating legislation to similar effect.

   Under-regulated, and for some time after a licensing régime has established itself for a newly acknowledged profession, the Courts obviously face a difficult task in assessing the appropriate standard of care and skill to be required of practitioners for the purposes of negligence liability. For an example of a Court tackling this task reasonably and constructively, see the recent midwifery case of *Carere v. Cressman* (2002), 2002 CarswellOnt 1238, 12 C.C.L.T. (3d) 217 (Ont. S.C.J.).

2. A notable "Canadian" monograph on this subject is J.J. Morris, **Canadian Nurses and the Law**, 2nd edition, 1999. Also worthy of note are Grant and Ashman, "Nurses' Practical Guide to the Law", (1997) and still useful, though somewhat dated, M. Philpott, "Legal Liability and the Nursing Process" (W.B. Saunders & Co., Canada Ltd., 1985).

3. This expansion, and resultant encroachment on what have traditionally been the preserves of physicians, inevitably conduce to "turf wars", especially where the phenomenon of the nurse-practitioner is concerned. A preliminary skirmish in this impending conflict is *Atcheson v. College of Physicians & Surgeons (Alberta)* (1994), 21 C.C.L.T. (2d) 166 (Alta. Q.B.).

4. In provinces where such persons are statutorily recognized as having legal decision making status: an issue discussed in Chapter 23, *post.*

5. Chapter 4, *supra.*

6. See *Ciarlariello v. Schachter* (1993), 15 C.C.L.T. (2d) 209 (S.C.C.), as considered in Chapter 4.

7. As in *Allan v. New Mount Sinai Hospital* (1981), 125 D.L.R. (3d) 276 (Ont. C.A.); and see *B. (N.) v. Hôtel-Dieu de Québec* (1992), 86 D.L.R. (4th) 385 (Que. S.C.).

8. In provinces where "living wills" or health-care directives enjoy legal recognition, provision may be made by a person, while of sound mind, which may reduce or eliminate such difficulties when mental incapacity supervenes: see Chapter 23.

9. *Reibl v. Hughes,* [1980] 2 S.C.R. 880; *White v. Turner* (1981), 31 O.R. (2d) 773 (H.C.), affirmed (1982), 47 O.R. (2d) 764 (C.A.); and see generally Chapter 4.

10. "Informed Consent — Ethical Considerations for Physicians and Surgeons": Royal College of Physicians & Surgeons of Canada, Biomedical Ethics Committee, September 1987.

11. [1974] 5 W.W.R. 311 (Alta. T.D.).

12. (1987), 49 Man. R. (2d) 20 (Q.B.), affirmed (1989), 57 Man. R. (2d) 140 (C.A.), leave to appeal refused (August 17, 1989), Doc. 21454 (S.C.C.).

13. (1987), 49 Man. R. (2d) 20 (Q.B.) at 33.

14. E.g., *Lavere v. Smith's Falls Public Hospital* (1935), 26 D.L.R. 346 (Ont. C.A.).

15. E.g., *Sinclair v. Victoria Hospital Ltd.* (1942), [1943] 1 W.W.R. 30 (Man. C.A.), *Harkies v. Lord Dufferin Hospital,* [1931] 2 D.L.R. 440 (Ont. S.C.).

16. *Supra,* note 11.

17. (1971), [1972] 2 W.W.R. 495 (B.C. S.C.).

18. *Ibid.,* at 499.

19. See *Bugden v. Harbour View Hospital,* [1947] 2 D.L.R. 338 (N.S. S.C.): and the Australian case of *Henson v. Perth Hospital* (1939), 41 W.A.L.R. 15.

20. E.g., *Barker v. Lockhart,* [1940] 3 D.L.R. 427 (N.B.C.A.).

21. (1980), 30 O.R. (2d) 691 (H.C.).

22. [1975] 2 S.C.R. 663.

23. (1976), 66 D.L.R. (3d) 530.

24. (1986), 1986 CarswellOnt 1846, [1986] O.J. No. 619.

25. See *Frandle v. MacKenzie* (1988), 47 C.C.L.T. 30 (B.C. S.C.), varied (1990), 5 C.C.L.T. (2d) 113 (B.C. C.A.): [failure to keep proper count of sponges]: and *Savoie v. Bouchard* (1982), 23 C.C.L.T. 83 (N.B. Q.B.), varied (1983), 26 C.C.L.T. 173 (N.B. C.A.), in which the defendant scrub-nurse incautiously injured the surgeon during an operation on a patient with Hepatitis B.

26. A subject beyond the scope of this book, but which is engagingly discussed by Philpott, *op. cit.,* note 2, *supra.*

27. (1976), [1977] 1 W.W.R. 468 (Man. Q.B.).

28. See *Henson v. Perth Hospital, supra,* note 19; and *Farrell v. Regina (City),* [1949] 1 W.W.R. 429 (Sask. K.B.), for examples of this stern principle in a nursing context.

29. On this subject generally, readers should be aware of the invaluable volume by Rozovsky L. and Inions N.J., "Canadian Health Information" (Toronto: Butterworths, 2002) 3rd ed.

30. [1970] S.C.R. 608.

31. A list of useful precepts for this purpose is given in J.J. Morris, *op. cit.,* note 2, *supra,* at 83ff.

32. (1978), 2 C.C.L.T. 170, 77 D.L.R. (3d) 161 (S.C.C.).

33. Mr. Justice Haines of the Ontario High Court in *Kolesar v. Jeffries* (1974), 9 O.R. (2d) 41 (H.C.) at 48.

34. *Ibid.,* at 47-8.

35. (1983), 23 C.C.L.T. 254 (Ont. H.C.), affirmed (1985), 33 C.C.L.T. 56 (Ont. C.A.).

36. (1983), 23 C.C.L.T. 254 (Ont. H.C.) at 290.

37. (1981), 17 C.C.L.T. 1 (B.C. S.C.).

38. A valuable recent contribution to the literature on this subject is G. Hunt (ed.), "Ethical Issues in Nursing": (Routledge, 1994). The essay therein by P. Wainwright, "The observation of intimate aspects of care: privacy and dignity", is of particular interest in the present context.

39. The leading authority on this issue is generally acknowledged to be the judgment of Vice-Chancellor Sir Robert Megarry in the English case of *Coco v. A.N. Clark (Engineers) Ltd.* (1968), [1969] R.P.C. 41 (Eng. Ch. Div.), where at p. 48, he endorsed the "reasonable person" test as explained in our text.

10

COMPENSATION FOR MEDICAL INJURIES: AN UNCERTAIN FUTURE

SUMMARY

This chapter deals with an evaluation of the current fault-based system of compensation for victims of medical accidents and reviews a number of policy options and alternatives to the current system. The chapter begins by explaining the broad nature of accident compensation systems of each province. It shows that fault or tort liability is one component of a system that includes a broad diversity of private and public compensation systems such as workers compensation, automobile no-fault schemes, criminal injury compensation schemes, federal income replacement schemes such as unemployment insurance and Canada Pension Plan, health care, social assistance, private insurance and charitable institutions. It is pointed out that medical accident victims must, however, place heavy reliance upon the tort system. The chapter then reviews the advantages and disadvantages of tort as a mechanism to provide compensation to injured patients and to enhance and maintain standards of medical care. Various options to the current system are reviewed, including the reform of tort law, the no-fault option, first party life and disability insurance, and the current system of accident compensation and prevention in Sweden. Finally the findings and recommendations of the 1990 *Report to the Conference of Deputy Ministers of Health of the Federal/Provincial/Territorial Review on Liability and Compensation Issues in Health Care* are considered.

CASE STUDY: *FERGUSON v. HAMILTON CIVIC HOSPITALS* (Ontario, 1985)[1]

The plaintiff, Ferguson, 58, underwent bilateral carotid arteriography to determine if his eye trouble (amaurosis fugax) was an early sign of carotid artery stenosis. The arteriogram negated that initial diagnosis. In the recovery room, he complained of symptoms which later developed into incomplete quadriplegia. He was left with some limited sensation and mobility in his arms but none in his legs. He lost all sexual function and was rendered incontinent. His condition was permanent and irreversible. The plaintiff sued, alleging negligence in the performance of the test and on the basis of the informed consent doctrine. He had not been told that the procedure entailed the risk of a stroke, the very risk that materialized. The trial judge ruled that the defendant-physicians were not liable. Negligent performance of the test was not proved, and although the defendants ought to have disclosed the risk of stroke, their failure to do so did not cause the injury. The reasoning was that whether the plaintiff was informed of the risk or not, a reasonable person in his circumstances would have consented to the procedure. The judge ruled that if liability had been established, damages would have totalled $385,000. At the close of his judgment, the trial judge, Mr. justice Krever, stated:

> I must add a personal note. In the conclusion to the reasons for judgment of Linden J. in *Davidson v. Connaught Laboratories et al.* (1980), 14 C.C.L.T. 251, there is to be found . . . an eloquent expression of concern about the requirement of our law that fault exist as a condition precedent to the receipt of compensation in matters of this kind. I cannot leave this case without following Mr. justice Linden's example. I confess to a feeling of discomfort over a state of affairs, in an enlightened and compassionate society, in which a patient, who undergoes a necessary procedure and who cannot afford to bear the entire loss, through no fault of his and reposing full confidence in our system of medical care, suffers catastrophic disability but is not entitled to be compensated because of the absence of fault on the part of those involved in his care. While it may be that there is no remedy for this unfortunate and brave plaintiff and that this shortcoming should not be corrected judicially, there is, in my view, an urgent need for correction.[2]

The plaintiff appealed to the Ontario Court of Appeal, on behalf of which, Mr. justice MacKinnon (then the Associate Chief Justice of Ontario) stated:

. . . for the very full and thoughtful reasons given by the learned trial judge the appeal is dismissed. We would not want to leave this case without adding that we are in complete sympathy and agreement with the penultimate paragraph of the learned trial judge's reasons. OHIP is the product of a socially conscious society, but we agree that in situations such as the instant one "an enlightened and compassionate society", to use the words of the learned trial Judge, should do more.[3]

1. INTRODUCTION

It is an inevitable consequence of our health care system that some patients are injured in the course of their medical treatment. Some medical accidents are caused by the action or inaction of physicians. Of those, some are caused by culpable or blameworthy conduct such as negligence, whereas others are caused by innocent conduct such as an error of judgment or misadventure. The incidence of medical accidents seems to be rising and governmental financial restraint and increased workloads are not likely to reverse this trend. We have seen in the chapters on negligence that the law of torts (wrongs) differentiates between medical accidents caused by fault or breach of duty and accidents caused by a physician's error of judgment or misadventure. Physicians must pay compensation to the victim of a medical accident only if the plaintiff proves that her injury was caused by the defendant-physician's fault. A prodigious amount of time, effort and expense is incurred in determining if the cause of a medical accident was blameworthy or innocent conduct on the part of the physician.

Recently, some alarm has been expressed about our fault-based compensation system. Since the late 1970s and early 1980s, the amounts of damage awards have risen dramatically. This was a direct consequence of a trilogy of Supreme Court cases in 1978 which revamped the method of calculating damages.* Through the course of the 1980s and 90s, claims increased with a consequent increase in settlement and judgment awards. As a result physicians are paying higher liability insurance premiums to the Canadian Medical Protective Association** and to other liability insurers.

These developments have led to a closer and more critical evaluation of the tort system by both physicians and the general public. The tort system is, however, only one compensatory mechanism in a diverse and complex range of private and public accident compensation systems. It is useful to

---

* For a further discussion of the "trilogy" and damages see Chapter 6.

** The C.M.P.A. is not technically an insurance corporation. It is a mutual defence organization that operates similarly to a liability insurer.

sketch the broad picture before focussing upon compensation of the victims of medical accidents.

2. ACCIDENT COMPENSATION: THE BROAD PICTURE

The accident compensation system is essentially the same in each province. From an historical perspective, its modern development began in the late 19th and early 20th centuries when the courts developed the basic proposition of fault liability; that a defendant is liable in damages for injury or death caused by conduct falling below the standard of a reasonably careful person. This fundamental fault principle has significant emotional and moral appeal. It provides a defensible rationale for shifting the loss from a morally innocent plaintiff to a morally culpable defendant. The injured person is compensated for her loss; and not only is the defendant punished for blameworthy conduct, but is also, along with the general public, deterred from acting in a similar manner in the future. The twin pillars of the tort system are compensation and deterrence.

The 20th century evolution of tort law was strongly affected by two factors: immense societal change and liability insurance. The development in the 20th century of a complex and highly integrated industrial, commercial and technological society brought with it a dramatic increase in accident rates. Automobiles, mass transportation, urbanization, mass consumption of consumer products, new leisure activities and the development of a sophisticated health care system have created a more accident-prone society. An increased risk of personal injury and accidental death seems to be an inevitable and unavoidable incident of social progress. As this social and technological revolution has progressed, the courts have held firm to the fault principle. The concept of care was utilized to balance the defendant's interest in freedom of action with the plaintiff's interest in security of the person. The duty of care now extends to virtually all persons involved in any activity creating a risk of personal injury or death. This includes all health care professionals and institutions. The corollary of the expansion and development of the fault principle was the expansion of and reliance upon liability insurance. People insure against the risk that they will be found liable for injuries arising through their fault. Liability insurance has mutual advantages: the defendant is saved from financial ruin and the plaintiff is assured of receiving damages, at least to the limit of the liability insurance policy. It is therefore more accurate to refer to the tort system as a "fault/insurance system."

Despite the rapid expansion of the fault principle and the heavy reliance upon liability insurance, large numbers of accident victims fall outside the scope of the tort system. Some are not injured through fault; others fail to recover damages because of practical difficulties in the operation of the tort system. It has become increasingly apparent through the course of this century that fault is too narrow a concept to provide the security to accident victims that a compassionate and humane society deems appropriate. It became increasingly apparent during the course of the twentieth century that fault was too narrow a concept to provide the security to accident victims that a compassionate and humane society deemed appropriate. The trend in the last century was towards greater collective security which was at odds with the highly individualistic nature of tort liability. Consequently the twentieth century witnessed a series of public and private initiatives to increase the compensation for accident victims. Initiatives at the provincial level included Workers' Compensation, which replaces the fault system with no-fault benefits for accident victims in the work place; no-fault automobile accident insurance which in some provinces adds no-fault benefits to the tort system, and in other provinces displaces the tort system entirely and Criminal Injuries Compensation which supplements the tort system with no-fault benefits for the innocent victims of criminal violence. On the federal level, Unemployment Insurance, Canada Pension Plan and Veterans Pensions and Allowances provide some income replacement benefits. Insured health services, social assistance and private employee benefits, accident and life insurance and charitable institutions complete the picture.

The result is that each province has an accident compensation system which is comprised of a poorly coordinated, unrelated mixture of fault, no-fault, welfare and private schemes. They display no consistent philosophy and provide an uneven range of benefits, the receipt of which depends more on particular eligibility requirements than upon the need of individual accident victims. This should come as no surprise. The development of the various compensatory vehicles was piecemeal, an *ad hoc* response to particular needs perceived over time. The current uncoordinated jumble was unavoidable. What it does evidence, however, is a clear policy that those who suffer personal injury should not be left to bear their loss alone. There is a clear sense of community responsibility to those who are the random and inevitable victims of social progress.

3. COMPENSATION FOR THE VICTIMS OF MEDICAL ACCIDENTS

Medical accident victims do not normally fare well under the various provincial accident compensation systems. Those systems favour victims of work-related and automobile accidents, and the victims of criminal violence. There is little protection for a person such as the plaintiff in *Ferguson v. Hamilton Civic Hospitals*. Mr. Ferguson may have been eligible for short-term unemployment sickness benefits and for a Canada Pension Plan disability pension and most of his medical and health costs would be met by the provincial health insurance plan; but unless he had personal wealth or extensive private or employee related first-party disability insurance, he would be saved from destitution only by the support of family and friends or the provincial social assistance and welfare programmes. Like many victims of medical accidents, his only chance for adequate compensation was to prove negligence in a civil action against the physicians and the hospital that provided his health care. Mr. Ferguson brought such an action and lost. Consequently, he received no compensation and he suffered the financial burden of his own lawyer's fee. Fortunately, the Court ruled that he did not have to pay the defendant's legal costs.

It is this kind of harsh result which led the trial judge and the Ontario Court of Appeal to urge that a compassionate and humane society provide some compensation to the victims of non-negligent medical accidents. This challenge certainly provides sufficient reason to make a careful appraisal of the tort system as it operates in the health care field.

4. MEDICAL ACCIDENTS AND THE FAULT SYSTEM: AN APPRAISAL

Strong views are held in the legal profession about the tort or fault system. There are those who view it as an essential legal phenomenon, a reflection of a civilized society and a repository of important cultural and societal values including personal responsibility for one's own actions. The critics condemn it as a compensatory system which is arbitrary, expensive, slow, unpredictable and administratively complex. They argue that there must be a better way to deal with injuries caused by medical accidents. The debate is of such importance to physicians in particular and to the health care system in general that we pause to summarize the main arguments of the proponents and opponents of the fault system.

(a) In Defence of the Fault System

The key premise of those who favour the fault system is that it serves a variety of important functions in the field of health care and that it is a mistake to isolate one function and attack the system solely on that basis. It is said that the functions of tort law include the compensation of accident victims, the punishment and deterrence of unacceptable conduct, the appeasement and vindication of the accident victim, and the education of physicians as to societal rules relating to professional conduct. The tort system is in essence a multi-functional system. Each facet will be considered in turn.

(i) *Compensation*

The tort system offers complete compensation to those patients injured by the fault of physicians. It is the only compensatory scheme of accident compensation which purports to make a full indemnity for all the patient's losses. In a trilogy of cases in 1978 the Supreme Court expressed a strong desire for complete compensation for pecuniary losses, including loss of income and future care costs. The Court was less committed to the full compensation of non-pecuniary losses such as pain, suffering and permanent disability; limiting such non-pecuniary damages to $100,000 as adjusted by inflation from the date of the judgment. At present, that ceiling is approximately $280,000. The Court feared a great escalation in these awards if no limit was set. The award of damages is made in one lump sum which is non-reviewable. This has the administrative advantage of finality and, once awarded, encourages rehabilitation, self-sufficiency and independence. An added attraction of the tort system is that it is administered and controlled by judges who are independent and impartial. As such they are more insulated from governmental policy and financial restraint than public sector compensation schemes.

(ii) *Punishment*

The fault system imposes a penalty on the physician who causes injury by breaching legal rules of professional conduct. The wrongdoer is called to account for her actions, and the award of damages is a punishment for unacceptable conduct. This function is also seen as specific deterrence, that is, it ensures that the defendant does not act in a similar manner again.

(iii) *Deterrence*

The imposition of liability on negligent physicians deters others from similar conduct. Thus, the fault system acts as a general deterrent. The deterrent impact of tort law reduces the number of medical accidents that would otherwise occur. Accident prevention is an extremely important goal, and the legal duty of care is instrumental in maintaining safety standards.

(iv) *Appeasement and Vindication*

Tort law provides a civilized process enabling an injured person to force a physician to account for her actions. The legal action provides a release for the plaintiff's anger, pain and bitterness and a degree of psychological comfort to the injured person. Tort law is a particularly useful vehicle to achieve these goals because the tort action is instigated by the individual initiative of the injured patient. The patient does not need to rely upon the actions of governmental bureaucracies for appeasement or a sense of vindication.

(v) *Education*

Tort law instructs physicians on the professional standards to which they are held accountable. Tort law dictates the need for consent and care, both in treatment and in providing information to patients. It may happen that individual cases come to the attention of the medical profession and that medical practice is changed as a consequence. In the 1950s, the Supreme Court of Canada's decision in *Anderson v. Chasney*[4] led to a change in medical practice by deciding that the failure to use sponges with tapes and to perform a sponge count in a tonsillectomy was negligent. The recent development of the doctrine of informed consent is also illustrative of this role of tort law.*

The proponents conclude that the fault system is a valuable compromise among important and sometimes competing social values and that *as a whole* it performs a useful function in society.

(b) The Fault System Under Attack

Over the last thirty years, the fault system has become the subject of much criticism. The major criticism focusses on the two major aims of tort law: compensation and deterrence. The critics point out quite correctly that the fault system cannot be justified solely in terms of appeasement and education alone. The criticism questions the *deterrent* impact of fault liability and its adequacy as a *compensatory* mechanism.

---

* However, doubt has recently been thrown on the ability of tort law to influence medical practice. A survey of physicians concluded that the Supreme Court decision in *Reibl v. Hughes*, [1980] 2 S.C.R. 880, 14 C.C.L.T. 1, 114 D.L.R. (3d) 1, 4 L. Med. Q. 209, 33 N.R. 361, which developed the informed consent doctrine, has had "little impact on medical practice." Robertson, "Informed Consent in Canada: An Empirical Study" (1984), 22 Osgoode Hall L.J. 139.

(i) *The Fault System as a Deterrent*

Many critics doubt the power of tort liability to deter negligent conduct and, thereby, maintain professional standards of care, knowledge and skill. The primary reason is the prevalence of liability insurance. In almost all medical malpractice cases, the physician does not personally pay the damages. The loss is not shifted on to the shoulders of the wrongdoer but is rather spread among all the members of the medical profession. There is disagreement over the extent to which liability insurance has reduced the deterrent power of tort law. Some would suggest that a system which exacts no personal penalty has no deterrent value at all, while others suggest that there is some residual deterrence and that it operates on three levels: the fear of adverse publicity if the physician is sued in negligence; the desire to avoid an adversarial trial; and the physician's wish to avoid damage to his reputation caused by a public declaration of his professional negligence.

The deterrent value of the fault action is an open question. It cannot be established conclusively one way or another. It is a matter of opinion and contention upon which strong views are held. It is, however, important to point out that the abolition of fault liability would not remove all incentives for safe conduct. The physician is governed by the criminal law and is subject to the disciplinary procedures of the College of Physicians and Surgeons. There is the threat of losing hospital privileges. Risk management and medical audit programmes in hospitals seek to encourage and maintain patient safety and assure quality care. The personal nature of the relationship between physician and the patient also encourages care. The pride that most physicians take in their professional reputations with their peers and their patients also provides an incentive for competence.

Only a physician can determine what motivates her to take care during the day-to-day routine of medical practice. We suspect it is more likely to be the individual physician's professional ethic and personal morality than any conscious fear of being sued. If one accepts the view that the deterrent value of tort law is minimal, the only significant rationale for fault liability remaining is compensation.

(ii) *Fault as a Compensatory Vehicle*

It is in the area of compensation that tort law has been subjected to its most vigorous criticism. We will briefly survey the individual arguments.

(A) The Irrationality of Fault as the Basis of Compensation

We spoke earlier of the apparent rationality and emotional appeal of the fault concept. It provides an emotionally satisfying and morally compelling reason to shift loss to the defendant. But, as we have noted, the practical reality of the system is quite different. All physicians are insured against liability. The loss is spread throughout the profession by way of annual insurance premiums. In a socialized health care system, where physicians are paid by the province, liability simply becomes another health care cost paid by the federal and provincial governments. Ultimately, the loss is spread among all taxpayers. Public money is being collected and distributed to victims of medical accidents who have been injured through the fault of physicians. There is no rational reason that such funds be paid on the basis of fault when the compensation is not paid by the wrongdoer. It is more reasonable to put the focus upon the injured patient and her needs, rather than upon the manner in which she suffered harm. It is this arbitrariness and irrationality of the fault concept which prompted the judges to speak out in the *Ferguson* case. They saw no valid reason to exclude Mr. Ferguson from a share of public money because he could not prove the fault of the defendants-physicians.

(B) The Cost of The Fault System

Chapter 1 described the course of a medical negligence action from the plaintiff's injury to final disposition by the Supreme Court of Canada. The individualistic determination of fault and the personal calculation of damage awards was seen to demand considerable time and energy. The result is that the fault system is very expensive. It is estimated that, of every dollar in premium paid to insurers, only about 50 cents is paid to victims of medical accidents. Fully 50 per cent of the premium is consumed in legal and administrative expenses. These high transaction costs are reflected in the Statements of Revenue and Expense found in the 2001 Report of the Canadian Medical Protective Association. In round numbers, the Association's total revenues in 2001 were $252,000,000. Of that, $153,000,000 paid awards and settlements.

(C) The Limited Range of Injured Patients Covered

The requirement that the plaintiff prove fault has effectively controlled the number of medical accident victims compensated. A recent study has indicated that only 10 per cent of injured patients with viable tort claims receive compensation from the tort process. Those who do not recover compensation include not only those who cannot prove fault but also those who do not initiate an action because of financial considerations, or ignorance of or discomfort with lawyers and the legal system.

(D) The Risks of Litigation

An important aspect of any compensation system is that it have some degree of certainty and predictability as to who will be paid compensation and how much they will receive. In many instances the payment of compensation in the fault system is uncertain, unpredictable and capricious. The adversarial process prevents lawyers from advising clients with any degree of confidence whether compensation will be paid, how much will be paid and when it will be paid. The system has been described as a "forensic lottery" in which a few winners achieve dazzling success while others are left in bewildered and bitter dismay.

We surveyed the reported decisions from 1995 to May 2002 in which counsel for the plaintiff argued for liability on the basis of the informed consent doctrine. One assumes that the claims were presented with a reasonable hope of success. The argument was successful in only 30 of 122 cases. There may be more unpredictability in a new doctrine such as informed consent, but of the other 92 cases there were only 17 cases where the plaintiff was successful on other grounds of liability such as negligent treatment. Overall the plaintiff was successful in only 47 of 122 cases. The 2001 report of the C.M.P.A. paints a similar picture. In 2001, a total of 1232 actions were concluded, most of which originated in prior years. The outcomes of those actions were: judgment for the plaintiff 2%; judgment for the physician 6%; settlement 32% and withdrawn or abandoned 60%. These numbers are also reflective of the five-year experience (1997-2001) which are: judgment for the plaintiff 2%; judgment for physician 7%; settlement 29%; withdrawn or abandoned 62%. The plaintiff is successful at trial or by settlement in only about a third of actions commenced. Given the great expense of civil litigation one might wish for greater certainty and the chance of more reliable prediction by plaintiff's counsel.

(E) Lump Sum Awards

We have noted earlier that most settlements before trial and all damage awards in negligence cases are made in a lump sum which is not reviewable in the future. The calculation of such a lump sum is a very difficult task when the plaintiff is seriously and permanently disabled. Loss of income must be calculated on the basis of working life expectancy and predictions of the plaintiff's likely work pattern and earning potential if she had not been injured. Future care costs require a consideration of life expectancy, future medical and care costs, and the plaintiff's long term medical prognosis. Non-pecuniary losses must be calculated to provide solace for pain, suffering and permanent disability. All of this must be projected into an unpredictable economic, social and political future and then be computed into a lump sum in current dollars. It is not surprising that one researcher commented that no matter "how scientific the evidence, how educated the experts, how judicious and fair the trier of fact the award will not mirror the plaintiff's actual future losses."[5]

In 1980, the Supreme Court of Canada pointed out the need to shift to some sort of system of periodic payments with future review, stating:

> . . . it is highly irrational to be tied to a lump sum system and a onceand-for-all award.
>
> The lump sum award presents problems of great importance. It is subject to inflation, it is subject to fluctuation on investment, income from it is subject to tax. After judgment new needs of the plaintiff arise and present needs are extinguished; yet, our law of damages knows nothing of periodic payment. The difficulties are greatest where there is a continuing need for intensive and expensive care and a long-term loss of earning capacity. It should be possible to devise some system whereby payments would be subject to periodic review and variation in the light of the continuing needs of the injured person and the cost of meeting those needs.[6]

As yet little legal change has taken place.*

(F) Delay

Delay is pervasive in the tort system and to a large extent it is institutional and not amenable to easy solution. The system of lump sum awards requires that the plaintiff's physical condition be stabilized before any serious talk of settlement can take place. In serious cases stabilization appears to take about one to two years. Further delay is caused by the adversarial process of civil litigation (described in Chapter 1). If the parties go to trial the situation is exacerbated. A case is unlikely to be tried earlier than three years from the date of the accident. Sometimes the delay is longer. We surveyed 120 cases from 1995 to May 2002** where the claim was based at least in part on the informed consent doctrine. The table below indicates the length of time between the date of the *medical accident* and the *trial*.

---

*   Manitoba and Ontario have passed legislation permitting periodic payments in certain circumstances. One should also note that structured settlements providing periodic payments are increasingly common.

**   Including almost all reported informed consent cases. A few are excluded because the date of the accident and/or trial is unknown.

Time Period (years) Between Date of Accident and Trial	Number of Cases
1	0
2	0
3	10
4	18
5	16
6	18
7	10
8	12
9	7
10	11
11	5
12	7
13	1
14	3
15	0
16	2
17	1
18	1
TOTAL	120

Of the 120 cases there have been, as of May 2002, 24 reported judgments on appeal. Others may be subject to an appeal which has yet to be decided and reported. The table below indicates the cumulative time of these cases from the date of the accident to judgment by the provincial court of appeal.

Time Period (years) Between Date of Accident and Judgment of Court of Appeal	Number of Cases
1	0
2	0
3	1
4	2
5	1
6	1
7	2
8	2
9	2
10	3

11	1
12	1
13	0
14	2
15	2
16	1
17	0
18	1
19	2
Total	24

Two informed consent cases were decided by the Supreme Court during this period. One was decided 10 years after the accident. The other took 19 years.

Such delay has a number of deleterious effects on injured persons. They need compensation immediately, not in the undefined and indefinable future. Most Canadian households rely on a regular injection of money, either weekly or monthly. Very few have the kind of reserves necessary to maintain themselves for prolonged periods. Thus, delay makes plaintiffs susceptible to pressure for premature and low settlements. It also impedes rehabilitation. There is little point in making a strong effort in that direction if its effect will reduce the final settlement or judgment. The anxiety and frustration of the legal process may cause compensation neurosis.* Finally, the delay may prevent a deserving plaintiff from proving her case. Over the years memories dim, witnesses move away or die, and at the end of the day the plaintiff may be unable to discharge her burden of proof.

Many critics conclude that the inability of tort law to compensate the victims of medical accidents promptly, cheaply and reliably dictates a careful examination of possible reforms.

5. MEDICAL ACCIDENTS: POLICY CHOICES

In its application to medical accidents the fault/insurance system is under substantial pressure. Claims against physicians are increasing. So are the number of judgments and settlements in favour of the plaintiff. Damage awards have increased as have the premiums physicians pay for liability insurance. The financial burden on the health care system has increased. There is every reason to believe that this trend will continue in

---

* A widely recognised condition arising after an accident and manifesting itself in anxiety, amnesia, irritability, intolerance and unwillingness or inability to return to employment. The condition may resolve itself when the claim for compensation is settled.

the foreseeable future. Added to the problems of cost are allegations that the concept of fault is increasingly out of touch with the modern health care system and is unable to fulfill its two major goals, the deterrence of negligent conduct and the compensation of medical accident victims.

Dissatisfaction on the part of physicians, the public and government with the fault/insurance system seems to be increasing. Chapter I noted the complexity of civil litigation and the discomfort and frustration with it expressed by physicians, whether involved as witnesses, defendants or experts. The physician's fear of public humiliation and damage to his reputation when sued for medical malpractice has also been noted. An ironical result of the system is that actions against the most negligent and incompetent members of the medical profession are the least likely to receive publicity. Those cases are usually settled in favour of the plaintiffs. The glare of publicity falls on the trial in which the defendant's negligence is not clear-cut and requires careful adjudication.

There is no doubt that the fault liability system benefits the few patients who successfully bring a civil suit. It does not, however, serve most consumers of health care well. We have noted the expense, delay and complexity of the system which by definition does not compensate many injured by medical accidents. Moreover, recent studies in the United States have indicated that the civil litigation process may have an *adverse* impact on the standard of medical practice. Involvement with the civil litigation *process* may cause serious stress which can result in some physicians avoiding certain kinds of patients, avoiding high risk procedures and suffering a loss of "nerve" and confidence in clinical situations.

If current trends continue, one may expect governments to become increasingly concerned about the costs of civil liability in an already burgeoning health care budget. This is particularly the case when it costs one dollar in administrative and legal expenses to deliver every dollar of compensation to the patient.

It seems likely that dissatisfaction with the fault/insurance system will continue and that careful consideration will be given to alternative approaches. The options for reform may be grouped into four categories: reform of the tort/insurance system; the no-fault option; first party life and disability insurance; and the Swedish model.

(a) Reform of the Tort System

There are many who continue to favour the tort system. That support is based upon its value as a multi-functional system which embodies important societal values such as responsibility for one's actions and which achieves, to some degree, its objectives of compensation, punishment, deterrence, appeasement and education. The most urgent need perceived by defenders of the fault system is the relief of the financial pressure on the system. This may be achieved in two ways: the curtailment of tort liability, and improvement in the cost-effectiveness of the fault system.

The curtailment of tort liability would require changes in the law to reduce the physician's exposure to liability and changes in damage assessment rules to reduce the amount of damage awards. Changes could be made to shorten the limitation period (the period of time within which a claim must be filed), to prevent double compensation when a successful plaintiff is also eligible for benefits from governmental or private compensation systems, to repeal pre-judgment interest legislation,* to abolish claims by members of the deceased or injured person's family for loss of care, guidance and companionship, and to change the rules of joint liability so that a defendant is liable only to the degree that her negligence caused the plaintiff's injuries.**

The lump sum damage award could be replaced by periodic payments coupled with review of the award if the plaintiff's circumstances change. Under such a scheme the Court would not be required to speculate on future losses. Legislated "caps" could be placed on damage awards. Changes such as these would reduce the financial burden of civil liability as fewer physicians would be liable for smaller amounts. This is an attractive option to the ultimate payer, the federal and provincial governments and to some extent to physicians. The interest of health care consumers, however, would not be advanced because a narrower band of medical accident victims would recover less.

Another way of relieving the financial pressure on the fault system would be to reduce the delay, complexity, and unpredictability of civil litigation. Procedural changes could be made to enhance the likelihood of settlement. The discovery process could be broadened to include witnesses. Special fast-track procedures developed for less complex cases. Reforming the procedural aspects of civil action would make the system less complex, less time consuming and consequently less expensive. Suggestions have also been made that medical malpractice cases no longer be resolved through the adversarial process. The legal system is becoming more receptive to alternative dispute settlement methods such as mediation, conciliation and arbitration. Colleges of Physicians and Surgeons now deal with minor complaints against physicians on the basis of investigation, concil-

---

* Recent legislation has imposed a liability to pay interest which would have accrued on the lump sum awarded at trial between the date of filing the claim and the judgment date.

** Presently, each defendant is fully liable for the whole amount of the plaintiff's loss; however, the plaintiff can recover no more than 100 per cent of the amount awarded.

iation and mediation. Medical negligence claims could also be processed in a less formal manner. Legislation could provide for arbitration before a board comprised of a lawyer, physician and layperson.

The basic assumption underlying all these reform proposals is that fault remains the most reasonable basis of accident compensation.

(b) The No-Fault Option

The attractiveness of the no-fault option normally depends upon one's perception of the deterrent effect of tort law and its role in maintaining high professional standards. If the deterrent role of tort law is regarded as minimal, it seems sensible to separate compensatory plans from safety incentives. A no-fault plan would provide compensation to all persons injured by a medical accident and the maintenance of high professional standards would be left to the criminal law, the College of Physicians and Surgeons, hospital committees, legislative safety rules and regulations, and personal and professional pride.

One proposal is to abolish the tort action as it applies to physicians and substitute a public no-fault compensation scheme providing compensatory benefits to all victims of medical accidents. This concept has been adopted in Quebec and Manitoba for all victims of automobile accidents. Benefits include income replacement, future care costs and moderate lump sums for physical disability. Premiums currently paid by physicians and hospitals to liability insurers would provide the primary funding for the scheme. The main disadvantage of this approach is that it is difficult to justify special treatment for victims of medical accidents. For this reason it has been argued that the issue of compensation for medical accident victims must not be decided in a vacuum. That is because compensation for accident victims is not simply a health care problem. It is a societal problem and the remedy must encompass all accident victims. Some call for a universal no-fault accident compensation plan. This would involve the rationalization and integration of all federal and provincial schemes of accident compensation into one publicly administered scheme. This option was exercised in New Zealand in 1974.

The New Zealand Accident Compensation Corporation administers a scheme which provides income security, future care and rehabilitation benefits, and compensation for permanent disability. No civil action is permitted in respect of any accidental personal injury or death. In determining eligibility for benefits, the Corporation does not concern itself with how, when, where or why the accident occurred. The Injury Prevention Rehabilitation and Compensation Act of New Zealand specifically covers medical misadventure as a compensable event. The definition of "medical misadventure" is drawn quite narrowly to contain eligibility within strict limits and to rule out a civil action. Medical misadventure covers both "medical mishap" and "medical error." A medical mishap means an adverse consequence of treatment caused by a health care professional which is both rare in occurrence and severe in consequence. It is rare if it occurs in fewer than 1/100 cases. It is severe if it results in death, in hospitalization for more than 14 days or in a significant disability lasting more than 28 days. "Medical error" is the failure to observe a standard of care of skill reasonably to be expected in the circumstances. Claims relating to a lack of informed consent or a failure to diagnose are not covered unless accompanied by negligence. These definitions insulate the medical profession from civil action, but the Corporation has the power to refer matters to the appropriate professional body for disciplinary action.

Another no-fault option is that which has been adopted by many Canadian provinces in the automobile accident and criminal injuries field. All victims of automobile accidents and violent crime are eligible for no-fault benefits. However, injured persons may have resort to the fault system if they deem it to be advantageous. These so called "add on" plans provide some compensation to all, but retain fault which provides more generous compensation to some. In Canada, some automobile no-fault schemes are operated by the private sector and some by public corporation. The private sector plays no part in criminal injuries compensation. This approach has also been adopted in Quebec in respect of those who suffer injuries from vaccination, and is capable of extension to all victims of medical accidents. Modified no fault is a variation of this concept. It calls for the payment of no fault benefits up to a certain threshold beyond which a tort action is available. The threshold may be set at a monetary amount or by some description of sufficiently grave and serious disability. Such a system is currently in operation in Ontario for injuries caused by automobile accidents. These compromises between fault and no-fault are open to a number of criticisms. Not only do they create disparity among classes of accident victims, but they also create a disparity among members of the same class by paying unequal compensation on the basis of the way in which the injury occurred or its extent.

An argument against the no-fault options outlined is that they are inherently unfair because they single out those disabled by injury for special treatment. It is argued that differential treatment of disabled persons on the basis of the cause of the disability is fundamentally inequitable. Treatment of those disabled by illness, congenital defect or injury must be uniform; the only way to achieve this being through a publicly funded, comprehensive disability compensation scheme.

(c) First Party Life and Disability Insurance

Victims of medical accidents are forced to rely primarily upon fault liability for adequate compensation because most patients do not carry sufficient private first-party* life and disability insurance. If a person has adequate life and disability insurance, she does not need to resort to tort law or to any other component of the provincial accident compensation system. Payments from that system are more in the nature of a windfall. Insurance may be purchased either individually or more commonly through a group such as employees. An interesting comparison can be drawn with property damage. First party property insurance is pervasive. Almost all people insure their homes, automobiles and other personal property. If that property is damaged by the fault of another, a claim in tort for damages can be made. However, the more typical response is to make a claim on the owner's insurance policy. On the whole, we insure our property much more fully than we insure ourselves and our income earning capacity.

One option worthy of consideration is to require patients to purchase first-party life and accident insurance to cover the duration of their hospitalization. This approach is based on the theory that most medical accidents occur in hospitals. This insurance would cover income loss and future care costs up to a generous level. The fault system could be retained for the recovery of income loss beyond a ceiling and for non-pecuniary loss. The premium pool could be supplemented by hospitals and physicians to the extent of the drop in premiums paid to their liability insurance carrier. Insurance premiums should fall because insurers would be exposed to less risk. The insurance could be offered in co-operation with private sector insurance companies, or through a public corporation; or the provincial health care system could be used. This might create an acceptable compromise for those who wish to reform the fault system but are suspicious of public sector intervention and uncomfortable with the outright abolition of tort liability. The benefits of first-party insurance are reduced delays and expenses in fault-finding and damage calculation, and enhanced reliability and predictability of compensation. Special provision would have to be made for those who could not afford the insurance premium.

---

* First party insurance requires the insurer to pay the insured an agreed upon amount on the occurrence of a stipulated event. It is contrasted with third party liability insurance which requires the insurer to discharge the insured's liability by payment to a third person.

(d) The Swedish Model*

The Swedish system warrants separate consideration because it represents significant progress toward a balanced and integrated scheme that clearly identifies and addresses the critically important objectives of compensation, deterrence and accident prevention. The three features of the system corresponding to the stated objectives are: (1) no-fault patient accident insurance; (2) the Medical Responsibility Board; and (3) the establishment of procedures providing informational feedback for the purpose of accident prevention.

The Swedish no-fault accident insurance plan was instituted in 1975. It was motivated by dissatisfaction with the fault-based tort system (in particular, the notorious difficulty of proving negligence) which mirrored to a great extent the North American experience. The insurance plan is predominantly funded by the public sector, but is administered by the County Council Mutual Insurance Co. It pays compensation for all major medical injuries that are preventable or avoidable. Fault is not a relevant factor. The insurance plan is a payer of last resort. It covers those pecuniary and non-pecuniary losses that have not been met by other components of the Swedish social welfare system. Economic losses are compensated fully, and non-pecuniary losses are compensated on the basis of a schedule of disability. The fault-based tort system has not been abolished, but as a practical matter medical malpractice cases are quite uncommon. In recent years financial pressure on the scheme has increased. Premiums have increased and compensation payable to the patient has been reduced. More significantly, "major injury" has been redefined from an injury requiring a 14-day sick leave to one requiring a 30-day sick leave and a minimum 10-day stay in hospital related to the injury.

The Medical Responsibility Board (M.R.B.) reviews complaints against health care professionals, including physicians. The board has disciplinary powers and may impose penalties, which include issuing a warning, restricting the right to practice and referring a case to the courts. The certificate of practice can be recalled only if the complaint is made by the National Board of Health and Welfare. To this extent, the M.R.B. is similar to the disciplinary procedures of Provincial Colleges of Physicians and Surgeons. The primary difference is that the M.R.B. is a publicly funded, autonomous administrative body, with a permanent staff and significant lay representation on the board. The M.R.B. employs a staff of administrators, legal experts and professional health specialists. The M.R.B. makes

---

* The description of the Swedish system is drawn from Rosenthal, *Dealing with Medical Malpractice. The British and Swedish Experience* (1988).

its own investigation and research of the complaint and the case and recommendations for action are presented to the board by a medical expert on
the staff of the M.R.B. The board is comprised of four members of parliament, three union representatives, an employer's representative and a judge
who acts as chairperson. The union and employer's representative are
usually health care professionals. The board appears to be well accepted
by both physicians and the public.

The third important feature of the Swedish system is its role in accident
prevention. A great deal of information is gathered by the patient accident
insurers and the M.R.B. This information is used to identify relationships
between medical accidents and certain procedures, hospitals, or geographic
areas. Information is fed back to the medical profession in a variety of ways
including the Swedish Medical Association journal, and the M.R.B. journal.

The Swedish system is not a panacea, but it does provide an interesting
and useful model for dealing with medical accidents in an integrated,
rational and fair manner. The accident insurance plan operates on the basis
of injured persons' needs and provides reliable and predictable compensation targeted at the most seriously injured. Tort law is not abolished but
is reduced in practice to an insignificant role. The M.R.B. addresses directly
the need for public accountability and the maintenance of high standards
of professional conduct. The haphazard and doubtful deterrence of tort law
is bolstered by the work of the board. It is the potential for accident
prevention, however, which is the most appealing feature of the scheme.
Accident prevention cannot be effective without clear information on the
pattern and causes of medical accidents. The accident insurance scheme
and the M.R.B. can provide that kind of information base.

6. THE REPORT ON LIABILITY AND COMPENSATION IN HEALTH CARE: TOWARDS A CANADIAN SOLUTION

In 1987, the Conference of Deputy Ministers of Health in Canada
appointed Robert Prichard, of the University of Toronto, to conduct a
Federal/Provincial/Territorial Review on Liability and Compensation Issues in Health Care. In 1990, the *Report on Liability and Compensation
Issues in Health Care* was issued. It is a document of major importance on
questions of accident compensation and health care. Its recommendations
were supported unanimously by the Advisory Committee which assisted
the Chairperson in preparing the Report. The Report falls into three parts.
The first presents findings on the current system. The second makes rec-

ommendations for reforming the tort litigation system and enhancing the accountability and responsibility of health care institutions. The third addresses the need to compensate the large number of injured patients who do not receive tort compensation.

(a) Principal Findings

The Report confirmed a number of the concerns about and criticisms of the current fault/insurance system that have been outlined earlier in this chapter. It found that there had been a significant growth in claims between 1971 — 1988, an increase comparable to rates of growth in the United States and Great Britain. There was also a consequential growth in insurance costs, which alarmingly grew at a faster rate than the underlying growth in claims. The Report found that this growth in claims and insurance costs was not due to any significant change in legal doctrine and was greater than in most other professions. The Report also confirmed the deficiencies of the fault system as a compensatory device. The great administrative expense was noted. Although insurance costs exceed two hundred million dollars annually, only 250 injured patients (10 per cent of those with viable tort claims) were compensated. Other problems such as delay and unpredictability were also confirmed. Interestingly, the Report did conclude that tort law, on balance, is an important vehicle of accident prevention and quality control and that the fault system should not be abolished. Finally, the Report sounded an alarm. It anticipated an inexorable growth in claims in future years, which would create a significant financial burden for the health care system. It noted that there were no significant or permanent impediments to growth and that statistics show that currently many patients who have claims are not suing. These findings support the view that some reform is necessary in order to avert an insurance crisis.

(b) Recommendations on Reform by the Current Fault/ Insurance System

The Report recommends a variety of changes in the tort system to improve its accessibility, efficiency and fairness. Recommended changes to tort law include a more rational system of limitation periods, improvements in the calculation of damages, periodic payment of damages and controls on double recovery from the tort system and other public and private compensatory schemes. Access to justice could be enhanced by greater use of contingent fee arrangements, greater availability of expert witnesses, the maintenance of access to legal aid, the retention of the rule as to costs and improved education of the public as to rights and remedies.

Further, important recommendations relate to questions of insurance and to a much greater collective responsibility of health care institutions as opposed to individual liability. The latter point is a reflection of the fact that medical care is a team enterprise for which collective responsibility is an appropriate response.

(c) No Fault Compensation for Serious Avoidable Health Care Injuries

The Report recognized that an increase in the accessibility, cost effectiveness and efficiency of the tort system would not solve all problems of medical injury, compensation and prevention. It may, to some extent, exacerbate problems by encouraging and facilitating more claims. Two key issues must be resolved. First, some mechanism must be found to limit the growth in tort claims and the quantum of damages. Second, a caring and compassionate society must do more to compensate a broader range of injured patients. The Report suggested that these objectives could be achieved by the implementation of an alternative no fault system for patients suffering serious avoidable injury in the course of health care.

The recommended scheme would cover significant losses generated by avoidable injuries, including vaccine, blood-product-related and pharmaceutical injuries. It would be targeted at those most seriously injured by setting a minimum threshold of injury. In the case of income earners, it would be permanent partial disability or a total loss of income earning capacity for eight weeks. In the case of non-earners (children, students, homemakers, elderly), the threshold of significant loss would require either permanent partial disability or substantially complete impairment of functions for at least eight weeks. The scheme would cover rehabilitation costs, income replacement, and future health and home care costs not covered by provincial plans. A moderate ceiling amounting to two times the average industrial wage would be placed on lost income. Limited recovery of non-pecuniary losses (pain and suffering, etc.) would be calculated by applying a scheduled percentage of permanent disability against a fixed amount. Other compensation benefits would be made by periodic payments. This scheme would be a payer of last resort; all other sources of compensation (*e.g.* private insurance benefits or other governmental benefits) must be collected in advance of entitlement under the scheme.

It is important to note that this proposed scheme is an alternative to the tort system. It is not an "add on" or modified system which allows the claimant to recover no fault benefits as well as any supplementary benefits that tort law may offer. At an appropriate point, when a claimant has sufficient information about a potential tort claim, an irrevocable choice must be made either to receive no-fault benefits or to sue in tort. Under no circumstance would a patient be permitted to first sue in tort and then if unsuccessful recover no fault benefits. This is crucial to the achievement of the objectives outlined earlier. The purpose is to create a substantial incentive to injured claimants to opt for guaranteed, fast and moderate no-fault benefits rather than take the chance of a higher pay off under the expensive, slow and unpredictable tort system. The theory is that the incentives to quality care provided by the tort system will remain, but that in practice less reliance will be placed on it, thereby easing financial pressures on physicians and their insurers. Patient compensation will not be sacrificed, given the new no fault benefits.

These proposals, which appear to draw on the Swedish model are open to criticism. The retention of fault guarantees that injured patients will not be compensated equally. Those recovering under the fault system will receive more generous compensation than those who receive no fault benefits. Those who are less impressed with the contribution of fault liability to the quality of care will favour the abolition of fault and a redirection of resources to a comprehensive no fault scheme which treats all injured patients in the same manner. Furthermore, the addition of a no-fault scheme to compliment the current fault system is a very expensive option requiring scarce federal and provincial funding. Given current financial conditions in Canada, the re-allocation of existing resources in a more equitable manner may be a more appealing approach. No action has been taken to implement this Report. In the short run we may see some reform of tort rules and procedures but we are unlikely to see the implementation of a no fault scheme until a crisis of significant proportion is reached. Nevertheless, the Report is an invaluable addition to our understanding of the current system and the policy debate on future directions.

7. CONCLUSION

In conclusion we return to the case of *Ferguson v. Hamilton Civic Hospitals* and the judicial challenge that an enlightened and compassionate society — should do more for injured patients such as Mr. Ferguson. If we accept that view, then we must determine how best to do so in a manner that not only ensures fair compensation but also fulfills the equally important objectives of accident prevention and safety. There is no doubt that the medical profession will be called upon to play a central role in making this determination.

NOTES

1. (1983), 40 O.R. (2d) 577, 23 C.C.L.T. 254, 144 D.L.R. (3d) 214 (H.C.), affirmed (1985), 50 O.R. (2d) 754, 33 C.C.L.T. 56, 18 D.L.R. (4th) 638 (C.A.).
2. *Ibid.,* (1983), 40 O.R. (2d) 577 (H.C.), at pp. 618-19.
3. *Supra,* note 1, (1985), 50 O.R. (2d) 754 (C.A.), at p. 755.
4. 57 Man. R. 343, [1949] 2 W.W.R. 337, [1949] 4 D.L.R. 71 (C.A.), affirmed [1950] 4 D.L.R. 223 (S.C.C.).
5. Manitoba Law Reform Commission "A Study of Damage Awards in Personal Injury and Death Cases" Working Paper 3, prepared by Professor P. Carlson, 1984 at p. 6.
6. Mr. Justice Dickson (as he then was), in *Andrews v. Grand & Toy Alberta Ltd.,* [1978] 2 S.C.R. 229, [1978] 1 W.W.R. 577, 3 C.C.L.T. 225, 83 D.L.R. (3d) 452, 8 A.R. 182, 19 N.R. 50, at p. 236 [S.C.R.].

11

THE PHYSICIAN'S OTHER DUTIES: GOOD FAITH, LOYALTY AND CONFIDENTIALITY

SUMMARY

The physician's duty to preserve the confidences of his patient, and to keep secret all matters learned within the doctor/patient relationship, is an ancient obligation both ethical and legal. As this chapter shows, it has in general been religiously observed by physicians down the centuries, and defended by them on occasion with great fortitude. So it is not surprising that there is little case-law on the subject, and little guidance as to the remedies which the law affords to the patient whose confidences have been betrayed. There is much more discussion in the law-books about the *exceptions* to the physician's duty of confidentiality — in other words, the circumstances in which countervailing considerations of law, policy or commonsense have seemed to our judges or legislators to outweigh the duty of secrecy and to require the reluctant physician to disclose what he knows.

These and related matters make up the greater part of this chapter. It concludes with a discussion of that very important document, the patient's record, and of the circumstances in which it may, or sometimes must, be laid open to the perusal of persons other than the physician or institution who compiled it. The confidentiality of the record is generally treated as enjoying the same measure of sanctity as any other information gleaned within the doctor/patient relationship. In the latter part of the chapter, attention is given to recent changes in the law, some effected judicially and some by statute, which have greatly augmented the rights of patients to gain access to their

"own" medical records, and in some provinces have given new "teeth" to patients' rights to have the confidentiality of their health information jealously preserved.

1. THE DUTY TO PRESERVE CONFIDENTIALITY

Quite distinct from the physician's duty of care and skill to the patient is another duty or complex of duties, with deep and ancient moral roots. Hippocrates enjoined his fellow physicians to preserve professional confidences as "holy secrets", and so, in our own day, does Rule six of the C.M.A. Code of Ethics. As a matter of professional ethics, this obligation is a fundamental precept. From a pragmatic point of view, it is an essential prerequisite to that frank doctor-patient communication without which such a relationship cannot work. Physicians down the centuries have in general shown a faithful observance of their responsibilities in this regard, and no doubt their scrupulousness in this matter has been prompted more by ethical considerations (and sometimes the fear of professional sanctions) than the prospect of lawsuits. Yet the threat of civil liability for the unprivileged disclosure of professional confidences is a very real one, and must now be examined.

Two sorts of problem attend the question of civil liability for the unprivileged disclosure of medical secrets. First, there is the very basic question of what remedies the law affords to the disgruntled patient. This most basic of questions does not admit of an easy answer in Canadian law, since the "common law" upon which it is founded has been remarkably slow to develop any protection for "privacy" interests. Secondly, the obligation of confidentiality has always been seen as a *qualified* one, whether as a matter of ethics or of law. The "Father of Medicine" himself was careful in drafting his famous Oath to confine the physician's duty of secrecy to those matters "that ought never to be published abroad", and the modern Canadian Code of Ethics likewise acknowledges exceptions, commanding secrecy "except where the law requires." In truth, most of the case-law in this area (and it is not extensive) deals with the exceptions engrafted upon the rule of nondisclosure, rather than the rule itself. Indeed, there is not a single Canadian case which has awarded damages or an injunction against a physician for the wrongful disclosure of professional confidences. And while there is a strong consensus among legal scholars that such an action might succeed on appropriate facts, there is considerable disagreement as to the variety of lawsuit which might appropriately be used to that end. While avoiding the deeper waters of academic controversy, this must logically be the first question for us to address.

Our legal system is not, of course, entirely closed to innovation, nor even particularly hostile to it. But in an old-established and slowly evolved area like the law of civil liability, a plaintiff's chances of securing an effective remedy are overwhelmingly enhanced if he can bring his complaint within the scope of some well-recognized and developed "cause of action", previously known to the law. When the complaint is that of a patient affronted by his physician's alleged breach of professional confidence, that is by no means a straightforward task.

There is in our law a phenomenon known as the *action for breach of confidence,* which has generated much litigation in recent times, mostly in the realm of commercial information, but not exclusively so. Whenever a person receives information in confidence, or which he ought to realize is imparted confidentially, the courts may invoke this principle to restrain the improper divulging of such confidential information. The principle applies not only to control the behaviour of the original recipient of that information, but also that of anyone who may by accident or design become privy to it. There are questions, to be sure, about the precise circumstances under which information will be regarded as clothed in confidentiality for the purposes of this action. But none of these questions is of any interest in a medical context, where every physician surely knows that all medical and personal information about his patient, or his family for that matter, is imparted in confidence. So does not this old-established cause of action afford a simple and obvious basis upon which to sue the physician who discloses professional secrets?

That it is neither simple nor obvious was stressed by an Ontario judge in *Damien v. O'Mulvenny*[1] in 1981. The defendant doctor diagnosed a venereal infection in one of his patients, the plaintiff, and allegedly — for the matter was never to be formally determined — disclosed this information to the plaintiff's employer, who dismissed him. The only point ever resolved in the case, as events transpired, was that the case was far too complex in point of law to be submitted to a jury trial. The problem was that actions of this type are "equitable" — that is, they trace their ancestry and evolution to the old Court of Chancery; and that Court, for historical reasons, never awarded damages. Accordingly, it is doubted by scholars to this day whether a patient, seeking monetary compensation from a doctor who has flouted his professional confidences, has any hope of recovering damages in the action for breach of confidence, however extreme the embarrassment that has been caused. One must conclude that the action for breach of confidence, which sounds the most promising action to bring against a doctor who discloses patients' secrets, is really the most speculative.

In four provinces of Canada, the total absence of any developed common law remedy for violations of a person's privacy has prompted the legislature to pass a Privacy Act. The provinces that currently enjoy such a statute are British Columbia (which enacted its Privacy Act in 1968), Manitoba (1970), Newfoundland (1981) and Saskatchewan (1974).[2] All make it a tort (that is, a wrong actionable at the suit of the individual affected), giving rise to a remedy in damages, to violate the privacy of another person; though British Columbia, Saskatchewan and Newfoundland insist that the violation be "wilful" if it is to be actionable. All these statutes leave it up to the courts to determine what exactly does amount to an invasion of privacy. Though it is never wise to "second-guess" the pattern of judicial law making, it is hard indeed to imagine any judge denying that such an invasion or violation occurs when a doctor reveals confidential information about a patient without lawful excuse. In the provinces where they apply, these statutes seem to provide the simplest and most straightforward avenue of recourse against a doctor who has in this way broken his professional traditions and duties.

In provinces not favoured with such legislation, though, the lawyer for the affronted patient will have to show considerable resourcefulness if she is to find a suitable legal vehicle for securing damages from the delinquent physician.[3] One method is to sue for breach of contract. It can be argued strenuously that in every contract for professional services entered into between doctor and patient there is an implied or tacit undertaking by the physician faithfully to preserve the patient's confidences. The breach of such an implicit contractual duty gave a remedy in damages to the plaintiff in the old Scottish case of *A.B. v. C.D.*,[4] in 1851. An elder of the Presbyterian Church was naturally aghast when only six months after their marriage, his wife gave birth to a child. He sought the opinion of the defendant, a doctor, as to whether the infant had been born prematurely, or after a full-term gestation. The doctor, inclining to the latter view, disobligingly informed not only the abashed father but also the authorities of the Church, who then expelled the father from the congregation. His action for breach of contract against this gratuitously indiscreet physician was unanimously upheld. That there have been no reported cases of this type in more recent times would seem to be simply a function of the extreme rarity of actions of any kind, brought against indiscreet physicians; a phenomenon which may be thought to reflect well upon the medical profession.*

---

* But see p. 224, *post*. Another possible explanation is that under a state-financed "Medicare" system, it is debateable whether there is a true contract between physician and patient. Also, it is important to remember that if the patient's confidences are violated by someone other than "his" physician

An alternative line of approach may be found in the tort of negligence, at which we have already looked extensively. This was the approach used by the successful plaintiff in *Furniss v. Fitchett,* (New Zealand, 1958).[5] Mrs. Furniss was examined by her family physician during a time of extreme marital strain, and (without saying so to her) he diagnosed her as suffering from paranoia, and in need of psychiatric help. He then drafted a memorandum to this effect, and handed it to her husband, (who was also Dr. Fitchett's patient), to be used by his solicitor in impending matrimonial proceedings! When the document was produced in court, and she learned for the first time of its contents, she sustained severe and debilitating nervous shock.* She brought action against Dr. Fitchett, initially both for libel (complaining that the offending document was defamatory), and for negligence, (and perhaps breach of contract too). The claim in libel was wisely dropped when Dr. Fitchett entered a "plea of justification", and proposed to prove, as he very probably could, that his accusation or diagnosis of paranoia was true and accurate. The judge was attracted by the idea of deciding the case in breach of contract, as in *A.B. v. C.D.*, which we have already examined. He expressed a clear opinion, in passing, that Mrs. Furniss would have won her case on that ground. However, since counsel had not pursued this line of reasoning, he elected instead to decide the case in the tort of negligence. Taking this line, he had no difficulty in deciding that Mrs. Furniss should win her case and receive damages. Dr. Fitchett ought, as a reasonable physician, to have foreseen that his memorandum would be produced in court, that it would take Mrs. Furniss completely by surprise, and that it might well cause trauma to her nervous system. In these circumstances, standard negligence doctrine as explained in *M'Alister (Donoghue) v. Stevenson*** imposed upon him a duty of care — a facet of his general duty of professional care to his patient — to refrain from making his diagnosis public in this way. His very ability, as a physician, to foresee the likely medical consequences to his patient of his

---

— for example by some specialist who has been asked for a second opinion — the existence of a contract between him and the defendant may be even more doubtful.

* The concept of "nervous shock" may well strike modern physicians as a preposterous one, but though embarrassingly unscientific, it is a legal term of art too well-rooted in our law (since the late nineteenth century) to be easily extirpated. It is deemed by lawyers to be present when events work upon the nervous system of an individual as to cause something more than a purely "emotional" reaction — more than mere embarrassment, annoyance, fear, or disgust, but some recognized form of mental disorder, or some discernible and substantial physical symptoms. Though scientifically indefensible, this concept is regularly used by the courts to draw the line in determining when damages shall or shall not be awarded.

** [1932] A.C. 562 (H.L.). See also Chapter 5.

indiscreet revelations, fixed him with this duty, and its breach warranted an award of damages to the lady whose confidence he had betrayed.

Two points of importance require brief mention at this juncture. Had Mrs. Furniss sustained an emotional upset falling short of "nervous shock" (as explained somewhat shamefacedly in the last footnote but one), she could not have succeeded in the tort of negligence, for that tort takes no account of merely "emotional" sufferings: though she might still have prevailed in contract, a context in which such harm is at least sometimes (though very sparingly) redressed. Best of all, of course, would be a Privacy Act claim, (*supra*) in those provinces which have such a statute; though in the absence of any case-law applying a provincial Privacy Act in a medical disclosure context, it is difficult to predict with confidence how, or at what monetary level, a court would put a pecuniary value on the patient's purely emotional sufferings.

One other point of importance can be gleaned from *Furniss v. Fitchett.* The judge in that case paid considerable attention to the Ethical Code of the medical profession, but stressed that while breaches of that code might be persuasive evidence of actionable negligence, they would never be conclusive in that regard.

Legal scholars reading this text will perhaps comment that the causes of action which have here been described do not form a complete list of the possible methods of suing a doctor who breaches her duty of professional secrecy or confidence. They may object that the torts of libel and slander* should have been more extensively touched upon, as should the rare and interesting tort postulated in *Wilkinson v. Downton.*** In a work of the present nature, no apology will be made for omitting these esoteric issues of law, which whatever their potential are largely or even wholly untried in the context of medical confidentiality. One area of law, however — until recently, amorphous and speculative in the extreme — must be mentioned at this juncture; namely, the action for "breach of fiduciary duty", arising out of a "fiduciary relationship." The law has long recognized that certain relationships — not a closed or finite list, but certainly including, among others, lawyer-client relationships and doctor-patient ones too — are of such a kind as to give rise to special obligations of conscientious and selfless behaviour. The key to recognizing fiduciary relationships is the extreme vulnerability of one person to another, created by the former's reliance upon and trust in the other's dutiful behaviour. In such a case, over

---

* These torts of "defamation" award damages to persons whose reputation and standing in the community have been harmed by untrue statements, whether written or oral.

** This tort consists in the doing of any wilful act calculated to cause physical harm or psychological trauma to another person, which in fact does cause such harm.

and above any legal duty of care and skill suggested by the ordinary law of negligence, fiduciary duties arise — obligations of good faith and scrupulous honesty and openness; and obligations too of undivided loyalty and commitment, unqualified by any element of clandestine self-interest or any competing loyalty to any other person or entity.

In recent years, the Supreme Court has repeatedly revisited the law of fiduciaries,[6] and has made clear what until recently was in doubt: that monetary damages are available as a remedy for harm done by a faithless fiduciary, including, where appropriate, punitive damages.[7] Though examples are happily rare, one can imagine a variety of forms of inappropriate conduct by a physician which might in this way generate a remedy for "breach of fiduciary duty." Inappropriate use of undue influence to secure legacies from a patient would clearly come under this rubric, as would those cases where a physician has taken sexual advantage of a vulnerable patient. In *Norberg v. Wynrib*,[8] decided by the Supreme Court of Canada in 1992, an elderly physician secured sexual favours from the plaintiff, a young woman, in exchange for inappropriate prescriptions of fiorinal, to which she was addicted. While a majority of the Court based its judgment upon familiar principles of assault and battery, (rejecting the patient's supposed consent as having been induced by the gross inequalities in the power relationship between the parties), two of the judges explicitly preferred to ground their conclusions upon the breach of the defendant doctor's fiduciary duty.

There seems no reason to doubt that other, less lurid forms of misconduct by physicians will in future be open to redress by an action for breach of fiduciary duty. Breaches of professional confidence, including the unprivileged revelation of patient information and professional confidences, certainly seem well within the potential scope of this developing remedy, as do, incidentally, those situations of divided loyalty (between patient and hospital, perhaps) which were adverted to in Chapter 6. This is an area of lively development in the law, which those who legally represent physicians will do well to watch with close attention.

We must mention finally that cause of action sometimes called "breach of statutory duty." It will sometimes happen that a statute, or some regulation made under its auspices, will direct the gathering or recording of information by a given body or institution, and expressly or impliedly forbid the divulgence of any information therein contained, except under carefully specified conditions. Such a statute may, exceptionally, provide expressly for a civil action for damages to lie at the suit of anyone who suffers when such a prohibition is flouted. Where the statute is silent upon that question,* however, difficult questions of law have arisen. But after many years of confused and confusing legal debate, the Supreme Court of Canada finally laid the law to rest in 1983,** dispelling any idea that the breach of a statute automatically amounted to a tort, or gave a civil remedy in damages. Rather, said the Supreme Court, the infringement of a statute is just one of the many items of evidence which in any given case may stiffen the Court's resolve to impose liability in the ordinary tort of negligence.

Neither the tort of negligence, the action for breach of contract, lawsuits for breach of confidence or fiduciary duty, nor any of the other more *recherché* remedies which an unhappy patient may attempt, offer him a perfect or invariably reliable remedy. Each has its drawbacks, especially when it comes to the question of what sorts of harm, if any, can be assuaged in damages in each instance. The remedies offered by some provincial legislation sound promising, but are wholly untried. For this reason, many welcomed the suggestion of one eminent authority, back in 1980, that a new *kind* of remedy should be created by provincial statute, specifically to address the issue of breaches of medical confidentiality. The Krever Commission† urged

> That a statutory right be created permitting a patient whose health information has been disclosed without his or her authorization, to maintain a civil action for the greater of his or her actual damages or $10,000.00 against:
>
> (a) any health care provider or other person under an obligation to keep health information about the patient confidential, who unjustifiably discloses his or her health information to a third person; and
>
> (b) any person who induced anyone under an obligation to keep health information about a patient confidential, unjustifiably to disclose his or her health information.

After long delay, some provinces[9] have now enacted legislation responsive to these suggestions and imposing penalties, indeed, which are significantly more draconian than those suggested. These statutes will be considered later in this chapter, after we have reviewed other developments concerning access to the medical record.

---

* Canadian examples are to be found in Ontario regulations passed under that province's *Mental Hospitals Act*, its *Public Hospitals Act*, and its *Venereal Diseases Prevention Act*.

** In *R. v. Saskatchewan Wheat Pool*, a case about beetle-infested grain, which nonetheless laid down principles of very general application.

† Report of the Commission of Inquiry into the Confidentiality of Health Information (Ontario, 1980). Commissioner, Mr. Justice H. Krever: Vol. I, pp. 15, 530-1.

2. EXCEPTIONS TO THE DUTY OF NON-DISCLOSURE

As noted at the beginning of this chapter, the physician's duty to preserve his patient's medical and personal secrets is a qualified one. Indeed, there are very few cases which deal squarely with the duty of confidentiality itself, or the civil remedies available to give "teeth" to that duty. Far more plentiful are those cases which take the duty for granted, but concentrate on the various exceptions or qualifications imposed upon it by the law. These exceptions may conveniently be allotted to two categories; revelations or disclosures made by a doctor in a court of law, and those made outside a court.

(a) Disclosure Within a Court of Law

The starting point for any discussion of this issue must even today be the ancient dispute known as the *Duchess of Kingston's Case*, decided by the House of Lords in 1776.[10] The Duchess was on trial for bigamy, the allegation being that she had "married" the Duke of Kingston while still married to a certain Mr. Hervey, (later, Earl of Bristol). Mr. Caesar Hawkins, physician to the accused lady, was asked whether as her surgeon he knew whether any marriage had been entered into between Mr. Hervey and his patient. Mr. Hawkins replied with dignity "I do not know how far any thing that has come before me in a confidential trust in my profession should be disclosed, consistent with my professional honour." Lord Mansfield, one of the great figures of judicial history, spoke authoritatively and in words which as a general proposition of law have never since been doubted:

> . . . A surgeon has no privilege where it is a material question, in a civil or criminal cause, to know whether parties were married or whether a child was born, to say that his introduction to the parties was in the course of his profession, and in that way he came to the knowledge of it. I take it for granted that if Mr. Hawkins understands that, it is a satisfaction to him and a clear justification to all the world. *If a surgeon was voluntarily to reveal these secrets, to be sure he would be guilty of a breach of honour, and a great indiscretion; but to give that information in a court of justice, which by the law of the land he is bound to do,* will never be imputed to him as any indiscretion whatever.[11]

Now these words, seeming to view the threat to the patient's privacy as merely a corollary to the paramount concern to preserve the physician's honour, may have a distinctly antique tone to modern ears. But the basic premise, of course, is that the Court's concern to elicit the truth overrides all other interests, whether of doctor or patient, and dispels any contention that the physician should enjoy a legally recognized "privilege" to take refuge in silence. Mr. Hawkins was obliged to speak, and did so, with devastating effect. His professional successors ever since, and both in England and Canada, have been similarly obliged. Refusal to testify, or to answer a question deemed permissible by the judge, would be deemed a contempt of court, and bring down criminal penalties upon the physician who refused.

A survey of Ontario physicians[12] conducted in 1971 showed apparently widespread (40 per cent) unawareness of this stern rule. And whether aware or not, 75 per cent of those who responded indicated that if pressed to give evidence which would divulge confidential information about a patient, they would refuse to do so (though most would do so if, and only if, the patient consented.) This suggests a commendably stoic resolution on the part of the medical profession to adhere to its ethical precepts even when the lawyers, and the courts, adjudge those precepts to be of less importance than the integrity of the courtroom process. Plainly, there is the potential here for conflict between the legal and medical professions. Yet in practice, such antagonism has been minimized by the respect accorded to medical sensibilities by the judges.

Both in England and in Canada there have been cases in which the judges have exercised a discretion to absolve doctors from answering questions which might elicit confidential information. As a matter of general principle, a judge may always refuse to allow a question to be put which is irrelevant, and is by accident or design calculated to prejudice a party or a witness. The question — and it is a difficult one — is whether the judge's discretion is more extensive than that. Can the judge grant the privilege of silence to a physician who demurs for ethical reasons to reveal a patient's medical secrets, even though the question at which the physician bridles has some potential relevance? As a matter of judicial courtesy, some judges will defer to the sensibilities of a physician witness and invite counsel not to press such embarrassing enquiries. Some counsel, as a matter of courtesy or prudence, will comply. But does a Canadian judge have in the last analysis this right to forbid such questions, and so grant a privilege of silence to physicians where the matters under scrutiny are potentially relevant?

"Probably not", is the answer. Yet, there are instances in recent times when judges have shown great reluctance to apply the *Duchess of Kingston's Case* and its "no privilege" rules to conscientious medical witnesses. The leading cases in this category are all, it seems, from Ontario. One example will suffice. In *Dembie v. Dembie* (1963),[13] a case involving a matrimonial dispute, the husband's counsel called the wife's psychiatrist as a witness. In language not unlike that of Mr. Hawkins, 187 years before, the psychiatrist declined to testify unless the judge insisted. Mr. Justice Stewart, despite the courteous remonstrations of counsel for the husband, did not insist, but said instead:

> ... I think it is inimical to a fair trial to force a psychiatrist to disclose the things he has heard from a patient, and, in addition to that, I think it rather shocking that one profession should attempt to dictate the ethics of another, which the courts are doing when they see fit to state what a doctor will say and what he will not. They are forcing a breach of oath, and the legal concept that the doctor is not breaching it, that he shall not disclose anything a patient shall tell him unless mete to do so, the idea that it is mete when he gets in the witness box is nonsense, and I have no intention of forcing Doctor [K] to repeat what his patient told him.[14]

Despite cases of this kind, it seems clear that if the stark ruling in the *Duchess of Kingston's Case* has been eroded at all, such erosion has been only vestigial, and any extension of the process — any attempt, in other words, to create any general privilege of non-testimony for the physician in a court of law — will meet with stiff judicial resistance. As we have seen, any such privilege seems to have only the most tenuous and precarious foothold in Canadian law,* and seems also to be confined to cases of psychiatric evidence, as distinct from evidence dealing with general medical matters.

Indeed some have argued that there may be good reasons for allowing the privilege of silence to psychiatrists, at least on a discretionary basis, while still denying it to other physicians; so fundamental is the attainment of total openness, confidence and candour to any purposeful interaction between psychiatrist and patient. It may be thought, however, that in the last analysis the psychiatrist's situation differs only in degree from that of his professional brethren; and that the best solution for Canadian legislatures would be to create by force of statute a judicial discretion to confer a privilege of silence wherever the public interest in the preservation of medical confidentiality seems to outweigh any public interest in unrestrained courtroom disclosure. That is the course which has been recommended both in England and in Canada by various law reform agencies;**

---

* Except in Quebec, where the *Medical Act*, R.S.Q. 1977, c. M-9, s. 42 makes doctors non-compellable.

** For example, the Law Reform Commission of Canada Report on Evidence (1975); and the reports of the English Law Reform Committee on Privilege in Civil Proceedings (1976) and of the Federal/Provincial Task Force on Uniform Rules of Evidence (1982).

a course less absolute than that adopted in Quebec, where the physician's right to silence is unqualified,* and not in the discretion of the judge; and far less absolute than in France, where the physician has a positive obligation of secrecy, so sternly maintained that not even the consent of the patient, it seems, can release him from its bonds.

The foregoing analysis of the physician's position within a court of law may be seen as somewhat daunting. There is, however, one matter which requires further and more specific mention — the topic of peer review procedures which, in varying forms and guises, have become a universal and important mechanism for quality assurance in modern Canadian health care administration. There has been some debate as to whether the participants in such procedures maybe compelled to testify as to matters learned by them in that context; and whether indeed documents and records arising out of such proceedings may be the object of subpoena. While there are still some who would argue for the right of the patient (and indeed of the public at large) to compel production of such information, the dominant view — and surely the more correct and more politic one — is that the absolute frankness and thoroughness, necessary to make peer review a useful exercise, can only be achieved while the secrecy of such procedures is secure. While the position in most Canadian provinces remains obscure upon this issue, two provinces, Manitoba and Alberta, have by their respective legislation[15] gone some way towards achieving this goal. Both provide that no participant in any hospital committee concerned with the advancement of medical education or the improvement of hospital care and practice shall be compelled to answer any question pertaining to its deliberations; nor shall he be compelled to produce any documents relating to its deliberations or findings. In this context at least, then, a physician may (unless of course he wishes to testify) take refuge in that privilege of silence which, as we have seen, is ordinarily denied to him in the courtroom.

(b) Disclosure Outside a Court of Law

(i) *Statutory Duties of Disclosure*

The general rule of ethics and law which forbids revelation of a patient's confidences and medical secrets is one scrupulously observed by most physicians. But there are certain situations where provincial statutes, passed in deference to compelling reasons of public safety or at least public policy, authoritatively qualify the physician's duty of silence and direct

---

* *Supra*, two notes previously.

him to reveal specified types of information to some public official or registry.

Among the earliest such statutes were Venereal Disease Prevention Acts, typically requiring a physician who diagnoses one of the specified infections to report his finding to the appropriate provincial health authority. In each province there will nowadays be found a multiplicity of like statutes, requiring notification of various medical conditions, usually, though not invariably, contagious ones; and it would be impossible in this book to list them all. If one may judge from the paucity of recorded prosecutions brought against doctors for allegedly flouting these enactments, the medical profession in each province seems well-informed as to its responsibilities under these various statutes, which ordinarily make it a punishable offence to fail to make the required report.

It is worthy of note that whether or not the particular statute actually says so, physicians will not be convicted under legislation of this kind unless the offence was intentional. This was established in the case of *R. v. Gordon* (Ontario, 1923).[16] Dr. Gordon was prosecuted for failing to report to the local health authority that his patient, a young boy, had diphtheria; such a report being required by the Public Health Act of Ontario. The local medical officer of health, who visited the patient the following day, had no difficulty making the correct diagnosis. Yet Dr. Gordon was acquitted. The judge held that an honest but erroneous diagnosis could not form the basis for a successful prosecution. This would be so, almost certainly, even if the misdiagnosis was negligent. What is required for a conviction is a knowing and wilful failure to comply with the statute.

Not all statutes of this kind are designed to curb the spread of disease. Some are directed against other social ills, and there is a growing number of statutes across Canada which require physicians to report to child protection agencies any suspected cases of child abuse. Some provinces, too, require physicians to report to the provincial Registrar of Motor Vehicles the name, address and clinical condition of any patient of driving age whose condition may make it dangerous for him to operate a motor vehicle. Obviously, information so garnered remains confidential and is not for public viewing. The disclosure is only "privileged" as between the physician in question and those whose job it is to carry out the purpose of the statute.

It is interesting to speculate upon the potential civil liability, in the tort of negligence, of a physician who fails to report to the appropriate quarter such information as may be required by one of these statutes. Suppose, for example, that a patient prone to frequent black-outs, or to epileptic seizures, is overcome by such a condition while driving, and severely injures a pedestrian. While there is as yet no case-law directly on point, the expanding scope of modern Canadian negligence law makes it quite conceivable that the stricken driver's physician might, even without regard to the statute, be held to have broken a duty of care owed to the pedestrian or other road-user who was injured. The breach of the statute, in those provinces where the reporting of unfit drivers is mandated, would certainly fortify the Court's resolve to make the physician liable in such a case. However, it is probable that if the physician involved in such litigation could show that he warned his patient not to drive, and that he had no reason to believe that the patient would disregard that advice, the physician would escape negligence liability on grounds of "remoteness of damage."*

(ii) *Where Countervailing Public Interest Dictates Disclosure*

The physician who learns that a patient has committed or is about to commit a serious criminal offence is confronted with a genuine ethical dilemma. Should he go to the police with such information, learned within the doctor-patient relationship? The answer favoured by the legal text-books nowadays is to urge doctors — as a matter of good conscience and public-spiritedness, and not of any legal duty   to put the public interest ahead of any professional scruples about confidentiality, and report the information with dispatch. There is in fact no legal duty** to assist the police at all, though it is an offence actively to obstruct their investigations. It is generally agreed, however, that a public-spirited doctor would not be liable to his patient if he volunteered information to the police about the latter's actual or intended crimes. If a physician in such a situation has anything to fear, it is not the censure of the courts, but the ethics and discipline committee of his own professional organization, which may quite properly consider it debateable whether the ethical duty of confidentiality should always, at least in such a forum, be deemed automatically subservient to considerations of "the greater public good." This troubling question has yet to be addressed in Canada.

Disturbing data emerged in Ontario in 1978, disclosing the apparent ease with which the R.C.M.P. had been garnering medical information about patients from physicians or other hospital personnel in that province. Some 368 instances of such behaviour were brought to the attention of the Krever Commission,[17] and sternly criticized not only by the Commissioner, but by the judges too, in a case arising out of the Commission's work.[18] No doubt the giving out of medical information on most if not all of these

---

* See Chapter 6, 3(b) "Remoteness of Damage: the Issue of Proximate Cause."
** With one rather esoteric exception. The Canadian *Criminal Code* (s. 50) makes it a crime not to forward to the authorities information concerning anticipated acts of treason.

occasions was done in the (erroneous) belief, on the part of the health-care professional concerned, that there was a legal duty positively to assist the police in this way. The litigation attending the Krever Commission inquiry did contain one crumb of comfort for physicians who committed such indiscretions; the police, it was held, could not be compelled to divulge the names of their informants, who were clothed in "police-informer privilege." But if ever their identity did come to light, no immunity would attach to them in the context of professional disciplinary proceedings, nor in any civil suit brought by the patient whose right to confidentiality had been violated in this way.

There is one situation, however, which requires special mention because by the express provision of the *Criminal Code* of Canada, a duty to assist the police is created. Sections 254-8 inclusive of this federal statute deal among other things with the taking of blood samples in cases where an accused person is suspected of operating a motor-vehicle, aircraft or vessel while under the influence of alcohol. A police officer may require such a suspect to submit to a testing of his breath or his blood. Where a blood sample is required, its abstraction must be done by or under the direction of a qualified medical practitioner, and it is an offence for a suspect to refuse to submit to such testing. In the event that the suspect does not consent, however, the physician should *not* proceed unless and until a warrant has been obtained from a justice to proceed with such testing. Such a warrant will only be issued when the justice has reason to believe that a physician (not necessarily the one who is asked to take the blood sample) has verified that the condition of the suspect will not be endangered by the taking of the blood. And it will only be issued when the justice is satisfied that a physician has determined that the suspect is so physically or mentally incapacitated (by intoxication, injury or otherwise) from himself giving or refusing consent. The physician, however public-spirited, who proceeds to abstract blood samples, or even to furnish to the police, without a warrant, blood-specimens taken for sound medical reasons, over the objections of an alert and non-consenting person, will expose himself to civil liability in battery (see Chapter 2), negligence (Chapters 5-8) and perhaps other torts as well.

The physician who conducts blood tests with the consent of the suspect is protected from civil liability, it seems, even though that consent might under ordinary circumstances be of questionable value, given the suspect's impaired or otherwise clouded mental acuity. A similar protection avails the physician who acts upon one of the warrants, discussed above. These protections are enshrined in s. 257 of the *Criminal Code*, which in view of its importance is here reproduced in full:

257. (1) *No qualified medical practitioner or qualified technician is guilty of an offence only by reason of his refusal* to take a sample of blood from a person for the purposes of section 254 or 256 and no qualified medical practitioner is guilty of an offence only by reason of his refusal to cause to be taken by a qualified technician under his direction a sample of blood from a person for such purposes.

(2) *No qualified medical practitioner* by whom or under whose direction a sample of blood is taken from a person pursuant to a demand made under subsection 254(3) or a warrant issued under section 256 and no qualified technician acting under the direction of a qualified medical practitioner *incurs any criminal or civil liability for anything necessarily done with reasonable care and skill* in the taking of such a sample of blood. [Emphasis supplied]

We have spent some time in considering the extent of the physician's latitude or privilege in assisting the police, because it is a familiar dilemma confronting physicians, and one which as can be seen does not admit of simple answers. Another ethical and legal puzzle, of particular importance at the moment, is the question of whether a physician who diagnoses a condition in his patient which may imperil a third party, is at liberty to warn that third party and so forestall any harm. Suppose, for example, that a patient is diagnosed as having syphilis, or AIDS. The physician will be under a statutory obligation, as we have seen, to report his findings to the appropriate authority. Once done, this may be sufficient to discharge the physician's obligations. But not necessarily. While most people, informed that they are afflicted with communicable disease, will take all appropriate measures and advice to protect those close to them, a physician may encounter a patient whose bitterness or amorality suggests a real danger that the infection will be passed on to some identifiable third person. In such a case, the physician who warned the prospective victim would probably not be exposed to civil liability at the suit of his patient, for giving such timely warning.

Authority on the question is scarce. One distinguished Canadian authority has offered this prudential conclusion:

The best advice for the Canadian doctor is to avoid divulging information about the patient's venereal disease to those who might be infected unless there is no other way to protect them.[19]

As basic advice, in the absence of clear guidance in the case law, this is probably the best that can be offered. But it will be noted that the final words — "unless there is no other way to protect them" — leave open the question postulated above, as to what to do with the determined or indifferent carrier of a contagion. It is entirely possible, indeed, that a doctor who failed to warn an identifiable prospective third-party victim, in such an extreme and time-sensitive situation, might be liable in an action for negligence by that third party, for any damage sustained by him! This has actually occurred in the United States.

In *Tarasoff v. Regents of University of California* (California, 1976),[20] the facts disclosed that a young man had been referred to psychotherapists employed by the university hospital, and attended there as a voluntary outpatient. He informed his therapist that he was going to kill a young woman — not named by him, but readily identifiable — as soon as she returned from her vacation. The therapist initially took measures to secure the committal of this alarming patient to a mental hospital, but his efforts were frustrated by the actions of other psychiatrists, who had taken the view that the patient was not in need of confinement. No one attempted to warn the girl or her parents. No sooner had she returned from her vacation, than the patient went to her home and killed her. The California Supreme Court noted that there was abundant American case-law in which physicians had been held liable for failing to warn members of a patient's family of his contagious condition, and noted that the patient's mental condition in this case had presented a danger quite as real as any infectious disease, to his identifiable prospective victim. A majority opinion of the Court observed:

> We conclude that a doctor or a psychotherapist treating a mentally ill patient, just as a doctor treating physical illness, bears a duty to use reasonable care to give threatened persons such warnings as are essential to avert foreseeable danger arising from his patient's condition or treatment.[21]

It was urged upon the Court that the professional divulgence of threats by such a patient as this would discourage other such persons from seeking therapy, or giving expression freely to their hostile feelings — in itself, an important part of the therapeutic process. But the Court remained persuaded that in such circumstances as had here arisen, the first and dominant duty of the defendant psychotherapists was to warn the prospective victim. Their failure to do so exposed them to liability in damages. It is not fanciful to suppose that where (as in *Tarasoff*) the substantial and imminent danger presented by a patient to an identifiable person is known to a physician, Canadian courts too might impose a duty to warn that prospective victim, a duty outweighing and displacing the physician's ordinary obligation to preserve the patient's confidences.

Mention should be made at this juncture of a difficult English case, *X v. Y*, (1988).[22] Employees of a health authority supplied to a newspaper reporter, for a cash reward, information obtained from hospital records, which identified two general practitioners who were carrying on their practices despite having contracted AIDS. The newspaper, having carried a story exposing the suppression of this "scandalous" situation by the health authorities, now proposed to identify the two physicians, and the hospital which was treating them, in a follow-up article. The plaintiff health authority successfully applied for an injunction to prevent its publication, as being an unlawful disclosure of confidential information. The judge stressed the peculiar need for confidentiality in AIDS cases,* since absolute secrecy is essential if infected persons and those at risk are to present themselves for diagnosis, and such diagnosis is obviously the essential prerequisite for counselling, still society's most powerful weapon in seeking to control the spread of the disease. At the same time, the curiosity of the media for information about (and from) the sufferers of this disease has led to distressing acts of intrusiveness on the part of the press, at least in Britain. The judge granted an injunction to restrain the proposed newspaper article, stressing not only the crucial need to preserve the confidence of patients, but also the need to uphold and enforce the loyalty of those personnel, from senior surgical staff to laboratory technicians and porters, who necessarily or inevitably gain access to the medical secrets of patients. On the facts, no countervailing argument of public policy or public interest could be allowed to override the interests, both public and private, which dictated absolute confidentiality.

(iii)   *Where the Patient Expressly or Impliedly Consents*

Sometimes, a patient will request his physician to disclose confidential information to someone else — an insurer, perhaps, or another doctor, or a current or prospective employer. The physician who complies with this request does not break any duty to his patient, of course, though in case of misunderstandings it would be prudent for the physician to get the request or consent in writing, before releasing the information. No doubt, too, the patient may qualify the consent given to such release, requiring the physician not to release intimate or embarrassing items of no legitimate concern to the intended recipient. This, however, may create for the physician a dilemma seemingly not yet resolved by the courts. A partial and selective account of the patient's condition may be quite as misleading as an outright falsification; and the physician may well recoil at the prospect of involvement in what may seem to him to be a deception. It is said upon some

---

* AIDS was still not a reportable disease in the United Kingdom.

authority* that a physician cannot refuse to divulge information when the patient so requests, however obnoxious such disclosure may be to the physician's sense of what is proper. The right of secrecy is, after all, the patient's right, and may be waived by him if he chooses to make his condition known. It is quite another matter, however, to say that a patient may, by a selective and qualified consent, involve his physician in a process of duplicity; and it can confidently be surmised that no court would compel a physician to disclose distorted versions of the medical facts, however insistent the patient.

It does seem, however, that other and purely professional scruples, which make a physician reluctant to reveal to a patient diagnostic information which might be therapeutically counter-productive, will not be allowed to prevail over the physician's duty to comply with the patient's request for disclosure. The matter, however, cannot be regarded as free from doubt, since in recent years the Supreme Court of Canada, while greatly enlarging the physician's duty to inform the patient of the nature and risks of treatment** has been careful to preserve to physicians a discretion to withhold such information where professional judgment suggests that its revelation would do more harm than good. Quite probably, then, a physician who for sound medical reasons, as distinct from merely ethical persuasions or considerations of personal kindness, declines a patient's request to make full disclosure to a third party, will not be compelled to do so.

There are situations in which a physician, without expressly being told so by the patient, can properly infer that the latter consents to revelations of confidential information. An obvious example of such "implied consent" is the privilege rightly assumed by physicians to seek second opinions or specialist advice from professional colleagues, concerning the patients in their care: or that of the physician to write out prescriptions which may unavoidably disclose to the pharmacist the nature of the patient's ailment. Again, though, it must always be remembered that the right of confidentiality is the patient's, so that even sensible consultations of this kind may be forbidden if the patient expresses such a wish.

The real problems arise when a physician is asked by persons not involved in the care of the patient, for information concerning him. In particular, how much can legitimately and safely be divulged to family-members? Writing in 1954, a distinguished Canadian judge and legal

---

* Even in Quebec, where the physician's statutory privilege of silence has been deemed by the judges to be subject to the patient's right to insist on disclosure.

** See Chapter 4 and especially the case of *Reibl v. Hughes.*

scholar, later Chief Justice of Manitoba,** answered this question in language compounded of commonsense and caution:

> There is the case, too, of responding to inquiries made by near relatives. A man has an operation. His anxious wife asks the doctor about the case. Is the doctor bound to get his patient's express consent before he answers an inquiry of that sort? To ask the question is to answer it. If in the ordinary case doctors insisted on observing such extreme precautions their public relations would suffer badly. No doctor could carry on his practice successfully if he could not answer normal inquiries of that sort without securing express permission from his patient in each case. *Unless, therefore, the circumstances are unusual and of such a character as to put the doctor on his guard, I* suggest that there is an implied consent for the doctor ordinarily to answer proper inquiries made by near relatives. [Emphasis supplied].

Subject always to the obvious qualification that the patient may expressly forbid the imparting of information to any particular member of his family, this quotation still seems accurately to reflect both the state of the law and those principles of good sense by which most physicians guide themselves in these matters.* To divulge medical confidences beyond the ambit of the immediate family, however, in circumstances where there is neither express consent nor any positive legal duty to do so, is to invite liability, as cases like *Damien v. O'Mulvenny* and *A.B. v. C.D.*, both discussed earlier in this chapter, make clear.

3. CONFIDENTIALITY AND PATIENT RECORDS

The importance of properly-kept medical records, whether compiled in a hospital or the office of a private practitioner, has already been stressed more than once in this book. It cannot be emphasized too strongly. One noted authority[23] has described such records as "the foundation of good hospital, medical and nursing care." In any medical litigation context, the state of the record is the most potent objective evidence of the quality of

---

** Hon. Samuel Freedman, "Medical Privilege", (1954) 32 Canadian Bar Review 1, at 19.

* A situation of some difficulty arises when the patient is the child of a broken marriage, and where a parent without custody rights seeks information as to the child's welfare. Where a divorce has been granted or divorce proceedings are pending, a non-custodial parent with access rights has a right to be given such information under the *Divorce Act* of Canada, s. 16(5); and there is a growing trend for provincial legislation to make similar provision for information to be imparted where the parent seeking it is merely separated from the custodial spouse, always provided that he or she has access rights [as in the *Family Maintenance Act* of Manitoba, and the *Children's Law Reform Act*, of Ontario.] It seems clear, then, that the physician may by virtue of these statutes feel free to provide medical information to such a parent, provided only that the latter can prove that he or she has been granted access rights.

care the patient has received. A record disfigured by voids, contradictions or equivocations invites a Court to fill those *lacunae,* and resolve those doubts, with inferences adverse to those medical professionals who were responsible for that record. Worse, a sloppily maintained record obviously conduces to substandard treatment, and subverts the process of informed and purposeful communication between all those physicians and other health-care professionals who may become involved in the patient's treatment. For these and other reasons, going both to the standard of patient care and the credibility of the physician in a court of law, full, accurate and honest maintenance of patient records is a task of the very first importance.

The record itself, whether it be a hospital or an office record, does not of course belong to the patient. As a document, it belongs to the institution or the physician, as the case may be. But insofar as it records confidential medical matters, or other secrets vouchsafed within the context of the doctor/patient relationship, the patient obviously has legitimate and serious concerns in preserving its confidentiality, so far as the law will allow. Generally speaking, and as one would expect, the legal rules governing this question closely parallel those considered earlier in this chapter, placing qualified restraints upon those physicians who would speak from their own knowledge, unassisted by documentary reminders, about confidential matters concerning their patients.

The fact that the hospital or physician owns the record — the actual physical document — is not, then, a particularly important legal conclusion. It begs more questions than it answers, and the questions were until recently attended with a good deal of difficulty.

To pose the obvious question first — does the patient have a right to see his own record or his own file? In former times, the answer was that ordinarily, no such right existed. True, the owner of the file was at liberty to grant a patient access to his or her record, but equally clearly, that owner was at liberty to refuse access, with or without giving reasons. Some provinces[24] passed legislation providing that hospitals might disclose a patient's records to him, but this type of statutory authorization always seemed rather superfluous, merely declaratory of a power which the hospital enjoyed anyway, as owner of the document. Only in these provinces — Alberta, Quebec and Nova Scotia — was mandatory disclosure of the record provided for: and even in those provinces, a patient confronted with a reluctant or stubborn record-owner would have to seek a court order, requesting a judge to order disclosure of the contents of the file.

There was in fact only one situation in which a patient might insist upon access to his record, without being subject to the sufferance of the document-owner or the discretion of a court. That was when the patient had actually begun a lawsuit by filing a Statement of Claim. Once that was done, rules of legal procedure in every province would make available to him the process known as "discovery of documents", and at that juncture production of the hospital record, or the physician's file, might be demanded by the patient as of right, since such documents would obviously be germane to the impending litigation. Otherwise, except of course where statutes dictated otherwise, the courts were adamant in their insistence that no patient had an enforceable right to see his other medical record.[25] When reasons were given for this inflexible stance, they tended to dwell upon the supposed incapacity of patients to understand the complexities of medical science and notation, and upon the danger that patients might be confused or needlessly alarmed by what they did not comprehend. Worse still, it was argued, patients might be encouraged, by what they saw, to bring groundless, costly and futile lawsuits against health-care providers.

This rule of non-disclosure, and the reasoning which supported it, were not without their critics. The Report of the Krever Commission* of 1980 concluded after careful deliberation that access by a patient to his hospital record should be the general rule.[26] In Ontario, that recommendation produced a swift and constructive response: but elsewhere in Canada, the position remained virtually stagnant.

Then along came a single case which entirely altered the picture. The case was *McInerney v. MacDonald* (New Brunswick, 1992)[27] and it ultimately yielded a unanimous judgment in the Supreme Court of Canada which in clear and emphatic terms both asserted and defined the patient's right of access to his or her medical record.

Mrs. MacDonald, the plaintiff, had been treated by various physicians over the years, most of whom prescribed thyroid pills. But when she eventually consulted Dr. McInerney, she was advised to desist from those pills. She did so, and as she followed Dr. McInerney's medical advice, and felt her health improve, became increasingly curious and concerned about the competency of the medical advice and treatment she had received in the past. Accordingly, she asked Dr. McInerney if she might glance through her file, which of course was composed of the notes of a succession of her previous medical advisers. Politely, scrupulously but firmly, Dr. McInerney replied that she would reveal everything on the file which had been entered by herself, but was not ethically at liberty to disclose entries made by her predecessors, unless of course their permission could be obtained. Mrs. Macdonald sought a court order compelling production and disclosure of the whole file. The New Brunswick courts showed surprising boldness in

---

* Report of the Commission of Inquiry into the Confidentiality of Health Information, Ontario 1980. Not, of course, to be confused with that other great Commission of Inquiry which recently investigated the safety of Canada's blood supply.

granting that order, and this progressive stance was endorsed by the Supreme Court of Canada. Mr. Justice LaForest, speaking for the Court, stressed the "fiduciary" nature of the doctor-patient relationship,[28] involving mutual obligations of openness and candour. Because of this, it should be held that while the file might belong to the doctor (or clinic, or hospital), the information it contained should be regarded as being held in a sort of trust for the patient. For this reason, a patient should ordinarily be treated as having a legal right of reasonable access to "his" health care records, even though they would remain technically the property of the physician or institution. True, it was said, the doctor's obligation to disclose the record was not absolute. Where, on sound medical grounds, the physician believes it is not in the patient's best interests to inspect his or her medical records, or believes the production might put some other party at risk, they may be withheld. Under such circumstances, the patient may be compelled to seek a court order for their production, but, as the Court stressed, the burden will in future lie upon the reluctant physician to justify his refusal.

Mrs. MacDonald's successful action in this way not only secured her access to her own complete file, but clarified and enhanced the rights of every Canadian patient to all health-care records compiled under his or her name. The whole battery of reasons which had supported the stubborn old rule of secretiveness, was clinically dissected, exposed as specious or impolitic, and replaced with a new philosophy of openness and candour, better suited to cultivate mutual trust between patients and their health care providers. Now that a mere request to one's physician would ordinarily be enough to secure access, the amount of futile litigation would surely decrease, said the Supreme Court: for the old system, by forcing patients to file Statements of Claim before they could insist upon seeing the record, had surely produced much futile litigation, the hopelessness of which had often become evident when, but only when, the file was ultimately produced.

McInerney has no doubt demanded, and demands still, a measure of adjustment by physicians and hospitals alike. Physicians will no doubt wish to redouble that anxious care with which they make notations, and sedulously avoid expressions which might give needless offence or concern. They will also need clear policies as to the conditions under which access will be granted, and the measure of supervision, interpretative assistance and professional explanation which should be provided to patients as they try to peruse their records. Hospitals, too, will need to evolve protocols for dealing with patients' requests and demands to see their records, and to photocopy them — another privilege recognized by the Supreme Court in *McInerney*. Overall, however, we may confidently suppose that the health care professions will accept the new order as being salutary and non-threatening, just as they have accepted, generally with equanimity, those other judicial assertions of patient autonomy which have so changed the face of medical jurisprudence in recent decades.

In the three prairie provinces, as we cryptically noted earlier (*supra*, at p. 218), such adjustments are firmly enjoined by statute law, in the shape of new Personal Health Information legislation.[29] While these statutes vary considerably in their terminology, the essential aims of all three are the same. Each is concerned with protecting all health-related information concerning individual patients. To that end, they define broadly what personal health information encompasses, identify the agencies, facilities and persons (such as physicians and hospitals) who compile and keep that information, and designate such persons variously as "trustees" or "custodians" of such information. Having done that, the statutes are in large measure "declaratory" of the common law, in that they essentially repeat and reinforce, with the full weight of statute, what cases like *McInerney v. MacDonald*, which we have already considered, lay down about patients' rights to access their own health records. Further, the statutes minutely regulate the manner in which health care information may be collected, and the purposes for which such collection may and may not be carried out. They then reinforce the patient's right to insist upon the secrecy of such data, laying out with great specificity the narrow circumstances under which such information may be disclosed, and specifying too the mode and circumstances under which it may be destroyed. Nothing in the statutes erases or diminishes the rights of the patient as previously identified by the general law, as discussed earlier. But the patients' rights are given new "teeth", in two ways. The statutes direct an official, variously referred to as an "ombudsman" (Manitoba) or "commissioner", to oversee the operation of the Acts, receive and investigate complaints, and refer matters for prosecution where appropriate; and they provide for severe penalties for those who violate their statutory obligations: fines of up to $50,000 for each day that an offence continues, plus (in Manitoba) a possible period of up to 2 years in prison. In all these ways, the three "prairie" health information statutes unequivocally lend weight to the stance long adopted by the common law, and emphatically insist on the strict obligation of health-care providers — and those whom they employ or engage as information managers — to preserve zealously the secrecy of these highly sensitive data. Every health care professional is strenuously advised to study and reflect upon the legislation in force in his or her particular jurisdiction.

It may well be asked, at this juncture, why so much fuss is being made about these documents which collectively make up the medical record. The answer lies in the legal rules governing the admissibility of evidence, and prescribing the weight to be accorded to items of evidence, once admitted.

In former times, courts were extremely reluctant to allow any medical records to be brought before them by either side in a case. Such documents were thought, not without reason, to infringe two fundamental principles of the law of evidence, the "Hearsay Rule" and the "Best Evidence Rule", both of which, in essence, denied the admissibility of "second-hand" evidence to prove factual contentions, when the first-hand evidence of the people involved might be made available, tendered under oath and verifiable by cross-examination. For better or worse, statutes in most provinces have expressly made the hospital and office records of patients admissible as evidence for either side in a lawsuit, provided always that those records were made more or less contemporaneously with the events they recorded, and made in the "usual and ordinary course of business." Even in those few provinces which lack a statute to this effect, the case law has tended uniformly to favour the admission of such records.

The important 1970 decision of the Supreme Court of Canada in *Ares v. Venner*[30] made it clear that hospital records — including such nurses' notes as were in issue in that case — are admissible in evidence so long as they were made contemporaneously by someone having a duty to make them. Further, the Supreme Court said that such a record might not just be admissible, but received as prima facie proof of the facts stated in it. Thus anyone wishing to challenge such factual assertions would have to call as a witness, and then cross-examine, the person who made the entry in question. In other words, a physician who has made an entry upon the record, an entry to which he does not now subscribe, will bear the burden of persuading the Court that the record is *not* an accurate reflection of what really happened. Worse, if an annotation potentially embarrassing to a physician is made upon the record by another physician or a nurse, such data may prove very difficult to displace in the courtroom. The moral is that the physician should carefully check the record for perceived inaccuracies, bearing in mind that under *Ares* v. *Venner,* statements of subjective opinion expressed therein are seemingly just as admissible as are notations of facts and events. There is lively debate among legal scholars as to the propriety and wisdom of this latter innovation in *Ares*. But the authority of *Ares* remains unshaken on this point. In these circumstances the prudent physician, appreciating its implications, will discuss with the person who made them any entries in the record, whether recording facts or expressing opinions, with which he disagrees: and will try without any effort at concealment openly to record upon the record the emergence of such disagreement and the fact of the resultant discussion, together with an outline of the conflicting positions in issue.

NOTES

1. (1981), 34 O.R. (2d) 448, 19 C.C.L.T. 48, 128 D.L.R. (3d) 258 (H.C.).
2. See also the 1975 Quebec Charter of Human Rights & Freedoms, s. 5 and Art. 1053 of the Quebec *Civil Code*.
3. A particularly broad-ranging and diversely-based claim is to be found in the Saskatchewan case of *Peters-Brown v. Regina District Health Board* (1996), 31 C.C.L.T. (2d) 302, [1997] 1 W.W.R. 638 (Sask. C.A.)
4. (1951), Session Cases (D. 14) 177 (Scotland, Court of Sess.).
5. [1958] N.Z.L.R. 396 (C.A.).
6. Notably in *International Corona Resources Ltd. v. Lac Minerals Ltd.*, [1989] 2 S.C.R. 574; *Canson Enterprises Ltd. v. Broughton & Co.*, [1991] 3 S.C.R. 534; *M. (K.) v. M. (H.)* [1992] 3 S.C.R. 6; *Norberg v. Wynrib*, [1992] 2 S.C.R. 226, additional reasons at [1992] 2 S.C.R. 318; and *Hodgkinson v. Simms*, (1994), 22 C.C.L.T. (2d) 1 (S.C.C.).
7. *Norberg v. Wynrib*, [1992] 2 S.C.R. 226, additional reasons at [1992] 2 S.C.R. 318.
8. *Ibid.*
9. *Personal Health Information Act*, S.M. 1997, c. 51; *Health Information Protection Act*, S.S. 1999, c. H-0.021 — (passed but not yet proclaimed in effect.) *Health Information Act*, S.A. 1996 c. H-4.8, now R.S.A. 2000, c. H-5. The purpose and effect of these statutes is considered in section 3 of this chapter.
10. (1776), 20 State Tr. 355 (H.L. (E.)).
11. *Ibid.*
12. 1971 Osgoode Hall Medical Legal Questionnaire.
13. (1963), 21 R.F.L. 46 (Ont. S.C.).
14. *Ibid.*, at p. 50.
15. See *Alberta Evidence Act*, R.S.A. 1980, c. A-21, s. 9; *Manitoba Evidence Act*, R.S.A. 1987, c. E150 (also C.C.S.A., c. E150), s. 9.
16. (1923), 54 O.L.R. 355, 42 C.C.C. 26, [1924] 2 D.L.R. 358 (S.C.).
17. Report of the Commission of Inquiry into the Confidentiality of Health Information (Ontario, 1980). Commissioner, Mr. Justice H. Krever.
18. *Canada (Solicitor General) v. Ontario (Royal Commission of Inquiry into Confidentiality of Health Records)* (1979), (sub nom. *Inquiry into Confidentiality of Health Records in Ontario, Re*) 24 O.R. (2d) 545, 13 C.P.C. 239, 98 D.L.R. (3d) 704, 47 C.C.C. (2d) 465 (C.A.), reversed [1981] 2 S.C.R. 494, 23 C.R. (3d) 338, 23 C.P.C. 99, 128 D.L.R. (3d) 193, 38 N.R. 588, 62 C.C.C. (2d) 193.
19. Picard, *Legal Liability of Doctors and Hospitals in Canada*, 2nd ed. (1984), at p. 21.
20. 551 P.2d 334, 131 Cal. Rptr. 14 (U.S. Cal., 1976).
21. *Ibid.*

22. [1988] 2 All E.R. 648 (Q.B.).
23. Rozovsky, L.E., "The Canadian Patient's Book of Rights" (Doubleday Canada Ltd., 1980), at p. 74.
24. Alberta, Quebec and Nova Scotia. In British Columbia, a slender stream of reported judgments had tended to assume a similar discretionary jurisdiction to grant patient requests for production of records.
25. See, for example, *Andrée v. Misericordia General Hospital* (1979), [1980] 2 W.W.R. 380 (Man. Q.B.).
26. The College of Physicians and Surgeons of Ontario, in a 1981 Report following hard upon the heels of the Krever Commission, urged its members to provide all reasonable medical information which a patient might request, while Regulation 448, s. 27, passed under the *Health Disciplines Act* of Ontario, ordered that it was "unprofessional conduct" for a physician to fail to provide any "report or certificate" requested by a patient, unless some reasonable cause could be advanced for withholding it.
27. (1992), 12 C.C.L.T. (2d) 225 (S.C.C.).
28. As discussed earlier in this chapter.
29. The citations for these important statues are provided in note 9, *supra.*
30. [1970] S.C.R. 608, 73 W.W.R. 347, 12 C.R.N.S. 349, 14 D.L.R. (3d) 4.

12

PUBLIC HEALTH LAW*

SUMMARY

Public health legislation has been enacted in all ten provinces, three territories, and federally. This legislation is directed toward the prevention, treatment, and suppression of communicable diseases such as HIV/AIDS and tuberculosis, and grants remarkably wide powers to ministers of health, medical health officers, and other health authorities by way of subordinate legislation or regulations.

This chapter focuses on the most important duties of medical health officers, the duties to report and to maintain confidentiality. The problem of contact notification is examined, and the possibility of managing contact notification through mediative processes is canvassed. Next, the chapter reviews the powers of medical health officers to examine, enter, detain, isolate, and close places. Finally, both public health law and criminal law penalty provisions are outlined, with examples from case law.

1. INTRODUCTION

The prevalence of Human Immuno-Deficiency Virus ["HIV"] and Acquired Immune Deficiency Syndrome ["AIDS"] in society has led to increased concerns about the health of the public. The number of people who have tested positive for HIV in Canada was 50,259 at December 31, 2001, while 18,026 cases of AIDS were reported in Canada as of December 31, 2001.[1] In 2000, 1,694 cases of new, active, and relapsed tuberculosis

---

*   This chapter written by Jennifer L. Schulz, Adjunct Professor, Faculty of Law, University of Toronto; Assistant Director, LL.M. in ADR Program, Osgoode Hall Law School, York University; Doctoral Candidate, Faculty of Law, University of Toronto. The author wishes to acknowledge two people for their invaluable research assistance. Thanks go to Ms. Gemma Smyth for collecting legislation and for her insights regarding public health law and mediation; and to Ms. Jackie Missaghi for updating legislation and gathering new cases.

["TB"] were reported.[2] These numbers, great as they are, do not represent the total picture however, as they do not include HIV-infected people who have not been tested, and any other unreported cases of communicable disease.

Increasingly, concerned citizens, disease sufferers, and governments are calling for better protection of public health. In Canada, that protection comes in the form of provincial, territorial, and federal public health legislation. Public health acts have been enacted in all jurisdictions, and are directed toward the prevention, treatment, and suppression of communicable diseases. Although most deal with all communicable diseases in a single statute, some provinces — British Columbia, New Brunswick and Newfoundland and Labrador — have also enacted legislation specifically designed to check the spread of venereal diseases ["VD"]. In addition, there is a federal statute that addresses communicable diseases, although its scope does not extend to sexually transmitted diseases.

All Canadian jurisdictions impose the duty to seek medical treatment upon any person who knows or has reason to suspect that s/he is infected with a communicable or sexually transmitted disease. In Alberta,

> Every person who knows or has reason to believe that the person is or may be infected with a communicable disease . . . shall immediately consult a physician to determine whether the person is infected or not, and if the person is found to be infected, shall submit to the treatment directed and comply with any other conditions prescribed by the physician until the physician is satisfied that the person is not infectious.[3]

In British Columbia, "an infected person must conduct himself or herself in a manner that does not expose other persons to the infection, and take and continue adequate treatment",[4] and in Prince Edward Island, the obligation to seek medical treatment applies not only if one knows or has reason to believe that s/he might be infected, but also when s/he suspects that s/he might be a carrier.[5] In the Northwest Territories and in Nunavut, persons must place themselves under the care of a physician, undergo the treatment directed by the physician, and follow whatever course of action is prescribed by the physician or by the Medical Health Officer.[6] Similarly, patients in Saskatchewan, New Brunswick, and Newfoundland and Labrador must also report their diseases and submit to treatment immediately.[7]

2.   DUTIES OF MEDICAL HEALTH OFFICERS

Public health legislation grants medical health officers, who are duly qualified medical practitioners, both duties and powers. The two primary duties placed upon medical health officers are: (a) the duty to report all known and suspected cases of communicable and venereal disease; and (b) the duty to keep confidential all reports and communications related to such diseases.

(a) The Duty to Report

In all provinces, and in the Yukon, Northwest Territories, and Nunavut, medical health officers must report all known or suspected cases of specified communicable diseases.[8] In addition to medical health officers, nurses and midwifes have duties to report communicable diseases in Alberta.[9] In Saskatchewan, Ontario, Newfoundland and Labrador, and Nova Scotia, teachers and principals have duties to report;[10] hotel-keepers must report in Newfoundland and Labrador;[11] and householders in British Columbia and Nova Scotia must report communicable diseases other than venereal disease.[12] Many of the statutes have a reporting section similar to section 22(1) of Alberta's *Public Health Act*, which provides:

> Where a physician, a health practitioner, a teacher or a person in charge of an institution knows or has reason to believe that a person under the care, custody, supervision or control of the physician, health practitioner, teacher or person in charge of an institution is infected with a communicable disease prescribed in the regulations for the purposes of this subsection, the physician . . . shall notify the medical officer of health. . . .[13]

However, there are differences across the country in what information medical health officers are duty bound to report. In Quebec, Ontario, and New Brunswick, the names of persons infected with venereal disease must not be reported.[14] While in British Columbia, the names of those infected must be provided,[15] and in Saskatchewan names and addresses must be reported.[16] In Newfoundland and Labrador, names and addresses must be reported for TB, but not for VD,[17] and in Nova Scotia, names and addresses of TB and VD sufferers must be reported,[18] but those who have tested HIV-positive pursuant to non-nominal testing will not have their names reported.[19] In Ontario, those who "may be infected with an agent of a communicable disease" must also be reported.[20]

In all provinces and territories, persons who have a communicable disease must submit to treatment. If the infected person refuses to submit to treatment, then more information is often reportable. For example, although names are not normally reported in Quebec, if the patient does not follow treatment, the patient's name will be reported.[21] Similarly, in Ontario, Newfoundland and Labrador, and New Brunswick, names and addresses must be reported if the patient refuses treatment.[22]

(b) The Duty of Confidentiality

The duty imposed upon medical officers of health to maintain confidentiality is necessary in order to encourage affected persons to attend and submit to treatment, and is taken very seriously. For example, in British Columbia, medical health officers can forfeit their offices if they breach confidentiality,[23] in Nova Scotia, all venereal disease-related proceedings are to take place *in camera*, with no written report,[24] and in Newfoundland and Labrador, if a person reveals that a patient has a venereal disease, the person is subject to a $200 fine, and in default, imprisonment for up to six months.[25]

The duty to maintain confidentiality is described in Ontario in the following manner: "no person shall disclose to any other person the name of or any other information that will or is likely to identify a person in respect of whom an application, order, certificate or report is made in respect of a communicable disease, a reportable disease, a virulent disease."[26] Similar provisions are found in British Columbia and Quebec.[27]

In other provinces, confidentiality requirements are slightly relaxed. For example, in Newfoundland and Labrador, the duty to preserve secrecy is described as follows:

> A person engaged in the administration of this Act shall preserve secrecy with regard to all matters which may come to his or her knowledge in the course of that employment and shall not communicate that matter to another person except in the performance of his or her duties under this Act or when instructed to do so by a medical health officer, or the minister.[28]

Thus, some disclosure is permitted. Similarly, in New Brunswick, information and records with respect to infectious disease are privileged and not admissible in evidence in any court, "except as and to the extent that the Minister directs."[29] In Prince Edward Island, although secrecy is required, "nothing in this section prevents the divulging of information to the extent that the Chief Health Officer directs in the best interest of that person or the public."[30]

Even more disclosure is permitted in other provinces. In Nova Scotia, TB sufferers must provide their name, address and occupation,[31] and the names of HIV-positive people will be reported where "the Health Unit Associate Director, after consultation with the physician of the positive person, is of the opinion that the protection of the public health requires it."[32] In Nova Scotia, a person who requests nominal HIV testing and tests positive must provide: (a) his or her name; (b) the risk factors that may have caused the HIV infection; (c) the date or dates on which and the location or locations where the positive person may have received blood or other tissues; (d) the positive person's history of donations of blood or other tissues; (e) confirmation that partners have been notified; and (f) any other epidemiological information required.[33] Similarly, in Alberta, the medical officer of health may demand information from the patient about the disease, its suspected source(s), and the name(s) and addresses of anyone exposed by the person to the disease.[34]

3. NOTIFICATION

(a) Contact Notification

Contact notification is legislated in certain provinces, and requires infected persons to notify others who have been in contact with them and might therefore be at risk for similar infection. It is a problematic issue because the same public health legislation that requires contact notification also requires medical health officers to maintain confidentiality. This medical-legal issue is further exacerbated by the fact that although disclosure might save the lives of third parties, Canadian medical and nursing codes of ethics stipulate that, unless otherwise required by law (e.g. reporting suspected cases of child abuse), divulging patient information without consent is prohibited. However, the fact that some jurisdictions now require contacts to be notified suggests that despite the importance of confidentiality in matters of public health, there is a compelling case to breach confidentiality when a third party is in imminent danger of contracting a life-threatening disease, such as HIV/AIDS.

As noted above, in Nova Scotia, a person who requests nominal HIV testing and tests positive must provide proof that sexual partners have been notified. Nova Scotia public health legislation requires that the positive person:

(a) notify partners in accordance with partner notification guidelines approved by the Health Unit Director; or

(b) transfer responsibility for partner notification to a physician or public health nurse who will notify partners on behalf of the positive person in accordance with partner notification guidelines approved by the Health Unit Director, in which case the positive person shall make all reasonable efforts to provide the names and other relevant information about every partner of the positive person to the physician or public health nurse.[35]

British Columbia, Alberta, and Saskatchewan also require contact notification.[36] In Saskatchewan, if patients do not inform contacts themselves, physicians or nurses will, without revealing who exposed the contacts to infection, and will also provide counselling.[37] In British Columbia, any contacts notified must also submit to an examination.[38] In Newfoundland and Labrador and Alberta,[39] contacts *may* be notified, and in Newfoundland and Labrador disclosure to household members for the protection of health is permitted.[40] In Quebec, it is prohibited to engage in the process of contact notification.[41]

(b) Managing Contact Notification through Mediation

Contemplating disclosure of one's illness to others can be very traumatic. Patients may conflict with medical health professionals over whether to notify contacts, and how to do so. One way to mange the difficult process of contact notification is through mediation. Mediation is "[t]he intervention in a negotiation or a conflict of an acceptable third party who has limited or no authoritative decision-making power, but who assists the involved parties in voluntarily reaching a mutually acceptable settlement of issues in dispute."[42] Mediators could assist patients and health care professionals negotiating or disputing over how best to notify contacts. Mediation, as a confidential, consensual process, might even be used to facilitate information exchange between patients and contacts, thereby helping to manage the highly stressful process of contact notification.

The process of notifying contacts would be made less difficult if personnel trained in mediative techniques were located in hospitals and clinics. These trained personnel could facilitate early, effective responses to conflict between patients, staff, and partners, and help with contact notification. If a mediation session between a medical officer of health, the infected person, and his or her contacts was arranged, the process of disclosure could be mediated in a controlled, safe environment.[43] Plans of action could be agreed to, testing could be scheduled, counselling could be arranged, and follow-up could be outlined. Especially for patients and/or contacts who were not comfortable dealing with governmental or formal health channels, a mediative intervention might prove effective. Eventually it might be possible to implement voluntary, systemic mediation programs that could also assist with the risks and ethical dilemmas attendant upon contact notification.[44]

At minimum, any mediative initiative in the contact notification context must provide counselling referrals,[45] guarantee confidentiality, and involve care providers in a consensus-based, patient-focussed process. Once those goals were accomplished, the benefits of mediative approaches for managing contact notification would be numerous. Because mediation is participant-determined, mediative interventions could be creative, collaborative resolutions to conflict that recognised the complexities of contact notification and balanced the interests of all those involved. Approaches that encouraged voluntary disclosure would be more effective in controlling the spread of HIV/AIDS, and when contacts were notified in a respectful, managed manner, the trauma to them would be lessened. Mediative approaches to the management of contact notification could prove successful in Canada, especially if bolstered by increased public health education and awareness of the benefits of conflict resolution processes.

4. POWERS OF MEDICAL HEALTH OFFICERS

In addition to their duties to report disease and keep information confidential, medical health officers have been granted wide powers, the most important of which are the powers to: (a) examine, (b) enter, (c) detain, (d) isolate, and (e) close places.

(a) The Power to Examine

The power to examine is very wide. Federally, medical health officers have the power to examine for both contagious and dangerous diseases.[46] In Nova Scotia, any medical health officer may examine any person, with or without consent, in order to ascertain whether the person is infected with tuberculosis or a venereal disease.[47] In Saskatchewan, the power to examine includes the power to take specimens,[48] and in British Columbia, the power to examine includes the power to take specimens and X-rays.[49] In Manitoba and Alberta, a person could be obliged to submit to examination even if not infected. The Manitoba legislation provides that a medical officer of health can "order any person whom he has reason to believe might be suffering from a communicable disease to submit to a medical examination."[50] The Alberta legislation stipulates that:

> Where a medical officer of health knows or has reason to believe that a person may be infected with a communicable (or sexually transmitted) disease...that person shall, at the request of the medical officer of health, submit to any examinations necessary to determine whether the person is infected with the disease.[51]

In other words, medical health officers need only have reason to believe the person has a disease in order to examine the person — a wide power that carries the risk of discriminatory application. Those who engage in high-risk behaviours for HIV/AIDS, such as homosexual sex, intravenous drug use, and prostitution could be subjected to random medical examinations simply because of a medical health officer's discriminatory suspicion of infection.

A more measured approach is illustrated by Ontario and Newfoundland provisions. In Ontario, the power to examine is restricted to cases in which there are "reasonable and probable grounds" to believe that a communicable disease exists or may exist.[52] In Newfoundland and Labrador, medical health officers require "reasonable grounds for believing that a person is or may be infected with or has been exposed to a communicable disease"[53] before the medical health officer may direct that person to submit to an examination.

(b) The Power to Enter

In addition to their power to examine, medical health officers are allowed to enter private residences in order to examine those they suspect are infected with a communicable or venereal disease. This is further evidence that medical health officers possess wide, police-like powers under public health legislation. In New Brunswick, medical health officers may:

> for any of the purposes of this Act, and in case of emergency at any hour of the day or night, as often as he or they think necessary, enter into and upon any premises and examine the same.[54]

Similarly, in Alberta, Quebec, Nova Scotia, the Northwest Territories, Nunavut, and the Yukon, medical health officers may enter places without warrants. In Manitoba, medical health officers may enter at all reasonable times without the consent of the owner and take samples of food, clothes, and bedding.[55] In Saskatchewan, medical health officers may enter into a residence at any reasonable time, require a person to submit to being examined by a physician, and may call for the assistance of a peace officer.[56] In the Yukon, Northwest Territories, and Nunavut, a medical health officer actually has "all the powers of a peace officer while acting in his or her capacity as a Health Officer."[57]

The power to enter is akin to the exercise of police power, yet victims of infectious diseases are not criminals. Given that unauthorised entry is not permitted by the criminal law, it seems overbroad that so many Canadian jurisdictions allow such unfettered entry for public health purposes. Some form of control before medical health officers can exercise the power to enter is preferable, and is illustrated in the legislation of three provinces. In Prince Edward Island, medical health officers may enter without consent and seize items, but only upon the written authority of the Chief Health Officer.[58] In Ontario, a medical officer of health has the power to enter, but not without the consent of the occupier,[59] and in British Columbia, medical officers of health require a warrant to enter a private dwelling.[60]

(c) The Power to Detain

The power to detain restricts freedom of movement in order to prevent the spread of infectious disease, and therefore public health legislation affords wide powers of detention to medical health officers. The power to detain can be used to enable the health officer to complete an examination, so for example in Ontario, Quebec, and Prince Edward Island, there is power to detain by court order or by a judge.[61] In Alberta, health officers can apply to a judge to extend the period of detention for up to seven days,[62] and in Newfoundland and Labrador, anyone who is infected with a communicable or venereal disease can be removed to and detained in a hospital until "no longer a danger to the public."[63] The New Brunswick and Nova Scotia statutes make special provision for the detention by a judge of anyone afflicted with tuberculosis, "for such period not exceeding one year."[64]

In most cases, however, it is those who fail to comply with an order of a medical health officer who are taken into custody and detained in hospital for treatment. The law allows the detention of recalcitrant patients who refuse to obey an order, submit to examination or treatment, or to follow directions concerning conduct. For example, in Alberta, certificates can be issued against recalcitrant patients and then the patients can be apprehended, examined, treated without consent, and detained,[65] and in New Brunswick, if a patient has TB and will not seek treatment, a judge can order detention in a sanatorium.[66] Federally, if a person is requested to undergo an examination and refuses, detention "for a period not exceeding the incubation period prescribed for that disease" may be ordered.[67]

A more measured response than detaining patients is ordering them to adhere to proper conduct. In that regard, Ontario's *Health Protection and Promotion Act* empowers the minister to make an order requiring a person to conduct himself in such a manner so as not to expose another person to infection.[68] If such a person is unwilling or unable to conduct himself accordingly, he may be detained "for a period of not more than four months."[69] In British Columbia and Newfoundland and Labrador, the person may be "detained in a place of detention for a period not exceeding one year."[70] These provisions recognize the importance of personal conduct in AIDS prevention, and highlight the wide, police-like powers of medical health officers.

The powers of medical health officers under public health legislation are in some cases even wider than *Criminal Code*[71] powers. In *Chambers v. B.C. (Attorney General)*,[72] the British Columbia Court of Appeal held that an HIV-positive sex worker could not be detained under the *Criminal Code* because of her illness or disease. A person can only be detained under the *Criminal Code* if the significant threat that person poses is with respect to criminal conduct. Since the sex worker's conduct was not criminal — it is not a criminal offence to be HIV-positive nor to engage in prostitution — she did not pose a significant threat related to criminal activity. Therefore, the custodial order made against her was unreasonable and she was granted a discharge.

> The appellant should not be detained under the *Criminal Code* because she is physically ill. . . . If she is considered a menace because of her physical condition, s. 7 of the *Health Act* may be invoked. It was not the intent of Parliament that the *Criminal Code* be used to confine persons who may develop AIDS or for that matter any other communicable disease.[73]

Chambers v. B.C. (Attorney General) illustrates the wider power of detention available through public health legislation as compared to criminal law.

(d) The Power to Isolate

Closely related to the power to detain is the power to isolate or quarantine. The power to isolate is generally reserved for recalcitrant patients who are later released when they are no longer infectious. In most jurisdictions, one can also apply for the cancellation of an isolation order. In New Brunswick, medical health officers may "isolate persons affected with communicable diseases",[74] and in Nova Scotia, when a communicable disease prevails in a house or place, the medical health officer may "send the person so diseased to a hospital or may restrain him and others exposed to the disease from intercourse with other persons and may prohibit ingress or egress from the house or place."[75] If a district is declared to be under quarantine in the Yukon Territory, a health officer is empowered to prevent the entrance or exit of persons and to detain them for observation and surveillance.[76] Similarly, in the Northwest Territories and Nunavut, where an area has been declared a quarantine district, medical health officers have the power to isolate.[77] Pursuant to the *Quarantine Act*, the federal government has the power to quarantine persons with infectious, contagious, and dangerous diseases,[78] recalcitrant patients can be quarantined for the length of the incubation period prescribed for the disease in question,[79] and, persons may also be quarantined if recently "in close proximity to a person who may have or may be the carrier of an infectious or contagious disease."[80]

(e) The Power to Close Places

Finally, medical health officers have the power to close places to prevent the spread of communicable diseases. In Quebec, any institution, educational facility, or meeting place may be closed on account of an epidemic or a real or apprehended danger.[81] If the health minister of Newfoundland and Labrador has reason to believe that a communicable disease threatens to become epidemic, then the minister may close schools and prohibit public gatherings "as in his judgment may be necessary to stamp out the infection or contagion."[82] The Chief Health Officer of Prince Edward Island may "close any school, church, or place used for public gathering or entertainment where he considers it necessary to prevent the occurrence or spread of communicable disease."[83]

5. PENALTY PROVISIONS

(a) Public Health Law

The public health laws of all Canadian jurisdictions contain penalty provisions for breach of their requirements. Every jurisdiction imposes a fine for breach of statutory requirements, although the maximum amount varies. In Nova Scotia, if a patient refuses to submit to a TB exam, there is a $50 fine.[84] In Alberta, the fine for breach of a statutory provision is not more than $100 for each day the offence continues.[85] In Newfoundland and Labrador, if a person with a communicable disease fails to comply with a health order, the fine is also $100.[86] However, if the person does not submit to treatment or examination upon discovering a venereal disease, the fine is $500, or imprisonment for a maximum of 6 months.[87]

In some provinces, the fines are larger. In Quebec, individuals who breach the Act are liable, for each day the offence continues, to a fine of not more than $1,400, and corporations are liable for a fine of not more than $7,000.[88] The Ontario Act allows a fine of up to $5,000 for every day or part of a day that an individual's offence occurs or continues.[89] However, where the offence is committed by a municipality or corporation, "the maximum penalty that may be imposed for every day or part of a day on which the offence occurs or continues is $25,000."[90] In Saskatchewan the maximum fine for a first offence is $75,000 and for a second offence, the maximum fine is increased to $100,000.[91]

Some jurisdictions allow for incarceration. In the Northwest Territories, Nunavut, and the Yukon, the penalty is a fine not exceeding $500, or imprisonment for a term not exceeding six months, or both.[92] In Manitoba, the penalty for breach of the *Public Health Act* is a fine not exceeding

$5,000, or imprisonment for no more than three months, or both.[93] In Prince Edward Island, the penalty is a fine not exceeding $5,000, or imprisonment for a maximum of six months, or both.[94] In British Columbia, the *Health Act* provides for a fine of not more than $200,000, or imprisonment for not longer than 12 months, or both,[95] while the *Venereal Disease Act* provides for a fine of not more than $100 or imprisonment for up to a year.[96] Offences committed under the federal *Quarantine Act* are punishable on summary conviction.[97]

Finally, in New Brunswick and Newfoundland and Labrador, if the person affected by the venereal disease is under 16 and does not comply with treatment, the person's mother or father can be liable. The parent will be subject to the penalties provided by the Acts unless the parent proves that s/he did everything reasonably within her or his power to cause the child to comply.[98] The position is similar in Ontario and Saskatchewan.[99]

Despite the ample penalty provisions available to medical health officers under public health legislation, public health law penalty provisions are not always effective. The limited role of public health law is illustrated by *Ontario (Chief Medical Officer of Health) v. Ssenyonga*.[100] Ssenyonga was the subject of a legal proceeding under Ontario's *Health Protection and Promotion Act*. The minister of health applied for a restraining order that Ssenyonga, known to be HIV-positive, abstain from sexual activity. Although the order was granted, Ssenyonga ignored it, assured future female sexual partners that he was free from disease, and infected at least three of them with HIV. Unfortunately, the efficacy of restraining orders, and of public health law generally, is dependent upon the goodwill of the person subjected to the order, which offers little comfort in cases like *Ssenyonga*.

(b) Criminal Law

In the *Criminal Code*[101] there are three sections that provide penalties for those who transmit communicable diseases to others: sections 180, 221 and 273.

(i) *Section 180*

Section 180 of the *Criminal Code* outlines the offence of committing a common nuisance: "Every one who commits a common nuisance and thereby (a) endangers the lives, safety or health of the public, or (b) causes physical injury to any person, is guilty of an indictable offence and liable to imprisonment for a term not exceeding two years."

In an Ontario case, *R. v. Thornton*,[102] the accused was convicted of committing a common nuisance for knowingly donating HIV-infected blood to the Red Cross, thereby endangering the lives of the public at large. Galligan J., for the Ontario Court of Appeal, stated: "When the gravity of the potential harm is great — in this case 'catastrophic' — the public is endangered even where the risk of harm actually occurring is slight, indeed, even if it is minimal."[103] Thornton had a duty to disclose to the Red Cross that his blood contained HIV antibodies, and by not doing so he committed common nuisance which endangered the life, safety and health of the public. Thornton's conviction and sentence of 15 months incarceration were upheld by the Supreme Court of Canada.

Conversely, in *R. v. Ssenyonga*,[104] the court held that Ssenyonga's unprotected sexual relationships with three women did not endanger the health of the public. Ssenyonga had previously been subject to a public health order to abstain from sexual intercourse.[105] However, he ignored the order. Three female complainants consented to unprotected sexual intercourse with Ssenyonga, and he infected all three with HIV. A preliminary inquiry was held to establish whether Mr. Ssenyonga should stand trial for: (i) criminal negligence causing bodily harm, (ii) aggravated sexual assault, (iii) administering a noxious thing, and (iv) common nuisance. The preliminary inquiry found that Ssenyonga should stand trial for (i) criminal negligence causing bodily harm and (ii) aggravated sexual assault.

The judge was not satisfied that there was sufficient evidence to show that the ejaculation of semen during sexual intercourse was committed with the intent to endanger life, and therefore Ssenyonga did not have to stand trial for the administration of a noxious thing. More controversially however, the preliminary inquiry judge found that Ssenyonga did not have to stand trial for committing the offence of common nuisance.

The *Ssenyonga* court distinguished *R. v. Thornton* and found that Ssenyonga did not commit a common nuisance endangering the health of the public. The court found that Ssenyonga did not offer himself to the general public, but rather to three specific women. "Certainly the complainants are members of the public but I cannot accept that they, from a legal perspective, represent the community as a whole. The offence of common nuisance is, in my view, not appropriate based on the evidence presented on this preliminary inquiry."[106] As a result, Ssenyonga was discharged on the counts of committing the offence of common nuisance contrary to s. 180 of the *Criminal Code*, but still had to stand trial for criminal negligence causing bodily harm and aggravated sexual assault.

More correctly, in *R. v. Hollihan*,[107] it was decided that having unprotected sex with one woman without disclosing HIV-positive status was enough to endanger the public. Hollihan was guilty of committing the offence of common nuisance. The Newfoundland provincial court came to the conclusion that even though there was only one complainant, that complainant was a member of the public. It did not matter whether unprotected sex was with one or more members of the public because unprotected sex endangered the person and anyone with whom the person subsequently became intimate. The seriousness and essence of the offence was the wilful act of endangerment.

Finally, there is the case of John Lyristis of Newfoundland. He currently faces the charge of committing a common nuisance and endangering the lives, safety or health of the public for refusing to treat his tuberculosis.[108] Lyristis was isolated from the general public pursuant to public health legislation due to his reluctance to attend medical appointments and refusal to take medication. A judicial order required him to take his medication, and when he continued to refuse, Mr. Lyristis was criminally charged with committing a common nuisance, thereby endangering the public. The result of his 2001 trial remains unknown because there is a publication ban on the case.

(ii) *Section 221*

Section 221 of the *Criminal Code* outlines the offence of committing criminal negligence causing bodily harm to another person. Section 221 states: "Every one who by criminal negligence causes bodily harm to another person is guilty of an indictable offence and liable to imprisonment for a term not exceeding ten years." Criminal negligence is established when the accused "shows wanton or reckless disregard for the lives or safety of other persons."[109]

There are not many cases where section 221 has been used to punish those who transmit communicable diseases. There is an unreported case from Nova Scotia in which an HIV-positive man pled guilty to the offence of criminal negligence causing bodily harm and was sentenced to three years in prison.[110] In another case, *R. v. Mercer*,[111] the accused pled guilty to charges of criminal negligence causing bodily harm in transmitting HIV to two women. He was sentenced to 27 months in prison, but the Crown successfully appealed his sentence. Given that Mercer knew he was HIV-positive, had unprotected sex with two women, assured both women that any protection was unnecessary, and both women became HIV-positive, the court found that it was one of the worst cases of criminal negligence and that the appropriate sentence should be 11 years. Finally, there is the *Ssenyonga*[112] case. The reader will recall that at the conclusion of the preliminary inquiry in his case, Ssenyonga was required to stand trial for criminal negligence causing bodily harm. Unfortunately however, Ssenyonga passed away due to AIDS before a verdict was reached. Had Ssenyonga lived, the Crown would likely have secured a conviction for criminal negligence causing bodily harm because DNA testing had linked Ssenyonga's peculiar strain of HIV to the complainants, and all other previous sexual partners of the complainants had been tested and none were HIV-positive. However, Ssenyonga's death put an end to the case.[113]

(iii)   Section 273

Section 273 of the *Criminal Code* provides the final criminal penalty provision that may be used against those who knowingly spread communicable diseases. Section 273 outlines the offence of aggravated sexual assault: "every one commits an aggravated sexual assault who, in committing a sexual assault, wounds, maims, disfigures or endangers the life of the complainant." The use of section 273 to punish those who inflict others with HIV again involves the notorious case, *R. v. Ssenyonga*.[114]

Ssenyonga was charged and tried on three counts of aggravated sexual assault. His lawyer moved that the charges of aggravated assault be dismissed on the ground that the complainants freely and voluntarily engaged in sexual intercourse with the accused without the use of a condom. The Crown argued that although the complainants consented to unprotected sex with Ssenyonga, he committed fraud by not informing them of his HIV-positive status. The Crown argued that Ssenyonga's fraud vitiated the complainants' consent. The court however granted defence counsel's motion and all three charges of aggravated sexual assault were dismissed.

The motion to drop the charges of aggravated assault was granted because the court found that Ssenyonga did not commit fraud. And, since there was no fraud, there was nothing that vitiated the complainants' consent. There could only be fraud as to the "nature and quality of the act" if the complainants did not understand what they were consenting to. Ssenyonga's sexual partners knew they were consenting to unprotected sex. Because the three women were under no misapprehension as to the nature of the acts in which they were engaging, there was no fraud, and Ssenyonga was not guilty.

Fortunately, in the subsequent case of *R. v. Cuerrier*,[115] the Supreme Court of Canada specifically did not follow the decision in *Ssenyonga*. Cuerrier had unprotected sex with two women without informing them of his HIV-positive status, although he had been explicitly instructed by a public health nurse to inform all prospective partners and to always use a condom. The complainants consented to unprotected sex with Cuerrier, and at the time of trial, had not tested positive for HIV. Both complainants testified at Cuerrier's trial for aggravated sexual assault that they would not have consented to unprotected sex had they known he was HIV-positive. At trial, Cuerrier was acquitted. The trial judge felt that the complainants' consents were not vitiated by fraud. The British Columbia Court of Appeal dismissed the Crown's appeal, so the Crown appealed to the Supreme Court of Canada. The Supreme Court allowed the Crown's appeal and ordered a new trial.

The Supreme Court found that a more flexible concept of fraud in sexual assault cases should be employed; it was no longer necessary to consider whether the alleged fraud related to "the nature and quality of the act." The essential elements of fraud are dishonesty, which can include non-disclosure of important facts, and deprivation or risk of deprivation. As such, the Supreme Court found that if an accused dishonestly concealed or failed to disclose HIV-positive status, putting the complainant at significant risk, it could constitute fraud, which could vitiate consent to sexual intercourse. Cuerrier's failure to disclose his HIV-positive status was dishonest and resulted in deprivation because it put the complainants at significant risk of suffering serious bodily harm or death. In such circumstances, a positive duty to disclose exists; without disclosure of HIV status there can be no true consent to sexual intercourse. The Supreme Court of Canada noted:

> It was also argued that criminalizing non-disclosure of HIV status will undermine the educational message that all are responsible for protecting themselves against HIV infection. Yet this argument can have little weight. Surely those who know they are HIV-positive have a fundamental responsibility to advise their partners of their condition and to ensure that their sex is as safe as possible. It is true that all members of society should be aware of the danger and take steps to avoid the risk. However, the primary responsibility for making the disclosure must rest upon those who are aware they are infected. I would hope that every member of society no matter how "marginalized" would be sufficiently responsible that they would advise their partner of risks. In these circumstances it is, I trust, not too much to expect that the infected person would advise his partner of his infection.[116]

Although interveners argued that the criminal law was not the best tool to deal with the transmission of HIV, the Supreme Court found that where public health initiatives fail to provide adequate protection to individuals, the criminal law can be effective.

> It was forcefully contended that these [public health] endeavours may well prove more effective in controlling the disease than any criminal sanctions which can be devised. However, the criminal law does have a role to play both in deterring those infected with HIV from putting the lives of others at

risk and in protecting the public from irresponsible individuals who refuse to comply with public health orders to abstain from high-risk activities. This case provides a classic example of the ineffectiveness of the health scheme. The respondent was advised that he was HIV-positive and on three occasions he was instructed to advise his partner of this and not to have unprotected sex. Nevertheless, he blithely ignored these instructions and endangered the lives of two partners.[117]

In the end, a new trial was ordered for Cuerrier. In the new trial the Crown will have to prove that the complainants would have refused to engage in unprotected sex with Cuerrier if they had been advised of his HIV-positive status, and the court will have to determine whether a reasonable person would find Cuerrier's actions to be dishonest.

The Supreme Court of Canada's statement in *R. v. Cuerrier* that there is a duty to disclose one's HIV-positive status was followed in the subsequent case of *R. v. Maisonneuve*.[118] The Quebec Provincial Court held that the accused had a duty to disclose his HIV-positive status to a woman with whom he had unprotected sex. It is likely that all future prosecutions under section 273 of the *Criminal Code* for aggravated sexual assault will result in decisions like *Maisonneuve*, and not like *Ssenyonga*.

6. CONCLUSION

All Canadians have responsibilities to report communicable and venereal diseases if they suffer from them, and medical officers of health must report any instances of communicable and venereal diseases they come across. However, when reporting diseases, medical health officers have a duty to respect the confidentiality of Canadian citizens. Requirements vary, but generally speaking, if patients comply with treatment, little information about them is revealed to public health authorities. If infected patients have had contact with others, contact notification is required in some jurisdictions, and mediation might be one way to manage the stressful process of informing others that they too may be infected.

In order to prevent, treat, and suppress communicable diseases such as tuberculosis and HIV/AIDS, medical health officers in all ten provinces, three territories, and federally have the power to examine, enter, detain, isolate, and close places. These remarkably wide, police-like powers could infringe individual patient liberty and other rights guaranteed by the Canadian *Charter of Rights and Freedoms*. As a result, the powers of medical health officers are vulnerable to constitutional challenges as violations of the *Charter*. However, since the powers are rarely enforced, and no constitutional challenges have been mounted, it remains to be seen whether the powers are unconstitutional in their breadth. Similarly, it remains to be seen if public health legislation has the potential to impact upon the spread of communicable diseases, particularly HIV/AIDS.

All public health legislation provides penalties for those who breach the statutes, and for those who have the criminal intent to infect others, the *Criminal Code* provides three different punishments. There appears to be justification for criminally sanctioning those who, like Ssenyonga, purposefully transmit or attempt to transmit HIV to others. However, for those who do not have such intent, the more measured response of public health legislation is appropriate.

> . . . public health laws can be an alternative to criminalization because they are, in general, better adapted to the particular facts of each case. They have the requisite flexibility for personalizing interventions, they respect confidentiality, and they are less likely to stigmatize. Contrary to criminal proceedings, they make it possible to proceed from less coercive to more restrictive measures.[119]

Penal responses can be counterproductive in their harshness. Infected individuals may neglect to report communicable diseases for fear of punishment. This makes treatment impossible, and increases the chances of the disease spreading to other individuals. It may be prudent to negotiate testing and treatment on people's own terms, taking their realities into account. "In the present context, the governing moral principle for assessing testing policies should be that interventions aimed at protecting health must exhaust the range of measures that can be taken to do things for people before state power is used to begin doing things to people."[120] Ultimately, it is not the resort to criminal law, or even public health law, that can effectively modify human behaviour. Education and public awareness offer the only real hope of preventing the spread of communicable diseases and HIV/AIDS.

NOTES

1. "HIV Infection Reporting in Canada" (April 2002) HIV/AIDS Epi Update. See Health Canada's Website at: www.hc-sc.gc.ca/pphb-dgspsp/publicat/epiu-aepi/hiv-vih/hivrep__e.html

2. "Tuberculosis in Canada 2000 Pre-Release" (2000). See Health Canada's Website at: http://www.hc-sc.gc.ca/pphb-dgspsp/publicat/tbc00p/index.html

3. *Public Health Act*, R.S.A. 2000, c. P-37, as amended, s. 20(1).

4. *Venereal Disease Act*, R.S.B.C. 1996, c. 475, s. 3(3).

5. P.E.I. Reg. EC 330/85, s. 4.

6. R.R.N.W.T. 1980, Reg. 212, s. 3. The Nunavut regulations are the same as the N.W.T. regulations.

7. *Public Health Act, 1994*, S.S. 1994, c. P-37.1, as amended, s. 33(1); *Health Act*, R.S.N.B. 1973, c. H-2, s. 16 and s. 19(3); *Venereal Disease Act*, R.S.N.B., 1973, c. V-2, s. 3; *Communicable Diseases Act*, R.S.N.L. 1990, c. C-26, s. 15; and *Venereal Disease Prevention Act*, R.S.N.L. 1990, c. V-2, s. 3(1).

8. *Public Health Act*, R.S.Y. 1986, c. 136, s. 2(a)(i); *Public Health Act*, R.S.N.W.T. 1988, c. P-12, s. 25(1)(a)(i); and Nunavut's *Public Health Act*, which is identical to *Public Health Act*, R.S.N.W.T. 1988, c. P-12.

9. *Public Health Act*, R.S.A. 2000, c. P-37, as amended, s. 22(2).

10. *Public Health Act, 1994*, S.S. 1994, c. P-37.1, as amended, s. 32(1)(c); *Health Protection and Promotion Act*, R.S.O. 1990, c. H.7, s. 28; *Communicable Diseases Act*, R.S.N.L. 1990, c. C-26, s. 5; and *Health Act*, R.S.N.S. 1989, c. 195, s. 70(2).

11. *Communicable Diseases Act*, R.S.N.L. 1990, c. C-26, s. 3(1).

12. *Health Act*, R.S.B.C. 1996, c. 179, s. 80; and *Health Act*, R.S.N.S. 1989, c. 195, s. 64(1).

13. *Public Health Act*, R.S.A. 2000, c. P-37, as amended, s. 22(1).

14. *Public Health Protection Act*, R.S.Q. 1977, c. P-35, s. 5; *Health Protection and Promotion Act*, R.S.O. 1990, c. H.7, s. 39; and *Venereal Disease Act*, R.S.N.B. c. V-2, s. 7(1).

15. *Venereal Disease Act*, R.S.B.C. 1996, c. 475, s. 2.

16. *Public Health Act, 1994*, S.S. 1994, c. P-37.1, as amended, s. 32(3).

17. *Communicable Diseases Act*, R.S.N.L. 1990, c. C-26, s. 4(1); *Venereal Disease Prevention Act*, R.S.N.L. 1990, c. V-2, s. 17.

18. *Health Act*, R.S.N.S. 1989, c. 195, s. 75(1) for TB and s. 92(1) for VD, but not HIV.

19. *Reporting Requirements for HIV Positive Persons Regulations*, O.I.C. 2000-101 (March 8, 2000), N.S. Reg. 31/2000, s. 7(3). 'Nominal testing' refers to HIV testing in which results can be linked to the person tested by the person's full name. 'Non-nominal testing' refers to HIV testing in which results can be

linked to the person tested by a code known only by that person and the physician performing the test.

20. *Health Protection and Promotion Act*, R.S.O. 1990, c. H.7, s. 26.

21. *Public Health Protection Act*, R.S.Q. 1977, c. P-35, s. 6.

22. *Health Protection and Promotion Act*, R.S.O. 1990, c. H.7, s. 34(1); *Venereal Disease Prevention Act*, R.S.N.L. 1990, c. V-2, s. 11(1); *Venereal Disease Act*, R.S.N.B. 1973, c. V-2, s. 7(2).

23. *Venereal Disease Act*, R.S.B.C. 1996, c. 475, s. 12.

24. *Health Act*, R.S.N.S. 1989, c. 195, s. 99.

25. *Venereal Disease Prevention Act*, R.S.N.L. 1990, c. V-2, s. 14(1).

26. *Health Protection and Promotion Act*, R.S.O. 1990, c. H.7, s. 39(1).

27. *Venereal Disease Act*, R.S.B.C. 1996, c. 475, s. 12; *Public Health Protection Act*, R.S.Q. 1977, c. P-35, s. 7.

28. *Venereal Disease Prevention Act*, R.S.N.L. 1990, c. V-2, s. 15.

29. *Health Act*, R.S.N.B. 1973, c. H-2, s. 33; and *Venereal Disease Act*, R.S.N.B. 1973, c. V-2, s. 22.

30. *Public Health Act*, R.S.P.E.I. 1988, c. P-30, s. 22(1)(b) and s. 22(2)(b).

31. *Health Act*, R.S.N.S. 1989, c. 195, s. 75.

32. *Reporting Requirements for HIV Positive Persons Regulations*, O.I.C. 2000-101 (March 8, 2000), N.S. Reg. 31/2000, s. 7(5)(b).

33. *Reporting Requirements for HIV Positive Persons Regulations*, O.I.C. 2000-101 (March 8, 2000), N.S. Reg. 31/2000, s. 7(2).

34. *Public Health Act*, R.S.A. 2000, c. P-37, as amended, s. 31(2).

35. *Reporting Requirements for HIV Positive Persons Regulations*, O.I.C. 2000-101 (March 8, 2000), N.S. Reg. 31/2000, s. 10.

36. *Venereal Disease Act*, R.S.B.C. 1996, c. 475, s. 5(6); *Public Health Act*, R.S.A. 2000, c. P-37, as amended, s. 56(1); and *Public Health Act, 1994*, S.S. 1994, c. P-37.1, as amended, s. 5 and s. 33(4)(b).

37. *Public Health Act, 1994*, S.S. 1994, c. P-37.1, as amended, s. 6 and s. 38(1)(h).

38. *Venereal Disease Act*, R.S.B.C. 1996, c. 475, s. 5(6).

39. *Venereal Disease Prevention Act*, R.S.N.L. 1990, c. V-2, s. 14(3); *Public Health Act*, R.S.A. 2000, c. P-37, as amended, s. 56(3).

40. *Venereal Disease Prevention Act*, R.S.N.L. 1990, c.V-2, s. 14(3).

41. *Public Health Protection Act*, R.S.Q. 1977, c. P-35, s. 7.

42. C. Moore, *The Mediation Process*, 2nd ed. (San Francisco: Jossey-Bass, 1996) at 15.

43. In order to effectively mediate a contact notification case, it is likely that the mediator would have to play a directive role and allow a public health official to be present at the session. See A. Thrush, "Public Health and Safety Hazards Versus Confidentiality: Expanding the Mediation Door of the Multi-Door Courthouse", [1994] **Journal of Dispute Resolution** 235 at 252.

44. The author is indebted to Ms. Gemma Smyth for many of these ideas.

45. Nova Scotia already requires counselling for HIV-positive patients. See *Reporting Requirements for HIV Positive Persons Regulations,* O.I.C. 2000-101 (March 8, 2000), N.S. Reg. 31/2000, s. 5 and 6.

46. *Quarantine Act,* R.S.C. 1985, c. Q-1, s. 8(1) and s. 11, respectively.

47. *Health Act,* R.S.N.S. 1989, c. 195, for TB: s. 76(1); for VD: s. 93; and for school children: s. 73(1).

48. *Public Health Act, 1994,* S.S. 1994, c. P-37.1, as amended, s. 38(2)(e)(ii).

49. *Health Act,* R.S.B.C. 1996, c. 179, s. 70(1), s. 11, and s. 65.

50. *Public Health Act,* R.S.M. 1987, c. P210, as amended, s. 12(c).

51. *Public Health Act,* R.S.A. 2000, c. P-37, as amended, s. 31(1).

52. *Health Protection and Promotion Act,* R.S.O. 1990, c. H.7, s. 22(2)(a).

53. *Communicable Diseases Act,* R.S.N.L. 1990, c. C-26, s. 15; and *Venereal Disease Prevention Act,* R.S.N.L. 1990, c. V-2, s. 7(1).

54. *Health Act,* R.S.N.B. 1973, c. H-2, s. 16(1).

55. *Public Health Act,* R.S.M. 1987, c. P210, as amended, s. 12(a) and (b).

56. *Public Health Act, 1994,* S.S. 1994, c. P-37.1, as amended, s. 38(2)(e)(i), s. 53(1)(a), and s. 55(1).

57. *Public Health Act,* R.S.Y. 1986, c. 136, s. 15; *Public Health Act,* R.S.N.W.T. 1988, c. P-12, s. 22(1); and Nunavut *Public Health Act,* R.S.N.W.T. 1988, c. P-12, s. 22(1).

58. *Public Health Act,* R.S.P.E.I. 1988, c. P-30, s. 15(b).

59. *Health Protection and Promotion Act,* R.S.O. 1990, c. H.7, s. 41(7).

60. *Health Act,* R.S.B.C. 1996, c. 179, s. 61.

61. *Health Protection and Promotion Act,* R.S.O. 1990, c. H.7, s. 35; *Public Health Protection Act,* R.S.Q. 1977, c. P-35, s. 12; and *Public Health Act,* R.S.P.E.I. 1988, c. P-30, s. 19(1). Also, in P.E.I. the medical officer of health can order children to be detained from attending school — see *Public Health Act,* R.S.P.E.I. 1988, c. P-30, s. 12(1).

62. *Public Health Act,* R.S.A. 2000, c. P-37, as amended, s. 30(3).

63. *Communicable Diseases Act,* R.S.N.L. 1990, c. C-26, s. 15(2)(a); and *Venereal Disease Prevention Act,* R.S.N.L. 1990, c.V-2, s. 7(3)(a).

64. *Health Act,* R.S.N.B. 1973, c. H-2, s. 26(5); and *Health Act,* R.S.N.S. 1989, c. 195, s. 80.

65. *Public Health Act,* R.S.A. 2000, c. P-37, as amended, s. 39.

66. *Health Act,* R.S.N.B. 1973, c. H-2, s. 26(5).

67. *Quarantine Act,* R.S.C. 1985, c. Q-1, s. 8(2).

68. *Health Protection and Promotion Act,* R.S.O. 1990, c. H.7, s. 22(4)(h).

69. *Health Protection and Promotion Act,* R.S.O. 1990, c. H.7, s. 35(7).

70. *Venereal Disease Act,* R.S.B.C. 1996, c. 475, s. 6(6); and *Venereal Disease Prevention Act,* R.S.N.L. 1990, c. V-2, s. 5(4).

71. *Criminal Code,* R.S.C. 1985, c. C-46.

72. *Chambers v. British Columbia (Attorney General)*, [1997] BCJ No. 1497, 1997 CarswellBC 1318 (C.A.).

73. *Chambers v. British Columbia (Attorney General)*, [1997] BCJ No. 1497, 1997 CarswellBC 1318 (C.A.), at para. 26.

74. *Health Act*, R.S.N.B. 1973, c. H-2, s. 19(3)(d).

75. *Health Act*, R.S.N.S. 1989, c. 195, s. 66(1). Also, s. 69 of the same Act grants medical health officers the power to prevent children from going to school.

76. *Public Health Act*, R.S.Y. 1986, c. 136, s. 3(2)(a) & (b). Section 2(a)(iii) of the same Act grants a general power of isolation to medical officers of health.

77. *Public Health Act*, R.S.N.W.T. 1988, c. P-12, s. 25(1)(a)(ii); and Nunavut's *Public Health Act*, which is identical to *Public Health Act*, R.S.N.W.T. 1988, c. P-12.

78. *Quarantine Act*, R.S.C. 1985, c. Q-1, s. 13(1) and s. 14(1).

79. *Quarantine Act*, R.S.C. 1985, c. Q-1, s. 8(2).

80. *Quarantine Act*, R.S.C. 1985, c. Q-1, s. 8(1).

81. *Public Health Protection Act*, R.S.Q. 1977, c. P-35, s. 17 and 18.

82. *Communicable Diseases Act*, R.S.N.L. 1990, c. C-26, s. 31.

83. *Public Health Act*, R.S.P.E.I. 1988, c. P-30, s. 13, and see s. 14 for the power to close places generally.

84. *Health Act*, R.S.N.S. 1989, c. 195, s. 76(4).

85. *Public Health Act*, R.S.A. 2000, c. P-37, as amended, s. 73(2).

86. *Communicable Diseases Act*, R.S.N.L. 1990, c. C-26, s. 15(6)(a).

87. *Venereal Disease Prevention Act*, R.S.N.L. 1990, c. V-2, s. 3(3) and s. 7(2).

88. *Public Health Protection Act*, R.S.Q. 1977, c. P-35, s. 71.

89. *Health Protection and Promotion Act*, R.S.O. 1990, c. H.7, s. 101(1).

90. *Health Protection and Promotion Act*, R.S.O. 1990, c. H.7, s. 101(2).

91. *Public Health Act*, R.S.S. 1994, c. P-37.1, as amended, s. 61.

92. *Public Health Act*, R.S.N.W.T. 1988, c. P-12, s. 23; Nunavut *Public Health Act*, which is identical to *Public Health Act*, R.S.N.W.T. 1988, c. P-12, s. 23; and *Public Health Act*, R.S.Y. 1986, c. 136, s. 20.

93. *Public Health Act*, R.S.M. 1987, c. P210, as amended, s. 33(1).

94. *Public Health Act*, R.S.P.E.I. 1988, c. P-30, s. 20.

95. *Health Act*, R.S.B.C. 1996, c. 179, s.104. Section 104(2)(b) of the same Act notes that if the offence is continuing, the fine is $200,000 for each day the offences continues, or imprisonment for not longer than 12 months, or both.

96. *Venereal Disease Act*, R.S.B.C. 1996, c. 475, s. 14.

97. *Quarantine Act*, R.S.C. 1985, c. Q-1, s. 22(1).

98. *Venereal Disease Act*, R.S.N.B. c. V-2, s. 13; and *Venereal Disease Prevention Act*, R.S.N.L. 1990, c. V-2, s. 19.

99. For Ontario, see *Health Protection and Promotion Act*, R.S.O. 1990, c. H.7, s. 23; for Saskatchewan, see *Public Health Act, 1994*, S.S. 1994, c. P-37.1, as amended, s. 39, which requires that parents ensure that their children comply

with public health orders if the children are less than 14 years old, or older than 14 but less than 18 and cannot understand the orders.

100. *Ontario (Chief Medical Officer of Health) v. Ssenyonga* (April 16, 1991), Doc. R.E. 545/91, [1991] O.J. No. 544 (Gen. Div.).

101. *Criminal Code*, R.S.C. 1985, c. C-46.

102. *R. v. Thornton* (1991), 3 C.R. (4th) 381 (Ont. C.A.), affirmed [1993] 2 S.C.R. 445.

103. *R. v. Thornton* (1991), 3 C.R. (4th) 381 (Ont. CA), affirmed [1993] 2 S.C.R. 445 at 389 [C.R.].

104. *R. v. Ssenyonga* (1992), 73 C.C.C. (3d) 216 (Ont. Prov. Div.).

105. *Ontario (Chief Medical Officer of Health) v. Ssenyonga* (April 16, 1991), Doc. R.E. 545/91, [1991] O.J. No. 544 (Gen. Div.).

106. *R. v. Ssenyonga* (1992), 73 C.C.C. (3d) 216 at 224 (Ont. Prov. Ct.).

107. *R. v. Hollihan*, [1998] NJ No. 176, 1998 CarswellNfld 349 (Prov. Ct.).

108. M. Friscolanti, "Man Jailed for Skipping TB Treatments" (December 8, 2001) **National Post.** This case has not been reported.

109. *Criminal Code*, R.S.C. 1985, c. C-46, s. 219.

110. *R. v. Scott William Wentzell* (1989), unreported, Nova Scotia.

111. *R. v. Mercer* (1993), 84 C.C.C. (3d) 41 (Nfld. C.A.), leave to appeal refused (1994), 86 C.C.C. (3d) vii (note) (S.C.C.).

112. *R. v. Ssenyonga* (1992), 73 C.C.C. (3d) 216 at 224 (Ont. Prov. Ct.).

113. The *Ssenyonga* case is the subject of a book by J. Callwood, *Trial Without End* (Toronto: Albert A. Knopf Canada, 1995). The title reflects the complainants' frustration that, because Ssenyonga's death precluded conviction and sentence, they were left with no sense of closure.

114. *R. v. Ssenyonga*, [1993] O.J. No. 1030, 1993 CarswellOnt 96 (Gen. Div.).

115. *R. v. Cuerrier*, [1998] 2 S.C.R. 371, [1998] S.C.J. No. 64, 1998 CarswellBC 1772, 1998 CarswellBC 1773.

116. *R. v. Cuerrier*, [1998] 2 S.C.R. 371, [1998] S.C.J. No. 64, 1998 CarswellBC 1772, 1998 CarswellBC 1773, at para. 144 [S.C.J.].

117. *R. v. Cuerrier*, [1998] 2 S.C.R. 371, [1998] S.C.J. No. 64, 1998 CarswellBC 1772, 1998 CarswellBC 1773, at para. 141 [S.C.J.].

118. *R. v. Maisonneuve* (October 20, 2000), Doc. 550-01-003220-995 (Que. Prov. Ct.).

119. "The Montreal Model: Public Health and People with HIV/AIDS Who Do Not Take Precautions" (1999), 4 **Canadian HIV/AIDS Policy & Law Newsletter**.

120. B. Hoffmaster & T. Schrecker, "An Ethical Analysis of HIV Testing of Pregnant Women and Their Newborns" (1999), 4 **Canadian HIV/AIDS Policy & Law Newsletter.**

13

MENTAL HEALTH LAW

SUMMARY

What makes mental health law unique in the field of health law generally is that its its main purpose is to provide a framework for compulsory delivery of medical services. Historically, the two main compulsory features of mental health law have been involuntary hospitalization and treatment without consent of the patient. While the rights of persons with mental illness have assumed a significantly more prominent role in recent decades, compulsion remains central to the concerns of mental health law. This has a number of implications.

First, mental health is largely governed by statutory rather than common law, since statutes are required to authorize intervention in the lives of individuals who are not seeking it, and to establish procedural and substantive limits on that intervention. In Canada, health is a matter of provincial jurisdiction. Consequently, different mental health statutes exist in each provincial and territorial jurisdiction. While they share many of the same features, significant differences exist. In fact, the differences may be greater in the early part of the 21st century than has been the case for many years.

Second, mental health law is a source of ongoing public controversy. The tension between a civil liberties, or patients' rights, perspective and what might be termed a treatment needs approach to mental health continues to characterize the debate in this field. The first, which finds some support in provisions of the *Canadian Charter of Rights and Freedoms*, continues to be influential. Nevertheless, recent statutory reforms in several provinces have responded more to the concern that law should facilitate treatment for persons with serious mental illness. The link in public opinion between the problem of urban homelessness and untreated mental illness, and the increased political weight of advocacy organizations representing families of persons with mental illness, have contributed to these developments.

This chapter starts by looking at the issues of involuntary committal, and treatment without consent. With both, the variety in terminology between provincial statutes is striking. Nevrtheless, committal procedures and criteria operate in a roughly similar fashion from jurisdiction to jurisdiction. Differences between provinces on the issue of consent to treatment, however, are marked, and range from recognition of involuntary patients' right to refuse treatment in Ontario, to the denial of any such right in B.C. and Newfoundland.

From there, the discussion moves to consideration of "community treatment orders", an innovation in the laws of Saskatchewan and Ontario intended to require compliance with treatment plans on the part of persons with mental illness living not in hospital, but in the community. The purpose is to maintain persons with chronic illness on a stable course, and prevent their falling prey to the "revolving door syndrome" in mental health care. Whether this innovation will succeed is a matter of speculation, but there are reasons to query its potential. This section also examines leaves of absence from hospital, a measure intended to achieve similar goals.

The chapter then provides an overview of liability issues of particular concern to mental health practitioners, including liability for injuries caused by persons with mental illness in a physician's care, and the duty to disclose threats to third parties made by patients in the course of therapy. This is followed by a brief discussion of forensic psychiatry, and other ways in which the criminal justice and civil mental health systems interact.

The chapter concludes by touching on the role of advocacy of legal rights for those with mental illness as a factor that contributes to making mental health service delivery more just and humane, and to diminishing discrimination against the mentally ill in Canadian society.

1. INTRODUCTION

(a) An Overview of Canadian Mental Health Law[1]

Canadian mental health law is difficult to summarize neatly, because each province has its own statutory regime for mental health service delivery. This follows from Canada's constitutional architecture, which leaves the greater part of health care within provincial jurisdiction. This means that there can be as many as ten possible answers to any question going to the details of how mental health law operates in Canada, and ultimately no substitute for consulting the legislation of the particular province with which one is concerned.[2] Despite its variety, mental health law in Canada does have a common overall shape. This can largely be attributed to two related characteristics of mental health law.

(1) its compulsory purposes;
(2) the context provided by the *Canadian Charter of Rights and Freedoms.*

First, it is significant that mental health *is* governed by legislation. This speaks to what makes it somewhat unique as an area of health law: its reliance on compulsion. Common law principles governing health care assume a standard model in which patients seek treatment for illness, and enter into voluntary arrangements with clinicians. To the extent that a person with mental health problems does the same, those same common law principles apply to the care they receive. The fact that the presenting problem manifests itself in psychological rather than physiological symptoms makes no difference, and would not itself necessitate a separate legal regime.

However, major mental illnesses, including schizophrenia, bipolar disorder and depression, often render those that experience them unaware of their illness and of treatment options. In serious form, these illnesses may cause behaviours that pose risks of harm to the person, and to others. Canadian society has long insisted on intervening in the lives of persons with mental disorders in order both to protect their safety and that of the public, and to facilitate their treatment. Historically, the two principal means of intervention have been involuntary committal to a psychiatric hospital setting, and the provision of psychiatric treatment without the patient's consent. These measures require statute law both to grant the authority to intervene in a compulsory fashion, and to limit the scope of this authority. While provincial mental health statutes deal with various other matters in the delivery of mental health services, their *raison d'etre* remains this framework of lawful compulsion.

Second, the compulsory nature of mental health law means that the *Charter of Rights and Freedoms* is an important contextual factor in its ongoing development. The *Charter* became part of Canada's Constitution in 1982. As such, it is binding on all laws enacted by Parliament and the provincial legislatures. This includes mental health statutes.

Involuntary hospitalization and treatment without consent implicate several individual rights guaranteed in the *Charter*. Section 7 of the *Charter* reads as follows:

> 7. Everyone has the right to life, liberty and security of the person and the right not to be deprived thereof except in accordance with the principles of fundamental justice.

Involuntary committal is a limit on "liberty." Treatment without consent is a limit on the right to "security of the person", which goes to an individual's physical integrity. The reference to "principles of fundamental justice" is understood as including a requirement of due legal process whenever the state seeks to limits the rights of life, liberty or security of the person. At minimum, then, section 7 supports claims to meaningful procedural rights on the part of persons subject to committal, or to treatment without consent.

Section 9 of the *Charter* guarantees freedom from "arbitrary detention." Section 10 provides a right, on detention, "to retain and instruct counsel without delay" and to be informed of that right. Section 12 provides a guarantee against "cruel or unusual treatment or punishment." Any of these rights might have general or specific application in the mental health setting.

Section 15 of the *Charter* prohibits laws that discriminate, including on the basis of "mental disability":

> 15(1) Every individual is equal before and under the law and has the right to the equal protection and equal benefit of the law without discrimination and, in particular, without discrimination based on race, national or ethnic origin, colour, religion, sex, age or mental or physical disability.

To the extent a law establishes a unique regime for dealing with health care for persons with mental illness, it could be vulnerable to challenge under section 15.

Charter rights are not understood to be absolutes. All are subject to section 1 of the *Charter*, which allows them to be balanced against the interests of the larger community:

> 1. The *Canadian Charter of Rights and Freedoms* guarantees the rights and freedoms set out in it subject to such reasonable limits

prescribed by law as can be demonstrably justified in a free and democratic society.

What impact has the *Charter* had on Canada's mental health laws? To date, the impact is not as great as some had hoped, and others feared. The number of *Charter* challenges have been surprisingly few, and fewer still have succeeded. No *Charter* cases concerning provincial mental health laws have gone to the Supreme Court of Canada, so there have been no judicial statements with national application. The most significant *Charter* case to date is *Fleming v. Reid*[3] in Ontario, which effectively established the patient's right to refuse psychiatric treatment in that province. Otherwise, Canadian courts have generally deferred to choices made by the legislatures in mental health matters. Still, the *Charter* is important to the overall context in this area. It serves as a backstop, or a floor of protection for individual rights. Any significant development in mental health legislation must take the *Charter* into consideration.

(b) The Historical and Social Context

Laws do not exist in a vacuum. They embody the values of the society they are intended to serve. In few areas is this truism more apt than in mental health. The history of Canadian mental health law reflects many issues of value and external influences, including social attitudes to persons with mental illness, developments in research and clinical practice, and fluctuating levels of public resources committed to health care services.

For a long period extending through the 1950s, Canada's laws dealing with mental health were largely concerned with facilitating the placement of persons with mental illness and other mental disabilities in large institutional facilities, for indefinite periods of time. This started to change in the 1960s. A reaction against discovered neglect and abuse of institutionalised populations and a growing consciousness of civil rights issues generally, contributed to the adopting of legal protections of the rights of persons with mental disabilities. These protections contributed to the move away from large institutional facilities to community living, which itself coincided with the arrival of new anti-psychotic medications.

Throughout this period and up to the present day, the question of the appropriate balance between compulsion and individual rights in the mental health system has been controversial. While many views have been influential, two opposed perspectives have predominated. They will be termed here the "patients' rights" and the "human needs"[4] positions. Both positions take a critical stance with respect to contemporary mental health laws, but for different reasons.

Proponents of a patients' rights approach (who comprise former involuntary patients, civil libertarians, and others) question the compulsory features of the law, believing that these should be minimized, if not eliminated. They hold that legal coercion stigmatizes persons with mental illness, and contributes to their dis-empowerment within the system, and society at large. They reject as paternalistic the involuntary committal of persons for anything other than demonstrated dangerousness to third parties, as well as the imposition of treatment over a patient's competent refusal.

Proponents of the human needs' approach (comprised largely of family members of persons with serious mental illness, and much of the psychiatric community) emphasize the need for law that facilitates the treatment of persons with serious mental illness. They oppose legal standards that limit involuntary hospitalization to situations involving imminent physical danger, and obstruct or delay treatment for persons whose stated refusal of treatment is, in their view, merely a symptom of their illness. Human needs' proponents hold that serious mental illness renders its sufferers unable to exercise meaningful liberty, while laws compelling them to receive care and treatment are a needed tool for restoring that liberty.

These thumbnail sketches no doubt do injustice to both positions. For one thing, they obscure the common ground they share (by most people who take a serious interest in mental health issues in Canada): the desire to improve the lives of persons with mental illness, to advocate for compassionate social responses, and to greatly enhance social and medical services available in the community. Nevertheless, it is important to recognize the heated political debate which surrounds discussions of the role of mental health law.

The debate is relevant to recent developments in mental health law. It could be argued that a high water mark for the patients' rights approach was reached in the early 1990s. In 1987, the Uniform Law Conference of Canada, an intergovernmental body that drafts model statutes in areas of common interest to all provinces, adopted a Uniform Mental Health Act.[5] The draft Act incorporated significant rights protections. In 1991, judicial decisions were rendered in two successful *Charter* challenges to mental health legislation.[6]

In the latter part of the 1990s, things changed. Concerns over untreated mental illness in the community received greater attention in media and public discussion. Human needs proponents attacked what many called the "revolving door syndrome" in mental health care: persons with mental illness being involuntarily committed to hospital just long enough to be stabilized on medications, being discharged back into the community, ceasing to take prescribed medications, and deteriorating to a point where they again required hospitalization. They pointed to strict committal criteria in mental health laws as a contributing factor. Many commentators attributed a significant part of the homelessness problem in Canada's cities to the revolving door phenomenon.

This perspective has achieved success in recent reforms to several provincial statutes. In B.C. in 1998, a reform package relaxed committal criteria, and made predictions of treatment non-compliance a consideration in maintaining a patient's involuntary status.[7] In Ontario, a more comprehensive set of legislative amendments followed in the wake of a highly publicised act of violence. In 1995, Brian Smith, a popular Ottawa sports broadcaster, was shot and killed outside the television station where he worked. His assailant was an individual with chronic paranoid schizophrenia who had been hospitalised on several occasions, but was then living in the community and untreated. The Ontario government responded by enacting *Brian's Law* in late 2000.[8] It too relaxed committal criteria. A central feature of the legislation is the "community treatment order" (CTO), a measure intended to compel treatment compliance by persons living in the community. Saskatchewan, the only other province to do so, had adopted a CTO scheme in 1996.

Whether these amendments reflect a new direction in Canadian mental health is not yet clear. They do mean, however, that the diversity in provincial mental health laws is likely as great as it has been in many years. This may allow in coming years for a useful comparison of the differing approaches. For the purposes of this chapter, it somewhat complicates things. In the sections which follow, the intention is to discuss both what is common to mental health law across the country, and what distinguishes some provincial approaches from others.

2. INVOLUNTARY COMMITTAL

(a) Voluntary Status

The majority of in-patients in Canadian mental health hospital facilities are there voluntarily. As such, they have the same rights in law as anyone receiving in-patient medical services in a non-psychiatric facility. Most provincial mental health statutes make reference to a discretionary authority in facility directors to admit patients on a voluntary basis, considering such factors as whether the facility offers therapeutic programs appropriate to the particular diagnosis. This makes it clear that individuals do not have a right to be admitted on request. Voluntary patients in a mental health facility have the right to discharge themselves at any time. Manitoba and Prince Edward Island, however, provide that clinical staff may detain a voluntary patient seeking to be discharged for the purpose of permitting a physician to assess the patient for committal. Without express authority of this kind, the detaining of a voluntary patient who wishes to leave hospital would constitute false imprisonment.

(b) Involuntary Committal: Procedural Aspects

The legal effect of involuntary committal is that the committed individual can be physically prevented from leaving hospital premises. This is authority for secure or locked wards that prevent egress. It may serve as authority for other limited forms of restraint intended for the same purpose. Involuntary status also serves as authority for issuing a warrant to apprehend and return a patient who has "eloped" from hospital. Nevertheless, the fact that a person is involuntarily committed does not mean that they must at all times reside in secure premises. See, for example, the discussion of "leaves of absence" in part 4, "Community Treatment", p. 286.

Civil committal has substantive and procedural aspects. The former refer to the substantive criteria for committal, i.e., the facts and findings which the law requires to be present in order to hospitalize an individual on an involuntary basis. Procedure sets out the steps which must be taken to effect committal, or to bring it to an end.

Committal procedure is similar in all provinces. It has three principal stages:

(1) apprehension for purposes of assessment;
(2) involuntary committal;
(3) tribunal review of committal initiated by the patient.

(i) *Apprehension for Purpose of Assessment*

Every province provides that a single physician may complete a certificate authorizing short-term involuntary hospitalization for mental examination and assessment purposes. The physician must state an opinion that the person's condition satisfies the criteria for committal (see below). The opinion must be based on observation of the individual, not merely reports given to the physician by other persons. This initial certificate serves as authority to apprehend and detain the individual in a hospital setting for a period set out in the statute, generally between 48 hours and one week.

Police officers have authority to apprehend an individual and bring them to an appropriate facility for assessment, without first obtaining a physician's certificate. Generally, this authority requires that officers form a reasonable belief that the person is mentally disordered and poses a danger to self or others, based either on direct observation or on information provided by third parties.

Most provinces also provide for an application to court for an order to apprehend a person for examination and assessment, based on information showing that the individual is likely mentally disordered and a danger to self or others. This less frequently used recourse may be appropriate where police or medical personnel have experienced difficulty gaining access to the individual, or are reluctant to do so.

(ii) *Committal, or Involuntary Admission to Hospital*

With the exception of Quebec, every Canadian province provides for committal on the basis of certificates completed by two physicians who have assessed the individual as meeting substantive committal criteria, based on direct observation. Some provinces require that at least one of the certifying physicians be a psychiatrist. The certificate completed in the community authorizing apprehension for assessment can serve as one of the two certificates, so long as it has not expired.

The initial committal period is generally between two weeks and one month. Renewal certificates can be completed using the same committal criteria, in order to extend involuntary status for additional and increasing periods (e.g., in B.C., one month, three months, and every six months thereafter). In Saskatchewan, renewals must be completed every 21 days — any longer period of detention must be made by court order. The time-limited nature of certification, and the need for renewal certificates, ensure that every patient's case will be periodically assessed. If at any point during a committal period a patient's condition improves to the point of no longer meeting the committal criteria, this should result in discharge, or in changing involuntary status to voluntary.

In Quebec, civil committal requires a court order.[9] In this respect, Quebec's mental health law is similar to that of most American states.

(iii) *Tribunal Review of Committal*

Every provincial statute allows for involuntary patients to apply for a review of their status by an independent administrative tribunal, generally once in every committal period. The tribunals are known by various names, including Review Panels in Alberta and B.C., the Administrative Tribunal of Quebec, and Ontario's Consent and Capacity Board. Depending on the province, the tribunal may or may not have decision-making power with respect to matters other than committal, such as authority for treatment decisions. In general, the review tribunals operate as three member panels, one of whom is a psychiatrist not affiliated with the detaining hospital. Principles of administrative law require panel hearings to be conducted in a procedurally fair and unbiased manner. Hearings are generally held in or near the hospital in question.

The review tribunals generally employ the statutory criteria for committal in deciding whether an individual should be discharged or continue to be involuntarily detained. In 1998, however, B.C. added a requirement that review panels take into consideration a patient's history of mental disorder, previous hospitalizations, and compliance with treatment plans following discharge. This is a clear signal from legislators that a prediction of treatment compliance is a relevant factor for review panels, even though this is not an explicit part of the initial committal criteria. An interesting argument might be made about whether a prediction of non-compliance in the community based on these prescribed factors could override a finding that an individual patient seeking discharge did not otherwise meet the criteria for committal.

The existence of tribunal review is an important due process right of patients. Because committal occurs on the basis of medical opinion alone (other than in Quebec), the recourse to tribunal review might well be found by Canadian courts to be required as a matter of fundamental justice under section 7 of the *Charter*. Judicial review or appeal from a tribunal decision is available to the patient, and to the hospital or the attending psychiatrists.

Involuntary patients may apply for *habeas corpus* before a superior court, as an alternative means of challenging their detention. This is a rarely pursued recourse given the availability of tribunal review, and the expense and formality of court proceedings.

(c) Involuntary Hospitalization: Substantive Committal Criteria

Canada's provincial mental health statutes all employ substantive committal criteria which combine at least these two features:

(1) the presence of a mental disorder, causing

(2) a risk of harm to self or to others — what will be termed here the "harm criteria."

These requirements ensure that neither every person diagnosed with a mental disorder, nor every person believed to be dangerous, is committable under mental health laws. Only persons exhibiting harmful behaviour as a consequence of mental disorder may be committed. There is a surprising degree of variation among provinces in the terms used to describe the requisite mental disorder, and degree of harm for committal.

(i) *Existence of Mental Disorder*

Several provinces use as a basis the somewhat detailed functional definition of "mental disorder" drafted for the Uniform Mental Health Act. The Alberta statute, for example, reads:

> "[M]ental disorder" means a substantial disorder of thought, mood, perception, orientation or memory that grossly impairs
>
> > (i) judgment,
> > (ii) behaviour,
> > (iii) capacity to recognize reality, or
> > (iv) ability to meet the ordinary demands of life.

Ontario, however, simply uses the term "mental disorder", defined as "any disease or disability of the mind."

Each of the definitions captures the major mental illnesses of schizophrenia and serious mood disorders, which comprise the great preponderance of diagnosed conditions among committed patients across Canada. With B.C.'s removing "mental retarded" from its definition of "person with a mental disorder" in 1998, no province expressly lists intellectual disability as a basis for committal. Several jurisdictions, in fact, expressly exclude intellectual disability from committal. Prince Edward Island uniquely cites mental disorder resulting from alcohol or drug abuse in its committal criteria.

One issue is whether a particular definition requires that a certifiable mental disorder be treatable. If one justification for the compulsory features of mental health law is that society has an obligation to treat individuals whose illness prevents them from otherwise obtaining treatment, it might be thought that only persons who have disorders amenable to psychiatric treatment should be subject to detention. The B.C. statute does in fact make treatablity a requirement for committal:

> "[P]erson with a mental disorder" means a person who has a disorder of the mind that requires treatment and seriously impairs the ability
>
> > (a) to react appropriately to the person's environment, or
> > (b) to associate with others.

"Treatment" is then defined as "safe and effective psychiatric treatment."[10] The meaning of the latter term is clearly subject to evolution in medical knowledge. Courts and tribunals called on to interpret such phrases can be expected to rely heavily on expert opinion concerning the state of such knowledge. A requirement of treatability suggests that a mental condition for which no known treatment is available cannot serve as the basis for civil committal. Arguably, personality disorder of the nature of sociopathy falls in this category. Notoriously difficult to treat, and associated by many in the psychiatric community with disruptive conduct harmful to a therapeutic environment, the B.C. definition may serve to exclude this group from the civil system.

Acting under Ontario's broad definition of "mental disorder" authorities have effected the civil committal of a paedophile nearing the end of his criminal sentence, on the basis that he continued to pose a danger to the community.[11] Persons committed for such disorders as anti-social personality or paedophilia will often be competent to refuse treatment, potentially raising a host of difficult issues (see part 3, "Consent to Treatment", p. 278).

Most provinces include in committal criteria a statement that the individual in question cannot be appropriately admitted or treated on a voluntary basis. Such a statement serves to ensure that committal will only be used in the last resort, when a person who otherwise meets committal criteria refuses admission or is incapable of consenting to a voluntary admission.

Saskatchewan, alone among Canadian jurisdictions, includes in its committal criteria the requirement that the individual be incapable of giving or withholding consent to treatment.[12] This is an interesting technique for avoiding dilemmas involving the obtaining of treatment consent from competent patients. This issue is discussed in part 3, p. 278. The Saskatchewan approach is a different means of ensuring that involuntary committal is closely connected to active treatment of mental disorder.

(ii) Harm criteria

(A) The Issue

The appropriate choice of statutory "harm criteria" has long been a source of controversy. What is not controversial is that every Canadian jurisdiction makes imminent, serious bodily harm, whether directed by the person with a mental disorder at self or at others, a basis for committal. This certainly covers risks of non-trivial physical harm to third parties, and of suicidal and serious self-mutilating behaviour. This level of harm will be called the "dangerousness" standard.

Most of the debate concerns how far the law should depart from the dangerousness standard in protecting persons with a mental disorder from harming themselves. This issue largely concerns two questions:

(a) should protection extend beyond serious *physical* harm?
(b) should protection extend to harm that is not imminent, but is likely to occur if no intervention occurs in the meantime?

The latter question is especially pertinent to the "revolving door" issue: that is, should persons who do not pose an imminent danger to themselves when taking medications under a treatment plan become committable when they cease complying with that plan?

(B)   The *Charter of Rights and Freedoms*

No Canadian court has yet found that the dangerousness standard is the minimum basis for involuntary committal required by the Constitution.[13]

To date, only two significant *Charter* cases have dealt with harm criteria. In *Thwaites*,[14] the Manitoba Court of Appeal struck down statutory criteria that stated a person could be certified when, in the opinion of a physician, he or she "should be confined as a patient at a psychiatric facility." The Court ruled that this breached the prohibition on arbitrary detention in section 9 of the *Charter* because it did not establish objective criteria related to mental condition and risk of harm. Justice Philp stated: "I do not think it can be said that, in the absence of a 'dangerousness' or like standard, the provisions impair as little as possible the right of a person 'not to be arbitrarily detained.'"[15] The Manitoba Legislature then amended the statute to include the standard of a "likelihood of serious harm." This standard was subsequently upheld.[16]

The committal criteria in B.C.'s *Mental Health Act* were challenged in 1993 in *McCorkell v. Riverview Hospital*.[17] The petitioner argued that the statute violated sections 7 and 9 of the *Charter* by authorizing committal where a person "requires care, supervision and control in a Provincial mental health facility for his own protection or for the protection of others." He argued that only criteria based strictly on dangerousness could be justified under the *Charter* as the standard for restricting an individual's liberty. Justice Donald of the B.C. Supreme Court rejected this argument. In particular, he rejected the plaintiff's attempt to draw an analogy between criminal law, in which the state's power to restrict liberty is circumscribed by extensive substantive and procedural protections for accused persons, and mental health law:

> Statutes dealing with criminal law are penal in nature; incarceration is a punishment of culpable individuals and serves the objectives of public safety and denunciation of crime. The Mental Health Act involuntarily detains people only for the purpose of treatment; the punitive element is wholly absent.[18]

Citing the Manitoba cases, Justice Donald continued:

In the Manitoba legislation, "serious harm" is not qualified; it can include harms that relate to the social, family, vocational or financial life of the patient as well as to the patient's physical condition. The operative word in the British Columbia act is 'protection" which necessarily involves the notion of harm.... The Manitoba cases dealt initially with a statute that had no criteria at all, then with an amended statute with criteria remarkably like British Columbia's act which passed a Charter examination.[19]

The decisions in *Thwaites* and *McCorkell* only have binding force in Manitoba and B.C., respectively. Taken together, and in the absence of other decisions, they describe the following situation: while mental health statutes must set out objective harm criteria for committal, and not leave this as a mere matter of medical judgment, considerable leeway exists with respect to the level of harm which will justify committal.

(C) Harm Criteria in Provincial Statutes

Where a particular jurisdiction lies along the spectrum of harm criteria involves both the wording used in the mental health statute, and judicial interpretation of that wording. Courts have varied considerably in their interpretations. As a general rule, it appears that a dangerousness standard is not presently employed by any province.

Several jurisdictions use statutory criteria that specify that the requisite harm must be physical in nature. Prior to 2000, Ontario's statute used these criteria:[20]

[that the person] is suffering from a mental disorder of a nature or quality that likely will result in

(d) serious bodily harm to that person,
(e) serious bodily harm to another person, or
(f) imminent and serious bodily impairment of that person.

While this might suggest a dangerousness standard, this wording was interpreted broadly to support the continued committal of a patient because, if released, she would return to poor eating habits that might result in a stroke.[21] This would not seem to fit the usual understanding of "imminent" physical impairment. In *Brian's Law*, Ontario removed the word "imminent" from this provision.

Several provincial statutes, including Quebec's, do not specify bodily or physical harm, but use the words "danger" or "dangerous." The Alberta statute, for instance, states that a physician may certify a person with a mental disorder who is "in a condition presenting or likely to present a danger to the person or others." In 1985, a court ruled that this phrase, minus the words "or likely to present", required that the harm be almost immediate, and rejected the idea that a deterioration in condition to a point of dangerousness that might take several weeks was sufficient for committal.[22] The legislature then inserted the phrase cited. More recent Alberta decisions suggest that expected consequences of a patient's ceasing to take medications may be a sufficient basis for a finding of danger.[23]

Several provinces, including Manitoba, Saskatchewan, B.C. and Ontario, have recently adopted a significantly lower threshold than dangerousness for committal. The standard refers to "substantial mental or physical deterioration." This clearly permits intervention at earlier stages of illness to prevent deterioration of the individual's health and well-being.

Section 20(1.1) of the Ontario statute establishes an alternative basis for committal to the "serious bodily harm" standard:

> 20(1.1) The attending physician shall complete a certificate of involuntary admission or a certificate of renewal if, after examining the patient, he or she is of the opinion that the patient,
>
>   (a) has previously received treatment for mental disorder of an ongoing or recurring nature that, when not treated, is of a nature or quality that likely will result in serious bodily harm to the person or to another person or substantial mental or physical deterioration of the person or serious physical impairment of the person;
>
>   (b) has shown clinical improvement as a result of the treatment;
>
>   (c) is suffering from the same mental disorder as the one for which he or she previously received treatment or from a mental disorder that is similar to the previous one;
>
>   (d) given the person's history of mental disorder and current mental or physical condition, is likely to cause serious bodily harm to himself or herself or to another person or is likely to suffer substantial mental or physical deterioration or serious physical impairment;
>
>   (e) has been found incapable, within the meaning of the Health Care Consent Act, 1996, of consenting to his or her treatment in a psychiatric facility and the consent of his or her substitute decision-maker has been obtained

Section 20(1.1) creates a class of persons subject to civil commitment that might be termed the "treatable, chronically mentally ill." For members of this class, the history of their mental disorder, and of its treatment, serves as a significant predictor of harm. This largely replaces the need for the observation of present harmful behaviour.

Committal under this "past history" provision turns on the individual's having already been found incapable of consenting to psychiatric treatment, and the consent of his or her substitute decision maker having been obtained. This seems intended to avoid the problem of a competent refusal of treatment, discussed in part 3 below.

3. CONSENT TO TREATMENT

Can involuntarily committed patients refuse psychiatric treatment? This is one of the most vexed issues in mental health law. Patients' rights advocates argue that the right to refuse treatment should be available to persons with mental illness on the same basis as for all consumers of health care. Not to recognize the right to refuse in the psychiatric setting is, they maintain, to discriminate on the basis of disability, contrary to section 15 of the *Charter of Rights and Freedoms.*

For advocates of a human needs approach, recognizing a right of involuntary patients to refuse psychiatric treatment imposes a barrier to providing treatment needed to restore patients to health and autonomy. Moreover, it can result in the situation of having persons detained in hospital due to illness, without being able to be able to be treated — in effect, turning a psychiatric facility into a jail.

In Canada, there is no single answer to the question of whether involuntary patients have a right to refuse treatment. In fact, there are at least four distinct approaches taken by Canadian provinces. Only one of these approaches, that employed in Ontario, recognizes a right to refuse treatment for involuntary patients that corresponds to the common law right to refuse medical treatment. This resulted from a decision of Ontario's highest court in *Fleming v. Reid.* This decision applies only to Ontario law, and no similar challenges have yet come forward in other provinces. To understand the Ontario approach, and the contrasting positions of other provinces, it seems helpful to begin with a review of the general law of consent to treatment.

(a) General Principles Governing Consent to Treatment

The following established principles of Canadian law dealing with consent to treatment provide a context for understanding differing statutory approaches to the issue of consent to psychiatric treatment. These principles are discussed in significantly greater detail in other chapters.

1. Every individual has the right to be free from interference with his or her physical integrity. Any such interference, including medical treatment, is unlawful unless the individual has consented to it.
2. The right to consent to medical treatment includes the right to refuse treatment. An individual has the right to refuse treatment

for subjective reasons of her own choosing, irrespective of what others might view as being in her best interests, even to the point of self-harm or death.

3.   The right to consent to or refuse treatment, is premised on having the mental capacity, or competence, to give a valid consent. Competence to consent to medical treatment means the ability to understand the nature and consequences of the proposed treatment, and the consequences of not receiving the treatment. This implies that the individual needs to have some understanding of their own medical condition.

4.   If a person is incompetent to make treatment choices, then health professionals may provide treatment without consent in emergency circumstances only. An emergency is understood as involving an urgent risk to life or of serious bodily harm. Few situations involving psychiatric treatment would qualify as an emergency in this sense.

5.   In the absence of an emergency, treatment can be provided to an incompetent person only if lawfully authorized. For this purpose, provincial statutes establish rules for recognizing a substitute decision-maker (SDM) for an incompetent individual.

With respect to the last point, significant legislative reform has taken place in Canada in recent years. Several provinces have overhauled their laws dealing with adult guardianship and substitute decision-making in health care. The reforms have addressed a number of gaps and difficulties in this area. Prior to statutory reform, it was often unclear who, if anyone, had lawful authority to consent to medical treatment for an incompetent individual, in the absence of a court order. Court orders were rarely obtained. Physicians faced uncomfortable choices between not treating, obtaining an informal consent from a patient's spouse or near relative, or proceeding to treat without authority — all done in the hope the issue of consent would never come under close scrutiny.

Reform statutes have, among other things, achieved the following: established priority lists of family members, in descending order of relationship to the individual, who can assume the SDM role without the need to go to court; imposed restrictions on health care decision-making by SDMs, requiring them to obtain judicial approval for particularly invasive treatments; and identified the criteria on which SDMs should base treatment decisions.[24]

One important reform goal has been to enhance the opportunities for competent adults to pre-plan for future periods of incompetence. Several provinces now give legal recognition to documents such as personal directives and representation agreements. These instruments authorize individuals to set out binding wishes with respect to treatment decisions in periods of incompetence. For much the same reason, the reform statutes generally require SDMs to base their decisions on any known previously expressed competent wishes of the now incompetent individual.

(b) Consent to Psychiatric Treatment

Two issues from the foregoing discussion have particular relevance to the area of mental health. The first is the relationship between treatment competence and the right to refuse medical treatment. Only persons who are competent can exercise the right. Many persons who meet the criteria for involuntary admission to a psychiatric facility will, as a result of mental disorder, lack treatment competence.

Much of the debate over the consent issue is really a disagreement over whether there is ever such a thing as a *competent* refusal by an involuntary patient. Many people who oppose recognition of a right to refuse treatment believe that major mental illness makes it impossible for an individual to understand that he or she is ill and in need of treatment. In their view, only a naive or shallow understanding of mental illness would suggest otherwise.

Canadian law, however, rejects global assumptions about decision-making competence. It views competence as a mutable quality that must be assessed with respect to the specific activity in question. A person may be incompetent for one purpose, such as making a will, but competent with respect to another, such as health care. As a consequence, and as a matter of principle, competence to consent to treatment must be assessed independently from the issue of whether the individual otherwise meets statutory criteria for involuntary status. Moreover, most provincial health care consent statutes have confirmed the common law presumption of competence.

The second issue worth emphasizing is that a competent refusal of medical treatment may be expressed in two ways: (1) a competent person may refuse a course of treatment at the time it is proposed; or (2) a person may express a wish while competent to refuse treatment, should they later become incompetent. Given the episodic nature of much mental illness, the availability of legal techniques for pre-planning treatment choices has particular significance.

The key question to ask is whether a particular mental health statute provides for overriding an involuntary patient's *competent refusal* of proposed psychiatric treatment, in that individual's best interests. Canadian jurisdictions employ four principal responses to this question:

(1) A right to refuse treatment (Ontario)

(2) No right to refuse treatment (B.C., Newfoundland)

(3) A right to refuse, subject to a "best interests" override (Alberta, Manitoba)

(4) Excluding treatment competent individuals from committal (Saskatchewan)

(i) *Ontario: Recognition of a Right to Refuse Treatment*

Fleming v. Reid involved previously expressed treatment wishes. The Ontario statute at that time required that consent to treat an incompetent involuntary patient be obtained from his or her SDM. The statute obliged the SDM to act on treatment wishes of the person expressed at a time of competence.

In *Fleming*, the patient had stated, while competent, his wish to refuse the medications which his attending psychiatrist later proposed. The SDM, in this instance the province's Public Trustee, acting under statutory obligation, refused to give its consent. The hospital applied to the Review Board to override the refusal, pursuant to a provision in the *Mental Health Act* that obliged the Board to make a treatment decision based on the patient's best interests. The Ontario Court of Appeal struck this provision down as a violation of "security of the person" in section 7 of the *Charter*. The Court found that the statute denied the patient's right to refuse treatment by making it subject to a best interests test. Moreover, it did so without any hearing into whether the patient's competent wishes should be honoured, irrespective of what might be thought to be in his best interests:

> The right to personal security is guaranteed as fundamental in our society. Manifestly, it should not be infringed any more than is clearly necessary. In my view, although the right to be free from non-consensual psychiatric treatment is not an absolute one, the state has not demonstrated any compelling reason for entirely eliminating this right, without any hearing or review, in order to further the best interests of involuntary incompetent patients in contravention of their competent wishes. To completely strip these patients of the freedom to determine for themselves what shall be done with their bodies cannot be considered a minimal impairment of their Charter right. Safeguards can obviously be formulated to balance their wishes against their needs and ensure that their security of the person will not be infringed any more than is necessary. Recognizing the important objective of state intervention for the benefit of mentally disabled patients, nonetheless, the overriding of a fundamental constitutional right by the means chosen in this Act to attain the objective cannot be justified under s. 1 of the Charter.[25]

While this passage implies that a scheme which balanced a patient's competent refusal against their "needs" or best interests might be constitutional, other statements by the Court were less ambiguous about the status of the right to refuse. This included a statement that a hearing into a previously expressed refusal of treatment should be limited largely to whether the previously expressed wishes still pertained to the treatment decision at hand:

> [T]here may be questions as to the clarity or currency of the wishes, their applicability to the patient's present circumstances, and whether they have been revoked or revised by subsequent wishes or a subsequently accepted treatment program. The resolution of questions of this nature is patently a matter for legislative action. But, in my respectful view, it is incumbent on the legislature to bear in mind that, as a general proposition, psychiatric patients are entitled to make competent decisions and exercise their right to self-determination in accordance with their own standards and values and not necessarily in the manner others may believe to be in the patients' best interests.[26]

Ontario law now incorporates the *Fleming* principles.[27] The Consent and Capacity Board has no power to override a competent treatment refusal by an involuntary patient. The following case study illustrates how these principles are being applied.

CASE STUDY: *STARSON v. SWAYZE*[28]

> Starson had been found not criminally responsible by reason of mental disorder with respect to charges of uttering death threats, and was detained in a provincial mental health facility pursuant to an order made under the *Criminal Code of Canada*. (see Forensic Psychiatry issues, part 6 below). He refused psychiatric treatment proposed by his attending psychiatrists. They applied to the Consent and Capacity Board for an order that Starson was incapable of making treatment decisions. The Board granted the order. The Ontario Superior Court allowed Starson's appeal of the Board's decision. The Ontario Court of Appeal upheld the Superior Court decision. Justice Malloy of the Superior Court found Starson to be "exceptionally intelligent", and an expert in physics. Although he lacked formal academic credentials, he maintained contact with leading physicists around the world, and had co-authored an article with one of them. He had been hospitalized for bipolar affective disorder several times in the preceding 15 years. The Court found that Starson understood the information relevant to making a decision about his treatment, including the likely consequences

of refusing treatment — i.e, indefinite detention. Although he did not agree with the psychiatrists that he had a mental illness, Starson knew he had mental "problems." Starson correctly testified that none of the medications previously prescribed for him had improved his condition, and he objected to their side-effects. In particular, he said that the medications made it impossible for him to work on issues in physics, his one great passion. The Board had ruled on what it viewed as being in Starson's best interests, but that was an improper basis for its decision. The question in law was whether Starson was competent to make the decision to refuse treatment, and the evidence showed he was:

"He understands the information relevant to that decision and its reasonably foreseeable consequences. He has made a decision that may cost him his freedom and accelerate his illness. Many would agree with the Board that it is a decision that is against his best interests. But for Professor Starson, it is a rational decision, and not one that reflects a lack of capacity. And therefore it is a decision that the statute and s. 7 of the Canadian Charter of Rights and Freedoms permit him to make."[29]

[Appeal to the Supreme Court of Canada was heard on January 15, 2003, and judgment reserved.]

Applications may be made to Ontario's Consent and Capacity Board to challenge a patient's competence, or whether a previously-expressed refusal remains applicable to current circumstances. In *Conway v. Jacques*,[30] the Ontario Court of Appeal overturned a decision of the Board which was based on speculation about what the patient would have chosen, had he anticipated changed circumstances concerning newly available medications. The Court stressed that once a previously expressed competent wish no longer applies, the appropriate test for the Board to apply is what is in the patient's best interests. The Court lamented that several years had passed while the case moved through the Board and the judicial system, during which the patient remained untreated.

(ii) *No Right to Refuse Treatment (British Columbia and Newfoundland)*

B.C. and Newfoundland stand at the opposite end of the spectrum from Ontario on the issue of consent. Both provinces maintain the approach that was long used in Canada: the directors of psychiatric facilities may authorize treatment for involuntarily committed patients without obtaining consent. Section 31 of the B.C. statute states that "treatment authorized by the director is deemed to be given with the consent of the patient." Further, the *Health Care (Consent) Act,* which essentially codifies the common law on consent to treatment, is expressly stated not to apply to involuntary patients in psychiatric hospitals.

Under this model, there is no requirement to assess an involuntary patient's treatment competency, nor is there any role for an SDM to make treatment decisions on the patient's behalf. This does not mean, of course, that informal practices of assessing competence, respecting patients' treatment wishes, and working with family members cannot be employed.

The B.C. statute provides involuntary patients the right to request a second opinion on proposed treatment. On receiving the second opinion, the director "must consider" whether to make changes in the psychiatric treatment authorized for the patient, but need not do so.

This approach ensures that treatment can be provided to involuntary patients with a minimum of procedural delay. Given that it involves the clearest denial of a right to refuse treatment, it might seem the most vulnerable to *Charter* challenge on *Fleming*-like grounds. The decision in *McCorkell* dealing with committal criteria, which emphasized the therapeutic purposes of mental health law, may signal a different judicial view in B.C.

(iii) *Right to Refuse, Subject to "Best Interests" Override (Alberta, Manitoba)*

This approach recognizes the distinction between treatment competence and incompetence, as well as the right of a competent patient to state a refusal of proposed treatment. However, the hospital board or attending physician may apply to the Review Panel for a review of the refusal. The Review Panel must act in what it believes to be the patient's best interests, and on that basis may override the refusal and order that the proposed treatment be administered. This is quite similar to the pre-*Fleming* system in Ontario.

This model involves significantly greater procedural rights for an involuntary patient around treatment decisions than is the case in B.C. and Newfoundland and Labrador. Nevertheless, the statute provides for overriding a competent refusal in the patient's best interests. For this reason, this model is also potentially vulnerable to a *Charter* challenge.

(iv) *Saskatchewan*

As earlier stated, Saskatchewan includes treatment incompetence in its substantive criteria for involuntary hospitalization. This effectively avoids the consent to treatment dilemma. That is, any person who is treatment competent cannot be involuntarily hospitalized. The question of respecting or overriding a competent refusal does not arise. This model would seem to satisfy any *Charter* concerns. One possible disadvantage, and perhaps the reason why other jurisdictions have not yet followed Saskatchewan, is that it means certain persons with mental illness who present a danger to others will not be committable. Only should they become incompetent, or commit an offence which brings them under the *Criminal Code*, will it be possible to detain them.

(c) Non-Psychiatric and Exceptional Treatments

Statutory provisions that authorize treatment of involuntary patients without consent apply to treatment directed at mental disorder or its symptoms. Medical treatment for unrelated physiological matters, such as dental surgery, must be provided to an involuntary patient on the same basis as to any other person: with the patient's consent, or if incompetent, by consent of an SDM or in an emergency. Should this limit not be expressly stated in the statute, it should follow from the fact that both detention and nonconsensual treatment are premised on the existence of mental disorder and the need to facilitate its treatment.

Special prohibitions or protections may exist with respect to treatments that are more invasive or controversial than standard psychiatric therapy. These may prevent SDMs from consenting on a patient's behalf, or impose additional obligations in the authorizing process. For example, Alberta prohibits "psychosurgery" unless both the patient and the review panel agree to it.[31] Ontario's *Health Care Consent Act* excludes medical procedures done for research or tissue transplant purposes, and non-therapeutic sterilization, from its substitute decision-making provisions. Electro-convulsive therapy ("ECT") is not singled out in provincial statutes for particular attention, but hospital and Ministry policy often imposes additional precautions, such as obtaining a second opinion.

(d) "Ulysses Agreements"

The idea of pre-planning one's treatment choices for periods of future incompetence was discussed above with respect to its use as a way of refusing unwanted treatment. The possibility also exists that an individual could use pre-planning tools to facilitate treatment at a future time when the individual is no longer competent but is objecting to treatment. Referred to as a "Ulysses Agreement", this could permit a person who knows she is prone to experience episodes of mental illness to "contract" to enter a psychiatric hospital facility, or to receive treatment during such an episode, even if she was then objecting to admission or treatment.

Despite considerable discussion about Ulysses agreements, it is not at all clear that there is much demand to use them. For one thing, there would be few circumstances in which such a document could accomplish what would not be achievable under a mental health statute. Second, questions about whether circumstances have changed since the plan was drawn up would be particularly serious where a person is now objecting to medical interventions.

4. COMMUNITY TREATMENT OPTIONS

Saskatchewan and Ontario have incorporated "community treatment orders" (CTOs) into their mental health statutes.[32] Based on models in several U.S. states, where it is commonly referred to as "outpatient committal", the CTO is intended to impose a duty to comply with psychiatric treatment on mentally ill individuals living in the community. The idea is to break the connection between involuntary hospitalization and non-consensual psychiatric treatment, and by addressing the problem of treatment non-compliance to keep persons healthy and in the community.

This section provides an overview of how the Ontario CTO provisions operate, and notes certain ways in which the Saskatchewan scheme differs. Questions about the potential effectiveness of CTOs will be briefly discussed. The section concludes by looking at leave of absence provisions, which have similar purposes to the CTO.

(a) Community Treatment Orders

The CTO scheme has its own substantive "committal" criteria. The statutory criteria in Ontario require that in order to issue a CTO: (1) the subject of the CTO must have previous involvement with the mental health system; (2) the subject must meet substantive criteria for mental disorder and risk of harm; and (3), it must be possible to put a "community treatment plan" in place for the subject.

The target group for CTOs is the "revolving door", or chronic client. In order to be subject to a CTO, a person must have been hospitalized on at least two occasions or for 30 days or more within the preceding three years. The legislation does not limit the previous hospitalizations to involuntary committals. Therefore, individuals who voluntarily admit themselves to psychiatric facilities may make themselves eligible for later CTO committal.

Second, the physician issuing the CTO must form the opinion, based on an examination of the individual, that he is at risk of *becoming* committable to hospital if he does not receive treatment in the community. That is, the individual must meet the statutory criteria for a psychiatric *assessment*; and the physician must form the opinion that "if the person does not receive continuing treatment or care and continuing supervision while living in the community, he or she is likely" to meet involuntary committal criteria.

Third, the CTO must include a "community treatment plan." The issuing physician has several responsibilities with respect to the plan. She must: develop the plan in consultation with the individual and any health practitioners intended to be involved in providing care in the community; ensure that the services set out in the plan are available in the community; and, assess the individual as being capable of complying with the treatment plan. Further, "the person or his or her substitute decision-maker [must consent] to the community treatment plan in accordance with the rules for consent under the Health Care Consent Act." Other provisions set out certain required elements of a community treatment plan.

The issuing physician has several additional obligations. She must ensure that the individual has consulted with a "rights adviser", and that copies of the CTO get to appropriate parties, including any health practitioners named in the plan. Further, the physician is made responsible for "general supervision" of the CTO.[33]

The CTO expires after six months, unless it is renewed. Express obligations are placed on the individual to comply with the community treatment plan, or on their SDM to make "best efforts" to obtain the individual's compliance. Should the individual fail to comply, or should he or the SDM withdraw consent to the community treatment plan, the physician may issue an "order for examination", which serves as authority to apprehend the person and bring him or her to the physician for an examination.

The Saskatchewan scheme differs from Ontario's in the following respects. A person is eligible for CTO committal if she has been hospitalized in a psychiatric facility on three occasions, or for a cumulative total of 60 days in the preceding two years. Only persons who are incompetent to consent to treatment can be the subject of a CTO, and no provision is made for a requirement to obtain the consent of a substitute decision-maker. This is consistent with the province's criteria for civil committal. However, some degree of mental competence must be present — like Ontario, Saskatchewan makes it a requirement that the issuing physician find the person able to comply with the CTO. A CTO must be "validated" by a second physician. It remains in effect for three months, and is renewable.

The differences between the two provinces on the consent issue are important, and clearly relate to the general issue of consent to mental health treatment in each jurisdiction. As noted, in Ontario, a competent refusal of treatment cannot be overridden. The implications for the CTO scheme in Ontario are problematic. In effect, any person who is treatment competent must "consent to be ordered" to comply with a treatment plan. This suggests that the CTO is not an "order" in the usual legal sense, and has limited compulsory force.

It might be argued that a consensual CTO is a form of contract whereby an individual binds himself to follow a certain course of conduct, with sanctions or penalties should he fail to do so. Consent to health care is not, however, conceived as creating a contractual relationship. Consent to treatment can be freely withdrawn at any point prior to the treatment's actually being provided. The Ontario legislation expressly allows for a treatment competent person to withdraw consent to a CTO at any time. It does, however, impose a statutory sanction on withdrawal of consent: on being notified of withdrawal from the CTO, the attending physician may issue a CTO warrant to apprehend the person for an examination.

(b) Discussion of CTO Effectiveness

The CTO experiment in Ontario and Saskatchewan is still in its early days. There are reasons, however, for questioning whether the CTO mechanism is capable of meeting the goals intended for it. This issue is distinct from the criticism of CTOs made by supporters of patients' rights, which go to extending compulsion into the community, and the stigma which they believe attaches to CTO subjects.

The problem is this: in what way will the CTO contribute to reducing the problem of non-compliance with psychiatric treatment by persons living in the community? The short answer is that it compels compliance. But is this true? As noted, in Ontario, the issuing of a CTO depends on consent. Beyond this, however, is the issue of sanction. Most "orders" with legal force are backed by sanctions for non-compliance. It is not at all clear that this is the case with CTOs.

One usual means of enforcing an order, the contempt power of the superior courts, is not available. CTOs are issued by physicians, not by courts, and neither province provides for a CTO to have the force of a court order. The penal nature of a contempt recourse would, in any event, seem wholly inappropriate to a therapeutic measure like the CTO.

It might be thought that non-compliance with a CTO would be sanctioned by involuntary committal to hospital. However, neither the Saskatchewan and Ontario statutes goes so far. Arguably, as a matter of principle, they could not go that far. Hospital committal depends on a person's meeting committal criteria related to mental condition and therapeutic need. It should not be available for failure to comply with an order, regardless of whether a person meets committal criteria. That could amount to arbitrary detention, contrary to the *Charter*.

The only sanction for non-compliance with a CTO is the physician's power to issue a form of warrant, authorizing police officers to convey the non-compliant person for purposes of a mental examination. This is not insignificant. A frequent complaint of family members of chronically mentally ill persons is the difficulty they encounter in obtaining help, including from police, to get their unwilling relative to a physician or to hospital when symptoms of acute illness appear. Nevertheless, it is questionable to what degree this authority changes the dynamics of community mental health treatment.

The success of CTOs may largely depend on their being part of a comprehensive plan that puts in place significant treatment resources, including ready contact with and support from health care professionals. Planning and support of this kind appears to be intended by the legislation. There is an irony here: the obligations taken on by the issuing physician and other professionals involved in the community treatment plan may be more important than any "obligation" to comply with the plan assumed by the client. Persons with mental illness often complain that it is difficult to obtain services in the community. The CTO provisions almost imply a "right to treatment" for CTO subjects that has not otherwise had a firm foundation in Canadian law. It is unlikely that the individual CTO client will be in a position to enforce this "right." Compliance with these obligations will largely be a matter of professional ethics and program management.

If CTO schemes work only to the degree the client is provided with comprehensive treatment and support services, it seems reasonable to ask whether the success is due more to the program than to the CTO itself. Would similar results be achieved for persons provided with those services irrespective of whether they were provided in conjunction with a CTO?[34]

(c) Leaves of Absence

A different means of maintaining a person on a treatment program in the community is a leave of absence from hospital for involuntary patients. Several provinces, including Manitoba and B.C., have enhanced statutory leave provisions to permit psychiatric facilities to gradually reintroduce involuntary patients into the community while remaining subject to committal and the authority of the facility. Leaves of absence are granted on conditions, often including compliance with a treatment plan. If a patient ceases to comply, or starts to decompensate, they can be brought back to hospital under the continuing involuntary status.

The leave of absence approach has advantages over the more complex CTO. The starting place is hospital and in-patient treatment, rather than an effort to enforce compliance on an individual living in the community who may not meet standard committal criteria.

One legal issue is whether, in some circumstances, a leave might be inconsistent with ongoing involuntary committal. The concern from a civil liberties perspective is that extended leaves of absence might too easily be used as a means of retaining control over individuals who, in fact, no longer meet the criteria for involuntary committal. To date, however, Canadian courts have not been receptive to this argument. In an Alberta case, a patient with an extensive history of self-mutilation argued that repeated leaves which only required him to spend weeknights in hospital were inconsistent with his meeting Alberta's dangerousness criteria for committal. The court disagreed, finding no presumptive inconsistency between a leave of absence and continued certification. The judge commented:[35]

> The granting of leaves of absence on a regular basis allows [the patient] a degree of freedom and human dignity, while at the same time decreasing the likelihood that he will harm himself.

A similar ruling was made in an Ontario case in which a patient argued that because he had received repeated leaves, even though the statute permitted only one leave, he should be declared discharged from involuntary status. The judge described leaves of absence as "a win-win situation", the benefits of which should not be lost by too technical an interpretation of the statute.[36]

5. TORT LIABILITY ISSUES

The general principles of medical malpractice and of negligence, discussed in detail elsewhere in this volume, apply in the mental health field. To reiterate, the required elements of an action in negligence are: the existence of a duty of care, the breach of the standard of care, and injury caused by the breach. The factual circumstances which may give rise to findings of liability for negligence are infinite. The key factor is that conduct which falls below the acceptable standard of care for the profession in question may give rise to liability. Standards of care evolve with professional knowledge and practice.

This section examines a few issues of potential negligence that tend to be specific to mental health. These relate to responsibility of clinicians for a patient's actions that cause injury to that person or to third parties. Tort law, in general, does not hold one person responsible for the actions of another. The difference here is that the harmful conduct results from illness, and is often beyond the wilful control of the patient. The clinician may incur liability for failing to protect a patient from self-harm, or a third party from the patient.

While potential liability lies in these areas, few cases in Canada have found health professionals and mental health facilities liable to patients, their families, or to third parties. A number of factors may explain this. Canada remains a significantly less litigious society than the United States. Canadian courts have also shown considerable deference to the clinical judgment of professionals, partly out of a recognition that mental health is a difficult area of practice, characterized by uncertain diagnosis and prediction. Moreover, courts have acknowledged the value of therapeutic approaches that impose lesser degrees of control over patients. Judges have expressed reluctance to make findings of liability that might cause clinicians to increase behavioural controls out of an overabundance of caution.

(a) Liability to Patients

Lawsuits have been brought in Canada against hospitals and individual physicians with respect to suicides or attempted suicides committed by patients. The actions have been brought by family members or, in the case of failed suicide attempts which resulted in injury, by patients themselves. Plaintiffs have claimed that physicians negligently failed to diagnose suicidal conditions, failed to commit suicidal patients to hospital, or otherwise failed to ensure patient safety. In 1973, the Supreme Court of Canada confirmed a trial court's finding of liability under Quebec's *Civil Code* against a hospital and psychiatrist with respect to a suicide.[37] However, in most subsequent cases, courts have found for the defendants.

CASE STUDY: *GANGER (GUARDIAN AD LITEM OF) v. ST. PAUL'S HOSPITAL*[38]

In this B.C. case, a person with suicidal ideation was voluntarily admitted to the open psychiatric ward of a general hospital. The attending psychiatrist testified that he would have committed the patient had the patient not agreed to remain in hospital. Three days later, on an unescorted trip to the hospital's cafeteria, the patient jumped from an upper floor window, sustaining catastrophic injuries. The patient sued the psychiatrist and the hospital. He alleged that the psychiatrist had been negligent in not appreciating the seriousness of the suicide risk, and in failing to commit him to a locked ward, or otherwise making sure he could not wander away without escort. Despite evidence from two psychiatric experts to the effect that the attending psychiatrist had breached the standard of care for emergency psychiatry, the trial judge dismissed the action. The Court of Appeal, by a 2-1 majority, upheld this decision. Justice Huddart stated:[39]

> In a case such as this it is important to distinguish an error in judgment from breach of a duty of care. All who are called upon to predict human behaviour recognize the near impossibility of doing so with any confidence. If an attempt at suicide may be said to establish an error in judgment on the part of anyone charged with assessing the risk of that very event who does not anticipate it, then errors in judgment are endemic in the assessment of the risk of suicide. The evidence is clear that an error in the assessment of the risk of an attempt at suicide is as likely as not. Even the best judgment of a skilled psychiatrist will frequently be wrong.

She cited with approval the following statement from a 1977 Ontario case:[40]

> It seems to me as well that, where a Court is called upon to analyze the judgment of a therapist who concluded that his patient was not suicidal, regard must be had to the undoubted advantage he enjoyed in his direct relationship with the patient at the time, over those who would attempt to second-guess him after the event.

Justice Huddart acknowledged that the crisis intervention method used on the hospital's open ward placed emphasis on patients' exercising decision-making responsibility, and that this approach involved a degree of risk, but concluded "[e]ven if it can be said that this practice is fraught with danger, I can think of no alternative that a reasonable person would utilize in order to avoid the risk of suicide while ensuring appropriate treatment for those suffering from depression who, overall, present a 5-15% risk of attempting suicide."[41]

(b) Liability to Third Parties: *Tarasoff* and the Duty to Warn

Are psychiatrists or other therapists liable for the failure to disclose threats made by a patient to harm another individual? This issue raises the conflict between the duty to maintain therapist-patient confidentiality and a duty to warn the threatened individuals.

The most famous case in this regard is the California Supreme Court decision in *Tarasoff v. Regents of University of California*.[42] In *Tarasoff*, a patient under the care of a psychologist confessed to the psychologist his intention of killing a particular young woman. The psychologist contacted the police. They questioned the patient, but concluded they were unable to detain him. Two months later, the patient killed the woman. The psychologist was found liable for failing to warn the murder victim or her family about the patient's stated intention. The Court recognized the value of maintaining patient confidentiality for encouraging candid communications by patients, but concluded that in the circumstances of the case, confidentiality should have given way to the need to protect the victim's safety.

The status of *Tarasoff* in U.S. law is unclear. Most commentators agree that it represents the high water mark in finding liability against a therapist for breach of a duty to warn third parties. Later case law has tended to limit the scope of *Tarasoff*. American courts have stressed that *Tarasoff* involved a specific threat concerning a specific individual. They have tended not to hold therapists liable for failing to diagnose patients as dangerous, or for not disclosing general threats of harm not directed at identifiable individuals.

The situation in Canada is also uncertain. To date, no physician or psychiatrist has been found liable for a failure to warn third parties of a threat of harm posed by a patient. Courts have, however, implied that the principle of *Tarasoff* would apply in similar circumstances. The most significant such statement comes from the Supreme Court of Canada in a 1997 case, *Smith v. Jones*.

CASE STUDY: *SMITH v. JONES*[43]

Mr. "Jones" (a pseudonym assigned by the courts) was accused of the aggravated sexual assault of a prostitute. Defence counsel referred Jones to Dr. Smith, a psychiatrist, for psychological examination. Counsel wanted Dr. Smith's opinion to assist in preparing Jones' case, and for possible submission to the court at the sentencing stage. Solicitor-client privilege therefore extended to the psychiatric examination and opinion. Aware that his communications with Dr. Smith were covered by solicitor-client privilege, Jones told him that the assault in question had been a "trial run" for the kidnapping and murder of prostitutes. He gave details of the planning he had undertaken to commit this and future offences. Dr. Smith diagnosed Jones as having multiple paraphilias, including sexual sadism and an anti-social personality disorder. He advised defence counsel that he considered Jones to be dangerous. Jones pled guilty. Prior to sentencing, Dr. Smith asked defence counsel if he was going to make the trial judge aware of his psychiatric opinion. On being told no, Dr. Smith proceeded to apply to court for an order permitting him to disclose the information in his possession.

The Supreme Court of Canada ruled that while solicitor-client privilege is a fundamental right in the Canadian justice system, it must give way, in limited circumstances, to the interests of public safety. Such circumstances exist where there is a clear risk to an identifiable person or group of persons, where the risk goes to serious bodily harm or death, and the danger is imminent. The Court found all three factors to be present in this case, and affirmed a lower court order authorizing Dr. Smith to disclose his opinion and the statements made to him by Jones to Crown counsel and the police. A minority of the Court thought that disclosure should be limited to the psychiatric opinion, and not extend to Jones' self-incriminating statements with respect to the offence with which he was charged.

The majority commented on the *Tarasoff* line of cases. They noted that in the U.S., *Tarasoff* has been limited to a "specific threat to a specific victim", but added:[44]

> There is much to commend these well-reasoned American decisions. Yet they lead me to believe that two observations should be made. First, it will not always be necessary to identify a specific individual as the victim. Rather it may be sufficient to engage the duty to warn if a class of victims, such as little girls under five living in a specific area, is clearly identified. Second, although Moore J. speaks of the patient "verbaliz[ing] his intentions", I believe it is more appropriate to speak of a person making known his or her intentions. While speech is perhaps the most common means of making intentions known, it is certainly not the only manner of indicating a clear intention. It could be accomplished soundlessly yet with brutal clarity by thrusting a knife through a photograph of the intended victim.

This would seem to be a clear endorsement of the idea that *Tarasoff*-liability is recognized in Canadian law.

Three points are worth noting about the decision in *Smith v. Jones*. First, the case concerns solicitor-client privilege, the strongest form of privilege recognized in Canadian law. It applies to disclosure of privileged communications by counsel, as well as any expert retained by counsel. By extension, the "public safety exception" recognized in *Smith* would almost certainly apply to the legally weaker physician-patient privilege.

Second, the Court did not conclude that Dr. Smith was under a *duty* to disclose the information concerning Jones' dangerousness, only that he was permitted to do so. It simply did not address this important issue. The question of whether there is a legal duty to disclose remains undecided.

Third, the Court said that while Dr. Smith was prudent to seek a court order permitting disclosure, this would not be necessary in all cases. Particularly in urgent situations, disclosure of information protected by solicitor-client privilege could be made to public authorities or an intended victim without court order. The Court warned, however, that care should be taken to disclose "only that information which is necessary to alleviate the threat to public safety."[45]

(c) Liability to Third Parties in Non-*Tarasoff* Circumstances

Liability to third parties for harms caused by a patient with a mental illness might arise in circumstances not involving disclosure of privileged communications. Again, however, few cases have been brought in Canada against physicians or hospitals, and fewer still have succeeded.

In the 1992 Alberta case *Wenden v. Trickha*,[46] a hospital and a physician were sued by persons injured in a motor vehicle accident caused by the faulty driving of a voluntary mental patient. The plaintiffs alleged that the defendants acted negligently by not placing the patient under increased supervision, or preventing him from leaving the hospital in a condition in which he posed a danger to the public. The trial judge dismissed the claim. He noted that the patient had been calm prior to leaving the hospital's psychiatric unit, that he had been under "close" observation (every 15 minutes), and that no one knew his car was parked at the hospital.

The plaintiffs also alleged that the psychiatrist should have diagnosed the patient as dangerous, and committed him to hospital. The Court of Appeal, in affirming the trial court's dismissal of the lawsuit, said that involuntary status would not necessarily have made a difference. The Court added:

> In most cases medical science is totally unable to predict which patients are dangerous and which are not. . . . The hospital and the physician did not think that the patient was such a danger, and so none of them could honestly have signed such a certificate. And for the reasons given above, that belief that he was not dangerous was not negligent.[47]

This is a significant hurdle for plaintiffs to get over in any case involving a claim of a failure to diagnose dangerousness.

6. FORENSIC PSYCHIATRY

The forensic psychiatric system deals with persons who commit criminal offences as a consequence of mental illness. Canada's forensic law was overhauled in 1992, partly as a result of the *Charter* decision in *R. v. Swain*.[48] Prior to 1992, the Criminal Code provided for a plea of "not guilty by reason of insanity" ("NGRI"). If found NGRI, the accused individual was automatically and indefinitely detained in hospital on a "Lieutenant Governor's warrant", meaning that release from hospital depended ultimately on a decision of the provincial Cabinet.

In *Swain*, the Supreme Court of Canada ruled that the NGRI process violated sections 7 and 9 of the *Charter*. Parliament responded by introducing a new Part XX.1 into the *Criminal Code* to govern this area. The term "insanity" and the finding of NGRI were replaced by "not criminally responsible by reason of mental disorder" ("NCRMD"). The legal test is that the accused did not appreciate "the nature and quality of the [criminal] act or omission or [know] that it was wrong."[49] In addition to NCRMDs, the forensic system also deals with individuals found unfit to stand trial due to mental illness.

A person found NCRMD is not subject to automatic detention in hospital. The trial judge must make a finding that, due to mental disorder, the accused represents a significant threat to public safety at the time of sentencing, in order to order detention in hospital. Thereafter, decision-making authority over the individual's continued detention lies with Review Boards established by each province. Review Boards must conduct periodic hearings for each patient.

The Supreme Court considered the constitutionality of this scheme in *Winko v. Forensic Psychiatric Institute*.[50] The Court ruled that "dangerousness", in the sense intended by the phrase used in the *Code*, of posing "a significant threat to public safety", is the appropriate basis for forensic committal. This standard corresponds to the federal government's constitutional jurisdiction over the criminal law. It has national application. The Court ruled that an NCRMD person is entitled to an absolute discharge from custody when he or she is found to no longer pose a significant threat to public safety. Short of an absolute discharge, Review Boards may order conditional discharges from hospital detention, which permit a return to the community on conditions, such as working with a treatment team.

The *Criminal Code* provisions do not authorize psychiatric treatment of NCRMD persons. Therefore, the authority to treat, including any authority to treat where the individual is unable or unwilling to consent to psychiatric treatment, falls to be determined by the provincial mental health law in the province where the individual is detained. For this reason, forensic patients are often certified under mental health statutes as well as being detained pursuant to the *Criminal Code*. Forensic psychiatric facilities are provincially operated, either as free-standing hospitals or as forensic units in mental health hospitals.

Winko also argued that as an NCRMD person, he remained subject to indefinite detention, and might well be detained beyond the maximum sentence he could have received had he been found guilty of the criminal offence. This, he claimed, constituted discrimination based on mental disability contrary to section 15 of the *Charter*. The Court ruled, however, that because the system is based on individualized assessment of the person's mental condition, it does not rely on stereotypes of mental illness and so is not discriminatory.

Forensics is not the only way in which mentally ill individuals in the criminal justice system may come under the authority of provincial mental health law. Prisoners who develop a mental illness while incarcerated may be transferred to secure psychiatric hospital facilities. Such transfers are provided for under mental health statutes.

Another route has recently been authorized by the Supreme Court. In *R. v. Knoblauch*,[51] the Court ruled that a conditional sentence may include an order that the accused person reside in a secure psychiatric facility. Conditional sentences allow a judge to order that a custodial sentence of less than two years be served in the community, rather than in jail. One of the criteria for giving a conditional sentence is that it not expose the community to a risk of harm.

In *Knoblauch*, the accused was convicted of possessing an "arsenal" of explosives. The trial judge found that while he did not meet the NCRMD criteria, he did have a mental disorder. It would be preferable that he receive treatment in hospital rather than go to jail. Knoblauch was dangerous, but he would not present a risk to public safety so long as he resided in a secure hospital setting. Moreover, a secure psychiatric facility could be viewed as being in the "community." A majority of the Supreme Court agreed. Much of this seems arguable. In effect, the Court used a criminal sentencing option to commit an individual to hospital. Whether this decision leads to many more such "committals" remains to be seen.

7. ADVOCACY AND RIGHTS OF PERSONS WITH MENTAL ILLNESS

In *Swain*, Chief Justice Lamer of the Supreme Court made an oft-cited statement about discriminatory attitudes toward the mentally ill:

The mentally ill have historically been the subjects of abuse, neglect and discrimination in our society. The stigma of mental illness can be very damaging. The intervener, CDRC, describes the historical treatment of the mentally ill as follows:

> For centuries, persons with a mental disability have been systematically isolated, segregated from the mainstream of society, devalued, ridiculed and excluded from participation in ordinary social and political processes.

The above description is, in my view, unfortunately accurate and appears to stem from an irrational fear of the mentally ill in our society.[52]

Most persons with mental illness, and the people who support and work with them, whether family members, health care professionals, social workers, or legal advocates, would agree. Still, progress has been made. The best marker of that progress is the degree to which the isolation and segregation that feeds fear and neglect is replaced with inclusion in the community. More effective medications with fewer side-effects, psychosocial rehabilitation, and semi-independent housing options with nursing and social worker support, are all playing an important role.

Legal rights and advocacy also have a significant contribution to make. A legal right is a claim to be noticed, to be taken seriously, not to be taken for granted. This chapter has mentioned a number of rights which Canada's laws accord persons with mental illness, including procedural protections with respect to compulsory interventions in their lives. There are other rights which now commonly appear in mental health statutes that could be mentioned: rights to be advised of one's rights when admitted involuntarily to hospital; to communicate freely with the outside world; and not to be subject to physical restraints unless strictly necessary for personal safety. Moreover, everyone is protected from discrimination on the basis of mental disability, pursuant both to provincial human rights laws and section 15 of the *Charter*.

As significant as these legal protections may be, they are often only as meaningful as there are advocates available to assist persons with mental illness in putting them forward. Several provinces support advocacy services for the mentally ill, through such measures as legal offices located at hospital sites, or the Psychiatric Patient Advocacy Office in Ontario. Alberta has a statutory office of the Mental Health Patient Advocate which investigates complaints made by involuntary patients. In other provinces, the Office of the Ombudsman plays a similar investigative and reporting role.

The increasing acceptance of the role of advocacy in mental health systems is a strong statement about their willingness to be transparent. Transparency in turn speaks to the goal shared by so many, to reduce the degree to which mental illness is a source of discrimination in Canadian society.

NOTES

1. The following sources have proved helpful in the preparation of this chapter, and are recommended for further reading:

    J. Gray, M. Shone and P. Liddle, *Canadian Mental Health Law and Policy* (Toronto: Butterworths, 2000); A. Kaiser, "Mental Disability Law" in T. Caulfield, J. Downie and C. Flood, eds., *Canadian Health Law and Policy* (Toronto: Butterworths, 2002), pp. 251-330; G. Robertson, *Mental Disability and the Law in Canada*, 2nd ed., (Toronto: Carswell, 1994); K. Brown and E. Murphy, "Falling Through the Cracks: The Quebec Mental Health System", (2000) 45 **McGill Law Journal** 1037-1079.

2. The ten provincial (and two territorial mental health statutes) are the following: *Mental Health Act*, R.S.A. 2000, c. M-13 (Alberta); *Mental Health Act*, R.S.B.C. 1996, c. 288 (British Columbia); *Mental Health and Consequential Amendments Act*, S.M. 1998, c. 36 (Manitoba); *Mental Health Services Act*, R.S.N.B. 1973, c. M-10 (New Brunswick); *Mental Health Act*, R.S.N. 1990, c. M-9 (Newfoundland); *Hospitals Act*, S.N.S. 1989, c. 208 (Nova Scotia); *Mental Health Act*, R.S.O. 1990, c. M.7 (Ontario); *Mental Health Act*, S.P.E.I. 1994, c. 39; *Civil Code of Quebec*, R.S.Q. 1991, c. 64, ss. 10-31, and *An Act Respecting the Protection of Persons Whose Mental State Presents Danger to Themselves or to Others*, R.S.Q., c. P-38.001 (Quebec); *Mental Health Services Act*, S.S. 1984-85-86, c. M-13.1 (Saskatchewan); *Mental Health Act*, R.S.N.W.T. 1988, c. M-10 (Northwest Territories, and Nunavut); *Mental Health Act*, S.Y. 1989-90, c. 36; all as subsequently amended. Hereinafter, these statutes will frequently be referred to as "the statute" or "mental health statute" of the specified province(s).

3. *Fleming v. Reid* (1991), 82 D.L.R. (4th) 298, [1991] O.J. No. 1083, 1991 CarswellOnt 1501 (C.A.).

4. "Human needs" is a term coined by Gray, Shone and Liddle, *supra* note 1, who are proponents of this position. Kaiser, *supra* note 1, writes more from a patients' rights position, which he prefers to term an "equality rights" perspective.

5. This can be found on-line at http://www.chlc.ca/en/us/index.cfm?sec=1&sub=1m1. The optimism that lay behind this project has not been fulfilled – to date, Prince Edward Island, in 1994, is the only province to enact this model legislation.

6. *Fleming, supra,* note 3, is one of these decisions. The other is *R. v. Swain*, [1991] 1 S.C.R. 933, which struck down those parts of the *Criminal Code of Canada* dealing with persons found "not guilty by reason of insanity." See discussion in Section VI, Forensic Psychiatry.

7. *Mental Health Amendment Act, 1998*, S.B.C. 1998, s. 35, amending the B.C. statute, c. 35.

8. *Brian's Law (Mental Health Legislative Reform) 2000*, S.O. 2000, c. 9, amending the Ontario statute, *supra* note 2.

9. *Civil Code of Quebec*, *supra* note 2, Article 30.

10. Treatability also appears in the committal criteria, which state in s. 22(3)(c)(i) of the B.C. statute, *supra* note 2, that the person "requires treatment in or through a designated facility."

11. *Starnaman v. Penetanguishene Mental Health Centre* (1995), 24 O.R. (3d) 701 (C.A.).

12. Saskatchewan statute, *supra* note 2, s. 24(2)(a):
   "[the physician] has probable cause to believe that:
      (ii) as a result of the mental disorder the person is unable to fully understand and to make an informed decision regarding his need for treatment or care and supervision."

13. A dangerousness standard for committal applies in the area of forensic psychiatry, governed by *Criminal Code of Canada*. See discussion in part 6 of this chapter.

14. *Thwaites v. Health Sciences Centre Psychiatric Facility* (1988), 40 C.R.R. 326 (Man. C.A.).

15. *Ibid.* at 332.

16. *Bobbie v. Health Sciences Centre* (1988), 49 C.R.R. 376 (Man. Q.B.).

17. *McCorkell v. Riverview Hospital* (1993), [1993] B.C.J. No. 1518, 1993 CarswellBC 188 (S.C.).

18. *Ibid.*, para 45.

19. *Ibid.*, para 58.

20. Ontario statute, *supra* note 2, s. 20(5).

21. *B. (L.) v. O'Doherty* (April 14, 1986), Kurisko D.C.J. (Ont. Dist. Ct.).

22. *M. v. Alberta* (1985), 63 A.R. 14 (Q.B.).

23. See for example, *T. (B.) v. Alberta Hospital* (1997), [1997] A.J. No. 894, 1997 CarswellAlta 1224 (Q.B.).

24. See generally R. Gordon & S. Verdun-Jones, *Adult Guardianship Law in Canada* (Scarborough, Ont.: Carswell, 1992). Examples of recently introduced substitute decision-maker legislation include, in Ontario, the *Substitute Decisions Act*, 1992, S.O. 1992, c. 30, as amended, and the *Health Care Consent Act*, 1996, S.O. 1996, c. 2, Schedule A, and in B.C., the *Adult Guardianship Act*, R.S.B.C. 1996, c. 6, proclaimed February 28, 2000 by B.C. Reg 12/00.

25. *Supra*, note 4 (QL), p.16.

26. *Ibid.*, p. 15.

27. Provisions on consent, the obligations of substitute decision-makers with respect to consent, and the applications which can be made to the Consent and Capacity Board are found in the *Health Care Consent Act*, *supra* note 24.

28. (2001), [2001] O.J. No. 2283, 2001 CarswellOnt 2053 (C.A.), leave to appeal

allowed (2002), 2002 CarswellOnt 1101, 2002 CarswellOnt 1102 (S.C.C.). Appeal to the Supreme Court of Canada heard, and judgment reserved, on January 15, 2003.

29. *Ibid.*, para 14.

30. (2002), [2002] O.J. No. 2333, 2002 CarswellOnt 1920 (C.A.).

31. Alberta statute, *supra* note 2, s. 29(5).

32. Ontario statute, *supra* note 2, section 33. For Saskatchewan, see *Mental Health Services Amendment Act*, 1993, S.S. 1993, c. 59, as amended by *Mental Health Services Amendment Act*, 1996, S.S. 1996, c. 17.

33. The attending physician is relieved of liability for any "default or neglect" of other persons providing treatment under the plan (33.6(1)). By implication, the physician appears not to be relieved of liability for default or neglect in his or her own responsibilities under the plan. Other health practitioners providing treatment under the plan "are responsible for implementing the plan to the extent indicated in it."

34. For further discussion of the CTO, see the author's "A New Direction for Mental Health Law: *Brian's Law* and the Problematic Implications of Community Treatment Orders", in T. Caulfield and B. Von Tigerstrom, eds. *Health Care Reform and the Law in Canada: Meeting the Challenge* (Edmonton: University of Alberta Press, 2001), pp. 187-222.

35. *W. (E.) v. Alberta Hospital (Edmonton)* (1999), [1999] A.J. No. 868, 1999 CarswellAlta 710 (Q.B.) (per Lee, J.), para 67.

36. *L. (A.J.) v. Kingston Psychiatric Hospital* (1999), [1999] O.J. No. 4306, 1999 CarswellOnt 3719 (S.C.J.), affirmed (2000), 2000 CarswellOnt 3428 (C.A.) (per Belch J.), para 29 [O.J. No.].

37. *Villemure v. L'Hôpital Notre-Dame* (1972), [1973] S.C.R. 716.

38. (1994), [1994] B.C.J. No. 2458, 1994 CarswellBC 2450 (S.C.), affirmed (1997), 40 B.C.L.R. (3d) 116 (C.A.).

39. *Ibid*, para 157 (per Huddart J.A.).

40. *Haines v. Bellissimo* (1977), 18 O.R. (2d) 177 (H.C.) at 190-91.

41. *Ganger*, para 186.

42. 551 P.2d 334 (U.S. Cal., 1976).

43. [1999] 1 S.C.R. 455

44. *Ibid.*, para 68.

45. *Ibid.*, para 96.

46. *Wenden v. Trikha* (1991), 8 C.C.L.T. (2d) 138 (Alta. Q.B.), amended (1991), 118 A.R. 319 (Q.B.), additional reasons at (1992), 1 Alta. L.R. (3d) 283 (Q.B.), affirmed (1993), 14 C.C.L.T. (2d) 225 (Alta. C.A.), leave to appeal refused (1993), 17 C.C.L.T. (2d) 285 (note) (S.C.C.).

47. *Ibid.*, at

48. *Supra*, note 6.

49. *Criminal Code of Canada*, R.S.C. 1985, c. C-46, s. 16(1).

50. *Winko v. Forensic Psychiatric Institute*, [1999] 2 S.C.R. 625.

51. *R. v. Knoblauch*, [2000] 2 S.C.R. 780.

52. *Supra*, note 6, at para 39.

14

ISSUES IN REPRODUCTIVE CHOICE: PART 1

SUMMARY

This chapter is concerned with the interface between the physician's role as genetic counsellor and the patient's right to make informed reproductive decisions. Perceived grievances by patients have led to the emergence of a new category of civil wrong — the *torts of wrongful birth and wrongful life*. A wrongful birth action is brought by the parents of a disabled child, who allege that the negligence of the defendant-physician caused the child's birth. The parents do not assert that the physician caused the handicap, but that he deprived them of the right to exercise an informed reproductive choice. Their claim is that if the physician had furnished the appropriate information, the child would not have been born. Five kinds of scenarios that lead to wrongful birth suits against physicians are presented. Although the tort of wrongful birth is well entrenched in the common law, only a minority of courts (none in Canada) have recognized the tort of wrongful life — the label for a cause-of-action brought in the name of the handicapped child herself, whose grievance is her very existence.

Wrongful birth/life claims are thus particular types of negligence actions. (As explained in Chapter 4, a physician's breach of the legal duty to obtain informed consent is actionable not by suing for battery but rather by suing for medical negligence.) Since the case law in this area was developed in the United States, the leading American cases are reviewed. The growing body of Canadian jurisprudence is also considered.

1. GENETIC COUNSELLING/SCREENING AND PRENATAL TESTING: THE TORT OF WRONGFUL BIRTH

When a person's death is caused by the negligent conduct of another, his next-of-kin may file a civil suit claiming damages for the tort of *wrongful death*. In recent years, courts in common law jurisdictions have recognized a new category of civil wrong — *the tort of wrongful birth*. A wrongful birth action, which is brought by the parents of a disabled child, alleges that *the negligence of the defendant-physician caused the child's birth*. The plaintiffs do not assert that the defendant caused the handicap. The essence of their claim is rather that the child would not have been born but for the physician's negligence. Their legal grievance is the child's very existence.

This new category of medical malpractice is an outgrowth of advances in human genetics, which have dramatically increased reproductive options. At the *pre-conception* stage, genetic counselling and testing enable physicians to advise patients regarding the risks of bearing offspring with various genetic disorders. If the wrongful birth suit alleges pre-conception negligence, the parents claim that the child would not have been conceived had the physician informed them that they were at risk to bear a handicapped child. At the *post-conception* stage, prenatal diagnostic techniques (e.g. amniocentesis, fetoscopy, and ultrasound) allow physicians to detect genetic and congenital anomalies. If the wrongful birth suit alleges post-conception negligence, the parents claim that they were precluded from exercising their right to abortion by the physician's failure to inform them of the risk that the fetus might be impaired. As will be noted, birth defects allegedly caused by drugs ingested in pregnancy on medical recommendation may also trigger a wrongful birth (and/or wrongful life) claim. Although here the defect is not genetic, the rationale is essentially the same: that the child's handicaps are traceable to the defendant's negligence.

The tort of wrongful birth is an outgrowth of the doctrine of informed consent. As the cases indicate, the physician must disclose sufficient information to enable the patient to make an informed reproductive choice. The following American cases illustrate various scenarios giving rise to wrongful birth suits. (We separately consider the tort of *wrongful life*, in which the action is brought in the name of the handicapped child — unlike the tort of *wrongful birth* in which the plaintiffs are the parents. The two actions are often combined in the same law suit: the parents suing for wrongful birth and their handicapped child suing for wrongful life.)

Most of the reported American wrongful birth cases involve an appeal by the plaintiff-parents from the decision of the trial court granting the defendant-physician's motion for summary judgment. As the scenario is played out, once the plaintiffs' case has been presented the defence responds not by introducing evidence but rather by the argument that, even if the allegations are all true (which the defence does not admit), they are not sufficient to establish a viable claim. In other words, the defendant contests the very concept of a wrongful birth action. When the plaintiffs appeal the granting of the motion, the court assumes that the facts as alleged in the statement-of-claim are all true in order to resolve the question whether a suit for wrongful birth is a legally recognized cause-of-action. If the court concludes that the evidence, if true, is sufficient to establish the tort of wrongful birth, then the motion is accordingly reversed and the case returned for trial. It is then up to the plaintiffs to prove the case. (The same process also occurs in wrongful life cases.)

2. THE TORT OF WRONG BIRTH: LEADING CASES

(a) Pre-Conception Negligence: Failure to Alert Plaintiffs of Their Risk of Bearing a Child with a Congenital/Genetic Disease

(i) *Park v. Chessin (New York, 1978)*[1]

Mrs. Park's first child died of polycystic kidney disease five hours after birth. Concerned that the disease might recur in future offspring, she and her husband consulted their obstetrician. According to their testimony, his response was that the disease was not hereditary and that the odds that the couple would conceive a second child so afflicted were "practically nil." Thus reassured, they bore a second child who succumbed to polycystic kidney disease at the age of two. The plaintiffs alleged that they would not have conceived the second child had they been correctly informed that polycystic kidney disease was an inherited condition.

The plaintiffs appealed the decision by the trial court to grant the defendant's motion for summary judgment. The New York Court of Appeal ruled in the plaintiffs' favour — that the case go forward because proof that the defendant did in fact fail to advise the couple of the risk to future offspring would thereby render him liable for the child's wrongful birth.

(ii) *Schroeder v. Perkel (New Jersey, 1981)*[2]

The plaintiffs were the parents of two children afflicted with cystic fibrosis. The first child suffered in infancy from a digestive disorder diagnosed as colic by the family physician. When the symptoms persisted, the parents were referred to the defendants (pediatricians), who diagnosed the child's condition as a malabsorption syndrome caused by an intolerance for fats. They ruled out CF by relying upon a stool test that had been done by the family physician. The diet that they prescribed (low in starch and high in protein) relieved her symptoms for four years. It did so because the same diet is indicated for patients with CF.

When the child's condition worsened, the defendants referred her to a specialist in digestive disorders. He diagnosed CF by performing a sweat chloride test: a simple, reliable procedure derived from evidence that the perspiration of cystic fibrosis patients contains an abnormally high concentration of salt. Unfortunately, Mrs. Schroeder was eight months pregnant when the diagnosis was confirmed. Two weeks after the birth of their second child, a sweat chloride test revealed that he too bore the disease. The second child was the subject of the wrongful birth claim.

The defendants admitted that a stool test was not the correct or preferred procedure for diagnosing CF. Had they performed a sweat chloride test on the first child, the result would have confirmed that both parents were carriers and that there was a 25% risk of the disease in future offspring.

Mrs. Schroeder testified that she would not have conceived another child had she known that her first child had CF. When that child's diagnosis was confirmed, Mr. Schroeder promptly underwent a vasectomy. She testified that because CF could not be detected in utero (which is now no longer the case), she carried the second pregnancy to term only because its advanced stage precluded abortion.

The New Jersey Supreme Court reversed the trial court's granting of the motion for summary judgment. In its view, evidence that the defendants had negligently failed to diagnose the first child's condition in time to prevent the second pregnancy or its timely abortion was sufficient in law to permit recovery for the wrongful birth of the second child.

(b)   Pre-Conception Negligence: Failure to Inform Plaintiffs of the Risks of Birth Defects from Prescription Drugs Resulting in the Birth of a Handicapped Child

(i)   *Harbeson v. Parke-Davies Inc. (Washington, 1983)*

A neurologist had prescribed Dilantin for the control of Mrs. Harbeson's epileptic seizures. She and her husband (a soldier) later consulted three physicians at a military medical facility as to whether the drug had teratogenic properties. Although advised that it could cause cleft palate and temporary hirsutism, none of the physicians conducted literature searches or otherwise sought data regarding Dilantin and other birth defects. Had they been diligent, they would have learned of a correlation between the drug and fetal hydantoin syndrome. Relying upon their assurances the Harbesons bore two children a year apart, and after the second child's birth both were diagnosed with the syndrome. The evidence of the medical witnesses was that:

> They suffer from mild to moderate growth deficiencies, mild to moderate developmental retardation, wide-set eyes, lateral ptosis, hypoplasia of the fingers, small nails, low-set hairline, broad nasal ridge, and other physical and developmental defects.

The parents testified that they would not have had children had they been advised of the correlation between Dilantin and fetal hydantoin syndrome. (Their medical witnesses satisfied the Court that the Dilantin had caused the anomalies.)

As in the *Park* and *Schroeder* cases, the plaintiffs claimed that the defendants' negligence had led them to bear handicapped children. After hearing the evidence, the trial court certified questions of law regarding the viability of the tort of wrongful birth for consideration by the Washington (State) Supreme Court. The Court responded by ruling that the parents had a valid claim for the wrongful birth of their two children.

What factually distinguishes the *Harbeson* case from the other wrongful birth cases canvassed here is that the handicap is directly attributable to treatment provided by the defendants. The other cases involve hereditary (e.g. Down syndrome) or congenital (e.g. rubella) factors over which the defendants had no control. But either the way the result is the same: but for the physician's negligence a disabled child would not have been born. (The Manitoba *Lacroix* case, which is noted in this chapter, also involved drugs prescribed in pregnancy that resulted in harm to the subsequently born child.)

(c) Post-Conception Negligence: Failure to Recommend and Consequently Perform Amniocentesis Resulting in the Birth of a Handicapped Child

(i) *Berman v. Allan (New Jersey, 1979)*[4]

During her pregnancy Mrs. Berman was under the care of the defendants (obstetricians), and at the age of 38 she gave birth to a child with Down syndrome. At no time did the defendants inform her that amniocentesis was warranted because of her maternal age. Mrs. Berman claimed that, if so advised, she would have undergone the procedure and that the finding of Down syndrome would have led her to abort the fetus.

The summary judgment for the defendants was reversed by the New Jersey Supreme Court on the grounds that since Mrs. Berman was at heightened risk to bear a Down syndrome child because of her age, the defendants were indeed under a legal duty to advise her regarding the options of amniocentesis and abortion. Hence, the Court concluded that liability for wrongful birth was the appropriate remedy against the defendants if the trial court accepted the parents' testimony.

(ii) Goldberg v. Ruskin (Illinois, 1984)[5]

The birth of a child afflicted with Tay-Sachs disease prompted the Goldbergs to file a wrongful birth action against their obstetrician. (Tay-Sachs is a progressive, degenerative disease of the nervous system, in which the child suffers eventual blindness, deafness, paralysis, seizures, and mental retardation. Life expectancy is from two to four years.) They alleged that the defendant had failed to warn them about the disease — most of whose victims are the offspring of Jewish parents of eastern European background — and to advise them that amniocentesis could detect its presence in utero. They asserted that, if properly advised, Mrs. Goldberg would have undergone amniocentesis and aborted the affected fetus.

The trial court certified a question for an intermediate appellate court* as to the viability of a cause-of-action for wrongful birth. The Court ruled that proof that the defendant had failed to inform the plaintiffs about the disease amounted to negligence because Jewish couples of Eastern European ancestry are known to be at particular risk to bear a Tay-Sachs child. According to the Court, a physician is liable under a wrongful birth claim when he fails "to advise parents of the risks of abnormality or of the availability of tests to detect abnormality." (What if the plaintiffs had not had an obviously Jewish name like Goldberg? Even so, it does not necessarily follow that the physician would escape fault for not knowing or suspecting that they were Jewish. The reason is that when pregnancy is contemplated or occurring, a family history should include questions about ethnicity and race. Since Tay-Sachs is but one of a number of genetic disorders associated with ethnicity or race, physicians should as a matter of routine seek this information unless it is otherwise obvious.)

---

*   An intermediate appellate court hears appeals from trial courts, and its rulings are appealed to the state supreme court.

(d) Post-Conception Negligence: Failure to Diagnose Congenital Condition that Results in the Birth of a Handicapped Child

(i) *Jacobs v. Theimer (Texas, 1975)*[6]

When Mrs. Jacobs became unwell and was hospitalized during her first trimester of pregnancy, she asked her physician if her illness was German measles (rubella). Without investigating the matter, he assured her that it was not German measles. But it was and seven months later she bore a child with severe birth defects. The parents sued the physician for his failure to diagnose rubella and to advise them of the substantial risk of birth defects. They claimed that but for the defendant's negligence, they would have aborted the fetus.

The defendant's motion for summary judgment was granted by the trial court but then reversed on appeal. The Texas Supreme Court ruled that proof that the defendant had failed to diagnose the rubella would constitute negligence. In that event, since the parents would have been deprived of knowledge that would have led them to obtain an abortion, the defendant would be held responsible for the wrongful birth of the physically impaired child.

(The Canadian case, *Arndt v. Smith*, which falls under this sub-heading, will be considered shortly.)

3. THE ESSENTIAL ELEMENTS OF THE TORT OF WRONGFUL BIRTH

The plaintiffs in a wrongful birth suit must prove: (1) that the defendant-physician breached the *legal duty* of care that she owed to them; (2) that the defendant was the *cause* of their consequent harm; and (3) that the harm warrants compensation by the award of a measurable amount of *damages*.

(a) Duty

The physician's legal duty to inform her patient about the risks of genetic/congenital anomalies derives from the *informed consent* doctrine. The physician is duty bound to respond fully and frankly to the patient's questions. When the Parks queried Dr. Chessin about polycystic kidney disease, the physician breached his legal duty by his negligent failure to respond with accurate information. In addition, the physician must volunteer information that a reasonable patient would consider *material* to her treatment decision. Even if the patient has omitted to inquire, the duty of reasonable care obliges the physician to provide information that the patient should be aware of. The Goldbergs never questioned Dr. Ruskin about Tay-Sachs disease. The Court nonetheless concluded that since the disease occurs primarily in Jewish infants of Eastern European ancestry, the physician owed a duty of disclosure to the Goldbergs. The Illinois court traced that duty to the fact that "the physician is learned, skilled, and experienced in subjects of vital importance to the patient but about which the patient knows little or nothing."

In either scenario — whether the physician is faulted for speaking wrongly (e.g. Dr. Chessin) or for remaining silent (e.g. Dr. Ruskin) — the breach of the duty to inform means that patients are deprived of information crucial to reproductive decision-making.

A physician's duty to her patient may require her to obtain relevant data from other persons. Consider, for example, a physician who artificially inseminates her patient with donor sperm, which results in a child disabled by a genetically transmitted disease. The physician confines the donor-screening process to a general inquiry about medical and genetic history. She neglects to perform readily available chromosomal and biochemical analyses that would have detected the genetic trait in question and thereby screened out the donor candidate. The parents respond by launching a wrongful birth action against the physician. They allege that restricting the donor-screening process to history-taking was negligent, given the known risk of transmission of infectious and genetic diseases.

What if a case were to arise (none has as of yet to our knowledge) in which there was persuasive medical evidence that a reasonably prudent physician would have performed the tests, and that the results would have disqualified the donor candidate? The court would no doubt conclude that the defendant-physician had breached her *duty* of care to her patient and was therefore accountable to the parents for the wrongful birth of their handicapped child.

(b) Causation

In several wrongful birth cases, the defence was based on the uncontested fact that the defendant-physician did not cause the child's birth defects. In response, the courts have explained that the argument misconstrues the nature of the wrongful birth suit. In such cases, the parents' grievance against the defendant-physician is not that she caused the child's condition. The claim is that *the defendant caused the child's birth* because her negligence deprived the parents of information that would have led them either to avoid conception (pre-conception negligence) or to terminate the pregnancy (post-conception negligence). What the principle of causation means in the context of wrongful birth is that, but for the defendant's negligence, the child would never have been born. In that sense, the wrong caused by the defendant is the very existence of the handicapped child. As the Court stated in the *Harbeson* case, the causation question in wrongful birth cases is whether: "but for the physician's negligence, the parents would have avoided conception, or aborted the pregnancy, and the child would not have existed."

When a wrongful birth suit is grounded in *post-conception* negligence (e.g. failure to recommend amniocentesis or to diagnose rubella), the core of the parents' grievance is that the defendant denied them the opportunity to abort the fetus. They must consequently prove that if they had been properly advised, the pregnancy would have been terminated. In Canada, the doctrine of informed consent mandates a so-called *modified objective* test of causation.* In this context, the issue is not whether the plaintiffs would have opted for abortion had they been properly informed by the defendant-physician. Rather it is whether reasonable parents so informed and standing in their shoes would have done so. In other words, the subjective approach asks what the actual parents would have done, whereas the objective approach asks what reasonable parents would have done if situated in their precise circumstances. Admittedly, there is no clear-cut boundary between the two formulations since the objective test incorporates factors directly bearing upon the plaintiffs' situation. More often than not, parents have overcome the hurdle by satisfying the courts that a reasonable couple in their circumstances would not have chosen to give birth to a handicapped child. (Although, as we see when we turn to the *Arndt v. Smith* case, the Supreme Court of Canada ruled that the trial judge had properly applied the test when concluding that a reasonable patient in the plaintiff's circumstances would have continued the pregnancy.)

What about a case of *pre-conception* negligence? We have considered the *Schroeder* case, in which the plaintiff-wife was eight months pregnant when she learned that her first child was afflicted with cystic fibrosis. (Recall that she testified that more timely discovery would have led to an abortion.) What if she had acquired that knowledge when two months pregnant but had refused to terminate the pregnancy because of a principled opposition to abortion? Assume that the defendant's response is that her claim should be barred because she had forsaken the opportunity to prevent the harm occurring — that if she had obtained an abortion she would not have borne a child that she knew would be afflicted. When this issue has arisen in American cases, the courts have disallowed the defence, reasoning along the following lines:

---

* See Chapter 4.

When a wrongful birth results from post-conception negligence, the defendant-physician is the legal cause of the harm because his conduct precluded abortion. As a result, the plaintiff must prove that she would have availed herself of the abortion option. But that is not the case here. Unlike a post-conception scenario, the plaintiff's grievance does not hinge upon a lost abortion opportunity. Her complaint is different — that if she had been properly advised, she would not have conceived. Her grievance is thus based upon a lost opportunity to prevent conception. She would not have conceived but for the defendant's negligence, but once that happened she cannot be penalized for her principled refusal to terminate the pregnancy.

(c) Damages

(i) *Wrongful Birth Cases*

In the first reported wrongful birth case, *Gleitman v. Cosgrove* (1967),[7] the New Jersey Supreme Court denied recovery to the parents by ruling that the public policy supporting the preciousness of human life, however handicapped, barred the awarding of tort damages "for the denial of the opportunity to take an embryonic life." The Court refused to accept the parents' contention that their child was an injury inflicted upon them by the defendants (obstetricians), who had assured Mrs. Gleitman that her German measles would not affect her pregnancy. The Court was repelled by the notion that damages should be awarded for the very existence of the plaintiffs' child, notwithstanding his grievous handicaps.

The New Jersey Supreme Court has since repudiated that position (in the aforementioned 1979 *Berman* case), and its turnabout reflects the fact that the wrongful birth action has become well entrenched in American case law. In rejecting the policy argument that grounded the decision against Jeffrey Gleitman's parents, the courts in subsequent wrongful birth cases have reasoned that the preventable birth of a severely handicapped child unquestionably constitutes a harm inflicted upon the parents.

(ii) *Wrongful Life Cases*

When the *parents* sue, the term *wrongful birth* applies. When the *child* is the plaintiff, the case is labelled as a *wrongful life* action. In most cases, the parental claim for wrongful birth is paired with the child's claim for wrongful life. In a wrongful birth suit, parents seek damages for the special costs of caring for the child and sometimes for the stress and grief they experience because of the child's circumstances. In a wrongful life suit, the child seeks damages for the pain and suffering of her impaired existence and for life-long medical costs.

Wrongful life claims have met with scant success in the United States as the courts are inclined to the position that the child has not sustained legally cognizable damages, which they explain as follows. When a plaintiff wins a negligence action, the court must compensate her for the *harm* caused by the defendant. The plaintiff is entitled to damages only if she proves that, on account of the defendant's negligence, she is worse off than she was before the harm occurred. In theory, the damages award is designed to restore the plaintiff to her pre-negligence state (although in the event of death or severe permanent injury, the harm is admittedly incapable of full redress).

The computation of damages accordingly requires a comparison between the plaintiff's pre-negligence state and her impaired post-negligence condition. Since the child's pre-negligence state is non-existence, there is no basis for a before-and-after comparison. It is therefore impossible to weigh the difference in value between the child's impaired life and the utter void of nonexistence. In short, how can one say that a person is worse off for having been born? The sentiment was expressed by the New York Court of Appeal in a 1978 case, *Becker v. Schwartz:*[8]

> Whether it is better never to have been born at all than to have been born with even gross deficiencies is a mystery more properly to be left to the philosophers and the theologians.

Aside from the lack of a yardstick to measure damages (the argument continues), there is another damages-related consideration that precludes recovery by a wrongful life plaintiff. The plaintiff's grievance is her very existence. The law suit filed in her name asserts that by being brought into the world she is entitled to compensation from the defendant-physician, who is responsible for the fact that she lives. In response, most American courts have ruled that the recognition of a wrongful life claim would be tantamount to a judicial declaration that there are severely handicapped children whose lives are without value or purpose and who consequently are better off dead.

The English courts have likewise spurned recognition of wrongful life claims for the same reasons noted in the American cases. In *McKay v. Essex Area Health Authority* (1982), the Court of Appeal stressed the insoluble problem of assessing damages in such cases:

> The only loss for which those who have not injured the child can be can be held liable to compensate the child is the difference between its condition as a result of their allowing it to be born alive and injured, and its condition if its embryonic life had been ended before its life in the world had begun. But how can a court of law evaluate that second condition and so measure the

loss to the child? Even if a court were competent to decide between the conflicting views of theologians and philosophers and to assume an "afterlife" or non-existence as the basis for the comparison, how can a judge put a value on the one or the other?[9]

In the few Canadian wrongful life claims that have gone to trial, all have been rejected. In 1999 Justice Jewers of the Manitoba Court of Queen's Bench dismissed a wrongful life suit in the case of *Lacroix (Litigation Guardian of) v. Dominique*.[10] The basis of the claim was that the child's mental disability and dysmorphic features were caused by anticonvulsant drugs prescribed by the defendant-neurologist during the pregnancy of her epileptic mother. (A suit for wrongful birth was also filed by the parents, but it was denied by Justice Jewers because it had not been brought within the two year period stipulated in the Limitation of Actions Act.)

Mrs. Lacroix was afflicted with temporal lobe epilepsy and in 1980 was referred by her family physician to the defendant, who proceeded to treat her with Tegretol and Mebaral. By 1982 she and her husband were ready to have children, and consequently they met with the defendant to discuss their concern whether the medication could affect fetal development. Justice Jewers found that the defendant had not advised them of the teratogenic effects of the drugs, and that "if the doctor had fulfilled his duty of care to the mother, the child would not likely have been born." Their first child was born in 1983 and was unaffected by the drugs. However, the plaintiff, who was born in 1984 and whose handicaps were attributed by the Court to the medication, requires lifetime care and supervision. Regarding the defendant's "duty to warn", Justice Jewers concluded:

> It is common ground that the defendant had a duty to warn Mr. and Mrs. Lacroix about any added risk to a fetus involved in the taking of the medication. It also appeared to be common ground that a patient in the position of Mrs. Lacroix had a 90% chance of giving birth to a normal child. Dr. Chudley, the medical geneticist who testified, said that the state of knowledge in 1982 of the medical profession concerning the teratogenic effects (birth defects) of Tegretol and Mebaral should have been disclosed to a woman who was contemplating pregnancy in 1982. He quoted...the committee on drugs of the American Academy of Pediatrics (1979) that no woman should receive anticonvulsant medication unnecessarily and that, when a woman who has epilepsy and requires medication asks about pregnancy, she should be advised that she has a 90% chance of having a normal child but that the risk of congenital malformations and mental retardation is two to three times greater than the average. . . .

Still, Justice Jewers denied the wrongful life claim and his ruling was affirmed in 2001 by a three-judge panel of the Manitoba Court of Appeal.[11] The Court did little more than quote extensively from the *McKay* case and adopt its position on the impossibility of measuring damages for wrongful life. In 2002 the Supreme Court of Canada denied an application by the couple to hear the case, thus foregoing the opportunity to settle the Canadian law on wrongful life. As it now stands in Manitoba, a child such as Donna Lacroix is dependent upon the diligence of her parents to file suit before the limitation period has expired. If they fail to do so, then a law suit cannot be brought in the child's name notwithstanding evidence of negligence by the physician that would have been sufficient to win an action for wrongful birth.

Although the Canadian courts have slammed the door on wrongful life claims, a minority of American courts have ruled otherwise.[12] The decisions agree with the majority view denying recovery for the child's pain and suffering. They acknowledge that such damages are incapable of measurement because there is no rational way to compare non-existence with the pain and suffering of the child's impaired life. But they have awarded damages for medical and associated costs. The line of reasoning is much the same in the various cases and can be summarized as follows:

> The reality of the wrongful life claim is that a handicapped child exists, and that its existence is attributable to the defendant's negligence. We concede that comparing the value of an impaired life to that of the void of non-existence is a task beyond human judgment. But it is neither necessary nor just to retreat into meditation on the mysteries of life. The reality is that the child will require medical care and social services for its lifetime. Our allowance of damages is based upon the child's financial needs, not on the belief that non-existence is preferable to an impaired life. To be blunt the question is, Who will pay? Our answer is that the defendant-physician must pay, since but for him such expenses would not be incurred.

Finally, it should be noted that an Ontario trial judge has recently expressed reservations about the rejection of wrongful life claims in Canada. In the case of *Petkovich (Litigation Guardian of) v. Olupona*, Justice Gans of the Ontario Superior Court of Justice dismissed a motion to strike out the wrongful life claim of the minor plaintiff as disclosing no reasonable cause of action.[13] The child was afflicted with Spina bifida and hydrocephalus, and the statement of claim alleged that the condition should have been detected during two ultrasound procedures and that, if so, the pregnancy would have been terminated. As he acknowledged:

> There is no doubt that a wrongful life claim raises a number of difficult, complex and fundamental issues which have indeed been rejected by a number of courts in a multitude of jurisdictions. . . .

He was nevertheless prepared to leave the question open and to allow the matter to proceed to trial. Since the claim was limited to the economic cost of caring for the plaintiff from the age of 18 to his death, Justice Gans was of the view that the "philosophical condundrum" of the sanctity of life and existence versus non-existence need not be confronted. And whatever the ultimate result of the case, this is the first sign of a backing away from the judicial consensus that the tort of wrongful life has no place in Canadian law. (The parents had filed their own claim for wrongful birth, which was not in issue at this stage of the proceedings.)

4. THE TORT OF WRONGFUL PREGNANCY

Although the tort of wrongful pregnancy is conceptually different from the tort of wrongful birth, it merits a brief discussion because its legal basis also centres upon a child born to the plaintiff(s). The label *wrongful pregnancy* (or *wrongful conception*) has been attached to cases in which parents claim compensation from a physician for the wrongful birth of a *healthy* child. The typical scenario is that of a negligently performed sterilization, whether female or male, which results in an unintended pregnancy and birth. (There are also rare cases of botched abortion in which the fact is discovered too late for a second procedure. These are of course wrongful pregnancy — not wrongful conception — cases; it is only the sterilization cases for which the terms are used interchangeably. But whether failed sterilization or abortion, the cases fall under the same legal category.)

Wrongful pregnancy cases thus involve negligently performed surgery, not the negligent withholding or disclosure of information that underlies the tort of wrongful birth. In a wrongful pregnancy case, the parents have an unplanned healthy child.* In a wrongful birth case, the parents have a planned albeit unhealthy child. (In the former case, the physician is sued for the negligent performance of a medical procedure. In the latter case, the physician is sued for the negligent failure to obtain informed consent.)

An illustrative case is *Cataford c. Moreau*,[14] a 1978 decision by the Quebec Superior Court. The defendant-surgeon negligently performed a sterilization procedure upon Mrs. Cataford, the mother of 10 children. Four

---

* As defined in Black's Law Dictionary: "Wrongful conception. Also known as wrongful pregnancy, it is a claim by parents for damages arising from the negligent performance of a sterilization procedure or abortion, and the subsequent birth of a child."

months later she became pregnant and in due course delivered her 11th child. She was then successfully sterilized. The Court awarded damages for the inconvenience of the pregnancy and for the pain occasioned by the birth and the second sterilization procedure. The parents had also claimed damages for the cost of maintaining the child until adulthood. The Court refused to award such damages, not because it denied the validity of the claim in principle but because it determined that the family's social allowances would cover the cost of the child's upkeep.

In the United States the tort of wrongful pregnancy is as well embedded in case law as is the tort of wrongful birth. In the former cases, the American courts have uniformly rejected the defence that the parents could have resolved the unwelcome situation by opting for abortion or adoption. The courts have ruled that the decision to avoid conception cannot be translated into a duty to dispose of the fetus or the child once born. But there is no consensus on the parental claim for damages for the cost of rearing the unplanned child to adulthood. Some courts deny the claim altogether, while others allow recovery for all child-rearing expenses. Others adopt a middle ground position: permitting recovery for child-rearing costs offset by an amount that represents the benefit that the parents derive from the child. In the *Cataford* case, the Court indicated its support for the middle ground position.

There is a Canadian case which involved a new twist to a claim for wrongful pregnancy (and an equally new twist to a claim for wrongful life). In *Cherry (Guardian ad litem of) v. Borsman*,[15] a mother and grievously handicapped daughter sued the physician for a failed abortion that led to the child's birth. The defendant had miscalculated the progression of the pregnancy and failed to extract the fetus because he used too small a curette. By the time an ultrasound confirmed the pregnancy, it was too late for an abortion. The B.C. Supreme Court* judge found that the botched abortion initiated a chain of events that damaged the fetus and led to the birth of a child afflicted with mental retardation and cerebral palsy. This is the only reported wrongful pregnancy case in which the child was born handicapped, and it is the only "wrongful life" case in which the defendant-physician did in fact *cause* the child's handicaps. In that sense, it is not a wrongful life case as that concept has been legally defined. Thus, in awarding damages to the mother (for wrongful pregnancy) and to the child (for wrongful life), the Court was dealing with a bizarre fact situation that took it outside the defined parameters of wrongful pregnancy and wrongful life actions.

Although the tort of wrongful pregnancy is recognized on this side of the Atlantic Ocean, it has been extinguished in Great Britain. In a 1999

---

*   In B.C., the Supreme Court is the highest level trial court.

case called *McFarlane v. Tayside Health Board (Scotland)* (1999), the Judicial Committee of the House of Lords slammed the door on wrongful pregnancy claims by ruling that damages should never be awarded for the birth of a healthy child.[16]

5.   CANADIAN CASES ON WRONGFUL BIRTH/LIFE

(a) *Arndt v. Smith* (Supreme Court, 1997)[17]

When Carole Arndt was 12 weeks pregnant she contracted chicken pox, which prompted her to ask her physician (the defendant) about risks to the fetus. Although the defendant advised her that there was a small chance of skin and limb abnormalities, she did not inform her of the risks of cortical atrophy and mental retardation. Although aware of these more serious risks, the defendant did not disclose them to the plaintiff because "it was not, in her view, appropriate to unduly worry an expectant mother about an improbable risk and one for which she [the defendant] would not advise therapeutic abortion." The patient carried on with the pregnancy, giving birth in 1986 to a daughter born with congenital varicella syndrome, which prevents her from swallowing, burping, or vomiting. Because the walls of her pharynx cannot move food into the stomach, Miranda can feed only by way of a tube passing through her mouth and down her esophagus. According to medical experts, she would likely spend a substantial part of her life in hospital and die before her 30th birthday.

In 1991 statements of claim by the parents for wrongful birth and the child for wrongful life were filed against Dr. Smith in the B.C. Supreme Court. The latter was dismissed by the judge on the public policy grounds already noted. Regarding the parents' cause-of-action, the judge recognized in principle the tort of wrongful birth as he held that:

> There is a duty on a physician to warn his or her obstetric patients of all material risks faced by their unborn fetuses, thus enabling such patients to consider the option of a therapeutic abortion.

He found that the defendant's omission to inform the plaintiff of all material risks associated with her condition was "classic medical paternalism" and that such failure amounted to "medical negligence." However, he went on to rule that even if fully informed of the risks to the fetus, a reasonable patient in Ms. Arndt's situation would have carried through with the pregnancy. The judge cited a 1984 article that summarized the state of medical opinion at that time, in which the author stated:

> What advice should be given to the pregnant woman who has contracted varicella in the 1st or 2nd trimester of pregnancy? One can only state that

there is probably a very small risk for the birth of a child with the congenital varicella syndrome and that there is no convincing indication for therapeutic abortion.

Furthermore, the plaintiff had experienced four failed pregnancies (miscarriages and stillbirths), and she and her husband very much wanted a child. The judge also stressed that Ms. Arndt was sceptical about mainstream medicine and had planned for a natural childbirth with the aid of a midwife; she had even rejected an ultrasound scan (which admittedly would not have detected the incipient varicella syndrome). In addition, she could not have obtained an abortion until around the 15th week of pregnancy, when the procedure is more risky than a first trimester abortion. Of course, the issue was not whether Ms. Arndt would have opted for abortion if fully informed of the risks to fetal development. Rather, it was whether a reasonable patient in her situation — a planned pregnancy, a "very small risk" factor, and the option of a second trimester abortion — would have made the same decision. In other words, the plaintiff had to prove causation: that the defendant caused the child's birth because, if properly informed, a reasonable patient in her circumstances would have terminated the pregnancy. But the judge did not see it her way.

On appeal, a three-judge panel of the B.C. Court of Appeal reversed the decision and ordered a new trial because it was not satisfied with the trial judge's handling of the modified objective test. Each justice wrote a separate opinion, and Justice Lambert posed a question crying out for resolution: what happens if some reasonable patients in the plaintiff's position would have opted for abortion whereas others would not? Unfortunately, this pressing question was ignored when the case went to the Supreme Court, which overturned the Court of Appeal and reinstated the dismissal of the law suit. According to the high court:

> [I]t is appropriate to infer from the evidence that a reasonable person in the plaintiff's position would not have decided to terminate her pregnancy in the face of the very small increased risk to the fetus posed by her exposure to the virus that causes chickenpox.

(b) *S. v. S.* (Manitoba, 1994)[18]

Although *Arndt* was the first reported Canadian case on point, a number of *wrongful birth* cases had already been settled out of court. One such case involved a Winnipeg couple whose son was born in 1989 with Down syndrome, heart defects, visual impairment, and deafness. (The statement of claim was filed within the two year statutory period.) By the age of five, the child was still in diapers and could only eat baby food. The plaintiffs

— the husband is an ophthalmologist and his wife a public health nurse — alleged that the defendant, a family physician, had advised them that the results of a maternal serum alpha fetal protein (AFP) test indicated no fetal defects. The test in fact revealed that the 33-year-old pregnant patient was in the same risk category for Down syndrome as a 37-year-old: a risk factor of one to 189. The test results had come back to the physician with a yellow marker calling her attention to that risk factor, but for unexplained reasons she did not see it until some time after she had already assured the couple that the AFP results were normal. When she finally saw the marker, she said nothing to the plaintiffs, apparently relying on the odds that the child would not be afflicted.

The plaintiffs sued for damages to cover the extraordinary costs of raising the child (including round-the-clock care). As an alleged post-conception tort, it was claimed that if properly informed, the couple would have opted for amniocentesis and then abortion. The case was settled for an undisclosed sum on the morning that the trial was scheduled to begin.

We turn now to some other cases that went to trial.

(c) *H. (R.) v. Hunter* (Ontario, 1996)[19]

In *Hunter*, an action for negligence was brought against two physicians alleging their failure to refer the plaintiff for genetic consultation. As a result she bore two children (two years apart) afflicted with Duchenne muscular dystrophy, the same disease that had caused her brother's death. The plaintiff alleged that, if there had been the referrals, she would have averted the births either by way of contraception or abortion. An Ontario civil jury ruled in the plaintiff's favour. (That settled the matter of liability because the only issue in the reported judgment was the measure of damages.)

(d) *Krangle (Guardian ad litem of) v. Briscoe* (British Columbia, 1997)[20]

In this case a justice of the B.C. Supreme Court (trial division) awarded damages to the plaintiffs for the costs of rearing their six-year-old son who was born with Down syndrome. Mrs. Krangle was 36 years old and expecting her first child when she consulted Dr. Merrill, a family physician. The defendant conceded that he did no genetic counselling or testing, nor did he advise the patient that there was an increased risk of chromosomal abnormality because of her age. He conceded that amniocentesis would have diagnosed Down syndrome and that Mrs. Krangle would have opted for abortion. Although awarding damages to the parents, the judge dismissed an action brought in the child's name on the grounds that the defendant caused him no physical harm. (In other words, the Court accepted the wrong birth claim but denied the wrongful life claim.)

(e) *Jones (Guardian ad litem of) v. Rostvig* (British Columbia, 1999)[21]

In another case before the B.C. Supreme Court, the judge dismissed an action for wrongful life brought on behalf of an infant born with Down syndrome. The plaintiff was 35 years old when her son was born. Her complaint was that the defendant had failed to alert her to pre-natal testing (a mid-trimester amniocentesis) which would have indicated Down syndrome and prompted her to obtain an abortion. One presumes that a wrongful birth claim by the parents had also been filed but the only issue here was the child's claim. And that was emphatically rejected by the judge because of the "conceptual and philosophical" obstacles to holding that a child had been legally wronged because the negligence of the defendant had caused his very existence.

(f) *Mickle v. Salvation Army Grace Hospital, Windsor* (Ontario, 1999)[22]

In this case Justice Zuber of the Ontario Court of Justice dismissed an action for wrongful birth brought by the parents of a seven-year-old child born with CHILD syndrome (an acronym for congenital hemihypoplasia ichthyosis erythroderma and limb deficiencies). The defendants were a radiologist and ultrasound technician. The judge described the child's condition:

> Sarah has intense and wide-spread reddening of the skin on her right side. Her right shoulder is not normally developed. She has an extremely short right arm and a paddle-like right hand. Her right leg is extremely short and has a rotated foot. She has no effective hip on the right side. . . . She has been fitted with a right leg prosthesis, which enables her to walk. Since she has no effective right hip she walks by swinging the right leg prosthesis around rather than by extending it forward. . . . As a result, walking becomes a more difficult exercise than what otherwise would be the case.

Still, she had a normal life expectancy and academically was "at the top of her class." According to her second grade teacher, Sarah was "spunky and assertive, has an engaging personality and interacts well with both children and adults."

It was alleged that the defendants had negligently failed to detect the condition in utero and that if informed the plaintiff would have exercised her right to abortion. A routine or Level 1 ultrasound had been performed on the plaintiff, which according to the judge was appropriate for a low risk patient. The crux of the complaint was that the right side abnormalities were not detected because not all the limbs were examined. However, the medical witnesses appearing for the defence pointed out that professional guidelines at that time did not require that all limbs be examined during a routine obstetrical ultrasound. Justice Zuber accepted that evidence and consequently found no negligence by the technician and radiologist.

That should have ended the matter, given that a wrongful birth claim is premised upon a finding of negligent nondisclosure. Be that as it may, the judge went on to say that even if negligence had been proved, he would have ruled against the plaintiff on the issue of causation. (Recall that the plaintiff must prove that if there had been disclosure, a reasonable patient in her circumstances would have aborted the pregnancy. In his view, a reasonable patient with knowledge of the deformities would have carried the pregnancy to term. From that standpoint it follows that the actual failure to inform is beside the point; it hasn't caused the birth of a disabled child because the child would have been born in any event.

Justice Zuber accordingly posed the question: if the ultrasound had revealed a significant asymmetry between the left and right side limbs, would a reasonable patient in the plaintiff's shoes have chosen abortion? As he saw it:

> (T)he condition of asymmetrical limb development is a very long way from those very tragic cases in which it is revealed that the fetus is devastatingly disabled, both mentally and physically. In these circumstances, I cannot conclude that a reasonable woman in Kelly Mickle's circumstances would choose abortion. Thus, in my view, apart altogether from the issue of negligence, this action must fail.

Given that the question of causation was irrelevant once the case was dismissed for the failure to prove negligence, why did the judge pursue the matter? I suggest that the answer lies in the final paragraph of his decision:

> To characterize Sarah's existence as a form of harm would be an extraordinary denigration of the value of her life. The acceptance of such a notion would surely also denigrate the value of the lives of all those who suffer from serious disabilities. I am unable to characterize the presence of this bright, beautiful, courageous (albeit seriously physically challenged) child as a form of harm that should be translated into an assessment of general damages.

This may be a noble sentiment, but still it is another indication of the flaw in the reasonable patient (so-called modified objective) test that was noted by Justice Lambert of the B.C. Court of Appeal in the *Arndt v. Smith* case. Justice Zuber himself recognized the difficulty when the court is confronting a wrongful birth claim:

> In a conventional *Reibl v. Hughes* case,* a court is asked whether a reasonable patient in the circumstances of the plaintiff would elect a form of treatment, balancing the prospect of cure or improved health against the risks of a worsened condition. In a case such as the one before me, the balance is between the burdens both financial and emotional that may be imposed on the mother and the continued life of the unborn child — a far different comparison. In a conventional case one is able to proceed on the basis of common values. . . . However, in cases such as the one before me, it is difficult to find any common or shared values.

Given that this was not a black and white case — either minimal handicap on the one hand or devastating mental and physical handicap on the other — the application of the reasonable patient standard is but the judicial pretence of objectivity. For how can a court conclude one way or the other when as here a case falls in the grey area?

6. SUMMING UP

The well entrenched tort of wrongful birth serves notice to physicians that they are duty bound to provide their patients with sufficient information to enable them to make informed procreative choices. The physician's duty stems from the patient's legal right to prevent the conception and birth of handicapped offspring. This is not to suggest that the physician is an insurer; liability is not imposed merely because her patient has borne a child with genetic or congenital defects. The physician is answerable in law only if the plaintiff-patient can prove that the child would not have been born but for her negligent disclosure or negligent withholding of information. The implication for the practitioner of reproductive medicine, whether generalist or specialist, is that the best safeguard against a wrongful birth claim is an understanding of the medical and clinical aspects of human genetics and teratology.

Still, there are health caregivers and laypersons who do not regard diagnostic and genetic testing before and during pregnancy as medical progress pure and simple. Dr. Everett Koop, the Surgeon General of the United States in the Reagan administration, repeatedly referred to pre-natal

---

* This landmark case is discussed in Chapter 4.

testing as "search and destroy missions." Brian Wilson, a prominent government minister in England, has condemned as "grotesque" the use of amniocentesis to "eliminate" the majority of fetuses diagnosed with Down syndrome.[23] Mr. Wilson, who has a child with the syndrome, has deplored the fact that about 1,800 abortions per year are performed in Great Britain for fetal abnormalities. Similar expressions of discontent have been recorded in Canada as elsewhere. When the Manitoba case of *S. v. S.* was in the news, the media reported that a number of physicians in the province admitted that they omit to inform pregnant patients about pre-natal testing because of their opposition to abortion. Surely this is unconscionable. Physicians are free to believe what they will about abortion and other contentious matters, but they are not free to hold their patients hostage to beliefs that subvert informed reproductive decision-making. If a physician cannot in good conscience support the patient in this regard, then his clear duty is to facilitate transfer to a colleague who will.

Finally, we note the unlikelihood that legal liability in regard to genetic screening will be confined to the filing of wrongful birth and wrongful life suits. The very nature of genetic screening is bound to impact upon the physician's duty to maintain patient confidentiality because genetic information enables a physician "to predict, intervene, and prevent heritable disorders not only in the individual, but in the patient's nuclear and extended family as well."[24] It is true that Canadian law does not regard the physician's duty to keep silent as sacrosanct; consider, for example, that child welfare statutes typically require health caregivers to report suspected cases of child abuse. But it remains to be seen whether the law will move to impose a duty upon physicians to breach confidentiality in compelling cases in which patients refuse to permit disclosure of genetic information that might prevent harm to blood relatives or impact upon the patient's spouse. In other words, should physicians owe a duty of disclosure to third parties in such cases? (In the *Tarasoff* case, which is discussed in Chapter 10, the Supreme Court of California ruled that when a patient informed a therapist of his intention to kill a young woman, the therapist should have breached confidentiality and alerted the intended victim to the threat. However, she was not warned and was killed by the patient, and the Court imposed liability for nondisclosure. It remains to be seen whether the law will follow suit in cases of genetic nondisclosure.) In a time of legal uncertainty, it is pertinent to quote the conclusion of a Canadian lawyer on the subject of confidentiality and familial access to genetic information:[25]

What must be considered is the patient's duty in all this. The patient does have an ethical duty to inform familial relations when there is a risk to their well-being, and the physician should counsel the patient to fulfil that duty. In fact, this may be the only course of action the physician can take in this matter and know that it will not be followed by a statement of claim.

NOTES

1. *Park v. Chessin*, 386 N.E.2d 807 (U.S. N.Y., 1978).
2. *Schroeder v. Perkel*, 432 A.2d 834 (1981).
3. *Harbeson v. Parke-Davies Inc.*, 656 P.2d 483 (U.S. Wash., 1983).
4. *Berman v. Allen*, 404 A.2d 8 (1979).
5. *Goldberg v. Ruskin*, 471 N.E.2d 530 (1984).
6. *Jacobs v. Theimer*, 519 S.W.2d 846 (1975).
7. *Gleitman v. Cosgrove*, 227 A.2d 689 (1967).
8. *Becker v. Schwartz*, 386 N.E.2d 807 (U.S. N.Y., 1978) [reported together with *Park v. Chessin*, note 1].
9. *McKay v. Essex Area Health Authority*, [1982] 2 W.L.R. 890.
10. *Lacroix (Litigation Guardian of) v. Dominique*, [1999] 12 W.W.R. 38 (Man. Q.B.), affirmed (2001), 202 D.L.R. (4th) 121 (Man. C.A.), leave to appeal refused (2002), 2002 CarswellMan 89, 2002 CarswellMan 90 (S.C.C.).
11. *Lacroix (Litigation Guardian of) v. Dominique*, (2001) 202 D.L.R. (4th) 121 (Man. C.A.), leave to appeal refused (2002), 2002 CarswellMan 89, 2002 CarswellMan 90 (S.C.C.). This is the only wrongful life case that has been heard by a provincial court of appeal.
12. The first case to recognize a wrong life action was *Curlender v. Bio-Science Laboratories*, 165 Cal. R. 477 (1980). The intermediate appellate court based its decision on the proposition that there should be a remedy for every wrong committed.
13. *Petkovich (Litigation Guardian of) v. Olupona* (2002), [2002] O.J. No. 1269, 2002 CarswellOnt 1081 (S.C.J.).
14. *Cataford c. Moreau* (1978), 7 C.C.L.T. 241, 114 D.L.R. (3d) 585 (S.C.).
15. *Cherry (Guardian ad litem of) v. Borsman* (1990), 5 C.C.L.T. (2d) 243 (B.C. S.C.), additional reasons at (1991), 5 C.C.L.T. (2d) 243 at 298 (B.C. S.C.), varied (1992), 12 C.C.L.T. (2d) 137 (B.C. C.A.), leave to appeal refused [1993] 2 S.C.R. vi.
16. *McFarlane v. Tayside Health Board (Scotland)*, [1999] 4 All E.R. 961 (H.L.). Notwithstanding the breadth of the *McFarlane* ruling, in 2002 the Court of Appeal carved out an exception in a case called *Rees v. Darlington Memorial Hospital NHS Trust*, in which a 'severely visually handicapped' woman bore a healthy child after a negligent sterilization procedure. The Court ruled that damages were allowable for the extra costs of raising the child resulting from her disability. The Court reasoned that, if damages were permitted for the extra costs of raising a disabled child, then the same rule should apply when the extra costs involved a disabled parent raising a healthy child. See **NLJ Practitioner**, February 22, 2002, at 281-2.
17. *Arndt v. Smith* (1997), 148 D.L.R. (4th) 48 (S.C.C.).
18. **Winnipeg Free Press**, September 6, 1994, at A1.

19. *H. (R.) v. Hunter* (1996), 32 C.C.L.T. (2d) 44 (Ont.).

20. *Krangle (Guardian ad litem of) v. Brisco* (1997), [1997] B.C.J. No. 2740, 1997 CarswellBC 2543 (S.C.), additional reasons at (1998), 1998 CarswellBC 1784, [1998] B.C.J. No. 1954 (S.C.), reversed (2000), 2000 CarswellBC 458, [2000] B.C.J. No. 465 (C.A.), leave to appeal allowed (2000), 2000 CarswellBC 2330, 2000 CarswellBC 2331 (S.C.C.), reversed (2002), [2002] S.C.J. No. 8, 2002 CarswellBC 64, 2002 CarswellBC 65. The case did go to the Supreme Court but only on the question of damages. See (2002), [2002] S.C.J. No. 8, 2002 CarswellBC 64, 2002 CarswellBC 65.

21. *Jones (Guardian ad litem of) v. Rostvig* (1999), [1999] B.C.J. No. 647, 1999 CarswellBC 595 (S.C.).

22. *Mickle v. Salvation Army Grace Hospital, Windsor* (1999), 166 D.L.R. (4th) 743 (Ont. Gen. Div.).

23. **The Daily Telegraph**, April 14, 2001, at 1.

24. L. Elias, A clinical approach to legal and ethical problems in human genetics. 39 **Emory Law Journal** 811 (1990).

25. J. Miller, Physician-patient confidentiality and familial access to genetic information. 2 **Health Law Journal** 141 (1994). This article is an excellent introduction to the subject matter. The Health Law Journal is published by the Health Law Institute, University of Alberta.

15

ISSUES IN REPRODUCTIVE CHOICE: PART 2

SUMMARY

The focus of this chapter is upon the following topics:

1. *Sterilization*. A mentally competent adult may consent to contraceptive sterilization and spousal consent is not legally required. A mentally handicapped adult can lawfully consent so long as she understands the nature and consequences of the surgery and the connection between sexual intercourse, pregnancy, and birth. In a 1986 case, *Re Eve* the Supreme Court prohibited the contraceptive sterilization of mentally handicapped persons who lack the mental capacity to consent. The ruling in *Eve* is contrasted with British and American cases that permit the procedure when there is compelling evidence that it will serve the incompetent person's best interests.

2. *Abortion*. The landmark 1988 *Morgentaler* case is summarized. In *Morgentaler*, the Supreme Court ruled that the *Criminal Code* provisions on abortion were invalid as a breach of the *Charter of Rights and Freedoms*. The decision left a gap in the law which the Court invited Parliament to fill, but that has not happened. In any event, there is still the issue of accessibility to abortion services.

3. *Maternal-Fetal Conflict*. Medical technology and knowledge have enabled physicians to bestow upon the fetus the status of patient. What happens when the physician comes to believe that one of his patients (the pregnant woman) is putting the other patient (the fetus) at risk? Is legal intervention ever warranted to protect a fetus from the pregnant woman? Issues are considered under three topic headings: the status of the fetus at common law; court-ordered obstetrical interventions; and substance abuse and pregnancy.

The chapter does not consider *non-coital (artificial) reproduction* issues — e.g. artificial insemination, surrogate motherhood, and in vitro fertilization — because federal regulation awaits enactment in Canada. However, that may not be long in coming; in May 2002, Health Minister Anne McLellan introduced the Assisted Human Reproduction Act. The proposed legislation stems from a longstanding interest and concern in the social policy issues stemming from clinical applications of non-coital reproduction. Amongst its provisions are prohibitions on the following: creating a human clone or transplanting a human clone into a human being; doing anything to "ensure or increase the probability that an embryo will be of a particular sex, or that would identify the sex of an in vitro embryo, except to prevent, diagnose or treat a sex-linked disorder or disease"; and paying for a woman to assume the role of a surrogate mother. (Surrogate motherhood desrcibes a scenario in which a woman who is artificially inseminated hands over the child to the sperm donor and his partner; since the ban applies only to commercial surrogacy, it leaves room for altruistic surrogacy.)

Advances in reproductive technology have prompted articles in Canadian law journals, reports on artificial insemination by the British Columbia Royal Commission on Family and Children's Law (1975) and the Saskatchewan Law Reform Commission (1981), and the *Report on Human Artificial Reproduction and Related Matters* (1985) by the Ontario Law Reform Commission. And in 1993 the federal government released *Proceed with Care: The Final Report of the Royal Commission on New Reproductive Technologies.*

1. STERILIZATION

(a) Eugenic Sterilization

The sterilization of mental incompetents for so-called *eugenic* indications is a black mark in medico-legal history.* In the early 20th century eugenics was proclaimed as the new science that would improve the human

---

* The literature on the eugenics movement is enormous. An excellent introduction to the subject is D.J. Kelves, *In the Name of Eugenics* (Albert A. Knopf, New York, 1985).

race by manipulating hereditary factors. Eugenicists zealously embraced biological determinism, believing that environmental factors counted for nothing and that heredity explained everything from mental illness, mental deficiency, epilepsy, and pauperism to prostitution, criminality, and addiction to alcohol and other drugs. The so-called science of eugenics amounted to the blind application to human behaviour of the principles of plant genetics formulated in the 19th century by Gregor Mendel. (An Austrian monk, Mendel crossbred peas for 40 years and is rightfully regarded as the pioneer geneticist.)

In the United States and England, eugenicists lobbied for state action to discourage the breeding of the "genetically unfit." Although the English eugenicists were unable to translate their ideas into public policy, their American colleagues met with stunning success. In 1907 a eugenic sterilization statute was enacted in Indiana, and by the 1930s 29 state legislatures had followed suit. All provided for the involuntary sterilization of mentally retarded persons, although two-thirds restricted the law's coverage to inmates of public institutions. A number of the statutes also covered persons labelled as mentally ill, epileptic, hereditary criminal, sex offender, moral degenerate, and syphilitic.

Many of the statutes have been repealed and those still found in state legislation are pretty much of a dead letter. Yet as recently as 1976, the North Carolina Supreme Court endorsed the practice of eugenic sterilization. In the case of *In re Moore's Sterilization*,[1] the Court ruled that a county social services department had the authority to order the sterilization of a minor (age unstated) whose I.Q. was under 40. The Court found the procedure warranted because there was uncontradicted evidence that unless sterilized, the minor "would procreate a child or children who would probably have serious physical, mental, or nervous diseases or deficiencies."

What about Canada? Eugenic sterilization laws were enacted in Alberta in 1928 and British Columbia in 1933 (both were repealed in the early 1970s). The law was of limited effect in B.C., but it was otherwise in Alberta. Alberta's *Sexual Sterilization Act* established a four-member Eugenics Board, stipulating that two members must be medical practitioners. The board was empowered to order the sterilization of mental hospital inmates who were: *psychotic*, afflicted with *neurosyphilis* and not responsive to treatment, *epileptic* with psychosis or mental deterioration, and suffering from *Huntington's Chorea*. The patient could consent "if capable of giving consent." Otherwise, the Act required spousal consent or the consent of parent or guardian if the candidate were unmarried or a minor, except that the consent requirement was waived for those with Huntington's Chorea. The surgery was authorized when an inmate was proposed for release and the board determined that the patient might safely be discharged if the danger of procreation with its attendant risk of multiplication of the evil by transmission of the disability to progeny were eliminated.

The Act was amended in 1937 to extend the board's jurisdiction to institutionalized *mental defectives* — but without a family consent requirement. As the statute directed, sterilization became a condition for the institutional release of mental patients and those diagnosed as mentally deficient. The inclusion of mental defectives in 1937 made children particularly vulnerable. From 1939 to 1953, 30% of the patients sterilized were between the ages of 10 and 15. The figure rose to 40% in the period from 1959 to 1972. The policy that institutional release was conditional upon sterilization was also expressed in the B.C. law, which applied to any inmate of an institution who

if discharged therefrom without being subjected to an operation for sexual sterilization, would be likely to beget or bear children who by reason of inheritance would have a tendency to serious mental disease or mental deficiency.

An unpublished study of the workings of the Alberta law revealed that it led to the sterilization of some 2,500 patients (of whom 65% were female).[2] Throughout the lifetime of the Act, native people were sterilized in disproportionately high number in comparison to population size. The figures for the board's final three years (1969-72) are particularly striking. Even though only 3% of Albertans were native, they totalled 25% of those sterilized. The study also found that throughout the history of the Act, those of British and West European ancestry were under-represented whereas those of Eastern European descent were over-represented. For example, from 1939-43, 35% of the procedures were performed on Eastern European ethnics, who formed but 15% of the general population. (Although the figures alone do not prove discrimination, they strongly hint at it.) The fact that the Alberta and B.C. statutes institutionalized the violation of human rights was sufficient reason to warrant their repeal. But beyond that, the statutes lacked scientific underpinning. The authors of a genetic critique of the Alberta statute observed shortly before its repeal:[3]

From a genetic point of view the act is antiquated, because it singles out in a rather incoherent way partly genetically induced and partly environmentally induced syndromes, which in the opinion of the modern geneticist constitute only minor contributions to the genetic burden of the population.

Alberta's foray into eugenic sterilization was in the news in 1996 when the Court of Queen's Bench awarded damages of $740,000 to Leilani

Muir, 51, who was institutionalized at the age of 10 in an Alberta training school for the mentally deficient and sterilized four years later.[4] All she was told was that she was undergoing a routine appendectomy (which was done), but the entire length of both fallopian tubes was also removed during the surgery. The reason for her sterilization was to prevent transmission of mental deficiency to any progeny. Yet there was no indication of mental defect and no psychometric testing or investigation was undertaken before she was sterilized. (As it turned out, she was not mentally defective but within the normal range of intelligence.) She left the school when she was 20 years old, against the advice of the medical staff, and it was not until years later during her marriage that she learned that she could not bear children.

Since the province admitted liability, the only issue before the Court was the measure of damages for wrongful confinement and sterilization. The law suit was not contested because it was indisputable that there had been no proper assessment of the plaintiff's mental state before she was institutionalized and then sterilized. As the judge found:

> The circumstances of Ms. Muir's sterilization were so high-handed and so contemptuous of the statutory authority to effect sterilization . . . that the community's, and the court's, sense of decency is offended. The court finds that Ms. Muir was improperly detained during this decade. . . . The standard of care practiced in justifying the Plaintiff's classification as mentally sub-normal, and her subsequent sterilization, fell substantially below the standard that I believe would have been expected of a specialist psychiatrist practicing at that time.

Over the next three years the Alberta government paid out $142 million to settle claims brought by 958 sterilization victims.

Sweden and Switzerland also have sorry histories of eugenic sterilization. A statute was enacted in the Swiss canton of Vaud in 1928, which according to a Swiss historian was applied primarily to female mental patients. The historian stated in 1997 that the practice was still continuing.[5] In Sweden, about 60,000 women were reported sterilized from 1936 to 1976.[6] Laws were also enacted in Denmark in 1929 and Norway, Belgium, Finland, Estonia, and Iceland in the 1930s.

Finally, even a cursory account of eugenic sterilization cannot avoid reference to the Third Reich. In 1933 (the year in which the B.C. statute was enacted), Adolf Hitler presented the German people with the Law for the Prevention of Hereditarily Diseased Offspring. The grounds for compulsory sterilization included: congenital mental deficiency; schizophrenia; manic-depressive insanity; and inherited epilepsy, blindness, and deafness. The Nazis set up 250 Hereditary Health Courts to administer the law, each staffed by two physicians and a jurist. By the outbreak of war in 1939, roughly 400,000 Germans had been sterilized.[7] Since 1907 there have been about 65,000 eugenic sterilizations in the United States, with more than one-third occurring in California.

(b) Contraceptive Sterilization

If a mentally competent adult chooses to undergo sterilization as a means of birth control, the law will not stand in his or her way. However, Canadian law has yet to address the question whether a mature minor can consent to contraceptive sterilization. It is arguable that on public policy grounds the minor should be required to wait until adulthood. (*Contraceptive sterilization* is distinguished from *therapeutic sterilization*, which is indicated for health reasons. As we shall see, the distinction between the two is not always that clear-cut.)

Consider a 20-year-old patient who asks to be sterilized because her intention is to shun marriage and children in pursuit of a career. If satisfied that she is mentally competent — that she understands the nature and consequences of the surgery — her physician is free to comply. What if the patient is married and insists that the procedure be kept secret from his or her spouse? In no province is there a legal requirement of spousal consent as a precondition to the sterilization of a married person. In any event, a provision to that effect would no doubt be stricken as a breach of the *equality rights* guarantee in the *Charter of Rights and Freedoms* (section 15). Even so, the physician may choose to withhold her services if her moral principles cannot abide the patient's insistence upon nondisclosure. The physician may likewise decline to sterilize her 20-year-old patient if she doubts the wisdom and maturity of her judgment. (In either case, the unwilling physician is ethically bound to make a referral since the patient is lawfully entitled to undergo the surgery.)

The fact of mental handicap is not in itself incompatible with informed consent to contraceptive sterilization. Notwithstanding her disability, a mentally handicapped adult is allowed to consent so long as she understands not only the nature and consequences of the surgery but also the connection between sexual intercourse, pregnancy, and childbirth. However, the physician is well advised to obtain a psychiatric finding of mental competency before proceeding.

What about parental consent to contraceptive sterilization when the individual, whether adult or minor, clearly lacks the mental capacity to consent? In the past, physicians routinely complied with parental (and institutional) requests for the procedure. They did so even though the legality of the surgery was clearly questionable, given that non-consensual contraceptive sterilization would normally amount to the tort of battery. In Ontario nearly 300 "mentally retarded" minors were sterilized in 1976, according to a Community and Social Services Ministry study that examined health insurance billings. In Quebec, 170 obstetricians and gynaecologists responded to a survey (a 46% return rate) seeking data on sterilizations performed between 1976-8 on "mentally retarded" adults and minors. The respondents reported carrying out 517 procedures. Since provincial statutes did not forbid the practice, physicians presumably assumed that they were acting within the law. Be that as it may, the Supreme Court banned the non-therapeutic sterilization of mental incompetents in the 1986 case, *Eve*, to which we now turn.

(i) *The Case of Eve, Re (Supreme Court of Canada, 1986)*[8]

The issue before the Supreme Court in the *Eve* case was the legality of contraceptive sterilization of mentally handicapped persons lacking the capacity to consent. In 1979 the Family Court in Prince Edward Island refused an application by the mother of a 24-year-old woman (whom the court dubbed "Eve") for authorization to consent to a tubal ligation for her daughter. Eve was attending a school for retarded adults, and her widowed mother was prompted to consider sterilization when her daughter formed a friendship with a male classmate. The judge described her condition:

> Eve suffers what is described as extreme expressive aphasia. She is unquestionably at least mildly to moderately retarded. She has some learning skills, but only to a limited level. She is described as being a pleasant and affectionate person who, physically, is an adult person, quite capable of being attracted to, as well as attractive to, the opposite sex. While she might be able to carry out the mechanical duties of a mother, under supervision, she is incapable of being a mother in any other sense. . . . (S)he would have no concept of the idea of marriage, or indeed the consequential relationship between intercourse, pregnancy, and birth (and she) is incapable of effective alternative means of contraception. . . .

The case was not finally resolved until seven years later, when by unanimous judgment the Supreme Court expressly prohibited the non-therapeutic sterilization of mental incompetents. In the Court's view, the procedure was a "grave intrusion" upon human rights when compared to its "highly questionable advantages." The Court found it "difficult to imagine a case in which non-therapeutic sterilization could possibly be of benefit" to a mental incompetent. The judgment stressed that "the importance of maintaining the physical integrity of a human being ranks high in our scale of values, particularly as it affects the privilege of giving life." The Supreme

Court consequently concluded that no court could "deprive a woman of that privilege for purely social or other non-therapeutic purposes without her consent."

The Supreme Court was confronted in *Eve* with an issue involving the judicial wardship role: the time-honoured responsibility of the courts (its so-called *parens patriae* jurisdiction) to protect the rights and welfare of mental incompetents. The judgment reflects the Court's position that authorizing the non-therapeutic sterilization of a mentally incompetent person would amount to the betrayal of a vulnerable person whom the judiciary was duty bound to protect.

The Supreme Court was mindful of the abuses committed in the name of eugenic sterilization. After commenting at length on the American experience, it prefaced its reference to the Alberta and B.C. statutes by observing that the decision to sterilize a mentally incompetent person "involves values in an area where our social history clouds our vision and encourages many to perceive the mentally handicapped as somewhat less than human." Still, eugenic sterilization was not at issue in *Eve*, as the question was not whether it was in the best interests of the human gene pool that Eve be sterilized. The case was rather about non-consensual *contraceptive* sterilization: whether the interests of Eve herself would be best served by depriving her of what the Supreme Court referred to as the "great privilege of giving birth." But as the Court indicated, the spectre of eugenic sterilization was a major reason why an application to sterilize a mental incompetent had to be approached with the utmost caution. That history lesson aside, the Court found ample grounds to justify its position, emphasizing the following factors:

1. There is considerable evidence that non-consensual sterilization produces a "significant negative psychological impact on the mentally handicapped."
2. There is no evidence that the stresses of pregnancy, delivery, and birth are greater for the mentally handicapped than for other women.
3. Although there are mental incompetents who are unfit parents, that kind of social inadequacy is not limited to the mentally handicapped.
4. Finally, from a human rights standpoint the prospect of unfit parenting does not warrant a response as drastic as non-consensual sterilization.

The Court conceded that the sterilization of mental incompetents was on occasion warranted on therapeutic grounds, adding that "this, of course, does not allow for subterfuge or for treatment of some minor medical problem." The Court defined therapeutic sterilization as surgery necessary for the "physical or mental health" of the patient. Although acknowledging that it was no easy matter to distinguish between non-therapeutic and therapeutic sterilization, the Court offered no guidance in this regard beyond its comment that the decision by the British Columbia Court of Appeal in a 1985 case, *K., Re*,[9] was "at best dangerously close to the limits of the permissible."

In that case, the parents of an epileptic and severely mentally handicapped 10-year-old, whose developmental level was that of a two-year-old, had filed a petition seeking judicial authority to consent to a hysterectomy. There was psychiatric testimony that she suffered a phobic aversion to the sight of blood, and that it was predictable that she would react with unmanageable hysteria to menstrual flow. A pediatric neurologist, who had treated the girl since birth, testified that she could not experience a loss of "gender identity" since she could comprehend neither menstrual function nor the loss of her uterus. (The reason for his testimony was that studies indicate that menstruation reinforces gender identity, which is an aspect of training for the severely handicapped.) There was also evidence that a desensitization programme was not a viable option, given that it had taken the child four years to learn how to use a spoon. The trial judge denied the petition and the parents appealed.

The B.C. Court of Appeal was persuaded by the medical evidence that the proposed surgery would clearly promote the child's best interests and was therefore therapeutic in nature. It accordingly reversed the lower court decision and granted the petition. Stressing that its ruling did not signify approval for the contraceptive sterilization of mental incompetents, the Court forcefully stated that:

> To have insisted on a meaningless retention of the right to reproduce would have been, in the circumstances of the case, a direct breach of the right of infant K to be protected against unnecessary pain and suffering.

By characterizing the *K.* case as "dangerously close to the limits of the permissible", the Supreme Court has served notice of the restricted sense in which it is prepared to recognize a sterilization procedure as "therapeutic." However, the high court's view is not shared by the Canadian Medical Association. In 1985 (one year before the Supreme Court's ruling in *Eve*), the CMA's General Council issued a policy statement regarding the sterilization of mentally handicapped persons lacking the capacity to consent. The CMA's position is that the procedure is permissible if the following clinical criteria are satisfied:

1. the patient is apparently fertile; and
2. there is clear benefit to the patient in that the overall benefit outweighs the trauma experienced as a result of the operation; and

3. alternative, less permanent methods of contraception are inappropriate for the individual.

By endorsing a best interests test, the CMA guidelines bypass the definitional muddle of a therapeutic-versus-non-therapeutic dichotomy. The CMA's position is in line with the admittedly overbroad definition of health formulated by the World Health Organization — "a state of complete physical, mental, and social well-being." (In *Eve*, the Supreme Court explicitly labelled social factors as non-therapeutic.) The CMA's approach also accords with that of the B.C. Court of Appeal, which declared in the *K.* case that:

> The test is not whether the operation is "therapeutic" or "non-therapeutic" but whether the anticipated benefits flowing from the operation are such that they exceed the harm or risk of harm to infant K.

Although not the law in Canada, the policy position endorsed by the CMA and the B.C. Court of Appeal is in effect the law in Great Britain. Six months after its decision in *Eve, Re*, the Supreme Court received a stunning rebuke from the highest court in Great Britain, the Judicial Committee of the House of Lords. In *B. (A Minor), Re* (1987),[10] the Law Lords authorized surgery to occlude the fallopian tubes of Jeanette, a 17-year-old whose mental development was that of a child of five and who could speak in sentences of only one or two words.

The girl was living in a residential facility where she had begun to make provocative approaches to male staff members and residents. She had been found in a "compromising situation" in a bathroom, which led her caretakers to express concern about pregnancy. Their plan was to transfer her to an adult training centre in two years' time, where she would receive less supervision than in the residential facility. There was uncontradicted testimony from three medical witnesses — a psychiatrist, an obstetrician/gynecologist, and a pediatrician — that Jeanette could not comprehend pregnancy and childbirth, that she was totally incapable of caring for a child, and that contraception was not a viable option. The witnesses testified that it was in the girl's best interests to be allowed as much freedom as possible, but that the greater the freedom then obviously the greater the risk of pregnancy (a consideration that the Supreme Court of Canada would presumably reject as an impermissible social factor).

In spelling out that its primary responsibility was to safeguard the incompetent's best interests, their Lordships took pains to emphasize the issue at stake:

> This case is not about sterilization for social purposes; it is not about eugenics;
> it is not about the convenience of those whose task it is to care for the ward

or the anxieties of her family; and it involves no general principle of public policy. It is about what is in the best interests of this unfortunate young woman and how best she can be given the protection which is essential to her future well-being so that she may lead as full a life as her intellectual capacity allows.

Because it found uncontroverted evidence that for Jeanette pregnancy would amount to an "unmitigated disaster", the Court unanimously authorized her sterilization. In the course of its judgment, the Law Lords took strong exception to the ruling in *Eve*. The high court of Great Britain scorned the high court of Canada's outright ban on non-therapeutic sterilization, branding the decision as "totally unconvincing and in startling contradiction to the welfare principle which should be the first and paramount consideration in wardship (guardianship) cases." It labelled the distinction drawn in *Eve* between therapeutic and non-therapeutic sterilization as "meaningless" and "quite irrelevant to the welfare principle." The Law Lords emphatically rejected the "sweeping generalization" pronounced in *Eve* that a mentally incompetent person's best interests could never be fostered by non-therapeutic sterilization:

> To say that the court can never authorize sterilization of a ward as being in her best interests would be patently wrong. To say that it can only do so if the operation is "therapeutic" as opposed to "non-therapeutic" is to divert attention from the true issue, which is whether the operation is in the ward's best interests, and remove it to an area of arid semantic debate as to where the line is to be drawn between "therapeutic" and "non-therapeutic" treatment.

In *Eve* the Supreme Court of Canada referred to childbirth as a "basic right", from which it followed that sterilization "removes from a person the great privilege of giving birth." In *B. (A Minor), Re*, the Law Lords responded with the scathing comment that:

> To talk of the "basic right" to reproduce of an individual who is not capable of knowing the causal connection between intercourse and childbirth, the nature of pregnancy, what is involved in delivery, unable to form maternal instincts or to care for a child, appears wholly to part company with reality.

Although the Law Lords opted for a "best interests" test, they offered no guidelines to facilitate its application in later cases. But there already was a precedent to that effect in the United States, a 1981 ruling by the New Jersey Supreme Court in the case of *In re Grady*.[11] (The case was cited by the Supreme Court in *Eve* but it chose to reject its approach.) In *Grady* the Court ruled that it was a judicial — not parental — function to determine the need for contraceptive sterilization, and that the judge "must be satisfied that sterilization is in the best interests of the incompetent person." The Court ordered that the following procedures be applied whenever the issue was judicially considered (leaving room for additional factors deemed relevant by the judge):

1. That the judge appoint an independent guardian to represent the incompetent, and that the guardian be given full opportunity to present evidence and to cross-examine witnesses at the hearing.

2. That the judge arrange for independent medical and psychological evaluations by qualified professionals, and further that the judge not rely solely upon the testimony of expert witnesses summoned by the party petitioning for sterilization.

3. That the judge meet with the person to obtain her own impressions of competency, and that she be convinced that "the individual lacks capacity to make a decision about sterilization and that the incapacity is not likely to change in the foreseeable future."

4. That the judge be persuaded by clear and convincing proof that sterilization serves the best interests of the incompetent, and that she accordingly consider the following factors:

    (a) "The possibility that the incompetent can become pregnant." (Fertility can be presumed in the absence of evidence to the contrary.)

    (b) "The possibility that the incompetent will experience trauma or psychological damage" in the event of pregnancy and/or birth, and conversely the possibility of such harm from the sterilization procedure.

    (c) "The likelihood that the person will voluntarily engage in sexual activity or be exposed to situations where sexual intercourse is imposed upon her."

    (d) The incompetent's inability to "understand reproduction or contraception and the likely permanence of that inability."

    (e) "The feasibility and medical advisability of less drastic means of contraception, both at the present time and under foreseeable future circumstances."

    (f) "The advisability of sterilization at the time of the application rather than in the future."

    (g) "The ability of the incompetent person to care for a child, or the possibility that the incompetent may at some future date be able to marry and, with a spouse, care for a child."

    (h) "A demonstration that the proponents of sterilization are seeking it in good faith, and that their primary concern is for the best interests of the incompetent person rather than their own or the public's convenience."

The detailed guidelines mandated in the *Grady* case are in effect an elaboration of the clinical criteria contained in the policy statement issued in 1985 by the CMA. (The *Grady* guidelines include the CMA's criteria — that the incompetent is apparently fertile, that she will clearly benefit from the procedure, and that less permanent methods of contraception are not feasible.)

It is certainly arguable that the incompetent's social well-being is a relevant factor if the determination of her best interests is the litmus test. Nonetheless, the law in Canada is otherwise, given the Supreme Court's narrow definition of "therapeutic" — physical and mental, but not social, well-being. Still, it would seem that there is no clear dividing line between social and mental well-being because whatever enhances the former is bound to exert a corresponding effect upon the latter. But the Supreme Court has not seen it that way.

On the other hand, the Court did not permanently shut the door to contraceptive sterilization of mental incompetents. Although ruling that judges currently lack that power, it left room for the enactment of provincial legislation to that effect. However, it was quick to add that the statute would have to contain sufficient safeguards to withstand scrutiny under the *Charter of Rights and Freedoms* (although it offered no model that would meet with its approval). What, then, if a provision were enacted with the kind of stringent safeguards mandated by the New Jersey Supreme Court in the *Grady* case? Perhaps the Court might allow it to stand on *Charter* grounds and perhaps not. The point is that the decision in *Eve* is not necessarily the last word on the subject of non-voluntary sterilization, particularly since none of the nine judges who unanimously decided that case is still on the bench.

How then should a physician respond when asked to sterilize a mentally handicapped person? As explained under the previous subheading (*Contraceptive Sterilization*), she is lawfully entitled to comply so long as the patient is mentally competent to consent to the surgery, notwithstanding her mental disability. But what if the person is mentally incompetent to consent? From a legal standpoint, one can say that the physician should stay her hand unless the procedure complies with the Supreme Court's definition of "therapeutic." But as we have seen, the definition says nothing more than that the surgery be considered necessary for the "physical or mental health" of the patient. All we know is that the facts in *Eve* do not satisfy such nebulous criteria, whereas the facts in *K.* barely make it. In sum, the Supreme Court has failed to provide clear markers to guide physician decision-making regarding the sterilization of mental incompetents. Unless confident that her case falls within the parameters of the ill-defined *Eve* standard, the physician is well advised to proceed only with the backing of a court order. Caution is warranted because the physician who sterilizes a mentally incompetent patient could find herself defending a civil suit for battery. (Although that contingency would arise only if the patient, or someone acting on her behalf, were to contest the legal validity of the procedure.) In any event, if uncertain about the patient's mental status the physician should arrange for a psychiatric assessment of competency.

Finally, one must consider the impact of treatment alternatives to surgical sterilization. There is Norplant, a set of tubes implanted under the skin which release a hormone that can prevent conception for five years. There is also Depo Provera, an injectible contraceptive; one injection is effective for three months. Because they offer less invasive and non-permanent options to surgical sterilization, these procedures leave open the possibility of reassessing the patient's circumstances at a later date. Although in *Eve* the Supreme Court dealt only with surgical sterilization, the comments voiced by the justices about discriminatory treatment of the handicapped would not appear to countenance the non-consensual resort to Norplant and Depo Provera. On the other hand, the ethical implications of non-consensual treatment are somewhat blunted by the less drastic nature of these alternatives. Still, it remains to be seen whether the law will allow their use for non-consenting patients.

(ii) *The Case of Adam Crockett (British Columbia, 2002)*

In 1997, when he was 21 years old, Adam Crockett* underwent a bilateral orchidectomy at a hospital in Nanaimo, British Columbia. Adam has the mental age of a five-year-old and the surgery was performed at the behest of his then single mother, who feared that the aggressive behaviour exhibited over the years by her hyperactive son could turn sexual. After he reached puberty he would get sexually aroused without knowing why. His mother recalled:[12]

> When my daughter brought friends over, he'd hug them and grab them. Once he rubbed a young child against himself. He didn't know what he was doing. He just knew it felt good.

Her concern was that an unwanted sexual advance could lead to his institutionalization, and she also wished to ensure that he never father a child as he could never develop parenting skills. As his legal guardian, she mistakenly assumed the right to consent to the surgery on his behalf. Five

---

*   Adam has a different surname from his mother and Adam is not his real name. He was given that name by the court (presumably because the young lady in the landmark case was called Eve).

years later Sandra Crockett found herself in the B.C. Supreme Court* facing a lawsuit by the provincial public guardian. The urologist who castrated Adam and the hospital were also named as co-defendants. (The urologist had previously been reprimanded and fined by the B.C. College of Physicians and Surgeons for performing an act prohibited by the Supreme Court in the *Eve* case.) According to the public guardian, the surgery was not only "unlawful, unethical, high-handed, arrogant, and demeaning", but also placed Adam at risk for early aging and osteoporosis.[13] Ms Crockett reacted defiantly to the lawsuit, saying that since the surgery her son needed less supervision because it had curbed his aggressive tendencies. The case did not go to trial because the urologist and hospital agreed to a financial settlement (paid into a trust for Adam). Ms Crockett has since expressed regret for her son's castration:[14]

> I realized he does have early signs of aging. I was never told (by the urologist) about all of the different things, osteoporosis, any of the risks involved in this except that it would sterilize him and reduce his aggression.

The media attention focused on the case prompted comments by disability rights advocates deploring the actions of Adam's mother and lauding the Supreme Court ruling in *Eve*. For the first time since *Eve* was decided, Canadians were reminded that the law does not allow for the non-therapeutic sterilization of mental incompetents. Recall that the Supreme Court defined therapeutic sterilization as necessary for the "physical or mental health" of the patient. Although it is arguable that institutionalization for sexual aggression would impair Adam's mental health, there are surely alternative means that could have been tried before resort to such an extreme remedy as castration. In any event, the restricted interpretation applied to "therapeutic" by the *Eve* court would not countenance Adam's surgery even if drugs or methods of behavioral control were tried and found wanting.

On the other hand, even if the litmus test were best interests (as in *B. (A Minor), Re* and *Grady*), sterilizing Adam to prevent his fathering a child would not qualify. The public guardian had decried the loss of Adam's "opportunity to become a parent", yet it is a role that he could neither fulfil nor even comprehend. That said, it must be acknowledged that, since fathering a child would have no direct impact upon his life, his best interests are not served by stripping him of that "opportunity." Although its eventuality could cause stress to his family, that would not be sufficient grounds to justify sterilization. If, however, the concern were mothering — not fathering — a child by a mental incompetent, one could argue that what is

---

* In B.C. the Supreme Court is the highest level trial court.

not in the best interests of an Adam is in the best interests of an Eve. In other words, quoting from the *Grady* guidelines, the question would be "the possibility that the incompetent will experience trauma or psychological damage" during pregnancy and/or childbirth. But as it now stands, that concern has no legal standing in Canada. As the Alberta Law Reform Institute put it in a 1988 report on sterilization:[15]

> The *Eve* decision means that the message "we will not risk letting you have babies" of the eugenic sterilization days has changed to the message "we insist you risk having babies" of the modern era.

2. ABORTION

(a) The Case of Regina v. Morgentaler (Supreme Court of Canada, 1988)[16]

In 1985 the Canadian Medical Association issued a policy statement on abortion, reiterating the stance it had maintained since 1971. Calling for the removal of the *Criminal Code* restrictions on access to abortion, the CMA argued that "such an elective surgical procedure should be decided upon by the patient and the physician(s) concerned."

Three years later, the Supreme Court aligned itself with the CMA policy when it handed down its momentous ruling in the case of *R. v. Morgentaler*. In *Morgentaler*, the high court invalidated as unconstitutional the *Criminal Code* regulations on legal access to abortion. (The decision was announced less than a week after the 15th anniversary of *Roe v. Wade*, the case in which the U.S. Supreme Court ruled that state laws restricting access to abortion were unconstitutional.)

The case arose in 1983 when Dr. Henry Morgentaler and two medical colleagues opened a Toronto abortion clinic. The Crown responded by indicting them on a charge of conspiracy "to procure the miscarriage of female persons", contrary to section 251 of the *Criminal Code*. The Crown was prompted to act because the three accused had issued a challenge to Canada's abortion law on two fronts: (1) the clinic was not a legally recognized abortion facility; and (2) their stated policy was to bypass the therapeutic abortion committee procedure mandated by law. (Section 251 prohibited abortion except under stipulated conditions, which the three accused contemptuously vowed to ignore.)

Dr. Morgentaler was no stranger to the criminal courts, since the trial marked the fourth occasion upon which he was prosecuted for his defiance of the Canadian abortion law. Juries in Montreal had acquitted him in three cases and the Toronto jury followed suit. However, the acquittal was overturned by the Ontario Court of Appeal, which ordered a new trial. That decision was appealed by the three physicians to the Supreme Court, whose decision was handed down 38 months after the jury acquittal. Although the Court did not set the direction for any Canadian abortion law of the future, its repudiation of the *Criminal Code* provisions did mark the road that could not be taken. Although section 251 is history, its content and constitutional defects are worth a brief review.

By a 5-2 margin, the Court declared the law null and void for breaching the guarantee of "security of the person" as enshrined in section 7 of the *Charter of Rights and Freedoms*. Enacted in 1969, the now defunct Criminal Code provisions had directed that an abortion could be lawfully performed only under the following conditions:

> The procedure had to be carried out in an "accredited" hospital, defined as "a hospital accredited by the Canadian Council on Hospital Accreditation in which diagnostic services and medical, surgical, and obstetrical treatment are provided." (According to *The Badgley Report*, a federal government study of the workings of the abortion law that was published in 1977, 58% of Canadian hospitals were ineligible for accreditation as abortion facilities.)

> The applicant had to have her case presented to an accredited hospital's therapeutic abortion committee. The committee had to be composed of at least three qualified medical practitioners. Committee approval required that a majority certify in writing that in its opinion, "the continuation of the pregnancy . . . would be likely to endanger her life or health."

The law's policy was set not only by what it provided but also by what it failed to provide. Although legal access to abortion was dependent upon committee approval, the *Criminal Code* did not require accredited hospitals to appoint committees. In effect if not by design, the result for women across Canada was a glaring inequality of access to abortion services. Statistics Canada reported that by 1982, only 46% of accredited hospitals nationwide had established therapeutic abortion committees. (There were no statistics on point since that date.) An Ontario study found that although 54% of accredited hospitals had committees in 1986, 12 of the 95 hospitals with committees had performed no abortions during that year. Legal abortions were unavailable in Prince Edward Island and the procedure was notably difficult to come by in Newfoundland and Saskatchewan.

Although "life or health" were the stated bench marks for committee approval, the *Criminal Code* neglected to define *health*. Consequently, there was no uniform standard for assessing the legal grounds for abortion. There were committees that applied the World Health Organization's overly broad formulation — health defined as "a state of physical, mental, and social well-being" — which in effect translated into abortion-on-demand. Some committees confined their focus to physical and mental health, whereas others considered only physical health. And there were committees that applied different standards for married and unmarried women.

In short, even where committees were in place, there was no uniformity in approach because there was no clearly articulated policy to guide decision-making. Gross disparity was predictable since the only guideline available to the committees was the amorphous "life or health" standard.

Another constitutional defect of the law was that the bureaucratic procedure mandated by the *Criminal Code* caused women to experience varying periods of delay before the abortion could be carried out. Delay was exacerbated by a factor that the Crown acknowledged in its written argument in the *Morgentaler* case:

> The evidence discloses that some women may find it very difficult to obtain an abortion; by necessity, abortion services are limited, since hospitals have budgetary, time, space, and staff constraints as well as many medical responsibilities. As a result of these problems a woman may have to apply to several hospitals.

The *Charter* case against the abortion law was forcefully presented by Chief Justice Dickson. He ruled that section 251 infringed upon the *Charter's* section 7 guarantee of "security of the person" by violating the bodily integrity of the woman seeking abortion "at the most basic physical and emotional level." The reason was that the law forced her to carry her unwanted pregnancy to term unless she satisfied "criteria entirely unrelated to her own priorities and aspirations." She was threatened in a physical sense because the decision-making power was not hers. She suffered emotional stress arising from the anxiety experienced while waiting out the committee's decision.

(b) The Law and Abortion: What Next?

By expunging the *Criminal Code* provisions the Supreme Court tossed the abortion issue into Parliament's lap, but our federal lawmakers have yet to respond to that challenge. Still, the criminal law aside, the provinces are entitled to regulate the medical practice of abortion since health care matters fall under their jurisdiction. But provincial action is subject to scrutiny under the *Charter* in line with the *Morgentaler* precedent. In response to the decision in *Morgentaler*, pro-life activists have turned to lobbying for provincial restrictions upon access to abortion. The proposed restrictions have included: "de-insuring" abortion procedures under provincial health care systems, thereby denying access to women unable to afford the cost; restricting the procedure to hospitals; and requiring the consent of two physicians as a pre-condition to payment by provincial health plans.[17]

Although the first two proposals have met with political success, they have not survived legal challenge. In Nova Scotia, legislation was enacted to "prohibit the privatization of the provision of certain medical services in order to maintain a single high-quality health care system for all Nova Scotians." The statute provided that "designated medical services" (including abortions) could be performed only in approved hospitals; that the health insurance plan would not reimburse for abortions performed elsewhere; and that a fine set between $10,000-$50,000 be levied against physicians performing abortions outside approved facilities. Dr. Morgentaler challenged the law by opening a clinic in Halifax and was charged with 13 counts of unlawful abortion. However, a Provincial Court judge ruled that the Act was unconstitutional — not on *Charter* grounds but because the enactment of criminal law is the exclusive mandate of Parliament. For that reason, the Nova Scotia legislature lacked the authority to impose restrictions on abortion under threat of penalty. The decision was affirmed by the Nova Scotia Court of Appeal.[18]

In British Columbia, a regulation was enacted that de-insured the abortion procedure unless performed in an approved facility and necessitated by a significant threat to the patient's life. As in the Nova Scotia case, the B.C. Court of Appeal ruled that the provincial action was an unconstitutional invasion of Parliament's exclusive jurisdiction over criminal law matters.[19]

A lesson learned from the abortion experience in the pre-1988 era is that legal entitlement to abortion does not necessarily guarantee its ready availability. Although Parliament is empowered to define the status of abortion in the *Criminal Code*, it cannot compel the provinces to provide the clinical facilities to offer the procedure. (In a 1988 policy statement, the CMA endorsed free-standing abortion clinics.) Ten years after the *Morgentaler* decision, the Canadian Abortion Rights Action League released a study indicating that there was still no uniform nationwide access to therapeutic abortion. It need hardly be said that this will not happen until the medical profession across Canada is committed to accessibility. But as law professor Sandra Rogers has noted:

> Retiring physicians are not being replaced with young doctors prepared to offer the service. Few medical schools offer training in abortion procedures or they provide training on an elective basis only. The current generation of young physicians has no memory of the terrible impact illegal abortion procedures had on women, and perhaps therefore a limited commitment to

providing the procedure. The level of violence against abortion providers also seriously discourages their participation.[20]

In 1998 the World Health Organization reported that annually about 20 million women obtain illegal abortions and that about 80,000 die in the process.[21] (In Latin America, thanks to the Roman Catholic Church's ban on birth control and contraceptive sterilization, abortion is the leading cause of death for women of child-bearing age.) And aside from mortality, there is awesome morbidity. The vast majority of criminal abortions happen in third world countries where, to state the obvious, the procedures are not performed by qualified physicians (or even nurses) in clinical conditions. The simple truth is that the law is not a magic wand. It cannot prevent abortion; it can only drive it underground.

The tenacity of these millions of unfortunate women can be explained by the concept of the "crime tariff." A tariff operates according to plan when the demand for the foreign product/service in question is elastic — such that the consumer will forego the purchase of the import because its cost has been inflated by the tariff. But when the demand is inelastic — when the consumer insists upon gratification whatever the cost or risk — the crime tariff comes into play. It does so in the context of a buyer-seller relationship. Since the buyer has a need that cannot be satisfied within the law, sellers will emerge from the shadows to fill the need outside the law. The inelasticity of the demand also means that the buyer is more willing to accept an inferior product/ service, and nowhere is this more true than in the context of abortion:

> Women . . . who want an abortion do not care what the market price is. Here the anticompetitive effect of the crime tariff operates not only on price but also on service. When women cannot generally get abortions from those who are in the best position to do a satisfactory job — the members of the medical profession — they are driven to accept a product of inferior grade and qualify from the hole-in-the-corner abortionist. They buy injury and even death from sellers who would be driven out of the market overnight if they did not have the protection of the crime tariff.[22]

In short, the historical record is clear that, however one addresses the social problem of unwanted pregnancy, the criminal law has no business forbidding women access to abortion. And none have learned that lesson better than the physicians and nurses in third world countries who try their best to patch up the casualties of the unwinnable war against abortion.

Finally, bear in mind that Parliament has the power to influence provincial action by attaching conditions to federal grants for provincial health care delivery. Its implications for access to abortion were noted in 1992 by then law professor Ann McLellan (later the federal minister of justice and then health in the Chretien cabinet):[23]

> Significant limitations may exist on provincial jurisdiction over the nature and delivery of health care in Canada, due to the federal government's cost-sharing arrangements, which are accompanied by federally imposed standards in relation to, among other things, accessibility. For a province to "de-insure" a procedure which is found to be "medically required" by a woman's physician or to limit its availability to only those circumstances in which the life of a woman is threatened, would call into question a province's commitment to reasonably accessible health care. The federal government would probably, therefore, be justified in refusing further funding for such a province.

3. MATERNAL/FETAL CONFLICT

(a) Introduction

We are accustomed to regard abortion as the setting in which an adversarial relationship between the fetus and the pregnant woman is played out in the realms of law and public policy. However, in recent years, medical advances have set the stage for new arenas of so-called maternal-fetal conflict. On the one hand, there are technologies for visualizing the fetus, detecting abnormalities, and possibly even correcting them before birth. On the other hand, there is growing concern with substance abuse in pregnancy as we learn more about the detrimental effects upon the fetus of drugs such as alcohol, tobacco, and cocaine. Medical technology and knowledge have thus enabled physicians to bestow upon the fetus the status of patient. But what happens when the physician comes to believe that one of his patients (the pregnant woman) is putting the other patient (the fetus) at risk? Is legal intervention ever warranted to protect a fetus from its pregnant host?

According to a prominent Canadian medical ethicist, Edward Keyserlingk, the answer is a resounding Yes. In his article, "Fetal Surgery: Establishing the Boundaries of the Unborn Child's Right to Prenatal Care",[24] he posed the question:

> What, if any, court-imposed medical interventions in utero performed upon the unborn child and in that child's interest, could be considered morally and legally acceptable in the event of a refusal by a pregnant woman.

By referring to the fetus first as an "unborn child" and then immediately thereafter as a "child", he was already flagging his outlook. I have summarized it as follows:

In the event of conflict "between the unborn child's rights to life, avoidable defects, and quality of life, and the woman's rights to physical integrity and autonomy", it is the rights of the former that must prevail. The pregnant woman who does not choose abortion has assumed a duty of care to the fetus such that she is duty-bound "to avoid acts known to be likely to cause serious injury or disability to her unborn child, and to provide or seek adequate and reasonable affirmative prenatal health care." If necessary, the law should intervene to protect fetal rights. For example, judges should be empowered to order the detention of an alcohol/drug addicted pregnant woman in order to "cure her habit and protect her unborn child." Such measures are called for because "the unborn child's interest in having its long-range health protected can justify and outweigh the temporary inconvenience and deprivation of liberty which would be imposed upon the pregnant woman." Regarding prenatal testing, a woman whose pregnancy is known to be at high risk and who refuses to undergo prenatal diagnosis should be subject to a court order mandating the procedure. There may even be cases warranting court-imposed fetal surgery: to correct a urinary tract blockage or to combat life-threatening fetal red blood cell deficiency by means of an intrauterine transfusion. Furthermore, in the event of defects that in medical judgment require pre-term delivery for ex utero correction, such as obstructive hydronephrosis/hydrocephalus, refusal of treatment would justify court-ordered pre-term delivery.

Professor Keyserlingk is not the only proponent of fetal protection to endorse a wide range of state-mandated pre-natal interventions. According to American law professor John Robertson:[25]

> Pregnant women may be prohibited from using alcohol or other substances harmful to the fetus during pregnancy, or be kept from the workplace because of toxic effects on the fetus. They could be ordered to take drugs, such as insulin for diabetes, medications for fetal deficiencies, or intra-uterine blood transfusions for RH factor. Pregnant anorexic teenagers could be force fed. Prenatal screening and diagnostic procedures, from amniocentesis to sonography or even fetoscopy, could be made mandatory. In utero surgery for the fetus to shunt cerebro-ventricular fluids from the brain to relieve hydrocephalus could also be ordered. Indeed, even extra-uterine fetal surgery, if it becomes an established procedure, could be ordered if the risks to the mother were small, and if it were a last resort to save the life or prevent severe disability in a viable fetus.

The fetal rights perspective finds literary expression in *The Handmaid's Tale*, authored by the renowned Canadian novelist, Margaret Atwood. The novel depicts a society in which most women are sterile, and the few who are fertile are allotted reproduction as their sole function. As one handmaid describes her lot in life: "We are two-legged wombs, that's all; sacred vessels, ambulatory chalices." Atwood's novel in turn calls to mind a 1987 case, *U.A.W. v. Johnson Controls*, in which a U.S. Circuit Court of Appeals upheld the "fetal protection policy" of an automotive battery plant that had barred women whose infertility was not medically documented from jobs carrying a risk of exposure to lead. The Court ruled in the face of uncontested evidence that not one child born to female employees had exhibited ill effects traceable to lead exposure. On appeal, the U.S. Supreme Court reversed by holding that the policy discriminated against women because men were not barred from employment even though the evidence indicated that exposure to lead also had a debilitating effect on the male reproductive system.[26]

In the United States, the law has been implicated in two additional arenas of so-called maternal-fetal conflict: substance abuse in pregnancy and the refusal to undergo a Caesarian-section when medically recommended (for the sake of the patient as well as the fetus). In Canada, there has not been the same rush to invoke the heavy hand of the law on behalf of fetal rights, although a British Columbia case involving a court-ordered Caesarian-section will be considered in due course.

(b) The Status of the Fetus at Common Law

Traditionally, the common law has adhered to the position that only persons have rights and that the fetus, whatever its stage of gestation, is not a person. This time-honoured view is starkly illustrated by the 1970 California *Keeler* case.[27] When Keeler learned that his ex-wife was pregnant by her boyfriend, he forced her car off the road and shoved his knee into her abdomen with the express purpose of killing her 34- to 36-week-old fetus. (As he shouted while assaulting her: "I'm going to stomp it out of you.") She was rushed to hospital where a Caesarian was performed, but the fetus was delivered stillborn because its skull was fractured. Keeler was charged with murder, the State alleging that he did "unlawfully kill a human being, to wit Baby Girl Vogt." (Vogt was the boyfriend's surname.)

In quashing the indictment, the Supreme Court of California ruled that, since the baby was born dead, Keeler could not be convicted of murder. If the legislature had changed the common law (as many states have done by defining the killing of a fetus by a third party, outside the abortion context, as murder or manslaughter), then Keeler would have been held accountable for the death. Because there was no such statute in California, the common law applied. And at common law an infant could not be a homicide victim unless it had emerged from the womb as a living being, regardless of how long it lived afterwards.

The legal authority for the ruling in *Keeler* can be traced as far back as the 17th century, when the common law on "abortional homicide" was stated by the Lord Chief Justice of England, Sir Edward Coke:

> If a woman be quick (16-18 weeks gestation) with childe, and by a potion or otherwise killeth it in her womb, or if a man beat her, whereby the child dieth in her body, and if she is delivered of a dead child, this is a misdemeanour and no murder. But if the child be born alive and dieth of the poison, battery, or other cause, this is murder; for in the law it is accounted a reasonable creature when it is born alive.

In short, abortion was murder only if the fetus was born alive, and that meant that every part of it must have come from the mother before its killing could constitute a felonious homicide. The common law was reiterated in an 1834 English case, *R. v. Brain*,[28] in which the jury was instructed that the accused could not be convicted of infanticide unless it was proved that the infant

> has been wholly born and was alive — it is not essential that it should have breathed at the time it was killed; as many children are born alive and yet do not breathe for some time after their birth.

Turning to Canada, the *Criminal Code* contains a precise definition of a human being, which in simply a codification of the common law. According to section 223:

> A child becomes a human being within the meaning of this Act when it has completely proceeded, in a living state, from the body of the mother whether or not: (a) it has breathed, (b) it has an independent circulation, or (c) the navel string is severed.
>
> A person commits homicide when he causes injury to a child before or during its birth as a result of which the child dies after becoming a human being.

As the *Code* indicates, an injury inflicted on a fetus (or the pregnant woman) can trigger a homicide prosecution, but only if the fetus dies after having emerged from the womb in a living state. The principle is illustrated by a 1987 Manitoba case, *R. v. Prince*,[29] in which the female accused was convicted of manslaughter for stabbing a woman who was six-months pregnant, causing her to go into premature labour and deliver a living child who died about 20 minutes after birth. (If the child had been stillborn, the result would have been the same as in the *Keeler* case.)

The same principle explains the result in *R. v. Sullivan*,[30] a 1991 decision by the Supreme Court which ruled that two lay-midwives could not be convicted of the *Criminal Code* offence of *causing death by criminal negligence*. After five hours of second stage labour, the head emerged but there were no further contractions. An ambulance was called and the baby delivered in hospital but it showed no signs of life and could not be resuscitated. The issue before the Court was whether a partially born full-term fetus was a person in the eyes of the criminal law. (The *Criminal Code* provision on criminal negligence refers to the death of a "person", whereas section 223 defines when a child becomes a "human being." According to the Court, the terms are synonymous and therefore section 223 defines a person in terms of the criminal negligence statute.) The Court went on to rule that, because the child aspirated and was born dead, it was not a "person" whose death could support a conviction for culpable homicide. Although it was still alive in the birth canal, it was dead by the time it had completely extruded from its mother's body. In short, the accused could not be convicted of the offence because the stillborn child did not satisfy the *Criminal Code* definition of a person.

The lack of common law protection accorded the fetus is not restricted to the realm of criminal law. The legal distinction between fetus and person has also surfaced in cases involving applications by child welfare agencies under child protection provisions, which grant the power to apprehend a "child in need of protection." Consider the 1990 Ontario case of *A., Re*,[31] in which the Children's Aid Society sought an order from the Family Court to detain a pregnant woman in hospital until her child's birth. (Under the Ontario *Child Welfare Act*, a "child" is defined as "a person actually or apparently under the age of 16.")

The woman had toxaemia and there was concern that she might develop eclampsia, thereby putting at risk both her life and that of the fetus. It was the agency's contention that she was not receiving "proper medical care and attention in preparation for the birth of the child." The agency was quite familiar with the family because of the recent apprehension of their four grossly neglected children who had been living in a house that was (to put it mildly) a pig sty. The father, who had a long criminal record for violent offences, had been diagnosed by psychiatrists as exhibiting an anti-social personality disorder (in lay language, a psychopath or sociopath). The judge ruled that the denial of legal status to the fetus precluded the agency from intervening on its behalf. To the same effect is the decision in a 1988 English case, *F. (in utero), Re*, in which a child welfare agency sought the confinement of a pregnant woman because of her alleged bizarre behaviour.[32] The Court denied the petition not only because a fetus is not a child but also on the pragmatic ground that "there would be insuperable difficulties if the Court sought to enforce any order in respect of the unborn child against the mother."

In sum, then, from the law's standpoint the key is live birth. In a 1933 case, *Montreal Tramways Co. v. Léveillé*, the Supreme Court of Canada considered a tort action launched by a child who had been injured in utero by a third party.[33] Although the Court acknowledged that the weight of judicial opinion in the common law world denied the right of a child when born to maintain an action for pre-natal injuries, it ruled that henceforth an action for such injuries could be brought on behalf of the child so long as the child was born alive. As the Court expressed it:

> If a child after birth has no right of action for pre-natal injuries, we have a wrong inflicted for which there is no remedy. . . . If a right of action be denied to the child it will be compelled, without any fault on its part, to go through life carrying the seal of another's fault and bearing a very heavy burden of infirmity and inconvenience without any compensation therefor.

The direction set by this case is now the law in all common law jurisdictions, and it explains why there are cases in which Canadian courts have ruled that prenatal neglect — in particular, substance abuse in pregnancy — is relevant to the question whether a newly-born child is in need of protection pursuant to child welfare legislation. An illustrative case is *Children's Aid Society of Kenora (District) v. L. (J.)* (Ontario, 1981).[34] An infant born with fetal alcohol syndrome was apprehended in hospital; the petitioning agency sought an order declaring the child "in need of protection" under the Ontario Child Welfare Act. (The mother did not help her cause by showing up drunk at the court hearing.) In granting the petition, the Family Court judge reasoned that the child was

> in need of protection prior to birth by reason of the physical abuse of the child by the mother in her excessive consumption of alcohol during pregnancy, and by her neglecting or refusing to obtain proper remedial care or treatment for the child's health. . . . [Evidence that the child was] in need of protection prior to birth is not essential to the finding that the child was in need of protection at the time of apprehension and at the time of the hearing — however, it is an important factor to be considered in determining the best interests of the child.

Note that the Court did not hold that a fetus fell under the statutory definition of a child. Rather it ruled that the prenatal neglect bore on the question whether the child (no longer a fetus) was "in need of protection" from its mother.

A half century after its ruling in *Montreal Tramways*, the Supreme Court had occasion to revisit the issue of fetal rights in another civil case, *Tremblay c. Daigle*.[35] The parties had cohabitated for several months, and shortly after the relationship ended Ms. Daigle resolved to have an abortion. Her ex-boyfriend responded by obtaining a court-ordered injunction prohibiting the procedure. The Quebec Court of Appeal affirmed the order but an appeal to the Supreme Court was expeditiously heard and decided. (Although in the meantime Ms. Daigle had defied the order and secured an abortion.) In any event, the Supreme Court unanimously ruled in her favour. It concluded that the fetus had no legal rights — either at common law or by statute in Quebec — that could justify the injunction. The Court also reiterated its position that, although injury to a fetus caused by the negligence of third parties is actionable, the right to sue does not arise until the infant is born alive.

(c) Court-Ordered Obstetrical Interventions

(i) *The American Experience*

In a 1987 article in the New England Journal of Medicine, the authors documented 21 American cases in which courts were petitioned by hospitals to order obstetrical interventions upon women refusing treatment deemed necessary for fetal survival (most often Caesarian-section but also three cases of intrauterine transfusion for Rh sensitization). Petitions were granted in all but three of the cases. All 21 women were being treated in teaching hospital clinics or were on public assistance. Sixteen were either black, Asian, or Hispanic. In every case, physicians testified that dire consequences to the fetus, and usually to the pregnant patient, would follow from the treatment refusal.[36] Still, the outcome of four of these cases belies the adage that the doctor always knows best.

In a Georgia case, *Jefferson v. Griffin Spalding County Hospital Authority*,[37] an out-patient who was 39 weeks pregnant was advised that she had a complete placenta previa; that it was "virtually impossible" that the condition would correct itself before delivery; that it was 99% certain that the child would not survive vaginal delivery; and that the odds of her surviving vaginal delivery were no better than 50%. The refusal by the Jeffersons to consent to the procedure was based upon their religious belief that the Lord had healed her body and that the Lord's will would determine the child's fate. The hospital responded by seeking a court order to compel Mrs. Jefferson to submit to ultrasonography and to a C-section if the test indicated that the placenta was still blocking the birth canal. Uncontested medical testimony led to the granting of the order. Surprisingly, the ultrasound "showed the placenta had moved — a most unusual occurrence." Mrs. Jefferson went on to have an uncomplicated vaginal delivery, an outcome that the medical witnesses had written off as "virtually impossible."

There is a New York case in which a hospital's petition for a court-ordered C-section was denied, even though the medical witnesses predicted dire consequences unless authorized to act. According to the witnesses, the fact that the umbilical cord was wrapped around the fetus's neck was a clear and unambiguous indication for an emergency Caesarean. The patient's refusal (it was her 10th pregnancy) was based upon her belief in "natural childbirth" and an intuition that the delivery would be problem-free. The patient's intuition was vindicated as she vaginally delivered a healthy baby.[38]

In another New York case the patient rejected the surgery on religious grounds, even though hypertension and preeclampsia had led her physician to believe that vaginal delivery would endanger both her and the fetus. She likewise defied a court order and had a successful home delivery.[39]

In a Michigan case the patient, who had a placenta previa, defied a court order that she submit to a C-section. She went into hiding and delivered vaginally with no complications, much to the surprise of the medical witnesses who had predicted dire consequences if she were allowed to have her way.[40]

The judges (invariably male) who have ordered non-consenting female patients to submit to surgical procedures have taken a step that is unprecedented in the history of the common law. They have proceeded on the theory that, if a parent cannot refuse treatment necessary to save her child's life, she likewise cannot refuse treatment necessary to save the life of her "unborn child." However, the reasoning is seriously flawed because the two scenarios are simply not comparable. When a court intervenes to save a child's life, as when a neonate is apprehended because the Jehovah's Witness parents refuse to consent to a blood transfusion, the treatment does not compromise the mother's bodily integrity. Consider, moreover, a child who is at grave risk and whose only hope for survival is a bone marrow transplant from a loving parent, who nonetheless refuses to consent. It is inconceivable that a court would compel the parent to undergo the procedure, no matter how dire the consequences for the child. (Yet, whether the patient refuses to donate tissue or submit to a Caesarian, in either case she is refusing an invasive and somewhat risky procedure that is deemed medically necessary to save the life of another.) In short, the cases of mandated obstetrical interventions stand for the proposition that the power of the state to protect the fetus exceeds the power of the state to protect living children.

Finally, the cases clearly illustrate the inadequacy of an emergency judicial hearing as a fact-finding mechanism. In the typical case, the patient is without legal counsel and the only evidence before the court is that of the physicians seeks the court order. And the emergency nature of the proceedings means that the judge has no time to research the legal issues. (An English case on point is discussed shortly.)

If such cases are still happening, they are rare events. The likely reason is that the policy of bringing the courtroom into the operating room has been condemned by a number of American medical bodies, including the American Medical Association and the American College of Obstetricians and Gynecologists. In particular, it is pertinent to refer to the 1990 AMA Board of Trustees Report, which was adopted by the AMA's House of Delegates. Titled, "Legal Interventions During Pregnancy", the Report delivered a stinging rebuke to the policy of court-ordered obstetrical interventions.[41] Amongst its "adverse consequences", the Report decried the effects on the patient-physician relationship, concluding that the "distrust factor" would lead women either to withhold information or "to reject medical or prenatal care altogether." The Report also stressed that the physician's duty is not to dictate patients' decisions but rather to provide sufficient information to enable them to make informed and thoughtful treatment choices.

(ii)   *The English Experience*

In a 1992 case, *S. (adult: refusal of medical treatment), Re*, a judge of the Family Division was called upon to decide whether a hospital could lawfully compel a mentally competent 30-year-old patient to submit to an emergency C-section.[42] The patient had been admitted to hospital with ruptured membranes and in spontaneous labor; she was six days past the expected due date. She and her husband (described as born-again Christians) had refused the surgery on religious grounds, prompting the health authority to apply for a declaration authorizing the hospital to proceed without consent. At 1:30pm the matter was brought to the attention of the judge, who convened an emergency hearing before 2pm The only witness was the patient's physician (called P by the judge), whose evidence was summarized by the judge:

> Her situation is desperately serious, as is also the situation of the as yet unborn child. The child is in what is described as a position of "transverse lie", with the elbow projecting through the cervix and the head being on the right side. There is the gravest risk of a rupture of the uterus if the section is not carried out and the natural labour process is permitted to continue. The evidence of P is that we are concerned with "minutes rather than hours" and it is a "life and death" situation. He has done his best, as have other surgeons and doctors at the hospital, to persuade the mother that the only means of saving her life, and also I emphasize the life of her unborn child, is to carry out a Caesarian section operation. P is emphatic. He says it is absolutely the case that the baby cannot be born alive if a Caesarian operation is not carried out.

At 2:18pm the judge granted the declaration, saying only that: "I wholly accept the evidence of P as to the desperate nature of the situation." His rush to judgment precluded the appointment of legal counsel for the patient.

Five years later the Court of Appeal ruled in a case called *M.B. (Caesarian Section), Re*, which involved a patient (40 weeks pregnant) who had consented to a C-section but then refused consent to anesthesia because of a "needle phobia."[43] The Court ruled that her refusal could be overridden because the phobia had rendered her "temporarily incompetent." However, the Court went out of its way to affirm that a competent patient is entitled to refuse any medical treatment for the benefit of the fetus. In the words of Lady Justice Butler-Sloss:

> The law is, in our judgment, clear that a competent woman who has the capacity to decide may, for religious reasons, other reasons, or for no reasons at all, choose not to have medical intervention, even though...the consequences may be the death or serious handicap of the child she bears or her own death. The fetus up to the moment of birth does not have any separate interests capable of being taken into account when a court has to consider an application for a declaration in respect of a cesarian section operation. The court does not have the jurisdiction to declare that such medical intervention is lawful to protect the interests of the unborn child even at the point of birth.

Since the Court of Appeal has reiterated its position in later cases, the law is clear in England that, if mentally competent, a pregnant patient cannot be treated without consent, regardless of the perceived risk to her and the fetus.

(iii) *The Canadian Experience: Baby R., Re (British Columbia, 1988)*[44]

In Canada, the issue has arisen only once — in the *Baby R.* case. Three hours after the patient was admitted to hospital to give birth, the obstetrician on call advised her to undergo a C-section because the fetus was in a footling breech presentation with one limb exposed. Her refusal prompted him to contact the Family and Child Services Department, which responded by apprehending the "unborn child." The social worker informed the obstetrician that he was authorized "to do what was required medically for the child" but added that he was "not consenting to any medical procedure to be performed on the mother." (How the fetus could be treated without invading the patient's body was a question that the social worker did not address.)

The agency assumed the authority to apprehend by a provision in the Child and Family Services Act that a "child in need of protection" includes one who is "deprived of necessary medical attention." (The Act defines "child" as "a person under 19 years old.")* The claimed deprivation was the patient's refusal to consent to the surgery, which according to the agency had the effect of depriving the "unborn child" of the care needed to deliver him without harm. After being informed of the apprehension and viewing ultrasound images, the patient responded: "Go ahead, cut me open." A healthy male infant was then delivered. The patient's appeal of the apprehension order was denied by the Provincial Court. Although the judge could have rested his ruling on his finding-of-fact that the patient had consented (albeit it is arguable that her consent was coerced), he nonetheless went out of his way to justify the order:

> This is not a case of women's rights. Mrs. R consented without coercion or threat to the operation. It is clear that this child was in the process of being born, and the intervention and redirection of its birth were required for its survival. Under those circumstances, namely where the baby is at or so near term and birth is imminent, the failure to provide necessary medical attention to prevent death or serious injury is sufficient to allow the Superintendent to invoke the procedure of apprehension.

The judgment was reversed on appeal by a justice of the B.C. Supreme Court,** who emphatically ruled that there was no legal basis for the apprehension because a fetus is not a child within the meaning of the Act:

> While the law recognizes fetal rights, the rights have always been held contingent upon a legal personality being acquired by the fetus upon its subsequent live birth. Until then, the fetus is not recognized as a person. . . . (The agency's powers) to apprehend are restricted to living children that have been delivered. Were it otherwise, then the state would be able to confine a mother to await her delivery of the child being apprehended. For the apprehension of a child to be effective, there must be a measure of control over the body of the mother. Should it be lawful in this case to apprehend an unborn child hours before birth, then it would logically follow that an apprehension could take place a month or more before term. Such powers to interfere with the rights of women, if granted and if lawful, must be done by specific legislation, and anything else will not do.
>
> What then of a legislative remedy? That is not a foreseeable option, given the decision by the Supreme Court of Canada in the case of the pregnant solvent abuser (to which we shortly turn).

---

* 19 is the age of majority in B.C.

** As previously noted, in B.C. the highest level trial court is called the Supreme Court. It has an appellate division which heard the case.

(d) Substance Abuse in Pregnancy

(i) *The American Response*

In the United States, the heavy hand of the criminal law has been brought to bear upon the social problem of substance abuse in pregnancy. It is primarily cocaine — heroin to a lesser extent — that has been targeted by the criminal justice system, accompanied by a barrage of media presentations on the detrimental effects of illicit drugs on the developing fetus. (At the same time the more catastrophic effects of alcohol on the fetus are by and large ignored, as is the connection between cigarette smoking and prematurity.) The resort to legal sanctions has assumed a variety of forms. Women convicted of minor non-drug offences that would ordinarily not result in jail time are incarcerated for the duration of the pregnancy in order to protect the fetus (a slender hope given the ready availability of illicit drugs in penal facilities). From 1985 to 1998, at least 240 women in 35 states were prosecuted for using illegal drugs during pregnancy; the charges included drug possession, drug distribution, delivery of a controlled substance to a minor, criminal child abuse, and criminal child neglect.[45] (A large number of the cases were from predominantly black counties in Florida and South Carolina.) The child abuse/neglect prosecutions have proceeded on the basis that the meaning of "child" in child welfare statutes includes an "unborn child." The theory behind prosecutions for "delivery of a controlled substance to a minor" is that cocaine passed into the newborn's body before the umbilical cord was severed. However, in 1992 the Supreme Court of Florida reversed a conviction in such a case by ruling that the legislature did not intend the statute to apply to the birthing process,[46] and appellate courts in Michigan and Georgia have ruled likewise.

In a 1996 case, *Whitner v. State of South Carolina*,[47] the Supreme Court of South Carolina upheld an eight year sentence imposed on a mother who had pleaded guilty to criminal child neglect for causing her baby to be born with cocaine metabolites in its system. There are also cases in which women in labour have been asked by their physicians about illicit drug use in pregnancy, and their positive responses have prompted notification to the police.

The shortsightedness of the punitive approach to substance abuse in pregnancy has been stressed in public statements by such professional bodies as: the American Medical Association, the American Academy of Pediatrics, the American Nurses Association, the American Public Health Association, and the American Society of Addiction Medicine Inc. Regarding the aforementioned Report of the AMA Board of Trustees, the Board of Delegates declared that:

Criminal sanctions or civil liability for harmful behaviour by the pregnant woman toward her fetus are inappropriate.

Pregnant substance abusers should be provided with rehabilitative treatment appropriate to their specific physiological and psychological needs.

(iii) *The Canadian Response: The Case of* Winnipeg Child & Family Services (Northwest Area) v. G. (D.F.) *(Supreme Court of Canada, 1997)*[48]

Although the criminal law has not been invoked in Canada against a pregnant drug abuser, a case arose in 1996 when Winnipeg Child and Family Services (CFS) applied to the Court of Queen's Bench for an order to force a 21-year-old aboriginal woman (called Ms G.) into a treatment program. At the time, she was five months pregnant with her fourth child and addicted to glue sniffing. Two of her children had been born with fetal alcohol syndrome and were permanent wards of the state.

The Court heard from Dr. Albert Chudley, Head of the Section of Genetics and Metabolism at the Winnipeg Health Sciences Centre, and his testimony is summarized as follows: Organic solvents used by chronic sniffers are neurotoxic to the fetal brain. Children exposed in utero to such substances may exhibit central nervous system dysfunction, developmental delay, attention deficit disorder, and microcephaly. Experimental studies have confirmed that chronic exposure to solvents can lead to retardation of fetal growth/development and to fetal death. Although the critical period for the development of the central nervous system in humans is in the first 16 weeks after conception, the central nervous system is, however, sensitive to a variety of toxic exposures until birth. Therefore, any reduction of toxic exposure during pregnancy would reduce the damage to the central nervous system. (The woman's attorney had argued that since his client was five months pregnant, there was no point to the order because whatever damage could be done to the fetus would have already occurred. That claim was effectively demolished by Dr. Chudley.)

Justice Shulman of the Court of Queen's Bench ordered that she be placed in the custody of CFS and detained in a health centre for treatment until the child's birth. He justified the order on two grounds: that Ms G. was a "mentally disordered" person under the *Mental Health Act*; and that since she was incompetent to care for herself, he was invoking the *parens patriae* jurisdiction of the court (the traditional power of the courts to protect citizens incapable of protecting themselves). He did not address the issue of fetal rights but simply focused upon Ms G., holding that it was necessary to restrain her because she was causing "very serious mental and physical damage to herself."

Two days after the Q.B. ruling, a justice of the Court of Appeal ruled that Ms G. could not be forced into treatment pending the outcome of her appeal; and five weeks later the Court of Appeal reversed the custody order in a unanimous judgment written by Justice Twaddle. The Q.B. judge had rejected the testimony of two psychiatrists that Ms G was not mentally disordered, and the Court of Appeal concluded that his contrary finding was not supported by the evidence. So much then for the mental health rationale.

The Court of Appeal then went on to confront the issue of fetal rights. Justice Twaddle explained that although a child can sue for harm caused in utero, the point is that the child must be born alive before it can do so. The reason is that in law the fetus is not a person and only persons have rights. Justice Twaddle also expressed public policy reasons against forced state intervention in a case such as that before it:

> By restraining this mother from sniffing solvents, we may induce other expectant mothers, fearing state intervention in their conduct, to avoid detection by not seeking desirable pre-natal care. There is a public interest in having expectant mothers receive proper pre-natal care. This public interest militates against recognition of fetal rights.

CFS promptly appealed but it was not until 13 months later that the Supreme Court issued its judgment, affirming Justice Twaddle's ruling by a 7-2 margin. (Notwithstanding the Court of Appeal's ruling, Ms G. had voluntarily chosen to continue treatment in hospital, and when discharged she went to live with her sister and expressed the determination to turn her life around. CFS was quick to provide supportive services, including a homemaker and periodic visits by a public health nurse. She did stop sniffing and her son was born at nine months with no apparent impairment; soon after she and his father were married. The day after the Supreme Court released its decision, the media reported that a battery of tests performed on the child, then 11 months old, found no sign of symptoms exhibited by the offspring of solvent abusers.)

Writing for the majority Justice McLachlin (now the Chief Justice) stated that the appeal raised two issues: (1) does tort law permit an order detaining a pregnant woman involuntarily in order to protect the fetus from conduct that may cause it permanent harm?; and (2) in the alternative does the power of a court to make orders for the protection of children (its so-called *parens patriae* jurisdiction) permit such an order?

The first issue was framed in terms of tort law, which deals with situations where one person has harmed another person. However, as Justice McLachlin explained, the order of detention by Queen's Bench Justice Shulman could not be supported as an injunction to restrain tortious conduct because Canadian law does not recognize the fetus as a legal person. Simply put, the fatal flaw was that the action was commenced and the injunctive relief sought before the child's birth.

It was not simply the common law tradition denying personhood to the fetus that prompted the Court's rejection of injunctive relief in the *G.* case. There were also pressing questions of public policy regarding the implications of state intervention into the lifestyle choices of pregnant women that could impact upon the fetus. To begin with:

> The potential for intrusions on a woman's right to make choices concerning herself is considerable. The fetus' complete physical existence is dependent on the body of the woman. As a result, any intervention to further the fetus' interests will necessarily implicate, and possibly conflict with the mother's interests. Similarly, each choice made by the woman in relation to her body will affect the fetus and potentially attract tort liability.

Justice McLachlin took note of the Canadian Royal Commission's 1993 report on New Reproductive Technologies, titled *Proceed with Care*, quoting the following passage:

> From the woman's perspective...considering the interests of the fetus separately from her own has the potential to create adversary situations with negative consequences for her autonomy and bodily integrity...(and) ignores the basic components of women's fundamental human rights — the right to bodily integrity, and the right to equality, privacy and dignity.[49]

She proceeded to dismiss the claim by CFS that the intrusions would be minimal because the duty of care could be narrowly defined in terms of

> activities that have no substantial value to a pregnant woman's well-being or right of self-determination and that have the potential to cause grave and irreparable harm to the child's life, health and ability to function after birth.

As Justice McLachlin responded:

> The problem with this test lies in the terms 'substantial value' and 'well-being or right of self-determination.' They are vague and broad and may not be adequate by themselves to narrowly confine the duty of care. What does substantial value to a woman's well-being mean? What does a woman's well-being include? What is involved in a woman's right of self-determination — all her choices, or merely some of them? And if some only, what is the criterion of distinction? Although it may be easy to determine that abusing solvents does not add substantial value to a pregnant woman's well-being and may not be the type of self-determination that deserves protection, other behaviours are not as easily classified. At what point does consumption of

alcohol fail to add substantial value to a pregnant woman's well-being? Or cigarette smoking? Or strenuous exercise? No bright lines emerge to distinguish tortious behaviour from non-tortious once the door is opened to suing a pregnant mother for lifestyle choices adversely affecting the fetus.

She added that lifestyle "choices" such as alcohol/drug abuse and poor nutrition may not result from the kind of free choice capable of effective deterrence by tort law. In that regard, she quoted from a law review article:[50]

[W]omen do not abuse drugs out of a lack of care for their fetuses. Drug abusing pregnant women, like other drug abusers, are addicts. People do not want to be drug addicts. In addition, a product of addiction is the inability to control in-take of the substance being abused. . . . Treating pregnant substance abusers as fetal abusers ignores the range of conditions that contribute to problems like drug addiction and lack of nutrition, such as limited quality pre-natal care, lack of food for impoverished women, and lack of treatment for substance abusers.

Pursuing the point, Justice McLachlin stressed that imposing tortious liability upon pregnant women for lifestyle-related fetal damage could be counterproductive in at least two ways:

First, it may tend to drive the problems underground. Pregnant women suffering from alcohol or substance abuse addictions may not seek prenatal care for fear that their problems would be detected and they would be confined involuntarily and/or ordered to undergo mandatory treatment. As a result, there is a real possibility that those women most in need of proper prenatal care may be the ones who will go without and a judicial intervention designed to improve the health of the fetus and the mother may actually put both at serious health risk. Second, changing the law of tort as advocated by the agency might persuade women who would otherwise choose to continue their pregnancies to undergo an abortion.

The public policy reasons for denying intervention grounded in tort law were also invoked against the resort to *parens patriae* jurisdiction as a means of restricting the liberty of substance abusing pregnant women. Justice McLachlin acknowledged the power of the courts to step into the shoes of the parent and act for the best interests of the child. But historically that jurisdiction has never been extended to cover the fetus:

The parens patriae power over born children permits the courts to override the liberty of the parents to make decisions on behalf of their children where a parental choice may result in harm to a child. The only liberty interest affected is the parent's interest in making decisions for his or her child. By contrast, extension of the parens patriae jurisdiction of the court to unborn children has the potential to affect a much broader range of liberty interests. The court cannot make decisions for the unborn child without inevitably making decisions for the mother herself. The intrusion is therefore far greater than simply limiting the mother's choices concerning her child. Any choice concerning her child inevitably affects her. For example, to sustain the order requested in the case at bar would interfere with the pregnant woman's ability to choose where to live and what medical treatment to undergo. The parens patriae jurisdiction has never been used to permit a court to make such decisions for competent women, whether pregnant or not.

In conclusion, Justice McLachlin suggested that the changes to the law sought by CFS were "best left to the wisdom of the elected legislature." Still, it is difficult to imagine that a statute restricting the liberty of a mentally competent pregnant woman for the sake of her fetus would pass Constitutional muster. Such a law most likely would be struck down by the Supreme Court as a breach of the woman's right to liberty under section 7 of the *Charter of Rights and Freedoms* (the same result would doubtless apply to a state-imposed obstetrical intervention against the will of a competent patient). Furthermore, if in either case the woman were not competent, the current direction of Canadian law would allow intervention only for the primary purpose of safeguarding the welfare of the woman herself and not the fetus.

In his dissenting opinion, Justice Major (joined by Justice Sopinka) opined that the position adopted by the Supreme Court in the landmark *Montreal Tramways* case* dictated a recognition of state intervention in the instant case:

> It seems fundamentally unfair and inexplicable for this Court to hold that a foetus, upon live birth, can sue for damages to recompense injuries suffered in utero, yet have no ability to obtain a remedy preventing that damage from occurring in the first place. This is the one of the clearest of cases where monetary damages are a singularly insufficient remedy. If our society is to protect the health and well-being of children, there must exist jurisdiction to order a pre-birth remedy preventing a mother from causing serious harm to her foetus. Someone must speak for those who cannot speak for themselves.

In the dissenters view, it therefore followed that judicial intervention was warranted "in extreme cases, where the conduct of the mother has a reasonable probability of causing serious irreparable harm to the unborn child. . . ."

---

* See p. 356.

Although Justices Major and Sopinka envisioned the courtroom as a haven "for those who cannot speak for themselves", Justice McLachlin and six others have spoken otherwise — and the majority rules.

So much, then, for the Winnipeg case of the pregnant solvent abuser.[51] A few months before the Supreme Court's ruling, The Society of Obstetricians and Gynecologists of Canada issued a policy statement against the imposition of treatment upon pregnant women.[52] As an alternative, it urged physicians to improve their communication and counselling skills with their patients in order to ensure the best possible outcome for their pregnancies. The statement also questioned whether a line could be drawn separating cases where intervention was warranted from those where it was not. The law is not a vaccine that can solve every social problem, and the SOGC is right to avow that state compulsion is not the way to deal with the ravages inflicted on fetal development by all too many unfortunate women (and surely one cannot ignore the men in their lives who also bear responsibility for these tragic situations). That said, there is still a clear role for the state — as forcefully called for by the Canadian Royal Commission in *Proceed with Care*:

> All provinces/territories ensure that they have in place: a) information and education programs directed to pregnant women so that they do not inadvertently put a fetus at risk; b) outreach and culturally appropriate support services for pregnant women and young women in potentially vulnerable groups; c) counselling, rehabilitation, outreach and support services designed specifically to meet the needs of pregnant women with drug/alcohol addictions.[53]

Although much has been done in the decade since the Commission spoke, much still remains to be done. Although the Supreme Court was right to reject coercive state action, it is unsettling that Justice McLachlin did not acknowledge the horrific social cost wrought by the Ms G.'s of this world. Amongst aboriginal communities in particular, fetal alcohol syndrome (FAS) is a scourge that shows no signs of abatement. (Alcohol was also part of Ms G.'s life on the streets and her two apprehended children were afflicted with FAS.) Two of the intervenors were aboriginal child and family service agencies, who urged the Court to sanction state intervention as a means of combatting substance abuse in pregnancy. They argued that legal coercion would be consistent with the aboriginal world view which places a higher value upon connectedness and community than upon autonomy. And although I for one would not fault the Court for its view that autonomy must hold the trump card, there is much to be said for the despair expressed by a columnist in the *National Post* when the Supreme Court released its decision:

To rejoice over this verdict is morally ignorant. To believe that we have solved something here is morally blind. We have solved nothing. The slaughter of human potential continues.[54]

(e) The Supreme Court and the Dobson case

Finally, by another 7-2 margin the Supreme Court ruled two years later in *Dobson v. Dobson (Litigation Guardian of)* that a mother could not be held liable for damages to her child that were caused in utero by her negligent driving.[55] Mrs. Dobson was 27 weeks pregnant when she collided with another vehicle, and her son was delivered by Caesarian section later that same day. He suffered permanent physical and mental impairment, including cerebral palsy. The legal issue was whether he had the legal capacity to bring a tort action against his mother for her negligent driving which occurred while he was in utero. The trial court answered in the affirmative and so did the New Brunswick Court of Appeal; but the Supreme Court ruled otherwise. Speaking for the majority, Justice Cory acknowledged that, if the child had been born to a pregnant passenger instead of the driver, he would have had standing to sue. As he explained: "when a child sues some third party for prenatal injury, the interests of the newborn and the mother are perfectly aligned." In such a case the law does not address the "physical unity of a pregnant woman and her fetus, or the postnatal conflict of interest between mother and child."

He went on to hold that the imposition of maternal tort liability for prenatal negligence was precluded for two reasons. To begin with, the imposition of a duty of care upon a pregnant woman toward her fetus or subsequently born child would result in "very extensive and unacceptable intrusions into (her) bodily integrity, privacy, and autonomy rights." Such a result "could render the most mundane decision taken in the course of her daily life . . . subject to the scrutiny of the courts."

In addition, there was the impossible task of formulating a judicial standard of conduct for pregnant women. Chief Justice Hoyt of the New Brunswick Court of Appeal had adopted the view that because a pregnant driver owes a general duty of care to the public, she surely must owe that same duty to her subsequently born child. He was quick to add, however, that the action would not be allowed if the activity in question was "peculiar to parenthood" or involved a "lifestyle choice", (this distinction was in effect the basis of the dissenting opinion by Justices Major and Bastarache). But Justice Cory disagreed:

A compromise judicial solution, based on the murky distinction between "lifestyle choices peculiar to parenthood" and a "general duty of care" owed to third parties, is simply too vague to be manageable, and will inevitably lead to inequitable and uncertain results.

He also rejected a so-called "motor vehicle exception" as is found in Great Britain under the Congenital Disabilities Act. The statute exempts mothers from tort liability for injuries caused to their children in utero with the exception of injuries sustained prenatally by negligent driving. Although not averse to the exception, Justice Cory concluded that this was a matter for the provincial legislatures and not for the courts.

In sum, the Court was of the view that allowing the claim for compensation by the Dobson child would constitute a severe intrusion into the lives of pregnant women with potentially damaging effects upon the family itself. (Recall that Justice Cory had suggested that imposing tortious liability upon a mother for prenatal injury affecting her subsequently born child would produce a "post-natal conflict of interest between mother and child.") Yet there was no conflict of interest in this case because compensation would have been paid by Mrs. Dobson's motor vehicle insurance coverage. If anything, denying the claim has caused irrevocable harm to the Dobson family by leaving it without a legal remedy for an injury caused to one member of the family by another.

NOTES

1. *In re Moore's Sterilization*, 221 S.E.2d 307 (U.S. N.C. S.C., 1976).
2. T. Christian, The mentally ill and human rights in Alberta: a study of the Alberta Sexual Sterilization Act. (Unpublished and undated.) The author is former dean of the University of Alberta Law Faculty.
3. K.G. McWhirter & J. Weijer, J. (1969). The Alberta Sterilization Act: a genetic critique. 19 **University of Toronto Law Journal** 431 (1969).
4. *Muir v. Alberta* (1996), [1996] A.J. No. 37, 1996 CarswellAlta 495 (Q.B.).
5. **Winnipeg Free Press**, August 29, 1997, at B3.
6. **Ibid.**
7. R. Proctor, **Mental Hygiene** (Harvard U. Press, Cambridge, 1989), at 95-117. With the outbreak of war, Hitler's eugenic plans for Germany shifted to 'euthanasia.'
8. *Eve, Re* (1986), 31 D.L.R. (4th) 1 (S.C.C.).
9. *K., Re* (1985), 19 D.L.R. (4th) 255 (B.C. C.A.), leave to appeal refused [1985] 4 W.W.R. 757 (S.C.C.).
10. *B. (A Minor), Re*, [1987] 2 All E.R. 206 (H.L.).
11. *In re Grady*, 426 A.2d 467 (1981).
12. **The Globe and Mail**, June 1, 2002, at A21.
13. **Canadian Press**, May 29, 2002.
14. **Canadian Press**, June 21, 2002.
15. Institute of Legal Research and Reform (Alberta Law Reform Institute), **Sterilization Decisions: Minors and Mentally Incompetent Adults** (Report for Discussion, #6, 1988), at 37.
16. *R. v. Morgentaler* (1988), 37 C.C.C. (3d) 449 (S.C.C.).
17. A. McLellan, Abortion and the Law in Canada. In J.D. Butler & D.F. Walbert (eds.), **Abortion, Medicine, and the Law** (4th ed.) (Facts of File, New York, 1992) at 354.
18. *R. v. Morgentaler* (1991), 283 A.P.R. 361 (N.S. C.A.), affirmed [1993] 3 S.C.R. 463.
19. *British Columbia Civil Liberties Assn. v. British Columbia (Attorney General)*, [1988] 4 W.W.R. 100 (B.C. S.C.).
20. S. Rogers, State intervention in the lives of pregnant women. In Downie & Caulfield (eds.), **Canadian Health Law and Policy** (Butterworths, Toronto, 1999), at 287.
21. **The Globe and Mail**, March 21, 1998.
22. H. Packer, **The Limits of the Criminal Sanction** (Stanford U. Press, 1968), at 280-1. And if a desperate woman cannot find or afford to pay an abortionist, she may risk death or injury by resorting to self-induced abortion.
23. *Supra* note 13, at pp. 355-6.
24. T. Keyserlingk, Fetal surgery: establishing the boundaries of the unborn

child's right to prenatal care. In C. Nemrod & G. Griener G. (eds.), **Biomedical Ethics and Fetal Therapy**. (Wilfred Laurier U. Press, Montreal, 1989).

25. J. Robertson, The right to procreate and in utero fetal therapy. 3 **Journal of Legal Medicine** 333, 354-5 (1982).

26. *U.A.W. v. Johnson Controls*, 111 S. Ct. 1196 (1991).

27. *Keeler v. Superior Court*, 470 P.2d 617 (1970).

28. *R. v. Brain* (1834), 172 E.R. 1272.

29. *R. v. Prince* (1988), 44 C.C.C. (3d) 510 (Man. C.A.).

30. *R. v. Sullivan*, [1991] 1 S.C.R. 489.

31. *A., Re* (1990), 28 R.F.L. (3d) 288 (Ont. U.F.C.).

32. *F. (in utero), Re*, [1988] 2 All E.R. 193 (C.A.).

33. *Montreal Tramways Co. v. Léveillé*, [1933] 4 D.L.R. 337 (S.C.C.).

34. *Children's Aid Society of Kenora (District) v. L. (J.)* (1981), 134 D.L.R. (3d) 249 (Ont. Prov. Ct.).

35. *Tremblay c. Daigle* (1989), 62 D.L.R. (4th) 634 (S.C.C.).

36. V.E.B. Kolder et al., Court-ordered obstetrical interventions. 316 **New England Journal of Medicine** 1192 (1987).

37. *Jefferson v. Griffin Spalding County Hospital Authority*, 274 S.E.2d 457 (1981).

38. J. Gallagher, The fetus and the law — whose life is it anyway? **Ms. Magazine**, September 1984, at 62.

39. N. Rhoden, The judge in the delivery room: the emergence of court-ordered Cesarians. 74 **California Law Review** 1951, 1959 (1986).

40. **Detroit Free Press**, June 29, 1982, at A3.

41. AMA Report, Legal Interventions During Pregnancy. 264 **Journal of the American Medical Association** 2663 (1990).

42. *S. (adult: refusal of medical treatment), Re*, [1992] 4 All E.R. 671.

43. *M.B. (Caesarian Section), Re*, [1997] 8 Med. L.R. 217.

44. *Baby R., Re* (1988), 15 R.F.L. (3d) 225 (B.C. S.C.).

45. C. Marwick, Challenging report on pregnancy and drug abuse. 280 **Journal of the American Medical Association** 1039 (1998).

46. *Johnson v. State*, 602 So.2d 1288 (1992).

47. *Whitner v. State of South Carolina*, (1996).

48. *Winnipeg Child & Family Services (Northwest Area) v. G. (D.F.)*, [1997] 3 S.C.R. 925.

49. (Ottawa, Minister of Government Services, 1993), vol. 2, at 957-8.

50. J.E. Hanigsberg, Power and procreation: state interference in pregnancy. 23 **Ottawa Law Review** 53 (1991).

51. In the most recent English case to affirm a patient's right to refuse a Cesarian-section, the Court of Appeal adopted the reasoning of the majority in the *G. (D.F.)* case while rejecting that of the minority. See *St. George's Healthcare NHS Trust v. S.*, [1998] 3 All E.R. 673.

52. **The Globe and Mail**, June 24, 1997, at A8.
53. *Supra* note 49, at 964-5.
54. **National Post**, November 8, 1997, at D7.
55. *Dobson v. Dobson (Litigation Guardian of)*, [1999] 2 S.C.R. 753.

16

DEFINING DEATH IN LAW AND MEDICINE

SUMMARY

When is a person legally dead? The common law (judge-made law) traditionally defined death as the irreversible cessation of cardio-pulmonary functioning. It did so because that was how physicians traditionally determined death. The resort to heart/lung criteria was appropriate before the era of artificial life-support and organ transplantation. Even now, unless the patient is connected to a ventilator (respirator), the physician will pronounce death in accordance with the common law criteria. As the irreversible cessation of cardio-pulmonary activity will be quickly followed in the natural course of events by the irreversible cessation of all brain functioning. In other words, the common law test is sufficient to pronounce brain death when the patient is not artificially ventilated.

When a brain-dead patient is maintained on a ventilator, she is not dead in common law terms because there is cardio-pulmonary functioning. In 1987, the Canadian Medical Association published its Guidelines for the Diagnosis of Brain Death. In outlining the criteria that establish the clinical diagnosis of brain death, the CMA explained that a brain-death standard was necessitated by "the development of techniques for the ventilatory and circulatory support of critically ill patients."

It is not only mechanical ventilation that has rendered the common law test a medico-legal anachronism. A patient cannot qualify as a cadaver organ donor until pronounced legally dead. Thus, adherence to the common law test for ventilated, brain-dead patients dooms their use as organ donors. In short, mechanical ventilation and organ

transplantation have dated the common law test in favour of a brain-centred definition.

1. INTRODUCTION

When is a person legally dead? Is it when he stops breathing and his heart ceases to beat? Or is the determinative test the death of his brain? Can a person be pronounced dead according to medical criteria and yet remain alive in the eyes of the law? Consider the manslaughter case of *Kitching and Adams (R. v. Kitching)*,[1] a 1976 decision by the Manitoba Court of Appeal.

In the late evening of July 23, 1975, a Winnipeg bar patron, Donald Junor, 26, suffered massive brain damage when assaulted by the two accused. On arrival in hospital at 1 a.m. he was examined by the emergency room resident, who was unable to detect respiration or heart beat. However, after seven minutes of CPR a pulse was obtained and artificial respiration established. The patient, who remained unconscious and unresponsive to pain, was admitted to the intensive care unit and placed on life-support.

At 7am the ICU attending physician examined the patient. He found that when removed from the ventilator, Junor breathed spontaneously although his breathing was shallow and inadequate. He entered on the patient's chart: "Patient deeply comatose and unresponsive to deep pain. Pupils dilated and unresponsive to light. No oculo-cephalic reflex. Limbs flaccid. Has fibrillating movements left side of tongue."

At 11:30pm he wrote on the patient's chart: "Totally unresponsive. Cranial nerve areflexia. No spontaneous respiration after five minutes off ventilator. Both EEGs reported verbally as electro-cerebral silence. Now fulfils generally accepted criteria for irreversible coma."

At 11am the following day (July 25), a neurologist concluded that Junor had suffered total brain death, noting on his chart: "In addition to findings yesterday, he has no spontaneous respiration and no brainstem reflexes."

One hour later Junor had a cardiac arrest, but his bodily functions were maintained in order to allow for the removal of his kidneys for transplantation. When that was accomplished, the ventilator was switched off at 2:10pm. The EKG continued to monitor cardiac activity for 12 minutes, and it was not until his heart stopped at 2:22pm that the patient was pronounced dead.

The two accused went to trial on a charge of manslaughter, where the Crown's case was that their assault upon Junor was the cause of his death. The defence was based upon the centuries-old common law (judge-made law) definition of death. *The common law test ignores the brain and focuses upon heart/lung functioning by defining death as the permanent cessation of blood circulation and respiration.*

In summary, the defence was as follows: The legal cause of Junor's death was the cessation of artificial life-support following the removal of his kidneys. Even if Junor were brain-dead before 2:10pm on July 25, he remained alive in the eyes of the law until his cardio-pulmonary systems ceased functioning. Even though the assault admittedly caused Junor to suffer total brain death, that act was not the legal cause of death. Instead, the victim's death was caused by the medical decision to shut off his ventilator, thereby bringing about death in accordance with the common law criteria. In short, it was the transplant team — not the defendants — who bore legal responsibility for Junor's death because it was they who directly killed him!

This defence was rejected by the trial judge and the jury went on to convict the defendants of manslaughter. Their appeal was dismissed by the Manitoba Court of Appeal. In its reasons for judgment, the Court side-stepped the issue of when the deceased had legally died. Although it stated that "by traditional criteria there is no question that Mr. Junor was alive when his kidneys were removed," it proceeded to deny the defence by invoking the common law principle of *concurrent causation*. This principle holds that an accused need not be the sole cause of death so long as his act significantly contributed to the victim's demise. The issue was therefore whether the injury inflicted by the accused was a major factor leading to Junor's death. According to the Court:

> Even if it could be shown that the actions of the doctors constituted an operative cause of Junor's death — and [we] emphasize that [we] do not suggest that the evidence would support such a conclusion — still that would not exonerate the accused unless the evidence left a reasonable doubt that the accused's actions also constituted an operative cause of the deceased's death. On that question, the evidence was overwhelming. Whether or not the kidneys had been removed, the deceased could not have lasted more than a short period of time even with artificial assistance.

It is true that the Court cannot be faulted for resolving the case by applying the long-standing doctrine of contributory causation. Still, it is regrettable that it chose to ignore the opportunity to question the utility of a definition of death that, in the era of organ transplantation and artificial life-support, is focused upon the cessation of cardio-pulmonary functioning. It is to that question that we now turn.

2. DEATH AT COMMON LAW

Although the common law measure of death is currently condemned as an anachronism, it had weathered the storms of time over generations of medical practice. As Benjamin Franklin observed in the 18th century: "Nothing in this world can be said to be certain except death and taxes." Law and medicine were in harmony because the medical pronouncement of death was likewise focused upon the absence of cardio-pulmonary functioning.

Time-honoured practice called for the physician to pronounce her patient dead when she found no pulse and a hand mirror held to the mouth failed to cloud over. As the physician knew, no pulse signified no detectable heartbeat and a clear glass meant no respiration. (In Shakespeare's *King Lear*, the king cradles his slain daughter Cordelia in his arms and cries out: "She's gone forever. I know when one is dead and when one lives. She's dead as earth. Lend me a looking glass; If that her breath will mist or stain the stone, Why, then she lives."[2]) In the 19th century the invention of the stethoscope made proof of death even more certain, since it permitted the detection of heartbeat with enhanced sensitivity.

Well into the 20th century the common law test provoked no dissent from the medical community. Until the advent of the intensive care unit with its mechanical life-support apparatus, the common law prescribed suitable criteria for measuring death. At the same time, its focus upon the heart and lungs was compatible with the perception that the organ that uniquely defines a living person is the brain, and that the death of the brain marks the end of life. It is true that generations of songwriters and poets have consecrated the heart as the core of one's being. Such lyrical mythology aside, physicians and laypersons alike have traditionally had an intuitive sense of death as a loss of total organic functioning. That perception was noted by the U.S. President's Commission for the Study of Ethical Problems in Medicine and Biomedical and Behavioral Research in its 1981 report, *Defining Death: Medical, Legal, and Ethical Issues in the Determination of Death*.

> Although absence of breathing and heartbeat may often have been spoken of as "defining" death, a review of history and of current medical and popular understanding makes clear that these were merely evidence for *the disintegration of the organism as a whole*. (Emphasis added.)

The Commission's comment addressed the fact that a patient who satisfied the common law test would rapidly suffer total brain death in the natural course of events. As every physician and nurse knows, when her patient stops breathing, the heart will fail — and when the heart stops pumping oxygenated blood to the brain, the whole brain will inevitably die within minutes.

The spotlight that the common law directed upon the heart and lungs can therefore be interpreted as setting the stage for a brain-centred definition of death. This is not to suggest that the conscious purpose of the judges who declared the common law was to establish criteria enabling physicians to determine brain death. It is doubtful that their formulation, however defined, reflected any clear-cut conception of death. All that they knew (because physicians told them so) was that, if there was no cardio-pulmonary functioning for a matter of minutes, then the person was dead.

Be that as it may, the courts had to furnish a workable death-defining standard that would facilitate the medical pronouncement of death. While the intuitive sense of the judges may have been that death meant "the disintegration of the organism as a whole", the medical tools traditionally available to make that solemn pronouncement required the law to define death as the termination of blood circulation and respiration. In fact, it was not so much a matter of defining death, strictly speaking, as of stipulating the criteria enabling the physician to declare the patient dead. In other words, the only way to prove "the disintegration of the organism as a whole" was by focusing upon the heart and the lungs. (If dispatched to a hospital in the twilight zone and confronted with a patient who had no heart-lung functioning but who could either recite Shakespeare or merely babble incoherently, no one — whether judge, physician, or peasant — would have concluded that the patient was dead.)

This explains why a 1952 Kentucky case, *Gray v. Sawyer*,[3] merits censure for abysmal lack of imagination and common sense. Issues of survivorship and inheritance obliged the Court to decide whether a husband and wife had died simultaneously, or whether one had predeceased the other. Their automobile had been demolished by a locomotive at a grade crossing. The husband's body was horribly mangled and his wife was decapitated. According to an eyewitness, her head was lying about 10 feet from her body, "which was actively bleeding from her neck and blood was gushing from her body in spurts." This evidence led the Court to rule that the victims had not died simultaneously but rather that the wife had outlived her husband for a fleeting moment. As the Court explained, the gushing of blood in spurts indicated a heart beat; and at common law she was not dead until her heart stopped beating, even though her head was lying 10 feet away.

It is understandable that the Court interpreted the common law rule in a rigid and uncalled-for literal sense. For it took its guidance from the medical witnesses, who testified that the decapitated victim was not dead until her heart had stopped beating. The decision reflects the reality that until the advent of mechanical ventilation, distinguishing the functioning of the brain from that of the heart and lungs was foreign to both the judicial and medical experience with death.

On the other hand, there is a 1988 murder case from British Columbia in which the trial judge rightly preferred the Common Law definition of death on the issue of causation. In *R. v. Green and Harrison*,[4] the co-accused were charged with the first-degree murder of one Frie who was shot three times in the head. Green's defence was that Frie was already dead when he "pumped two bullets into him." There was evidence that Harrison fired the first shot to the top of Frie head. As Justice Wood of the B.C. Supreme Court (trial division) summarized the evidence relating to Green's claim:

> The evidence establishes that three bullets were fired into the head of Mr. Frie. All three individually were fatal wounds in the sense that no amount of treatment could have saved Mr. Frie's life if any one — and only one — had been inflicted alone. As I understand it, all three bullets severely damaged the base of the brain and/or brain stem from which the respiratory function is controlled. As a consequence with the first shot fired, whichever one it was, Mr. Frie likely ceased breathing. The evidence however is also capable of supporting the conclusion that his heart would have continued to beat for anywhere from three to five minutes after the first shot. The opinion of (a medical witness) to this effect is supported by his finding that all three bullet tracks showed evidence of arterial bleeding, a phenomenon which can only occur as long as the heart beats.

Green's defence was that if Frie was already dead when he shot him twice, then he could be convicted of attempted murder at best (an accused can be convicted of attempted murder if he shoots a corpse believing that the person is alive). Green's defence counsel thus argued that the jury should be instructed that his client could not be convicted of murder unless the Crown proved beyond a reasonable doubt that Frie was not brain dead when the second and third shots were fired. Although Justice Wood had no quarrel with the brain death definition of death, he concluded that it was "a completely impractical standard to apply" to the case before him. As he explained:

> If the onus is on the Crown to satisfy this jury beyond a reasonable doubt that Mr. Frie was still alive — that is to say that his brain function had not irreversibly ceased — when the accused Green "pumped" two bullets into him, it can be seen that such an onus would be impossible to discharge — unless someone had happened along with an EEG monitor and applied same

to Mr. Frie either before or immediately after the two shots allegedly fired by Green.

The judge concluded that he would instruct the jury that as a matter of law the victim "was alive so long as any of his vital organs — which would include the heart — continued to operate." In short, the jury could acquit only if the Crown could not prove that none of Frie's vital organs continued to function before the second and third shots were fired.

In the result both accused were convicted as charged. It was the Crown's theory that they were joint accomplices, in which case Green's argument on causation would be irrelevant. The reason is that, if they acted in concert, they would be equally responsible for the totality of their acts. Since there was strong evidence that they had planned the killing together, this alone was enough to warrant conviction. Because jurors cannot be questioned about their deliberations, one cannot know to what extent, if any, the causation argument played in the process leading to their guilty verdict. At the end of the day, the judge cannot be faulted for his pragmatic approach to the causation issue.

3. DEATH, ORGAN TRANSPLANTATION, AND THE COMMON LAW

The utility of the common law criteria depended upon the link connecting cardiopulmonary functioning to that of the brain. Neither function could survive without the other. But that link snapped when the sophisticated life-support technology of intensive care medicine entered the health care mainstream. The reason it happened is that life-support measures enable the maintenance of a brain-dead patient's blood circulation and respiration. In strict common law terms, a patient is alive so long as the heart and lungs continue to function; and it matters not that cardio-pulmonary functioning is artificially maintained. After all, a polio victim in an iron lung — which was simply a primitive ventilator — was no less alive at common law because she could not breathe on her own.

In the *Kitching and Adams* case, the defence correctly pointed out that a brain-dead patient cannot be presumed dead in strict common law terms until the ventilator is switched off and his heart stops beating. But when mechanical life-support is terminated, the cessation of oxygenated blood flow rapidly causes his vital organs to deteriorate. It follows that with the advent of organ transplantation, adherence to the common law standard would preclude the use of brain-dead donors. In other words, the reason that the brain-dead patient must be defined as legally dead is that the transplant surgical team cannot do its job unless life-support remains in place.

The medical necessity to redefine the law was spelled out in 1968 by the *Ad Hoc Committee of the Harvard Medical School to Examine the Definition of Brain Death*. As it observed in its report, *A Definition of Irreversible Coma*:[5]

> From ancient times down to the recent past it was clear that, when the respiration and heart stopped, the brain would die in a few minutes; so the obvious criterion of no heart beat as synonymous with death was sufficiently accurate. In those times the heart was considered to be the central organ of the body; it is not surprising that its failure marked the onset of death. This is no longer valid when modern resuscitative and supportive measures are used. These improved activities can now restore "life" as judged by the ancient standards of persistent respiration and continuing heart beat. This can be the case even when there is not the remotest possibility of an individual recovering consciousness following massive brain damage.

In its report, the Harvard Committee presented the first set of neurologically precise and reliable criteria for diagnosing the irreversible loss of all brain functioning. It was not until this breakthrough occurred that a viable alternative to the common law standard became feasible. Although mechanical life-support measures had rendered the common law a medico-legal anachronism, brain death could not be entrenched in law until medicine could prove brain death in fact. Once such medical criteria were in place by the late 1960s, the law was ready for reform. In the United States in particular, the state legislature soon became the forum for the repeal of the common law definition of death.

4. DEATH AND LEGISLATION

In 1970, Kansas adopted the first brain death statute in North America. Although most states have followed suit, only one Canadian province has seen fit to supplant the Common Law by legislative enactment. On June 19, 1975, the Manitoba *Vital Statistics Act* was amended to provide:[6]

> For all purposes within the legislative competence of the legislature of Manitoba, the death of a person takes place at the time at which irreversible cessation of all that person's brain function occurs.

The Manitoba provision is in accord with that of the American statutes, all of which require the death of the *whole* brain — not merely cerebral death. (This explains why a patient in a permanent vegetative state is not legally dead. Although irreversibly unconscious because of the absence of cerebral functioning, the patient lives in the eyes of the law because of residual brain stem activity.)

Even though the other nine provinces have not seen fit to follow the Manitoba lead, physicians across Canada do not hesitate to apply the brain death standard that guides their Manitoba colleagues. In 1987 the Canadian Medical Association published its Guidelines for the Diagnosis of Brain Death.[7] (The guidelines were formulated by a subcommittee of the Canadian Congress of Neurological Sciences.) In outlining the criteria that establish the clinical diagnosis of brain death, the CMA explained that a brain-centred standard was necessitated by "the development of techniques for the ventilatory and circulatory support of critically ill patients."

The CMA guidelines reflect the overwhelming consensus in Canadian medical circles that the death of the whole brain marks the end of life, notwithstanding that mechanical life-support maintains cardio-pulmonary activity. As we have noted, the common law's heart/lung criteria are sufficient to determine death for the patient who is not artificially ventilated. In such event, the physician still applies brain-centred criteria because she knows that total brain death quickly and inevitably ensues when the non-ventilated patient loses cardio-pulmonary functioning. In that sense, medical practice across Canada carries on as if the brain death standard were the law of the land. This is illustrated by provincial human tissue legislation, which grants the legal authority for cadaver organ donation. Except in Manitoba (whose human tissue law echoes the definition of death contained in its *Vital Statistics Act*), the legislation does not define death. In virtually identical language, the statutes provide under the heading, Determination of Death:

> For a post-mortem transplant, the fact of death shall be determined by at least two physicians in accordance with accepted medical practice.

When a mechanically ventilated brain-dead donor outside Manitoba is ready for organ removal, the surgeons do not stay their hands because the patient is alive in strict common law terms. If that brain-dead patient is not an organ donor candidate, her physician likewise does not hesitate to disconnect the ventilator even though the patient is not dead in strict common law terms. In either case, physicians act in accordance with "accepted medical practice" — that when a ventilated patient is brain-dead, she is legally dead, the common law notwithstanding. Since provincial attorneys-general have never questioned such medical practice, it follows that the brain-centred definition of death has found acceptance in both Canadian medicine and law.[8]

5. DEATH, PARLIAMENT, AND CRIMINAL LAW

Manitoba entrenched brain death as its legal standard on June 19, 1975, five weeks before Donald Junor's admission to hospital. Why then did the Manitoba Court of Appeal not resolve the *Kitching and Adams* case by ruling that Junor was brain-dead and hence legally dead *before* his kidneys were removed? Although the Court could have done so, it was not bound to that result because, as specified in the Constitution Act (1867), Parliament has exclusive power to legislate in relation to criminal law. Recall that the Manitoba statute explicitly recognizes its Constitutional limitation by stating that its application is confined to matters that fall within the "legislative competence" of provincial authority.

This explains why provincial statutes authorizing cadaver organ donation cannot guarantee immunity from criminal prosecution to physicians who pronounce death "in accordance with accepted medical practice." Provincial law is empowered to set a standard to determine death for the purpose of cadaver organ donation, but it cannot in the process stipulate the definition of death in a criminal case. That privilege is reserved for Parliament or for a court hearing a criminal case. Although the Manitoba statute could not define death in criminal cases, the Court in the *Kitching and Adams* case could have followed its lead by incorporating its focus upon whole brain death as an updated common law definition of death in the area of criminal law. However, as we have seen, the Court chose to steer clear of the issue of precisely when the victim had legally died.

On the other hand, the question of defining death in a criminal law context was directly confronted by a Massachusetts appellate court in a 1977 case. In *Commonwealth v. Golston*,[9] the accused answered a charge of murder by raising the identical defence heard the previous year by the Manitoba Court of Appeal. The Massachusetts court chose to redefine the common law test to accord with brain death and duly affirmed Golston's conviction. Since common law is after all judge-made law, the Court chose to exercise its authority to refashion the common law measure of death. If the Manitoba court had been so inclined, it likewise could have redefined the common law to align with the province's brain death statute.

(Bear in mind that an accused can be convicted of causing death even if the victim is taken off life-support while still alive. The principle is illustrated by *Matter of J.N.*, a 1979 decision by the District of Columbia Court of Appeals.[10] An 85-year-old mugging victim was pronounced dead 15 minutes after all "heroic measures" were stopped. As the Court acknowledged: "All agree that under any legally accepted definition of death, the victim was not dead when the heroic measures were discontinued." In affirming the conviction, the Court held that "the physician's act in discontinuing heroic measures was a reasonable medical procedure and did not insulate defendant from liability for murder." In other words, the notion of contributory causation — which was applied in the *Kitching and Adams* case — is sufficient to establish that an accused has caused death when his victim's condition warrants the cessation of life-prolonging measures.)

In any event, the resort to judicial precedent is hardly the preferred approach to settling public policy matters of such magnitude as the legal definition of death. There are two compelling reasons why the issue is better suited for resolution in a legislative forum than in an adversarial courtroom proceeding: (1) narrow rules of evidence restrict the scope of information that can be presented to the court; and (2) interested third parties are generally not allowed to present evidence because that privilege is confined to the contesting parties. It is not surprising that the Law Reform Commission of Canada (LRCC) focused attention upon the question of legally defining death, and it is to the LRCC's proposal that we now turn.

6. THE LAW REFORM COMMISSION OF CANADA PROPOSAL

In its 1981 report, *Criteria for the Determination of Death*, the LRCC endorsed a legislative solution to the issue at hand. It recommended that Parliament enact the following amendment to the *Interpretation Act* so that for all purposes within the jurisdiction of Parliament:

(1) A person is dead when an irreversible cessation of all that person's brain functions has occurred.

(2) The irreversible cessation of brain functions can be determined by the prolonged absence of spontaneous circulatory and respiratory functions.

(3) When the determination of the prolonged absence of spontaneous circulatory and respiratory functions is made impossible by the use of artificial means of support, the irreversible cessation of brain functions can be determined by any means recognized by the ordinary standards of current medical practice.

The 1981 report was preceded by a 1979 working paper, which set the groundwork for a co-operative medico-legal inquiry into the advisability of a federal brain death statute. In May 1979, *Canadian Doctor* published a review of the LRCC's tentative proposal.[11] It was accompanied by a questionnaire jointly prepared by the LRCC and the journal, to which the readership was invited to respond. There were 444 respondents, of whom 89% agreed that brain death criteria should be formalized by Parliament. In 1980 the Canadian Medical Association expressed its support for the

LRCC's model statute, which was the product of lengthy consultation with individual physicians and medical bodies, including the Canadian Neurological and Neurosurgical Societies.

The proposal is to be commended because its structure underscores the distinction between *the standard or definition of death* (section 1), and *the tests or criteria for proving death as so defined* (section 2).

Section 1 defines death as the irreversible cessation of all brain functioning. Neocortical or cerebral death is not sufficient to establish brain death. The death of the higher brain may well lead the physician to terminate artificial life-support on the grounds that continued treatment is medically pointless. But a patient whose higher brain functions have been destroyed is not legally dead until the brain stem has also ceased to function. When life-prolonging treatment is halted because of neocortical (cerebral) death — as in the case of a patient in a permanent vegetative state — the reason is not that the patient is already dead but rather that she should be allowed to die. To reiterate, the focus of section 1 is upon the death of the whole brain.

Sections 2 and 3 specify the means whereby brain death is proved. If the patient is not ventilator-dependent, then section 2 authorizes the physician to determine brain death "by the prolonged absence of spontaneous circulatory and respiratory functions." When the patient is on artificial life-support, section 3 requires that brain death be determined by neurological examination of the brain itself. Section 3 wisely refrains from mandating specific neurological criteria to determine brain death because the criteria could change over time. It simply requires that whatever tests are employed be "recognized by the ordinary standards of current medical practice."

When compared to the common law, the LRCC proposal does not present a competing definition of death. The reason is that the traditional common law criteria did not really define death at all, even though judges and legal dictionaries referred to the criteria as the "definition" of death. In truth, the common law's direction amounted only to an assurance that when a person stopped breathing and her heart ceased to beat, death (whatever that meant) was imminent. What the common law really provided was merely a *test* — the permanent cessation of blood circulation and respiration — that for generations was sufficient to prove "the disintegration of the organism as a whole." Simply put, the common law did not define death; it merely provided a test to prove its occurrence. This is all that the common law had to offer, but until the mid-20th century it was enough. On the other hand, section 1 of the LRCC's model statute does contain a definition of death — the irreversible cessation of all brain functions. It then goes on in sections 2 and 3 to stipulate the two tests that enable that definition to be satisfied. As figure 1 illustrates, the entire common law formulation is wholly incorporated in the section 2 test.

LRCC MODEL STATUTE

Section 1 — DEFINITION OF DEATH

Irreversible Cessation of all Brain Functions

Tests or Criteria to Prove Section 1

Section 2	**Section 3**
Prolonged Absence of Spontaneous Circulatory & Respiratory Functions	When Artificial Means of Support, then Neurological Testing of Brain

COMMON LAW TEST

Prolonged
Absence of
Spontaneous
Circulatory &
Respiratory
Functions

7. CONCLUSION

One might suggest that death-defining statutes should be enacted at the federal and provincial levels, and that the LRCC proposal serve as the model. The Uniform Law Conference, a joint federal-provincial body empowered to formulate and propose legislation for uniform adoption, is a mechanism in place that could set that process in motion. However, its agenda has yet to address the question as to when a person is legally dead. The following factors explain why brain death legislation has not been given priority by federal and provincial lawmakers:

1.   The Canadian medical community overwhelmingly endorses the brain death standard, even though it is not the official law of the land (Manitoba aside).

2. This consensus has not altered medical practice, since proving brain death by neurological examination of the brain is indicated only for patients who are being artificially ventilated. In the vast majority of cases, the physician can determine that her patient is brain-dead by confirming the same clinical signs that counted for her forbears: that the patient has stopped breathing and has no heartbeat.

3. The primary reason for a brain death standard is to facilitate cadaveric organ donation, and physicians (whether in Manitoba or elsewhere in Canada) already apply brain death criteria to organ donor candidates.

4. Brain death criteria are also applied across Canada to artificially ventilated patients who are not organ donor candidates. If the neurological evidence is that the patient is brain-dead, then all treatment will be discontinued because the patient will be deemed a corpse. No less than their Manitoba colleagues, physicians elsewhere in Canada act on the premise that a brain-dead patient with (artificially maintained) cardio-pulmonary functioning is legally dead.

5. Hence the conclusion that the enactment of federal and provincial legislation is not necessary because the medical profession already functions as if the brain death standard were the law, and the provincial attorneys-general are content to leave well enough alone.

One cannot imagine that a Canadian court would follow the sorry example of the Kentucky court that ruled that a decapitated accident victim was alive during the fleeting moments that her heart continued to beat. It is also inconceivable that a physician would be charged with murder or manslaughter for disconnecting a brain-dead patient's ventilator. Nor is it likely that a disgruntled parent or husband would file a wrongful death suit against the physician who took his brain-dead child or wife off life-support. And it is highly improbable that the defence raised in the *Kitching and Adams* case will ever be replayed in a Canadian courtroom. Nonetheless, a vague sense of uncertainty in medical circles is warranted until the legal system officially discards the common law heart/lung criteria.

Beyond the notion that the law should be certain, there is the argument that a matter of such profound significance as the legal definition of death should not be resolved by the law's passive, off-the-record acceptance of the medical definition of death. A legal definition of death should be proclaimed by the law and not delegated by the law to medicine. And in the process of carrying out that task, our lawmakers would also provide a forum for the education of the public on an issue that affects us all as mortal beings.

Finally, we note a 1989 case that calls to mind a line from the Scottish poet Robert Burns — "the best laid plans of mice and men." In *Kepler v. Georgia International Life Insurance Co.*,[12] a Florida appellate court affirmed a trial court decision dismissing an action by a widow seeking to recover the proceeds of her late husband's life insurance policy. Mr. Kepler was a life insurance agent who had purchased a 15-year term policy for himself in 1972. Its effective date was April 19, 1972; and hence its expiration date was April 19, 1987. Although the policy had actually been issued a few weeks after its effective date, Mr. Kepler had backdated it to the day before his April 20th birthday in order to qualify for a lower annual premium.

On May 28, 1986, Mr. Kepler suffered a massive cardiac arrest which left him in a persistent vegetative state. Ten months later Mrs. Kepler petitioned the court for an order authorizing the discontinuance of food and hydration. The order was granted on April 9, 1987 and although it was immediately complied with, the patient was not pronounced dead until April 29, 1987. Not surprisingly, the insurer denied the widow's claim on the grounds that her husband had died ten days after the expiration of the policy.

At trial it was the contention of the plaintiff that her husband had actually died on May 28, 1986, the date of his cardiac arrest. Although his treating physician testified that Mr. Kepler "died" in the sense that his heart stopped on that date, he admitted on cross-examination that the patient's brain stem activity meant that he was not then dead for legal and medical purposes. The trial court denied the claim and its ruling was affirmed on appeal. In recognizing the distinction in law and public policy between a dead patient and a living patient in a persistent vegetative state, the appellate court concluded:

> While the plaintiff's argument would provide a comforting solution to this case, it would create numerous problems in other cases. During the last eleven months of his life, the plaintiff would deem Mr. Kepler dead for purposes of life insurance, but not for purposes of medical insurance, disability insurance, and numerous other legal rights. . . . We are not empowered to create a legal purgatory which would provide life to Mr. Kepler for those problems requiring life, and also permit death for those problems for which death would be more desirable. While the life insurance policy involved in this case does not define "death", we do not find that term to be ambiguous under the specific facts of this case. Legally, Mr. Kepler can die only once. In this case, under any acceptable definition of "death", Mr. Kepler did not die before the expiration of his life insurance policy. We cannot rewrite the contract between the parties.

NOTES

1. *R. v. Kitching* (1976), 32 C.C.C. 2d 159 (Man. C.A.), leave to appeal refused (1977), 32 C.C.C. (2d) 159n (S.C.C.).

2. **King Lear**, 5.3, 264-7.

3. *Gray v. Sawyer*, 247 S.W.2d 496 (1952).

4. *R. v. Green* (1988), 43 C.C.C. (3d) 413 (B.C. S.C.).

5. Ad Hoc Committee of the Harvard Medical School to Examine the Definition of Brain Death, A Definition of Irreversible Coma 205 **Journal of the American Medical Association** 205, 337 (1968).

6. R.S.M. 1987, c. V60, s. 2.

7. CMA Position: Guidelines for the Diagnosis of Brain Death 136 **Canadian Medical Association Journal**, 136, 200A-200B (1987).

8. Although the concept of brain death is well settled in law and medicine, concerns have been expressed about its theory and practice. See RD Truog, Is it time to abandon brain death? 27 **Hastings Center Report** 29 (1997).

9. *Commonwealth v. Golston*, 366 N.E.2d 744 (1977).

10. *Matter of J.N.*, 406 A.2d 1275 (1979).

11. J.-L. Baudouin (1979. Definition of death. 45 **Canadian Doctor** 47 (1979).

12. *Kepler v. Georgia International Life Insurance Co.*, 538 So.2d 940 (1989).

17

ORGAN AND TISSUE DONATION

SUMMARY

All provinces have enacted human tissue legislation to facilitate organ/tissue donation. The statutes provide for both *post-mortem* (cadaveric) and *inter vivos* (live donor) donation. The provisions on *post-mortem* gifts are basically identical across Canada. The statutes all stipulate that an adult may consent that her body or body parts be made available for therapeutic, educational, and research purposes. According to the statutes, such consent 'is binding and is full authority' for carrying out the donor's directive. (Before turning to the material on *post-mortem* organ donation, the reader should be familiar with the discussion on the legal definition of death in the previous chapter.)

When the deceased leaves no direction for *post-mortem* donation or is a minor, consent may be obtained from the patient's family. The statutes contain a priorized list of persons permitted to consent on behalf of the deceased. Heading the list is the patient's *spouse*. If there is no spouse or the spouse is not readily available, any *adult child* may consent. If there is no adult child at hand, either *parent* may consent. If there is no parent at hand, an *adult sibling* may consent. If there is no adult sibling at hand, any *adult next-of-kin* may consent.

Regarding *inter vivos* donation, mentally competent adults are permitted to donate both regenerative tissue (e.g. bone marrow) and nonregenerative tissue (a kidney, portion of a lung, or lobe of a liver). Particular attention is paid to the P.E.I., Manitoba, and Quebec statutes because they contain provisions on *inter vivos* donation by minors.

The chapter also considers the so-called *required request* provision (found in the Manitoba and Nova Scotia statutes), which imposes a duty to seek permission from

next-of-kin for post-mortem donation when the deceased had left no direction. The *opting-in* and *opting-out* procedures for post-mortem organ retrieval are briefly considered, as is the controversy over the use of anencephalics as organ donors.

1. INTRODUCTION

In 1954 a dramatic new chapter opened in medicine when surgeons at the Peter Bent Brigham Hospital in Boston performed the first successful kidney transplant. The donor and recipient were 23-year-old male identical twins. The ensuing decades were a checkered history of triumph and tragedy on the transplant front, but by the 1980s the art of organ transplantation had finally come of age — thanks to improved surgical techniques, a clearer understanding of the body's immune system, and the development of new immuno-suppressive drugs.

The phenomenon of cadaveric organ donation led to two major responses by the legal system: (1) fine tuning the traditional definition of death; and (2) creating a mechanism to facilitate the harvesting of cadaveric body parts. The first step was necessary because the common law defines death as the irreversible cessation of cardio-pulmonary functioning. The common law notwithstanding, the medico-legal definition of death in Canada is brain-oriented, even though Manitoba is the only province that has seen fit to alter the common law by legislating a brain death standard. The province was moved to respond because mechanical ventilation, reliable tests for proving brain death, and the feasibility of cadaver organ donation had rendered the common law criteria a medico-legal anachronism. The Manitoba statute was thus prompted by the demand that the law accommodate medical progress by defining an artificially ventilated, brain-dead organ donor candidate as legally dead. Although in this respect the law has spoken officially only in Manitoba, the brain death standard has received the law's unofficial off-the-record endorsement across Canada. As a matter of unstated policy, provincial attorneys-general do not contest the legality of cadaveric organ donation because they recognize the inadequacy of the common law formula for the artificially ventilated patient.*

Except for Quebec, all provinces have enacted statutes called Human Tissue or Human Tissue Gift Acts, which authorize the removal of cadaveric body parts for transplantation (or the donation of the deceased's body for medical research/education).** The reason for the legislation is that at

---

* See previous chapter.
** In Quebec the legislation is found in the *Civil Code*.

common law, a person had no right to control the disposition or use of her body after death. She could provide for the post-mortem donation of her body for therapeutic, research, or educational purposes; but her family was not legally bound to honour her directive. In fact, there was no clear Common Law authority enabling the deceased's family to consent to the use of the remains for such purposes even if the family were so inclined.

The necessity to fill the gap in the law prompted action by the Uniform Law Conference, a joint federal-provincial body whose mandate is the formulation of model provincial legislation. In 1965 the Conference adopted the Uniform Human Tissue Act, which provides for *post-mortem* organ donation. In 1971 the act was amended to encompass *inter vivos* gifts (gifts by living donors). Except for Quebec (which will be considered separately), the provinces have patterned their legislation after the model act; and the nine statutes are sufficiently uniform to permit the following general summary. However, the statutes of three provinces — Manitoba, Prince Edward Island, and Nova Scotia — contain provisions on *inter vivos* donation by minors that warrant separate treatment, as do the so-called "required request" provisions on *post-mortem* donation which are found in P.E.I. and Manitoba.

2. THE PROVINCIAL LEGISLATION

(a) Inter Vivos Gifts

(i) *Defining Tissue*

Except for the Manitoba and Prince Edward Island statutes, the others provide in identical language that *tissue* "includes an organ, but does not include any skin, bone, blood, blood constituent or other tissue that is replaceable by natural processes of repair." The statutes were drafted at a time when the *kidney* was the only non-regenerative organ that one could donate without compromising health (the donation of a lobe of the lung or liver has now become accepted practice). To reiterate, except in Quebec, Manitoba, and P.E.I., the *inter vivos* provisions in Canadian human tissue legislation regulate only non-regenerative organ donation. Regenerative tissue donation (skin, bone, blood, etc.) is covered by the common law, which clearly permits the practice when the donor is a mentally competent adult. (Regenerative tissue donation by minors will be considered shortly.)

The Manitoba and P.E.I. statutes define tissue to include both regenerative and nonregenerative tissue but exclude "spermatozoa or ova, an embryo or fetus, or blood or blood constituents." The excluded body parts are thus covered by the common law (allowing donation by mentally competent adults).

(ii)   *The Statutory Requirements*

According to the Saskatchewan *Human Tissue Gift Act*:[1]

Any person who has attained the age of majority, is mentally competent to consent, and is able to make a free and informed decision, may, in a writing signed by him, consent to the removal forthwith from his body of the tissue specified in the consent and its implantation in the body of another living person.

That provision appears in substantially the same form in the human tissue acts of other provinces. However, Ontario sets the age at 16, and there are also the special provisions on minors in the Manitoba, Quebec, and P.E.I. statutes which are considered shortly.

Although physicians as a matter of practice accept only in-family *inter vivos* donors, none of the statutes prohibits donation from an adult to an unrelated recipient. Nonetheless, there are legitimate reasons for this medical policy. There is the legitimate fear of commerce in human tissue, which is not only unethical but also illegal (except for blood and blood constituents the statutes prohibit the sale of tissue). Moreover, there is a shrinking need for living donors because new immuno-suppressive drugs have appreciably improved the success rate of cadaveric donation.*

(iii)   *The Manitoba, P.E.I., and Quebec Statutes*

The scope of the Manitoba *Human Tissue Act* was confined to *post-mortem* organ donation until 1987, when it was amended to encompass *inter vivos* gifts. The Act stipulates three age categories for living donors:[2]

Persons who are *"18 years of age or over* and able to make a free and informed decision" may consent to the removal of both regenerative and non-regenerative tissue for therapeutic, educational, or research purposes.

Persons who are *"under the age of 18 years but not under the age of 16 years"* may consent to the removal of both regenerative and non-regenerative tissue for therapeutic purposes, but only under the following conditions:

1. A physician not associated with the tissue recipient certifies in writing that in her opinion the donor "understands the nature and effect of the procedure authorized by the consent."

---

*   As one would expect, the situation is different for minor donors, as shortly explained.

2. The donor and recipient are members of the same *immediate family* (parent or step-parent, or sibling or half-sibling).
3. Consent is obtained from the donor's parent or legal guardian.

Persons who are *"under the age of 16 years"* may consent to the removal of *regenerative tissue* for therapeutic purposes but only under the following conditions:

1. The recipient would "likely die" without the transplant.
2. The donor and recipient are members of the same immediate family.
3. The transplant is recommended by a physician not associated with the recipient.
4. The donor's parent or legal guardian consents to the procedure.
5. The transplant is approved by the Court of Queen's Bench (which is the highest level trial court in the province).

In summary, provided that the stipulated procedures are followed, a minor in Manitoba who has attained the age of 16 is allowed to donate non-regenerative or regenerative tissue. Prior to the age of 16, he cannot donate the former but only the latter.

The P.E.I. statute has two age categories for *inter vivos* donation: persons who are 16 years of age and over and persons who are under 16 years of age.[3] Regarding the former, a person who "understands the nature and consequences of transplanting tissue . . . in another living body" may donate both *regenerative* and *non-regenerative* tissue. Regarding the latter, a person who "understands the nature and consequences of transplanting tissue" may consent to the removal of *regenerative* tissue. However, a minor under 16 who does not have the mental capacity to consent may still donate *bone marrow* to a "biological brother or biological sister." Whenever the proposed donor is under 16, there must be approval not only by "a parent or guardian" but also by a panel of three or more persons appointed by the Minister of Health and Social Services to conduct an "independent assessment" (one of whom must be a physician). The persons conducting the independent assessment cannot approve the procedure unless they determine that:

1. The transplant is the "medical treatment of choice."
2. "All other members of the family of the donor have been eliminated, for medical or other reasons, as potential donors."
3. The donor has not consented because of coercion or inducement.
4. The removal of the tissue does not create "a substantial health or other risk to the donor."

Thus, in P.E.I. any mentally competent person over 16 may donate both regenerative and non-regenerative tissue. A mentally competent minor under 16 may donate regenerative tissue with the consent of his parent/ guardian and the consent of an independent assessment panel; a mentally incompetent minor (lacking the mental capacity to consent) may donate bone marrow with the same two consents.

In Quebec, the authorization for *inter vivos* donation is contained in two brief paragraphs in the *Civil Code*:[4]

> A person of full age who is capable of giving his consent may alienate a part of his body *inter vivos*, provided the risk incurred is not disproportionate to the benefit that may reasonably be anticipated.

> A minor . . . may, with the consent of the person having parental authority . . . and with the authorization of the court, alienate a part of his body only if that part is capable of regeneration and provided that no serious risk to his health results.

In sum, in Quebec an adult is authorized to donate both regenerative and nonregenerative tissue whereas a minor is restricted to the donation of regenerative tissue.

(iv) *The Minor Transplant Donor*

In seven provinces the donation of non-regenerative tissue is restricted to mentally competent adults, whereas Ontario, Manitoba, and P.E.I. grant the privilege to minors over the age of 16. (Still, consider the hypothetical case of a minor who wishes to donate a kidney to an identical twin but is excluded because of his age in seven provinces, and a minor under 16 in like circumstances who is excluded in the other three. The minor could petition the court for authority to donate by pleading section 15 of the *Charter of Rights and Freedoms*, which bans discrimination based on age. The petitioner could present a compelling argument that there is no countervailing public policy to counter judicial approval of the donation in this ideal kind of transplant case — in which tissue rejection and the lifelong use of immuno-suppressive drugs are not factors because the donor and recipient are identical twins.)

Regenerative tissue is covered in the Quebec, Manitoba, and P.E.I. statutes, which permit donation by minors. In the other seven provinces, it is necessary to turn to traditional common law principles to determine the legality of regenerative tissue donation by minors.

As noted, except in Quebec, P.E.I., and Manitoba, the *inter vivos* provisions in provincial legislation only regulate non-regenerative tissue donation. Regenerative tissue donation is therefore covered by the common law, which allows the procedure when the donor is a mentally competent adult. An unsettled issue is whether common law principles permit parents to authorize the procedure when the proposed donor is a minor. The common law empowers a child's parents to consent to medical treatment for the minor's benefit. However, the courts have not addressed the question whether that authority extends to parental consent for a procedure that offers no direct benefit to the minor. (The focus here is upon the minor who lacks the mental capacity to decide for herself; the mature minor as regenerative-tissue-donor-candidate is considered shortly.) In British Columbia and Ontario — the provinces that have pediatric bone marrow clinics but whose human tissue acts do not address donation by minors — the hospitals in question do not seek court orders before accepting children as young as pre-schoolers as bone marrow donors. Instead they are satisfied to act upon parental consent.

(As we have seen, physicians in Manitoba could not lawfully act in such circumstances without a court order because their human tissue law requires court approval for regenerative tissue donation by a child under 16. The Manitoba law reflects the policy that parents cannot be permitted on their own authority to subject a child to an intrusive medical procedure in order to benefit a sibling. Although the P.E.I. provision does not mandate judicial oversight, it does require approval by an "independent assessment" panel.)

Is this policy of acting upon parental consent compatible with legal principles? With the exception of the *emergency* and *mature minor rules*,* the common law requires parental (or guardian) consent for the medical treatment of minors. Bone marrow clinics that use minors as donors are acting upon the consent of parents who are authorizing a surgical procedure upon a child that is not for her direct benefit. Given that the parental right to consent to medical treatment is predicated upon the assumption that the parents will promote the child's best interests, the question of concern from the common law standpoint is: Of what benefit is the transplant to the donor? Or to put it differently, given the lack of direct benefit to the minor donor, does the law permit her to undergo an invasive medical procedure whose purpose is to benefit another?

The parents presumably would argue as follows. The benefit to the donor is the prevention of a death in the family; the donor has a vested interest in the welfare of her sibling because her own well-being is symbiotically tied to the well-being of the family unit. Furthermore, the anticipated benefit to her sibling far outweighs any short-term discomfort she

_____

* See Chapter 3.

may experience from the bone marrow extraction. In any case, since the tissue is regenerative it is not as if she were donating a kidney.

Recall that Quebec permits a minor to donate regenerative tissue, subject to parental and court approval. An illustrative case (unreported) is that of *In the Matter of Real and Ginette Faucher* (1980). The petitioners were the parents of Glenn, 15, and Mona, 14. Mona was suffering from acute lymphoblastic leukaemia (ALL), and the petition was accompanied with an affidavit from her hemotologist to the effect that her "only hope for survival" lay in receiving a bone marrow transplant from her brother. A consent form was signed by Glenn, indicating that he had been informed by physicians at the Montreal General Hospital of "the nature, risk, and consequences of the operation and that no serious risk to my health will result therefrom." The judge readily gave the go-ahead.

If a court case were to arise involving the issue of regenerative tissue donation by a minor — aside from Quebec, P.E.I., and Manitoba, where the procedures set out by statute must be followed — it is improbable that judges applying the common law would ban the procedure because of the absence of direct therapeutic benefit to the minor donor. We turn to consider the question as it might arise in the other seven provinces.

To begin with, what if the proposed donor could qualify as a mature minor? In three provinces, legislation enables mature minors to consent to medical treatment: In Ontario (under the *Consent to Treatment Act*), British Columbia (under the *Infants Act*), and New Brunswick (under the *Medical Consent of Minors Act*).* The Ontario and B.C. statutes do not require the minor to be of any particular age in order to qualify, so long as the minor has the mental capacity to consent to treatment. However, the B.C. statute requires that the treatment must be "in the minor's best interests." In New Brunswick, where 16 is the age of consent to medical treatment, a mature minor under 16 likewise can consent to treatment but only with a "best interests" requirement. The statutes, which provide the legal basis for regenerative tissue donation by mature minors, leave two questions open: is the donor consenting to "treatment" and (if in British Columbia and New Brunswick**) does the procedure serve the minor's "best interests"? There is no doubt but that the courts would answer both questions in the affirmative. Still, since the statutes do not address the subject of tissue donation by mature minors, it is advisable for the hospitals involved to secure judicial approval before proceeding.

---

*   See Chapter 20.

**   This discussion is purely theoretical with respect to the New Brunswick statute because there is currently no pediatric bone marrow clinic in the province.

In the other four province (which, like New Brunswick, do not currently have bone marrow facilities), it would be advisable to seek judicial approval and in all probability the Courts would find, as a matter of common law, that the mature minor rule is sufficient warrant to allow the procedure. In other words, whether by statute or at common law, a mature minor would likely be allowed to consent to donate regenerative tissue.

Secondly, what if the proposed donor could not qualify as a mature minor? The courts would in all probability unite compassion and reason by ruling that, as a matter of common law, the child as a family member benefits not only the recipient but also herself through her gift of bone marrow to her sibling. Thus, even if the minor were incapable of consent, the courts would likely ground approval by coupling parental consent with the benefit principle — that the minor's best interests are served by the in-family donation to her sibling.

The parental consent requirement would also enable the non-mature minor to serve as a bone marrow donor in Ontario, B.C., and New Brunswick, as their consent-to-treatment statutes only concern the waiver of parental consent for mature minors and have no application to the principle of parental consent for non-mature minors. Thus, the same common law principles would apply: that parental consent coupled with the best interests of the donor candidate are sufficient warrant to justify the procedure. Once again, we suggest that the hospital seek judicial approval before proceeding.

In sum, the compassion factor grounds our belief that, notwithstanding the absence of direct therapeutic benefit to the donor, judges would permit in-family bone marrow transplants from a child far too young to qualify as a mature minor. Compassion nonetheless does have its limits, as indicated by the blanket prohibition against non-regenerative tissue donation by minors in seven provinces, and by restrictions in the other three (Ontario, Manitoba, and P.E.I.) against donation by minors under the age of 16. Although the Manitoba and P.E.I. statutes show a willingness to bend the law when the stake is the loss of regenerative tissue, the provinces have all drawn a line at the permanent loss of tissue.

To return to the Manitoba statute, recall that minors "under the age of 16 years" may *consent* to donate regenerative tissue — but only to an immediate family member and only if the recipient would "likely die" without the transplant. The provision has no minimum age requirement; the litmus test is simply whether, whatever her age, the minor consents. But the younger the minor, the more likely that the pursuit of the consent requirement would degenerate into a charade. The common law has never regarded mere *assent* as tantamount to *consent*; simply because a person says Yes does not in and of itself establish consent to whatever is at issue. However, given the compelling circumstances — where a life hangs in the balance — Manitoba judges called upon to approve the procedure for younger children would be inclined to rationalize a finding of consent on humanitarian grounds.

But what if the child were so young that by no stretch of the law could a judge find consent? (The literature reports the use of bone marrow donors as young as one year old, and no ethical concerns have been voiced against using an infant donor to save a sibling's life.) In that event, the only legal recourse is to send the proposed donor out of province. Clearly, this flawed statute should be amended to provide that, when consent is unobtainable, the Queen's Bench Court shall consider the best interests of the proposed donor — and that the Court apply the test in light of the minor's status as a member of the proposed recipient's immediate family. Recall that the P.E.I. statute permits a minor under 16, who lacks the capacity to consent, to donate bone marrow with the approval of an "independent assessment" panel.

Finally, it is instructive to consider American cases dealing with kidney donation by minors. In 1957 three precedent-setting cases were decided in Massachusetts, each of which involved a hearing before a single justice of the state supreme court on the question whether a minor should be allowed to donate a kidney to an identical twin.[5] One set of twins was 19 (at that time the age of majority was 21), and the other two were 14. In each case, a psychiatrist testified that the healthy twin would suffer irreparable psychological harm if his sibling died because he was prevented from giving him a kidney. Each justice justified (rationalized) his decision by finding that such evidence proved that sufficient benefit would accrue to the proposed donor. What the justices meant by benefit was the prevention of distress caused by the death of a sibling, not the conferring of direct therapeutic gain to the donor.

In *Hart v. Brown* (1972),[6] the Connecticut Superior Court (highest level trial court) permitted the donation of a kidney by a seven-year-old girl to her identical twin, who had undergone a bilateral nephrectomy following a diagnosis of haemolytic uraemic syndrome. The judge was led to that result by evidence that a parental homograft (each parent had volunteered a kidney) would place the recipient at risk to suffer appalling side-effects from immuno-suppressive drugs — and that in any event the survival rate of a parent-donated kidney was only 37% after seven years. In stark contrast was testimony that since 1966 identical twin grafts were functioning at 100%.

His review of the medical testimony persuaded the judge to authorize the procedure on the grounds that there was "negligible risk" to the donor, and that an isograft (identical twin graft) was clearly in the recipient's best interests. As in the Massachusetts cases, the judge concluded that the donor would derive psychological benefit from the transplant. He based that finding on the testimony of a psychiatrist that she "would be better off in a family that was happy than in a family that was distressed", and that her sister's death would cause her to suffer "very great loss." Since the donor was only seven years old, it is arguable that the judge was really stretching the benefit rationale. Still, who would quarrel with the result — twins each with one kidney or one twin with both kidneys intact and the other twin dead or languishing on dialysis?

The use of minor transplant donors raises not only the issue of *benefit* but also that of *consent*. In each of the three Massachusetts cases, the Court ruled that the consent of the parents was not sufficient but that the donor must consent as well. (It was presumably the absence of direct therapeutic benefit that directed the justices to require the minor's consent, given that the law does not require the minor's consent when the treatment authorized by the parents is for his direct benefit.) In each case, there was a finding that the donor-twin understood the nature, risks, and consequences of the proposed surgery. Given the ages of the twins — one set was 19 and two were 14 — the findings can be viewed as satisfying the consent requirement of the mature minor rule, assuming that each of the justices was convinced that the choice was truly voluntary and not the product of open or subtle family pressure.

Although the judge in *Hart v. Brown* did not impose a consent requirement (hardly feasible for a seven-year-old), he did comment that, "insofar as she may be capable of understanding she desires to donate her kidney so that her sister may return to her." In light of the grim prognosis without the transplant, it is not surprising that the judge preferred as the outcome healthy seven-year-old twins, albeit each with one kidney. Simply put, what explains the judgment in this case is compassion, not reasoned analysis of the legal issues.

In summary, we think it helpful to the reader to present the following outline on the law relating to minor donors.

A. **Non-regenerative Tissue** (e.g. kidney).
1.   In seven provinces only an adult can donate.
2.   In Ontario, Manitoba, and P.E.I., (mature) minors over 16 can donate.
B. **Regenerative Tissue** (e.g. bone marrow).
1.   Human tissue legislation in Quebec, Manitoba and P.E.I. permits donation by minors, although in Manitoba and P.E.I. the consent requirement is more stringent when the minor is under 16.
2.   Consent to treatment legislation in New Brunswick, Ontario,

and B.C. provides the statutory basis for donation by mature minors. If the minor is not mature, authority could still be granted under the common law (that the best interests of the donor is promoted by serving as an in-family donor).

3.   In the other four provinces, one must turn to the common law.

(a) If the proposed donor has the mental capacity to consent, then the common law's mature minor rule is authority for allowing the procedure.

(b) If the proposed donor lacks the mental capacity to consent, a court could still authorize the procedure by applying the 'benefit' rule (that the best interests of the donor is promoted by serving as an in-family donor).

(b) Post-Mortem Gifts

(i) *The Statutory Requirements*

In all provinces save Quebec, the provisions for *post-mortem* donation are patterned after the Uniform Human Tissue Act. In virtually identical language, they provide that:

> Any person who has attained the age of majority may consent:
>
> (a) in a writing signed by him at any time; or (b) orally in the presence of at least two witnesses during his last illness; that his body or parts thereof specified in the consent be used after his death for therapeutic purposes, medical education, or scientific research.

A consent given by a person who has not attained the age of majority is valid for the purposes of this Act if the person who acted upon it had no reason to believe that the person who gave it had not attained the age of majority.

The statutes provide that such consent "is binding and is full authority" for proceeding in accordance with the donor's directive. What about minors or adults who have left no direction for post-mortem donation? Each statute stipulates that when such a person dies or death is imminent, the following priorized categories of persons are authorized to consent to post-mortem donation.

Heading the list is the patient's *spouse*, a term which is undefined in seven provinces. However, recent amendments in Ontario and Manitoba should be noted. In Ontario the reference is now to "spouse or same-sex partner", whereas in Manitoba it is to "spouse or common law partner."[7] (Since the Manitoba law had qualified the latter as an "opposite sex" couple, the amendment presumably removes that barrier.) In P.E.I. spouse includes "a common law spouse of the opposite sex" (unmarried but cohabiting).[8]

If there is no spouse or the spouse is not readily available, any *adult child* may consent. If there is no adult child or none is readily available, either *parent* may consent. If there is no parent or none is readily available, any *adult sibling* may consent. If there is no adult sibling or none is readily available, then any *adult next-of-kin* may consent.

What if a patient is survived by her parents and one consents although the other objects? Or what if the parents and adult children favour donation, but the spouse withholds consent? In each case, the objection prevails. The reason is that the statutes disallow post-mortem donation when a relative consents but an objection is voiced by "a person of the same or closer relationship" to the deceased.

On the other hand, consent by the closer relative will overcome an objection expressed by a family member lower down the chain. For example, spousal consent would legally override a parental objection. But in practice the parent likely would prevail. There is anecdotal evidence that hospitals will not proceed in the face of familial opposition, even though the dissenter is not legally entitled to enforce his will. In fact, even when the patient had made a legally binding *post-mortem* donation, there is further anecdotal evidence that an objection from within the family will be honoured. In either circumstance, whether explained by ignorance of the law or concern for the sensitivity of objecting relatives, health care providers are frustrating the intent of the legislation.

In Quebec the authorization for *post-mortem* donation is contained in the *Civil Code*, which stipulates that "a person of full age or a minor 14 years of age or over" may consent to the "removal of organs or tissues." A minor under 14 may donate with parental consent. The consent must be in writing or expressed orally before two witnesses. In the absence of such a direction, the statute permits donation if the physician secures the consent of the nearest relative of the deceased. Consent is not required when two physicians attest in writing "to the impossibility of obtaining it in due time, the urgency of the [recipient's] operation, and the serious hope of saving a human life or improving its quality to an appreciable degree."[9]

Note that in virtually identical language, the statutes contain the following conflict of interest provisions (quoting from the Ontario *Human Tissue Gift Act*).[10]

> No physician who has had any association with the proposed recipient that might influence his judgment shall take any part in the determination of the fact of death of the donor.

No physician who took any part in the determination of the fact of death of the donor shall participate in any way in the transplant procedures.

Finally, when does death occur for the purpose of post-mortem donation? Even though Manitoba is the only province with a statutory definition of death ("irreversible cessation . . . of all brain function"), the brain death standard applies throughout Canada. In the other provinces the human tissue acts do not define death but simply provide that for the purpose of post-mortem transplant: "the fact of death must be determined by at least two medical practitioners in accordance with accepted medical practice." And what that means is brain death.

However, in the United States there are transplant centres that have utilized so-called non-heart-beating donors (NHBD). The majority of such donors have suffered an irreversible cardio-respiratory arrest immediately before or shortly after admission to a hospital emergency department. Others are general ward patients who have suffered cardiac arrest secondary to catastrophic intercranial hemmorrhage.[11] This policy is, needless to say, quite controversial, and it remains to be seen whether it will be exported to Canada.

(ii) *Required Request*

Under the heading, *Physician's obligation to consider*, the Manitoba Act stipulates that when a patient dies without having consented to post-mortem donation, "the last physician to attend the deceased person before death" is instructed to determine whether the deceased is a suitable transplant donor candidate. If so, the physician is directed to "request permission from the deceased person's nearest relative to use the body . . . or to remove tissue . . . for therapeutic purposes." The duty is waived if the physician has reason to believe that donation "would be contrary to the (deceased) person's religious beliefs."[12]

Although a Manitoba physician in breach of the statute could in theory be prosecuted (as omission to comply with a statutory duty is a provincial offence), the likelihood of that happening is virtually nil. The reason is that, aside from the difficulty if not impossibility of enforcement, the legislative intent is not to threaten physicians. It is rather to impress upon them that they hold the key to relieving the current organ donor shortage. The aversion that many physicians (and nurses) express toward the practice of requesting permission from grieving families is understandable, but the evidence is that when asked most families will consent. Required request is a means of encouraging health care professionals to overcome their inhibitions and to work toward narrowing the gap between the supply of and demand for retrievable organs.

The only other province with a comparable provision is Nova Scotia. Under the heading, *Request for permission*, the act provides that upon the death of a patient who has not made a post-mortem direction, the hospital shall request consent for transplant purposes from the next-of-kin. The duty is waived when a physician determines that the body cannot be used for tissue donation or seeking permission is precluded by "the emotional and physical condition" of the next-of-kin.

As in Manitoba and Nova Scotia, nearly all the American states turned to required request provisions that likewise directed hospital personnel to initiate the proceedings. However, as Caplan stated in 1993 in reporting the results of studies on the impact of required request statutes:[13]

> [We] surveyed health departments, eye banks, organ procurement agencies, and hospitals in the first ten states to pass required request laws. While most reported an increase of 20% or more in the number of cornea, skin, and bone donors since the enactment of required request laws, the increase was still substantially less than the doubling predicted based on estimates of eligible donors. Organ donation increased 10-20% in four states surveyed while, in the remainder, the number of donors was constant or decreased. Other studies have shown small increases in organ donation rates and modest increases in tissue rates.

In 1994 the Pennsylvania legislature adopted a new approach — a "routine referral law", which requires hospitals to refers cadaveric organ donor candidates to their Organ Procurement Organization (OPO). (There are currently 59 OPOs operating in the United States. They co-ordinate activities relating to organ procurement in designated service areas, which may include a state or a portion of one or more states.) The Pennsylvania law requires trained OPO personnel to offer the option of organ donation to the families of candidates who had not signed organ donor cards. By 1997 organ donations had increased by 30% and are currently 50% higher than in 1994. New Jersey in 1995 and Delaware in 1998 enacted comparable legislation, but in any case the federal government has recently ordered that the practice of donor referral to OPOs be implemented nationwide.[14]

(iii)   *Opting-In Versus Opting-Out*

The Canadian system of organ retrieval reflects an opting-in policy. Donation requires the consent of either the deceased or his next-of-kin (with narrow exceptions discussed under this heading). In contrast, an opting-out (*presumed consent*) policy — which has been adopted in several countries, e.g. France, Spain, Belgium, Sweden, Austria, Portugal, Turkey, and Singapore — facilitates post-mortem donation by presuming the consent of the patient and family. In theory, the opting-out scheme is a more efficient mechanism of organ retrieval than the Canadian system. One presumes that the physician who can take as of right will take more than the physician who can take only with permission, and there is evidence that organ donation is about one-third higher where presumed consent is the law than where it is not.

The retrieval rate where presumed consent is the case varies from one country to another; it is dependent upon such variables as the fatal accident rate, population density, the number of available ICU beds, and the extent of collaboration between physicians and hospital administrations. The Belgian experience is instructive. Since 1986 a computerized registry system affords every citizen the opportunity to say Yes or No to post-mortem retrieval. The registry is only accessible to transplant teams which are obliged to access it before proceeding, and presumed consent applies when a potential donor has not registered.[15]

Although all Canadian provinces have adopted the opting-in principle (which is the case across common law jurisdictions), there are statutory exceptions to the general rule. We have seen that the Quebec *Civil Code* waives the consent requirement when neither spouse nor next-of-kin is on hand to consent, and the organ donation is urgently required to save the recipient's life. The authority has been invoked on rare occasions. In several provinces, the consent requirement is waived to enable the extraction of the pituitary gland at autopsy for use in the treatment of growth hormone deficiency. The proviso is useless because of evidence that a fatal neurological disorder (Creutzfeldt-Jakob disease) can be caused by a virus produced by the growth hormone extracted from the pituitary gland. In any case, patients are now being treated with artificial growth hormone.

In Manitoba, the statute waives the consent requirement to enable the *post-mortem* removal of "eye tissue" — unless there is reason to believe that "the deceased, if living, would have objected thereto; or that the nearest relative of the deceased objects thereto." In Saskatchewan, the *Coroners Act* authorizes the extraction at autopsy of a deceased's corneoscleral button if suitable for immediate transplant, subject to the same restriction as applies in Manitoba.

(iv) *Brain Death and Anencephaly*

The Manitoba statute provides that for the purpose of *post-mortem* transplantation, at least two physicians shall determine the "brain death" of the donor. Elsewhere in Canada, the law stipulates that for the purpose of *post-mortem* transplantation, "the fact of death shall be determined by at least two physicians in accordance with accepted medical criteria." Since "accepted medical criteria" follow the brain death standard — that the patient's whole brain (including the brain stem) must cease functioning — the practice is the same in all provinces: the patient must be pronounced brain-dead before he can qualify as a post-mortem donor.

Until the late 1980s, medical professionals had no quarrel with the concept of whole-brain death as the appropriate indicator for *post-mortem* organ donation. Whatever policies were considered to alleviate the perennial shortage of donor organs, there were no proposals calling for the relaxation of the brain death standard. However, as paediatric organ transplantation has become more feasible, that consensus has broken down because of the view that the organ shortage can be eased by a new donor candidate: the anencephalic.

In 1987 surgeons at Loma Linda University Medical Centre in California performed a heart transplant that captured global headlines. The recipient (dubbed Baby Paul by the media) had been diagnosed in utero as afflicted with hypoplastic left heart. Upon the availability of a heart donor in London, Ontario, Baby Paul was prematurely delivered by Cesarean section. The mother of the donor (Baby Gabriel) was eight months pregnant when an ultrasound revealed that the fetus was anencephalic. Rejecting the option of induced labour, she and her husband chose to carry the fetus to term so that it could serve as an organ donor. The day after her birth in Orillia, Baby Gabriel was transferred to Children's Hospital in London and attached to a ventilator. She was pronounced brain-dead when she failed to breathe after 10 minutes off the ventilator. Baby Gabriel was then flown to Loma Linda, where her heart was promptly removed and transplanted into the recipient who was only three hours old when the surgery was begun.

Although there are scattered references in the medical literature to anencephalic kidney donation,[16] it was the heart transplant in Loma Linda that propelled the question of the anencephalic-as-organ-donor into the public forum. The critical legal issue arises from the fact that the anencephalic is not dead according to the brain death standard. The term *"brain-absent"* has been coined to describe the anencephalic because its cranial vault is incomplete and all or most of its cerebral cortex is missing. (It is in a sense born into a permanent vegetative state.) However, it lives in the eyes of the law since the infant has residual lower brain activity such that it can maintain breathing for up to a few days. The dilemma is that in the process of dying, its vital organs will deteriorate from loss of oxygen as the infant's breathing becomes more compromised. As happened with Baby

Gabriel, the anencephalic must be mechanically ventilated — not for its benefit but rather to preserve its organs for the ultimate recipient.

As a donor candidate, the anencephalic must be declared brain-dead before its organs can be removed for transplantation. The troubling aspect of the Baby Gabriel case is that brain death was considered proved by a 10-minute lack of spontaneous respiration, notwithstanding that clinically accepted neonatal brain death criteria have yet to be formulated. The lack of such criteria has led to proposals that the brain death standard be amended to include the "brain-absent" anencephalic. Its proponents believe that provincial law should stipulate that an anencephalic at birth is deemed legally dead for the purpose of organ transplantation.

Still, provincial law cannot categorize an anencephalic as legally dead unless the province already has a precise definition of death. In other words, an anencephalic cannot be excluded from the whole-brain death standard if there is no such legal standard already in place. Manitoba aside, the provinces have thus far exhibited a marked legislative indifference to the question, When is a person legally dead? It is doubtful that the anencephalic-as-organ-donor issue is enough to transform that unconcern into legislative action.

The proposal to define the anencephalic as brain-dead has generated a heated response. Its opponents stress the so-called "slippery slope" argument: that its acceptance would set a dangerous precedent. They contend that once whole-brain death criteria are relaxed to include the anencephalic, there is the risk that other patient categories (e.g. permanent vegetative state) would in time be added to the list. Furthermore, as one critic has pointed out:

> Adding anencephalics to the category of dead persons would be a radical change, both in the social and medical understanding of what it means to be dead and in the social practices surrounding death. Anencephalic infants may be dying, but they are still alive and breathing. Calling them "dead" will not change physiologic reality or otherwise cause them to resemble those (cold and nonrespirating) bodies that are considered appropriate for post-mortem examinations and burials.[17]

In May 1988 Dr. Donald Hill, the chief of pediatrics at the Vancouver Children's Hospital, disclosed that the hospital would no longer provide life-support for anencephalics. The policy change was prompted by a case in which an anencephalic was ventilated for six days. Life-support was terminated at that point because there was no available recipient for its heart. According to Dr. Hill: "We have decided that until such time that there is a better definition (of brain death) that fits these infants, we won't accept a request to maintain these babies." Three months later the Loma

Linda University Medical Centre announced the suspension of its anencephalic/organ donor program. The decision followed 13 unsuccessful attempts to harvest organs, leading Loma Linda officials to conclude that the program had "failed dismally."

As it now stands, anencephalics are not serving as organ donors, but who can say whether and when this will change. Aside from the ethical issues, the technological stumbling block is that clinically accepted neonatal brain death criteria have yet to be formulated. An option that could be considered is the use of non-heart-beating donors (NHBD) that, as noted, has been adopted in some American transplant centres. In that event, the anencephalic would qualify as a donor when the heart stopped. Of course, the profound ethical questions raised by the Baby Gabriel case would remain. And though her life was but a fleeting moment Baby Gabriel has dramatized an issue that strikes at the heart of the interface between medical technology and human values.

NOTES

1. R.S.S. 1978, c. H-15, s. 4(1).
2. S.M. 1987-88, c. 39.
3. S.P.E.I. 1992, c. 34.
4. *Civil Code*, Book 1, Title 1, art. 19, 20.
5. The cases are discussed in W.J. Curran, A problem of consent: kidney transplantation in minors. 34 **New York University Law Review** 891 (1959).
6. *Hart v. Brown*, 289 A.2d 386 (U.S. Conn. Sup. Ct., 1972).
7. *Trillium Gift of Life Network Act*, S.O. 2000, c. 39, s. 1. Bill 34, *The Charter Compliance Act*, 3rd session, 37 Leg., Manitoba, 2002.
8. *Human Tissue Donation Act*, S.P.E.I. 1992, c. 34, s. 1.
9. *Civil Code*, Book 1, Title 1, art. 43, 44.
10. R.S.O. 1980, c. 210, s. 7(2), (3).
11. M.L. Nicholson et al., A comparison of the results of renal transplantation from non-beating, controversial cadaveric, and living donors. 58 **Kidney International** 2585 (2000).
12. S.M. 1987-88, c. 39, s. 4.
13. A. Caplan, Can we ever solve the shortage problem? 3 **Journal of Transplant Coordination** 51 (1993).
14. Interview with Mr. Howard Nathan, President, Gift of Life Donor Program, 201-2000 Hamilton Street. Philadelphia, PA.
15. J.R. Chapman et al., **Organ and Tissue Donation and Transplantation** (Oxford U. Press, New York, 1997), at 345.
16. Beginning with L.W. Martin et al., Hemotransplantation of both kidneys from an anencephalic monster to a 17 pound boy with Eagle-Barrett syndrome. 66 **Surgery** 603 (1966).
17. A.M. Capron, Anencephalic donors: separate the dead from the dying. 17 **Hastings Center Report** 5 (1987).

18

EUTHANASIA, ASSISTING SUICIDE, AND TERMINATION OF LIFE-PROLONGING TREATMENT: DEFINITIONS AND OVERVIEW

SUMMARY

This section presents an overview of what Dutch commentators refer to as MDEL, an acronym for medical decision-making at the end of life. The subject matter is introduced by five hypothetical case scenarios: (1) withholding life-prolonging treatment at the behest of a mentally competent patient; (2) withdrawing life-prolonging treatment from a mentally incompetent patient; (3) mercy-killing at the behest of a mentally competent patient; (4) mercy-killing of a mentally incompetent patient; and (5) aiding the suicide of a mentally competent patient. The physician acts lawfully in scenarios one and two; scenarios three and four are defined as murder and it is legally irrelevant that in scenario three the act was committed with the consent of the patient. Scenario five is defined as the crime of aiding suicide.

The first four scenarios were for some time conceptualized according to the following typology: (1) *passive voluntary euthanasia*; (2) *passive non-voluntary euthanasia*; (3) *active voluntary euthanasia*; and (4) *active non-voluntary euthanasia*. However, terminology changes over time and in common parlance the focus of the debate over the legalization of "euthanasia" has come to focus upon the third and fifth scenarios: either mercy-killing at the request of a mentally competent patient or the assisted suicide of such a patient. Instead of the term *passive euthanasia*, the first and second scenarios now come under the heading, *the termination of life-prolonging treatment*,

and thus fall outside the parameters of the current "euthanasia" debate.

1.   THE FIVE CASES OF DR. COMPASSIONATE

Case 1   A Case of Withholding Life-Prolonging Treatment at the Behest of a Mentally Competent Patient (Passive Voluntary Euthanasia)

Dr. C's patient is a 60-year-old male who has had six myocardial infarctions in the last nine years. He is on maximal therapy for congestive heart failure, which has afflicted him for about four years. He suffers from severe and persistent angina pectoris. Dyspnea has rendered him incapable of more than limited exertion, and he is reduced to a bed-to-chair existence. A recent heart catheterization and coronary angiography revealed end stage congestive cardiomyopathy with inoperable and severe triple vessel coronary artery disease.

Two months ago the patient suffered a cardiac arrest on the ward. He was resuscitated and started on anti-arrhythmic therapy. The therapy has only partially controlled his premature ventricular contractions and recurrent ventricular tachycardia.

After frequent discussion with Dr. C about his condition, the patient instructs her that he is not to be resuscitated in the event of another cardiac arrest. Although understandably depressed he is mentally competent, and Dr. C enters a DNR (do-not-resuscitate) order on his chart. A few days later his heart stops, and in accordance with the DNR order there is no attempt to resuscitate. Within minutes the patient is pronounced dead.

Case 2   A Case of Withdrawing Life-Prolonging Treatment of a Mentally Incompetent Patient (Passive Non-Voluntary Euthanasia)

Dr. C's patient is a 30-year-old male who was diagnosed with AIDS 18 months ago. In the past six months he was twice admitted to hospital for treatment of pneumocystis carinii pneumonia. Heightened confusion and significant weight loss preceded his current admission, which occurred after the patient overdosed on illegally obtained meperidine. His landlord found him unconscious and not breathing. On arrival at hospital he was intubated, mechanically ventilated, and transferred to the intensive care unit. His aspiration pneumonia has caused him to remain dependent on life-support. Beyond that, the overdose has resulted in anoxic brain damage, leaving him in a chronic vegetative state.

Except for his twin sister, the patient is estranged from his family. Dr. C advises her that since continued treatment is pointless, her brother should be allowed to die. Responding that her brother "no longer has a life", she agrees to the withdrawal of his life-support measures. After she bids him farewell and leaves the ICU, the ventilator (respirator)* is disconnected and within minutes the patient is dead.

Case 3 A Case of Mercy-Killing at the Behest of a Mentally Competent Patient (Active Voluntary Euthanasia)

Dr. C's patient is a 40-year-old male. His diagnosis is esophageal carcinoma with metastases to the regional lymph nodes and invasion into the thoracic spine. Neither curative nor palliative surgery is a feasible option, and the prognosis is death within three to six months. The tumour, which has proved resistant to radiotherapy treatment, is advancing and is associated with intractable bone pain. Neurosurgical pain-controlling procedures are not feasible, nor can narcotics alleviate the pain without rendering the patient stuporous. He is being tube-fed. The patient, who is fully aware of his condition, repeatedly beseeches Dr. C to "put me out of my misery". After agonizing reflection, Dr. C complies by administering a massive dose of sodium pentobarbital (to render him unconscious) followed by succinylcholine (which causes his death by respiratory paralysis).

Case 4 A Case of Mercy Killing of a Mentally Incompetent Patient (Active Non-Voluntary Euthanasia)

Dr. C's patient is a 40-year-male with the identical diagnosis as the patient in Case 3, although his prognosis is measured in weeks not months. The patient is bleeding from the site of the tumour and is frequently choking on his blood. He lies curled up in a fetal position, drooling and sobbing. He is compliant when treated but is verbally uncommunicative. He has neither family nor friends. Motivated by compassion, Dr. C ends his life in the same manner as in Case 3.

Case 5 A Case of Physician-Assisted Suicide

Dr. C's patient is the same as in Case 1. Responding to his persistent plea for help in committing suicide, she mixes a lethal dose of pentobarbital

---

* Since *ventilator* and *respirator* are synonyms for a mechanical breathing machine, the terms are used interchangeably in this text.

with liquid in a cup and, after giving him an antiemetic, hands him the fatal concoction. After expressing his gratitude he quickly ingests the contents, lapses into unconsciousness, and dies a quick and painless death.

2. COMMENTARY

This chapter introduces the subject matter of what Dutch physicians refer to as MDEL: Medical Decision-Making at the End of Life. As a shorthand expression covering Dr. C's five case scenarios, MDEL avoids the confusion occasioned by the term *euthanasia*, whose meaning has changed over time. In that regard, note that philosophers in particular have drawn a distinction between what they define as *active euthanasia* on the one hand and *passive euthanasia* on the other: active euthanasia is to *killing* as passive euthanasia is to *letting die*. According to that scheme, the first four of Dr. C's cases would come under the following respective headings: passive voluntary, passive non-voluntary, active voluntary, and active non-voluntary euthanasia.

However, that four-part classification scheme is currently dated, and in any event it is not followed in public discourse. That is not surprising, given that "euthanasia" has no fixed meaning and is neither a legal nor a medical term. Its roots rather lie in the realm of philosophy, where it conveys the notion of "an easy and painless death; a peaceful manner of dying."[1] The word derives from the Greek: "eu" which means well, and "thanatos" which means death; and it is really for each of us to decide what kind of death would fit that notion. To a young Winston Churchill, the ideal, albeit not peaceful, death was from a bullet in the heart while leading a cavalry charge. And for a quick if not dignified death, comedian/film maker Woody Allen recommends inhaling deeply while standing next to an insurance salesman.

In public discourse, the euthanasia debate has centred around the scenarios captured in Dr. C's third and fifth cases: the cases of active voluntary euthanasia and physician-assisted suicide. Henceforth, we use the term "euthanasia" in that dual sense: the mentally competent patient beseeching the physician either for the injection of a lethal drug or for a lethal drug to self-administer. As we see in Chapter 26, the Dutch euthanasia policy does not distinguish between lethal injection and assisting suicide cases; and in fact Dutch commentators have taken to using the acronym *EAS* (euthanasia and assisted suicide) as a shorthand expression of that policy in their English language publications.

Note that in recent years the phrase "passive euthanasia" has fallen by the wayside in favour of the "termination of life-prolonging treatment". As a shorthand expression, one might say "pulling the plug" or "letting die"

— or simply the withdrawal or withholding of life-prolonging treatment. Pulling the plug in a near literal sense — turning off the ventilator in Case 2 — is an example of withdrawal; and a DNR order (Case 1) is an example of withholding. (In the pursuit of semantic refinement, one could say that treatment withdrawn is treatment terminated and that treatment withheld is treatment foregone. That said, commentators commonly say "termination" when referring to either scenario. In any event, neither law nor medical ethics distinguishes between withholding and withdrawing treatment; if one is allowable then so is the other.)

The fifth case simply falls under the separate heading, aided or assisted suicide. In the withdrawal-of-treatment and mercy-killing cases (1, 3, and 4), it is the physician who performs the act that directly causes death. In Case 2 — the withholding-of-treatment — it is the physician who allows death to proceed. In these four cases the patient plays a passive role in the mechanics of death. However, in Case 5 it is the patient, albeit assisted by the physician, who performs the act that directly causes death.

Dr. C has acted lawfully by foregoing (withholding) life-prolonging treatment in Case 1 and terminating (withdrawing) life-prolonging treatment in Case 2. Case 1 is covered by the no-treatment-without-consent principle. Her mentally competent patient has the legal right to choose to die rather than to undergo CPR in the likelihood of another cardiac arrest. The patient's legal right to refuse treatment imposes a reciprocal legal duty upon Dr. C to comply, or to transfer the patient to another physician if she cannot in good conscience abide by his decision. Dr. C would be civilly liable in *battery* for resuscitating the patient in the face of his express refusal of such treatment.

The Case 2 scenario is within the law even though there is scant legal authority to that effect. What matters is that provincial attorneys-general do not question the legality of the medical practice of terminating life-support measures for mentally incompetent patients when the withdrawn or withheld treatment is considered to offer no reasonable hope of benefit. Their deliberate silence is widely and reasonably interpreted as the legal system's off-the-record acceptance of the medical practice of "passive non-voluntary euthanasia".

In the mercy-killing scenarios (Cases 3 and 4), Dr. C is guilty of murder under the *Criminal Code*. It is legally irrelevant that the deceased consented or even instigated the act (that it was voluntary on his part), or that the deceased was never consulted (that it was non-voluntary). In either case the law brands the act as murder. The illegality of the former is mandated by the long tradition of the common law, which is codified in section 14 of the *Criminal Code*:

No person is entitled to consent to have death inflicted upon him, and such consent does not affect the criminal responsibility of any person by whom death may be inflicted upon the person by whom consent is given.

In Case 5, Dr. C has breached section 241 of the *Criminal Code*, which defines the offence of "aiding suicide". The crime of aiding suicide is committed whether or not the person being assisted succeeds in his attempt. The maximum sentence is 14 years' imprisonment, although there is no mandatory minimum sentence. In fact, although neither suicide (for obvious reasons) nor attempted suicide is a criminal offence, anyone who knowingly helps the effort has committed the crime of aiding suicide. In short, it is a crime to assist someone to commit an act that for the latter is not a crime. (The crime of attempted suicide was removed from the *Criminal Code* in 1972. Although one who commits suicide is beyond punishment, the early common law decreed that his property be forfeited to the Crown and that he be denied burial in consecrated ground.)

In its 1995 report, *Of Life and death*, the Canadian Senate Special Committee on Euthanasia and Assisted Suicide provided the following examples of assisted suicide:

A physician gives a patient information about how to take a lethal dose of a drug and writes a prescription for the drug, knowing that it is the intention of the patient to kill himself with the drug. The patient takes the lethal dose and dies as a result.

A friend of a partially-paralysed woman goes to the pharmacy to get a prescription for barbiturates filled, brings them to her, pours them into her hand, and brings her a drink to wash down the pills. The woman takes the pills with the drink and dies as a result.[2]

As the Committee explained, in assisted suicide cases "the patient is the agent of death but death results from the assistance supplied by another person." These cases are thus distinguishable from mercy-killings, in which the direct act that causes death is performed by the accused. Therefore, a physician who gives a deliberate lethal injection to a patient commits the crime of murder, whereas the physician who gives lethal drugs to a patient for the purpose of enabling her to ingest them herself commits the crime of aiding suicide.

It is the distinction between acts of *commission* and acts of *omission* that explains the disparate legal classification of euthanasia (the lethal injection and assisted suicide scenarios) and the termination/foregoing of life-prolonging treatment. Euthanasia is criminalized because the patient's death is caused by a direct act of *commission*. The deliberate injection of a lethal drug clearly fits the category, as does its provision to the patient who performs the act that brings about death. In either case, the physician deliberately interrupts the disease process by an act that directly kills the patient (either by the physician's or the patient's hand). In that sense it is not the disease process that kills or causes the patient's death. Instead, the culprit is the physician.

In contrast, when the patient dies either because a DNR order precludes resuscitation or his ventilator is shut down, his death has not resulted from an act of commission. According to the conventional legal wisdom, his death has ensued from an act of *omission*. Omission means that the physician withholds or withdraws treatment to enable nature to take its course. When the treatment is omitted, it is the disease process that kills. In that sense, the physician has not killed or caused the patient's death. The culprit is the disease.

In Case 1, a treatment (resuscitation) was withheld. In Case 2, a treatment (artificial ventilation) was withdrawn. In neither case has Dr. C committed homicide; rather she has lawfully permitted the two patients to die natural deaths.

It is true that when Dr. C turned off the ventilator in Case 2, her conduct was not passive in the dictionary meaning of the term (physical inaction). In that semantic sense, the withdrawal of treatment in Case 2 is distinguishable from its withholding in Case 1. (If passivity means doing nothing, it is arguable that the physician is doing something, whether switching off a respirator or issuing a written or even verbal DNR order.) However, it is not semantics but rather social policy that guides the law. The policy is that the physician is not duty bound to provide non-beneficial treatment; and the Canadian courts have not questioned decisions by physicians to withhold or to withdraw life-prolonging treatment, either with or without patient consent.

Still, one can make too much of the distinction between commission and omission. What if an unscrupulous physician were to withhold antibiotics from a patient whose only medical problem was pneumonia and the patient consequently died? In the eyes of the law the physician is guilty of murder. The absurdity of the defence that there was no act of commission but merely an omission speaks for itself. The physician would be faulted because he was under a legal duty to act, and his failure to act — his omission — is what renders him culpable. After all, the notion of criminal neglect is based upon a failure to act (as when, for example, parents neglect to provide necessary medical care for their minor children).

In other words, it is not the fact of omission alone that determines why the scrupulous physician who withholds or withdraws life-prolonging treatment is not deemed the legal cause of her patient's death. Rather, what renders the omission lawful is that the physician was not under a legal duty to provide the treatment in question. As explained by the U.S. President's Commission for the Study of Ethical Problems in Medicine and Biomedical and Behavioral Research (in its 1983 report, *Deciding to Forego Life-Sustaining Treatment*):

> In a death following nontreatment, designating the disease as the cause not only asserts that a fatal disease process was present but also communicates acceptance of the physician's behavior in foregoing treatment. Conversely, if an otherwise healthy patient who desired treatment died from untreated pneumonia, the physician's failure to treat would be considered to have caused the patient's death.[3]

3. CONCLUSION

The law has in effect endorsed the Roman Catholic position on the termination/foregoing of life-prolonging treatment — a position grounded in the distinction between *ordinary* and *extraordinary* treatment. The former is defined by the Church as treatment offering "a reasonable hope of benefit for the patient". The latter is treatment that cannot offer such hope. If the treatment provides a net benefit, it is considered ordinary treatment and is morally obligatory. If it fails to benefit the patient, it is deemed extraordinary treatment and is not morally obligatory. Ordinary treatment must always be furnished, whereas extraordinary treatment may legitimately be withheld or withdrawn. (Bear in mind that the very notion of non-beneficial treatment is value-laden in its assumption that life is not always worth living; this issue is addressed under the topic heading of *Futility* in Chapter 22. Furthermore, in accordance with the no-treatment-without-consent principle, if a mentally competent patient says No, then it is beside the point whether the spurned treatment is "ordinary".)

What determines under which heading a treatment falls is not the specific nature of the treatment but rather the treatment's effect upon the patient. For example, dialysis is ordinary treatment when it benefits the patient and extraordinary treatment when it confers no benefit (or its burden outweighs its benefit). This distinction was accepted by the New Jersey Supreme Court in the landmark *Karen Ann Quinlan* case:*

> The use of the same respirator or like support could be considered "ordinary" in the context of the possibly curable patient but "extraordinary" in the context of the forced sustaining . . . of an irreversibly doomed patient.

---

* This case is discussed in Chapter 21.

In *Barber v. Superior Court* (1983),* a California appellate court rejected the ordinary/extraordinary terminology while still embracing the concept:

> The use of these terms begs the question. A more rational approach involves the determination of whether the proposed treatment is *proportionate* or *disproportionate* in terms of the benefits to be gained versus the burdens caused. (Emphasis added.)

We agree that the California court's terminology more clearly captures the essence of the treatment's impact upon the patient. As explained in the *Hastings Center Guidelines*:

> No treatment is intrinsically "ordinary" or "extraordinary". All treatments that impose undue burdens on the patient without overriding benefits or that simply provide no benefits may justifiably be withheld or withdrawn. While traditional definitions of "extraordinary" hinged on this comparison of benefits and burdens, the term has become so confusing that it is no longer useful.[4]

In any event, whether one says ordinary-extraordinary or proportionate-disproportionate, it is parallel to the distinction drawn in this book between *life-saving* and *life-prolonging* treatment. Treatment is life-saving when: (1) it is likely to help return the patient to his pre-morbid state; or (2) it provides a net benefit to the patient even though it cannot cure his condition (e.g. dialysis, insulin, or a quality of life deemed worth living by the patient whatever his prognosis). In contrast, treatment is life-prolonging when it arguably: (1) provides neither benefit nor burden; or (2) its burden outweighs its benefit.

The first life-prolonging category is illustrated by a patient in a permanent vegetative state (PVS). For this patient there is no benefit from artificial life-support because his total lack of awareness puts him beyond the benefit-burden equation. (Admittedly, there is a viewpoint that proclaims the absolute sanctity of human life such that even a PVS patient must be kept alive unless he had provided otherwise by way of a health care directive.)

The second category is illustrated by a ventilator-dependent mentally competent patient suffering from ALS (amyotrophic lateral sclerosis). The patient, who is totally paralysed, pleads for the termination of life-support because she can no longer abide the agony and humiliation wrought by the disease. In her case, the burden of treatment exceeds its benefit. Mechanical ventilation benefits the patient because (unlike the PVS patient) she is

---

* This case is discussed in Chapter 21.

mentally intact. But its beneficial effect is overcome by the burden of her misery, as indicated by her preference for death over life in her current state. For both her and the PVS patient, the ventilator is life-prolonging treatment because it fails to offer "a reasonable hope of benefit for the patient".

In the next chapter, we consider two cases — *Satz v. Perlmutter* (Florida, 1978) and *Nancy B. (B. (N.) v. Hôtel-Dieu de Québec)* (Quebec, 1992) — in which mentally competent patients obtained court orders compelling their caregivers to cease their efforts to keep them alive on mechanical life-support. For these patients their treatments were life-prolonging. There are other patients in their circumstances who prefer to live, so for them life-support is life-saving. Once again, the key is not the particular treatment at issue but the application of the benefit-burden scale to the patient. If competent the patient makes that determination; if incompetent others decide (with the guidance of a health care directive if the patient had the foresight to fill one out).

It is instructive to contrast the plight of Nancy B. with that of Sue Rodriguez, whose affliction with ALS prompted her to challenge the constitutionality of the Criminal Code prohibition against assisted suicide.* Because Nancy B. was dependent upon artificial ventilation, she could insist upon its removal. However, because Sue Rodriguez was able to breathe on her own, there were no life-support measures that stood as an impediment to her death. Thus, unlike the situation of Nancy B., there was no lawful way for a physician to help Sue Rodriguez die unless the Supreme Court was prepared to rule in her favour — but the Court denied her claim.

Another term, *life-extending* treatment, is occasionally used in later chapters as a shorthand expression for cases where the treatment may well be worth pursuing but where it is too early to tell whether it will offer significant benefit to the patient. In other words, it is the difference between potentially life-saving and most likely life-saving. An example is furnished by the 2002 case of *Alberta (Director of Child Welfare) v. H. (B.)*, in which a 16-year-old Jehovah's Witness stricken with leukemia refused blood products — a necessary component of the treatment regimen for the disease.** The medical evidence was that the odds of long-term survival with the conventional treatment (chemotherapy/blood) were between 40-50%. However, if she were in remission at the end of two cycles of chemotherapy, then a bone marrow transplant would increase the odds to 65%. When the case was in the courts, the spurned treatment was thus life-extending.

---

* The *Rodriguez* case is covered in Chapter 25.
** The *B.H.* case is considered in some detail in Chapter 20.

The law that has developed regarding the termination of life-prolonging treatment will be examined in the next five chapters. The virtual absence of Canadian law on the subject until the ruling in the *Nancy B. (B. (N.) v. Hôtel-Dieu de Québec)* case stands in marked contrast to American law, which has been grappling with the legal implications of "letting die" since the New Jersey case of *Karen Ann Quinlan* captured global headlines in 1975-6. The *Nancy B.* case dealt with the termination of life-prolonging treatment at the request of a mentally competent patient whereas *Quinlan* involved the termination of life-prolonging treatment of a mentally incompetent patient at the request of her parents. For two reasons — (1) that Canadian law has barely tackled the *Quinlan*-type scenario,* and (2) that Canadian medical practice nonetheless functions as if the American law on *Quinlan* and related cases was in effect the law in Canada as well — we devote Chapter 21 to the American jurisprudence on terminating life-prolonging treatment for mentally incompetent patients.

---

* The very few Canadian cases on point are covered in Chapters 22-23.

NOTES

1. Webster's New Twentieth Century Dictionary Unabridged (2nd ed.) (William Collins World Publishing Co., 1977).
2. Senate Special Committee on Euthanasia and Assisted Suicide, **Of Life and Death** (Minister of Supply and Services Canada, 1995), at 51.
3. U.S. President's Commission for the Study of Ethical Problems in Medicine and Biomedical and Behavioral Research. **Deciding to Forego Life-Sustaining Treatment** (U.S. Government Printing Office, Washington, D.C., 1983), at 69-70.
4. The Hastings Center, **Guidelines on the Termination of Life-Sustaining Treatment and the Care of the Dying** (The Hastings Center, New York, 1987), at 5.

19

THE MENTALLY COMPETENT ADULT PATIENT AND THE REFUSAL OF TREATMENT

SUMMARY

As explained in Chapter 2, a physician can lawfully treat a mentally competent patient only when there is consent to treatment. The physician who treats without consent commits the civil wrong (tort) of *battery*. The law does not waive the patient's right even if the treatment is necessary to maintain life.

In short, the *no-treatment-without-consent principle* provides legal grounding for the medical practice of complying with the demand of a mentally competent patient for the termination of life-prolonging treatment. Consider the patient whose prognosis is dismal and who decides that the burdens of treatment outweigh its benefits. When the patient withholds consent to continued treatment, her physician is legally obliged to stop treatment even though the result is the patient's death (or to transfer her to a physician who will do her bidding). The principle is illustrated by the *Nancy B. (B. (N.) v. Hôtel-Dieu de Québec)* case (Quebec, 1992), in which the patient was forced to seek judicial relief when her caregivers refused to turn off her respirator. The controlling factor in the *Nancy B.* case was not the patient's severe disability but rather that she was competent to withdraw consent to the treatment at issue. We consider American and English cases on the criteria for determining mental competency to refuse life-prolonging treatment because there are no Canadian cases on point.

1. INTRODUCTION

Consider a mentally competent patient who informs her caregivers that she no longer wishes to be kept alive by life-support measures. In that event, the physician is lawfully entitled to withhold or withdraw life-prolonging treatment and thereby hasten the patient's death. In fact, it is not so much the physician's right but rather her duty to comply. The controlling factor in such cases is not the nature and extent of the competent patient's condition but whether the patient has withdrawn consent to the treatment at issue. In the United States, the issue was first confronted in the 1970s in a number of cases in which the courts applied common law principles that are found in Canadian as well as American jurisprudence. Yet it was not until the 1992 Quebec case of *Nancy B. (B. (N.) v. Hôtel-Dieu de Québec)* that a Canadian court dealt with the question. Before turning to *Nancy B.*, we consider three precedent-setting American cases (all from 1978) which ruled that a mentally competent patient has a legally enforceable right to call a halt to life-prolonging treatment

2. THREE LEADING AMERICAN CASES

(a) Abe Perlmutter (Florida, 1978)[1]

Abe Perlmutter was a 73-year-old retired cabdriver afflicted with amyotrophic lateral sclerosis (ALS). Death was anticipated "within a short time" (not otherwise specified), and he was quite insistent that the ventilator be turned off. As he repeatedly said to his family and caregivers, "I'm miserable, take it out." Even though his wife and children supported his decision, the physicians (and hospital) refused to comply. That prompted him to petition the Florida District Court for an order to restrain the hospital from maintaining him on life-support against his will. He was interviewed at his bedside by the judge. Perlmutter told him that he wished to live but that he could not tolerate the agony and humiliation wrought by the disease, and that death "can't be worse than what I am going through now." According to the judge:

> The affliction has progressed to the point of virtual incapability of movement, inability to breathe without a mechanical respirator; and his very speech is an extreme effort.

The judge found him mentally competent to refuse treatment and ordered the hospital to yield to his demand. That happened the following day and Perlmutter died with his family at his bedside.

(b) Robert Quackenbush (New Jersey, 1978)[2]

A New Jersey hospital filed a petition in County Court seeking the judicial appointment of a guardian for a 72-year-old patient, Robert Quackenbush. Even though advised by his physician that he would be dead within three weeks unless his gangrenous legs were amputated, Quackenbush had nonetheless refused to allow the surgery. The petition alleged that the patient was mentally incompetent, thus requiring a guardian to consent on his behalf.

At the time of his hospital admission, Quackenbush had been living for 10 years as a semi-recluse in a trailer with his only known relative, an 83-year-old cousin. He was unwillingly brought by ambulance to the hospital emergency room at the behest of his neighbours. Although he refused treatment and behaved in a belligerent and rambunctious manner, he was admitted and assigned a treating physician. At the hearing on the petition, the physician — who referred to Quackenbush as a "conscientious objector to medical therapy" — testified that except for one brief hospitalization he had shunned medical treatment for the past 40 years. The patient's condition was described by the Court.

> Quackenbush has gangrene in both legs. On his left leg the skin is black from the knee down, is partially mummified; and the foot is dangling, about to fall off. On the left leg there is an open sore, which is draining fluid and in which the tibia and tendons are exposed. His right leg is in a similar condition except that the black skin and mummified condition extend from midcalf down. Neither leg has a normal pulse behind the knee or ankle, indicating total absence of blood flow. The blood is being seeded with bacteria from inflamed areas adjoining the gangrene. Cultures of the blood indicate the presence of gas-forming bacteria. Such bacteria can lead to gas gangrene, a more fulminating type infection than gangrene. The diagnosis is that the gangrene is caused by arteriosclerosis . . . inducing high fever, dehydration, and profound anemia.

The physician testified that, at the very least, the surgery would entail the amputation of both legs just above the knee. However, he acknowledged that it might prove necessary to remove both legs entirely, given that the extent of amputation could not be determined until the operation was underway. In either event, the fate reserved for Quackenbush was wheelchair confinement in a nursing home.

Testimony concerning the patient's mental state was elicited from two psychiatrists, one of whom was a witness for the hospital. He had seen Quackenbush on January 6, his opinion was that the patient was mentally incompetent to exercise an informed choice to refuse the surgery. The second psychiatrist testified as an independent witness called by the Court. On the basis of an interview on January 11, he concluded that the patient was mentally competent to refuse the operation.

On January 12 the judge conducted a 10-minute bedside interview with Quackenbush. He found him alert and responsive, as had the court-appointed psychiatrist who had examined him on the previous day. The judge accordingly denied the hospital's petition, thereby affirming Quackenbush's right as a mentally competent patient to choose death over a life that he did not consider worth living.

(c)   Rosaria Candura (Massachusetts, 1978)[3]

Rosaria Candura, 77, was readmitted to a Massachusetts hospital on account of gangrene in her right foot and lower leg. Months before, a toe and a portion of the foot had been amputated. At that time an arterial bypass had been performed to decrease the likelihood of the recurrence of the gangrene. But it did recur, and when she was readmitted to hospital her attending physician recommended amputation of the leg without delay. Although she initially agreed, she withdrew her consent on the morning scheduled for the surgery. She was discharged from hospital but returned two weeks later after a change of heart. Once again she reversed her position and this time persisted in her refusal, notwithstanding the entreaties of her physician and four adult children.

Mrs. Candura offered numerous reasons for the decision to surrender her life instead of her leg. She had been unhappy since her husband's death two years before and did not wish to burden her children. She had no desire to live as an invalid or in a nursing home. She was discouraged by the failure of prior surgery to arrest the gangrene and had no faith in a favourable outcome from future surgery. Mrs. Candura also indicated that she did not fear death but on the contrary welcomed it. Her daughter responded by filing a petition in Family Court for appointment as her mother's temporary guardian for the purpose of consenting to the surgery. The Court granted the petition and Mrs. Candura appealed. She had testified at the hearing on her daughter's application; and the intermediate appellate court* had this to say about her evidence, demeanour, and mental competence.

> She expressed a desire to get well but indicated that she was resigned to death and was adamantly against the operation. Her testimony, which was corroborated by that of several of the witnesses, showed that she is lucid on some matters and confused on others. Her train of thought sometimes wanders. Her

---

* An intermediate appellate court is a lower court of appeal in a state. An appeal from its decision would go to the state supreme court.

conception of time is distorted. But she has exhibited a high degree of awareness and acuity when responding to questions concerning the proposed operation. She has made it clear that she does not wish to have the operation even though that decision will in all likelihood lead shortly to her death. We find no indication in any of the testimony that that is not a choice with full appreciation of the consequences. The most that is shown is that the decision involves strong emotional factors, that she does not choose to discuss the decision with certain persons, and that occasionally her resolve against giving consent weakens.

The Court stressed that the relevant question was not whether she had made a *medically* rational choice. Even if irrational in that regard, it did not inevitably follow that she was incompetent in law. The issue was whether Mrs. Candura had the mental capacity to appreciate the nature of the proposed treatment and the consequences of her decision. The Court found:

> The fact that she has vacillated in her resolve not to submit to the operation does not justify a conclusion that her capacity to make the decision is impaired to the point of legal incompetence. Indeed, her reaction may be readily understandable in light of her prior surgical experience and the prospect of living the remainder of her life nonambulatory. Senile symptoms, in the abstract, may of course justify a finding of incompetence, but the inquiry must be more particular. What is lacking in this case is evidence that Mrs. Candura's areas of forgetfulness and confusion cause or relate in any way to impairment of her ability to understand that in rejecting the amputation she is, in effect, choosing death over life.

The Court admitted that Mrs. Candura's decision could reasonably be regarded as regrettable. Still, that was not the issue; rather the issue was whether her refusal was an informed choice. As the Court concluded: "On the record of this case, it is not the uninformed decision of a person incapable of appreciating the nature and consequences of her act." Whereupon it reversed the judgment of the lower court and dismissed the daughter's petition.

3. CANADIAN LAW — NANCY B. (B. (N.) v. HÔTEL-DIEU DE QUÉBEC) (QUEBEC, 1992) AND ROBERT CORBEIL (QUEBEC, 1992)[4]

Over a three-month period beginning in late 1991, the Canadian media accorded front page status to the story of Nancy B., a 24-year-old patient at the Hôtel-Dieu Hospital in Quebec City who had sought a court order to compel her caregivers to stop life-support measures. The case attracted nation-wide interest because it dramatically raised the question whether a Canadian hospital had the legal right to treat a mentally competent patient against her will.

Did the hospital have the right literally to force treatment down the patient's throat? That was the situation here, because Nancy B. was being kept alive by a ventilator whose removal she had repeatedly asked for. (This was, of course, the precise scenario in the *Perlmutter* case.) Although the media was quick to label it as a "right to die" case, the issue before the Quebec Superior Court was simply whether a mentally competent patient was powerless to enforce her refusal of life-prolonging treatment. As in the *Perlmutter, Quackenbush* and *Candura* cases, Nancy B.'s petition squarely addressed the consent doctrine: not the patient's right to die but the patient's right to refuse treatment.

Nancy B. was afflicted with Guillain-Barre syndrome, a neurological disease that in most cases results in complete recovery. Tragically, in her case it had caused total and permanent paralysis as well as weakness of the muscles required for breathing. She had been a quadriplegic since 1988 and over time had come to the considered judgment that her existence was intolerable and that she no longer wished to live. In February 1991 she accordingly asked her physician at the Hotel-Dieu hospital to stop treatment and let her die. Although she was pronounced mentally competent by a hospital psychiatrist, the physician refused to honour her stated refusal of treatment on the grounds that compliance was not only unethical but also illegal. Three months later the patient reiterated her demand but was again turned down, even though the psychiatrist confirmed his previous finding of mental competency.

The hospital's general director backed up the physician's refusal to do her patient's bidding by claiming that her stand was compelled by *Criminal Code* provisions against "euthanasia" and aiding suicide. Given the steadfast refusal of her caregivers to heed her wishes, Nancy B.'s only recourse was to petition for judicial relief.

Given the longstanding recognition of the no-treatment-without-consent principle in Canadian law, health lawyers and bio-ethicists were puzzled by the hospital's steadfast refusal to honour Nancy B.'s insistent demand for the withdrawal of her mechanical life-support. A mentally competent patient cannot be treated without consent, and the physician who nonetheless does so commits the tort of battery and the crime of assault. Aside from its secure basis in the common law, the principle is found in the Quebec *Civil Code* under the general heading, Integrity of the Person. As stated in article 19, "No person may be made to undergo care of any nature, whether for examination, treatment or any other act, except with his consent."

Nancy B. went to court to enforce her right to patient autonomy, her right as a mentally competent patient to say "hands off" to her caregivers. Her case invites comparison with *Malette v. Shulman*, a 1990 decision by the Ontario Court of Appeal, which ruled that the defendant-physician had committed a battery when he gave blood transfusions to an unconscious patient who had suffered life-threatening injuries in an auto accident.[5] Although Mrs. Malette had signed a Jehovah's Witness medical alert card specifying that no blood be administered under any circumstances, Dr. Shulman had refused to abide by its directive. It was beside the point that he saved her life and that the patient fully recovered from her injuries. As the Court explained its decision: "To deny individuals freedom of choice with respect to their health care can only lessen, and not enhance, the value of life." The Ontario Court went on to extol "the freedom of the patient as an individual to exercise her right to refuse treatment and to accept the consequences of her own decision."*

If a patient is lawfully empowered to refuse treatment that would *restore* health for religious reasons that are rejected by most Canadians, how can one deny the same right of refusal to a patient whose prospects were as grim as those facing Nancy B.? Moreover, Mrs. Malette was not mentally competent upon admission to hospital and thus not able to deal with her life-threatening situation in the here-and-now (albeit she was mentally competent when she signed the directive). Although she could not directly speak to Dr. Shulman, her opposition to blood transfusion was there for him to read. Still, it is not the prognosis nor the reason for the patient's decision that is controlling in either case. In the eyes of the law, what is compelling is that a mentally competent patient cannot receive treatment — whether life-saving (e.g. the *Shulman* case) or life-prolonging (e.g. the *Nancy B.* case) — unless she consents to that treatment.**

In January 1992 the case was resolved in Nancy B.'s favour by Justice Jacques Dufour of the Quebec Superior Court. During the trial he had met with Nancy for 10 minutes at her bedside where she told him:

> I am fed up with living on a respirator. It's not a life. I don't want to live on a machine any more. The only thing I have is the television and staring at the walls. It's enough. It's been two and a half years that I am on this, and I have given it my all.

---

* The *Shulman* case is also considered in Chapters 2 and 24.

** Life-prolonging and life-saving treatment are defined in Chapter 18.

Given the undisputed mental competence of the patient, Justice Dufour was bound to apply the forenamed provision in the Quebec *Civil Code* and to conclude that the petitioner "has the right to request that the respiratory support treatment be stopped." In brief but incisive comments, he also held that the *Criminal Code* did not impede the withdrawal of the treatment that was keeping her alive.

Five weeks after his decision the ventilator was disconnected when Nancy B. said it was time, and she died a quick and painless death. As noted, this was not a "right to die" case. The issue was whether the patient could be treated without her consent and the Court's response was a re-sounding No. It mattered not that the treatment was life-prolonging. As Justice Dufour in effect ruled, the very essence of the consent doctrine cannot tolerate an exception based upon the nature of the treatment that is being rejected in a particular case. In sum, 14 years after the rulings in the *Perlmutter, Quackenbush* and *Candura* cases, a Canadian court likewise affirmed the right of a mentally competent patient to refuse life-prolonging treatment.

Two weeks after the ruling by Justice Dufour, a colleague on the same court decided a case that oddly enough failed to attract the attention of the national media. In *Manoir de la Pointe Bleue (1978) Inc. c. Corbeil*, Quebec Superior Court Judge Rouleau considered an application by an extended care facility for a determination whether it lawfully could permit a 35-year-old quadriplegic resident to fast unto death. Sixteen months after he was paralysed from the neck down in an accident, Robert Corbeil stopped eating for the express purpose of bringing about his death. However, he wished to remain in the facility because of its familiar surroundings and its excellent care.

The judge ruled that the petitioner should continue to make food available to the patient but was not obliged to resort to the "degrading" recourse of forced feeding. In his view, the question was not whether Corbeil's resolve to die was reasonable but whether it was the informed decision of a mentally competent patient. Since only the patient could judge the quality of his life, his "balanced and clear-minded" decision to terminate that life must be honoured by his caregivers. In finding that the facility would commit no crime by honouring Corbeil's wishes (although he made no reference to particular *Criminal Code* provisions), the judge went out of his way to state that Corbeil's death would not constitute "euthanasia or mercy-killing."

Of course, what distinguishes *Corbeil* from *Nancy B.* and the can-vassed American cases is that a patient who is not being tube-fed and who stops eating is not rejecting life-prolonging medical treatment. Still, Robert Corbeil was seeking the same end as the patients in the other cases: the right to prevent his caregivers from interfering with his bodily integrity albeit at the cost of hastening his death.

4. COMMENTARY

The cases presented affirm the right of mentally competent patients to refuse life-prolonging treatment (and in *Corbeil* to refuse nutrition). In *Perlmutter* and *Nancy B.*, it was held that treatment (artificial respiration) must be *withdrawn* at the insistence of a mentally competent patient. In *Candura* and *Quackenbush*, it was held that treatment (surgery) must be *withheld* at the insistence of a mentally competent patient.

The rulings in these cases are hardly surprising. The reason is that American and Canadian medical jurisprudence have enshrined the principle that a mentally competent patient cannot be treated without consent, even if the patient's refusal will lead to her death.

Consider, for example, the frequent media accounts of mentally competent adult Jehovah's Witnesses who have chosen to die rather than submit to the transfusion of blood.* In such instances the physician deplores the death that will ensue from the patient's resolve to refuse life-saving treatment on religious grounds. But however compassionate, the physician will most likely stay her hand when confronted with the command that, in Jehovah's name, blood not enter the patient's veins. It may be that respect for the principle of patient autonomy is enough to ensure compliance with the patient's non-treatment decision. If not, there is the deterrence factor: that to act against her competent patient's rejection of treatment is to risk criminal prosecution for assault and civil suit for battery. Until 1987 the likelihood of legal repercussions was remote, given that there was no Canadian case of record in which a physician or hospital had been civilly sued or criminally prosecuted in such circumstances. However, that was the year of the *Shulman* case, which as we have seen set the precedent that a physician's right to treat a mentally competent patient hinges on the latter's continued consent. The tandem cases of *Shulman* and *Nancy B.* have thus served notice on Canadian health care providers that when the mentally competent patient says No, the law will affirm that No means No.

In sum, the mentally competent patient is at liberty to reject both life-saving and life-prolonging treatment. If it is the latter — if the patient's decision to terminate treatment is grounded in her belief that a tolerable existence is precluded by her medical condition (as in our four illustrative cases) — then it is describable as a so-called "right to die" case.

---

* What if the Jehovah's Witness patient is a minor? That question is considered in the next chapter.

On the other hand, when a Jehovah's Witness succumbs after refusing treatment that would have restored her health, her manner of death does not fit under the so-called "right to die" heading. In her case, the rejection of blood is not a statement that a life racked by bodily infirmity is no longer worth living. It is true that she rejects *life-saving* treatment — not because she wants to die but rather because it can only be had at the cost of eternal damnation for breaking faith. In contrast, the focus of this chapter is upon:

(a) mentally competent patients whom medicine is powerless to rescue from the misery of progressive degenerative disorders (e.g. *Perlmutter* and *Nancy B.*), or permanent and severe debilitation (e.g. *Candura* and *Quackenbush*); and

(b) who consequently reject *life-prolonging* treatment because death is considered a lesser evil.

When a patient such as Robert Quackenbush expresses his preference for death over the prolonged misery of a terminal or permanently debilitating disease, his decision reflects his conviction that the burden of treatment exceeds its benefit. It is true that the double amputation would have prolonged his life. But to Quackenbush, its beneficial effects were outweighed by the burden of existence as a legless and friendless nursing home patient. For the four patients whose cases we have canvassed, what medical science had to offer was not life-saving treatment. From their perspectives, it was merely life-prolonging treatment because it did not hold the promise of sustaining life that to the patient was worth living.

In none of the four cases did the courts ponder whether the treatments in question were life-saving or life-prolonging. In each case, the no-treatment-without-consent principle meant that the legally relevant question was whether the patient was mentally competent to refuse treatment. As we have seen, in each case the finding of mental competence led the Court to rule that the treatment could not be forced upon the unwilling patient. The state of the law was summed up in *Shulman*: "A conscious, rational patient is entitled to refuse any medical treatment and the doctor must comply, no matter how ill-advised he may believe that instruction to be."

On the other hand, the distinction between life-saving and life-prolonging treatment is legally relevant when the patient is mentally incompetent and has not signed a health care directive.* In the precedent-setting *Quinlan, Re* case (1976),** the New Jersey Supreme Court authorized the termination of artificial life-support measures because the treatment was life-prolonging (not life-saving) in the sense that it did not serve the pa-

---

*   See Chapter 24.
** See Chapter 21.

tient's best interests. When, however, the patient is mentally competent (or there is a *Shulman* scenario), then it is legally irrelevant whether the spurned treatment is seen to serve her best interests. That is because in such cases the sole question is whether the patient is exercising an informed choice. As the cases have consistently held, a patient cannot be treated against her will so long as she comprehends her condition, the perceived risks and benefits of the proposed treatment, and the likely consequences of her no-treatment decision.

5. MENTAL COMPETENCY TO REFUSE TREATMENT

As indicated, the patient's right to refuse treatment is conditioned upon a finding of mental competency/capacity. (For that matter, the concept of informed consent to treatment is likewise predicated upon the mental competency of the patient to decide for herself.) The law presumes that every (adult) patient is mentally competent and that it is for the health care provider to show otherwise in the particular case. The question of mental competence is decision-specific; does the patient retain the mental capacity to decide upon the particular treatment at issue? For example, a mentally handicapped patient who would be considered incompetent for certain purposes could still consent to a sterilization procedure if she understood the connection between sexual intercourse, pregnancy, and childbirth and also understood the nature, risks, and consequences of the procedure.

In any event, it must be understood that there are no definitive criteria that measure a patient's decision-making capacity. As explained in an article in the *American Journal of Psychiatry*:[6]

> The search for a single test of competency is a search for the Holy Grail. Unless it is recognized that there is no magical definition of competency to make decisions about treatment, the search for an acceptable test will never end. ... Judgments (about competence) reflect social considerations and societal biases as much as they reflect matters of law and medicine.

Furthermore, whatever the opinions of the medical witnesses in a particular case, the issue is one of legal status. It is for the court to assess competency and, although medical witnesses are invited to have their say, the court is not bound to abide by the thrust of their testimony. Medical judgment on the competency question may be definitive in the clinic setting, but it is not necessarily the last word in the courtroom setting. That is because the former is a medical enterprise and the latter is a legal enterprise.

Although the judges in the *Nancy B.* and *Corbeil* cases found that the patients were mentally competent, they did not discuss the criteria leading to that determination. Since there are no other comparable Canadian cases of record, our jurists have yet to grapple with the test for mental competency in so-called "right to die" cases. On the other hand, there are statutory definitions of mental capacity in provincial mental health acts and other statutes — e.g. the *Health Care Consent Act* (Ontario) and the *Health Care Directives Act* (Manitoba) both provide that a person has the capacity to consent to treatment who can "understand the information that is relevant to making a decision . . . [and is] able to appreciate reasonably foreseeable consequences of a decision or lack of decision."

In the few American cases on point, the courts favour criteria that are the mirror image of the informed consent doctrine: that the patient understand the nature of her medical condition and the reason for the proposed treatment; the risks, benefits, and likely consequences of the treatment; and the prognosis if the patient withholds consent to the treatment. In any event, it appears that this was the approach implicitly followed in the two Canadian cases: one knew that life-support was keeping her alive and the other knew that eating was keeping him alive, and both knew that by saying No they would die. (As we see in the next chapter, a patient's mental capacity is negated by a finding of *undue influence*. The reason is that — whatever the treatment decision — it must be the voluntary choice of the patient; and that choice is compromised if it is the product of coercion.)

In *Perlmutter* and *Nancy B.*, the hospitals conceded the mental competency of their recalcitrant patients. In *Candura* and *Quackenbush*, the hospitals adduced psychiatric testimony to contest the decision-making capacity of their patients. In *Candura*, the hospital called a psychiatrist, Dr. Kelley, who testified that the patient's ability to exercise an informed, rational choice was impaired by irrational and emotional factors. He also branded as "suicidal" her "unwillingness for whatever reason to consent to life-saving treatment." Yet he undercut the credibility of his assessment when he frankly admitted:

> You know, it really comes down to a philosophical difference. I hope there is no psychiatric argument in this case. It's the right of a patient to decide she wants to die, and I spend all my life trying to keep people alive. So I take quite a different view.

A second psychiatrist testified that Mrs. Candura was competent to refuse the surgery. When asked to explain why he disagreed with Dr. Kelley, he replied:

> I think it is just a personal philosophy type of thing where I believe the persons themselves ought to be given the benefit of the doubt as to what they want to do with their lives, whereas Dr. Kelley, I guess, is more protective. I can't really speak for him, but his general philosophy is different from mine.

Dr. Kelley's admission prompted the appellate court to conclude that "his opinion is not one of incompetency in the legal sense." It found that what he meant by rational choice was what he regarded as "the *medically* rational choice." The Court explained:

> The irrationality of her decision does not justify a conclusion that Mrs. Candura is incompetent in the legal sense. The law protects her right to make her own decision to accept or reject treatment, whether that decision is wise or unwise.

The Massachusetts court clearly understood that the question in such cases is not whether the patient retains the mental capacity to manage property or to execute a will. It is whether the patient understands the *nature* of the proposed treatment and that death is the *likely consequence* of her refusal. Furthermore, as shown by the *Quackenbush* case, a particular finding of incompetency does not preclude a contrary assessment at a later time. The judge in that case did not doubt the testimony of the psychiatrist who examined Quackenbush on January 6 and pronounced him incompetent. He summarized his evidence:

> The doctor's conclusions are that Quackenbush is suffering from an organic brain syndrome with psychotic elements. He asserts that the organic brain syndrome is acute and could be induced by the septicemia. He bases his opinion on the patient's disorientation as to place — not aware of being in a hospital; his disorientation as to the people around him — not aware of talking to a nurse and doctor during the interview; his visual hallucinations — seeing but not hearing people in the room who were not there, and the inappropriateness of his responses to the discussions on the gravity of his condition and what might result. He did acknowledge that the hallucinations could be induced by conditions related to the septicemia but concluded that Quackenbush's mental condition was not sufficient to make an informed decision concerning the operation.

On January 11 a second psychiatrist examined Quackenbush and pronounced him mentally competent to decide his fate. His testimony was summarized by the judge:

> At the interview the doctor and Quackenbush thoroughly discussed the patient's condition, illness, and ramifications involved in the options of having the operation. The doctor indicates that Quackenbush knows he has gangrene and fully appreciates the magnitude of his illness. Quackenbush told him he hoped for a miracle and that he is a coward about making decisions. The doctor found no hallucinations. He did find some fluctuations in mental lucidity. Quackenbush would lose his train of thought, and his discussion

would wander off, but the doctor says this is to be expected under the circumstances and is not a sign of mental incompetency. (The psychiatrist) is of the opinion . . . that Quackenbush has the mental capacity to make decisions, to understand the nature and extent of his physical condition, to understand the nature and extent of the operation, to understand the risks involved if he consents to the operation, and to understand the risks involved if he refuses the operation.

This finding of competency on January 11 was confirmed the following day by the judge, who interviewed Quackenbush at his bedside for 10 minutes. As he reported in his ruling (rendered the day after the interview):

During that period he did not hallucinate, his answers to my questions were responsive, and he seemed reasonably alert. His conversation did wander occasionally but to no greater extent than would be expected of a 72-year-old man in his circumstances. He spoke somewhat philosophically about his circumstances and his desires. He hopes for a miracle but realizes there is no great likelihood of its occurrence. He indicates a desire — plebian, as he described it — to return to his trailer and live out his life. He is not experiencing any pain and indicates that, if he does, he could change his mind about the operation.

The judge in effect ruled that a prior finding of incompetency does not preclude a subsequent determination that the patient was now competent to decline treatment. If a patient has the mental capacity to decide in the here-and-now, then her prior state of incapacity is beside the point. The reverse is also true — that the treatment preference of a mentally competent patient is not cancelled out by a subsequent determination of incapacity. The ruling in *Quackenbush* would thus stand even if the patient were later to revert to a state of incompetency. After all, when a competent adult Jehovah's Witness refuses blood, the physician cannot lawfully transfuse if the patient becomes unconsciousness (incompetent).

To reiterate, a treatment decision by a competent person survives a subsequent loss of mental capacity. Were it otherwise, the person's right to bodily self-determination would surely be compromised. That, of course, was the point of the ruling in *Malette v. Shulman*. The principle is also illustrated by the New York case of *Lydia E. Hall Hospital, Re*.[7] A 41-year-old hospital patient with end-stage-renal-disease made the decision to stop dialysis after three years of treatment. His nephrologist determined that he was mentally competent and that opinion was confirmed by a psychiatrist. The patient, who was "blind, totally incapacitated, crippled and racked with pain", signed a printed hospital form entitled "Basic acknowledgement of refusal to permit diagnostic or therapeutic procedure." The form read in part (in large capital letters):

ALTHOUGH MY FAILURE TO FOLLOW THE ADVICE I HAVE RE-CEIVED MAY SERIOUSLY IMPERIL MY LIFE OR HEALTH, I NEV-ERTHELESS REFUSE TO SUBMIT TO THE RECOMMENDED PRO-CEDURE.

Two days after signing the form, the patient stopped breathing and lapsed into a coma, whereupon the hospital petitioned for a court order allowing it to keep him on dialysis. In denying the petition the Court found that although currently incompetent, the patient had previously made "an informed, rational, and knowing decision" to forego dialysis. The treatment was accordingly withdrawn and the patient died with his family at his bedside.

To the same effect is a recent South Carolina case, *Harvey v. Strick-land.*[8] The plaintiff, an adult Jehovah's Witness, had signed two hospital forms refusing blood before undergoing surgery to remove a blockage in his carotid artery. After a post-operative stroke and blood clot, he underwent additional surgery during which he suffered massive blood loss. The vascular surgeon, who knew that the patient had signed the forms, nonetheless asked the unconscious patient's mother for permission to transfuse her son; although she initially refused she then consented. The patient was transfused and made a complete recovery. His law suit against the surgeon for battery was dismissed at trial, but the state supreme court reversed and ordered a new trial. It based its ruling upon the following provision in the South Carolina Adult Health Care Consent Act:

This chapter does not authorize the provision of health care to a patient who is unable to consent if the attending physician or other health care professional responsible for the care of the patient has actual knowledge that the health care is contrary to the patient's unambiguous and uncontradicted instructions expressed at a time when the patient was able to consent.

The Court concluded that the statute made it clear that

a patient's wishes against medical treatment or intervention, when made known to a physician prior to surgery, must be followed by the physician.

In the cases considered, the legally pertinent issue was not whether the patient had made the "medically sensible" decision. It was whether the patient had the *cognitive capacity* to understand her condition, the nature and consequences of the proposed treatment, and the attendant risks involved in either pursuing or foregoing the treatment. In each case the Court refused to mandate treatment because the patient was found mentally competent to reject further medical intervention.

On the other hand, consider the case of *Tennessee Department of Human Services v. Northern*, in which an intermediate appellate court ruled that a 72-year-old hospital patient (unmarried and with no close relatives) was mentally incompetent to refuse surgery to amputate her feet.[9] Both feet were severely necrotic and affected by wet gangrene. Surgery was risky (a 50% survival rate), but the probability of survival without amputation was reckoned at 5% to 10%. In its petition for a court order compelling surgery, the agency included a letter from Ms Norton's physicians. The letter asserted that the patient understood neither the severity and consequences of her disease process nor that the failure to amputate would most likely lead to death. The lower court granted the petition, which was upheld on appeal. The appellate judges interviewed the patient and found her "lucid and apparently of sound mind generally." But the Court added:

> [O]n the subjects of death and amputation of her feet, her comprehension is blocked, blinded or dimmed to the extent that she is incapable of recognizing facts which would be obvious to a person of normal perception. For example . . . the patient looked at her feet and refused to recognize the fact that the flesh was dead, black, shrivelled, rotting and stinking.

The patient was examined by a psychiatrist, who reported that she was "generally lucid and sane." He nonetheless concluded:

> She is functioning on a psychotic level with respect to ideas concerning her gangrenous feet. She tends to believe that her feet are black because of soot or dirt. She does not believe her physicians about the serious infection. There is an adamant belief that her feet will heal without surgery, and she refused to even consider the possibility that amputation is necessary to save her life. There is no desire to die, yet her judgment concerning recovery is markedly impaired.

Although it found that the patient lacked the mental capacity to refuse treatment, the Court took pains to point out that its decision was not based upon the notion that a person refusing treatment is incompetent merely because a "normal or rational" person would have chosen otherwise. In affirming the lower court's treatment order, the Tennessee appellate court stressed:

> [The decision] is based on the Court's finding that Miss Northern is unable or unwilling to comprehend even dimly certain very basic facts, without which no one, whether elderly lady, doctor, or judge, would be competent to make such a decision. These facts include the appearance of her feet, which

are disfigured, coal black, crusty, cracking, oozing, and rancid. Yet Miss Northern looks at them and insists that nothing is wrong. Also included is the fact that her doctors are of the opinion that her life is in danger, yet she has expressed no understanding of either the gravity or the consequences of her medical condition. Again, this Court respects Miss Northern's right to disagree with medical opinions and advice. Again, if this Court in good faith could find that she perceived as facts that her feet do look and smell as they do, and that her doctors are telling her that she needs surgery to save her life, we would not interfere with whatever decision she made regard-less of how much it conflicted with the substance of her medical advice or with what we ourselves might have chosen. But from our honest evaluation of the facts and evidence of this case, we have been forced to conclude that Miss Northern does not comprehend such basic facts and hence is currently incompetent to decide this difficult question.

Be that as it may, the fact that a patient is suffering from a severe mental illness does not necessarily preclude the decisional capacity to refuse a particular treatment. An English case on point is *C. (Refusal of Medical Treatment), Re.*[10] The 68-year-old patient was a chronic paranoid schizophrenic who had been institutionalized for about 30 years. He was found to have gangrene in the foot and a consultant vascular surgeon concluded that death was imminent unless the leg was amputated below the knee. Although Mr. C refused to consent to amputation, he did agree to "more conservative surgery" — debridement of the dead tissue. The surgery was successful, thus averting the prospect of imminent death. The patient's lawyer then sought an undertaking from the hospital that, if amputation were later deemed necessary (a possibility that could not be ruled out), it would not proceed without his consent. When it refused to provide that assurance, the lawyer petitioned the Family Division for an injunction to restrain the hospital from amputating the leg without the patient's express consent.

The legal issue was whether the patient was competent to refuse medical treatment, and the judge determined that competency entailed a three-stage process: comprehending and retaining treatment information, believing it, and weighing the information in terms of risks and needs. The patient was heard from and the judge had this to say about his testimony:

> Mr. C himself throughout the hours that he spent in the proceedings seemed ordinarily engaged and concerned. His answers to questions seemed measured and generally sensible. He was not easy to understand and the grandiose delusions were manifest, but there was no sign of inappropriate emotional expression. His rejection of amputation seemed to result from sincerely held conviction. He had a certain dignity of manner that I respect.

The judge's assessment of the medical witnesses led him to grant the injunction. As he concluded:

> I am completely satisfied that the presumption that Mr C has the right to self-determination has not been displaced. Although his general capacity is impaired by schizophrenia, it has not been established that he does not sufficiently understand the nature, purpose and effects of the treatment he refuses. Indeed, I am satisfied that he has understood and retained the relevant treatment information, that in his own way he believes it, and that in the same fashion he has arrived at a clear choice.

It has been said that competency is only questioned when the physician disagrees with the patient's decision. But leave it to a lawyer to argue that the disagreement itself could cause the patient to become incompetent. In a recent English case, *B. (adult: refusal of medical treatment), Re*, a 43-year-old quadriplegic (her condition caused by an intramedullary cervical spine cavernoma) sought a court order to compel her caregivers to accede to her repeated demands for the termination of artificial ventilation.[11] Eleven months before the hearing in the High Court Family Division, the lawyers for the NHS trust running the hospital had advised that it was lawful to stop treatment if she were competent, and three psychiatrists confirmed that she was indeed fully capable of so deciding. But her physicians refused to comply because of their "ethical objections to causing her death." At the hearing, the trust's legal counsel suggested that the patient (described as a "former social care professional") was incompetent because her anger over the frustration of her wishes could have rendered her unable "to balance matters in her mind." However, Judge Dame Elizabeth Butler-Sloss, President of the Family Division, gave short shrift to the argument:

> She is getting very annoyed because they won't listen to her. To suggest that her anger . . . should be treated as a loss of capacity is to underestimate the feelings of patients in hospital. She is angry with them for treating her in a paternalistic way, as though she isn't fit to make a decision. If you are lying there and not being listened to, I'm not sure this goes to lack of capacity. Serious frustration and anger are natural emotions. You have to go a long way to say that distorts capacity. You seem to be saying that if you want something and the doctors don't think it is a good idea because they want to do something else, the more you disagree the more you will be regarded as unable to make a decision. That is a dangerous concept. There is a very paternalistic element. It's a very "doctor knows best" concept. I really bridle at that as a member of the public as well as a judge.

In granting the petition, Dame Elizabeth ruled that the patient (called Ms B) had the necessary mental capacity to refuse continued treatment. She had met the patient at her hospital bedside and said of her:

> I would like to add how impressed I am with her as a person, with the great courage, strength of will and determination she has shown in the last year, with her sense of humor, and her understanding of the dilemma she has posed to the hospital. She is clearly a splendid person and it is tragic that someone of her ability has been struck down so cruelly.

But as Dame Elizabeth explained, it was the Court's duty to enforce the will of a mentally competent patient to say No to her care providers, however well intentioned their wishes to keep her alive. As she put it:

> One must allow for those as severely disabled as Miss B, for some of whom life in that condition may be worse than death. . . . We have to try inadequately to put ourselves into the position of the gravely disabled person and respect the subjective character of experience.

The lawyer for the hospital trust promptly announced that there would be no appeal, and that his client wished to express regret for any distress "however unintentionally caused" to Ms B in the course of resolving "this very difficult case."[12] The patient waited one month before giving the order to stop life-support and died a peaceful and quick death.

6. THE OUTCOME TRAP

In the *Candura* case, the psychiatrist whose finding of incompetency was rejected by the Massachusetts court had fallen into what is called the "outcome trap." In assessing competency, the proper focus is not upon the treatment decision but rather upon how the patient got there. However, Dr. Kelley worked backward from a treatment decision that he considered foolish/irrational and concluded — for that reason alone — that the patient was incompetent. He was rightly faulted because the key is process, not outcome.

In the *B. (adult: refusal of medical treatment), Re* case, a psychiatrist testified that the patient "was at the extreme end of competence, despite the limitations of her physical state and her environment in the ICU." Dame Elizabeth was in effect alluding to the outcome trap when she commented upon his evidence:

> He pointed out that one thing that struck him forcibly was that the clinicians started from the decision made by Ms B, and not from the assessment of her competence. They looked too much at the decision, which was contrary to their advice and which they would not endorse, and not enough at the sur-

rounding circumstances. The clinicians were not able to accept her views and deal with them. It was a fundamental principle that one should start with the individual's capacity to make decisions and values. There may have been some confusion over her values compared with other people's, and it was important to focus on the individual and respect that individual's values.

At the end of her judgment she returned to the clash of values between Ms B and her caregivers:

> Throughout the sad developments of this case, all those looking after Ms B have cared for her to the highest standards of medical competence and with devotion. They deserve the highest praise. Ironically this excellent care has to some extent contributed to the difficulties for the hospital. Ms B has been treated throughout in the ICU in which the medical and nursing team are dedicated to saving life, sometimes in adverse medical situations. As Dr C (the ICU physician in charge of her care) said, they are trained to save life. The request from Ms B, which would have been understood in a palliative care situation, appears to have been outside the experience of the ICU in relation to a mentally competent patient. It was seen by some as killing the patient or assisting the patient to die and ethically unacceptable.

One trusts that Dr. C and her colleagues now know that carrying out the patient's wishes was dictated by the legal and moral imperative that a mentally competent patient cannot be treated against her will even if death is the certain result. Presumably, they have also come to know that a patient cannot be pronounced incompetent simply because she has said No to life.

7. MENTAL COMPETENCY: THE PHYSICIAN'S RESPONSIBILITY

The patient's directive that treatment be terminated is legally binding only if she is mentally competent to make that decision. The treating physician is responsible for determining whether her patient is expressing an informed choice; and if she has any doubts on the matter, she is well advised to arrange a psychiatric consultation. (In fact, given the finality of a decision to stop life-prolonging treatment, it is prudent as a matter of course to call upon psychiatry to assess the patient's competency.)

Cases such as *Nancy B.* involve a process whereby a patient dies after her *voluntary* refusal of life-prolonging treatment. The point is that, unless the patient was mentally competent, her act of dying cannot be so categorized. When a physician turns off a respirator at the behest of a patient who is not mentally competent to order its removal, she has in effect abandoned the patient. That conduct puts her at risk to incur criminal and/or civil liability.

In a civil suit for wrongful death, the deceased's next-of-kin would have to prove not only the patient's incompetency but also that the physician was negligent in not knowing it. If the plaintiff proves her case, the measure of damages would depend upon the degree of harm caused by the physician's wrongful termination of treatment. The less favourable the patient's condition and prognosis, the less the amount of damages recoverable from the defendant. (What if, however, the defendant-physician offered the following defence: although I erred in pronouncing the patient competent, still his condition did not warrant continued life-support; in other words, even though he was in fact mentally incompetent, the decision to stop treatment was medically reasonable in the circumstances. In that event, the law suit would fail unless the plaintiff could prove that the patient's condition was not as hopeless as alleged by the defence.*)

The applicable *Criminal Code* offence (section 220) is a branch of manslaughter called *Causing Death By Criminal Negligence*. The *Code* defines criminal negligence as "wanton or reckless disregard for the lives or safety of other persons." This would oblige the Crown to prove beyond a reasonable doubt: (1) that the patient's incompetency was apparent; (2) that the defendant-physician's affirmative response exhibited reckless indifference; and (3) that she complied with the incompetent patient's request.

Or the physician might invite prosecution under section 215 of the *Criminal Code*, which falls under the heading, *Duties Tending to Preservation of Life*. The provision states:

> Everyone is under a legal duty . . . to provide necessaries of life to a person under his charge if that person is unable by reason of . . . illness . . . to withdraw himself from that charge, and is unable to provide himself with necessaries of life.

There is ample case authority for the principle that medical treatment falls under the heading of "necessaries of life." Therefore, if the Crown chooses not to press for a manslaughter conviction, it could still prosecute the erring physician under section 215 for breaching her legal duty to preserve her patient's life.

---

* The termination of life-prolonging treatment for incompetent patients is the subject matter of Chapters 21 and 22.

8. THE LEGAL BASIS OF THE RIGHT OF THE COMPETENT PATIENT TO REFUSE LIFE-PROLONGING TREATMENT

Although *Nancy B.* was the first case in which a Canadian court directly confronted the issue of whether a mentally competent patient could refuse life-prolonging treatment, a Saskatchewan trial court judge had recognized as far back as 1929 that there was no legal authority to compel treatment even when the patient's life was at stake. *Masny v. Carter-Halls-Aldinger Co.* was a negligence action, in which the plaintiff sued his employer for head injuries suffered at a building site when he was struck by a plank.[13] Although the judge found in the plaintiff's favour, he deplored his failure to submit to urgently recommended medical treatment. He summarized the evidence:

> After the plaintiff had been in the hospital for two months or more his medical advisers diagnosed his case as requiring a trepanning operation, for the purpose of removing the pressure from which the plaintiff was suffering because of a clot of blood in the vicinity of the brain. The evidence was that the operation is not a dangerous one. The plaintiff refused to submit to an operation and was adamant in his refusal. The medical men foresaw that results of the gravest kind would follow such refusal and they persisted in advising that such operation take place. The plaintiff's friends also pleaded with him to undergo the operation. Today the plaintiff is (humanly speaking) nigh to death's portal as a result of such refusal on his part.

The judge acknowledged the absence of legal authority to force treatment upon the mentally competent plaintiff, whom he described as a "self-made martyr going to a self-inflicted death." Because his viewpoint was that society owed a duty to protect "such a man from his own foolishness", he called upon the province to enact legislation "to prevent a recurrence of such a waste of life."

His plea notwithstanding, Canadian law has never seen fit to authorize intervention to overrule a competent adult patient's decision to forego life-prolonging treatment. As the Law Reform Commission of Canada (*LRCC*) stated in its 1982 working paper, *Euthanasia, Aiding Suicide and Cessation of Treatment*, such forbearance is clearly compatible with the common law principle that "the competent patient . . . is the absolute master of decisions regarding his own body."[14] The LRCC nonetheless advised that the *Criminal Code* should "clearly and formally recognize the competent patient's absolute right to refuse medical treatment or to demand its cessation."[15] The reason for its proposal is that there are *Criminal Code* provisions which — if read narrowly — would appear to prohibit patients such as Nancy B.

from ordering a halt to the treatment keeping them alive. In that case, the director of the Hotel-Dieu hospital had raised the spectre of the *Criminal Code* as justification for refusing to abide by her decision to terminate life-prolonging treatment. However, as the following commentary indicates, there was no substance to that concern.

Consider, for example, *section 14* of the *Criminal Code*, which provides that: "No person is entitled to consent to have death inflicted upon him, and such consent does not affect the criminal responsibility of any person by whom death may be inflicted on the person by whom consent is given." When the *Criminal Code* was first enacted in 1892, section 14 appeared in essentially its current form.[16] However, one cannot draw the inference that it was designed to encompass the facts of the *Nancy B.* case. The termination of life-prolonging treatment was not an issue a century ago when most deaths were caused by infectious diseases that physicians were by and large powerless to prevent. Section 14 is the codification of the long-standing common law rule that one cannot consent to being killed. It is therefore directed against what ethicists traditionally have referred to as *active voluntary euthanasia*: when a physician intentionally causes the death of a consenting patient by a direct act of commission (injecting a lethal drug). As a declaration of public policy, the consent of the patient is deemed legally irrelevant. It is highly unlikely that a jury would convict a physician in such a case but that is beside the point. If the physician has the intent to kill — with or without the consent of the patient — then her compassionate motive cannot ground a defence in law.

In sum, section 14 precludes a mercy-killing defence when a physician inflicts death by lethal injection upon a consenting patient, but it has nothing to do with the natural death of a patient who dies after life-prolonging treatment is terminated at her insistence. Since Nancy B. was asking to die a natural death, she would not have death inflicted upon her. Therefore, section 14 is inapplicable to her situation.

The same may be said for *section 216* of the *Code*, which provides that anyone who undertakes medical treatment is "under a legal duty to have and to use reasonable knowledge, skill and care in so doing." Bearing in mind the above-noted comments on patient autonomy by the Ontario Court of Appeal in the *Shulman* case, one is bound to conclude that Nancy B.'s caregivers had acted unreasonably in turning a blind eye to her repeated plea to turn off her respirator. In other words, when the mentally competent patient says No, the reasonable care that the law mandates is that the physician call a halt to the objectionable treatment. As the Court ruled in *Shulman*, the physician who continues to treat in such a case has committed a battery. It would also follow that the physician has likewise committed an assault under section 265 of the *Criminal Code*, as she has intentionally applied force to a nonconsenting person.

What about *sections 217 and 219* of the *Criminal Code*? The former states that: "Everyone who undertakes to do an act is under a legal duty to do it if an omission to do the act is or may be dangerous to life." According to the latter: "Every one is criminally negligent who in doing anything, or in omitting to do anything that it is his duty to do, shows wanton or reckless disregard for the lives or safety of other persons." If the person dies, the offence of manslaughter is committed (causing death by criminal negligence).

Consider the argument that because Nancy B.'s caregivers had undertaken to treat the patient, her ventilator could not be turned off (even at her request) because an omission to maintain the treatment would not simply endanger her life — it would end it! By complying with her wishes her caregivers would commit culpable homicide; their omission not only would entail a breach of legal duty but also clearly show "reckless or wanton disregard" for her life. In short, the breach of legal duty under section 217 would trigger a prosecution under section 219.

This argument misses the mark because it misstates the meaning of section 217, which has no bearing upon the instant case. The provision, which is found in essentially the same language in the 1892 *Code*, is a restatement of the common law rule that one who gratuitously undertakes rescue cannot unreasonably abandon the effort and leave the person in continuing peril.[17] Recall that our medical forbears of the late 19th century were by and large powerless to prolong the lives of their disease-stricken patients. The sophisticated life-support technology of our time was foreign to their world, and it takes a benighted imagination to conjure up this provision as an impediment to the will of the patient who seeks to opt out of unwanted life-prolonging treatment.

It follows that section 217 would apply to a medical treatment scenario only if a physician acted unreasonably in terminating the treatment keeping her patient alive. For example, the physician decides to take her patient off dialysis without the patient's consent solely because, in her view, the patient is a socially worthless alcoholic whose death from kidney failure would be no loss to society. Section 217 imparts a notion of abandonment, and in the medical context it would apply to our hypothetical case of the nonconsenting dialysis patient whose treatment is not terminated on sound medical grounds. (Of course, this scenario must be distinguished from the case of the mentally competent patient who insists that life-prolonging treatment be halted. As we well know, the physician is obliged to comply even though she regards the patient's decision as medically unwise.)

Furthermore, there is no authority for the proposition that a patient cannot release her physician from the duty to treat. Because the physician-patient relationship is contractual, the mentally competent patient is free to sever the connection. Beyond that, Canadian physicians are accustomed to terminate life-prolonging treatment in clinically appropriate cases, even when patients are no longer mentally competent to ratify the medical decision to accelerate the dying process. In so doing, they act on the assumption that their duty to treat is discharged when continued treatment becomes futile: no longer offering the patient a reasonable hope of benefit.* Although there is scant Canadian law to that effect, provincial attorneys-general have never seen fit to quarrel with such practice. If anything, the case for terminating life-prolonging treatment is even more compelling for those such as Nancy B., who are mentally competent and can directly speak for themselves.

The implication of the hospital's position in the *Nancy B.* case is that once treatment is initiated, the physician is locked into its perpetuation, no matter how grim the prognosis or how insistent the patient that the treatment be withdrawn. This absurd proposition is surely not the law. Aside from entrenching medical malpractice, it would cause the infliction of pain and suffering upon patients condemned to live even when they choose to exercise their right to refuse treatment that prolongs an intolerable existence. It is not surprising that Justice Dufour emphatically held that stopping Nancy B.'s life-support would not amount to wanton or reckless conduct:

> Can we consider as unreasonable behaviour that of a physician who interrupts the respiratory support of a patient at the patient's informed and free consent in order to let nature take its course. Can we say that such behaviour is wanton or reckless? I think not.

Leaving aside section 217, consider the contention that turning off a respirator is not an omission to treat but rather the commission of an act — from which it follows that Nancy B.'s death would constitute a criminally negligent act under section 219. However, one need not debate whether turning off a respirator is categorized as omission or commission. The distinction is beside the point for the simple reason that when Nancy B. rejected continued life-support, she thereby discharged the physician from her duty to treat. Since the physician was legally precluded from keeping her patient alive, her compliance with the patient's demand cannot be regarded as a criminally negligent act.

One can therefore conclude that the criminal law in Canada, as elsewhere in the common law world, draws a distinction in the medical context

---

* See the discussion on futility in Chapters 21 and 22.

between killing and letting die. The former is condemned by the law even if the act was prompted by the patient. On the other hand, the decision by a mentally competent patient to call a halt to life-prolonging treatment is legally protected because it is part and parcel of the no-treatment-without-consent principle.

Finally, there is the question of aiding or assisting suicide. As the hospital director indicated, there was concern that compliance with Nancy B.'s plea would implicate the hospital (and attending physician) in the crime of aiding a person to commit suicide. One is legally free to commit suicide, but anyone who helps her along the way commits the offence of aiding suicide under *section 241* of the *Criminal Code*. Was that the case here?

To begin with, Justice Dufour's decision was cited by Lord Goff of the House of Lords (Great Britain's highest court) in a 1993 case, *Airedale NHS Trust v. Bland*.[18] As His Lordship commented:

> I wish to add that, in cases of this kind, there is no question of the patient having committed suicide, nor therefore of the doctor having aided or abetted him in doing so. It is simply that the patient has, as he is entitled to do, declined to consent to treatment which might or would have the effect of prolonging his life, and the doctor has, in accordance with his duty, complied with the patient's wishes.

The issue has likewise been addressed by several courts in the United States that have heard petitions comparable to that presented by Nancy B. No such court has concluded that a patient's refusal of artificial life-support is tantamount to suicide. The judicial consensus is: 1) that the patient's intent is simply to exercise her legal right not to be treated without consent, and (2) that suicide is an inappropriate label because the patient dies a natural death attributable to the underlying disease process. In any event, it would mock the very doctrine of informed consent if the physician's compliance with the patient's refusal of life-prolonging treatment could be defined as the crime of aiding suicide.

In that regard, the Florida appellate court in the aforementioned *Perlmutter* case emphatically ruled that the patient's death could not be branded as suicide. As the Court noted, the patient's "basic wish to live" was not incompatible with his rejection of continued mechanical ventilation. Moreover, "the fact that he did not self-induce his horrible affliction" would preclude the label of suicide as attaching to his decision to halt treatment and allow death to occur from natural causes. It cannot be denied that such a patient foresees the virtually certain outcome of death following the termination of the scorned treatment. Yet, of the many American courts that have considered *Perlmutter* and *Nancy B.* scenarios, not one has seen fit to label a mentally competent patient's refusal of life-prolonging treatment as equivalent to a suicide bid. Justice Dufour saw it the same way in *Nancy B.*, stating that whereas suicide is not a natural death, "if the plaintiff dies after the respiratory support is stopped . . . it would be nature taking its course."

It thus follows that there is no substance to the claim by Nancy B.'s hospital that the *Criminal Code* stood as a barrier against compliance with her steadfast rejection of continued life-support. On the other hand, it is true that the law in Canada had not directly spoken to the issue until the decision in *Nancy B.* Nonetheless, in countless cases that have not gone to court, physicians have not hesitated to terminate life-prolonging treatment at the insistence of their mentally competent patients. They have rightfully assumed that the no-treatment-without-consent principle means precisely what it says: that a patient cannot be treated without consent, and that the consequences of withdrawn consent (whether the patient lives or dies) are beside the point. The willingness of physicians to honour treatment refusals of life-prolonging treatment is no doubt buttressed by the fact that Canadian law has never seen fit to quarrel with such matters. In other words, provided that the patient is fully aware of the consequences of her decision, it is her decision to make. Unfortunately for Nancy B., her caregivers refused to abide by a medical practice that their peers across Canada had reasonably come to regard as both ethically and legally binding.

In its 1982-3 working paper and report, *Euthanasia, Aiding Suicide and the Cessation of Treatment*, the LRCC recommended an amendment to the *Criminal Code* to spell out that sections 14 and 217 do not require a physician "to continue to administer or to undertake treatment against the express wishes of the person for whom such treatment is intended." As the LRCC forcefully stated, the halting of life-prolonging treatment at the behest of a mentally competent patient is clearly compatible with the Common Law principle that "the competent patient . . . (is) the absolute master of decisions regarding his own body." Yet because Parliament had not directly addressed the issue, it concluded that the *Criminal Code* should "clearly and formally recognize the competent patient's absolute right to refuse medical treatment or to demand its cessation."

Regrettably, Parliament has turned a blind eye to the LRCC's recommendations, as it did to Bill C-203. The latter (a private member's bill) covered the same ground as the LRCC's report in similar language — providing that the *Code* not be interpreted to require a physician "to commence or continue to administer surgical or medical treatment to a person who clearly requests that such treatment not be commenced or continued." The bill was shelved by a parliamentary committee meeting in private session.[19] (The same proposal appears in *Of Life and Death*, the 1995 report of the Special Senate Committee on Euthanasia and Assisted Suicide.)

Had Parliament responded favourably to the urging of the LRCC, Nancy B. would not have been forced to endure the months of added life that she found so intolerable. By 1982 the time had come, as the LRCC then proposed, to remove any doubt in the minds of tremulous health care professionals about whether a mentally competent patient had the right to decline life-prolonging treatment. Its failure to act then was inexcusable, as was its later failure to enact Bill C-203. After all, the decision by a Quebec Superior Court judge is scarcely a binding precedent, even in that province.[20] The door is thus left open for unduly cautious hospital attorneys to advise against honouring patient requests to terminate life-prolonging treatment in the absence of a court order.

It is true that since the ruling in *Nancy B.*, we have not heard of any such cases. Yet but bear in mind that if a patient does not legally contest the refusal to honour her wishes for the cessation of artificial life-support, the matter would not likely come to public attention. It is also true that the common law principle that a patient who rejects artificial life-support is not committing suicide (rather dying a natural death) is not directly applicable to the *Corbeil* case. Still, even if one accepts that Corbeil's intent was to commit suicide, his caregivers could be regarded as aiding that end (and thus committing the offence of aiding suicide under section 241 of the *Criminal Code*) only if they were under a legal duty to prevent him from carrying out his resolve. But in that case the judge ruled that the no-treatment-without-consent principle trumped the duty to force feed the patient to prevent his death.

Could a patient in Nancy B.'s predicament seek relief under the "liberty" and "security of the person" provisions found in section 7 of the *Charter of Rights and Freedoms?* Nancy herself could not have invoked the *Charter* because of a 1990 case in which the Supreme Court held that the *Charter* only binds public and quasi-public institutions that are part of the apparatus of government and that hospitals do not fall under that category.[21] However, in 1997 the Supreme Court ruled in the *Eldridge* case that hospitals do fall within the protections of the *Charter*.[22] In the post-*Eldridge* era, it would likely follow that a health care facility's refusal to honor a patient's decision to forego life-support measures would breach section 7 of the *Charter*. Of course, it would be a different matter if there were good grounds to question the mental competency of the patient.

9. THE SOCIAL POLICY IMPLICATIONS OF THE NANCY B. CASE

Although many were quick to applaud the ruling in the *Nancy B.* case as a ringing affirmation of the law's commitment to informed consent and patient self-determination, a different perspective was expressed within the disabled community. According to a spokesperson for the Canadian Disability Rights Council, the death of Nancy B. symbolized society's inability to deal with the suffering of the severely disabled. In his view, Nancy B. was "almost encouraged and supported by society to take her own life (and) was a victim of a society which believed her life was irrevocably ruined."[23] A spokesperson for the Canadian Paraplegic Association similarly commented that: "What concerns me is the ease with which people have accepted her life is worthless, to be so ready to help her die."[24] (The same reaction was voiced in disability circles in England when the Court ruled that the patient known as Miss B. could not be kept alive against her will. For example, a woman with spina bifida confined to a wheelchair said that the ruling sent the message that "living with a disability isn't worth it."[25])

There is a sense in which *Nancy B.* is a case of both tragedy and triumph. The tragedy is the death of a young woman who found her life not worth living because of permanent and total paralysis. The triumph is that she mustered the strength to sue for the right to control her destiny and to oblige her reluctant caretakers to bend to her will that she not be treated without consent.

Although it is not their intent, those who label Nancy B. as a victim are in effect stripping her of her humanity. The devotion and compassion of her physician, who could not abide her insistent wish to die, refutes the claim that she was a helpless pawn of a society that had written her off or that was eager to help her die.

Nancy B. had made it clear time and time again that life had nothing more to offer her and that there was nothing that could change her mind (including the option of ventilator support in the home setting).[26] As a mentally competent adult, she made the decision to enforce her right not to be treated without her continuing consent, and we should salute the courage and strongmindedness with which she pursued her conviction that it was not for others to force her to live a life that she had come to regard as a living hell. Her legacy is a judicial ruling that spells out that, no matter how disabled, a mentally intact patient does not surrender the right to control the course of her medical treatment.

Still, those who deplore Nancy B.'s decision are rightfully anxious about society's commitment to the welfare of the handicapped who live amongst us. Their concern — and fear — is that the lives of our disabled brethren will come to be disvalued in a society whose health care system is stretched thin by mounting costs.

There is also the spectre of Nazi Germany's misnamed Euthanasia Programme, in which 200,000 physically and mentally disabled German citizens were brutally murdered because Hitler had condemned them as "useless eaters."[27] And who can guarantee that this deplorable mind set will not become public policy in the 21st century, as our beleaguered health care system becomes increasingly more burdened by an aging population?

Yet the message that Nancy B. has bequeathed us stands in stark contrast to the Hitlerian notion that, because the value of the individual's life is measured by his social worth, marked disability is accordingly sufficient warrant for his death sentence. What we learn from Nancy B. is that a person, no matter how disabled, has the moral and legal right to be treated with respect and human dignity. Society has the moral duty to treat its less fortunate citizens with compassion, but it also has the duty to recognize their autonomy — their right to accept or to spurn ongoing medical treatment.

Advocates for the disabled are right to stress the unique worth of every individual, regardless of his/her degree of handicap. Still, it does not serve their cause to depict Nancy B. as the helpless pawn of a non-caring society. We do not honour her memory by portraying her as a victim stripped of control over her fate. Rather we honour it by remembering her as a courageous young lady who had the determination to fight for her right to say to her caregivers: You cannot continue to treat me without my consent and that you no longer have.

Nancy B. has shown us that not all who are afflicted are the same, that some who are severely disabled lose the will to live whereas others fight for life with grim determination. Nancy B.'s caregivers did their best to make her life bearable, but it was her entitlement to decide that her life was no longer worth living. We should salute her courage to make that choice, which was hers and only hers to make. Equally, we should pay homage to our severely disabled citizens who have the courage to refuse to call it quits.

The lesson from the *Nancy B.* case is that the moral society has a stake in both autonomy and compassion. A commitment to autonomy means that we respect the wishes of the severely disabled, whether they decide to reject the miracles of medical science that keep them alive or whether they decide to live on. After all, most of the gravely handicapped do not regard themselves as better off dead (as did Nancy B.), and we must do what we reasonably can to foster their will to live. A commitment to compassion means that we do whatever is humanely and fiscally possible to make life meaningful for our less fortunate brethren (for example, by the provision of personal care and support services in the home setting).

In that regard, it is pertinent to consider two American cases in which state supreme courts affirmed the right of mentally competent patients to compel the removal of mechanical ventilation. *McKay v. Bergstedt* (Nevada, 1991), involved a 31-year-old quadriplegic whose disability resulted from a swimming accident at the age of ten.[28] There is a troubling aspect to the case in that the patient's decision was prompted by the impending death of his father from lung cancer. His father was his sole caretaker, and the patient lived a reclusive life at home with no contact with social services or a disability support community. He was terrified at the prospect of being left alone in the world, and his devoted father supported his decision by saying that he and his son no longer felt that they could carry on the fight.

They were both dead by the time the Nevada Supreme Court heard the case; the patient's respirator had been disconnected soon after the trial court ruled in his favour, and his father died a week later. Although the high court affirmed his legal right to terminate life-prolonging treatment, it nonetheless expressed the concern that other options had not been explored. According to the Courts, if the patient were still alive, "it would have been necessary to fully inform him of the care alternatives that would have been available to him after his father's death." The Court deplored the absence of any counselling regarding alternative support measures because he "needed some type of assurance that society would not cast him adrift in a sea of indifference after his father's passing."

State v. McAfee, (Georgia, 1989), involved a 30-year-old patient who had been rendered quadriplegic following a motorcycle accident four years earlier.[29] He sought the court order to end a life that he found intolerable, but then something happened that turned his life around. The media coverage — which lauded the Georgia Supreme Court's ruling as a victory for patients' rights — prompted an engineer to contact McAfee and equip him with a voice-activated computer. The publicity also helped to mobilize the provision of other services for the patient, all of which gave him a new lease on life and prompted him to forego his court-ordered "right to die."

That No is not necessarily No — at least not yet — is the point of a paper published in *The New England Journal of Medicine* under the title, "When life support is questioned early in the care of patients with cervical-level quadriplegia."[30] Its focus is upon cognitively intact patients who are in the acute phase of a complete cervical spinal cord injury and who insist that artificial life-support be stopped. In such a case, the physician cannot in good conscience comply until the patient has come to understand the potential for long term rehabilitation. Moreover, the patient should be informed that contrary to popular belief, spinal cord injury does not usually lead to marital breakup, the cessation of work productivity, depression, or a poor quality of life. As the authors put it:

> The chief practical conclusion to be drawn is that decisions about life-support in an alert patient with a cervical spinal injury should . . . be delayed until the patient appreciates fully what life will be like after a full course of rehabilitation. Once patients are finished with intensive and acute care, they are far more likely to have the cognitive capacity to weigh the factors involved in such decisions.

If the patient has been exposed to options and still says No to life, then his care providers can in good conscience comply with his wishes. It is arguable that he must know what it is to live before he can decide that he would rather be dead. That said, the competent patient's right to refuse treatment is inviolable; and if he persistently refuses to consider living, then his wishes must be honored. Surely his caregivers must have some time to try persuading him not to die, but still they cannot persist beyond a reasonable time — which can only be measured on a case-by-case basis. (It is true that McAfee was not in the acute stage of his injury as he waited four years before going to court; but in all that time all he ever got was warehousing.)

In the aforementioned English case of *B. (adult: refusal of medical treatment), Re*,[31] it was argued by the NHS trust that the patient's steadfast refusal to enter a spinal rehabilitation unit was indicative of mental incapacity. As Dame Elizabeth noted, that view was expressed by a consultant surgeon in spinal injuries who had interviewed the patient:

> He accepted that Ms B had mental competence and his one reservation was his conclusion that she was unable to give informed consent, not because of a lack of capacity in general but (because of) her specific lack of knowledge and experience of exposure to a spinal rehabilitation unit and therefore to readjustment to life in the community. Without that opportunity, which might take up to two years to complete, Ms B did not have the requisite information to give informed consent.

However, Dame Elizabeth was quick to reject his position:

> On that aspect of his evidence, I have the gravest doubts as to its legal validity and indeed its practicality. Even in issues of the utmost significance and gravity, people including patients have to make decisions without experience of the consequences and his requirement is unrealistic.

Bear in mind that the Court was not dealing with a patient in the acute phase of disability. Ms B had been stricken in February 2001, but the case was not heard until March 2002. By August 2001, she had come to reject the option of transfer from hospital to a spinal rehabilitation unit, and she persisted in her wish that the ventilator be switched off. When asked by a lawyer for the NHS trust why she so adamantly rejected the rehabilitation option, she replied:

> I know what it has to offer and I know that what I want it cannot offer. It offers me no chance of recovery. That is not disputed by anyone.

In other words, this was not a spur of the moment decision explainable by the shock of finding oneself permanently paralyzed from the neck down. As was the case with her Canadian counterpart, Nancy B., Ms B had come to the considered decision that her life was no longer worth living. It is gratifying that most quadriplegics instead choose life, and although Dame Elizabeth emphatically ruled that Ms B's wish for death must be honoured she took pains to remark that:

> I hope she will forgive me for saying, diffidently, that if she did reconsider her decision, she would have a lot to offer the community at large.

Tragically, Ms B saw it otherwise; but then, as the now familiar adage has it: "Whose life it is, anyway?"

Finally, it is fitting to recall the sentiment of disability rights advocates that the decision in *Nancy B.* reflected the lack of commitment by society to its sorely afflicted brethren. We do not propose to consider whether that viewpoint is well taken. However, what is beyond debate is that the *McAfee* and *Bergstedt* cases serve notice that the right to refuse life-support measures is stripped of its moral force unless it transpires in a society willing to provide sufficient resources to give the patient a true choice as to whether to live or to die. Ms B was given that choice and it was her right to say No.

NOTES

1. *Satz v. Perlmutter*, 379 So.2d 359 (1980).
2. *In the Matter of Robert Quackenbush*, 383 A.2d 785 (1978).
3. *Lane v. Candura*, 376 N.E.2d 1232 (1978).
4. *Nancy B. (B. (N.) v. Hôtel-Dieu de Québec)* (1992), 69 C.C.C. (3d) 450 (Que. S.C.); *Manoir de la Pointe Bleue (1978) Inc. c. Corbeil*, [1992] A.Q. no 98, [1992] R.J.Q. 712 (S.C.).
5. *Malette v. Shulman* (1990), 72 O.R. (2d) 417 (C.A.).
6. L.H. Roth et al., Tests of competency to consent to treatment. 134 **American Journal of Psychiatry** 279 (1977).
7. *Lydia E. Hall Hospital, Re*, 455 N.Y.S.2d 706 (1982).
8. *Harvey v. Strickland* (July 1, 2002), No. 25491.
9. *Tennessee Department of Human Services v. Northern*, 563 S.W.2d 197 (1978).
10. *C. (Refusal of Medical Treatment), Re*, [1994] 1 F.L.R. 31.
11. *B. (adult: refusal of medical treatment), Re*, [2002] 2 All E.R. 449. C. Dyer, Woman makes legal history in right to die case. 324 **British Medical Journal** 629 (2002).
12. Paralysed women wins right to die. wysiwyg:/icwales.icnetwork.co...ectid=11725445&method=full&siteid=50082
13. *Masny v. Carter-Halls-Aldinger Co.*, [1929] 3 W.W.R. 741 (Sask. K.B.).
14. Law Reform Commission of Canada, **Euthanasia, Aiding Suicide and Cessation of Treatment**, Working paper 28 (Dept. of Supply and Services Canada, Ottawa: 1982), at 55.
15. *Ibid.*, at 57.
16. As stated in section 59 of the *1892 Code*: No one has a right to consent to the infliction of death upon himself; and if such consent is given, it shall have no effect upon the criminal responsibility of any person by whom death may be caused.'
17. As stated in section 214 of the *1892 Code*: 'Everyone who undertakes to do any act, the omission to do which is or may be dangerous to life, is under a legal duty to do that act, and is criminally responsible for the consequences of omitting, without lawful excuse, to perform that duty.'
18. *Airedale NHS Trust v. Bland*, [1993] 1 All E.R. 821 (H.L.). The *Bland* case is summarized in Chapter 22. The case scenario was different from that in *Nancy B.* The issue was whether tube feeding could be stopped for a patient in a permanent vegetative state.
19. **Toronto Globe and Mail**, Feb. 27, 1992, p. A21. Bill C-203 also contained a provision that the *Code* not be interpreted as requiring a physician 'to commence or continue to administer surgical or medical treatment to a person

where such treatment is medically useless and not in the best interests of the person.'

20. Of course, in Ontario there is the precedent-setting decision in the *Shulman* case. Although the Court did not refer to the *Criminal Code*, its decision left no doubt but that a patient cannot be treated without consent, even if the consequence is avoidable death.

21. *Stoffman v. Vancouver General Hospital*, [1990] 3 S.C.R. 483.

22. *Eldridge v. British Columbia (Attorney General)*, [1997] 3 S.C.R. 624.

23. **Winnipeg Free Press**, February 14, 1992, p. A2.

24. *Ibid.*

25. **Toronto Globe and Mail**, March 23, 2002, at A5.

26. Telephone interview with Nancy B.'s attorney, Anne Lapointe.

27. See R.J. Lifton, **The Nazi Doctors** (Basic Books, New York, 1986).

28. *McKay v. Bergstedt*, 801 P.2d 617 (1990).

29. *State v. McAfee*, 385 S.E.2d 651 (1989).

30. D.R. Patterson et al., When life support is questioned early in the care of patients with cervical-level quadriplegia. 328 **New England Journal of Medicine** 506 (1993).

31. *Supra* note 10.

20

THE MATURE MINOR PATIENT AND THE REFUSAL OF TREATMENT

SUMMARY

The focus of this chapter is upon the mature minor rule in Canadian law. The topic is introduced by summaries of five cases in which adolescents refused treatment for life-threatening conditions; four of the cases involved Jehovah's Witness minors refusing blood products as a necessary adjunct to chemotherapy. In three of these cases, the courts ruled that the patients were mature minors and therefore allowed to refuse blood. However, the decisions do not establish the precedent that — regardless of prognosis — a mature minor can refuse life-extending treatment measures. That is because in those three cases the prognosis even with conventional treatment was not favourable. Statutes dealing with the consent of minors to medical treatment are noted, as is the evolution of the common law in this area. Finally, two recent Alberta cases involving Jehovah's Witness minors are considered against the backdrop of the law summarized in the chapter.

1. FIVE CANADIAN CASES

(a) Lisa Dorothy Kosack (Ontario, 1985)[1]

The Children's Aid Society of Metropolitan Toronto applied to the Provincial Court (Family Division) for an order declaring a 12-year-old patient "in need of protection" under the Ontario *Child Welfare Act*. The agency acted to facilitate the provision of chemotherapy treatment for the child. The girl — whom the court referred to as L — was afflicted with acute myeloid leukaemia (AML). Her Jehovah's Witness parents were opposed to the treatment recommended by her physicians at the Hospital for Sick Children, and the patient likewise expressed her opposition to blood products.

The family resided in Winnipeg and when the disease was diagnosed in the spring of 1985, the parents were advised by local physicians that chemotherapy was imperative. Since the treatment would necessitate blood transfusions, the parents withheld consent. Aside from her objection to receiving blood, the girl also had expressed a strong aversion to the chemotherapy regimen because of its known side-effects. The family then travelled to Mexico, where "certain substances [not identified by the Court] provided a very brief period of stabilization." When the girl's condition began to deteriorate, the family went to Thunder Bay where chemotherapy was again proposed and again rejected. The family then consulted a Florida physician who placed the girl on a mega-vitamin regimen. This produced a brief period of stabilization, but then her condition turned for the worse. At that point the family's odyssey led to the Hospital for Sick Children in Toronto.

Once again the family was advised that chemotherapy offered the only hope for survival. The physicians proposed to administer daunomycin and cytosine-arabinoside. However, in addition to killing the tumour cells these drugs attack bone marrow, temporarily inhibiting the production of white and red blood cells and platelets. Hence the necessity to transfuse blood and blood products until the return of normal bone marrow function.

When the parents and patient refused to accept the proposed treatment, the hospital informed the Children's Aid Society. The agency promptly sought relief under the provincial *Child Welfare Act*, which defines "a child in need of protection" to include one whose parent or guardian refuses

> to provide or obtain proper medical...care or treatment necessary for the child's health or well-being, or refuses to permit such care or treatment...when it is recommended by a legally qualified medical practitioner.

At trial, the agency called two physicians from the Hospital for Sick Children to explain the recommended therapy. They testified that in their experience, 30% of patients had not relapsed after two-and-one-half years of treatment. The judge heard evidence concerning the severe side effects of the two drugs: nausea, vomiting, pain, and loss of hair. There was also evidence of the remote risk of sterility and death from heart failure. Judge Main was deeply impressed by the girl's impassioned and unwavering hostility to the proposed treatment:

> During this past week...L. has seen children who are undergoing chemotherapy treatment and have lost their hair, are crying from the pain, and are

begging not to have any further treatment. L.'s position is now, and has been from the day she saw a documentary on this disease, that she does not want any part of chemotherapy and blood transfusions. She takes this position not only because it offends her religious beliefs but also because she does not want to experience the pain and anguish associated with the treatment process. L. has told this court clearly and in a matter-of-fact way that, if an attempt is made to transfuse her with blood, she will fight that transfusion with all of the strength that she can muster. She has said that she will scream and struggle, and that she will pull the injecting device out of her arm and will attempt to destroy the blood in the bag over her bed.

The judge, who had no doubt that she meant what she said, described her in the following light:

> L. is a beautiful, extremely intelligent, articulate, courteous, sensitive, and...courageous person. She has wisdom and maturity well beyond her years, and I think it would be safe to say that she has all of the positive attributes that any parent would want in a child. She has a well thought out, firm and clear religious belief. In my view, no amount of counselling from whatever source...including an order of this court, would shake or alter her religious beliefs.

The judge denied the petition on the grounds that the agency had failed to prove that the child was "in need of protection." In so ruling, he stressed the odds against a favourable outcome from the proposed treatment as well as the patient's determined opposition to both chemotherapy and blood transfusions. He also faulted the treatment plan because it "addresses the disease only in a physical sense. It fails to address her emotional needs and her religious beliefs. It fails to treat the whole person."

Judge Main further noted that the parents had proposed a treatment alternative: that their daughter leave hospital and that a regimen of mega-vitamin therapy be initiated under medical and family supervision. On balance, he decided in favour of the family's treatment proposal, even though acknowledging the absence of evidence supporting the efficacy of the treatment:

> This child's life is equally in danger whichever path is taken, whether she is left here [in hospital] and subjected to [chemotherapy] treatment, or she is allowed to leave and be treated according to the beliefs and wishes of herself and her parents.
>
> During this treatment L. would be surrounded by her family, and she would be free to communicate with her God.... I believe that L. should be given the opportunity to fight this disease with dignity and peace of mind. That can only be achieved by acceptance of the plan put forward by her and her parents.

Lisa Kosack was treated as she and her family wished, and she died two weeks after the Court's decision.

(b) Adrian Yeatts (Newfoundland, 1993)[2]

Adrian Yeatts was 15 years old when diagnosed with acute B cell lymphocytic leukaemia (ALL). Four months later his condition took a rapid turn for the worse, leading Dr. Jardine, his oncologist/haematologist at the Janeway Child Health Centre in St. John's, to conclude that unless chemotherapy was quickly instituted his patient would be dead within one to two weeks. The parental and patient opposition to blood prompted the hospital to notify the Director of Child Welfare, who consequently sought a declaration that Adrian was "in need of protection" under the *Child Welfare Act*. At the time of the hearing in the Unified Family Court, the cancerous cells were multiplying every 18 to 36 hours, subject to short periods of remission of one to seven days. In summarizing the testimony of Adrian's physician, the judge stated:

> He was asked what the effect of intensive chemotherapy treatment would be, and he said nobody can be absolutely certain of that, but under the best conditions and in the best circumstances, it can be hoped that A. has a chance expressed in percentage terms of something between 10 or 20 and 40 percent. This is not a 10, 20 or 40 percent chance of complete recovery and cure. That is a chance that the... progress of the disease could be arrested to some degree.

Although Dr. Jardine testified that chemotherapy (with its attendant blood transfusions) was the best medical course under the circumstances, he nonetheless expressed his opposition to a court order requiring the patient to undergo the spurned therapy. As a proponent of a "holistic" approach toward the treatment of cancer, he stressed that any hope of success required a co-operative and positive frame of mind by the patient. Dr. Jardine opined that Adrian's suitability for the treatment would be drastically reduced by his religious convictions. In fact, he informed the Court that if the petition filed by the Director of Child Welfare were granted, he personally would refuse to administer blood products to his patient as a matter of professional conscience.

Although the patient did not testify, he submitted an affidavit in which he declared his belief "in the teachings of Jehovah's Witnesses, including those against blood transfusions." He also indicated an understanding of his precarious medical condition and that: "I know I could die if no blood is used." He emphatically added:

> But that is my decision. No one talked me into that. The way I feel is that if I'm given any blood, that will be like raping me, molesting my body. I don't

want my body if that happens. I can't live with that. I don't want any treatment if blood is going to be used, even a possibility of it. I'll resist use of blood.

In the result, the judge dismissed the petition on the grounds that the patient was a "mature minor" whose wish to receive medical treatment without blood products must be respected. However, he made it clear that his ruling was also underpinned by Dr. Jardine's testimony:

I am not satisfied that in this particular case the use of blood products as a follow-up to the chemotherapy is considered essential by the qualified medical practitioner from whom I have heard and in whom I have considerable confidence.

In short, it was not only the patient's refusal but also his physician's treatment philosophy that explains the decision in this case. There was no chemotherapy and Adrian died two months after the Court's ruling.

(c) Joshua Walker (New Brunswick, 1994)[3]

This is the third reported Canadian case involving a leukaemia-stricken Jehovah's Witness minor. The medical evidence was remarkably similar to that in the *Yeatts (Y. (A.), Re)* case, although in this case the hospital and the attending physician did not oppose the decision by the 15-year-old patient to reject blood products as part of the treatment regimen for his acute myeloid leukaemia (AML). In fact, they petitioned the Court of Queen's Bench for an order that the patient be declared a mature minor with the legal entitlement to refuse blood.

According to an affidavit filed on April 18, 1994, by Dr. Scully, Joshua's oncologist/haematologist at the St. John Regional Hospital:

When he was first admitted (on March 31, 1994), his blood platelets were very low and were counted at approximately 26 X 10 9/L which is far below the normal reading [level] of 150 to 450 X 10 9/L. Furthermore, his fibrinogen reading [level] which is a clotting factor, was extremely low and hence he presented with a very high risk of acute spontaneous haemorrhaging.

On April 13 Dr. Scully initiated a treatment regimen of chemotherapy and retinoic acid. Although there had been no prior need for administering blood, she stated in her affidavit that blood would be required within the next week to ten days. Yet, given her assessment that Joshua was a "mature individual" who understood the implications of his decision to refuse blood, she asked that the Court declare him a mature minor so that his decision to refuse blood could be lawfully honoured. Like her colleague in the *Yeatts* case, she endorsed a holistic approach linked to a positive mental attitude by the patient, "which requires that he has the utmost trust in his attending physician." She added that studies indicate that "treatment protocols tend to be far less effective" when the patient's mental attitude suffers from a lack of trust in his physician. She also echoed the sentiments of Dr. Jardine in the *Yeatts* case that she could not in good conscience transfuse the patient without his consent.

The patient also filed an affidavit in which he declared his adherence to the faith of his parents, and his understanding of his condition and the medical implications of his steadfast refusal to accept blood products. He forcefully stated his position:

> And it's because Jehovah has taught us not to take blood or blood products, and I'd never want it done to me, even if I might die, because it's wrong. If someone tried to force blood on me, I'd fight them as hard as I could, with all my strength, to keep them from putting the i.v. in me. And I'd scream and yell.

On April 20 the Queen's Bench Court ruled against the petitioners on the basis that if Joshua "is likely to die unless he receives transfusions, they must be given." There was an immediate appeal, and on April 25 the case was argued before the Court of Appeal. The case was decided that same day, the high court reversing the lower court decision and declaring that Joshua was a mature minor who accordingly could not be transfused without his consent.

In New Brunswick, the *Medical Consent of Minors Act* sets 16 as the age of consent to medical treatment.[4] However, the Act further provides that a minor under the age of 16 is empowered to consent to medical treatment if: (a) "the minor is capable of understanding (its) nature and consequences," and (b) the treatment "is in the best interests of the minor and his continuing health and well-being."

The Court grounded its decision in the fact that the evidence at trial was overwhelming that

> Joshua is sufficiently mature and that, in the circumstances, the proposed treatment (without blood products) is in his best interests and his continuing health and well-being.

Joshua Walker died on October 4, 1994, at home with his family and members of his Jehovah's Witness congregation at his bedside. (By the year 2000, the odds of long term survival for a patient with AML who was treated with blood products and chemotherapy had risen to about 50%. Since it was considerably less at the time of this case, the odds were weighed against Joshua Walker even without the blood issue.)

(d) H. (T.) (Ontario, 1996)[5]

This is another case involving a Jehovah's Witness teenager refusing blood, but the outcome was different from the previous cases. The patient (referred to by the Court as T.H.) was diagnosed with aplastic anaemia when she was 13 years old. The only available treatment was blood platelets along with either chemotherapy or bone marrow transplant. The girl and her mother were Jehovah's Witnesses, whereas the father was not. He supported the position of the child welfare agency to seek an order of protection so that she could be treated with blood products. An emergency hearing was held in Provincial Court the day after the diagnosis, and the patient's two treating physicians testified that she lacked the maturity to weigh and judge the reasonably foreseeable consequences of her decision. (Their reservations about her capacity to decide were confirmed by a child psychiatrist who had examined the patient at their request.) As noted by the judge:

> She is thirteen, and under tremendous pressure. She has had to answer very difficult questions, questions obviously that are of the most profound nature, and in my view at this point she is not — her expression of views is not adequate to express what might otherwise be regarded as an expression of refusal, capable of expression of refusal of consent.

Concluding that the patient was not a mature minor capable of deciding for herself, the judge made her a temporary ward of the agency to ensure that she be treated with blood products.

The order was appealed, although by the time it was heard the patient, who had responded well to treatment, had been discharged from hospital. Still, the appeal was heard by a judge of the Divisional Court because it raised *Charter* issues that might arise in a similar case in the future. In the result, the judge acknowledged an infringement of the girl's right to freedom of religion under section 2(a) of the *Charter*. But he ruled that the infringement was justified under section 1 of the *Charter* because the girl was not capable of making the decision to refuse the treatment necessary to save her life.*

---

* Section 1 provides that the rights and freedoms guaranteed in the *Charter* are "subject only to such reasonable limits prescribed by law as can be demonstrably justified in a free and democratic society." In other words, it was reasonable to limit her exercise of religious freedom because of her decisional incapacity to express it in the case at hand.

(e) Tyrell Dueck (Saskatchewan, 1999)[6]

Tyrell Dueck was 13 years old when diagnosed with osteogenic sar-coma at the Cancer Centre of the Royal University Hospital in Saskatoon. Although the faith of Tyrell's fundamentalist Christian parents did not preclude medical treatment, they nonetheless insisted on seeking alternative medicine. The Centre responded by taking legal action, and a court order was obtained declaring Tyrell a child "in need of protection" under the *Child and Family Services Act*. The treatment commenced and Tyrell completed all three cycles of his first course of chemotherapy and the first two cycles of the second course. When due for the third cycle, he informed the attending paediatric oncologist (Dr. Mpofu) that he would not consent to it nor to the impending surgery to amputate his leg. The boy also said that he believed that God had healed him.

A hearing was promptly convened before Justice Rothery in the Court of Quench's Bench (Family Law Division). The issue was whether Tyrell should remain under the protection order or whether he had sufficient mental capacity to enforce his non-treatment decision. The judge noted that the relevant factors were: the child's age, maturity, and capacity to appreciate and understand the treatment; and furthermore whether he had a sufficiently independent nature to speak his own mind.

Justice Rothery heard from a clinical psychologist (Dr. Nanson) and a child psychiatrist (Dr. Duncan). Dr. Nanson testified that when she and Tyrell spoke privately, he told her that this was the only time he had discussed his illness with anyone outside his family. He explained that "his father makes all the rules...(and) they are not negotiable." In fact, as he told her, he had never broken a rule. According to Dr. Duncan, the Dueck family structure was consistent with their Christian principles — that the parents tell the children what to do and that the children unquestionably obey.

Unlike the other cases canvassed here, religious conviction was not the cause of the conflict between patient and caregivers. It was rather that Tyrell agreed with his father that there was a preferable alternative to a final cycle of chemotherapy and the amputation of his leg. It was Dr. Mpofu's opinion that the odds for long term recovery with the conventional treatment stood at about 65%. However, Mr. Dueck had come to accept that an alternative-cancer-treatment centre, American Biologics Mexico Institute, had a 85%-90% chance of curing his son with a regimen of diet, herbs, multi-vitamins, and other unconventional treatments. And beyond the more favourable odds, the Institute had led Mr. Dueck to believe that amputation might not be necessary. He conveyed his feelings on the matter to his son who responded by saying No to Dr. Mpofu.

Dr. Duncan testified that although Tyrell had the capacity to decide on treatment, he could not provide an "informed consent." As the judge summarized his evidence:

> Dr. Duncan explained that what is missing for Tyrell is the ability to obtain the information on his own in the medical community. His father is screening the medical information. And his father's influence will continue to play a large part in Tyrell's decision-making. Tyrell's father is his authority figure.

Dr. Mpofu had informed the Court that the Mexican option was in truth no option, leading the judge to remark that: "Tyrell has been misguided by his father into placing his hopes for recovery on a cure that does not exist." As Justice Rothery went on to rule:

> On the evidence, I have no hesitation in concluding that Tyrell is not a mature minor. He is far from it. He is a boy deeply under the influence of his father. The information that his father gives him is wrong and could place the child in medical peril. Tyrell does not appreciate or understand the medical treatment he requires. And Tyrell does not appreciate and understand that if he discontinues his chemotherapy and refuses surgery, he will die within a year from the spreading cancer.

The order of protection was continued and Dr. Mpofu and his staff allowed to continue Tyrell's planned treatment. Mr. Dueck immediately vowed to appeal, but four days later the family's attorney informed the media that the cancer had spread to the lungs and that the hospital held out scant hope for Tyrell.[7] The stunning announcement brought a rapid halt to the legal battle, and within days he was being treated at the American Biologics Mexico Institute. Soon after Tyrell's arrival physicians at the Institute announced that they could find no evidence that the cancer had spread to his lungs, contradicting the finding of two teams of Saskatoon oncologists. The family settled in with the expectation that the Institute would accomplish the miracle that they incessantly prayed for. The treatment regime included shark cartilage, garlic, and laetrile (a substance derived from apricot pits that was totally discredited as a cancer-curing agent by controlled studies in the early 1980s).

But a miracle was not to be. The family remained at the Institute until their money — $65,000 (U.S.) donated by friends and strangers — ran out after three weeks. The family returned to Canada with the good news that the tumour was shrinking and that Tyrell would be receiving experimental cell therapy at an Ottawa hospital. Six weeks later Tyrell died of bone cancer in the palliative care unit of St. Paul's Hospital in Saskatoon.

The case had captured attention across Canada, launching a heated debate on whether it was right for the judiciary to step in and prevent Tyrell and his parents from deciding what was best. Of course, we can never know if Tyrell would still be alive if his family had not balked at carrying through with the chemotherapy and amputation. In any event, I'll leave the last word on this tragic case to an editorial that appeared in the National Post two days after Tyrell's funeral:

> There just aren't words enough for the contempt in which those who promote quackery should be held, and for their handmaidens — charlatans who dangle a cure through God's will, or the power of the supernatural, or in crystals or alternative therapy, or heaven forfend, high colonics, apricot pits, or mega-doses of vitamins.[8]

2.   PRELUDE TO THE COMMENTARY ON MATURE MINORS AND CANADIAN LAW

At common law there was a long-standing rule that minors could not consent to health care; consent to treatment was vested exclusively in the parents or guardians. The only exceptions were the *emergency* and *emancipated minor* rules (the latter referring to a minor living independently: e.g. being married or if unmarried in the work force and living on her own).

However, beginning in the 1960s statutes were enacted in a number of American states allowing unemancipated minors to consent to treatment for sexually transmitted disease. The statutes were not inspired by a rethinking of the traditional common law position that minors as a class lacked the mental capacity to authorize medical care. Instead they stemmed from the fear that adolescents with STDs would be inhibited from seeking treatment if obliged to inform their parents and secure their consent. The same concern explained the expansion of minor consent statutes to cover alcohol/drug abuse and mental health issues. And it was the spectre of teen pregnancy and self-induced/back alley abortion that prompted legislators to allow minors to access birth control and abortion without parental consent. To reiterate, this trend in American law did not reflect a dawning respect for adolescent autonomy but rather the view that access to medical treatment in these kinds of cases would promote the best interests of troubled minors — and by extension of society at large.[9]

The first reported Canadian case on access to abortion by a minor followed this trend. In *C. (J.S.) v. Wren* (Alberta, 1986), a 16-year-old girl obtained medical approval for a therapeutic abortion, and her parents sought an injunction to prevent it.* When it was denied they appealed, but the

---

*   This was at a time when the law allowed abortion only with the approval of a therapeutic abortion committee. The law was struck down in the *Morgentaler* case (see Chapter 15).

Alberta Court of Appeal affirmed the lower court ruling.[10] As the Court saw it, "the issue is simply one of the capacity to consent." Although acknowledging the parental right to control children, the Court noted that the trend of modern law was to exercise increasing restraint on parental power as children approached the age of majority. It concluded that the parents could not prevent the abortion because their daughter had "sufficient intelligence and understanding to make up her own mind." The Court of Appeal could have come to the same result by applying the best interests test, but it chose to hinge its decision on the maturity of the minor to decide for herself.

There are two factors that distinguish cases such as *Wren* from the five cases that introduce this chapter. First, the latter do not involve conflict between parents and children over the provision of treatment. Second, they feature the refusal of — not consent to — treatment by minors. When a minor seeks out medical care (as in the *Wren* case), one may presume that its provision will serve her best interests. On the other hand, it is questionable whether a minor's best interests are served when she rejects proffered treatment for a life-threatening condition. Of course, it is arguable that whatever inspired the recognition of the mature minor rule, its natural evolution is toward recognition of the right of a mature minor to decide for herself without her autonomy being subverted by third parties claiming that they know her best interests better than she.

Bear in mind that the term "mature minor" is a shorthand expression for one who has the mental capacity to make the treatment decision at hand. That said, it is relevant to address briefly the nature of adolescent decision-making and its fit within the law's understanding of mental competency. As explained in the previous chapter, the competency framework for medical treatment cases is cognition-based. It looks to knowledge and understanding: does the patient know/understand her medical condition; does she know/understand the nature of the proposed treatment and its risks and likely consequences; does she know/understand the risks and likely consequences of refusing the proposed treatment. What counts is not outcome but process — not what the patient decides but whether the patient is a free agent with the capacity to apply her values and preferences to the matter at hand.

If the cognition model of competency — which evolved with adult patients in mind — is not suitable for transfer to adolescents, then the risk of harm to an adolescent is surely greater when she withholds consent to treatment that serves her best interests than when she gives consent to such treatment. And the suitability of that transfer is indeed questionable. As a thoughtful commentator has written:

Decisional capacity can be even more difficult to assess in adolescents than in adults. Achieving the necessary maturity and understanding to make decisions about treatment is an incremental process that takes place over time, but progress is not necessarily constant, uniform or without setbacks. Nor do all adolescents mature at the same rate. Development is affected by the individual's environment as well as personal characteristics. Children's abilities to comprehend complex concepts, formulate a settled value system, understand death, and imagine their own futures develop with age and experience. It follows that their decision-making capacity (in the legal sense) will similarly evolve.[11]

The mature minor rule is, after all, about maturity. In that sense, the minor's cognitive understanding of the treatment at issue is not enough. Her decision must also reflect a sense of independence that is grounded in emotional, psychological, and social maturity. But given that there is evidence that adolescents are more subject to parental influence (and peer pressure) than adults, let us revisit the tragic case of Tyrell Dueck. The Court ruled that Tyrell lacked decision-making capacity because he had been "misguided by his father into placing his hopes for recovery on a cure that does not exist." But what if Tyrell had not been misinformed? What if he and his parents were Jehovah's Witnesses and he refused blood products, understanding full well that by so doing he would most likely die? Given the nature of his relationship with his father, how could one say that it would truly be *his* decision?

In the other cases canvassed, there is also a concern whether the adolescent patients were truly exercising decisional capacity. One cannot question the love and devotion of their parents, but still their parents were equally adamant that blood products not enter their bodies. Could these youngsters even allow themselves to ponder whether they would rather listen to their caregivers than to their parents? Could they live with the thought that by accepting blood they would break faith with the parents and church community that had helped shape their lives? And even if in such a case the adolescent had no inner doubts about her decision, who could say that as she matured into adulthood she would keep the faith that she had learned from her parents?

The complexity of the issues in this area of the law was spelled out in 1995 in *The Manitoba Law Reform Commission Report on Minor's Consent to Health Care*:

It is clear that the mature minor rule is firmly entrenched in Canadian common law. There are, however, some aspects of the rule that need further clarification. For example, maturity may involve more than an intellectual appreciation of the nature and risks of the medical treatment per se. The court may also consider ethical, emotional maturity, particularly in difficult and controversial areas such as contraceptive treatment, abortion and the treatment of sexually-transmitted disease. The welfare principle [that the mature minor cannot act against her best interests] has also yet to be tested. It may be seen as incompatible with mature, autonomous and independent decision-making. However, hard cases will test the extent of the court's commitment to the autonomy of mature minors. Some of those hard cases will centre on a mature minor's right to refuse beneficial and necessary treatment favoured by both parents and the medical establishment. It will arise when mature minors refuse life-saving treatment when the chances of success are good and the treatment is supported by parents and the medical professionals.

As we have seen and will see again when we consider the recent case of *Alberta (Director of Child Welfare) v. H. (B.)*, what makes hard cases even harder is when one or both parents support the minor's treatment refusal.

3. MATURE MINORS AND CANADIAN LAW

The cases that introduce this chapter address the claimed right of adolescents to refuse medical treatment for life-threatening conditions that their physicians believe afford the only hope for survival; and the reader may find that the law is not as clear-cut as in cases involving adults and pre-adolescents.*

The view has been expressed in Jehovah's Witness circles that the decisions in *Kosack (Children's Aid Society of Metropolitan Toronto v. K.)*, *Yeatts (Y. (A.), Re)*, and *Walker* vindicate the right of minors to refuse medical treatment on religious grounds. But a close reading of the facts of the three cases does not support that broad conclusion. For example, in *Kosack* (aside from the patient's rejection of blood products) there are three factors that explain the decision: (1) the chemotherapy treatment — with its grim side effects — would last for a considerable time, and even then the odds were against a favourable outcome; (2) it was anticipated that repeated blood transfusions would be necessary, the numbers ranging as high as 15 for one cycle of chemotherapy treatment; and (3) the family had an alternative treatment plan.

Judge Main clearly erred in finding that the family's proposal, a regimen of mega-vitamin therapy, was a viable medical option. There was then and currently is no medical evidence to support his opinion that the patient's life was "equally in danger whichever path is taken." Mega-vitamin therapy's proven success rate for acute myeloid leukemia is 0%.

---

* The former is the subject of Chapter 19 and the latter of Chapter 23.

At the time of the *Kosack* case the proven success rate for chemotherapy was 30% after two-and-one-half years (with most of the 30% going on to long term survival).

It is apparent, however, that the judge's ruling did not hinge upon the alternative treatment plan proffered by the parents. Had there been no such proposal, his decision in all likelihood would have been the same — given the patient's steadfast opposition to chemotherapy/blood products and his finding that she possessed "wisdom and maturity well beyond her years." Given the 70% odds against survival even with the conventional treatment, can one reasonably say that he should have decreed otherwise?

We have seen the same compelling variables repeated in the *Yeatts* and *Walker* cases: (1) an unfavourable prognosis even with aggressive medical management; (2) the breach of the patient's bodily integrity by not simply one but rather multiple transfusions over time; and (3) the patient's firm resolve to resist treatment believed to jeopardize his eternal salvation. Furthermore, the "holistic" treatment philosophy of Drs. Jardine and Scully was reason enough for the Newfoundland and New Brunswick courts to accept the treatment decisions of their minor patients. How could it be otherwise when a judge hears the treating physician express the professional opinion that, given the patient's frame of mind, his will to combat the disease would be adversely affected by the forcible administration of blood products?

In sum, the courts deciding the *Kosack, Yeatts* and *Walker* cases did not rest their rulings solely upon the mature minor rule. Even if the courts had found the patients lacking the mental capacity to decide for themselves, the aforementioned variables would have been sufficient warrant to rule against the spurned treatment. The cases set the legal precedent that the mature minor has the right to decide when the medical data indicate an "unfavourable" prognosis. However, they do not necessarily entrench the broader principle that, regardless of prognosis, the mature minor is legally empowered to refuse life-extending treatment. It remains to be seen whether the precedent will be broadened in future rulings to encompass scenarios in which the data indicate a relatively favourable outcome.

Child welfare legislation in every province authorizes the apprehension and treatment of children deemed "in need of protection" because they are not receiving essential medical services (whether caused by parental neglect or otherwise). This was the statutory mechanism that the petitioners sought to invoke in the *Kosack* and *Yeatts* cases. (Recall that in *Walker*, the hospital and treating physician sought a declaration that the patient be allowed to decide for himself as a mature minor.) In practice, the courts are disinclined to remove children from parental custody unless the circumstances clearly warrant legal intervention. Clearly, the more serious the child's condition and the more favourable the prognosis, the greater the likelihood of court-ordered treatment. Bear in mind that until the advent of the mature minor rule, the common law simply distinguished between two categories of persons refusing life-extending treatment on religious grounds: (1) mentally competent adults; and (2) minors: that is, anyone under the age of majority. The right of refusal was extended to the former but not to the latter, who would be treated even over parental objection.

The issue is whether the emergence of the mature minor rule in Canadian jurisprudence has changed matters when the minor is rejecting treatment that is likely to arrest a lethal disease process. In the *Walker* case, there was a concurring opinion in which the judge agreed that in the circumstances of the case the patient could not be forced to undergo blood transfusions. However, he expressed the view that the intent of the legislation regarding minors under the age of 16 was not to permit the refusal of treatment in a life-threatening situation. In other words, he regarded the legislation as empowering a minor under the age of 16 to consent to beneficial treatment but not to refuse such treatment. Given that the legislation stipulates that the treatment must be "in the best interests of the minor and his continuing health and well-being", the concurring judge considered that the rejection of treatment in a case with a favourable prognosis would subvert the intent of the law.

What then of a case with a favourable prognosis in which treatment is refused by a minor patient with the "maturity and wisdom" of a Lisa Dorothy Kosack. The renowned American jurist, Oliver Wendell Holmes, once commented that "the art of civilization is the act of drawing lines." At what point might a court decide that, however objectionable to the patient and her family, the treatment must go ahead?

Consider the hypothetical case of a 15-year-old Jehovah's Witness patient, who has acute lymphocytic leukaemia (ALL) with a favourable cell type and who fully understands the implications of her decision to refuse blood products as a necessary adjunct to chemotherapy. The provincial child welfare agency consequently seeks judicial authority to override her treatment refusal. Or consider a *Shulman*-like scenario in which a 15-year-old auto accident victim is brought to hospital in an unconscious state.* The provision of blood products is likely to ensure a full recovery, but it is brought to the treating physician's attention that the minor patient had signed a Jehovah's Witness medical alert card foreclosing that option.

---

* The case of *Malette v. Shulman*, in which a Jehovah's Witness patient won a judgment in battery against a physician who refused to abide by her medical alert card (refusing blood products "under any circumstances") and transfused her when she was unconscious, is discussed in Chapters 2, 19, and 24.

Assume in the first case that the court must decide whether to honour the treatment refusal. And assume in the second case that the minor is transfused and responds by suing the treating physician for the tort of *battery*.

In a province with no statutory provisions dealing with minors and treatment decision-making, the court would consider whether the minor's refusal of treatment fell under the common law mature minor rule. In Ontario, the minor would base her claim under the recently enacted *Health Care Consent Act*, which does not stipulate a fixed age at which a person becomes mentally competent to consent to treatment.[12] By omitting a specific age of consent, the Act in effect permits mature minors of whatever age to make their own treatment decisions.

Recall that in New Brunswick, the consent-to-treatment-requirement applies not only to adults but also to minors over the age of 16; however, a mature minor under 16 is allowed the same privilege only if two physicians certify that the treatment serves her "best interests" and "continuing health and well-being." In British Columbia, the *Infants Act* was amended in 1993 to provide that "a minor, regardless of age, may provide a valid consent to treatment."[13] However, the Act stipulates that the physician can act upon the consent of a mature minor only when she "has concluded that the treatment is in the minor's best interests." The effect of such a "best interests" equation is to undermine the patient's absolute right to decide because it grants veto power to the physician. There is also a "best interests" provision in the Alberta *Child Welfare Act* that will be considered in due course. There are no statutory restrictions on the minor's right to make medical treatment decisions in the other provinces.

On the other hand, in a 1998 case, *Kennett Estate v. Manitoba (Attorney General)*,[14] the Manitoba Court of Appeal opined that whatever the scope of the provisions in the Child and Family Services Act that deal with medical treatment for apprehended children, the Act

> does not replace the common law authority of a doctor to act upon the directions of a minor if the doctor believes the minor is capable of making mature decisions in his or her best interests.

In other words, the Court was prepare to apply the "best interests" gloss to the mature minor rule (it was speaking hypothetically because it was not dealing with an on-going treatment case). It also went out of its way to rule that the question was not one of age but rather of decisional capacity. Recall that the Ontario, New Brunswick, and British Columbia statutes likewise focus upon capacity and not a minimum age of consent.

It remains to be seen whether courts in provinces without statutory restrictions on the mature minor rule would deny its application when an adolescent who is considered competent withholds consent to treatment that is medically regarded as in her best interests. Who can say if the courts would be inclined to interpret the rule as enabling the patients in the two aforementioned hypothetical cases to renounce clearly beneficial treatment? The first case would present the court with the distasteful prospect of forcing a continuous series of invasive treatments upon the patient. That spectre might well stay the hand of a court otherwise inclined to mandate treatment, although evidence that the treating physician favours the regimen might sway the court to allow the chemotherapy.

Be that as it may, these factors would not come into play in our *Shulman*-like scenario, in which the court is confronted by a minor who is alive and well, was transfused but once and while unconscious, and is seeking damages for breach of her bodily integrity. In such a case, the court might well be inclined toward a ringing endorsement of the mature minor rule. However, if confronted by our ALL/chemotherapy case, the same court might withhold that endorsement because of its awareness that a ruling in the minor's favour would in effect amount to a judicially sanctioned death sentence. Or the court might reluctantly accept that result by ruling that, notwithstanding the favourable prognosis for the ALL patient, her rights must prevail. Suffice it to say that one cannot confidently predict the path that the law would follow in these heart-rending situations.

In conclusion, a court faced with either hypothetical fact scenario would have to decide whether a common law rule originally designed to facilitate access by minors to health care should be broadened to permit the rejection of potentially life-saving treatment. In the *Shulman*-like scenario, the court would have to consider issues arising under the *Charter of Rights and Freedoms*; the reason is that the Supreme Court ruled in the 1997 *Eldridge* case that its provisions apply to hospitals as public and quasi-public institutions that are part of the apparatus of government.[15] In the hypothetical case involving an ALL patient with a favourable cell type and a "children in need of protection" section of a *Child Welfare Act*, the *Charter* would also be implicated because a provincial statute is part of the apparatus of government. How might a court convened in emergency session decide the hypothetical case of *Jane Doe, Re* — a 16-year-old ALL patient with a favourable cell type who claims equal entitlement to her adult co-religionist's right to refuse blood? Perhaps the court would respond in the following fashion:

> The avoidable death of an adult Jehovah's Witness patient who refuses blood products is a regrettable but inevitable consequence of the no-treatment-without-consent doctrine. Given such dire consequences, society has the obligation to restrict the exercise of the right to refuse life-saving treatment to mentally competent adults. We do not say that

we would so rule in all cases involving minors. Suffice it to note that it is crucial to our ruling that the prognosis for Jane Doe is more favourable than that reported in the *Kosack, Yeatts*, and *Walker* cases. In any event, the law has traditionally drawn lines between adults and minors, and its application in this particular case is well warranted. If you are prepared to risk death for your faith, then you must wait until you cross the line into adulthood because until then the law is hesitant to trust your judgment.

We hold to this position, notwithstanding the rights and freedoms guaranteed under sections 2, 7, and 15 of the *Charter*. Section 2 protects "freedom of conscience and religion." Section 7 guarantees the right to "liberty and security of the person." And section 15 in part prohibits discrimination based on age and religion. We grant that our ruling breaches each of these *Charter* protections, but that is because the latter are overridden in the particular case before us by section 1, which provides that the rights and freedoms guaranteed by that document are "subject only to such reasonable limits prescribed by law as can be demonstrably justified in a free and democratic society."

We would not invoke section 1 if the patient were an adult, but we conclude that it is reasonable to limit the exercise of one's *Charter* rights to refuse life-saving treatment to an adult in the particular type of case before us. We do not ascribe to the view that a minor who refuses blood on religious grounds has been "brainwashed" by her parents. In fact, the evidence is that Jane Doe is an intelligent young lady who has not lightly come to her decision, and we are therefore tempted to conclude that she qualifies as a mature minor. It is, however, a fact of life that a minor is usually inclined to follow the faith of her parents; and even if the parents do not press the minor to keep the faith, the latter may nonetheless feel constrained to refuse blood because of the fear that by breaching faith she will compromise her and her family's standing in their religious community. Still, as it now stands, her position does appear rooted in her deep commitment to her faith such that we cannot say that she is of two minds on the question.

But at the end of the day is the nagging concern that in adulthood she may well come to turn from the faith of her parents. And even though she is an impressive young lady, we still question whether a 16-year-old has enough maturity and life experience to spurn the only medical treatment that can save her life. That is why we rule that Jane Doe must attain the status of adult before being allowed to decide for herself. However, we hasten to add that if a case arises in which the prognosis is considerably less favourable than it is for Jane Doe, we would not be so readily inclined to tip the delicate balance in favour of state intervention.

In 1986 an inquest was held in Winnipeg into the death of 15-year-old Daniel Kennett.[16] Kennett was a hemophiliac who died in hospital from internal haemorrhaging. As Jehovah's Witnesses he and his parents had steadfastly refused to authorize a life-saving blood transfusion. Kennett went into renal failure and died before the hospital could obtain legal authority to proceed. According to Provincial Court Judge Gyles, who did not question the legality of transfusing the youth against his express wishes:

> Before adulthood is attained, a parent should not be permitted to withhold life-saving medical or surgical treatment, even where the child appears to be in agreement with his parents wishes.

But the ethics of the 1980s are not necessarily the ethics of the first decade of the 21st century. Perhaps the court deciding the case of *Jane Doe, Re* would rule that the 15-year-old ALL patient has the legal right to refuse a treatment regimen that offers favourable odds of long term survival. A court so inclined would frame its judgment along the following lines:

> Although we regret the patient's resolve to refuse treatment that entails the administration of blood products, we rule that as a mature minor it is her legal right to so decide. The view that the minor's right to *consent to* medical treatment does not encompass the right to *refuse* treatment makes a mockery of the very concept of the mature minor. If a minor has the requisite mental capacity to decide the one, then surely she cannot be restrained from deciding the other. As the Ontario Court of Appeal stated in the *Shulman* case: "The right of self-determination which underlies the doctrine of informed consent also obviously encompass the right to refuse medical treatment."

> To reiterate, a ruling to the contrary would strike at the heart of the mature minor rule. It would in effect send the message: you are mature enough to decide for yourself when the court agrees with your decision but you are not mature enough to make a decision that the court regards as unwise. (One is here reminded of the cynic who claims that a physician will question her patient's mental competency only when she strongly disagrees with the patient's treatment choice.)

> Just as parents must learn that they are not free agents entitled to control their child's life until the very age of majority, so this court has decided that the time has come for the law to abandon its traditional paternalistic policy toward minors who, whatever the age, have the

mental capacity to make their own treatment decisions. In an ironic sense, that we deplore the decision of the minor in the case at hand ennobles the principle upon which she stands.

Once we grant the mature minor's right to decide for herself, we cannot restrict that right to cases in which we agree with her choice. If her right is to have any meaning it must be hers to exercise, and it is beside the point whether the court believes that she has made a wise or foolish decision. If her right to decide hinges upon whether the court endorses her stand, then the right becomes a shadow divested of any substance. The heart of the matter is whether Jane Doe has the mental capacity to make her own treatment decisions. Once we decide that question in the affirmative, we must stand back and respect her choice, albeit we do so with heavy heart.

Furthermore, we hold that the forced submission of the patient to the administration of blood products would violate her rights under sections 2, 7, and 15 of the *Charter*. The public policy reasons that inform our judgment in the common law sphere likewise support our conclusion that it would not be reasonable to invoke section 1 to deny Jane Doe her right to decide for herself.

Predicting judicial trends can be a risky business, and alas we have no crystal ball to inform us of the direction that the law will take when such a case inevitably arises. Suffice it to say that, as our analysis indicates, the *Charter* furnishes no guiding light. The court inclined to rule in the minor's favour would stand by her *Charter* rights, whereas the court inclined to rule against her would — in line with Justice Holmes' maxim that "the art of civilization is the act of drawing lines" — trump her *Charter* rights by invoking section 1.

In the cases canvassed so far, the impassioned opposition of the patient was a factor that could not be ignored; and one must acknowledge that even if a court were to authorize treatment in a particular case, the caregivers might well refuse to go ahead when confronted by a patient resolved to resist. Kosack, Yeatts, and Walker indicated that they would battle against being transfused with all the strength they could muster (and Walker was an athlete, a six-footer weighing 172 pounds). After all, a hospital is not a torture chamber; and the spectre of a patient kicking and screaming throughout a lengthy course of treatment might well be enough to render the law a dead letter. When Dr. Jardine was asked by the Newfoundland court whether he would administer a court-ordered transfusion to Adam Yeatts, he replied: "No, I personally would not do it." And Dr. Scully advised the New Brunswick court that: "I have assured Joshua Walker that

I would not under any circumstances administer a blood transfusion to him unless he should change his mind in that regard."

We have referred to the extent of invasiveness of the spurned treatment — e.g. one transfusion on one occasion as compared to multiple transfusions for each of several cycles of chemotherapy — as a variable distinguishing our *Shulman*-like scenario from the *Kosack, Yeatts,* and *Walker* cases. We have also considered the prognosis numbers game as another variable for consideration. However, it is in theory arguable that these two factors are irrelevant to the question whether the patient has the mental capacity to qualify as a mature minor. The argument is as follows:

> When a child care agency seeks a court order to force treatment upon a recalcitrant minor, the court must decide *either* that the order be granted (because the minor is not decisionally capable) *or* that the order be denied (because the minor is decisionally capable). Given that framework, the prognosis and the degree of invasiveness of the rejected treatment are simply beside the point. Is she mature or is she not: that is the question.

Still, there is the view that the mature minor rule was not designed to enable a patient to act against her best interests, and from that perspective the prognosis in particular would be a relevant factor in deciding whether to empower the patient to decline the treatment. As we see shortly when we consider an English case, *W. (A Minor), Re,* the fact that a court finds the patient to be a mature minor does not inevitably lead to a ruling in her favour.

In any event, it is pertinent to note that the road to maturity lies along a developmental continuum such that there is not a single magical moment in time when a minor is ready to don the decision-making mantle of responsible adulthood. Although the law may choose to define the issue in black-and-white terms, the reality of adolescent psychological development is a progression from black to grey to white. The cases we have considered are as heart-rending as any that a court confronts; and on the issue of decisional capacity a case falling in the grey zone might go either way, depending on such factors as the invasiveness of the procedure and the prognosis itself. In a case in which the judge finds that the minor does not clearly fall in either camp, her decision might well be influenced by the prognosis and invasiveness variables. In other words, a favourable prognosis and limited invasiveness might lead her to rule that the minor lacks the maturity to decide for herself. And a less sanguine prognosis coupled with a high degree of invasiveness might lead her to the opposite conclusion. (In either case, the judge might not even be consciously aware of the "extralegal" factors that have influenced her decision.)

On the other hand, the judge might acknowledge the minor's decision-making capacity but nonetheless compel treatment on the grounds that the mature minor rule was not formulated to enable a patient to reject "beneficial" treatment. Or, as we have seen, the judge could come to the same result by citing section 1 of the *Charter* as the legal rationale for court-ordered treatment. In either case, the judge would be invoking a public policy rationale to frustrate the patient's wishes — either by limiting the scope of the common law rule itself or else by overriding its application on *Charter* grounds.

We have thus far canvassed the issues raised when a minor is prompted by religious convictions to refuse the only treatment regimen that her physicians believe can stave off death. The patient wants to live but not at the cost of breaching faith. What if, on the other hand, the minor patient says No because she wants to die? In contrast to the Jehovah's Witness cases in which the patient wishes to live, but not at the price of receiving blood products, we turn now to scenarios involving minor patients who prefer to die rather than endure the relentless burdens of a debilitating disease.

Consider the following summary of a case history published in 1973 in the journal, *Pediatrics*. It appears in an article titled, "The Adolescent Patient's Decision to Die."[17]

> Karen, 13, was hospitalized in September 1968, following a three-week course of nephrotic syndrome. Her condition failed to improve and a renal biopsy the following April revealed "chronic, active glomerulonephritis." In August 1970 her deteriorating renal function necessitated a bilateral nephrectomy. The following month she received a kidney donated by her father and the transplant functioned well for several months. However, after severe protein-uria, the kidney ceased functioning in March 1971. Before the transplant and following its failure, Karen underwent thrice-weekly haemodialysis. She tolerated dialysis poorly, constantly suffering chills, nausea, vomiting, severe headaches, and fatigue.
>
> Within weeks of the transplant failure, Karen and her parents asked the medical staff to halt treatment and to let "nature take its course." A decidedly negative staff response led the family to agree to continue dialysis, medication, and diet therapy. The patient's renal incapacity returned to pre-transplant levels, and her life continued to be marked by social isolation, diet restriction, chronic discomfort, and fatigue. Karen was hospitalized in May after 10 days of high fever, and three days after admission the transplanted kidney was removed. Its pathology resembled that of her original kidneys, thereby suggesting the likelihood of a similar reaction in any subsequent transplant. Two weeks later Karen refused further dialysis. Although the medical staff reacted

with frustration and anger, her parents supported her decision. She was evaluated by a child psychiatrist who reported no evidence of psychotic thinking. He also concluded that her decision was the product of careful deliberation and that she knew that she was asking to die. She had established a relationship with the hospital chaplain and spoke to him following her decision to terminate dialysis. She told him that she did not believe in hell and that, even if there were no heaven, nothingness was preferable to the suffering that she would continue to endure. Nine days after her decision to come off dialysis, Karen died with her parents at her bedside. Shortly before her death, she told her father, "Daddy, I will be happy there (in the ground) if there is no machine, and they don't work on me anymore."

Since the hospital abided by her decision, it had no doubt been advised by its legal staff that even though Karen was a minor, she had the legal right to choose death over her tortured existence on dialysis. As noted, the mature minor doctrine has traditionally applied to the provision of beneficial medical treatment. It follows that the doctrine would accommodate a decision by a mature minor to refuse treatment that prolongs life but that she finds more burdensome than beneficial. Although perhaps unlikely to accept a mature minor's refusal of *life-saving* treatment, the law would most likely endorse a mature minor's decision to forsake *life-prolonging* treatment.* It is arguable that the law has rational grounds for limiting the right to reject life-saving treatment to competent adults. But if the prognosis is bleak and the treatment more burdensome than beneficial, there are no public policy grounds to preclude the law from granting to a mature minor the merciful release that it grants to an adult. That would be the case even if one or both of parents opposed her decision. Once the law concedes her right as a mature minor to decline life-prolonging treatment, then no one — neither physician, hospital, nor even parents — can lawfully stand in her way.

In 1994, a Florida social services agency intervened when a 15-year-old stopped taking his anti-rejection medication because of its intolerable side-effects — debilitating headaches, nausea, irritability, and hallucinations.[18] Benny Agrilo's second transplanted liver was failing, and he was adamant that he would not suffer the ordeal of a third transplant. The agency arranged for the police to apprehend him at home, where he was forcibly strapped to a stretcher and taken to hospital. He refused to co-operate and with his mother's support petitioned the Circuit Court to order his release. As Benny told the judge who attended at his bedside:

---

*   See Chapter 18 for the distinction between life-saving and life-prolonging treatment.

I'm tired of living in pain. I'd rather stay at home and live as close as I can
to a natural life. I know what I'm doing. I don't want to die. I'm not trying
to commit suicide. But I don't want to live like that.

In ordering Benny's discharge, the judge ruled that he was a mature
minor and therefore entitled to refuse what he had come to regard as
burdensome treatment. Benny had received his first liver transplant when
he was eight years old, and the second five years later. For nearly half his
life he had endured the side-effects of immuno-suppressive drugs, and the
judge no doubt recognized the reasonableness of his decision to call a halt
to treatment that had rendered his life unbearable. Benny went home where
a few weeks later he died peacefully with his family at his bedside.

Assume for the moment, however, that the judge believed that Benny's
decision was unreasonable (which was the position of his physician, a
renowned transplant surgeon). In that event would he have allowed a
decision to stand that he thought tragically misguided? Put differently,
would he have been able to isolate his personal opinion from his assessment
of the patient's decisional capacity? Who can say?

4. THE ENGLISH WAY

In 1991, the English Court of Appeal handed down its ruling in the
case of *W. (A Minor), Re*.[19] The patient was a 16-year-old anorexic and the
Court opened its judgment by commenting that: "Fate has dealt harshly
with W." That was surely no understatement. She was orphaned at the age
of eight, had a disastrous foster placement, finally found a haven where
she was well treated but then had to leave when her foster mother was
stricken with cancer in 1989. Two months later she suffered the loss of her
grandfather to whom she was deeply attached. In 1991 the severity of her
condition — she was 5'7" tall and her weight had fallen to 77 pounds —
led to her admission to an adolescent residential treatment unit.

The worsening of her condition over the next eight months prompted
her caregivers to solicit her consent to a transfer to a hospital specializing
in the treatment of eating disorders. But W refused, saying that she preferred
to stay where she was and that she would cure herself when she decided it
was time. A petition was then filed seeking judicial authority to effectuate
the forced transfer and treatment of the patient. The petition was granted
by the Family Division and affirmed by the Court of Appeal. In England
the age of consent to medical treatment is 16, and the Court of Appeal
agreed with the trial judge that W was of sufficient understanding and
intelligence to appreciate the treatment proposed and the likely consequences of its rejection. Given the finding of mental competency, one

would have expected the Court of Appeal to reverse the lower court. But the Court affirmed, justifying its ruling by invoking the *parens patriae* jurisdiction of the courts — their inherent long-standing power to step in to protect vulnerable persons (excluding mentally competent adults). Thus, even though parents cannot lawfully override the treatment decisions of their mentally competent 16-year-old children, the Court assumed that role in the instant case.

In effect, the Court of Appeal held that a minor of the statutory age of consent to treatment is entitled to exercise her right, but subject to judicial oversight. Its ruling would appear to frustrate the intent of Parliament that mentally competent 16-year-olds be allowed to make treatment decisions for themselves. Still, it is arguable that there is a role for the courts when a minor, even if deemed competent, is not deciding in a manner that accords with her best interests. Of course, the countervailing argument is that if the minor is over 16 and found to have decisional capacity, then it is not for the court to say that it knows better than the minor what is best for her.

In any event, it may happen that a Canadian court could likewise declare that a minor has decision capacity and then turn around and invoke its *parens patriae* jurisdiction to mandate treatment, as did the Court of Appeal in the *W. (A Minor), Re* case. Such an approach has already been hinted at by the B.C. Supreme Court. In a 1993 case, *Ney v. Canada (Attorney General)*,[20] Judge Huddard of the Supreme Court (trial division) acknowledged that whatever the common law and legislation have to say about adolescent treatment decision-making for a child, "the parens patriae jurisdiction of the court may override a minor's refusal to consent to treatment that is in the minor's best interests."

5. TWO RECENT ALBERTA CASES

Recall that in the *Walker* case, the Court of Appeal applied the best interests test in accordance with a statute providing that a minor under 16 could consent to medical treatment if: "the minor is capable of understanding (its) nature and consequences," and the treatment "is in the best interests of the minor and his continuing health and wellbeing." In that case the Court of Appeal found that the patient was a mature minor and that his refusal of blood products satisfied the mandated best interests test. In Alberta, section 2(d) of the *Child Welfare Act* directs decision-makers for the child to consider the "best interests of the child," adding that "if the child is capable of forming an opinion...the child's opinion should be considered by those making decisions that affect the child." (The proviso appears to leave no room for the mature minor rule as it says nothing about a child's decisional capacity.) In addition, the Act defines a child as "anyone under the age of 18." We turn now to two recent Alberta cases that have considered the statute in familiar territory — that of critically ill Jehovah's Witness minors refusing blood.

(a) Alberta (Director of Child Welfare) v. H. (B.)

When 16-year-old Bethany Hughes (called B.H. by the courts) was diagnosed with acute myeloid leukemia (AML), sub-type M-1, on February 13, 2002, she was quick to assert that chemotherapy was acceptable but not blood. Her Jehovah's Witness parents supported her decision. On February 15 her treating physician, Dr. Max Coppes (the head of the Oncology Department at the Alberta Children's Hospital) consulted with a number of physicians across the United States and Canada, one of whom is the leading authority in North America on the treatment of AML, sub-type M-1. All responded that his proposed treatment — four intensive courses of chemotherapy — was the best option, and that blood and blood products were a vital component of the treatment regimen because the chemotherapy would destroy the patient's healthy blood cells as well as the cancerous cells.

(i) *The hearing in Provincial Court*

On that same day, Judge Jordan of the Provincial Court held a hearing at the hospital to consider an application by the Director of Child Welfare that Bethany be subject to apprehension and treatment orders. At that time her father informed the judge that he had reversed his position and now believed that the Biblical provisions in question did not apply to blood transfusions.

At the hearing, physicians from Alberta Children's Hospital testified that a worldwide search for non-blood alternatives had proved fruitless. They also indicated that the odds of long term survival with the conventional treatment were between 40-50%. Moreover, if she were in remission at the end of two cycles of chemotherapy, then a bone marrow transplant would be considered. In that event, the odds for long term survival would hover around 65%.

Evidence that multiple transfusions were necessary prompted Bethany's lawyer to complain that the harm to his client's religious beliefs would be compounded with each transfusion. "It's an assault," he said. "If you are assaulted once, does that mean further assaults don't have consequences?" His central assertion was that she was a mature minor and hence lawfully entitled to refuse blood products. He advised the Court that she was a good student, was "bright and thoughtful," and attended church and church activities several times a week.

Bethany was questioned by the judge, who asked her how she would feel about her relationship with God if she were transfused against her will. She replied that like a rape victim she would not be held responsible by God for what happened, but that somehow — and she found it difficult to articulate — "it would still be a violation in His eyes." She added that she would be "different" to Him. Judge Jordan then asked her: "How do you reconcile that with a God who loves you unconditionally?" She replied that God did "love me unconditionally because I follow his principles...and He shows me his mercy and justice, because I follow all his principles."

Bethany's father was also heard from. He described his daughter as "child-like in some ways" and expressed the belief that she "does not understand what it is to die." Still, there were three physicians (two pediatricians and a child psychiatrist) who questioned her on February 16 and concluded that she was a mature minor. But according to the judge, the most persuasive evidence of Bethany's level of maturity was provided by Dr. Corrine Saunders (described by the judge as her "pediatric support physician"). Quoting from her testimony:

> [I do] not believe that B.H. understands on an experiential level what it is to die. She has never ndured the death of a child or even a close family member.... I think she hasn't had time or the disease has also not progressed to a frightening point where she feels physical vulnerability...but I don't think she is old enough or has experienced enough of ill health to experience the vulnerability and the moral questioning that goes along with (it)....

> I think B.H. is an imaginative child who has a very developed intellectual capacity. But who strikes me as quite young and not immature, but more childlike than other adolescents of her age. Which is actually her most charming feature. And I would be concerned that her childlike beliefs are not tempered by life's experiences and the complexities of theological argument and investigation, (which) would mean that she's being guided by her faith that is appropriate for her developmental level....

> The other thing that's operative with B.H. is the almost universal adolescent belief in their own immortality.... But it would certainly come out in the belief that I can't possibly die so I'm not worried about not accepting transfusions.... I don't think she knows what it's like to die and that worries me.

After reviewing this evidence, Judge Jordan concluded that Dr. Saunders "has serious reservations about whether B.H. is a minor of a sufficient level of maturity to make the medical decision to refuse treatment...." In the result the judge granted the apprehension and treatment orders, resting her decision on four grounds:[21]

1. Bethany could not be treated effectively without a treatment regimen including blood and blood products.

2. She was not a mature minor because she "has not had the life or developmental experience which would allow her to question her faith and/or its teachings.... Intelligence, thoughtfulness, exemplary behaviour and noble academic achievement are not sufficient when the magnitude of the decision faced by a 16-year-old involves a certain risk of death." Furthermore, she has led a "sheltered life" in her religious community, and "adherents to the faith do not question dogma or examine other points of view."

3. She agreed with Justice Clarke's decision in the *U.C. (Next Friend of)* case that section 2 of the *Child Welfare Act* superseded the common law. That said, the issue of decisional capacity was irrelevant because the litmus test was simply the best interests of the minor.

4. Although some of her *Charter* rights were violated, they were trumped by the reasonable limits proviso in section 1.

Bethany's father welcomed the decision, telling the media that his daughter "lived such an isolating controlled life — all her friends are Jehovah's Witnesses." He said that her life counted for more than the church's ban on blood transfusions.[22] His breach of faith opened a rift between him and his wife and two other daughters, 22 and 14, who joined their religious community in shunning all contact with him.* (The media reported that Bethany was alternating between expressions of hatred and love for her father.)

Two days later a Queen's Bench judge denied a stay of the lower court orders. As he put it: "If she doesn't have the treatment she will suffer irreparable harm. I acknowledge that there is a harm to religious beliefs but that has to be balanced with right to life." He said that the day before, the girl had received two transfusions which had improved her blood cell count, to which he added: "The harm has already taken place." Outside the courthouse her lawyer said to the media: "This ruling will mean that she will continue to receive blood transfusions imposed against her will by means of restraint and sedation. It will be devastating to her."[23]

---

* Shunning in this context means that the Jehovah's Witness community avoids all contact with the transgressor. He is in effect excommunicated, and his wife has filed for divorce.

(ii) *The appeal to the Court of Queen's Bench*

The appeal was heard on April 4 before Justice Adele Kent of the Court of Queen's Bench, who was told by the girl's lawyer:

> This case is about the state using a court order to hold her down in her bed. It's inhumane. She fights back with all she can to prevent the blood transfusions. Twelve times since February 18 that has happened and the court order makes her stay at Alberta Children's Hospital under the *Child Welfare Act*.[24]

He contended that there were alternative methods of treatment that did not involve blood products with "at least as high a potential success rate as the procedures now being used." The Child Welfare attorney responded that Calgary Children's Hospital had canvassed alternatives before concluding that the current regimen offered the best hope.

The lawyer for Mr. Hughes vigorously contested the assertion that his daughter was a mature minor. Counsel argued that she was being subjected to "undue influence that affected her decision on this life-saving matter" — that her mother, sisters, and the church elders were encouraging her "to die for her faith."

Assuming the absence of non-blood alternatives, the Q.B. judge was faced with a stark choice between relatively certain death if treatment were stopped and a reasonable hope, but certainly no guarantee, of life if the treatment continued. Six days after the hearing Justice Kent denied the appeal.[25] As she spelled out, there were the same four issues on appeal as had been considered by the trial court:

1. Is the treatment essential?

2. Is Bethany a mature minor?

3. Does section 2(d) of the *Child Welfare Act* replace the mature minor rule when a child refuses essential medical treatment?

4. Subject to the answers to the above questions, have any of Bethany's *Charter* rights been violated, and if so are any such violations justifiable under section 1?

(A) The Treatment Issue

Justice Kent dismissed the assertion by Bethany's lawyer that the team approach of her caregivers was explained by its lack of experience with her condition. As she indicated, the team approach to treatment of leukemia in children is standard policy across North America; and that the consensus amongst all those consulted by Dr. Coppes was that "the proposed course of treatment was the only course that held any expectation of curing the

AML M-1." She also rejected the submission that the treatment was "experimental."

(B) The Mature Minor Issue

On the one hand, Justice Kent faulted the lower court judge for finding that adherence to religious dogma affects decisional capacity. As she put it:

> To say that no Jehovah's Witness child who is of sufficient intelligence and ability to understand the consequences can refuse blood because it comes from a religious conviction which we believe is wrong creates a principle which may be used at other times in dangerous circumstances.

She did find that Bethany was a mature minor during the first few days after she was diagnosed with AML. (Recall that the three physicians who expressed the same opinion had seen her on February 16, three days after the diagnosis.) However, her review of the evidence led her to rule that "the undue influence put upon her in the last few weeks has taken away her ability to make an informed choice." In that regard, Justice Kent expressed particular concern about the actions of Bethany's mother. On March 4, Dr. Saunders had written on the patient's chart that her mother had attempted to remove the IV line giving blood. The judge also referred to the mother's affidavit, which she described as "intemperate." Mrs. Hughes had written that her daughter's "experimental" treatment bore "a chilling resemblance" to the "atrocities" committed by Nazi physicians. To emphasize her point, she appended a copy of the 1948 Nuremberg Code, which stipulated ethical guidelines for medical research on human subjects in light of the Nazi experience. In the judge's view: "If Mrs. H. truly believes what she says, then it is a very strong indication that she has no perspective on her child's current medical situation."

According to a hospital social worker, Bethany informed her that she had been instructed by her mother and lawyer to "fight" against the transfusions. The social worker added: "Once the mother began to attend during the blood transfusions, there was an immediate and noticeable deterioration of the child's behaviour." On March 28, the hospital restricted bedside visits to the patient's immediate family to halt the stream of visitors from her church.

Finally, Justice Kent quoted from a nurse's statement that on March 18: "She voiced disbelief that her death would result if she received no blood products." This led the judge to comment: "B.H. has not been allowed to look death in the face. Because of incorrect information and the behaviour of some around her, she now believes that she will not die if she does not have transfusions." In sum, for the reasons given her status under the mature minor rule had shifted over time.

(C) The Section 2(d) Issue

Agreeing with the lower court, Justice Kent placed the matter of Bethany's decisional capacity on the sidelines. As she expressed it: "Under the mature minor principle, it is B.H. who does the analysis. Under the legislation, it is the court and other people exercising authority who do the analysis." The only question was that of best interests, and "balancing all the factors, it is in B.H.'s best interests to have the treatment proposed by the hospital." Thus, whether or not she was a mature minor, she would be treated with blood against her will.

(D) The *Charter* Issue

Justice Kent held that any *Charter* violations of Bethany's rights were justified by section 1. In particular, regarding section 15 (the prohibition on age discrimination), she concluded that "age is used as a qualification for no other reason than to avoid or reduce the administrative burden of individualized testing." She cited as examples laws regulating voting, driving, drinking alcohol, marrying, and leaving school. In short, although section 2(d) of the *Child Welfare Act* breached section 15 of the *Charter*, it was saved under section 1 on the grounds of administrative efficiency.

(iii) *Commentary*

The Q.B. ruling is clearly flawed in upholding section 2(d) on *Charter* grounds. In my view, the argument from administrative convenience overlooks the fact that this kind of case is an exceedingly rare event compared to activities such as driving and marrying. As it now stands, the law in Alberta is that, however mature the minor, she is not allowed to control her medical care when others say that her decision does not accord with her best interests. Given a life-and-death situation as in this case, I believe that the decisional capacity of the minor should be very carefully scrutinized in accordance with a high threshold standard of competency; but if she passes the test then she should be allowed to lead her life as she sees fit.

That said, I acknowledge that in cases involving Jehovah's Witness minors, there is a genuine concern with respect to voluntary choice. In her ruling, Judge Jordan cited a 1993 English case, *E. (A Minor), Re*,[26] in which a judge of the Family Division found that a 15 1/2-year-old Jehovah's Witness stricken with leukemia (ALL) was not competent to refuse blood. She extracted the following excerpt from that opinion:

He is of an age and understanding at least to appreciate the consequences if not the process of his decision, and by reason of the conviction of his religion, which I find to be deeply held and genuine, says NO to a medical intervention which may save his life. What weight do I place upon this refusal? I approach this case telling myself that the freedom of choice in adults is a fundamental right. He is close to the time when he may be able to take those decisions.* I should therefore be very slow to interfere. I have also to ask myself to what extent is that assertion, "I will not have a blood transfusion," the product of his full but his free informed thought. Without wishing to introduce into the cases the notions of undue influence, I find that the influence of the teachings of the Jehovah's Witnesses is strong and powerful. The very fact that this family can contemplate the death of one of its members is the most eloquent testimony of the power of the faith. He is a boy who seeks and needs the love and respect of his parents whom he would wish to honour as the Bible exhorts him to honour them. I am far from satisfied that at the age of 15 his will is fully free. He may assert it, but his volition has been conditioned by the very powerful expressions of faith to which all members of his creed adhere. When making this decision, which is a decision of life or death, I have to take account of the fact that teenagers often express views with vehemence and conviction — all the vehemence and conviction of youth! Those of us who have passed beyond callow youth can all remember the convictions we have loudly proclaimed which now we find somewhat embarrassing. I respect this boy's profession of faith, but I cannot discount at least the possibility that he may in later years suffer some diminution in his convictions. There is no settled certainty about matters of this kind.

Justice Kent also cited this lengthy excerpt from *E. (A Minor), Re*, noting that it had been quoted in the lower court opinion. Evidently, the concerns expressed in the English case were shared by the two judges in this case. If, as Bethany's father insisted, hers is "an isolating controlled life", how could one assuredly say that she had the decision-making capacity to say No? How can one say that she was capable of speaking her own mind, when she surely knew that, if she broke faith, she would face bitter disappointment and ostracism by her mother, siblings, and the congregants of the church that encompassed all of her social life?

Furthermore, there is Bethany's comment to her nurse that she would not die if she did not receive blood. Even if one could factor out the exhortations of her mother and other co-believers to stand firm, her competency would still be called into question if she shared her mother's belief in non-blood alternatives. One of the elements of decisional capacity is an

---

* As we see in the *W. (A Minor), Re* case, in Great Britain 16 is the age of consent to medical treatment.

understanding of the risks of refusing the proffered treatment. A patient would not be considered incompetent for the sole reason that her refusal of life-extending treatment is prompted by her belief in divine healing. Provided that she understands the medical implications of her decision, she is free to put her trust elsewhere. Hers is an informed decision because she knows that she is placing faith above reasoned medical judgment.

But if her decision is based upon incorrect information (e.g. non-blood alternatives), then she is deficient with respect to an essential component of capacity/competency: not only an understanding of the risks of the treatment in question but also an understanding of the risks of spurning the treatment. It follows that if the reason for Bethany's rejection of blood is her belief in a non-existent treatment, then her decision is not informed. In sum, the believer in miracles is competent because she is aware of the medical risks of refusing treatment (albeit she believes that she will be saved by divine intervention). However, Bethany would not be competent if she were unaware of the medical risks of refusing blood because she had come to believe that she could be treated without it.

Bear in mind that whether the patient is consenting to treatment or refusing consent to treatment, the patient's choice has legal standing only if it is voluntary. It is one thing for a caregiver or anyone else to persuade a patient to reverse a treatment decision. One is entitled to suggest that the patient change her mind, provided that the patient is free to accept or reject that advice in the exercise of her own judgment. But it is another thing when a patient expresses a decision that is the product of coercion (the legal term is *undue influence*). When that happens the patient's decision is without legal effect because it is not voluntary.* In a 1992 English case, *T. (adult: refusal of treatment), Re*, the Court of Appeal ruled that a 20-year-old patient's refusal of blood was not legally binding because her will had been overborne by her Jehovah's Witness mother.[27] It is instructive to consider the observations of Lord Donaldson under the heading, "The vitiating effect of outside influence":

> A special problem may arise if at the time the decision is made, the patient has been subjected to the influence of some third party. This is by no means to say that the patient is not entitled to receive and indeed invite advice and assistance from others in reaching a decision, particularly from members of the family. But the doctors have to consider whether the decision is really that of the patient. It is wholly acceptable that the patient should have been persuaded by others of the merits of such a decision and have decided ac-

---

* Undue influence was a factor in the case of Tyrell Dueck, given the nature of his relationship with his father.

cordingly. It matters not how strong the persuasion was, so long as it did not overbear the independence of the patient's decision. The real question in each such case is: does the patient really mean what he says or is he merely saying it...to satisfy someone else or because the advice and persuasion to which he has been subjected is such that he can no longer think and decide for himself. In other words, is it a decision expressed in form only, not in reality?...

[T]he relationship of the "persuader" to the patient may be of critical importance. The influence of parents on their children...can be...much stronger than would be the case in other relationships. Persuasion based upon religious beliefs can also be more compelling and the fact that arguments based upon religious beliefs are being deployed by someone in a very close relationship with the patient will give them added force and should alert the doctors to the possibility — no more — that the patient's capacity or will to decide has been overborne. In other words the patient may not mean what he says.

In the *T. (adult: refusal of treatment), Re* case, the patient was 34 weeks pregnant when admitted to hospital after an auto accident, complaining of severe pain and difficulty in breathing. She was treated with antibiotics, oxygen, and Pethidine (demerol) after being diagnosed with pneumonia. The next afternoon she told a staff nurse that she did not want a blood transfusion. The nurse thought her comment strange — she said that it had come "out of the blue" — because there had been no discussion of a need for blood. Shortly afterwards she went into labour and was transported by ambulance to the maternity unit; she promptly indicated to the nurse-midwife that she did not want blood and signed a hospital form to that effect. (Her mother had been with her in the hospital and in the ambulance.) The baby was stillborn early the next morning; that same day she was transferred to intensive care because she had developed an abscess in her lungs. She was ventilated, sedated, and given paralysing drugs. The consultant anesthetist in charge of the ICU determined that she needed blood but hesitated because of her written refusal. Two days later her father and boyfriend petitioned a circuit judge for an order allowing blood. The order was granted after an emergency hearing and later affirmed by the Court of Appeal.

It was the family history that explained the finding of undue influence by the mother. The patient's parents had separated when she was three years old, in large part because the mother was a fervent Jehovah's Witness, whereas the father rejected the teachings of the sect. Although most of her childhood was spent in her mother's custody, she was not baptized into the faith. She had left home at the age of 18 and was living with her boyfriend when the accident happened; and there was no evidence that she had ever embraced the religion. As the circuit judge summarized the evidence:

She was incarcerated (sic) in this belief by her mother during her early teenage years; she has rejected that faith; her own view as expressed to the ante-natal clinic was that she had no religion; as she discussed with her father...she had ceased to be a Jehovah's Witness; she lived a life which is quite contrary to the practices and beliefs of the faith.... She gave no indication to her boyfriend or to her father that she had repented of her sinful ways and I have no evidence from the mother to suggest that she had; she (the patient) proclaimed herself to the staff nurse to be an ex-Jehovah's Witness.

Given that her refusals of blood were pronounced when she was in severe pain and being treated with narcotics, the Court of Appeal questioned whether she was competent to make that decision. But the Court went on to conclude that in any event "the influence of her mother was such as to vitiate the decision which she expressed."

The matrimonial history of father and mother suggests that Miss T's mother is a deeply committed Jehovah's Witness who would regard her daughter's eternal salvation as far more important, and more in her daughter's best interest, than lengthening her terrestrial lifespan. We do not know what the mother said to Miss T...but it appears to be the fact that on the two occasions when Miss T raised the issue of blood transfusions, she did so suddenly and "out of the blue" without any inquiry from hospital staff and immediately following occasions when she had been alone with her mother.

Recall that it was the overbearing presence of Bethany's mother that persuaded Justice Kent to rule that the girl was not competent to refuse blood. Yet aside from the mother, there is the church itself and its dominant role in the lives of its adherents. When a Jehovah's Witness minor is afflicted with leukemia, her religious community is quick to seize the case as a rallying point for the faithful and their commitment to the prohibition against blood. The stricken minor is cast in the role of a poster child who would rather die than forsake one of the bedrock principles of the faith. And if she dies she is celebrated by the faithful as a martyr. Consider the May 22, 1994 issue of *Awake!*, a Canadian semi-monthly Jehovah's Witness magazine. The front cover, under the caption "Youths who put God first", features the photographs of two adolescents whose cases we have canvassed, Adrian Yeatts and Lisa Kosack. The article's discussion of the former concludes:

By rejecting blood transfusions that could conceivably have extended his present life, Adrian Yeatts showed himself to be one of the many young people who put God first.

And the recounting of the latter's death concludes:

In so doing she joined the ranks of many other youthful Witnesses of Jehovah who put God first. As a result, she will, with them, enjoy the fulfilment of Jesus' promise: "He that loses his life for my sake will find it." — Matthew, 10:39.

Surely Bethany was aware that her mother, her sisters, her lawyer (who is an elder [clergyman] in the church and works for its central office in Georgetown, Ontario), and her social circle of fellow believers would have been crestfallen had she consented to receive blood. And she also knew that the church does not tolerate dissent, given the shunning (excommunication) of her father when he broke faith. During her hospital stay she received a steady stream of visitors from the church, and an elder told her that her case would be featured in a forthcoming issue of *Awake!* According to the Supervised Visit Report of May 21, when a meeting from the Kingdom Hall was piped into her room (which happened often), an elder was discussing Bethany's case with the congregation and directly encouraging her to remain steadfast. As recorded in the Supervised Visit Report of June 14, an elder gave Bethany a diary inscribed in gold lettering on the cover: "Zealous Kingdom Proclaimers: Personal Notes of Bethany Hughes, Program 2000-2003." It was intended for publication in the church's annual Year Book. Perhaps her will was not overborne by the faithful gathering around her in a contest pitting the church against the state — that her resolve to spurn blood when given the diagnosis was unshakeable and therefore not in need of constant encouragement. But, then, perhaps not. I suspect that even Bethany Hughes could not have truly known whether her decision was uncontaminated by the expectations of those closest to her. And perhaps one could say the same about the other Jehovah's Witness minors whose cases are canvassed in this chapter.

Because there is a legal presumption of mental capacity when the patient is an adult, the party claiming otherwise has the burden to prove incapacity. As we see, that hurdle was overcome in the *T. (adult: refusal of treatment), Re* case because the patient's previous history was devoid of any commitment to the Jehovah's Witness creed. Had Bethany been an adult, her previous history of devotion to the creed would have presented a formidable obstacle to proving incapacity. But when the patient is a minor, she has the burden of proving capacity and it is understandable that Justice Kent was not prepared to find that Bethany was truly expressing her own free will. In fact, given the enormous pressure placed upon her by her co-religionists, how could she have proven that her decision was not unduly influenced by the impassioned voices of others incessantly commanding her to say No to blood? After all, it is one thing to hold to this core tenet of the church when one's life is not in jeopardy. It is surely another to hold fast in the face of death. (In that regard, there is anecdotal evidence of Jehovah's Witnesses, both adults and minors, who have abjured the faith and consented to blood in life-threatening situations. There are also two reported American cases where adult patients refused consent to blood but readily volunteered that they would comply with a court order to that effect.[28] Given the mixed message — I won't say Yes but I invite you to say Yes — it is not surprising that in both cases the order was forthcoming.) Perhaps there is really no way of resolving the question whether the bedrock of Bethany's commitment was such that it did not require the support of others to remain firm. Justice Kent was not satisfied that this was the case and ruled accordingly. At the end of the day — when the question is whether a minor patient has the capacity to make treatment decisions — if she cannot persuade the court that the answer is Yes, then the court must answer No.

But still, whether or not Bethany could pass the mature minor test, there are other issues. As considered earlier in this chapter, two factors that should enter the treat-or-not-to-treat equation are the prognosis and the invasiveness of the treatment. If the prognosis was grim, let us say 10% chance of long term survival, then there would be little sense to force treatment that is unlikely to succeed even if it is questionable whether the minor is "mature" in the legal sense. Yet when diagnosed Bethany's odds fell around the middle of the prognosis continuum, 40%-50% — but increasing to 65% if she were in remission after her chemotherapy treatments and a bone marrow transplant could then be done. The odds were not greatly in her favour, but they were good enough to conclude that the conventional therapy had a reasonable likelihood of success.

The other variable is the extent of the bodily invasion and its impact upon the girl's physical, emotional, and spiritual integrity. Fourteen transfusions were required for the first cycle of chemotherapy treatments (the dozen referred to by her lawyer at the April 4 hearing were followed by two others soon after), and an estimated 18 transfusions were projected when her caregivers got the green light to proceed with the second cycle. (All told she received 38 transfusions.) Her lawyer characterized the forced transfusions as "inhumane", and he accordingly argued that they were precluded by section 12 of the *Charter*, which prohibits "cruel and unusual punishment or treatment." However, Justice Kent had no hesitation in finding that the treatments were not cruel and unusual. As she put it: "The restraint, sedation, and restricted visitation were measured responses to B.H.'s expressions of resistance necessary to effect safely the essential medical treatment."

Still, even if Bethany did not mount a vigorous resistance to the transfusions — as both Lisa Kosack and Joshua Walker had vowed to do if push came to shove — it is arguable that a patient does not have to kick and scream in order for the treatment to be labelled as cruel and unusual. There can be a quiet dignity to a patient receiving treatment that offends her physical, emotional, and spiritual integrity no less than would be the case if she fought like a tiger. But even if Justice Kent had accepted a section 12 argument, she no doubt would have trumped it by invoking section 1. As indicated earlier in this chapter, my inclination is to measure the variables — prognosis and invasiveness — each against the other, and the more favourable the prognosis the more weight I would assign it. (I am assuming here that the patient does not qualify as a mature minor, which in my view would settle the matter.) The poorer the prognosis and the more invasive the treatment, the more likely would I be inclined to prohibit blood. (This is why I agree with the decisions in the *Kosack, Yeatts*, and *Walker* cases.) Since the case of Bethany Hughes falls on a prognosis borderline, it is distinguishable on that ground alone from these other cases.

(iv) *Court of Appeal*

Justice Kent's decision was unanimously affirmed on April 26 by the Court of Appeal in a one page judgment. The Court ruled that there was ample evidence to support her finding that Bethany lacked decisional capacity, and therefore that it was unnecessary to consider whether section 2(d) of the *Child Welfare Act* "overrules medical decisions by a mature minor, or whether (it) contravenes the *Charter* if it does so."[29]

(v) *Follow-Up*

On July 3, 2002, *The Globe and Mail* reported under the headline, "Cancer's spread ends girl's fight over transfusions", that a provincial court judge had dismissed an application by the province to extend guardianship over Bethany Hughes.[30] The judge made her ruling after hearing from the girl's physicians that they had stopped giving blood and that palliative care was all they could now offer. In response, the Minister of Child and Family Services stated publicly that the province would seek control over the girl's treatment if her condition were to improve. On July 11 the Supreme Court announced its refusal to hear an appeal against the Court of Appeal decision; it gave no reasons for its ruling. The following day Bethany was discharged from the Alberta Children's Hospital; she then entered an unidentified cancer clinic where a physician had agreed to treat her without blood products. This courageous young lady succumbed to her disease on September 5, 2002, two weeks after her 17th birthday. The immediate cause of death was congestive heart failure, caused by the provision of chemotherapy without blood. Her aggrieved father told the media:

> I did what I think any decent father would do — try to save their child's life at any cost. I'd do it all over again. I have no guilt whatsoever, nor any regrets.[31]

(b)   U. (C.) (Next Friend of) v. Alberta (Director of Child Welfare)[32]

C.U. was baptized as a Jehovah's Witness in 1999 when she was 15 years old, and one year later she was scheduled for a dilation and curettage procedure (D&C) to control excessive menstrual bleeding. She was admitted to hospital with "dysfunctional uterine bleeding" and informed by the admitting gynecologist, Dr. Mah, that she might require blood transfusion during the surgery. C.U. produced an advance medical directive/release card prohibiting blood and indicated to Dr. Mah that it meant what it said. The physician replied that if she needed blood she would die if it were not given. When the girl did not respond, her physician notified Child and Family Services who in turn contacted a Provincial Court judge.

The judge conducted an emergency treatment hearing at the hospital. Dr. Mah testified that blood was required in about 20% of D&C procedures and that she would give blood only if necessary to save C.U.'s life. The patient was represented by two members of the faith (neither a lawyer), one of whom asked Dr. Mah whether there were drug alternatives to blood; she replied that they would not work quickly enough. The patient was questioned and reaffirmed her position, which was supported by her parents. The judge ordered that the patient be apprehended as a child "in need of protection" and that blood be given if necessary. However, he gave no reasons for his decision.

An appeal was dismissed five months later by Justice Clarke of the Court of Queen's Bench. He opened his opinion by stating that the apprehension and treatment orders of the lower court judge "had been completed" (blood transfusions were in fact administered). Be that as it may, C.U. was seeking a declaration that she was a mature minor and hence that the orders were a nullity.

Although Justice Clarke acknowledged that the Alberta Court of Appeal had applied the mature minor doctrine in the *Wren* case (granting a 16-year-old the right to an abortion against parental opposition),* he distinguished that case on the grounds that it dealt with consent to treatment

---

* For whatever (unstated) reasons, he declined to deal with the *Charter* arguments raised by C.U. — that the treatment order breached sections 2, 7, and 15.

whereas the case before him involved a refusal of treatment. Furthermore, it was his view that, whatever the common law had to say about mature minors, section 2(d) of the *Child Welfare Act* controlled the outcome of the case before him. He concluded that the Act was the binding authority insofar as it granted the courts the power to declare a child "in need of protection" whenever the parents withhold consent to necessary medical treatment. He also brushed aside the question of decisional capacity, presumably because his position was that, if there is a blanket rule that a minor is not allowed to refuse treatment on best interest grounds, then it is simply beside the point whether or not she falls under the mature minor rule. Justice Clarke cited the *W. (A Minor), Re* case in support of his decision.

In February 2003, a three-judge panel of the Alberta Court of Appeal denied the patient's appeal from the decision by Justice Clarke. As the Court held:

> The mature minor rule does not apply in child welfare proceedings in which a child refuses to consent to essential treatment recommended by a physician. While the court must consider the expressed wishes of a mature child, it is not bound to comply with those wishes. Instead, the best interests of the child govern.

Recall that in the *Hughes* case, the Court of Appeal had ruled that it was unnecessary to consider whether section 2(d) of the *Child Welfare Act* "overrules medical decisions by a mature minor" because of the evidence that Bethany lacked decisional capacity. In the *McGonigle* case, the Court has now answered that question by ruling that, even if the patient qualifies as a mature minor, a treatment refusal stands only if it accords with her "best interests."

6. LAST WORD

There is a viewpoint that runs along the following lines. The true test of the mature minor's right to make her own health care decisions will come only when a court deplores the decision in a particular case but nonetheless rules that the right cannot be subject to judicial veto power. If the law is prepared to grant the mature minor the right to decide for herself, then that right becomes an empty shell unless judges are prepared to accord the same respect to the treatment decisions that they deplore as to the decisions that they accept. Be that as it may, one must acknowledge that the courts face no challenge greater than that of confronting the awesome complexities of adolescent decision-making in the face of life-threatening illness.

NOTES

1. *Children's Aid Society of Metropolitan Toronto v. K.* (1985), 48 R.F.L. (2d) 164 (Ont. Fam. Ct.).

2. *Y. (A.), Re* (1993), 111 Nfld. & P.E.I.R. 91, 348 A.P.R. 91 (Nfld. U.F.C.)

3. *Walker (Litigation Guardian of) v. Region 2 Hospital Corp.* (1994), [1994] N.B.J. No. 242, 1994 CarswellNB 24 (C.A.).

4. S.N.B. 1976, c. M-6.1.

5. *H. (T.) v. Children's Aid Society of Metropolitan Toronto* (1996), 138 D.L.R. (4th) 144 (Ont. Gen. Div.).

6. *D. (T.T.), Re* (1999), [1999] S.J. No. 143, 1999 CarswellSask 160 (Q.B.).

7. **National Post**, March 22, 1999, at A1.

8. **National Post**, July 6, 1999, at A13.

9. A.R. Holder, **Legal Issues in Pediatrics and Adolescent Medicine** (2nd ed.) (1985), at 130.

10. *C. (J.S.) v. Wren* (1986), [1987] 2 W.W.R. 669 (Alta. C.A.).

11. J.M. Gilmour, Children, Adolescents, and Health Care. In J. Downie & T. Caulfield (eds.) **Canadian Health Law and Policy** (2nd edition, Butterworth Canada, 2002), at 210.

12. *Health Care Consent Act*, 1996, S.O. 1996, c. 2, Schedule A.

13. *The Infants Act*, S.B.C. 1993, c. 196 [now am. R.S.B.C. 1996, c. 223].

14. *Kennett Estate v. Manitoba (Attorney General)* (1998), [1999] 1 W.W.R. 639 (Man. C.A.).

15. *Eldridge v. British Columbia (Attorney General)* (1997), 151 D.L.R. (4th) 577 (S.C.C.).

16. H. Gyles, Report on the inquest into the death of Daniel Kennett. 7 **Health Law in Canada** 57 (1986).

17. J.E. Schowalter et al., The adolescent patient's right to die. 51 **Pediatrics** 97 (1973).

18. Winnipeg Free Press, June 14, 1994, p. A9.

19. *W. (A Minor), Re*, [1992] 4 All E.R. 627 (C.A.).

20. *Ney v. Canada (Attorney General)* (1993), 102 D.L.R. (4th) 136 (B.C. S.C.). The same view was expressed by the Queen's Bench judge in the *Alberta (Director of Child Welfare) v. H. (B.)* case which is discussed shortly.

21. *Alberta (Director of Child Welfare) v. H. (B.)* (2002), [2002] A.J. No. 356, 2002 CarswellAlta 1045 (Prov. Ct.).

22. **Canadian Press**, February 20, 2002.

23. **National Post**, March 12, 2002.

24. **Calgary Herald**, April 5, 2002.

25. *Alberta (Director of Child Welfare) v. H. (B.)*, 2002 ABQB 371 (Q.B.), affirmed 2002 ABCA 109 (C.A.), additional reasons at 2002 ABCA 216

(C.A.), leave to appeal refused (2002), 2002 CarswellAlta 862, 2002 CarswellAlta 863 (S.C.C.), reconsideration refused 2003 ABCA 6 (C.A.).

26. *E. (A Minor), Re* (1990), [1993] 1 F.L.R. 386 (Eng. Fam. Div.).

27. *T. (adult: refusal of treatment), Re*, [1992] 4 All E.R. 653.

28. *United States v. George*, 239 F.Supp. 752 (1965); *Powell v. Columbian Presbyterian Medical Centre*, 267 N.Y.S.2d 450 (1965).

29. (2002), [2002] A.J. No. 568, 2002 CarswellAlta 621 (C.A.), additional reasons at 2002 ABCA 216 (C.A.), leave to appeal refused (2002), 2002 CarswellAlta 862, 2002 CarswellAlta 863 (S.C.C.), reconsideration refused 2003 ABCA 6 (C.A.).

30. **The Globe and Mail**, July 3, 2002, at A9.

31. **Winnipeg Free Press**, Sept. 6, 2002, at A1.

32. *U. (C.) (Next Friend of) v. Alberta (Director of Child Welfare)* (2000), [2000] A.J. No. 1067, 2000 CarswellAlta 967 (Q.B.) (sub nom. *U. (C.) v. McGonigle*, 2003 ABCA 66.

21

THE MENTALLY INCOMPETENT ADULT PATIENT AND THE FOREGOING OF LIFE-PROLONGING TREATMENT: THE AMERICAN PERSPECTIVE

SUMMARY

Beginning in 1976 with the *Quinlan* case, appellate courts in roughly half the American states have ruled that life-prolonging treatment can be withdrawn or withheld from mentally incompetent adult patients. In stark contrast, the medical practice of foregoing life-prolonging treatment for such patients has generated scant law in Canada. (The only two Canadian cases on point are considered in the following chapter.) Yet, like their American counterparts, Canadian physicians routinely accelerate the dying process by foregoing such interventions as cardiopulmonary resuscitation (CPR) pursuant to a do-not-resuscitate (DNR) order, artificial respiration/ventilation, tube feeding, dialysis, and antibiotics.

In short, Canadian medical practice functions as if the leading American cases were in effect the law in Canada as well. We therefore think it instructive to devote a chapter to the American jurisprudence on the termination of life-prolonging treatment for mentally incompetent patients. (Moreover, we strongly recommend that this chapter be read before turning to the next chapter on the Canadian perspective.) Leading American cases are discussed, including *Quinlan* and the 1990 U.S. Supreme Court decision in *Cruzan*. In the process of developing a substantial body of case law, the American courts have grappled with a number of questions, which are considered in turn. What

medical indications are sufficient to enable physicians to withdraw or withhold life-support measures from incompetent patients? Who should be legally empowered to exercise "the right to die" on the incompetent patient's behalf? What standards apply to surrogate decision-makers? Is it permissible to hasten death by withholding nutrition and hydration? Is it lawful to let patients die pursuant to do-not-resuscitate (DNR) orders on their charts? Do patients or their surrogate decision-makers have a positive right to insist upon measures that their caregivers reject as medically futile? Finally, what is the legal basis for the cessation of life-prolonging treatment for incompetent patients?

Bear in mind that the focus of this chapter is upon mentally incompetent patients who do not have health care directives (popularly called "living wills") that are provided for by statute. Since most patients (be they American or Canadian) do not have such directives, the cases canvassed in this chapter are of obvious relevance to end of life decision-making for incompetent patients. Health care directives is the subject matter of Chapter 24.

1. THE TWO LANDMARK CASES

(a) Karen Ann Quinlan (New Jersey, 1976)[1]

On the night of April 15, 1975, Karen Ann Quinlan, 21, collapsed after a party and apparently ceased breathing for at least two 15-minute periods. On admission to hospital her condition was described as a "coma of unknown etiology." Her friends, who had summoned the police, provided scant information: and the history in the hospital records was essentially incomplete and uninformative. The emergency room physician reported normal vital signs, unreactive pupils, unresponsiveness to deep pain, a low blood oxygen level, and her legs in a rigid curled position. Because she could not breathe spontaneously, she was connected to a respirator.

Blood and urine tests "indicated the presence of quinine, aspirin, barbiturates...and traces of valium and librium." A physician who reviewed Karen's medical records concluded that the drugs were within "therapeutic range" and that the quinine was consistent with that used in mixed drinks. Karen had consumed several gin-and-tonics during that ill-fated party and (according to her date) had been "popping pills" earlier that day.

At 10 p.m. next day she was examined by a neurologist, Dr. Morse, who found evidence of decortication (a derangement of the cerebral cortex causing a physical posture in which the upper extremities are flexed and the lower extremities extended). An EEG indicated an abnormal electrical rhythm, which the neurologist considered "consistent with her clinical state." Other neurological tests — brain scan, cerebral angiogram, and lumbar puncture — were all normal in result. Dr. Morse was unable to obtain an adequate account of the circumstances prior to her admission, and the cause of her collapse and loss of spontaneous respiration has remained a mystery. He concluded that she had a lesion on the cerebral hemispheres and a lesion in the brain stem. At the trial he testified that, in the absence of a clear history, he had based his opinion regarding the brain lesion sites upon the patient's decorticate posturing and respiratory difficulty.

According to Dr. Morse, Karen was initially in a sleep-like unresponsive condition but soon developed "sleep-wake" cycles. She would blink and cry out but otherwise remained unresponsive to her environment. His opinion was that Karen was in a "chronic persistent vegetative state."

The attending physicians (Dr. Morse, and Dr. Javed, a pulmonary internist) could offer no hope to her parents that she would ever regain cognitive functioning. Attempts to wean Karen from the respirator proved futile, and her devoutly Roman Catholic parents reluctantly decided that artificial life-support measures be withdrawn so that she could die a natural death. On July 31 Karen's parents signed a written consent directing her attending physicians "to discontinue all extraordinary measures, including the use of a respirator." The document also released the physicians and hospital "from any and all liability." Although Drs. Morse and Javed had initially concurred with the parental decision, they backed off when their insurance company questioned the legality of the decision to stop life-support. The physicians, supported by the hospital, then informed the parents that they would comply only pursuant to a court order. On September 10, Mr. Quinlan filed a petition in the Superior Court, seeking appointment as Karen's guardian for the express purpose of directing the removal of her respirator.

The trial opened on October 20. Superior Court Judge Muir* heard from three neurologists who had examined Karen on October 2 in the presence of Drs. Morse and Javed. He summarized their evidence:

A general synopsis of their testimonies indicates that they found Karen comatose, emaciated, and in a posture of extreme flexion and rigidity of the

---

* Three years later it was Judge Muir who decided the *Quackenbush* case, which is discussed in Chapter 19.

arms, legs, and related muscles, which could not be overcome, with her joints severely rigid and deformed. During the examination she went through awake and sleep periods but mostly awake. The eyes moved spontaneously. She made stereotyped cries and sounds, and her mouth opened wide when she did so. Cries were evoked when there was noxious stimulation. She reflexed to noxious stimuli. Her pupils reacted to light and her retinas were normal. Her reflex activity, deep tendon reflexes, and plantar stimulation of soles of her feet could not be elicited because of the severe flexion contractures. She triggered the respirator during the entire examination except for the interval of removal. When she was removed from the respirator, with an oxygen catheter inserted through the tracheostomy, she breathed spontaneously and her blood gases were in the normal range. Her EEG showed normal electrical activity for a sedated person. (She was sedated for the EEG.)

All (the medical witnesses) agree she is in a persistent vegetative state. She is described as having irreversible brain damage; no cognitive or cerebral functioning; chances for useful sapient life or return of discriminative functioning are remote.

The Court also heard from a neurologist who had examined Karen on a separate occasion, and his testimony was summarized:

His description of Karen's posturing, reflexes, eyes, body movements, and other conditions did not vary significantly from the other experts. His diagnosis of the extent and area of the brain injury or lesion — in the cerebral hemisphere with brain stem involvement — essentially agrees with that of Dr. Morse. He described the upper brain area injury as a severe bilateral cerebral involvement with anoxia as the probable cause. He found a palmomental reflex, evidencing interruption in the brain stem fiber. He indicates the extensiveness of the reflex, a dimpling of the chin generated by stimulation of the palm, is greater than usually found because any stimulation along the entire arm generated it. He described her condition as a persistent vegetative state.

After a seven-day trial, Judge Muir denied the petition. The medical witnesses had all testified that Karen could not sustain life if removed from the respirator, and the judge ruled that he was duty bound to protect the life of a helpless and disabled person. Although admittedly in a permanent vegetative state, Karen was not brain-dead. Since she was legally alive, Judge Muir was not prepared to authorize an act that presumably would bring about certain death.

Mr. Quinlan appealed the decision to the Supreme Court of New Jersey. In March 1976 (11 months after Karen's admission to hospital), the Court reversed the trial judge's ruling. It held that Karen had a right to die that flowed from her *constitutional right of privacy*, and that the only way to guarantee that right was by enabling her father to assert it on her behalf. The Court concluded that artificial respiration could be terminated, provided that "there is no reasonable possibility of Karen's ever emerging from her present comatose condition to a cognitive, sapient state."

When the prognosis was confirmed respiration was stopped, but Karen confounded the medical experts by breathing on her own. (Apparently one of her physicians had secretly weaned her off the respirator.) Her birthdays were duly noted by the media and she lived on until June 11, 1985, when she died in a New Jersey nursing home of "respiratory failure following acute pneumonia." Throughout the years of daily vigil at her bedside, her parents did not object to tube feeding but were prepared to withhold antibiotics in the event that she contracted pneumonia. When that happened, their wish was honoured and their daughter allowed to die. Karen, who was 5'4" in height, weighed about 65 pounds at the time of death. Her bones had long since calcified into a rigid fetal position, and for 10 years her face had remained expressionless except for an occasional frown.

(b) Nancy Cruzan (U.S. Supreme Court, 1990)[2]

Nancy Cruzan, 25, was discovered lying face down in a ditch after her vehicle overturned on a winter's night in Missouri, and she was deprived of oxygen for at least 12-14 minutes before paramedics were able to restore her breathing and heartbeat at the accident site. She arrived in hospital in a coma, and in time she was diagnosed as in a permanent vegetative state. In 1987, four years after the accident, her parents asked the hospital administration to allow her to die by stopping her tube-feeding; and its refusal prompted the Cruzans to petition the Probate Court for authority to force compliance with their wishes.

According to the medical evidence, the accident had caused cerebral cortical atrophy which was irreversible, permanent, progressive, and ongoing. She was in a permanent vegetative state and aggressive treatment could prolong her life another 30 years. At the trial Nancy's roommate testified that a year before the accident, Nancy had confided to her that she would never wish to live as a "vegetable" and that "she knew it was usually up to the family whether you lived that way or not." However, the roommate acknowledged that on that occasion Nancy did not directly express her wishes on the withdrawal of life-prolonging hydration and nutrition.

The Probate Court judge granted the petition and the state attorney general appealed to the Missouri Supreme Court, which in a 4-3 decision reversed the order approving the termination of Nancy's artificial feeding. The majority concluded that her statements to her roommate were "unreliable for the purpose of determining her intent", and that no person could authorize the termination of life-prolonging medical treatment for an incompetent patient in the absence of "clear and convincing" evidence that such decision would accord with the previously expressed intent of the patient.* The Court stated that it was compelled to that result because of its commitment to the "absolute sanctity of human life."

The Cruzans appealed and again suffered a narrow defeat when the U.S. Supreme Court affirmed the Missouri Supreme Court decision by a 5-4 margin. The majority ruled that there was no denying Missouri's interest in "the protection and preservation of human life", and that "Missouri may legitimately seek to safeguard the personal element of the choice (between life and death) through the imposition of heightened evidentiary requirements."

Chief Justice Rhenquist ruled that a state is entitled to assert an "unqualified interest in the preservation of human life" by declining to make "quality of life" judgments. In other words, the states are free to choose to follow the New Jersey path (no such evidence required) or the Missouri path (such evidence required). Hence there is no constitutional bar to a state policy that life-prolonging treatment cannot be terminated for a mentally incompetent patient unless there is clear and convincing evidence that the patient would have wanted the particular treatment terminated. In that regard, he stressed that Nancy's comments to her roommate "did not deal in terms of withdrawal of medical treatment or of hydration and nutrition." Although the Chief Justice expressed concern for the tragic plight of the Cruzan family and did not question their love and devotion for Nancy, he was constrained to add:

> Close family members may have a strong feeling — a feeling not at all ignoble or unworthy, but not entirely disinterested, either — that they do not wish to witness the continuation of the life of a loved one which they regard as hopeless, meaningless, and even degrading. But there is no automatic assurance that the view of close family members will necessarily be the same as the patient's would have been had she been confronted with the prospect of her situation while competent. The State may choose to defer only to those wishes (of the patient while competent), rather than confide the decision to close family members.

---

*   The "clear and convincing" standard is not as onerous as the burden in criminal cases — "beyond a reasonable doubt". But it is more onerous than the civil standard of preponderance of probabilities. From judicial pronouncements one can infer that along a continuum it lies substantially closer to the criminal burden than to the civil burden.

In his dissenting opinion, Justice Stephens deplored the majority view for failing to respect "the best interests of the patient." He emphatically rejected its position that:

> A person's Constitutional right to be free from unwanted treatment is thereby categorically limited to those patients who had the foresight to make an unambiguous statement of their wishes while competent.... The Court's decision affords no protection to children, to young people who are the victims of unexpected accidents or illnesses, or to the countless thousands of elderly persons who either fail to decide, or fail to explain, how they want to be treated if they should experience a similar fate.

A similar concern was underscored by Justice Brennan in his dissenting opinion:

> Too few people execute living wills or equivalently formal directives for such an evidentiary rule to ensure adequately that the wishes of incompetent persons will be honoured. While it might be a wise social policy to encourage people to furnish such instructions, no general conclusion about a patient's choice can be drawn from the absence of formalities. The probability of becoming irreversibly vegetative is so low that many people may not feel an urgency to marshal formal evidence of their preferences. Some may not wish to dwell on their own physical deterioration and mortality. Even someone with a resolute determination to avoid life-support under circumstances such as Nancy's would still need to know that living wills exist and how to execute one. Often legal help would be necessary, especially given the majority's apparent willingness to permit States to insist that a person's wishes are not truly known unless the particular medical treatment is specified.

In sum, by a 5-4 margin the Supreme Court endorsed the position that a state *may* mandate — as a precondition for the termination of life-prolonging treatment for an incompetent patient — that when competent the patient had the foresight to predict her fate and specify with precision the particular treatments that would no longer be acceptable. However, the ruling left intact the line of cases beginning with *Quinlan*, in which about two dozen state courts have permitted surrogate decision-makers to authorize the termination of life-support measures for incompetent patients. What the Supreme Court ruled in *Cruzan* was simply that a state is not constitutionally obliged to march in step with the *Quinlan* line of cases.

The Cruzans responded to the Supreme Court ruling by petitioning the Probate Court to consider new evidence regarding Nancy's wishes. Co-workers testified as to conversations in which Nancy had stressed her abhorrence at living "like a vegetable", and the judge ruled that such evidence was sufficient to meet the clear and convincing standard even though Nancy had not specifically addressed the question of artificial nutrition and hydration. (One cannot help but wonder whether this was contrived testimony but its validity was not questioned. The state had proven its point and at this stage it was not prepared to contest the family's last ditch effort to end its nightmare.) There was no appeal and Nancy Cruzan died on December 26, 1990, 12 days after her feeding tube was removed.

2. COMMENTARY ON AMERICAN CASE LAW

In stark contrast to the United States, issues regarding the withholding/ withdrawing of life-prolonging measures for mentally incompetent patients have generated but scant law in Canada. Yet, like their American colleagues, Canadian physicians routinely accelerate the dying process by foregoing such interventions as CPR pursuant to a DNR order, mechanical ventilation, tube feeding, dialysis, and antibiotics. These medical practices reflect the assumption by physicians and nurses (and their institutions) that they act within the law when they hasten death for patients unable to speak for themselves. In that sense, Canadian caregivers function as if the general trend of American case law were the law in Canada as well. For that reason a survey of the American law is in order. (The Canadian jurisprudence is found in the following chapter.)

Although clinical practice has been influenced by the law that we here canvass, recourse to the courts is rarely invoked during the course of end-of-life decision-making. For one thing, the sheer volume of such cases is enough to preclude judicial sanction as the norm. As Justice Brennan noted in the *Cruzan* case:

> Of the approximately 2 million people who die each year, 80% die in hospitals and long-term institutions...and perhaps 70% of these after a decision to forego life sustaining treatment has been made.[3]

The cases that wind up in court are therefore but the very small tip of a very large iceberg. They happen in the rare instances in which there is irreconcilable conflict between physicians and the families of incompetent patients.* As in *Quinlan* and *Cruzan*, the reported cases typically involve families seeking to end life and physicians/health care facilities seeking to prolong life — or else the latter are willing to comply only when the family's wishes are buttressed by a court order. However, in recent years an opposite trend has emerged: so-called futility cases in which families oppose decisions to cease life-prolonging measures. Still, the absence of

---

* The role of the family in end-of-life decision-making is considered in the following chapter.

conflict between interested parties does not mean that the law is irrelevant. Physicians and health care facilities are prepared to forego life-support measures because they know that their actions are sheltered by a broad legal consensus which has evolved over the past three decades.

In any event, *Quinlan* is the first of a long line of American cases authorizing the medical practice of foregoing life-prolonging treatment for mentally incompetent patients. The cases have predominantly involved petitions by next-of-kin for judicial authorization to hasten death for incompetent loved ones. In the process, the courts have grappled with the following questions, each of which will be considered in turn:

(a) What medical indications are sufficient to enable physicians to withdraw or withhold life-support measures from incompetent patients?

(b) Who should be legally empowered to authorize the termination of treatment?

(c) What standards of surrogate decision-making should apply?

(d) Do patients or their surrogate decision-makers have a right to insist upon the continuation of life-prolonging measures deemed futile by the physicians?

(e) If the patient is not respirator-dependent, is it permissible to hasten death by removing or clamping the feeding tube?

(f) Do physicians/nurses act lawfully when death occurs without an attempt to resuscitate pursuant to a DNR order on the patient's chart?

(g) What is the legal basis for the incompetent patient's right to the foregoing of life-prolonging treatment?

(a) Medical Indications For Terminating Treatment

The trail blazing case is of course the 1976 decision by the New Jersey Supreme Court in *Quinlan*. Recall that the Court ruled that Karen's life-support apparatus could be removed so long as there was "no reasonable possibility" that she would ever emerge from her "present comatose condition to a cognitive, sapient state." The precedent set in *Quinlan* has been followed by most of the appellate courts that have considered the question whether a prognosis of *irreversible coma* or *permanent vegetative state* is sufficient in itself to warrant the termination of life-support apparatus at the request of family members. (As we have seen, there is a minority position that the Supreme Court in *Cruzan* allowed to stand along side the Quinlan-majority position.) In any event, the *Quinlan*-majority opinion reflects the public policy that indefinite life-support maintenance for such patients is neither morally nor legally obligatory. Given the prognosis of irreversible unconsciousness, continued treatment is generally regarded as a pointless exercise in futility.

From a medical standpoint, one must distinguish between a coma and a permanent vegetative state (PVS) because they define separate neurological states. The former refers to eyes-closed unconsciousness, whereas the latter refers to eyes-open unconsciousness because PVS patients have sleep/wake cycles, although there is no conscious awareness. (While the adjectives "persistent" and "permanent" are often used interchangeably for vegetative patients, the former is a diagnosis whereas the latter is a prognosis.) According to the Multi-Society Task Force on PVS of the American Academy of Neurology, the vegetative state is characterized by the following features:[4]

1. No evidence of awareness of self or environment and the inability to interact with others.
2. No evidence of sustained, reproducible, purposeful or voluntary behaviourial response to visual, auditory, tactile, or noxious stimuli.
3. No evidence of language comprehension or expression.
4. Intermittent wakefulness manifested by the presence of sleep-wake cycles.
5. Sufficiently preserved hypothalamic and brain-stem autonomic functions to permit survival with medical and nursing care.
6. Bowel and bladder incontinence.
7. Variably preserved cranial-nerve reflexes (pupillary, oculolocephalic corneal, vestibulo-ocular and gag, cough, sucking and swallowing) and spinal reflexes.

What about the legal response to patient conditions that fall short of permanent unconsciousness? In a 1985 case, *Conroy, Re*,[5] the New Jersey Supreme Court authorized the removal of an incompetent 84-year-old patient's nasogastric tube. Claire Conroy was a bedridden nursing home resident left severely demented by an organic brain syndrome. She was also afflicted with atherosclerotic heart disease, hypertension, and diabetes mellitus. Her left leg was gangrenous to the knee, and she had several necrotic decubitus ulcers on her left foot, leg, and knee. She required a urinary catheter, had no bowel control, and could not move from a semi-fetal position. Ms. Conroy was unable to speak and her limited ability to swallow necessitated the insertion of the feeding-tube. However, she could move her head, neck, hands, and arms to a limited extent. She could scratch herself and would moan when moved or fed or when she experienced pain. Her eyes would sometimes follow persons in her room, and she would smile on occasion such as when her hair was combed or her body rubbed. The prognosis was death in approximately one year. In the result, she died not long after her nephew (who had known her for over 50 years) sought a court order for the removal of her feeding-tube. The case nonetheless continued until its resolution by the Court that had decided *Quinlan* nine years earlier.

In the *Conroy* case, the high court of New Jersey ruled that an incompetent patient's life-prolonging treatment could be terminated even though the patient was not in a state of irreversible unconsciousness. The Court's basic premise was that "the goal of decision-making for incompetent patients should be to determine and effectuate, insofar as possible, the decision that the patient would have made if competent." It therefore concluded that life-support measures could be halted "when it is clear that the particular patient would have refused the treatment under the circumstances involved." In the absence of such evidence, the Court would permit the cessation of treatment only when: (1) the patient had a life expectancy limited to roughly one year; and (2) "the net burdens of the patient's life with treatment clearly and markedly outweigh the benefits that the patient derives from life."

The Court's approach was to extend to the health care context the two legal standards for managing domestic and property affairs for mentally incompetent persons: the *substituted judgment* test and the *best interests* test (which will be discussed shortly). The Court found insufficient evidence to apply the substituted judgment test (that Claire Conroy would if competent choose to die). Instead, it concluded that her feeding-tube could be removed on the basis of the best interests test (that for the patient herself, it was more burdensome than beneficial to be kept alive). The Court went out of its way to caution against misreading its ruling to mean that there are patients whose deaths are no loss to society:

> We expressly decline to authorize decision-making based on assessments of the personal worth or social utility of another's life, or the value of that life to others. The mere fact that a patient's functioning is limited or his prognosis dim does not mean that he is not enjoying what remains of his life, or that it is in his best interests to die. More wide-ranging powers to make decisions about other people's lives, in our view, would create an intolerable risk for socially isolated and defenceless people suffering from physical or mental handicaps.

The *Conroy* precedent has been followed in other jurisdictions. In a 1987 decision, *In the Matter of Beth Israel Medical Center*,[6] a New York trial court denied the hospital's petition for authority to amputate the gangrenous leg of a mentally incompetent 74-year-old patient. The patient,

Sadie Weinstein, a partially paralysed and aphasic nursing home resident, was admitted to hospital following her second stroke. (Two years earlier, she had suffered a massive cerebral occlusion that left her totally paralysed on her right side.) In hospital she was afflicted with an occlusion of the left iliac artery, and gangrene resulted from the impeded circulation in her left leg. Although not comatose, the patient had "very little cognitive functioning." She could no longer communicate in any manner and evinced no awareness of her surroundings. In summarizing the testimony of her attending neurologist, the judge stated:

> Though she may feel pain, she probably does not realize it as such. Her physical responses to external stimuli are at best haphazard. She is completely bed-bound and, since her latest episode affected her ability to swallow, she must be fed through a nasogastric (N/G) tube. In the neurologist's opinion, the patient presents a neurological condition which not only is irreversible but which can be expected to deteriorate further.

Evidence was presented by two surgeons — the acting chief of the surgery service at the hospital and a vascular surgeon from another hospital who was appointed by the judge to conduct an independent evaluation of the patient's need for surgery. They agreed that unless a mid-thigh amputation were promptly performed, sepsis would set in and cause her death within a matter of weeks. The surgeons concurred with the opinion of the patient's internist that she was a "poor or at best a fair risk" to survive surgery.

The patient's only relative was her sister, Lillian. Until her nursing home admission (occasioned by her first stroke), the patient and her sister had lived together all their lives. Their close relationship over a lifetime led Lillian to believe that, if mentally competent, her sister would choose to forego the surgery. For that reason, Lillian was adamantly opposed to the recommended amputation. As a matter of general policy, the judge stated that

> no life-shortening course of action should be contemplated unless the patient is, at the very least, suffering from severe and permanent mental and physical debilitation and with a very limited natural life expectancy.

He proceeded to deny the hospital's petition because there was "clear and convincing evidence that the burdens of continued life for this patient markedly outweigh the benefits that further life would bring." The judge took painstaking care to explain his decision:

> Ms. Weinstein is presently without any functioning intellect or meaningful awareness of life around her. Though not entirely comatose, she is, for all

practical purposes, merely existing. She cannot understand or speak. Her paralysis has left her immobile on her right (side) and her left side is now affected. Thus, she will never be able to move on her own. Even if she can withstand the surgery, her debilitated condition can only be expected to worsen.

Life has no meaning for her. She derives no physical or emotional pleasure of any degree, nor any intellectual satisfaction in her day to day existence. She will remain completely dependent on others. She will always need an N/G tube which, aside from its discomfort, poses a continuing risk of aspiration and pneumonia.

Of further importance in this matter was the opinion of the (vascular) surgeon who when asked, stated he would be reluctant to recommend surgery for this patient. He felt it was both medically and ethically unsound, since its net medical benefit would be marginal.

In sum, other than to afford this patient the potential for limited additional life, the proposed surgery offers her no other benefit. If performed it would not to any degree return this patient to an integrated functioning or cognitive existence. It would, at best, unnecessarily prolong the natural process of her dying. There is no human or humane benefit to be gained from subjecting Sadie Weinstein to the pain and body mutilation this surgery will present. She should be permitted to die with dignity.

In another 1987 case, *In re Guardianship of Grant*,[7] the Washington (State) Supreme Court ruled that life-prolonging treatment could be withheld from Barbara Grant, 22, who was in the advanced stages of Batten's disease, an inherited degenerative condition of the central nervous system. Most victims of the disease die in their teens or early twenties, and Barbara had followed its typical pattern. The disease process was described by the Court:

Victims of the disease usually start life as normal appearing children. The first symptom is a problem with vision, followed by epileptic seizures and a loss of motor control which cause the child to stagger. Later, the child has speech difficulties. Eventually, the child can no longer walk or talk and is completely blind. Batten's disease also causes severe mental retardation, with intellectual functions progressively failing. The child develops difficulty with swallowing, caused by a loss of voluntary muscle control. Brain control of the heart and lungs deteriorates, initially causing irregular heart rate and breathing, and finally, cardiac or respiratory arrest.

When she was 14, Barbara was admitted to a state institution for disabled children (Rainier School) because her parents could no longer care for her at home. By that time she was blind and moderately retarded. Seven years later her parents petitioned for a court order that "life support systems" be withheld in the event of either cardiac or respiratory arrest or the inability to swallow. They were moved to seek legal action because the institution's stated policy was to resort to all measures necessary to sustain life, however dismal the prognosis. (Shortly before they filed their petition, the medical nurse at the Rainier School had administered CPR and oxygen when Barbara experienced respiratory distress.) Barbara's condition at the time the petition was filed was summarized by the Court:

> She could not walk or feed herself, and had urinary and bowel incontinence. She could not turn from side to side in bed, lying most of the time on her right side with her hands clenched or crossed and tightly pulled to her chest. She could not sit up in a wheelchair by herself, had no control over her head and only limited use of her hands. She had to be tied in bed to be restrained from harmful movement caused by seizures. She had more and more difficulty swallowing food.

> Barbara's intellectual and cognitive functions had virtually disappeared. She was unable to respond to a standard intelligence test, and the psychologist at Ranier School estimated her mental age to be between 2 weeks and 1 (and) 1/2 months. Barbara had, at most, only a fleeting awareness of her environment. Although she could still respond to sound, she showed little if any awareness of music. She would occasionally smile or laugh, but at inappropriate times. She could still feel sensation and respond to touch, and occasionally differentiate between people she liked and disliked. However, she no longer responded at all to the presence of her father, mother, or brother, Edward.

The trial court heard from medical witnesses that Barbara was in the "terminal stages" of the disease. Her parents testified that they opposed intrusive medical treatment because it would serve only to delay her inevitable and imminent death. They asked that the Court prohibit the use of the following measures: cardio-pulmonary resuscitation, artificial respiration, intubation, and naso-gastric and intravenous feeding. The trial court denied the petition by ruling that it was "premature", as Barbara was not yet faced with the need for such intrusive medical procedures. It was reversed on appeal by the state supreme court on the grounds that

> a person has the right to have life-sustaining treatment withheld when he or she (1) is in an advanced stage of a terminal and incurable illness, and (2) is suffering severe and permanent mental and physical deterioration.

In sum, as the cases indicate it is not so much the particular prognosis that counts, but rather the question whether that prognosis is sufficiently grim to warrant the cessation of life-prolonging treatment (although as we shall see, the incompetent patient may in effect have a say in the matter because of a prior oral declaration or health care directive).

(b) Who Decides and By What Criteria?

In a 1993 law journal article, "The Legal Consensus About Forgoing Life-Sustaining Treatment: Its Status and its Prospects",[8] Professor Alan Meisel observed that

> a judicial consensus has emerged — reflecting a strongly held view in the medical profession — that decisions about life-sustaining treatment are best made in the clinical setting and that ordinarily the courts should not be involved.

The trend was set in *Quinlan*, where the New Jersey Supreme Court stated that as a general rule judicial involvement was not only unnecessary but also inadvisable in decision-making for mentally incompetent patients:

> We consider that a practice of applying to a court to confirm such decisions would generally be inappropriate, not only because this would be a gratuitous encroachment upon the medical profession's field of competence, but because it would be impossibly cumbersome. Decision-making within health care...should be controlled primarily within the patient-doctor-family relationship.

Eleven years later the New Jersey Supreme Court underscored that sentiment in two cases, *Peter, Re*[9] and *Jobes, Re*.[10] As it observed in *Peter*:

> Courts are not the proper place to resolve the agonizing personal problems that underlie these cases. Our legal system cannot replace the more intimate struggle that must be borne by the patient, those caring for the patient, and those who care about the patient.

And in *Jobes*:

> Normally those family members close enough to make a substituted judgment would be a spouse, parents, adult children, or siblings. Generally in the absence of such a close degree of kinship, we would not countenance health care professionals deferring to the relatives of a patient.... However, if the attending health care professionals determine that another relative, e.g., a cousin, aunt, uncle, niece, or nephew, functions in the role of the patient's nuclear family, then that relative can and should be treated as a close and caring family member.

The New Jersey position has found widespread support elsewhere. The American cases have by and large involved patients with next-of-kin, thus obviating the necessity to determine the appropriate surrogate for patients without available family. That issue is essentially unresolved, although there are indications that the courts will accept surrogates from friendship circles (e.g. for AIDS patients). On the other hand, if there really is no one who can assume the surrogate role, then the courts deem it advisable to seek judicial appointment of a guardian.

In sum, the cases reflect a judicial consensus that the hospital — not the courtroom — is the proper setting for the decision-making process for incompetent patients. Still, there is a role for the courts to play when there is no physician-surrogate consensus on the appropriate course of action. If, for example, there is irreconcilable conflict within the family or between the family and the health care team on the advisability of foregoing life-prolonging measures, then the courtroom becomes the appropriate forum for resolution.

Although decision-making is thus relegated to the clinical setting, the ultimate responsibility still rests with the attending physician. The reason is that American law reflects a judicial reliance upon the good faith judgments of physicians who do not choose to stave off death at all cost. New Jersey Supreme Court Justice Alan Handler has suggested that the decisions in the American right-to-die cases

> can be seen as a form of judicial deregulation, as a cautious withdrawal of judicial oversight from the decisions of private parties. They can also be seen as a form of delegation, entailing a deference to the medical and health-care professions, as a belief that the standards governing the doctor-patient relationship, and the procedures developed by hospitals are together sufficient to allow us to trust the resulting treatment decisions.[11]

(c)   Standards of Surrogate Decision-Making: Effectuating the Incompetent Patient's Wants or Needs

Regarding standards of treatment decision-making for mentally incompetent patients, there is a judicial consensus that if the patient when competent had indicated his treatment preferences, then his wishes must be followed. This is referred to as the *subjective standard*. If that is the situation in a particular case, then there is no need for surrogate decision-making (someone making a decision for the patient). That is because the patient will have made the treatment decision beforehand — either by way of oral instructions or a written health care directive. The former scenario is illustrated by the *Brother Fox (Eichner v. Dillon)* case (New York,

1981).[12] In 1979, Brother Joseph Fox, an 83-year-old member of the Roman Catholic Order of the Society of Mary, suffered a cardiac arrest during surgery to repair an inguinal hernia. He sustained severe brain damage, slipping into a coma and requiring artificial respiration. His attending physician informed Father Philip Eichner — his close friend for 26 years and the director of the school where Brother Fox had lived in semi-retirement — that his condition was hopeless and that there was no reasonable chance that he would ever regain consciousness.

The priest called in two neurosurgeons who confirmed that Brother Fox was in a state of irreversible unconsciousness. When Father Eichner then asked the hospital to stop life-support measures, it refused to comply without a court order. He promptly filed a petition seeking court appointment as guardian of the person of Brother Fox for the express purpose of directing the cessation of treatment. His petition was supported by all the patient's surviving relatives (10 nieces and nephews). It was also accompanied by affidavits from Brother Fox's attending physician and neurosurgeon, which stated that "diffuse cerebral and brain stem anoxia" had caused the patient to lapse into a "permanent vegetative state."

At the trial Father Eichner testified that he and Brother Fox had often discussed the *Quinlan* case, and that Brother Fox had expressed his agreement with the Roman Catholic position that in such cases a ventilator is "extraordinary" treatment. According to the Church, extraordinary means that the treatment offers no reasonable hope of benefit for the patient and may legitimately be withdrawn or withheld, even if it hastens death. Months before his surgery Brother Fox had remarked to Father Eichner that he would oppose such "extraordinary business" if he were ever in a hopeless condition. The point is that Father Eichner was not seeking the status of a surrogate decision-maker. Rather his role was that of a messenger — reporting the specific treatment direction of the patient who was no longer able to speak for himself.

The trial judge granted Father Eichner's petition but his decision was appealed by the hospital. However, before the case could be resolved Brother Fox died of congestive heart failure — five months after the surgery from which he never regained consciousness. His death notwithstanding, the appeal process continued because all parties agreed that the case presented questions that likely would recur. (Given the protracted nature of legal proceedings, it is not surprising that the patient died before the case was resolved. That has happened in many of the leading cases, including the aforementioned *Conroy* case.) Fourteen months after Brother Fox's death, the New York Court of Appeal* upheld the lower court's ruling on the following grounds:

1. A mentally competent adult patient has a common law right to refuse medical treatment.

2. This right is extended to an incompetent patient who when competent had expressed the view that his life should not be prolonged by artificial means, if and when his health were to fail and his prognosis was hopeless.

3. While competent Brother Fox had indicated his aversion to being kept alive in a Quinlan-type situation, and that precise contingency had arisen.

4. The sentiments expressed by Brother Fox to Father Eichner were "obviously solemn pronouncements and not casual remarks made at some social gathering."

5. The guardian was standing in for Brother Fox and in that capacity was seeking to enforce the patient's common law right to direct his future course of medical management, if and when he became incompetent to issue a direct order for the cessation of life-support measures.

The Court emphasized that it was not obliged to consider whether a decision to discontinue life-support measures could be made by someone other than the patient. The reason was that "Brother Fox made the decision for himself before he became incompetent." As the Court explained:

> He carefully reflected on the subject, expressed his views and concluded not to have his life prolonged by medical means if there were no hope of recovery. These were obviously solemn pronouncements and not casual remarks made at some social gathering, nor can it be said that he was too young to realize or feel the consequences of his statements. That this was a persistent commitment is evidenced by the fact that he reiterated the decision but two months before his final hospitalization. In sum, the evidence clearly and convincingly shows that Brother Fox did not want to be maintained in a vegetative coma by use of a respirator.

In short, the Court was satisfied from the evidence that Father Eichner was acting to enforce the very decision that the patient had projected before his surgery. Keep in mind that the Court would have come to the same result if the patient's wishes had been documented in his chart.

An illustrative case involving a written directive is *John F. Kennedy Memorial Hospital v. Bludworth* (Florida, 1984).[13] Admitted to hospital

---

* In New York, as throughout Canada, the Court of Appeal is the jurisdiction's supreme court.

for acute respiratory failure, chronic pulmonary interstitial fibrosis, and gastro-intestinal bleeding, the patient had stopped breathing and lapsed into a permanent vegetative state. The patient's wife applied for a court order allowing her to enforce the termination of artificial ventilation. She entered into evidence a document, entitled "Mercy Will and Last Testament", that the patient had executed six years earlier. It contained a provision that categorically rejected the use of "extraordinary life-support equipment such as a respirator" in the event that he were hopelessly and terminally ill. She also testified that as recently as two months before his admission to hospital, she had promised him that if he were hospitalized she would see that the document was entered on his chart.

Although the patient had died in the interim the case wound its way to the Florida Supreme Court, which ruled that the "living or mercy will" was "persuasive evidence of the incompetent person's intention and should be given great weight" by the surrogate decision-maker. Even though there was no living will — now called health care directive or advance directive — statute in Florida at the time, the Court nonetheless held that such a document could serve as the basis for a decision to terminate a PVS patient's life-prolonging treatment. (The legislature responded to the *Bludworth* decision by enacting a living will statute.*)

What, then, if the patient has not left oral or written instructions to guide specific treatment decisions at such time that the patient lacks decision-making capacity. In that event, medical ethicists posit two principles of biomedical ethics — *autonomy* and *beneficence* — as setting the standards of surrogate decision-making for patients unable to speak for themselves. The *substituted judgment* and *best interests tests* are the respective legal mechanisms that apply these principles on behalf of mentally incompetent patients. The former pursues the goal of patient autonomy because it seeks to implement the decision that the patient would make if competent to decide for herself. The latter is by definition a commitment to beneficence.

The majority view, beginning with the *Quinlan* case, is that the surrogate decision-maker should seek to apply the substituted judgment test and only turn to the best interests test when there is no evidence supporting the application of substituted judgment. (There is, of course, no room for the substituted judgment test when the patient was never competent — e.g. a young child or an adult with life-long severe mental disability.)

In stark contrast is the Missouri/New York approach (affirmed in *Cruzan*), which rejects the surrogate's role altogether by stipulating that

---

* There are now statutes in all 50 states (34 since 1984) which recognize the so-called living will, which is the subject of Chapter 24.

life-prolonging measures cannot be foregone for an incompetent patient unless, when competent, the patient had rejected the particular treatment in issue. This view applies whether or not the patient is in a permanent vegetative state. On the other hand, there is the Michigan/California approach which does not allow the surrogate to decide when the patient has a minimal degree of consciousness. If the patient had not rejected the particular treatment when competent, then the treatment cannot be stopped. The middle ground view — as illustrated by the state supreme courts of Kentucky and Maryland — is that the surrogate's empowerment is restricted to the substituted judgment test; if there is no evidence to support its application, the surrogate cannot resort to the best interests test as grounds for abating life-prolonging treatment. (These various positions will be considered forthwith.)

(i)   *The Substituted Judgment Test*

The consent requirement for medical treatment reflects the law's commitment to the goal of self-determination for the mentally competent patient. The substituted judgment test is designed to achieve that goal for the incompetent patient whose treatment wishes can be inferred, albeit not spelled out by the patient in accordance with the subjective standard. Substituted judgment is one step removed from a Brother Fox scenario in which the patient had clearly indicated his treatment preferences. It is only when there is no such direct evidence (the subjective standard) that it becomes necessary to turn to a surrogate decision-maker.

In effect, then, the test places the surrogate in the patient's shoes such that she is directed to decide as the patient would if he were competent to decide for himself. The question is whether the patient has left enough telltale evidence to enable the surrogate to infer his treatment choices. To that end it is incumbent upon the surrogate to flesh out the patient's wishes from whatever sources are relevant. In *Conroy*, the New Jersey Supreme Court suggested that evidence to support substituted judgment could "take the form of reactions that the patient voiced regarding medical treatment administered to others." Or it could be deduced from the patient's religious convictions or from his "consistent pattern of conduct with respect to prior decisions about his own medical care."

Although the substituted judgment test is enshrined in American case law, recall the *Cruzan* ruling that state courts are not obliged to allow that standard of decision-making for mentally incompetent patients. In *Cruzan* the Supreme Court held that the Missouri courts could enforce the rule that life-prolonging treatment be foregone only when there was "clear and convincing" evidence that the patient had in effect left instructions that covered the precise treatment in issue.

Missouri does not stand alone in its exclusive reliance upon the subjective standard for incompetent patients; its position was adopted by the New York Court of Appeals in the 1988 *O'Connor* case.[14] Mary O'Connor was a 77-year-old patient who was "profoundly incapacitated" and "severely demented." Her daughters (both nurses) had refused her hospital's request to institute artificial feeding by nasogastric tubing on the grounds that their mother would not wish her life prolonged in her current condition.

Their steadfast refusal prompted her caregivers to seek judicial authority to override their decision. The case for the daughters was as follows. The patient's working career had been in hospital administration, and she had cared for her husband and two brothers as they lay dying from cancer. That experience had often led her to express the sentiment that artificial means should not be used to sustain life; that if critically ill she would never want to be "a burden" or "lose her dignity." Her daughters testified that their mother had said that it was "monstrous to keep someone alive by using machinery and things like that when they were not going to get better", and that she "would never want any sort of life-support system."

The trial court denied the hospital's petition but its decision was reversed by the high court. Although the Court did not dispute the daughters' evidence, it preferred to base its ruling upon

> Our fundamental commitment to the notion that no person or court should substitute its judgment as to what would be an acceptable quality of life for another.

From that standpoint, "the inquiry must always be narrowed to the patient's expressed intent." What was fatal to the daughters' case was their admission that their mother had never specifically indicated a firm and settled commitment to refuse a feeding tube. The justices were thus let to conclude that there was no "clear and convincing" evidence of the patient's expressed intent that she should never be subjected to the particular treatment at issue.

In sum, the Missouri/New York position has no quarrel with the decision to halt treatment that maintains an incompetent patient's life, so long as there is clear and convincing evidence that when competent the patient had expressed that preference by accurately anticipating his future illness and precise course of treatment.

Still, it is only the Missouri and New York courts that reject surrogate decision-making altogether for incompetent patients. However, in two cases with remarkably similar facts, *Martin v. Martin* (1995)[15] and *Wendland v. Wendland* (2001),[16] the Michigan and California Supreme Courts respectively have ruled that only the subjective standard can apply to a patient who is not terminally ill and is minimally conscious.

In 1987, 36-year-old Michael Martin was involved in an auto accident that "significantly impaired his physical and cognitive abilities", leaving him unable to walk, talk, feed himself, or control his bladder and bowel. Five years later, when he was being treated for an obstructed bowel, his wife applied for a court order allowing her to direct his caregivers to withdraw the nutritive support provided by his gastrotomy tube. She acted to hasten his death on the grounds that he would not want to be kept alive in his current condition. His mother and sister objected and the case accordingly wound its way through the courts. Several therapists and laypersons testified at the trial that Martin had "an apparent limited ability to interact with others and to respond to simple yes or no questions with head nods." However, their testimony varied "with respect to the consistency and appropriateness of the perceived interactions and responses."

It was the contention of the patient's wife (and his two children and brother) that he was the kind of person who would have hated to live in a dependent state. Mrs. Martin testified that they had often talked about death and dying; that he had repeatedly told her that he could not endure a life of dependency, and that he would want to die if ever he had an accident from which he could not recover and "could not be the same person." She said that he had made her promise that she would not let him live like that, "because if you do, I'll haunt you every day of your life.'

The petition was granted and the patient's mother and sister promptly appealed. According to the intermediate appellate court, the issue was whether a gastrotomy tube could be removed

> from a conscious patient who is not terminally ill nor in a permanent vegetative state, but who suffers from a mixture of cognitive function and communication impairments that make it impossible to evaluate the extent of his cognitive deficits.

The Court answered in the affirmative and once again the patient's mother and sister appealed. This time they prevailed, the Michigan Supreme Court ruling that Mrs. Martin's testimony did not constitute clear and convincing evidence that her husband's pre-injury statements expressed his wishes to refuse life-prolonging treatment under his precise current circumstances. However, the Court went out of its way to say that it was expressing

> no opinion about the proper decision-making standard for patients...existing in a persistent vegetative state...or patients who are terminally ill.

In 1993, 42-year-old Robert Wendland rolled his truck at high speed while drunk and spent more than a year in a coma. Although he recovered a limited degree of cognitive awareness, he remained severely physically and mentally disabled. A medical report in 1995 summarized his condition as follows:

> [He has] severe cognitive impairment that is not possible to fully appreciate due to the concurrent motor and communications impairments...severe paralysis...severely impaired communication without compensatory augmentative communication system;* severe swallowing dysfunction, dependent upon non-oral enteric tube for nutrition and hydration; incontinence of bowel and bladder; moderate spasticity; mild to moderate contractures; general dysphoria; recurrent medical illnesses....

On three occasions his wife had authorized surgery to replace dislodged feeding tubes but the fourth time she refused. She had discussed his plight with their daughters and his brother, and all agreed that he would not wish to go on living. In 1995, two years after the accident, she petitioned for a court order to discontinue tube-feeding. As in *Martin*, it was the patient's mother and sister who opposed the petitioner, and the case dragged on until 2001 when the California Supreme Court ruled against the patient's wife.

Again as in the *Martin* case, there was evidence from the patient's family about his attitude toward life-prolonging medical care. According to his wife, her husband had told her on the occasion of her father's death that he would never want to die a lingering death attached to a respirator. His brother testified about a conversation in which he admonished Robert that his drinking could lead to an accident that would either kill him or leave him "laying in bed just like a vegetable." He said that Robert replied: "Don't let that happen. Don't let them do that to me." His daughter confirmed the conversation and added that

> if he could not be a provider for his family, if he could not do all the things he enjoyed doing, just enjoying the outdoors, just basic things, feeding himself, talking, communicating, if he could not do those things, he would not want to live.

The trial court denied the petition on the grounds that Mrs. Wendland had not proven by clear and convincing evidence that her husband desired to die or that stopping nutrition and hydration would serve his best interests. In affirming that decision the Supreme Court stressed that best interests was not the issue. Rather it was simply whether, as the trial court expressed

---

* "Augmented communication" refers to communication facilitated by a yes/no board, which pronounces the words when corresponding buttons are touched. The patient's answers were "extremely inconsistent".

it, the patient had articulated "the desire to have his life-sustaining medical treatment terminated under the circumstances in which he now finds himself." The high court agreed with the trial court that the patient's desire not to live "like a vegetable" did not prove the point. However, the justices were clear that its ruling did not affect patients who were terminally ill, comatose, or in a permanent vegetative state. (The Court briefly commented in a footnote that the patient had died while the case was before it but that the important issues it raised merited resolution.)

In a recent law journal article, Dr. Ronald Cranford, a prominent neurologist who testified in both cases, described Martin and Wendland as in a "minimally conscious state." He explained that such patients "have severely impaired consciousness, demonstrate limited and inconsistent signs of cognitive awareness, and thus are not in the persistent vegetative state." He referred to a consensus statement by the Aspen Neurobehavioral Conference Work Group, composed of professionals in the fields of rehabilitation and neurology, who define the minimally conscious state — for which they use the acronym MCS — as "a condition of severely altered consciousness in which minimal but definite behavioral evidence of self or environmental awareness is demonstrated."[17]

The rulings in *Martin* and *Wendland* reflect the position that unless the patient is terminally ill or in a permanent vegetative state, the onerous step of hastening death by stopping tube-feeding cannot be allowed in the absence of clear evidence that the patient would have wanted that to happen in his current condition.

One can understand the reluctance of the Michigan and California Supreme Courts to allow the substituted judgment test when the patient is not terminally ill or in a permanent vegetative state. A number of disability rights organizations filed friend-of-the-court briefs in both cases, raising the spectre of the proverbial slippery slope if families were allowed to direct the deaths of patients retaining some level of cognitive functioning, however minimal. Although the legitimacy of this concern cannot be denied, Dr. Cranford has a different perspective:

> The argument for requiring continued treatment of a minimally conscious patient ignores the pain and suffering the patient will undergo while his life is being prolonged. Vegetative patients experience nothing with or without life-sustaining treatment. In contrast, continued treatment of minimally conscious patients — precisely because they are conscious — may result in them suffering for years, or even decades, and probably being wholly unable to express adequately to anyone the depth of their pain, not to mention the elemental sense of frustration and loss.[18]

There was, after all, compelling and credible evidence that Martin and Wendland would not have wanted to be kept alive in their minimally conscious condition. As the trial judge in the *Wendland* case commented: "It can still be debated whether (Mr. Wendland's) life is being preserved or he is being sentenced to life by my order." Dr. Cranford found the life sentence metaphor quite apt:

> In Mr. Wendland's case, the "life sentence" is to an indefinite term in a prison of solitary confinement, unable to reach out to other persons, unable to express himself, unable to even move, possibly deeply frustrated by being stranded in a diminished life he never wanted, yet able to suffer to an extent ultimately known only by him. With the minimal degree of awareness that gives him the capacity for pain and suffering — the precise extent or nature of which is unknown to others — the minimally conscious patient poses a much stronger case for allowing death than the vegetative patient does due to the principle of mercy.[19]

Finally, there is a middle ground perspective that draws the line at substituted judgment, thereby rejecting the best interests test. In *Mack v. Mack* (1993),[20] the Court of Appeals of Maryland considered the case of a patient who had been in a permanent vegetative state for 10 years and whose wife — over the impassioned objection of his father — sought judicial approval for the removal of his feeding-tube. Since the patient had not signed a health care directive spelling out treatment directions to cover the case at hand, the Court held that his wife had the burden to prove by clear and convincing evidence that her husband would prefer death to his vegetative existence. Since there was no evidence whatsoever regarding his wishes about any life-and-death issues, the Court sustained the decision of the trial court that there was no legal basis for granting the petition. In the result, the Court rejected the best interests test because

> it lets another make a determination of a patient's quality of life, thereby undermining the foundation of self-determination and inviolability of the person upon which the right to refuse medical treatment stands.

In another 1993 case, *DeGrella v. Elston*,[21] the mother of a patient in a permanent vegetative state (likewise of 10 years' duration) also sought the removal of her daughter's feeding-tube. Unlike the *Mack* case, there was no family dispute but rather the refusal of the nursing home to act without a court order. The Kentucky trial court ruled in the mother's favour because there was "clear and convincing" evidence that her daughter had

> rejected during her lifetime...the principle that life must be maintained at any cost. To the contrary she expressed explicitly on many occasions her desire

that her life not be maintained if she would come under conditions which would require extraordinary means to preserve her life.

In affirming the decision the Kentucky Supreme Court took pains to stress that its ruling was not to be regarded as an endorsement of the "quality of life issue." As the Court put it:

> As long as the case is confined to substitute decision-making by a surrogate in conformity with the patient's previously expressed wishes, the case involves only the right of self-determination and not the quality of life. However, as evidence regarding the patient's wishes weakens, the case moves from self-determination toward a quality-of-life test. At the point where the withdrawal of life-prolonging medical treatment becomes solely another person's decision about the patient's quality of life, the individual's "inalienable right to life" as so declared in the United States Declaration of Independence...outweighs any consideration of the quality of the life, or the value of the life, at stake.

In sum, the *Mack* and *DeGrella* cases do not go so far as to require clear and convincing evidence that the patient while competent had rejected the precise treatment in issue. Although the Missouri/New York position leaves no room for surrogate decision-making whatever the patient's prognosis, the Maryland and Kentucky courts will allow a surrogate to make the decision that she believes the patient would have made. But in the absence of evidence supporting the resort to substituted judgment, the surrogate cannot go on to decide that it is in the patient's best interests to die even if the patient is in a vegetative state.

Since the precedent-setting *Quinlan* case, courts in roughly half the states have grappled with the fate of PVS patients and, as we have seen, not all have been prepared to allow death to proceed by way of the best interests test. Still, it is arguable that there is no earthly reason to ward off the death of a patient whose permanent loss of consciousness has deprived him of the essence of what it means to be a person. As Dr. Lawrence J. Schneiderman, a distinguished medical ethicist/physician, expressed it in an essay poignantly titled, *Exile and PVS*:

> Although modern neurology dismisses the possibility of suffering in permanently unconscious patients, they exist in a worst possible, dehumanizing condition — enslaved to perpetual inertness, emotionless, helplessness, unlike any other form of human existence, isolated from every human connection and communication — an exile, whether perceived or not.... If physicians find this view persuasive, then withdrawing life-supporting treatment from a patient in PVS becomes not merely ethically permissible, but an obligatory act of beneficence.[22]

Be that as it may, the prevailing direction of American law since the *Quinlan* case is that of acceptance of the long standing medical practice of turning to incompetent patients' families for guidance in end-of-life decision-making. The law's underlying rationale is that until the contrary is indicated, family members are in the best position to know what their loved ones would want or in the absence of that knowledge to know what serves their best interests.

Beyond that there is also a pragmatic consideration. Most mentally intact persons do not contemplate a future state of incompetency and specify — by oral statement or written directive — the circumstances in which they would choose death over life-support maintenance. Moreover, the sheer volume of nontreatment decisions for mentally incompetent patients precludes a general policy of prior judicial approval. Recall that, as noted by Justice Brennan in the *Cruzan* case, it is estimated that 70% of the 1.3 million in-hospital deaths in the United States per annum result from the foregoing of some form of life-prolonging treatment.[23] Furthermore, it would be cruel and pointless (both for patients and families), as well as fiscally irresponsible, for the law to insist upon aggressive treatment unto death for all those who have not specified their treatment preferences. In other words, the courts really have no choice but to relegate decision-making responsibility to the clinical setting.

As discussed in Chapter 24, an instructional directive (popularly referred to as a "living will") is a mechanism enabling a mentally competent person to anticipate a future state of incapacity by giving treatment directions that are binding should that contingency comes to pass. If the directions are sufficiently precise — "in the event that I wind up in a permanent vegetative state, I refuse tube-feeding because I regard that condition as incompatible with life" — then there is no need for a surrogate because the patient has made the decision for himself. Yet the living will is not a magic wand that will obviate the need for surrogate decision-making. For one thing, it is unlikely that the majority of health care consumers will fill out a treatment directive. (Recall that this point was stressed by Justice Brennan in his dissenting opinion in *Cruzan*.) For another, however detailed the instructions contained in such a document, there is no guarantee that the person will have foreseen the precise treatment decisions that need resolution. Furthermore, many of the standard form living wills contain vague language that provide precious little direction to surrogates and health care providers.

Still, even when the patient had not anticipated the precise treatment decision in issue (as in the *Brother Fox* and *Bludworth* cases), evidence sufficient to satisfy the substituted judgment test may not be that difficult to come by. After all, cases such as *Quinlan* and *Cruzan* have received extensive media coverage, and we have likely either expressed ourselves or heard others express sentiment such as: "No way would I want to end up like a vegetable or some other horrible state dependent on artificial life-support with no reasonable prospect for a tolerable life. If it ever happens to me, pull the plug." However, even such a remark would not be enough if it were a one-time casual utterance. That is because the courts have indicated that the substituted judgment test is operable only if the surrogate decision-maker is convinced that the patient herself would prefer the blessing of death to her current state.

As noted, the test is satisfied if there is indirect evidence of the patient's treatment preferences — e.g. the patient had led a vigorous life style and had often expressed the view that death was preferable to a life plagued by physical and/or mental disability. What if there is no such evidence, but a family member or a close friend avows with certainty and sincerity that she *knows* that the patient would prefer death to his current condition? The direction of American law is that the substituted judgment test can be satisfied by evidence based upon an intimate knowledge of the patient.

As the cases indicate, the grimmer the patient's prognosis the more likely that the law will accept indirect evidence that the patient would, if competent, reject life-prolonging treatment. Yet, however intimate the patient-surrogate relationship, there is surely some degree of guesswork involved when one must decide whether the silent patient would prefer death to his current state. For how can the surrogate know with certainty what the patient would have chosen if able to speak for himself. The doctrine of substituted judgment is thus not a panacea that guarantees that those who know us best will make the decisions that we would have made. (In Chapter 24 we return to the substituted judgment test in our discussion of the status of patients' advance directives in Canadian law.)

(ii) *The Best Interests Test*

As illustrated by the *Bludworth* case, the substituted judgment test is triggered by indirect evidence enabling the surrogate to determine the patient's wishes regarding life-prolonging treatment. However, substituted judgment is not appropriate when: (1) the patient while competent did not provide such evidence; or (2) the patient was never mentally competent (e.g. a child or severely mentally handicapped adult). In such circumstances, the surrogate must then determine the treatment course that in her view serves the patient's best interests.

On a case-by-case basis, it is likely that whatever the particular decision by way of substituted judgment, the same result would occur under the best interests test. In other words, when a surrogate applies substituted judgment (making the decision that she believes the patient would have made), she no doubt assumes that the decision also serves the patient's best interests because most people would act upon what they believe is best for themselves. Still, one must distinguish between the two tests, as each must stand or fall according to its own conceptual framework. In any event, if there is no basis upon which to apply substituted judgment, then it is idle to speculate as to the wishes of the patient. In that instance the only signpost available for guidance is the best interests test.

An illustrative case is *Torres, Re* (1983),[24] in which the Minnesota Supreme Court affirmed a lower court order to discontinue artificial respiration for a patient in a permanent vegetative state. There was no evidence before the trial court to indicate the treatment wishes of the 57-year-old patient (unconscious for eight months). The medical testimony was that there was no evidence of cortical function and only "very rudimentary evidence of low medullary brain stem function." The high court agreed with the trial judge that terminating life-support was in the patient's best interests.

A murder indictment against two Los Angeles physicians in a 1982 case, *Barber v. Superior Court*,[25] led to an affirmation of the best interests test by an intermediate appellate court. The patient, 55, had suffered a cardio-respiratory arrest following surgery for closure of an ileostomy. Three days later, the defendants (his surgeon and internist) informed the family that the patient had sustained severe brain damage, that he was in a deeply comatose state, and that the prognosis for recovery was "extremely poor." At the family's written request, his ventilator was disconnected, but the patient surprisingly breathed on his own. A few days later there was a further consultation with the family, after which the physicians ordered the withdrawal of the intravenous catheter providing hydration and nutrition. The patient died three days later. Alleging that the physicians had committed cold-blooded murder by starving their patient to death, the prosecuting attorney's office had them charged with murder.

The defendants then filed a motion with the appellate court for dismissal of the indictment, and the motion was granted. The Court ruled that by removing the ventilator and catheter, the defendants had not engaged in unlawful "affirmative action." On the contrary, their conduct was described as the lawful omission of continued "heroic treatment." A cardinal principle of the common law is that an accused commits an offence by way of omission only when his inaction constitutes the breach of a legal duty to act. In the Court's view: "the omission to continue treatment under the circumstances though intentional and with the knowledge that the patient would die was not an unlawful failure to perform a legal duty." The Court explained:

The question presented by this modern technology is, once undertaken, at what point does it cease to perform its intended function? A physician has no duty to continue treatment, once it has proved to be ineffective. Although there may be a duty to provide life-sustaining treatment in the immediate aftermath of a cardio-respiratory arrest, there is no duty to continue its use once it has become futile in the opinion of qualified medical personnel.

The Court reasoned that the issue was whether the proposed treatment was "proportionate or disproportionate in terms of the benefits to be gained versus the burdens caused." It defined proportionate treatment as that having "at least a reasonable chance of providing benefits to the patient, which benefits outweigh the burdens attendant to the treatment." The Court observed that a proposed treatment regimen could be painful and/or intrusive but still proportionate, provided that it held out hope of significant improvement for the patient. The Court added:

On the other hand, a treatment course which is only minimally painful or intrusive may nonetheless be considered disproportionate to the potential benefits if the prognosis is virtually hopeless for any significant improvement in condition.

In sum, *proportionate* treatment is legally required whereas *disproportionate* treatment is not. (The Court was in essence applying its own terminology to the terms, *ordinary* and *extraordinary* treatment, which we have explained in Chapter 18.) As the Court noted, how one categorizes the treatment "depends upon facts unique to each case, namely, how long the treatment is likely to extend life and under what conditions." In the case at hand, the Court dismissed the charges because the evidence indicated that the withdrawn treatments were disproportionate. Its ruling hence stands for the principle that when an incompetent patient's death is occasioned by the cessation of life-support measures, the physician acts within the law so long as the forsaken treatment was disproportionate.

Note that the principle is subject to the rider that if there is clear evidence that the patient would reject the treatment at issue — by way of either the subjective or substituted judgment standard — then the patient's wishes control the outcome.

Even if the treatment is considered "proportionate", its provision is trumped by evidence that from the patient's standpoint it is "disproportionate." In short, the principle strictly applies only to the application of the best interests test.

The ruling in the *Barber* case reflects the consensus that the surrogate decision-maker (whether judge, court-appointed guardian, next-of-kin, intimate friend, or physician) must seek to maximize the incompetent patient's welfare, assuming the absence of credible evidence sufficient to indicate what the patient herself would have chosen in the circumstances. In theory, the best interests test expresses a neat formula enabling the decision-maker to measure the benefits variable against the burdens variable. Yet benefits and burdens are not cut-and-dried concepts, and the perils of practice are illustrated by a judicial ruling that applied the best interests test to achieve a result that threatened to condemn a mildly retarded youngster to a drawn out death from a correctible heart defect.

In the 1979 case of *In re Phillip B.*,[26] a California appellate court (a sister court to that which decided *Barber*) ruled that the parents of a 12-year-old Down syndrome group home resident could lawfully withhold consent for life-saving heart surgery. Phillip Becker, whose I.Q. was about 60, could communicate verbally and function in a sheltered workshop setting. He was found to have a ventricular septal defect, and his parents were advised that without corrective surgery he would suffer progressive debilitation that would lead to death in about 10 years. (The Beckers had institutionalized Phillip at birth and visited him about twice a year.) The surgery carried a 5% mortality risk and post-operative complications were more likely for Phillip than for a normal child. If successful, the surgery would enable him to attain the normal life span of someone with the syndrome.

His parents explained their decision by invoking the concern that Phillip might outlive them and wind up warehoused in a state institution. The state child welfare agency responded by filing a neglect petition seeking judicial appointment of a guardian to authorize the surgery. The trial court rejected the petition; and its decision was affirmed by an intermediate appellate court, which ruled that the surgery was not in Phillip's best interests because of its mortality and morbidity risks.

The surgical risks notwithstanding, the decision is surely deplorable. Given Phillip's grim prognosis without heart surgery, the trial and appellate judgments appear indefensible; and one cannot help but suspect that the decision would have been otherwise had Phillip not been mentally handicapped. (Two years later a court awarded guardianship of Phillip to a couple who had been caring for him and who were anxious to proceed with the surgery if still medically indicated. They got the green light and the surgery corrected his heart defect.)

In *Conroy*, the New Jersey Supreme Court stressed its abhorrence of "decision-making based on assessments of the personal worth or social utility of another's life, or the value of that life to others." The *In re Phillip B.* case should keep us mindful of the risk that, even if not by design, the effect of a decision to halt or to deny treatment may be to sacrifice a vulnerable patient's welfare for the convenience of others.

The *In re Phillip B.* case also exposes the pitfall that confronts the decision-maker whose concern is with the patient's well-being and who seeks to determine, "Is the patient better off dead?" That after all is what the *best interests test* is all about: whether the burdens of the patient's medical care so overpower its benefits that a compassionate judgment favours death over life. Every physician knows that there is suffering that is worse than death, and that mercy and compassion often dictate the hastening of the dying process. The necessity for such decision-making cannot be denied. But then neither can the legitimacy of the nagging question, "How can one rest assured that a patient who cannot speak for herself is better off dead?"

In the aforementioned case of Sadie Weinstein (*In the Matter of Beth Israel Medical Center*), the New York court deemed it necessary to enumerate criteria for the assessment of the benefits-versus-burdens equation.[27] It stipulated the following factors:

1. the patient's age
2. her life expectancy with and without the contemplated procedure
3. the degree of current and future pain and suffering with and without the contemplated procedure
4. the extent of the patient's physical and mental disability and degree of helplessness
5. the quality of the patient's life without the procedure; and the extent, if any, of pleasure, emotional enjoyment, or intellectual satisfaction that she will obtain from prolonged life
6. the risks entailed from the contemplated procedure, as well as side-effects and degree of invasiveness
7. the views of the patient's family, close friends, and physician
8. the type of care required if life is prolonged as contrasted with the care that actually will be available for the patient.

In the Washington case (*In re Guardianship of Grant*),[28] the Court likewise sought to guide the surrogate seeking to determine whether it is in the incompetent patient's best interests to have life prolonged. Its nonexclusive list of factors was as follows:

> Evidence about the patient's present level of physical, sensory, emotional, and cognitive functioning; the degree of physical pain resulting from the medical condition, treatment, and termination of treatment, respectively; the degree of humiliation, dependence, and loss of dignity probably resulting from the condition and treatment; the life expectancy and prognosis for recovery with and without treatment; the various treatment options; and the risks, side effects, and benefits of each of these options.

Although there may be no quarrel with the criteria formulated in the *Sadie Weinstein* and *Grant* cases, we are still left with the uncertainty inherent in the application of the criteria to particular cases. How, for example, can one with reasonable certainty determine the degree of pain or humiliation borne by the patient who cannot articulate her feelings? Save for the case in which the prognosis is permanent loss of consciousness, there is no standard or formula that can neatly calculate the circumstances that clearly point to a patient's death as serving her best interests. As the New Jersey Supreme Court acknowledged in *Conroy*:

> We are aware that it will frequently be difficult to conclude that the evidence is sufficient to justify termination of treatment under the best interests test. Often, it is unclear whether and to what extent a patient such as Claire Conroy is capable of, or is in fact, experiencing pain. Similarly, medical experts are often unable to determine with any degree of certainty the extent of a non-verbal person's intellectual functioning or the depth of his emotional life.

Moreover, there is no instrument that can provide a reliable physiological measurement of pain. Nor can one neatly calculate the depth of emotional pain — the sense of helplessness, humiliation, and frustration, or the loss of pride, dignity, and independence — when the patient is unable to communicate her feelings. Human judgment is fallible and there are no guarantees that the good faith decisions of physicians will not cause some patients to live too long and others to die too soon.

Finally, bear in mind that more than medical judgment is involved when the physician, with or without input from the incompetent patient's family, decides to forego life-support measures that are not seen as benefitting the patient. The determination that prolonging a patient's life is an exercise in futility is a social value judgment that calls for the wisdom of Solomon, and as mere mortals even the most dedicated and conscientious physician is hard put to qualify for that role. It may sound hackneyed, but the inescapable conclusion is that the protection of the incompetent patient's best interests requires not only clinical acumen but also the integrity, wisdom, compassion, and common human decency of the physician. (The moral complexity of the matter is further addressed by the topic heading of *Futility*, to which we now turn.)

(d) That Troublesome "F" Word: Futility

According to Taber's Cyclopedic Medical Dictionary, treatment is defined as: "Any specific procedure used for the cure or amelioration of a disease or pathological condition." In that sense, it follows that the very notion of nonbeneficial treatment is an oxymoron because a procedure that fails to benefit the patient does not fall under the heading of treatment. In any event, whether we say that nonbeneficial treatment is not treatment or simply that it is treatment that is not working, in either case we are led to the conclusion that its provision is pointless.

Still, it must not be forgotten that to stop fighting for a patient's life is to act upon the value-laden judgment that the patient is better off dead.* In that regard, there is a viewpoint that challenges that very judgment — that foregoing life-prolonging treatment can ever serve an incompetent patient's best interests. Consider the following American cases.

In 1990 an article appeared in the New England Journal of Medicine titled, "Physicians' Refusal of Requested Treatment."[29] The patient, who was called Baby L, was a two-year-old girl born at 36 weeks and weighing 1970 grams. As described by the authors:

> The pregnancy was complicated by fetal hydronephrosis and oligohydramnios in the last trimester. Decelerations in the fetal heart rate and thick meconium below the vocal chords was noted at delivery. APGAR scores were 1 at 1 minute, 4 at 5 minutes, and 5 at 10 minutes. The infant was resuscitated, stabilized, and weaned from mechanical ventilation. Over a period of weeks the infant's respiratory function improved, but the neurologic condition remained very depressed, with no responsiveness except to pain.

> The infant underwent a gastrotomy at the age of one month, a Nissen fundoplication at four months, and a tracheostomy at seven months. There were intermittent episodes of aspiration and uncontrolled seizures. She was discharged after 14 months with 24-hour nursing care, but was readmitted within two weeks for recurrent pneumonia. During the next several months she was repeatedly hospitalized for pneumonia and septic shock. At the age of 23 months the child — having been readmitted with worsening pneumonia and sepsis — required mechanical ventilation and cardiovascular support. During those 23 months of recurrent pneumonia and four cardiopulmonary arrests, the mother had continued to demand that everything be done to ensure the child's survival.

When Baby L's caregivers informed the mother that further medical intervention was uncalled for because a child with such extensive neurologic deficits could only experience pain, she contacted an attorney who arranged a hearing in Probate Court. The attorney found a paediatric neurologist whose assessment of the case was as grim as that of Baby L's caregivers but who was prepared to manage the case aggressively. When

---

* We leave aside those cases in which death results from the application of the subjective or substituted judgment standard. The focus here is upon best interests.

the hospital agreed to the transfer, the judge terminated the legal proceedings. As the case summary concludes:

> Two years later she remains blind, deaf, and quadriplegic and is fed through the gastrotomy. She averages a seizure a day. Her pulmonary status has improved, but she continued to require intensive home nursing 16 hours a day. Her mental status remains that of a three-month-old infant.

In a 1991 Minnesota case, *Wanglie, Re*,[30] the caregivers of an 86-year-old PVS patient took the unprecedented step of seeking a court order in response to family insistence upon the maintenance of artificial ventilation. The patient's husband (her legal guardian) and adult children claimed that she would want to be kept alive as long as medically possible because of the family's shared religious conviction that only God could take life. Their unwavering refusal over several months to agree to the termination of life-support prompted the hospital to seek a judicial order from the Probate Court. (The hospital was prepared to transfer the patient elsewhere but no placement could be found.) For whatever reason, the hospital did not petition for an order authorizing the attending physician to disconnect the ventilator, but rather for an order to replace the husband as the patient's legal guardian, although it presumably planned to facilitate that result if the case went its way.

The hospital had framed the issue in narrow terms, and the Court responded in kind by denying the petition on the grounds that Mr. Wanglie was undeniably a devoted husband who was "dedicated to promoting his wife's welfare." Thus, the Court never squarely faced the question whether a patient's family could insist upon treatment that the caregivers regarded as futile. In any event, Mrs. Wanglie died four days after the Court's ruling, still connected to the ventilator.

The National Legal Center for the Medically Dependent and Disabled filed a friend-of-the-court brief in the 1993-4 Virginia case of *Baby K., Re*,[31] which it later lauded as "an important victory for infants with disabilities and their right to receive necessary acute care." That case arose when the mother of a newborn anencephalic insisted upon aggressive treatment because of her "firm Christian faith that all life should be protected (and that) God will work a miracle if that is His will." And if no miracle were forthcoming, it was her conviction that only God should determine the time of her daughter's death. The hospital physicians advised her that "no treatment existed for Baby K's anencephalic condition, no therapeutic or palliative purpose was served by the treatment, and that ventilator care was medically unnecessary and inappropriate." Her steadfastness prompted the hospital to seek a court order permitting the discontinuance of treatment for the infant. The father, who was not married to the mother, signed on as a co-petitioner.

The U.S. District Court denied the petition by ruling that stopping treatment would constitute child abuse in violation of a federal statute, the Emergency Medical Treatment and Active Labor Act (EMTALA), which prohibits discriminatory treatment against persons requiring emergency medical care. The hospital had contended that it was not in breach of the statute because emergency treatment for Baby K's respiratory distress could not cure her anencephaly. However, the Court accepted the argument that the emergency condition for which care was sought was not anencephaly but rather respiratory distress; and that the emergency treatment was not futile because it would resolve the patient's breathing crisis. At the time that the Court rendered its decision in July 1993, Baby K was nine months old, and required periodic ventilator support, which involved frequent transfers from nursing home (its permanent placement) to hospital. Seven months later the decision was affirmed by the U.S. Fourth Circuit Court of Appeals, which held that:

> In this case, where the choice essentially devolves to a subjective determination as to the quality of Baby K's life, it cannot be said that the continuation of Baby K's life is so unreasonably harmful as to constitute child abuse or neglect.

There is also a Minnesota case in which the National Legal Center for the Mentally Dependent and Disabled was denied standing to intervene, the trial judge ruling that the Center was essentially a stranger to the issue before the court. (The denial of standing is a court's way of telling the applicant that he has no interest in the matter before it and should consequently mind his own business.) The petitioners were the parents of a 34-year-old PVS patient who had been stricken at the age of 17. They had decided that once he had lived half his life in that condition, it was time to let him go. The judge granted their petition for the removal of his feeding-tube and the patient died days later with his parents at his bedside.

In a 1998 Louisiana case, *Causey v. St. Francis Medical Center*,[32] the family of a patient contested the attending physician's decision to stop dialysis and artificial ventilation. The 31-year-old patient was "comatose, quadriplegic and in end-stage renal failure." To begin with, the trial judge stated that he would not address the concept of futility because "focus(ing) on a definition of 'futility' is confusing and generates polemical discussions." Instead the judge considered "an approach emphasizing the standard of medical care", which led to the result that the physician was not legally bound to provide treatment that was "medically inappropriate."

Finally, there is a 1995 Massachusetts case, *Gilgunn v. Massachusetts General Hospital*,[33] in which a civil jury dismissed a law suit claiming damages for emotional distress brought by the daughter of a mentally incompetent elderly patient who had died after the termination of artificial life-support. Although the daughter had insisted that it was her mother's wish to be kept alive for as long as possible, the attending physician removed the ventilator because he and his medical colleagues were convinced that her mother would not emerge from her comatose condition. (He had also written a DNR order over the daughter's objection.) In dismissing the action, the jury found that although the patient would have wanted to be kept on life-support until she died, the treatment was "futile." It consequently concluded that her daughter was not entitled to recover damages for the unilateral action of the physician. There is no appellate decision because the jury verdict was not appealed, which means that the case does not establish a legal precedent. Still, as noted by the authors of an article about the case that appeared in the *Journal of Intensive Care Medicine*:[34]

> It does, however, indicate how a jury responded when asked to review and assess the value conflict between the family and the treating physician on the use of aggressive interventions for a comatose dying patient. The jury found that, given the circumstances, it was appropriate for the treating physician — even over the family's vehement protests — to withhold interventions deemed by the physician to be "futile."

These American cases (and there are others) address the troublesome question of *medical futility*. It was the debate sparked by the *Wanglie* case that introduced the term "futility" into the bio-ethics lexicon; and the issues first raised by *Wanglie* continue to attract the attention of medical and bio-ethics journals. Yet it is not as if the notion of futile treatment was suddenly discovered in the post-*Wanglie* era. Bear in mind that ever since the *Quinlan* case — when the New Jersey Supreme Court ruled that ventilator support could be withdrawn from a patient when there was no reasonable possibility of a "return to cognitive and sapient life" — the American courts have grappled with criteria to define when treatment no longer serves the best interest of incompetent patients. Although the courts have not articulated a concept of futility as such, their opinions are scattered with references to treatments described as "ineffective", "useless", "extraordinary", and sometimes even "futile."

However, it is only since the *Wanglie* case that caregivers and ethicists have come to grips with a concept that is more complex and troublesome than it appears at first blush. After all, if the concept of futility were that straightforward, there would be nothing to debate. If a treatment regimen is indeed futile, no one in her right mind would see the point of it. That is certainly true if it is physiological futility of which we speak. The Hastings Center Guidelines define "physiologic futility" in reference to treatment that is "clearly futile in achieving its physiological objective and so offers no physiologic benefit to the patient."[35] If, for example, a patient insists upon an antibiotic for a viral infection or interferon to treat his stomach cancer, his demand is senseless and rightly resisted as an exercise in futility. Yet, aside from obviously inappropriate treatment requests, there are cases in which physicians know from clinical experience that there are no available treatment options that offer any hope of arresting a disease process or staving off death. In other words, determinations that particular treatments are ineffectual may rest on solid physiological grounds.

However, beyond the straightforward physiological sense of the term, the futility of a particular treatment may be expressed in either *quantitative* or *qualitative* terms; and it is here that we cross over into the contested areas that have fuelled the so-called futility debate. Quantitative futility refers to therapies that are unlikely to produce their intended effects. Consider, for example, a published study titled "Outcomes of Cardiopulmonary Resuscitation in the Elderly", which concluded that CPR is "rarely effective for elderly patients with cardiopulmonary arrests that are either out-of-hospital, unwitnessed, or associated with asystole or electromechanical dissociation."[36] According to the study, of 116 patients aged 70 and over experiencing unwitnessed arrests, only one survived to discharge. There was also only one survival to discharge amongst 237 patients with asystole or electromechanical dissociation (terminal conditions). And only two of 244 patients with out-of-hospital arrests survived to discharge. Furthermore, of the 19 patients in the total pool of 503 who left hospital alive, nine had a broad range of functional and mental impairments.

What then of a patient who fits within one of the three categories but who is nonetheless resuscitated? If the patient beats the odds and survives to discharge, then in her case the treatment was surely not futile. The same can be said if she does not survive to discharge but the resuscitation enables her to bid farewell to friends and loved ones or otherwise find satisfaction in her remaining time.

The point is that quantitative futility refers to the high probability — rather than certainty — of a clinical conclusion. (If it were the latter, it would fit under the morally uncontested heading of physiological futility.) Hence, the prediction that a patient in a high risk category will not benefit from the treatment-in-question reflects a value judgment that fighting against the odds is not worth the effort. Yet it does not necessarily follow that this viewpoint is morally indefensible. There are, after all, considerations as measured by a utilitarian calculus (the philosophy of the greatest good for the greatest number). If it is necessary to administer aggressive treatment to 100 patients in order to benefit but one of their number, is that benefit outweighed by the harm inflicted upon the other 99? Moreover, does it represent a cost-effective application of scarce medical resources to devote so much time and effort with so little result? In this regard, it is pertinent to note that in 1992 the Clinical Ethics Committee of the Montreal General Hospital published its revised DNR-CPR guidelines, which incorporate the principle that patients and their families do not have the unlimited right to demand treatment. The guidelines accordingly stipulate that physicians act ethically when they refuse to administer CPR in cases where the therapy is likely to prove nonbeneficial or harmful to the patient.

If anything, the concept of qualitative futility is even more value-laden and hence controversial than its quantitative partner. It assumes two forms. On the one hand, there are cases in which the burden of the patient's existence is arguably regarded as of sufficient magnitude to warrant the foregoing of life-prolonging treatment. Such was the case of *Baby L*, whose caregivers went so far as to claim that it was unconscionable to strive to prolong a life of pain and suffering.[37] (The same dynamic occurred in the New Brunswick case of *Cara B. (New Brunswick (Minister of Health & Community Services) v. B. (R.))*, which is discussed in Chapter 23.)

On the other hand, there are cases in which life-prolonging treatment is branded as pointless because the patient is beyond both benefit and burden — the treatment cannot hurt a patient who is beyond hurting, but then again neither can it help. According to this perspective, the ventilator in *Wanglie* and the feeding-tube in *Cruzan* are not medically futile in the strict physiological sense of the term because they clearly could do what they were designed to do: breathe for and feed patients who cannot breathe and feed on their own. Nonetheless, they are exercises in futility because they cannot benefit such patients. In fact, the PVS patient is a paradigmatic example of the kind of case in which treatment cancels itself out because it neither benefits nor burdens. It is said that, in such cases, life-support measures have an "effect" but that, given the prognosis, their impact serves no rational end.

The meaning of the debate on qualitative futility is captured in the following comment by two physicians from the MacLean Center for Clinical Medical Ethics at the University of Chicago:

> A major source of controversy results from disagreements among different observers as to whether the predictable physiologic effect of a treatment is actually a benefit. For example, it is clear that, in general, tube feeding will predictably prolong the life of a permanently unconscious patient. However, whereas such a patient's family may believe that prolonging the life of their

relative is beneficial, the patient's physician may disagree. To assert that it is futile to provide tube feedings for a permanently unconscious patient is to assert that prolonging the patient's life is not a benefit. In such situations, claims of futility imply not that the therapy is ineffective, but rather that any effect is nonbeneficial. Thus the futility debate frequently reduces to: What effects count as benefits, and who decides which benefits are worth pursuing.[38]

As we have seen, that debate (although not expressed with the precise term futility) has been at the centre of legal attention in the United States since the Quinlan family sought judicial approval to direct the removal of their daughter's respirator. Beginning with *Quinlan*, many if not most of the American "right to die" cases have involved PVS patients whose health care facilities had contested the requests of family members to discontinue artificial ventilation or tube-feeding. (*Wanglie* was the first reported case of the reverse situation: the caregivers seeking to disconnect and the family striving to keep alive.) In most such cases, the institutions were not swayed by a commitment to maintaining life at all cost but rather by the absence of clear judicial authority to comply with the requests. Although the ruling in *Quinlan* has set the general direction of American case law on the termination of life-prolonging treatment for PVS patients, the U.S. Supreme Court ruling in the *Cruzan* case illustrates the lack of a uniform consensus on the futility of treating PVS patients. The absence of such a consensus is also indicated by the fact that throughout the United States (and Canada as well), PVS patients are actively treated and tube-fed. Still, without fanfare there are cases every day in which caregivers and families agree to forego life-prolonging measures for patients — both vegetative and otherwise — because keeping them alive is deemed an exercise in futility.

In sum, then, the reality of medical practice is that physicians are accustomed to rendering "letting die" decisions for their mentally incompetent patients (with family input if possible). Yet however imperfect the very concept of futility in both its qualitative and quantitative senses, we surely could not abide a commitment to the relentless application of medical technology regardless of prognosis. Such a policy would not only exact a fearsome toll in its impact upon patients and their loved ones but would also raise hard questions about the allocation of resources in an overburdened health care system. Be that as it may, there is the concern expressed by Professor Alan Meisel regarding the economics of health care in the United States that applies as well to Canada:[39]

> There is a fear, not totally unwarranted that physicians, on their own initiative or at the behest of health care administrators, will begin to make treatment

recommendations and decisions based on the financial interests of the health care institution, rather than the best interests of the patient. The fact that this motivation may be unconscious does not make it any less pernicious; indeed, it may make it more dangerous because it is harder to detect.

When Professor Meisel speaks of "financial interests", he is of course raising the spectre of rationing — a factor that was directly confronted by the English Court of Appeal in a 1995 case, *R. v. Cambridge Health Authority*.[40] This tragic case involved a 10-year-old girl afflicted with acute myeloid leukaemia, who had been treated with chemotherapy and a bone marrow transplant. When she suffered a relapse, the health authority refused to authorize a second attempt because of its cost (equivalent to $170,000 Canadian dollars) as weighed against the slim odds of survival. According to the health authority, she had only a 2.25% chance of recovery, although a paediatric oncologist testified that 10% was a more accurate estimate. The parents sought to compel the defendant to authorize the procedure, but the Court of Appeal turned them down, concluding that the health authority could not be faulted for considering other claims on its limited resources, particularly in light of the patient's unfavourable prognosis.*

In the result, it held that budgetary allocations was not a matter for the courts, but rather for the health authorities. The case clearly raised the question of futility: whether the proposed treatment was contraindicated because the odds were weighed heavily against remission. But at the same time there was the issue of rationing: the allocation of limited health care resources. Speaking for the Court, Sir Thomas Bingham MR reluctantly concluded:

> I have no doubt that in a perfect world any treatment which a patient, or a patient's family, sought would be provided if doctors were willing to give it, no matter how much it cost, particularly when a life was potentially at stake. It would however, in my view, be shutting one's eyes to the real world if the court were to proceed on the basis that we do live in such a world.... Difficult and agonizing judgments have to be made as to how a limited budget is best allocated to the maximum advantage of the maximum number of patients.

Questions of futility and rationing are not necessarily intertwined, as a decision to halt life-prolonging treatment on futility grounds may be unaffected by economic factors. But the point is that the spectre of rationing already haunts our health care system, and disabled health consumers in

---

* The extensive media coverage of the case prompted an anonymous donor to fund the patient's treatment, but not surprisingly it failed to save her life. See H. McConnell, Girl at centre of British health care storm dies of leukemia. *Medical Post*, June 4, 1996, at 56.

particular are not paranoid when they express concerns about the interconnection between medical judgments of futility and the high costs of life-prolonging care. This concern is no reason to combat the dying process to the bitter end when interested parties (caregivers and patients/families) agree that aggressive measures are no longer appropriate. But the spectre is not going away and it is better that we keep it in mind than bury it out of mind. (If it is arguable that futility decisions should not exclusively rest with physicians, an even stronger case can be made that decisions on rationing grounds can be made at the bedside only in accordance with policy directives hammered out by government.)

Although one may grant the unlikelihood of resolving the current debate on medical futility, it is an issue that cannot be ignored as we struggle to define the elements of a humane health care system for the 21st century. And as Dr. Steven Miles (who happened to be Helga Wanglie's treating physician) has noted:

> Regardless of its policy outcome, this important debate is leading to a reexamination of the nature of a patient's entitlement to health and of the ends of medicine.[41]

Along that line, Dr. Miles has grappled with the question, Whose burdens and whose benefits count? In his view, an ethic of "stewardship" required him to consider not only the benefit to Helga Wanglie from being kept alive but also the burden to the members of the insurance pool covering the cost of her care (which in Canada would simply be us taxpayers). In other words, is it time not only for caregivers but also for society generally to recognize limits on the kinds of treatment demands that the health care system can absorb? As the English court acknowledged in the *Cambridge Health Authority* case, the futility debate is really about rationing, about limiting expenditures in cases where the cost of therapy is high and the expected benefit is low. Needless to say, the futility debate can only gather momentum as our policy makers struggle to cut the ever burgeoning costs of medical care. (Questions of futility are implicated in two Manitoba cases which are considered in the next chapter.)

(e)   Removal of the Patient's Feeding-Tube

(i)   *The Case of Paul Brophy (Massachusetts, 1986)*[42]

In 1985, the wife of Paul Brophy, 48, a fireman and emergency medical technician, filed suit in Probate Court to compel her husband's physicians to remove or clamp his gastrotomy feeding tube. The irreversibly unconscious patient had been hospitalized 23 months earlier when he collapsed at home after complaining of a "splitting headache."

A neurological examination revealed subarachnoid bleeding in the posterior fossa surrounding the upper brain stem. An angiogram was accordingly performed, which detected an aneurysm at the apex of the basilar artery. In short, the patient had suffered a subarachnoid haemorrhage caused by a ruptured aneurysm. Brophy did regain consciousness and two weeks later, when the cranial swelling had subsided, underwent a right frontotemporal craniotomy. While awaiting the surgery he attempted to sit up to kiss one of his five daughters. When she admonished him for not lying still as ordered, he replied: "If I can't sit up to kiss one of my beautiful daughters, I may as well be six feet under."

Shortly after the surgery (from which Brophy never regained consciousness), several CT scans demonstrated extensive infarction of regions subserved by the left posterior cerebral artery and right temporal lobe. Although the patient was in a chronic vegetative state, his cerebral cortex was largely intact. His injury was confined primarily to the thalamus, which conducts impulses to the cortex; but the cortex cannot function without stimulation from the thalamus. He continued to breathe on his own, albeit through a tracheostomy tube. His other major organ systems all functioned normally.

At Mrs. Brophy's request the attending physician had entered a DNR order on her husband's chart. At the same time, the physician (and hospital) refused her plea to remove or clamp his feeding tube. At the trial Brophy's family presented evidence of his preference for death over an irreversibly unconscious existence. His wife testified that when discussing the *Quinlan* case, he had remarked: "No way do I want to live like that. That isn't living." His brother testified that Brophy had told him about rescuing the driver of a burning truck. The badly burned survivor lived three months and, according to the brother, Brophy rued his heroic deed and said to him: "If I'm ever like that, just shoot me, pull the plug." When Brophy was awarded a commendation for bravery for that incident, he tossed it in the trash, bitterly saying to his wife: "I should have been five minutes later. It would have been all over for him."

The trial court ruled against Mrs. Brophy and she appealed. In September 1986 — by which time Brophy had been in a permanent vegetative state for three-and-one-half years — the Massachusetts Supreme Court found in her favour, authorizing her to remove her husband to a facility that would undertake to discontinue his nourishment. The Court based its decision upon the substituted judgment test — that the evidence proved that Brophy would have opposed the prolongation of his vegetative existence by artificial feeding. (Had the case happened in Missouri or New York, which reject substituted judgment, Mrs. Brophy would have lost her case because her husband had never specifically expressed his abhorrence of being tube-fed whilst in a vegetative state.) Brophy was transferred to another hospital where he died eight days after his feeding-tube was removed.

(ii) *The Emerging Jurisprudence*

In the 1970s, the mechanical respirator/ventilator was the medical marvel that gave rise to the right-to-die cases in American courtrooms. In the mid-1980s, it was the feeding-tube that surfaced as a right-to-die symbol in the halls of justice. In the process, that symbol has evoked spirited debate in bio-medical ethical circles. Is the withholding of artificial nutrition and hydration from an incompetent patient — an act which is clearly designed to hasten death — a course of action that the law should never countenance, however dismal the prognosis?

Is it the first step down a morally treacherous Orwellian road — as in the second sense of the word *treacherous* in Webster's New Twentieth Century Dictionary: "having a false appearance of safety, honesty, etc.; deceptive; not to be depended upon; insecure?" Should the law enforce the moral position that grants a special entitlement to the symbolic role of feeding the helpless, such that its proponents can accept the shutting off of Karen Quinlan's ventilator and yet reject the removal or clamping of Paul Brophy's G-tube? Or is there no moral distinction between a feeding-tube and other kinds of medical treatment — e.g. mechanical ventilation, dialysis, and antibiotics — which are not obligatory when they fail to benefit the patient?

The nature of that debate is beyond our purview. It is enough to report that as typified by the *Brophy* case, the American courts have rejected the professed distinction between ventilator and feeding-tube (a position also endorsed by all nine Supreme Court justices in the *Cruzan* case). The American Medical Association has expressed the same view. In 1986 The AMA's Council on Ethical and Judicial Affairs adopted guidelines advising physicians that it is "not unethical to discontinue all means of life-prolonging medical treatment" — including "technologically supplied respiration, nutrition, or hydration" — for permanently unconscious and imminently dying patients.

In *Conroy* the New Jersey Supreme Court categorized the patient's feeding-tube as life-prolonging medical treatment that lawfully could be withdrawn. In 1987 the same Court ruled in the case of *Jobes, Re* that the husband of a 31-year-old nursing home patient, who had been in a persistent vegetative state for six years, could order the removal of her jejunostomy tube. In the 1987 Washington case, *In re Guardianship of Grant*, the Court concluded:

Nasogastric tubes and intravenous infusions are significantly different from typical human ways of providing nutrition. These procedures may be likened to the use of an artificial respirator; in each instance an artificial or mechanical device is required to prolong life because the body is unable to perform a vital bodily function on its own.

The direction that the courts have taken was emphatically stated in the first reported case to consider the issue. In *Barber v. Superior Court* (the California case of the murder indictment against the defendant-physicians for removing the moribund patient's feeding-tube), the prosecutor claimed that, unlike a ventilator, the provision of food and water was not medical treatment. The reason for the indictment was that "the patient did not die naturally of a terminal illness; he was dehydrated to death intentionally with death being as certain a consequence as if he was shot at point-blank range." The Court paid short shrift to that contention:

> The prosecution would have us draw a distinction between the use of mechanical breathing devices such as respirators and mechanical feeding devices such as intravenous tubes. The distinction urged seems to be based more on the emotional symbolism of providing food and water to those incapable of providing for themselves rather than on any rational difference in (the) cases.... Medical nutrition and hydration may not always provide net benefits to patients. Their benefits and burdens ought to be evaluated in the same manner as any other medical procedure.

According to the prosecutor in the *Barber* case, the withdrawal of food and fluids was tantamount to murder because the patient's death was not caused by the disease process but rather by starvation. However, as explained in Chapter 18, euthanasia — the deliberate lethal injection scenario that the criminal law defines as murder — is criminalized because the patient's death is caused by a direct act of commission. The physician deliberately interrupts the disease process by an act that directly kills the patient. In that sense, it is not the disease process that kills or causes the patient's death — rather the culprit is the physician. However, beginning with the *Barber* case, the American courts have in effect ruled that discontinuing artificial feeding is legally comparable to discontinuing artificial ventilation. In the former scenario it is the disease process that causes death because it prevents the patient from feeding on her own. In the latter scenario it is the disease process that causes death because it prevents the patient from breathing on her own. Thus, in either case, the patient's death is not caused by a direct act of commission but rather by the legally permissible foregoing of life-prolonging treatment.

(f) The No-Code (DNR) Order

In the case of *Matter of Dinnerstein* (Massachusetts, 1978),[43] an intermediate appellate court authorized the entry of a no-code (DNR) order on the patient's chart. The Court further held that judicial approval was not required because such cases present

> a question peculiarly within the competence of the medical profession of what measures are appropriate to ease the imminent passing of an irreversibly, terminally ill patient in light of the patient's history and condition and the wishes of her family.

The Court rejected the argument that "it is the duty of a doctor attending an incompetent patient to employ whatever... life-prolonging treatments the current state of the art has put in his hands." The Court explained that for patients who are irreversibly unconscious or in "the terminal stages of an unremitting, incurable mortal illness", resuscitation is powerless to "cure or relieve the illnesses which have brought the patient to the threshold of death." According to the Court, resuscitation in such cases "could aptly be described as a pointless, even cruel, prolongation of the act of dying."

In *In re Custody of a Minor* (1982),[44] the Massachusetts Supreme Court upheld a juvenile court ruling that a "no-code" be entered on the chart of a five-month-old infant. The patient suffered from severe congenital heart and lung malformations, and the prognosis was death within a year. The high court ruled that resuscitation was not in the infant's best interests as it would serve only to prolong his suffering.

In *Rasmussen by Mitchell v. Fleming* (1987),[45] the Arizona Supreme Court affirmed a ruling by a trial judge allowing the entry of a "do not resuscitate" order on the chart of a 74-year-old nursing home patient. According to the medical witnesses, the patient had been in a "nonverbal and essentially vegetative state since 1983." The high court affirmed that the patient's best interests were served by the DNR order.

These decisions are in harmony with *Quinlan* and the cases that have followed its precedent. If artificial ventilation may be *withdrawn* when it fails to benefit the mentally incompetent patient, then it likewise follows that resuscitation may be *withheld* in accordance with reasonable medical judgment. (A mentally competent patient is of course entitled to make that judgment for herself, either in direct conversation with her physician or by way of advance directive.)

Over the past few years, a growing number of states have enacted statutes to clarify the procedures for writing DNR orders. As Professor Meisel has observed, they cannot be interpreted as compelling the provision of CPR against medical judgment:

The purpose of DNR statutes is to provide physicians with assurances that it *is* permissible, and to provide individuals with a mechanism for implementing the right to refuse treatment — specifically, the right to refuse cardiopulmonary resuscitation. There is no basis in the history and purposes of these statutes...that they were intended to create a right to compel the provision of CPR. The decision whether CPR is to be offered is implicitly left to medical judgment.[46]

(g) The Legal Theory

The American courts have grounded the competent patient's right to refuse life-prolonging treatment in two unrelated principles: (1) the common law requirement that a competent patient cannot be treated without his consent; and (2) the constitutional right of privacy. The same principles serve to enshrine the right of an incompetent patient to the same privilege.

(i)   *A Common Law (Judge-Made) Right*

In the *Brother Fox (Eichner v. Dillon)* case, the New York Court of Appeals extended the competent patient's common law right to decline life-prolonging treatment to the incompetent patient. In the process, the Court rejected the argument that "whatever right the patient may have (to refuse such treatment) is entirely personal and may not be exercised by any third person once the patient becomes incompetent."

(ii) *A Constitutional Right of Privacy*

In *Quinlan*, the New Jersey Supreme Court noted that, if Karen were competent, she could without doubt exercise her constitutional right to refuse mechanical ventilation. The Court went on to conclude that her privacy right could be exercised on her behalf by a surrogate decision-maker. The Court explained:

> If a putative decision by Karen to permit this non-cognitive vegetative existence to terminate by natural forces is regarded as a valuable incident of her right to privacy, as we believe it to be, then it should not be discarded solely on the basis that her condition prevents her conscious exercise of that choice. The only practical way to prevent destruction of the right is to permit the guardian and family of Karen to render their best judgment...as to whether she would exercise it in these circumstances.

Although the courts have not ignored the common law approach that was followed in the *Brother Fox* case, they have tended to rely primarily upon the constitutional grounds first enunciated in *Quinlan*. Until the 1990

Cruzan case, the U.S. Supreme Court had refused to hear cases involving the termination of life-prolonging treatment for incompetent patients because of its policy position that the issues should be resolved at the state court level. Notwithstanding the *Cruzan* ruling, a reasonable inference to draw from its general policy of avoidance is that the Supreme Court endorses the impressive array of state court judgments that have permitted physicians to halt life-prolonging treatment for mentally incompetent patients. By leaving such judgments intact, the Court has in effect permitted the privacy doctrine to become firmly entrenched as the prevailing judicial doctrine in this area of the law.

NOTES

1. *Quinlan, Re*, 355 A.2d 647 (U.S. N.J. Sup. Ct., 1976).
2. *Cruzan v. Director, Missouri Health Department*, 497 U.S. 261 (U.S. Sup. Ct., 1990).
3. Of course, not all these cases involve mentally incompetent patients; and there are American cases (which are noted in Chapter 19) in which it was the patient who sought the foregoing of life-support measures. The focus in this chapter is upon patients who cannot speak for themselves and who have not left guidance by way of health care directives.
4. The Multi-Society Task Force on PVS. Medical aspects of persistent vegetative state, 330 **New England Journal of Medicine** 1499 (1994).
5. *Conroy, Re*, 486 A.2d 1209 (U.S. N.J., 1985).
6. *In the Matter of Beth Israel Medical Center*, 519 N.Y.S.2d 511 (1987).
7. *In re Guardianship of Grant*, 747 P.2d 445 (1987).
8 A. Meisel, The Legal Consensus About Forgoing Life-Sustaining Treatment: Its Status and its Prospects. 2 **Kennedy Institute of Ethics Journal** 309, 319-20 (1993).
9. *Peter, Re*, 529 A.2d 419 (1987).
10. *Jobes, Re*, 529 A.2d 434 (1987).
11. A. Handler, Social dilemmas, judicial (ir)resolutions. 40 **Rutgers Law Journal** 23-4 (1987).
12. *Eichner v. Dillon*, 420 N.E.2d 64 (1981).
13. *John F. Kennedy Memorial Hospital v. Bludworth*, 452 So.2d 921 (1984).
14. *O'Connor, Re*, 531 N.E.2d 607 (1988).
15. *Martin v. Martin*, 538 N.W.2d 399 (1995).
16. *Wendland v. Wendland*, Cal. Rptr. 2d 412 (2001).
17. L.J. Nelson & R.E. Cranford, Michael Martin and Robert Wendland: Beyond the vegetative state. 15 **Journal of Contemporary Health Law and Policy** 427, 428 (1999).
18. *Ibid.*, at 448.
19. *Ibid.*
20. *Mack v. Mack*, 618 A.2d 744 (1993).
21. *DeGrella v. Elston*, 858 S.W.2d 696 (1993).
22. L.J. Schneiderman, Exile and PVS. 20 **Hastings Center Report** 5 (1990).
23. Amicus Curiae for the American Hospital Association, cited in *Cruzan v. Director, Missouri Health Department*, 497 U.S. 261 (U.S. Sup. Ct., 1990).
24. *Torres, Re*, 357 N.W.2d 332 (1984).
25. *Barber v. Superior Court*, 195 Cal. Rptr. 484 (1983).
26. *In re Phillip B.*, 156 Cal. Rptr. 48 (1979).
27. *Supra* note 6.
28. *Supra* note 7.

29. J.J. Paris et al., Physicians' refusal of requested treatment. 322 **New England Journal of Medicine** 1012 (1990).

30. *Wanglie, Re*, No. PX-91-283 (1991).

31. *Baby K., Re*, 16 F.3d 590 (1994).

32. *Causey v. St. Francis Medical Center*, 719 So.2d 1072 (1998).

33. *Gilgunn v. Massachusetts General Hospital* (April 22, 1995), Doc. SUC92-480 (Super. Ct. Suffolk County, Mass.).

34. J.J. Paris et al., Use of a DNR order over family objections: The case of Gilgunn v. MGH. 14 **Journal of Intensive Care Medicine** 41, 45 (1999).

35. The Hastings Center, **Guidelines on the Termination of Life-Sustaining Treatment and the Care of the Dying** (The Hastings Center, New York, 1989), at 32.

36. D.J. Murphy et al., Outcomes of cardiopulmonary resuscitation in the elderly. 111 **Annals of Internal Medicine**, 199 (1989).

37. *Supra* note 29.

38. R.M. Taylor & J.D. Lantos, The politics of medical futility. 11 **Issues in Law & Medicine** 3 (1995).

39. A. Meisel, **The Right to Die: 1994 Cumulative Supplement No. 1**. (John Wiley & Sons, New York, 1994), at xxiv.

40. *R. v. Cambridge Health Authority*, (sub nom. *B, ex parte*) [1995] 2 All E.R. 129 (C.A.).

41. S.H. Miles, Medical Futility. 20 **Law, Medicine & Health Care** 310 (1992).

42. *Brophy v. New England Sinai Hospital Inc.*, 497 N.E.2d 626 (1986).

43. *Matter of Dinnerstein*, 380 N.E.2d 134 (U.S. Mass. C.A., 1978).

44. *In re Custody of a Minor*, 434 N.E.2d 601 (1982).

45. *Rasmussen by Mitchell v. Fleming*, 741 P.2d 674 (1987).

46. A. Meisel, **The Right to Die**, Volume 1 (2nd ed.) John Wiley & Sons, New York, 1995), at 553.

22

THE MENTALLY INCOMPETENT ADULT PATIENT AND THE FOREGOING OF LIFE-PROLONGING TREATMENT

SUMMARY

As of yet there are no Canadian appellate decisions addressing the foregoing of life-prolonging treatment for incompetent adult patients. Even so, physicians are not inhibited from withholding and withdrawing life-support measures in order to hasten the deaths of such patients. In any event, neither civil nor criminal law has imposed a duty upon physicians to furnish treatment that offers no reasonable hope of benefit for the patient. The role of the family in the decision-making process is considered, as is the legality of do-not-resuscitate (DNR) orders. The discussion of medical futility in the last chapter is continued here in the context of two Manitoba cases.

The focus of this chapter is upon mentally incompetent patients without health care directives; those with directives are considered in Chapter 24.

1. INTRODUCTION

In its 1982 working paper, *Euthanasia, Aiding Suicide and Cessation of Treatment*, the Law Reform Commission of Canada (LRCC) forcefully repudiated the view that "it is the doctor's solemn duty in the case of the incompetent patient to initiate and to continue treatment in all cases."[1] Its contrary position was clearly stated:

> Insistence on heroic but useless measures is no more justified for the incompetent patient than it is for the competent. In other words, an individual's incapacity should not serve as a basis or pretext for denying him the fundamental right or opportunity available to the competent patient to exercise

choice. It would be regrettable and absurd if, because a person is incompetent, his attending physician were legally obliged to continue or to undertake useless treatment and required to prolong his patient's suffering to no avail. It would be unthinkable that a person should lose his right to die with dignity as soon as one becomes incapable of expressing wishes.[2]

The LRCC also went out of its way to urge Canadian law to specify that a physician acts lawfully when he fails to take measures to prolong life "if these measures are useless or contrary to the patient's wishes or interests."[3] As it elaborated:

> The law must recognize what is now a medical and scientific reality. It must admit that the cessation or noninitiation of treatment which offers no chance of success is a good decision and one based on sound medical practice. Treatment is a measure designed to help the patient recover from his illness, to halt its progress at least temporarily or to relieve its symptoms. It is selected and administered in an effort to protect or to extend life.... The guiding principle for medical decision-making is not life in itself as an absolute value, but the patient's overall welfare. In most instances, this welfare imposes the maintenance of life, but this is not always the case. It is not the case when the prolonging of life has become purely artificial. In other words, it is not the case when treatment is diverted from its proper end and merely prolongs the dying process rather than life itself.[4]

Unfortunately, the LRCC's call for law reform has gone unanswered, in sharp contrast to the United States where a sizeable body of jurisprudence has been fashioned to permit the termination of life-prolonging treatment for incompetent patients.*

Still, there is a sense in which Canadian law has endorsed the LRCC's proposals by indirection, and what this means in terms of medical practice is considered in due course. As noted, the LRCC's working paper builds on the premise that physicians act within the law when they call a halt to life-prolonging treatment for incompetent patients. In that document it offered its view on two key policy questions: (1) Who Decides?, and (2) Under What Criteria?

As to the former, the LRCC indicated its firm opposition to the "judicialization" of the decision-making process. Its opinion was that court involvement is necessary only when there is unresolvable conflict within the patient's family or between family and physician.

> One would not wish to judicialize and hence to make adversarial a decision-making process which should be based more on consensus than confrontation.

---

* See Chapter 21.

A judicial decision is necessary when there is some conflict. It may be superfluous when it is used merely to formalize a decision which has already been made and which no one has challenged and which involves no real dispute, controversy, or conflict.[5]

The LRCC went on to suggest that the incompetent patient's physician should be the central figure in the decision-making process; that the physician consult with the family but that the ultimate responsibility must rest on her shoulders. In addressing the *What Criteria* question, it endorsed the *substituted judgment* and *best interests tests** as the proper standards to guide the decision-maker.

The working paper was followed up the next year with a report, also titled *Euthanasia, Aiding Suicide and Cessation of Treatment*,[6] which simply echoed the policy recommendations contained in the earlier document. Given the rarity of judicial involvement, it would appear that "cessation of treatment" cases in Canada are marked by the consensus model that the LRCC favours. (The rare case that winds up in court when the consensus fails will be considered in due course.)

Aside from the American case law canvassed in the previous chapter, there are now rulings from two Commonwealth jurisdictions that have fashioned common law principles to authorize the medical practice of abating life-prolonging treatment for mentally incompetent patients. The cases were decided in 1993 by the high courts of New Zealand and Great Britain, and we turn now to these two precedent-setting decisions.

2. TWO LANDMARK CASES

(a) *Auckland Area Health Board v. Attorney General* (New Zealand Supreme Court, 1993)[7]

The 59-year-old patient was admitted to hospital in July 1991 with Guillian-Barre syndrome, the same neurological disease that afflicted Nancy B.** He had suffered a complete absence of conduction along the nerves and degeneration of the nerve axons; the result was total denervation in a patient who could not communicate and who was described as being in a totally "locked in and locked out" state. By the following April all eight physicians involved in his case — four neurologists and four critical care specialists — concurred that the time had come to stop all life-support measures. His immediate family (wife and brother) and the hospital ethics committee agreed that the patient be allowed to die.

---

* The tests are discussed in Chapter 21.

** See Chapter 19.

Although his physicians were convinced that the decision to hasten death was medically and ethically appropriate, they hesitated to act because there was no clear legal authority that what they proposed to do was allowed by the criminal law. They accordingly followed the advice of the hospital's legal counsel to obtain a judicial declaration to that effect.

In the result, the New Zealand Supreme Court ruled that the physicians were under no legal duty to keep the patient on artificial life-support. As in the Canadian *Criminal Code*, the New Zealand Crimes Act contains a section that defines the duty to provide "necessaries of life." (The wording of the two provisions is virtually identical, which is not surprising as both were based upon the 1879 Draft Code written by the prominent English jurist, James Fitzhugh Stephen.) In any event, the provision in the Crimes Act states in pertinent part that a person is under a legal duty to provide necessaries of life (which according to case law includes medical treatment) to anyone under his charge who because of sickness is unable to obtain such necessaries for herself. And such person is "criminally responsible for omitting without lawful excuse to perform such duty if the death of that person is caused...by such omission...."

The key question, of course, was whether the incompetent patient's condition constituted a "lawful excuse" sufficient to discharge the duty to provide life-support. In resolving that issue the Court ruled that the cessation of treatment would constitute a "lawful excuse" if it complied with "good medical practice." What that entailed was spelled out as follows:

1. That the decision to stop treatment was in the patient's best interests.
2. That it would "command general approval within the medical profession."
3. That the patient's immediate family gave their informed consent to the decision.
4. That approval was secured from a "recognized ethical body."

Finally, the Court ruled that decisions in such end-of-life cases were not for the courts, but rather were the responsibility of physicians acting in concert with the families of their incompetent patients. In the result, the patient's life-support was stopped and he quickly died with his family at his bedside.

(b) *Airedale NHS Trust v. Bland* (House Of Lords, 1993)[8]

Amongst the scores of victims trampled in the Hillsborough Football Stadium disaster of 1989 was 18-year-old Anthony Bland. Although he survived, his injuries destroyed his higher brain functions and left him in a permanent vegetative state (PVS).* Three years later his parents and physicians decided that it was time to let him die, and that the way to accomplish that end was either to stop the nutrition and hydration supplied through his nasogastric tube, or else to withhold antibiotics in the event of infection. As in the New Zealand case, the caregivers were reluctant to act because there were no legal precedents allowing the termination of life-prolonging treatment for a mentally incompetent patient.

A petition was accordingly filed in the Family Division, seeking a declaration that Bland's caregivers could lawfully refrain from those two courses of action. The declaration was granted, affirmed by the three-judge panel of the Court of Appeal, and affirmed on further appeal by the Judicial Committee of the House of Lords (with the assent of all five law lords who heard the case). The law lords were quick to dispel the notion that life-prolonging treatment could not be halted for mentally incompetent patients. In the words of Lord Goff:

> There was no absolute rule that a patient's life had to be prolonged by medical treatment regardless of the circumstances.... Indeed it would be most startling and could lead to the most adverse and cruel effects upon the patient if any such absolute rule were held to exist.... Indeed if the justification for treating a patient who lacked the mental capacity to consent lay in the fact that treatment was provided in his best interests, it had to follow that the treatment might and ultimately should be discontinued where it was no longer in his best interests to provide it.... (I cannot) see that medical treatment was appropriate or requisite simply to prolong a patient's life, when such treatment had no therapeutic purpose of any kind, as where it was futile because the patient was unconscious and there was no prospect of any improvement in his condition.

The decision in the *Bland* case is in line with the sentiment expressed by the LRCC at the beginning of this chapter when it scorned the notion that "it is the doctor's solemn duty in the case of the incompetent patient to initiate and to continue treatment in all cases." The question, to which we now turn, is whether the same can be said for Canada, where there is no legal authority of comparable stature to that of the high courts of New Zealand and Great Britain.

3. CRIMINAL LAW IMPLICATIONS

In its aforenoted 1983 report, the LRCC recommended an amendment to the *Criminal Code* to clarify that physicians were not legally bound

---

* PVS cases are discussed in Chapter 21.

to continue to administer or undertake medical treatment, when such treatment has become therapeutically useless and is not in the best interests of the person for whom it is intended.[9]

The reason for its proposed amendment is found in the language of two sections of the *Criminal Code*. On the one hand, there is section 215: "Everyone is under a legal duty...to provide necessaries of life to a person under his charge if that person is unable by reason of...illness...to provide himself with necessaries of life." On the other hand, there is section 217: "Every one who undertakes to do an act is under a legal duty to do it if an omission to do the act is or may be dangerous to life." In theory a Crown prosecutor could indict a physician for manslaughter if his moribund patient died when life-prolonging treatment was either withheld — e.g. CPR, dialysis, or antibiotics — or else withdrawn — e.g. disconnecting the ventilator. The Crown's case would proceed along the following lines:

> A conviction of the physician for manslaughter can be supported on two grounds. Under section 215, the accused had an ill and helpless person under her charge and therefore was duty bound to maintain treatment because there is ample case law defining medical treatment as falling under the heading of "necessaries of life."

> Under section 217, a physician who undertakes treatment assumes a legal duty to preserve her patient's life at all costs. The accused's omission or failure to maintain treatment was "dangerous to life", as proved by the fact that her neglect directly caused her patient's death.

> Furthermore, section 219 provides that: "Every one is criminally negligent who in... omitting to do anything that it is his (legal) duty to do, shows wanton or reckless disregard for the lives or safety of other persons." The twin legal duties imposed by sections 215 and 217 mean that however grim the prognosis, the physician is obliged to keep her patient alive if the technology to do so is at hand. Section 219 clearly applies here because the accused breached her legal duty to treat and in the process clearly exhibited "wanton or reckless disregard" for the life of her patient. It follows that she has committed the manslaughter offence of causing death by criminal negligence under section 220.

There is an air of unreality to our hypothetical prosecution because no criminal charge has ever been filed in Canada against a physician for terminating her incompetent patient's life-support measures. In the previous chapter, we considered the first of two American cases in which that happened, *Barber v. Superior Court*, and in that case a California court dismissed murder indictments against two physicians who had withdrawn their irreversibly unconscious patient's ventilator and feeding tubes. (The other case, *State of Kansas v. Naramore*, is considered in Chapter 25.)

A Canadian case comparable to *Barber* would almost certainly result in the vindication of the accused. It is our view that the Canadian courts would no doubt reject the proposition that when treatment offers no reasonable hope of benefit to the patient, the physician is nonetheless locked into a *Criminal Code* duty to provide aggressive medical management until such time as the patient is pronounced brain-dead. Beginning with the *Quinlan* case, the American courts have enshrined the principle that a physician is not bound to preserve life when treatment no longer benefits her patients but serves only to postpone death. Even though there is scant Canadian case law (considered shortly), Canadian physicians no less than their American colleagues practice medicine in line with that principle. After acknowledging in its 1982 working paper that, without interference from the law, Canadian physicians daily "pull the plug" on incompetent patients, the LRCC commented.

> Many believe that there is no longer any problem: the practice is legal because it exists, because it occurs every day, and because the law has never seen fit to intervene. The law's silence is thus interpreted as an indorsement or tacit consent on its part.[10]

This observation is as true today as when it appeared in 1982. Our provincial attorneys-general have in effect adopted an unstated policy of noninterference in end-of-life medical decisions for mentally incompetent patients. There is, of course, the rider that the physician must be guided by the best interests of her patient (or previously known wishes of the patient), and that she act in accordance with accepted medical practice. In its 1982 working paper (and again in its 1983 report), the LRCC urged Parliament to state the law explicitly by *Criminal Code* amendment in order to lift the "veil of uncertainty" occasioned by its continued silence. Although that has yet to happen, Canadian care providers and hospitals have indicated their willingness to live with the law's off-the-record endorsement of the kind of medical practice endorsed by the LRRC in the working paper.

Even if the spectre of criminal prosecution can be discarded, what of the threat of a law suit for wrongful death when a physician foregoes life-prolonging treatment for an incompetent patient? Assume that the patient has left no health care directive (to guide surrogate decision-making), and that a disgruntled next-of-kin insists that her loved one be kept alive at all cost. Assume further that her lawyer sends a letter threatening the physician/health care facility with a medical malpractice claim for wrongful death if aggressive treatment is not maintained. One is prompted to respond that there is no duty to provide non-beneficial or futile care; but the response begs the question, How does one define a procedure as futile when it is keeping the patient alive? This issue, which was canvassed in the last chapter, confronted the Manitoba Court of Appeal in a bizarre case to which we now turn.

4. THE MANITOBA COURT OF APPEAL CASE OF CHILD & FAMILY SERVICES OF CENTRAL MANITOBA v. L. (R.)[11]

This 1997 case involved an infant who was a victim of shaken baby syndrome, and the question was whether his physician could enter a DNR order on his chart over the objection of the parents. The infant had been apprehended by Child and Family Services (CFS) at the age of three months, and at the time of judgment was eleven months old. According to the medical evidence before the trial court:

> The injuries inflicted upon D (the patient) have reduced him to a "persistent vegetative state." His brain has, quite literally, shrunk over the intervening months. His doctor says D is moving from one intermittent illness to another. Sooner or later he will be struck by a serious illness that will require intrusive heroic measures which, if successful, will only bring him back to his persistent vegetative state.

CFS agreed with the physician's call for the DNR order; but when the parents who were still his legal guardians, refused to consent, the agency sought judicial approval for the order. Its application was based on section 25(3) of *The Child and Family Services Act*, which stipulates that an agency may seek a court order "authorizing medical...treatment for an apprehended child where the parents...refuse to consent to treatment." The petition was granted at trial and the parents appealed. Although the three-judge panel (in a decision written by Justice Twaddle) overturned the ruling, it was no victory for the parents. That was because the Court of Appeal found that section 25(3) dealt only with treatment; and that since a DNR order was in the realm of non-treatment, the authority to issue the order lay not with the judiciary but rather with the attending physician. As Justice Twaddle concluded: "There is no legal obligation on a medical doctor to take heroic measures to maintain the life of a patient in an irreversible vegetative state." In fact, as he added:

> Indeed the opposite may be true.... (P)hilosophical arguments apart, it is in no one's interest to artificially maintain the life of a...patient who is in an irreversible vegetative state. That is unless those responsible for the patient

being in that state have an interest in prolonging life to avoid criminal responsibility for the death.

Although Justice Twaddle did not elaborate, he presumably had in mind the so-called "year-and-a-day rule", pursuant to which an accused could not be convicted of culpable homicide (whether murder or manslaughter) unless the victim died within a year and a day from the time of the assault. (This centuries' old common law rule was enshrined in section 227 of the *Criminal Code*; it was repealed two years after the decision in this case.) Although the police had yet to make an arrest for the assault against the infant, the case was still open at the time of the Court of Appeal's judgment. Since at that time a suspect could be charged with unlawful act manslaughter (assault causing death) if the patient died within a year and a day of the incident, the decision appears by implication to question the good faith of the parental objection to the DNR order. In any event, Justice Twaddle went on to say:

> [N]either consent nor a court order in lieu is required for a medical doctor to issue a non-resuscitation direction where in his or her judgment the patient is in an irreversible vegetative state. Whether or not such a decision should be issued is a judgment call for the doctor to make having regard to the patient's history and condition and the doctor's evaluation of the hopelessness of the case. The wishes of the patient's family or guardian should be taken into account, but neither their consent nor the approval of a court is required.

Although the Court was dealing with the question of a DNR order for a PVS patient, its ruling is not restricted to that particular fact scenario. It is true that Justice Twaddle specifically ruled that it lay within the physician's discretion whether to issue a DNR order for a PVS patient. And he elsewhere stated that a physician was not obliged to maintain the life of such a patient. If he had simply said that these facts — a DNR order for a PVS patient — were sufficient in themselves to decide the case without looking at broader issues, then that would support a narrow-based decision. But that he did not do. Instead he emphasized that the heart of the matter lay "in understand(ing) why authority for medical treatment is necessary." As he explained, consent is required in non-emergency settings only when the provision of treatment without it would constitute assault (or a battery in tort law). Hence it followed that there was "no need for a consent from anyone for a doctor to refrain from intervening," subject to the rider that

> [t]he only fear a doctor need have in denying heroic measures is the fear of liability for negligence in circumstances where qualified practitioners would have thought intervention warranted.

Since the ruling is grounded in the distinction between treatment and non-treatment, its range cannot be confined to the particular condition of the patient and the particular medical intervention at issue. As noted, the Court stressed that treatment involves physical contact with the patient. When there is non-emergency touching (treatment), then consent by patient or surrogate is necessary to negate assault/battery, whereas no such consent is required whenever the physician's action is not part of the treatment process. And that is the case when there is no physical contact with the body of the patient.

The Court's focus is not directed to the patient's medical condition nor to the treatment to be withheld or withdrawn. Rather it falls upon the crucial circumstance requiring consent — treatment that involves physical contact with the patient's body. It follows that if there is no such contact, then the physician can act unilaterally even if the patient is not vegetative and the treatment refrained from is other than CPR.

Moreover, it logically follows that if it is solely the physician's prerogative whether to refrain from a particular "treatment," it matters not whether the insistence upon it stems from the patient, let alone from a surrogate. If, as the Court ruled, a patient's legal guardians could not dictate the provision of treatment, then it would also be the case that no one else — even an adult or mature minor patient — could do so. To reiterate, that is because the only relevant concern is the reasonableness of the medical decision to forego life-support measures, and that can be contested only after the fact. (Notwithstanding the ruling in *L. (R.)*, there is anecdotal evidence that some Manitoba physicians act against their professional judgment by bowing to pressure from families to provide treatment for incompetent patients. The director of resident care at a longterm care facility in Winnipeg has acknowledged cases in which this has occurred, as have nurses at other such facilities. One presumes that this experience happens across the country.)

5. COMMENTARY ON THE MANITOBA CASE

(a) The PVS Patient

Surely, one must concede that the decision that a patient — however dismal the prognosis — is better off dead is one that cannot be taken lightly. Given that the Court in *L. (R.)* was asked to endorse a medical decision based upon quality-of-life grounds, it was surely incumbent upon it to address the profound ethical implications of the matter at hand. In the *Bland* case, the House of Lords devoted 46 pages to a painstaking analysis of the issues addressed by the proposed termination of artificial feeding for a PVS patient. In stark contrast, the Manitoba Court of Appeal disposed of the matter of withholding life-prolonging treatment from such a patient in one sentence:

> [P]hilosophical arguments apart, it is in no one's interest to artificially maintain the life of a...patient who is in an irreversible vegetative state. [The Court's reasons for judgment take up a scant two pages in the law reports.]

Yet when one is dealing with so-called "right to die" cases, the judging process surely requires the resolution of "philosophical arguments." If one decides, as did the Manitoba Court of Appeal, that the "life" of a PVS patient is not worth living, that is surely a philosophical judgment. Suffice it to say that the question warrants far more than the cursory treatment afforded by this court, whose rush to judgment stands in marked contrast to rulings in other common law jurisdictions which have given the attention that is deserved for resolving life and death matters.

(b) Touching versus Non-touching

L. (R.) is the only case in a common law jurisdiction in which an appellate court has ruled that consent to the termination of life-prolonging measures is not required so long as carrying out of the medical decision does not entail hands-on treatment. According to the Court, the only reason for the consent requirement to medical treatment is that, emergencies aside, nonconsensual touching of the patient's body constitutes the crime of assault. (It likewise is a battery in tort law.) The Court was led to conclude that, since omitting CPR means not touching, the physician could issue a DNR order for his PVS patient without securing consent from the legal guardians or the judiciary.

Once again, since consent is required only when there is physical contact with the patient, Justice Twaddle's ruling cannot be restricted to PVS patients and DNR orders. In sum, whatever the patient's medical situation, if treatment — whether CPR, dialysis, tube-feeding, mechanical ventilation, antibiotics, or whatever — is being foregone, then the physician can act unilaterally. And that is because, in Justice Twaddle's view "[t]here is no need for a consent from anyone for a doctor to refrain from intervening."

The Court thus confines the decision-making authority of patient/ surrogate to active interventions. Simply put, treatment requires consent but non-treatment — refraining from intervening — does not. The Court's definition of treatment can be contrasted with that found in "Tabor's Cyclopedic Medical Dictionary." The first entry under the heading of treatment defines it as "medical, surgical or psychiatric management of a patient." In that sense, a DNR order is part of the treatment plan.

That a DNR order is part of a treatment plan was assumed by a judge of the Ontario Divisional Court in a case heard but one month before the Manitoba ruling. In *London Health Sciences Centre v. K. (R.) (Litigation Guardian of)*,[12] the Court considered an application by the hospital for a declaration of criminal and civil immunity if life-support were withdrawn from an 83-year-old PVS patient. The submission referred to the proposed discontinuation of "ventilation, nutrition and hydration by artificial means" and to non-resuscitation in the event that the patient suffered "a cardiac or respiratory arrest either before or after such discontinuance." In the result, Justice McDermid rejected the application because he found that there were no legal obstacles to the proposed measures. He further remarked that:

> I have no hesitation in finding that the proposed plan of treatment, namely to withdraw artificial life-support from R.K. and to refrain from resuscitating him in the event of another cardiac or pulmonary arrest, is in his best interests.

It was plain to this Ontario judge that a treatment plan for a patient encompasses measures that will be taken as well as measures that will not be taken. For how else can one determine the care — the treatment — of the patient? To say that a non-treatment option is not part of the patient's treatment plan is to ignore the fact that treatment is about caring — and that caring sometimes means hands-on and sometimes means hands-off. Either way, the patient is being treated as a person for whom not doing may be just as beneficial as doing.

Even if, however, one were to accept Justice Twaddle's treatment versus non-treatment dichotomy, it would require further refinement. Given his standpoint, it really becomes a question of treatment versus the *withholding* of treatment and the *withdrawal* of treatment when it does not involve bodily contact. Thus, the import of his decision is that different legal implications may attach to withholding and withdrawing; that whereas consent is not required for withholding, there must be consent to withdrawal of treatment unless the procedure does not entail contact with the body of the patient.

In the *Bland* case, it was argued by the guardian *ad litem* for the patient that the proposed removal of his nasogastric tube and the discontinuance of artificial feeding were "positive acts of commission" and therefore tantamount to "euthanasia" (i.e. murder). The Court responded that "the failure to continue to do what you have previously done is...by definition an omission to do what you have previously done." Acknowledging that the "positive act of removing the nasogastric tube presents more difficulty,"

Lord Browne-Wilkinson offered pertinent comments about the artificiality of the distinction between life-ending acts of commission and omission:

> It is undoubtedly a positive act, similar to switching off a ventilator in the case of a patient whose life is being sustained by artificial ventilation. But...in neither case should the act be classified as positive, since to do so would be to introduce intolerably fine distinctions. If, instead of removing the naso-gastric tube, it was left in place, but no further nutrients were provided for the tube to convey to the patient's stomach, that would not be an act of commission. Again...if the switching off of a ventilator were to be classified as a positive act, exactly the same result can be achieved by installing a time-clock which requires to be reset every 12 hours; the failure to reset the machine could not be classified as a positive act. In my judgment, essentially what is being done is to omit to feed or to ventilate; the removal of the nasogastric tube or the switching off of a ventilator are merely incidents of that omission.

Justice Twaddle's ruling would thus allow a physician to act without the consent of patient/surrogate when ventilator support is terminated by not resetting the time-clock. In other words, if there is no touching then consent is not required. If, however, a sedating dose of morphine were indicated because the patient might otherwise gasp for breath, then consent (even if implied) would be required. These scenarios illustrate the peculiar nature of a ruling that takes the overall treatment plan for a patient and bisects it into treatment, which requires consent, and refraining from treatment, which does not.

As their lordships in *Bland* correctly noted, the distinction between commission and omission does not hinge upon whether the physician makes contact with the patient's body in the course of discontinuing life-prolonging treatment. Their conclusion is in accord with the overwhelming consensus of the courts (and medical ethicists) that there is no legal (or ethical) distinction between withholding and withdrawing life-prolonging treatment. In contrast, the import of the ruling in *L. (R.)* is that the physician who withdraws artificial life-support without the consent of patient or surrogate commits the crime of assault (and the tort of battery) only if removal entails the touching of the patient. But should legal principles follow from such a nit-picking distinction? As Lord Browne-Wilkinson pointed out in *Bland*, the caregiver can adopt procedures to obviate the need to touch the patient in the process of discontinuing life-support measures. Thus, the touching versus non-touching dichotomy lacks any ethical or — the case of *L. (R.)* aside — any legal relevance.

At the end of the day the question of patient/surrogate consent cannot be resolved on the narrow ground offered by Justice Twaddle. In a 1993 Supreme Court of Canada case, *Ciarlariello v. Schacter*,[13] the issue was whether the plaintiff had withdrawn consent to an angiogram that tragically resulted in rendering her a quadriplegic. In a unanimous ruling against the plaintiff, the Court held that although she had asked that the test be stopped, she had then consented to its resumption. Speaking for the Court, Justice Cory explained the core issue at stake:

> It should not be forgotten that every patient has a right to bodily integrity. This encompasses the right to determine what medical procedures will be accepted and the extent to which they will be accepted. Everyone has the right to decide what is to be done with one's own body.

Admittedly, our highest court was dealing with the question of whether a patient had been treated without her consent, and not whether the patient had the right to enforce treatment. Yet in either case — "do not treat me!" and "you must treat me!" — there are questions of patient autonomy and bodily integrity that cannot be ignored. At the dawn of a new millennium, the case of *L. (R.)* forces us to confront the kind of health care system that we want and that we can afford. And however we grapple with these questions, we can find precious little guidance in an equation that reduces itself to two variables: touching the patient and not touching the patient.

(c) The Right to Refuse versus the Right to Demand

With due respect to the Manitoba court, the fitting tension is not between non-touching and touching but rather between *negative* and *positive* rights. Case law in Canada and other common law jurisdictions has established the right of mentally competent patients (and when incompetent their surrogates) to refuse treatment. A patient's entitlement to freedom from unwarranted interference with her bodily integrity is a negative right — that she not receive hands-on treatment without consent. That is why Twaddle, J.A. rightly emphasized that non-emergency treatment without the consent of the patient or surrogate is unlawful. In contrast, a demand by patient/surrogate for a particular treatment is the assertion of a so-called positive right. As the authors of an article on medical futility put it:

> The law underlying the right to refuse treatment does not easily transfer to the right to receive treatment. The difference between the demands "don't touch me" and "you must touch me" is dramatic. The law has almost uniformly conceded the former but has only hesitantly recognized the latter, and only in situations related to public health and safety.[14]

Surely, there is more to the claimed right of a patient or surrogate to treatment — whether it be CPR, mechanical ventilation, tube-feeding, dialysis or whatever — than can be resolved by the simple invocation of a tension between touching and non-touching. Profound public policy concerns are implicated by medical decisions to withhold and withdraw life-prolonging measures; and it is here that we confront that troublesome "F" word — futility — and its quantitative and qualitative aspects.* The patient's right to refuse life-prolonging treatment follows from the recognition of patient autonomy as a core principle of medical law and ethics. The question here is whether the law's enshrinement of the patient's negative right to refuse treatment should be extended to include a positive right by the patient to demand treatment that is arguably futile, or for the patient's surrogate to demand such treatment on the grounds that this is what the patient would ask for if competent to speak for herself.

Although *L. (R.)* is the only Canadian appellate decision involving the withholding of CPR, the matter has been treated in the Joint Statement on Resuscitative Interventions issued in 1995 by the Canadian Medical Association, the Canadian Nurses Association, the Canadian Healthcare Association, and the Catholic Health Association of Canada. As the guidelines stipulate: "there is no obligation to offer a person futile or nonbeneficial treatment." Accordingly, CPR is not a reasonable option when "it offers no reasonable hope of recovery or improvement or because the person is permanently unable to experience any benefit."

As pointed out by Professor Joan Gilmour, the guidelines are ambivalent as to whether physicians should be entitled to direct DNR orders over the objection of patient or surrogate.[15] Although they provide that "as a general rule a person should be involved in determining futility in his or her case," the guidelines go on to say that CPR should not be a treatment option when the patient will almost certainly not benefit from it. This lack of clarity is no doubt a reflection of the complexities inherent in a dispute between the patient and/or family saying Yes to treatment and the physician responding by saying No.

That said, the question is whether the law has given a clear direction as to who wins that kind of conflict. As noted earlier, the LRCC suggested that the incompetent patient's physician should be the central figure in the decision-making process; that the physician consult with the family but that the ultimate responsibility must rest upon her shoulders. Although it left open resort to the courts in cases of conflict, we have seen that the Manitoba Court of Appeal deems that route unnecessary when the medical decision involves the foregoing of treatment. Yet another court faced with the same essential facts might have used the occasion to develop common law guidelines for the resolution of conflict — perhaps by prescribing a

---

* See Chapter 21 at pp. 533-42.

speedy hearing before a hospital review panel with final recourse to the courts if the matter cannot otherwise be resolved.

The import of the *L. (R.)* case is that there is no civil liability — and by implication, no criminal liability — when caregivers act upon the reasonable medical judgment that life-prolonging treatment is no longer warranted in the particular case. There is already an abundance of case law in common law jurisdictions to that effect although the cases have not involved the foregoing of treatment over family dissent. Beginning with the 1976 decision by the New Jersey Supreme Court in the *Quinlan* case, the cases have rather involved families seeking redress when health care facilities have declined to discontinue life-support measures.

Professor Meisel does not read the cases establishing the right of patients/surrogates to refuse life-prolonging treatment as enshrining their right to demand such treatment. In his view, to contend that the former

> creates a claim on the part of patients to require that life-sustaining treatment be continued against the will of the physician — in effect, a right on the part of patients or families to dictate to physicians what treatment they will administer — is to read the common law precedents out of context and far too broadly.[16]

In sum, although the law allows for the termination of life-prolonging treatment at the demand of patient/surrogate, this entitlement does not carry over to a legal mandate that life-prolonging treatment be maintained when insisted upon by patient/surrogate. And however dealt with in the future, it is questionable whether courts outside Manitoba will embrace the Manitoba Court of Appeal's touching versus non-touching dichotomy as a cut-and-dried solution to patient or surrogate demands for a positive right to treatment. The good news is that we now have an appellate ruling that allows physicians to forego life-prolonging treatment for patients who can no longer speak for themselves. The bad news is that by failing to cloak its judgment in a reasoned analysis, the Manitoba Court missed the opportunity to lead the way toward a Canadian jurisprudence on end-of-life decision-making in such cases. Canadian law still awaits a judicial framework of comparable stature to that which marks such precedent-setting cases as *Quinlan* and *Bland*.

6. THE SAWATSKY CASE

Notwithstanding the ruling in the *L. (R.)* case, one year later the wife of a mentally incompetent 79-year-old patient legally challenged the entry of a DNR order on his medical chart. In *Sawatsky v. Riverview Health Centre Inc.*,[17] Justice Beard of the Manitoba Court of Queen's Bench heard an application for an interlocutory injunction to put the DNR order on hold. In addition to Parkinson's disease, the patient had experienced multiple strokes and had chronic aspiration pneumonia and dementia. According to Riverview's medical director:

> Mr. Sawatsky is able to convey his wishes only on a very inconsistent basis, and mostly through non-verbal signals, and only for very basic needs. He has difficulty swallowing, difficulty speaking, and the strokes have resulted in impairment of his mental abilities.

The DNR order was based upon the medical judgment that in the event of a respiratory or cardiac arrest, CPR would most likely prove futile: either he would die notwithstanding the effort, or be reduced to a vegetative state. Riverview was not saying that CPR was doomed to fail — that there was no chance that it could bring the patient back from the brink of death. What it was saying was that, given his state of being, CPR was simply not worth doing if the patient arrested.

Justice Beard granted the injunction but was at pains to point out that her order did not address the merits of the case. Her stated intention was to clarify the situation, and she accordingly called for at least two independent medical opinions as to Mr. Sawatsky's condition and the advisability of the DNR order. Her expressed hope was that these additional reports would help resolve the conflict between Mrs. Sawatsky and her husband's caregivers.

Counsel for the Manitoba League of Persons With Disabilities, which was granted intervenor status in the *Sawatsky* case, raised the question whether a DNR order without the consent of patient or family breached sections 7 and 15 of the *Charter of Rights and Freedoms* — the former pronounces the right to life, liberty, and security of the person and the latter prohibits discrimination based on mental or physical disability. (Such discrimination is also the subject matter of provincial human rights statutes.) Justice Beard noted that the Court of Appeals judgment did not consider the *Charter*, and she left open the pursuit of *Charter* issues if the parties could not resolve their differences.

Six months after Justice Beard's ruling, the media reported that two independent medical assessments had concurred with the DNR order. One of the consultants stated that Mr. Sawatsky's Parkinson's disease has worsened and added: "I believe that should Mr. Sawatsky suffer a cardiac arrest in his present state, death in hospital would be inevitable even if he was successfully resuscitated."[18] Months later Riverview reluctantly agreed to Mrs. Sawatsky's request to move her husband to a home care setting, although the director commented that his condition "is so poor that there are few in the community able to take on his care."[19] Two weeks later

Andrew Sawatsky died at the Victoria General Hospital in Winnipeg (the cause of death was not reported by the media).

Although that marked the end of the *Sawatsky* case, what remains is the policy issue that it so dramatically raised: whether the law's recognition of the *negative right* to refuse treatment should be extended to include a *positive right* by patient or family to enforce a demand for treatment that the caregivers regards as "futile." The issue is whether the law should require physicians to act against their professional judgment that a demanded treatment will not benefit and might well harm the patient. Physicians would no doubt respond that a law that so commands clashes with the ethical commandment, "Primum non nocere" — Above all, do not harm your patient.

Yet it must be acknowledged that the physician's resolve to omit life-support measures for a mentally incompetent patient is not a purely medical decision. As indicated by the commentary on medical futility in the last chapter, such a decision reflects the value judgment that the patient's prognosis precludes aggressive measures to stave off death. Still, this kind of decision-making is standard procedure in hospital practice, and on any given day scores of patients across Canada die a quicker (and hopefully easier) death than they would if aggressive life-support measures were kept in place until the bitter end. That happens because it is senseless to keep patients alive for no other reason than that it can be done.

The *Sawatsky* case highlights a public concern about the spectre of undertreatment, and much of the media coverage portrayed the case as a David and Goliath encounter — an elderly and devoted wife singlehandedly seeking to save her husband from the clutches of an impersonal medical system. (For example, one front page article in The Globe and Mail was headlined, *Doctors won't save man despite wife's plea.*) In letters to the press and comments on radio talk shows, concerned Manitobans expressed agreement with Mrs. Sawatsky when she said about her husband, "They have written him off. The older you get, the more vulnerable you become, the more expendable you get." Her conflict with Riverview likewise prompted comments from the disabled community that unilateral DNR orders were an infringement of patients' entitlement to health care, which is why the Manitoba League of Persons With Disabilities sought intervenor status in the case.

These outpourings of concern occupy the converse side to the spectre of overtreatment — physicians using medical technology to drag out the dying process to no rational end. It was this legitimately perceived overuse of resources that spawned the so-called "right to die" cases beginning with

Quinlan,* which have affirmed the (negative) right of patients/surrogates to decline life-prolonging measures. The *Sawatsky* case is the flip side of the treatment coin, as Mrs. Sawatsky was in effect demanding that a positive right to treatment stand shoulder to shoulder with the negative right to refuse treatment. At least for now the law in Manitoba says No. Yet it may happen that in *Sawatsky* (or another case), the validity of a DNR order (or other non-treatment direction) will be contested on *Charter* and/or Human Rights grounds. If that comes to pass, then the judiciary will have to strike a balance in the particular case between two competing claims. There is the patient or family demanding the right to compel the reluctant physician to offer treatment. And there is the physician responding that there is no duty to do whatever the patient or family wants when clinical judgment dictates otherwise, and that compelling treatment in such circumstances undercuts the physician's commitment to professional integrity.

That the law has a stake in protecting medical integrity is evident from American cases that have allowed mentally competent patients to spurn life-prolonging treatment. In the process, the courts have weighed the patient's right of refusal against the state's interest in upholding the integrity of the medical profession. In determining that the patient's right of refusal is not trumped by this state interest, the courts have ruled along the following lines, quoting from the judgment of the Nevada Supreme Court in a 1990 case, *McKay v. Bergstedt*:

> Despite the medical profession's healing objectives, there are increasing numbers of people who fall in the category of those who may never be healed but whose lives may be extended by heroic measures. Unfortunately, there are times when such efforts will do little or nothing more than delay death in a bodily environment essentially bereft of quality. Under such conditions...the medical profession is not threatened by a competent adult's refusal of life-extending treatment.[20]

In 1992 the English Court of Appeal decided a case called *J. (A Minor), Re*.[21] The 16-month-old patient, who was in foster care, was afflicted with severe microcephaly (an abnormally small head, which is inevitably accompanied by brain damage), blindness, and severe forms of cerebral palsy and epilepsy. Since the consultant paediatrician was of the view that intensive therapeutic measures would not be medically appropriate if the infant were to suffer a life-threatening event, the local health authority sought a judicial declaration as to whether life-prolonging treatment could be withheld. In the result, the Court of Appeal held that it would amount to a

---

*   See Chapter 21.

judicial "abuse of power" to order a physician to act against her clinical judgment:

> If the court orders a doctor to treat a child in a manner contrary to his or her clinical judgment it would place the conscientious doctor in an impossible position. To perform the court's order could require a doctor to act in a manner which he or she genuinely believed not to be in the patient's best interests; to fail to treat the child as ordered would amount to a contempt of court. Any judge would be most reluctant to punish the doctor for such a contempt, which seems to me to be a very strong indication that such an order should not be made.

In short, even if the physician rues the patient's decision as medically unwise, her professional commitment to healing and caring is not compromised by the patient's overriding claim to bodily integrity. The *Sawatsky* case, of course, presents a different question: whether the profession is threatened by a demand for treatment that is opposed on futility grounds. Since Canadian, no less than American law, has a stake in the integrity of the medical profession, the question surely cannot be ignored as we ponder the ramifications of the decision by the Manitoba Court of Appeal in the *L. (R.)* case.

When the *Sawatsky* case hit the media, Mrs. Sawatsky was quoted as complaining that the Riverview physicians "were playing God" with her husband's life. That may be true, but the fact is that advances in medical technology have made that inevitable. A hundred years ago the medical profession could do precious little to keep patients alive, but the technology is now there to prolong dying beyond the point at which nature should be allowed to take its course. But still, it is no simple matter to determine when that point of no return has come such that it is time to call a halt to life-support measures. According to section 19 of the code of conduct of the College of Physicians and Surgeons of Manitoba: "Treatment that offers no benefit and serves only to prolong the dying process should not be employed." None would disagree with that mission statement, but still it begs the question as to when, in any particular case, the treatment is in fact non-beneficial and is only prolonging dying.

Finally, whatever one thinks of Mrs. Sawatsky's refusal to bow to medical judgment, we can all thank her for heightening public awareness of issues that affect us all as mortal beings. Her story has no villains, as those who disagreed with her refusal to abide by the DNR order were likewise motivated to do what was best for her husband. In any case, who ever said that playing God was easy?

7. THE ROLE OF THE FAMILY

Recall that in its 1983 report, *Euthanasia, Aiding Suicide and the Cessation of Treatment,* the LRCC concluded that the ideal decision-making model for incompetent moribund patients should reflect a consensus among the physician, other involved health care personnel, and the family. It also proposed that the physician should be the central figure in the decision-making process; that the physician consult with the family but that the ultimate responsibility must rest on her shoulders. This in effect appears to be the way it is when physicians and families discuss end-of-life care.

The reality of medical practice in health care facilities is that the incompetent patient's family is not invited to decide whether life-support measures should be foregone. It is the physician — not the family — who makes that decision. There will be discussion between physician and family; and the former may ask the latter for guidance, particularly for any known treatment wishes of the patient. If the patient had the foresight to prepare a health care directive, that will help facilitate the discussion and may in fact direct the outcome. Physicians certainly consult with families, but not in the sense of an equal partnership. What rather happens is that physicians usually guide families to agree with their medical judgment calls, whether it be to continue or to stop treatment. (Sometimes the dialogue is initiated by the family, who question the need to prolong the patient's dying.) In short, there is an ethic (or one could say, medical custom) that prompts physicians to consult with families. But the law does not question the assumption by physicians of the power — and the responsibility — of decision-making.

Bear in mind that as a general rule an adult patient's family has no legal standing to direct the course of treatment. (Even if an adult has a legal guardian, the law has not endowed the latter with the authority to make medical treatment decisions for the former.) In any case, the physician has an independent legal duty toward the patient that cannot be delegated to a third party. First, in the realm of tort law the fiduciary nature of the physician-patient relationship imposes a duty of care upon the physician toward her patient. Second, section 216 of the *Criminal Code* provides that anyone administering medical treatment is "under a legal duty to use reasonable knowledge, skill and care in so doing." The family thus has no entitlement to overrule the medical judgment that life-prolonging treatment be maintained or forgone. When a patient/physician relationship is formed, the ultimate treating responsibility rests with the physician. The physician — not the family — has undertaken the patient's care, and the responsibility rests with the physician to treat the incompetent patient in accordance with her best medical judgment (bearing in mind whatever wishes had been expressed by the patient).

Yet what if the patient had signed a health care directive appointing a family member — or anyone else for that matter — as a proxy?* In that event, the proxy is authorized to make treatment decisions if and when the patient loses decisional capacity. Or a statute may provide a priorized listing of family members who are empowered to make treatment decisions for an incompetent patient with no health care directive. For example, the Ontario Health Care Consent Act grants such right in descending order to the patient's spouse or partner, parent or child over 16, sibling, or other relative.[22]

It is arguable that the statutory grant of decision-making authority to the family/proxy does not fundamentally alter the physician's role. If the family/proxy demands that the patient be allowed to die, the physician cannot in good conscience acquiesce unless her judgment is that continued therapy is no longer medically reasonable (unless the family can satisfy the physician that the patient would not want to be kept alive in his current condition). In other words, if the family/proxy can satisfy either the subjective or substituted judgment test** — leading to the conclusion that the patient would not want to be kept alive in his current condition — then the physician acts lawfully when she stops life-prolonging treatment. Even if she believes that the treatment is serving the patient's best interests, evidence that the patient would not wish to be kept alive discharges her from her duty of care.

Nevertheless, it is one thing when the family/proxy has a fair idea that the patient would prefer death to his current condition, and another when it has no such idea but believes, however sincerely, that the patient is better off dead. If the conflict is over the perceived best interests of the patient (when there is no evidence of the patient's wishes), then the physician cannot simply acquiesce in the insistence by the proxy/family that the patient be allowed to die when the physician in good conscience believes that the patient's condition does not warrant the termination of life-prolonging treatment. At the end of the day, the physician's tort and criminal law duty of care hold the trump card. Admittedly, the courts have not dealt with a case on point. But it would seem unlikely that a physician would be faulted for treating when the family/proxy says No, and the physician reasonably believes that stopping treatment does not serve the patient's best interests.[23]

---

*   See Chapter 24.
**   The subjective and substituted judgment standards are explained in Chapter 21.

On the other hand, what if the Yes and No rules are reversed — the family or proxy insists upon aggressive measures that the physician rejects as medically unreasonable? As noted in our commentary on futility, Canadian law has yet to enforce a positive right to treatment and it matters not whether the demand comes from family/proxy or even from the patient. It may be that the physician will accede to an insistence upon treatment (particularly if it comes from the patient), but if that happens it is not because the physician is legally bound to that result.

But even when the opposition to halting life-prolonging treatment comes from just one family member, there is anecdotal evidence that health care facilities have directed compliance with the demands of the sole dissenter, particularly when the insistence upon treatment has been backed by a threatening letter from a lawyer. In such instances hospital attorneys have reacted to the spectre of a law suit by advising that life-support measures continue, notwithstanding the contrary views of the caregivers and other family members. Presumably, what explains these scenarios is uncertainty regarding hospital liability when life-prolonging measures are terminated over the objection of a family member.

A number of such cases has led to the coining of the term, "the daughter from California syndrome."[24] Assume an elderly widowed patient and the acquiescence by her in-town adult children in the medical recommendation to forego life-support measures. The daughter from California (or perhaps the son from a distant province), who has not seen the parent for years, appears on the scene and disrupts the management of the case by stridently demanding inappropriate aggressive care. The daughter's guilt feelings are reflected by acute denial as well as anger and resentment directed against the staff and her siblings. She threatens a law suit unless her parent is aggressively treated and a warning letter from an attorney duly arrives soon after she returns home. When the patient dies weeks or months later notwithstanding treatment, as often as not the daughter from California does not fly back for the funeral.

Yet what if the in-town siblings were not cowered into submission by the California sister, and the caregivers were thereby encouraged to dig in their heels and terminate life-support measures? If the California sister were to carry out her threat by filing a wrongful death action, she would have the burden of proving that the caregivers were medically negligent in foregoing life-prolonging treatment. We have noted that there is no criminal liability when the physician acts upon the reasonable medical judgment that aggressive treatment is no longer warranted, and the same principle holds when the physician is a defendant in a civil suit. My co-authors and I are not aware of any Canadian case in which a physician has been sued for wrongful death by a disgruntled member of the patient's family. (The first case in a common law jurisdiction in which a physician who terminated life-prolonging treatment was sued for wrongful death by an angry next-of-kin was *Gilgunn*, which is discussed in the previous chapter. In that case the jury ruled against the plaintiff.)

What about the patient who has no family (or significant other) and the physician's clinical opinion is that life-support measures should be stopped. The physician could request the hospital to petition for judicial approval of the decision to let the patient die. There is, however, no indication in the medico-legal literature that Canadian physicians seek the aid of the courts in that situation. Nor is there any reason that the physician should, so long as she is convinced that continued therapy is not called for.

Also note that, according to guidelines issued in June 1999 by the British Medical Association, physicians are entitled to overrule a family's insistence on keeping a patient alive if they (the physicians) believe that treatment is not benefitting the patient. Furthermore, the guidelines assure physicians that they need not seek a court order for a unilateral decision to withdraw or withhold treatment because "it is ultimately the doctor's call." But still, "the decision should be taken in a spirit of consensus and that will happen in the vast majority of cases."

In any event, there is data from the United States indicating that physicians do act unilaterally in such circumstances. In 1988, a Boston physician reported that over the previous 10 years there were 20 cases at the Massachusetts General Hospital in which physicians had written DNR orders for terminally ill incompetent patients despite family objections — 16 of which occurred over the last three of the 10 years. All the decisions were approved by the hospital's Optimum Care (Ethics) Committee on futility grounds.[25]

A more recent study reported the results of a survey of physicians practicing in adult intensive care units across the United States.[26] Of the 879 respondents, 726 acknowledged that they had withdrawn or withheld life-prolonging treatment on futility grounds. Of these 726, 219 (30%) had done so without the written or oral consent of patient or family, 120 (17%) without the knowledge of patient or family, and 28 (4%) despite objections from patient or family. Although there are no comparable Canadian studies, it is reasonable to assume that such cases are happening here. I am familiar with a Winnipeg case in which life-support was terminated for a vegetative six-month-old patient over the objection of the father who kept insisting that God would perform a miracle. And I know of a more recent Winnipeg case in which life-support was stopped for a 70-year-old patient with end-stage lung cancer where some (but not all) family members opposed the decision.

Finally, it is pertinent to refer to a "Model Policy on Appropriate Use of Life-Sustaining Treatment" developed in 1998 by the University of Toronto Joint Centre for Bioethics. Its stated focus is on situations where a patient or surrogate asks for treatment that the caregivers regard as "inappropriate." As the statement acknowledges: "There is no clearly established ethical and legal framework for this situation.' It goes on to propose an 11-step "process for decision-making" for such cases (noting that the order of steps 1-8 could be varied, that several steps could occur together, and that the patient's condition could preclude completing the process). The steps are as follows:

1. Interprofessional team consensus — on range of appropriate treatment
2. Communication
   a. of prognosis and wishes for treatment with patient, if possible
   b. explore why patient or surrogate wishes continuation of treatment
   c. discuss with patient or surrogate rationale for withholding/withdrawing life-support
   d. describe palliative measures
   e. offer hospital resources to assist family with their psychosocial, cultural, spiritual, and informational needs
   f. document communications in patient's health record.
3. Negotiation — of treatment plan mutually acceptable to physicians and patient or surrogate
4. Intensive Care Consultation — if ICU admission required.
5. Second Opinion — to be presented as option to patient or surrogate
6. Trial of Therapy — time-limited trial re step 3
7. Patient Transfer — option to be given patient or surrogate
8. Mediation
9. Arbitration — if mediation fails
10. Notice of Intention to Withhold or Withdraw Life-Sustaining Treatment — patient or surrogate should be given opportunity to challenge decision in court
11. Withholding/Withdrawal of Life-Sustaining Treatment — after ennumerated procedures followed.

8. THE LEGAL THEORY SUPPORTING THE TERMINATION OF LIFE-PROLONGING TREATMENT FOR INCOMPETENT PATIENTS

How would a Canadian court handle a petition by an incompetent patient's family for an order compelling compliance with their rebuffed demand that life-prolonging treatment be terminated? Assuming that the evidence was sufficient to satisfy the criteria for surrogate decision-making (either the subjective, substituted judgment, or best interests standards), the court would most likely grant the petition on the grounds that the incompetent patient, no less than the competent patient, has a right at common law to the cessation of non-beneficial life-support measures. Along the lines of the *Brother Fox* case,* the court could reject the claim that the right is entirely personal and only exercisable by the patient herself. (In Chapter 24 we consider the role of the *health care directive* as another avenue of approach toward the termination of life-prolonging treatment for the mentally incompetent patient.)

What about a constitutional right to the termination of life- prolonging treatment? In theory, the right would stem from the protection afforded "security of the person" in section 7 of the *Charter of Rights and Freedoms* — that the proviso protects the bodily integrity of an incompetent patient such that she has a constitutional right to die when life-prolonging treatment offers no reasonable hope of benefit. This approach would parallel the *Quinlan* precedent, which based the incompetent patient's right to die on a constitutional right of privacy. Since hospitals fall under the purview of the *Charter*, a constitutional argument is a viable option in such a case.

---

* The *Brother Fox* case is discussed in Chapter 21.

NOTES

1. Law Reform Commission of Canada, Working Paper 28: **Euthanasia, Aiding Suicide and Cessation of Treatment** (Minister of Supply and Services Canada 1982), at 57.
2. *Ibid.*, at 57-8.
3. *Ibid.*, at 66.
4. *Ibid.*, at 58-9.
5. *Ibid.*, at 64.
6. Law Reform Commission of Canada, Report 20: **Euthanasia, Aiding Suicide and Cessation of Treatment** (Minister of Supply and Services Canada 1983).
7. *Auckland Area Health Board v. Attorney General*, [1993] 1 N.Z.L.R. 235 (H.C.).
8. *Airedale NHS Trust v. Bland*, [1993] 1 All E.R. 821 (H.L.).
9. *Supra* note 6, at 32.
10. *Supra* note 1, at 29.
11. *Child & Family Services of Central Manitoba v. L. (R.)* (1997), 123 Man. R. (2d) 135 (C.A.).
12. *London Health Sciences Centre v. K. (R.) (Litigation Guardian of)* (1997), 152 D.L.R. (4th) 724 (Ont. Gen. Div.).
13. *Ciarlariello v. Schacter*, [1993] 2 S.C.R. 119.
14. W. Prip & A. Moretti, Medical futility: a legal perspective. In Zucker M.B. & Zucker H.D. (eds.), **Medical Futility and the Evaluation of Life-Sustaining Treatment** (Cambridge University Press, 1997), at 136.
15. Ontario Law Reform Commission, **Study Paper on Assisted Suicide, Euthanasia and Foregoing Treatment** (Ontario Law Reform Commission, Toronto, 1996), at 232-3.
16. A. Meisel, **The Right to Die**, Volume 2 (Wiley Law, 1995), at 540.
17. *Sawatzky v. Riverview Health Centre Inc.* (1998), [1998] M.J. No. 506, 1998 CarswellMan 515 (Q.B.).
18. Winnipeg Free Press, May 20, 1999, at A3.
19. Winnipeg Free Press, October 9, 1999.
20. *McKay v. Bergstedt*, 801 P.2d 617 (1990).
21. *J. (A Minor), Re*, [1992] 4 All E.R. 617.
22. The health care directive acts in Alberta, Newfoundland, Prince Edward Island, and Saskatchewan also provide a hierarchical list of substitute decision-makers empowered to make treatment decisions for an incompetent patient with no directive. The surrogate may also be consulted when there is a directive but instructions are unclear or inapplicable to the situation at hand, or when a proxy is unavailable or unable to decide. The priorized listing is headed by the spouse and then progresses down the line to adult children, parents, siblings, and finally other relatives. The Ontario provision differs in that after

spouse, it says parent or child.

See Chapter 17 where Human Tissue Acts provide priorized lists of relatives authorized to consent to post-mortem organ/tissue donation. The standard provision is that one turns to the spouse or partner, but if none or unavailable then to the next one down the chain (parent), but if none or unavailable then so on down the chain.

23. Section 25 of the Manitoba Health Care Directives Act — which states that "Nothing in this Act abrogates or derogates from any rights or responsibilities conferred by statute or common law" — can be read as affirming the tort and criminal law duties imposed upon physicians to act in the best interests of their patients (unless a patient when competent says otherwise). The Act allows a proxy appointed by the maker of a directive to make treatment decisions if and when the maker becomes incompetent. Yet section 25 in effect recognizes that the proxy's power cannot stand independently of the physician's legal responsibilities toward her patient. In any case, a provincial legislature cannot tamper with section 216 of the *Criminal Code* because criminal law is a matter of federal jurisdiction. The Manitoba statute is discussed in Chapter 24.

24. D.W. Molloy et al., Decisionmaking for the incompetent elderly: the daughter from California syndrome. 39 **Journal of the American Geriatrics Society** 396 (1991). Dr. Molloy authored the health care directive, "Let Me Die," which is considered in Chapter 24.

25. T.A. Brennan, Incompetent patients with limited care in the absence of family consent. 109 **Annals of Internal Medicine** 819 (1988).

26. D. Asch et al., Decisions to limit or continue life-sustaining treatment by critical care physicians in the United States: Conflicts between physicians' practices and patients' wishes. 151 **American Journal of Respiratory Critical Care Medicine** 288 (1995).

23

FOREGOING OF TREATMENT FOR NEONATES AND PRE-ADOLESCENTS

SUMMARY

This chapter opens with five reported Canadian cases involving young children in which treatment decisions were at issue. The famous English conjoined twins case is also considered. There are two features that distinguish these cases from those of adults and mature minors: (1) the younger the patient the less appropriate is the substituted judgment test for surrogate decision-making (which asks what the patient would want done in the current circumstances), thus leaving the best interests test as the appropriate test; and (2) the presence of one or two parents as the patient's legal guardian. Finally, with neonates in particular there is often the spectre of the uncertain prognosis, which no doubt complicates the decision-making process.

1. INTRODUCTION

The reader will note that the title of this chapter does not qualify the reference to treatment with the adjective "life-prolonging." As explained in Chapter 18, treatment is *life-prolonging* when it arguably provides neither benefit nor burden to the patient, or else its burden outweighs its benefit. Although this is an apt designation for the cases canvassed in the previous two chapters, one cannot say that it describes all the cases found in this chapter. In the *Dawson* case, the treatment at issue would stabilize the condition of a severely handicapped child; it would not cure his premorbid condition but would prevent his death. And given his quality-of-life, it would prove to his benefit. In the *Sheena B.* case, the treatment at issue held out the hope of full recovery. In these two cases, then, the treatment rejected by the parents is describable as *life-saving*. (As defined in Chapter 18, treatment is life-saving when it is most likely to benefit the patient.) In the *Paulette* case, the treatment spurned by the parents — a liver transplant — is describable as *life-extending*. (As defined in Chapter 18, treatment is life-extending when it may well benefit the patient but it is too early to tell.)

2. FIVE CANADIAN CASES

(a) Stephen Dawson (British Columbia, 1983)[1]

Two weeks after his birth in March 1976, Stephen Dawson contracted meningitis. The consequences were catastrophic: severe mental retardation, blindness (though with some light perception), cerebral palsy, and a seizure disorder. Hydrocephaly led to the placement of a ventriculo-peritoneal shunt when he was five months old. Stephen lived at home until 1978, when his parents placed him in Sunnyhill Hospital, a facility for chronically handicapped children.

In February 1983, Sunnyhill's medical director diagnosed a blocked shunt and consequently asked Stephen's parents to authorize remedial surgery. The Dawsons withheld consent on the ground that their son's life was so dismal that he should be allowed "to die with dignity." Their refusal triggered Stephen's apprehension by child welfare personnel acting under the authority of the B.C. Family and Child Services Act, which declares a child "in need of protection" when "deprived of necessary medical attention."

The Superintendent of Family and Child Service promptly filed an application for an order to carry out the surgery, which was denied by a provincial court judge. Two days later the case was retried by a Supreme Court judge,* who heard medical evidence that withholding the shunt revision would not necessarily lead to the child's death. But the witness added that the failure to shunt likely would cause further brain damage, reduced functional ability, and an increase in head circumference. In addition, there was evidence that Stephen's existence was not as grim as his parents had alleged. According to Sunnyhill's medical director:

> Stephen seemed happy, responded to others and smiled or laughed when stimulated. He seemed to be in contact with his surroundings and capable of rudimentary communication, such as babbling. He seemed to show some response to verbal interaction.

---

* In B.C. the Supreme Court is the highest level trial court.

There was testimony to the same effect from a Sunnyhill paediatrician and from Stephen's teacher for the previous six months. The judge quoted at length from the teacher's affidavit, in which she attested that:

> He obtained great pleasure and smiled a great deal in vocalizing sounds. Not only did he progress to the stage of removing his hands from his mouth, he also began to interact with his environment in various ways, including clapping on his chair tray and learning to work the levers on an electronic toy which would operate a fan or tape recorder. [H]e appeared to be emotionally well off in that he was able to both give and receive pleasure. In particular, he would smile and vocalize in response to social overtures, and he would also show great pleasure in being cuddled and being played with.

A three-day hearing culminated in the finding that Stephen fell within the "in need of protection" proviso in the *Family and Child Services Act*. The judge accordingly granted the application and within hours of the judgment Stephen's shunt was repaired. As he explained his decision:

> This is not a "right to die" situation where the courts are concerned with people who are terminally ill from incurable conditions. Rather it is a question of whether S[tephen] has the right to receive appropriate medical and surgical care of a relatively simple kind which will assure to him the continuation of his life, such as it is. I am satisfied that the laws of our society are structured to preserve, protect, and maintain life and that...this court could not sanction the termination of a life except for the most coercive reasons. The presumption must be in favour of life. Neither could this court sanction the wilful withholding of surgical therapy where such withholding could result not necessarily in death but in a prolongation of life for an indeterminate time but in a more impoverished and more agonizing form.

(b) Catherine Jacquet (Quebec, 1986)[2]

Catherine Jacquet was born in May 1982, and shortly before her second birthday it was determined that she was afflicted with sacrococcygeal teratoma, a rare form of pelvic cancer found only in infants. In June 1984 her malignant tumour was removed at the Montreal Children's Hospital, at which time it was ascertained that the cancer had spread to her liver.

The first of three series of chemotherapy treatments was initiated one month later. In January 1986, the child's treating physicians at the Montreal Children's Hospital proposed a fourth series. Catherine's mother and grandmother had agreed to the prior chemotherapy regimens. (Her mother, 21, was separated from her husband; the child had been in the grandmother's care and custody since birth.) This time they withheld consent.

The hospital responded by filing an application under the Quebec *Public Health Protection Act*, which authorizes court-ordered medical treatment when a parental refusal to so provide "is not justified in the child's best interests." The child's mother and grandmother defended their position on two grounds:

(1) The chemotherapy treatments had already caused untold physical and emotional suffering as well as severe side effects: constant nausea, loss of hair, a bloated liver, loss of hearing, and a 50 per cent reduction in renal function (the hearing and renal damage were likely to be permanent).

(2) The hospital acknowledged that the treatments afforded only a 10-20% chance of arresting the disease process.

A Superior Court judge granted the hospital's petition. That decision was overturned by the Quebec Court of Appeal, which ruled that the hospital had failed to prove that the family's decision was contrary to the child's best interests. The Court in effect adopted the family's position by emphasizing that: (1) the prior treatments had caused the child to suffer pain "exceeding human endurance," and (2) even with further chemotherapy treatment, the odds were heavily weighted against a successful outcome. The Court noted that there was no reliable statistical basis for the alleged 10-20% survival rate. According to the evidence, the figures were extrapolated from a sample of cases of adult patients with testicular cancer of the same histological type as that afflicting Catherine. Furthermore, her physicians had admitted that they really had no idea of the odds favouring survival because of the profession's limited experience with children suffering from sacrococcygeal teratoma.

(c)   K'aila Paulette (Saskatchewan, 1990)[3]

When K'aila Paulette was 10 months old, he was found to have biliary atresia. His First Nations parents were advised that a liver transplant offered his only hope for survival and that otherwise he would be dead within six months to one year. The data indicated a 70-75% survival rate in the first post-transplant year (assuming the availability of a liver), diminishing to 60-65% after five years. The parents opted against the surgery for two reasons: their spiritual belief that organ transplantation violated the workings of nature; and the hard and uncertain road that their son would travel were he to become a liver recipient candidate. Dr. Jones, the paediatric gastroenterologist consulted by the parents, was prompted by their refusal to notify child welfare; the Department of Social Services petitioned the Provincial Court for temporary custody for the purpose of consenting to the procedure. According to the judge (who, in summarizing the mother's position, was presenting the father's as well):

> The mother feels that the transplant is an extraordinary feat of medical science, which attempts to prolong life in the face of inevitable death. She fears condemning her son to a life of being vulnerable to infectious diseases which are relatively benign for the general population. She is concerned that medical scientists can only base their prognosis for the future of transplant recipients on the past seven years experience. She does not want her child to suffer when she knows that his inevitable death will be relatively painless under a care program. She feels it is wiser and kinder to her child to allow his death to be dignified. She clearly does not want to lose this child, but she has resigned herself to that fact. She asks, "Are these extraordinary medical procedures for prolongation of life the way society is supposed to deal with questions of life and death."

Although Dr. Jones testified that the parental stance was unreasonable because, in his view, the benefits from a transplant outweighed the risks, the Court heard otherwise from three of his specialist colleagues (one of whom was the child's treating physician). They testified that they could not fault the parental decision, given the uncertain course of the surgery as well as the potentially severe side-effects of immuno-suppressive drugs (e.g. cancer, delayed growth, hypertension, and kidney fibrosis). In essence, it was the lack of medical consensus favouring the transplant that persuaded the judge to deny the petition:

> Survival necessarily entails an uncertain quality of life. The child will be very susceptible to infection. The child will suffer the surgery and the known side-effects of the follow-up drug therapy. Death may be avoided and life may be prolonged in the short term. There are no guarantees.... The parents have chosen a course of treatment which they recognize will not avoid the death of the child. This course of treatment is clearly recognized by the medical community as being acceptable in this situation. In fact, the majority of the doctors who testified...are not critical of the parents' choice....

Another factor explaining the result was that the judge saw the parents as an intelligent couple who were devoted to their son and who had rejected the transplant option only after the most painstaking and thoughtful consideration. Six weeks after the ruling, K'aila died peacefully in his mother's arms.

Some months later the case was featured on the CBC television series, *Man Alive*, in a segment titled, *A Choice for K'aila*. The Paulettes presented as thoughtful, articulate, and loving parents, who addressed both spiritual and medical concerns in explaining their heart-wrenching decision. According to the mother:

> My misgivings came from a recognition that in this life our physical being is intimately connected with our spiritual being and what's more, putting part of somebody else from another body that had another spiritual identity connected with it, putting that into his body, just the possible implications of that were really disturbing to me.

However, she was also careful to weigh the benefits-versus-burdens equation:

> Is this going to give my son a chance to heal, to become well and whole again? If so, it's really worth looking at. But from what I learned about the aftermath, the effects of the drugs on his body, his body would be like a war zone for the rest of his life.

The spiritual and medical aspects were also expressed by the father:

> All that we have here on this Mother Earth is a blessing and gift of the Creator. To me there is a fundamental order that I strongly believe in.... If the Creator had meant it to be that we can take another liver and put it into another person's body and there's no complications whatsoever, nothing whatsoever, you sew up the person and everything is all right, everything check's out — but that's not the case.

In a thoughtful article in the *Health Law Journal*,[4] Jocelyn Downie suggests that the fundamental question raised by the *Paulette (P. (F.))* case is: "Should First Nations parents be held by non-First Nations people to non-First Nations standards of necessary medical treatment?" (It is true that the Court vindicated the parents' non-treatment decision, but in all likelihood that was only because of the supportive medical testimony. As Downie comments, "If the Paulettes had only been able to find traditional healers to endorse their decision...they might not have won their case.") As she explained, her posed question addressed the self-government debate: "If First Nations people have never lost their sovereignty, then...they should be left alone to determine an appropriate standard of (medical) care for First Nations children." If that is not the case, however, then they stand on equal footing with religious and cultural sub-communities which are not considered exempt from the law's commands — as illustrated by the many cases involving Jehovah's Witness parents whose children are apprehended when they refuse to consent to blood transfusions. One such case — *Sheena B. (B. (R.))* — is shortly considered.

The ruling in *Paulette* is echoed in a 1997 English case, *T. (Wardship: Medical Treatment), Re.*[5] The case involved a refusal by the parents of a

17-month-old son to consent to a liver transplant. The medical evidence was that without the surgery he would die within a year. The parents had withheld consent because they believed that his quality of life would be unacceptable if the surgery went ahead. However, the trial court ordered the transplant by applying the best interests test. In reversing the ruling, the Court of Appeal emphasized that the welfare of the child could not be considered apart from the feelings and predicament of the mother, who would have the burden of care for years to come. It therefore concluded that the transplant was not in his best interests. In the view of a commentator on the *Paulette* and *T* cases:

> These cases are extremely significant ones. There was no other potentially available therapy available in either instance. It was therefore a balancing of quality- and quantity-of-life factors, with the views of the parents bearing heavily on the former. In so far as the parents are very likely to be the only proposed carers for the child post-transplant, the decisions displayed substantial deference to parental discretion....[6]

Surely from the child's standpoint, a post-transplant life of uncertainty serves his best interests more than does his impending death. It was for that reason that three years later the Court of Appeal ordered the separation of conjoined twins over parental opposition in a celebrated case that we consider shortly. Still, the rulings in the *Paulette* and *T. (Wardship: Medical Treatment), Re* cases do reflect a heightened sensitivity to the burden of long term caring that will fall upon parents who sincerely believe that their child should not have to bear the prospects of a life marked by peril and uncertainty.

(d)   Cara B. (New Brunswick, 1990)[7]

Cara B. was born with an encephalocele and in the first 10 months of life developed hydrocephalus and twice contracted meningitis. The hydrocephalus left her with an enlarged head, atrophied brain, and periodic convulsions. At the age of 10, she was blind, unable to feed herself, and could not stand, walk, or crawl. When she contracted meningitis for the third time, her parents refused to consent to antibiotics to treat an infection in the area of the shunt draining fluid from her skull. Their refusal prompted the Minister of Health and Community Services to petition the Family Division of the Court of Queen's Bench for custody and authorization to treat the infection. The parents had withheld consent because they believed that the gravity of their 10-year-old daughter's condition did not warrant aggressive life-prolonging measures. The child's neurosurgeon (who had treated her since birth and who supported the parents' decision) filed an affidavit with the Court in which he stated that: "In my opinion, Cara will never experience any further development, (and) further treatment will serve only to prolong Cara's suffering."

However, the judge who heard the petition emphatically rejected the position of Cara's parents and the neurosurgeon. The parents had introduced in evidence a law journal article by a Canadian bio-ethicist recommending against life-prolonging treatment for an "infant with an encephalocele, a condition in which all or most of the brain is missing." The judge not only took issue with that viewpoint but also expressed astonishment that "such a philosophy can be expressed by a professor." In granting the petition the judge ruled that he was bound to that result by sections 7 and 15 of the *Charter of Rights and Freedoms*. (Section 7 provides that "everyone has the right to life, liberty, and security of the person." Section 15 is the equality provision and bans discrimination based on various grounds, including "mental or physical disability.")

His view of the case was that he was being asked to "approve of illegal discrimination" because "the parents and the neurosurgeon want to discriminate against the girl because she is severely mentally retarded and neurologically handicapped." Hence he interpreted the *Charter* as foreclosing any consideration of the question whether life-prolonging treatment would serve only to prolong Cara's suffering. In other words, no matter how dismal the future prospects of the patient, the parents were stripped of the right to withhold consent to treatment. All that mattered was that their refusal was explained by her mental/physical disability, and that amounted to discrimination which could not be legally countenanced.

Yet even if one does not quarrel with the end result, the judge can be faulted for basing his ruling on *Charter* grounds. The reason is that the *Charter* can be invoked only in response to direct or indirect state action, which does not characterize the non-treatment decision by the child's parents. In any event, it is doubtful (even if the *Charter* were implicated in a particular case) that courts at the appellate level would interpret sections 7 and 15 as a mandate for aggressive treatment regardless of prognosis and against the wishes of parents whose refusal could not be regarded as an abnegation of their duty to promote their child's best interests.

Notwithstanding his misapplication of the *Charter*, the judge could have come to the same result if satisfied by the evidence that the parental decision did not serve the child's best interests. On the other hand, a different judge might well have held that the decision of Cara's parents was supportable on best interests grounds. As we have seen in our all too brief consideration of the concept of *qualitative futility*,* it is an awesome

---

* See Chapter 21.

task indeed to decide that a patient who cannot speak for herself is better off dead. Be that as it may, the antibiotics were administered; but Cara's condition deteriorated and she died two weeks after the Court's ruling.

(e) Sheena B. (Supreme Court, 1995)[8]

Sheena B. was born four weeks prematurely on June 25, 1983, and was transferred to the Sick Children's Hospital in Toronto, where she was treated with parental consent for a number of ailments. On July 30 her haemoglobin level dropped to such an extent that her attending physicians opined that she might require a blood transfusion to treat potentially life-threatening congestive heart failure. The refusal to consent by her Jehovah's Witness parents prompted notification to the Children's Aid Society, which petitioned for a hearing in the Family Division of Provincial Court. Temporary wardship was granted to the agency, and the order was extended in mid-August when the hospital's head of ophthalmology testified that he suspected that Sheena had infantile glaucoma and recommended exploratory surgery under general anaesthesia (necessitating a blood transfusion). Custody of the infant was returned to the parents after the eye surgery, and they appealed the rulings of the Provincial Court. It was not until eleven years later that the case was finally resolved by the Supreme Court, which upheld the custody orders. (This case is of course distinguishable from the other four cases in that Sheena B.'s parents were not objecting to the treatment regimen as a futile attempt to ward off the ravages of a disease process. There was no conflict between their treatment goal for their daughter and that of her caregivers. Their only quarrel was that it must not involve the use of blood products. The case is presented here, however, because it implicates the same overriding issue presented in the other cases: the resolution of treatment conflict between parents and caregivers.)

In dismissing the parents' claim that the custody orders had violated their right to liberty under section 7 of the *Charter*, the Court ruled that:

> While the right to liberty embedded in section 7 may encompass the right of parents...to choose among equally effective types of medical treatment for their children, it does not include a parents' right to deny a child medical treatment that has been adjudged necessary by the medical profession and for which there is no legitimate alternative. The child's right to life must not be so completely subsumed to the parental liberty to make decisions regarding that child. Although an individual may refuse any medical procedures upon her own person, it is quite another matter to speak for another separate individual, especially when that individual cannot speak for herself. Parental duties are to be discharged according to the "best interests" of the child. The

exercise of parental beliefs that grossly invades those best interests is not activity protected by the right to liberty under section 7. There is simply no room within section 7 for parents to override the child's right to liberty and security of the person.

The Court also found that the parents' freedom of religion, guaranteed under section 2(a) of the *Charter*, did not include the "imposition of religious practices which threaten the safety, health or life of the child."

3. IN RE A — THE CONJOINED TWINS CASE (England, 2001)[9]

In 2000, the English Court of Appeal decided a case involving six-week-old conjoined twins that captured international media attention. The twins, who were joined at the lower abdomen, were born in Malta; and the parents followed the advice to take them to London for a medical consultation. The medical evidence was that one twin (whom the Court called Jodie) appeared to have a "normal brain" and that if separated she would require reconstructive abdominal surgery that would enable her to lead a "more or less normal life." However, the evidence regarding her sister (whom the Court called Mary) was of severe abnormality in three key respects: (1) she had a poorly developed "primitive" brain; (2) her heart was "very enlarged, almost filling the chest with a complex cardiac abnormality and abnormalities of the great vessels;" and (3) there was "a virtual absence of functional lung tissue (severe pulmonary hypoplasia)." The Court addressed the dilemma arising from the medical evidence:

> The unique and the crucial feature of the case is that the twins share a common aorta. That enables Jodie's heart to pump the blood she oxygenates through Mary's body as Mary's heart and lungs have no capacity to sustain life. She would have died probably in the womb but certainly a birth but for the life-sustaining support she received from her sister. The sad fact is that she lives on borrowed time, all of it borrowed from her sister. She is incapable of independent existence. She is designated for death. Doing the work for two imposes a terrible stain on Jodie's heart. It is common ground that her heart will fail and she will suffer a cardiac arrest. She is not expected to live more than three to six months, or perhaps a little longer. Mary's death will inevitably follow hers.

The case was in the courts because the devoutly Roman Catholic parents withheld consent to the surgery. When they had learned that both could not survive, they preferred that the matter rest in God's hands. When the trial court sanctioned the surgery, the parents appealed. And although the Court of Appeal expressed its respect and sympathy for the parents' predicament, it concluded that the matter was out of their hands. (The stance of the parents was supported by the Church; the Vatican offered free hospice care for the twins in Rome and English's top Roman Catholic Prelate publicly urged the Court of Appeal to respect the parental wishes.)

There were two major issues before the Court, the first of which was the application of the best interests test to the facts of the case. After noting that "the worthwhileness of the treatment is a legitimate factor to weigh," it went on to say:

> For the reasons given the treatment is not worthwhile for Mary for one cannot escape from the fact that Mary has always been fated to an early death; her capacity to live has been fatally compromised. Though Mary has a right to life, she has little right to be alive. She is alive because and only because to put it bluntly but nonetheless accurately she sucks the lifeblood of Jodie and her parasitic living will soon be the cause of Jodie ceasing to live. Jodie is entitled to protest that Mary is killing her. Nobody but the doctors can help Jodie. Mary sadly is beyond any help.

Not surprisingly the Court concluded that:

> The best interests of the twins is to give the chance of life to the child whose actual bodily condition is capable of accepting the chance to her advantage even if that has to be at the cost of the sacrifice of a life which is so unnaturally supported.

The other issue was whether the surgeons could lawfully separate the twins because a direct effect of the surgery would be to end Mary's life by the severance of the shared aorta. Although such a direct killing would ordinarily constitute murder, the Court invoked the defence of medical necessity to justify the procedure. The Court thus allowed the surgery to proceed. It took 20 hours and although Mary quickly died Jodie survived; the media reported that she had made a strong recovery and that the surgeons were optimistic about her future.

The case has provoked voluminous commentary and there are many thoughtful voices on both sides of the question whether the law should have respected the parental wishes. None has been more eloquent than Canadian law professor Allan Hutchinson who has concluded that:

> Where the moral dilemma is so acute and the right solution so elusive, it will always come down to who has the final say. In a case such as Mary and Jodie's — thankfully rare — the parents should get the first and last word. Judges should resist becoming moral prophets. When there is no genuine

consensus on what to do, parents are as likely to get it right (or wrong) as anyone else.[10]

4. THE BEST INTERESTS TEST

Although parents do not hold life and death authority over their children, the law is loath to interfere with their health care decisions for their offspring. Nevertheless, as evidenced by the abundance of cases in which courts have ordered blood transfusions over parental objection, the law will not hesitate to intervene when a child's health is clearly jeopardized by a parental failure to provide medical treatment. One example amongst many is the *D., Re* case (Alberta, 1982).[11] A child born after 38-weeks gestation was found to have a severe respiratory infection and Group B streptococcal septicemia. Although the family physician and two pediatric consultants urged an immediate blood transfusion, the Jehovah's Witness parents withheld consent. The day after his birth the Court allowed the transfusion. Another illustrative case — in which religion was not a factor — is *Goyette, Re* (Quebec, 1982),[12] where treatment was ordered under the same statutory provision at issue in *Couture-Jacquet*. The parents of a two-year-old with Down syndrome had withheld consent for heart surgery; although the surgery entailed serious risk, the child was otherwise certain to die. A Superior Court judge ruled that the proposed surgery was feasible, necessary, and in the child's best interests.

The decisions in *D., Re* and *Goyette* illustrate the law's public policy in this arena of parental/state conflict. As expressed by an Ontario judge in a 1981 case:

> While I have great sympathy for persons who hold...honest and sincere beliefs that certain medical practices are abhorrent and ineffective, this does not give them the right to reject a treatment which any reasonable parent would recognize as the only hope of preserving life.[13]

As noted, that policy was affirmed by the Supreme Court of Canada in the *Sheena B.* case, which rejected an appeal by Jehovah's Witness parents against a court order allowing their infant child to receive a blood transfusion. Clashes between law and religion are regrettable, and the sect of Jehovah's Witnesses has sought to minimize such encounters by establishing a hospital liaison committee network that functions in 164 Canadian and American cities. A 24-hour emergency hot line telephone number provides information about medical centres that offer "bloodless medicine and surgery" and also lists 16,000 physicians available for consultation and patient transfer.* The sect has also produced a five-point medical treatment protocol for Jehovah's Witnesses, which suggests that health care personnel consider the following options:

1. "Pursue nonblood medical alternatives...."
2. "Consult with other doctors experienced in nonblood medical management at the same facility...."
3. "Contact local Hospital Liaison Committee for Jehovah's Witnesses to locate cooperative doctors at other facilities for consultation on alternative medical care."
4. "Transfer patient, if necessary, to cooperative doctor or facility before the patient's condition deteriorates."
5. "In a rare situation, if the above steps have been exhausted and governmental intervention is deemed necessary, the patient, the parents, or the guardian should be notified as soon as possible of such intended action."

The first of the protocols can rightly be viewed as a moral imperative binding upon health care providers. Still, as the fifth protocol acknowledges, there will be the "rare situation" in which the clash between law and religion cannot be avoided. One hopes that such cases can be kept to a minimum, but cases in which physicians face an emergency situation requiring immediate action and/or there are no non-blood alternatives are bound to occur. If the patient is a competent adult, her refusal of blood products is legally binding. If the minor patient is a neonate or otherwise incapable of deciding for herself, then the courts will affirm the state's authority to intervene.

Of course, whatever prompts the parents to withhold consent, the litmus test is the best interests of the child. In that regard, the *Dawson* court cited a 1981 English case, *B. (A Minor), Re*,[14] as a precedent for its ruling. In fact, the B.C. judge quoted almost the entire three-page opinion in his decision. In that case, the English Court of Appeal considered the plight of a 10-day-old infant with Down syndrome, whose parents had withheld consent to surgery to repair her duodenal atresia (blockage of the upper small intestine). The Court ordered the surgery because it concluded that it was in the child's best interests to live. In coming to that result the Court stated that the question was whether

the life of this child is demonstrably going to be so awful that in effect the child must be condemned to die, or whether the life of this child is still so imponderable that it would be wrong for her to be condemned to die.

---

* The Canadian hot line number is 1-800-265-0327.

From there it went on to conclude:

> There may be cases, I know not, of severe proved damage where the future
> is so certain and where the life of the child is so bound to be full of pain and
> suffering that the court might be driven to a different conclusion, but in the
> present case the choice which lies before the court is this: whether to allow
> an operation to take place ...or whether...to terminate the life of a mongoloid
> child because she also has an intestinal complaint. Faced with that choice I
> have no doubt that it is the duty of this court to decide that the child must
> live.

If the patient's legal guardians (usually parents) withhold consent to
beneficial treatment, then the physician is duty bound to seek judicial
authority to override their decision if she cannot persuade them otherwise.
In every province there is child welfare legislation allowing the apprehension of "a child in need of protection", which is defined to include the
provision of necessary medical treatment. As generally happens, the child
is returned to parental custody upon completion of the treatment (unless
there is an issue of child abuse or parental unfitness).

In 1971, a Down syndrome neonate with duodenal atresia was allowed
to die at Johns Hopkins Hospital in Baltimore after the parents refused
consent for surgery. Although vehemently opposed to the decision, the
physicians and hospital acquiesced. Food and water were withheld, and the
infant lingered for 15 days before dying. The case was widely publicized
but produced no reaction from the medico-legal community. In 1976 a
similar case caused a contrary response from St. Joseph's Hospital in
London, Ontario. When the parents of a three-day-old Down syndrome
infant with duodenal atresia refused consent for remedial surgery, the
hospital notified the Children's Aid Society. That same evening a judicial
hearing was convened in the hospital boardroom. The Family Court judge
found that the proposed treatment was in the infant's best interests and
consequently authorized the surgery, which was performed the following
day.

The Ontario case symbolized the raised consciousness that emerged
in the mid-1970s on the medical practice and legal implications of terminating life-extending treatment for neonatal patients. Although the Johns
Hopkins incident had cast the first public gaze upon such cases, the issue
did not spark public debate until 1973 when an article titled, "Moral and
Ethical Dilemmas in the Special Care Nursery," was published in the New
England Journal of Medicine.[15]

Written by two Yale-affiliated paediatricians, Dr. Raymond Duff and
Dr. A.G.M. Campbell, the paper revealed that 43 of the 299 deaths occurring in the intensive care nursery at Yale-New Haven Hospital from 1970

to 1972 had resulted from the termination of life-support measures. The diagnoses included: chromosomal disorders, chronic cardiopulmonary disease, myelomeningocele, and multiple congenital anomalies. In all 43 cases, "parents and physicians in a group decision concluded that prognosis for meaningful life was extremely poor or hopeless, and therefore rejected further treatment." The authors concluded with the expectation that by publishing their findings: "Perhaps more than anything else, the public and professional silence on a major social taboo and some common practices has been broken further."

This truly seminal article clearly accomplished its purpose. It provoked a deluge of commentary in the media and in medical, bioethics, and law journals. And it no doubt played a role in the emergence of a new rights issue in the 1970s — the right to treatment of neonatal patients. In the process, the consciousness triggered by Duff/Campbell has led to a new ethic: that the neonate as patient has the same moral and legal right to treatment that serves her best interests as does any older patient. However, the age factor highlights two matters that have particular relevance to cases involving children and neonates: the presence of a legal guardian and the all too often uncertain prognosis (particularly in cases of prematurity). These issues will be addressed in turn.

5. THE PARENT AS LEGAL GUARDIAN

Save for the exceptions carved out by the *emergency* and *mature minor* doctrines,* a physician cannot treat a child without the consent of the parents who are her natural and legal guardians. In that capacity, parents are obliged by the *Criminal Code* to furnish "necessaries of life" (e.g. medical treatment) for their children. Moreover, child welfare statutes in every province authorize the apprehension and court-ordered treatment of children whose parents fail to provide necessary medical attention.

The parental duty is to procure health care that is reasonable and appropriate, and the courts traditionally defer to parental judgment and intervene only when there is evidence that the withholding of treatment places the child's life or health in jeopardy. The duty owed to the ailing child by her parents mirrors the duty owed to the child by her physician. Given the physician's independent duty to her patient, she cannot comply with a parental demand to withdraw or withhold treatment unless she concludes that their decision is in the child's best interests. If she cannot in good conscience endorse their judgment or convince them otherwise, her legal duty is to request remedial action by the child welfare authority.

---

* See Chapter 20.

The principle is illustrated by the innumerable cases of court-ordered blood transfusions for minors over the objections of their Jehovah's Witness parents, and the issue at the constitutional level has now been settled by the Supreme Court in the *Sheena B.* case.

Consider the converse situation: parents insist upon aggressive management which the physician believes is contraindicated because of the child's dire prognosis. Is the physician legally entitled to act unilaterally if the parents remain steadfast and the conflict is not resolved by the child's death? As noted in the previous chapter, Canadian law has yet to recognize a *positive* right to treatment: that physicians can be compelled to bestow therapy that they regard as medically unreasonable. It may well happen that a case will arise in which parents seek a court order to enforce their demand for life-prolonging treatment, or a health care facility deems it advisable to petition for judicial authorization to forego treatment demanded by parents. A dispute of this nature would no doubt place the court in an awkward position as it hears distraught parents plead for their child's life. On the other hand, since the concern at stake is the child's best interests, a course of treatment considered uncalled-for by medical witnesses coupled with an unfavorable prognosis would provide sufficient legal grounds to call a halt to life-support measures, notwithstanding parental objection.

This scenario unfolded in a recent English case, *A National Health Service Trust v. D.*[16] The trust applied for a declaration in Family Court that in the event of a cardiac/respiratory arrest, it should be allowed to withhold CPR and mechanical ventilation for an 18-month-old patient. The infant was born at 31 weeks by emergency Caesarian section necessitated by pre-eclampsia. In detailing the patient's medical history, the judge noted:

> At approximately 90 minutes of age, he required endotracheal intubation by reason of increasing respiratory disease due to surfactant deficiency because of prematurity. Unfortunately, he developed the well-recognized complication of ventilator-induced lung injury. Ante-natal scan findings, confirmed on day one, were consistent with the diagnosis of Dandy-Walker syndrome and lissencephaly, both involving brain structure abnormality, which is irreversible. These abnormalities are associated with neurological handicap and severe developmental delay.

Furthermore, there was evidence of hepatic and renal dysfunction and congestive heart failure. Yet however dismal the child's condition, the parents insisted upon aggressive case management, whereas the infant's caregivers were strongly of the view that palliative care was called for. In the judge's view:

> Having regard to the minimal quality of life that the child had in the short life span left to him through his irreversible and worsening lung condition, any possible very limited short-term extension that mechanical ventilation might give him had to be weighed...against the pain and suffering caused by further mechanical ventilation.

It was clear to the judge that, notwithstanding the wishes of the parents, a course of palliative care accorded with the best interests of the child. He accordingly granted the declaration.

6. THE UNCERTAIN PROGNOSIS

In the *Couture-Jacquet* case, the Quebec Court of Appeal ruled that the child's dismal prognosis could not justify the ordeal of another course of chemotherapy. But what if there had been credible medical evidence of a survival rate of 70-80%, or perhaps a 50/50 chance of a successful outcome? In either case, the court likely would have ruled in the hospital's favour. The point is that treatment can be said to offer no reasonable hope of benefit only if a dim prognosis is relatively clear. But in the practice of neonatal medicine in particular, physicians are continually confronted with uncertain prognoses. Consider a case from a Winnipeg intensive care nursery whose kind of uncertainty is no doubt familiar to neonatal caregivers across Canada.*

> A 740-gram female infant was born at 25 weeks to a 19-year-old unwed mother (her first pregnancy) by emergency Caesarean section for abruptio placenta. The infant was asphyxiated at birth, with Apgars of 2 at one minute and 6 at five minutes. She was intubated in the caseroom and transferred to the intensive care nursery. A chest x-ray at 12 hours of age revealed evidence of moderate to severe respiratory distress syndrome. A patent ductus arteriosus was found when she was five days old, which led to a course of Indomethacin therapy. Therapeutic failure necessitated surgical ligation of the ductus when she was ten days old.
>
> When she was seven days old, cerebral ultrasound detected a Grade II intraventricular haemorrhage bilaterally. She also suffered several pneumothoraces, requiring the insertion of chest tubes. When she was two weeks old, followup cerebral ultrasound indicated progression of the ventricular bleeding — to a Grade III on the right side and a Grade IV on the left. The ventricles were dilated, and the head circumference was increasing. When she was four weeks old, a chest X-ray showed chronic changes consistent with early bronchopulmonary dysplasia. The head circumference continued to increase de-

---

* This case example was provided to the author by a neonatal nurse.

596   Canadian Medical Law

spite attempts at medical management. Consultation with a neurosurgeon led to the placement of a ventricular peritoneal shunt, which functioned adequately. At ten weeks of age, the infant remained ventilator dependent with significant bronchopulmonary dysplasia. An ophthalmological examination found signs of Grade III retinopathy of prematurity bilaterally.

At this stage, the infant's prognosis is uncertain. Assuming aggressive management, the most optimistic outcome is mild spasticity and visual impairment — but no mental handicap. Conversely, the end result could be devastating: chronic ventilator dependency, blindness, mental retardation, cerebral palsy, and seizures.

What if the infant were now to exhibit signs of sepsis? Should antibiotic therapy be started? In the aforementioned English case, *B. (A Minor), Re*, the Court ordered surgery because the neonate's prognosis was "still so imponderable." However, the English court suggested that it would not have mandated treatment if the evidence had indicated a case "of severe proved damage where the future is so certain and where the life of the child is so bound to be full of pain and suffering."

In the Winnipeg case, an antibiotic was administered because the physician and mother viewed the treatment issue in the same light as did the court in *B. (A Minor), Re*. They risked the burdens of continued therapy because the infant's prognosis was "still so imponderable." It will be years before the caregivers can say from the vantage point of hindsight whether their decision was medically warranted. The law obviously does not demand that kind of wisdom. What it does demand is a decision that is reasonable and proper, given the circumstances of the case. Uncertainty of prognosis is one variable in the best interests equation; and the lower the odds of long term benefit, the more likely will the law accept the legitimacy of the decision to let the infant die.

6. THE CANADIAN PEDIATRIC SOCIETY GUIDELINES

In 1986, the Canadian Pediatric Society issued a statement on "Treatment Decisions for Infants and Children." Although acknowledging that treatment ordinarily serves the patient's best interests, the statement recognized four circumstances sufficient to suspend the physician's duty to prolong life:

When there is irreversible progression of disease to imminent death.

When treatment will clearly be ineffective or harmful.

When life will be severely shortened regardless of treatment and when non-treatment will allow a greater degree of caring and comfort.

When the patient's life will be filled with intolerable and intractable pain and suffering.

The law cannot quarrel with the C.P.S. guidelines (which were reaffirmed in 2000), given that each is grounded in the principle that the duty to prolong life is discharged when treatment no longer serves the "best interests" of the patient. Inherent in a best interests assessment is the application of a quality-of-life standard, which is morally and legally permissible so long as its focus is patient-centred. The use of social worth criteria — measuring the value of the patient's life to society against the burdens society will bear to support that life — is legally indefensible and rightly evokes the spectre of Hitler's so-called "euthanasia program."* Only if the physician's focus is patient-oriented can the decision to let die be regarded as a benevolent, merciful, and lawful response to the plight of an infant or child patient whose bleak prognosis tips the balance from the struggle for life to the resigned acceptance of death.

---

* The Nazi euthanasia program is summarized in Chapter 26.

ENDNOTES

1. *British Columbia (Superintendent of Family & Child Services) v. D. (R.)*, [1983] 3 W.W.R. 618 (B.C. S.C.).
2. *Couture-Jacquet v. Montreal Children's Hospital* (1986), 28 D.L.R. (4th) 22 (Que. C.A.).
3. *Saskatchewan (Minister of Social Services) v. P. (F.)*, [1990] 4 W.W.R. 748 (Sask. Prov. Ct.).
4. J. Downie, A choice for K'aila. 2 **Health Law Journal** 99 (1994).
5. *T. (Wardship: Medical Treatment), Re*, [1997] 1 All E.R. 906.
6. D. Price. *The Legal and Ethical Aspects of Organ Transplantation.* (Cambridge U. Press, 2000), at 441-2.
7. *New Brunswick (Minister of Health & Community Services) v. B. (R.)* (1990), 106 N.B.R. (2d) 206 (Q.B.).
8. *B. (R.) v. Children's Aid Society of Metropolitan Toronto* (1995), 122 D.L.R. (4th) 1 (S.C.C.).
9. *In re A (Children) (Conjoined Twins: Surgical Separation)*, [2001] 2 W.L.R. 480.
10. A. Hutchinson, *Nightmare choice for parents.* **Toronto Globe and Mail**, Sept. 27, 2000.
11. *D., Re* (1982), 30 R.F.L. (2d) 277 (Alta. Prov. Ct.).
12. *Goyette, Re*, [1983] C.S. 429 (Que. S.C.).
13. *R. v. Cyrenne* (1981), 62 C.C.C. (2d) 238 (Ont. Dist. Ct.).
14. *B. (A Minor), Re*, [1981] 1 W.L.R. 1421.
15. R.S. Duff & A.G.M. Campbell, Moral and ethical dilemmas in the special care nursery. 289 **New England Journal of Medicine** 890. (1973).
16. *A NHS Trust v. D.*, [2000] 2 F.C.R. 577.

24

PATIENTS' ADVANCE (HEALTH CARE) DIRECTIVES

SUMMARY

The advance (health care) directive is a mechanism enabling a mentally competent person to plan for a time when he may lack the mental capacity to make medical treatment decisions. It comes into effect only when he becomes incompetent to speak for himself. The advance directive is a more sophisticated concept than that of the living will, although the two terms are often confused. A *living will* is a document in which the person makes an anticipatory refusal of life-prolonging measures during a future state of mental incompetency. On the other hand, an advance directive is not restricted to the rejection of life-support measures; its focus is upon treatment preferences, which may include asking for as well as refusing treatment. The advance directive assumes two forms: the *instructional directive* (in which the maker* spells out specific directions to govern his care in more detail than generally found in the living will); and the *proxy directive* (in which he appoints someone as his medical care agent to make treatment decisions on his behalf). One can fill out both directives, or simply one or the other. The pros and cons of the advance directive are considered.

1. INTRODUCTION

In 1995 the Journal of the American Medical Association published an article, "Determinants in Canadian Health Care Workers of the Decision to Withdraw Life-Support From the Critically Ill."[1] The objective of the far ranging study there summarized was to examine the attitudes of intensive care physicians, medical house staff, and nurses toward the termination

---

* We use the term "maker" to refer to the person signing an advance directive.

of life-support. The nine co-authors (who conducted the study for the Canadian Critical Care Trials Group) surveyed 1,361 respondents from across Canada, who were presented with 12 clinical scenarios and directed to rank the importance of 17 "determinants of withdrawal of life-support" for each of the hypothetical cases. They were also asked to select the level of care for each case, ranging from comfort measures to aggressive high-tech intervention. To avoid the effects of patient and family preferences, the scenarios all involved mentally incompetent patients with no advance directives and no families available for consultation. The 17 factors included: likelihood of surviving current episode, likelihood of long-term survival, premorbid cognitive function, age, socioeconomic status, premorbid physical condition, premorbid emotional function, alcohol abuse, drug abuse, and religious affiliation. Overall, the respondents rated the first four as the most important. However, in choosing the level of care for the 12 patient scenarios, the same option was selected by more than half the respondents in only one of the cases; and opposite extremes of care were chosen by more than 10% of the respondents in eight of the cases.

The data led the authors to conclude that "the most striking and important finding in our study is the variability in respondents' choice of level of care for the same scenario." Although deploring the impact of idiosyncratic values upon life-and-death decision-making, the authors acknowledged that clinicians cannot ignore their social, moral, and religious values. However, they suggested that there was a mechanism — the advance directive — that could move the locus of decision-making further toward the patient.

That sentiment was echoed by Dr. Thomas Todd, chairman of the Canadian Critical Care Trials Group, who commented to the media that advance directives "would be a lot of help" to hospital staff, although he added that vaguely worded directives fail to provide sufficient guidance to caregivers and thus simply complicate the decision-making process.[2] And one of the study's co-authors, Dr. Deborah Cook, was quoted in the media as saying that advance directives "can have their shortcomings", and therefore that patients should discuss the details of their directives with their physicians and family members so that they "can make intelligent choices about what is best for them."[3]

What precisely is an advance directive? Is it the same thing as a living will? Is it a legally binding document? What are its implications for health care professionals? It is to these questions that we now turn.

2. THE FIRST GENERATION DIRECTIVE: THE LIVING WILL

In the 1930s, a Chicago attorney, Luis Kutner, drafted a document that he called a "living will", so named because it stated the signer's anticipatory refusal of life-prolonging measures in the event that he became mentally incompetent to express his wishes during a terminal illness. While a number of individuals signed living wills — the second of whom was the Hollywood film star, Errol Flynn — they did not receive public distribution until Kutner made the document available to the New York-based Euthanasia Educational Council in 1968. However, it was not until the *Karen Quinlan* case* in 1976 that the living will fully entered public consciousness; within six months of the decision the Council received 600,000 requests for Kutner's brainchild.

Living wills were also formulated by other so-called "right to die" organizations, although their wording differed little from that of the Council's version which states in pertinent part: "If there is no reasonable expectation of my recovery from physical or mental disability, I, _____, request that I be allowed to die and not be kept alive by artificial means or heroic measures." Other standard form living wills direct that treatment be halted when the patient's condition is "incurable" or when treatment "would serve only to prolong dying."

The concept of the living will was embraced by health care consumers haunted by the spectre of the *technological imperative* and the related notion of *vitalism* — that the wonders of modern medical science are there to be used and in particular must strive to stave off death for as long as possible because life, however lived, is always preferable to death. Another factor adding to consumer anxiety was the American media reporting of cases in which physicians/hospitals insisted upon the maintenance of life-support measures, regardless of prognosis, as a defensive measure against the fear, however unfounded, that letting patients die would lead to lawsuits by disgruntled relatives for wrongful death.

In Canada the question of living wills was addressed by the Law Reform Commission of Canada in its 1983 report, *Euthanasia, Aiding Suicide and Cessation of Treatment.*[4] Although the Commission had no quarrel with the widespread revulsion against overtreatment, it nonetheless cautioned the provinces against the enactment of living will statutes:

> We believe that it would risk the reversal of the already-established rule that there should be no duty to initiate or maintain treatment when it is useless to

---

* See Chapter 21.

do so. The living will approach begins from the opposite principle, since it requires that the (incompetent) patient's wishes be formally expressed in writing in order to authorize the physician not to prolong that patient's agony and death.

With due respect, this perspective failed to appreciate that living will statutes do not compromise the principle that there is no legal duty compelling physicians to maintain non-beneficial life-support measures for mentally incompetent patients. Rather, what living will legislation truly compromises is the physician's unfettered discretion to impose such treatment when the patient is mentally incompetent to indicate otherwise. In a sense, the living will is a challenge to the traditional nature of the physician/patient relationship, in which it is the physician who has wielded control. When legally recognized as an enforceable document, the living will confers a right that the law had heretofore not conferred upon the patient — the right to anticipate his medical future and to direct his treatment outcome.

In short, living will legislation is not grounded in the premise that, unless the patient has spoken, his physician cannot call a halt to life-prolonging treatment. A physician is not legally precluded from discontinuing treatment that fails to benefit a mentally incompetent patient, but without a legally enforceable direction she cannot be obliged to exercise that option. Simply put, a living will statute is designed to grant the patient the authority to direct the physician as to when the time has come to let him die. Still, the patient can provide clear direction on the course of his medical management only when he has anticipated the precise nature and development of his current or future illness. Even if legally recognized, a living will binds the physician only when the patient's condition conforms to that spelled out in the document. In other words, a stipulation that "heroic measures" be omitted when the patient's condition is "incurable" provides precious little direction to caregivers; such wording neither precisely defines the patient's medical state nor specifies the medical interventions that are not to be used.

The dilemma faced by health caregivers confronted with a standard form living will is illustrated by the New York case of *Evans v. Bellevue Hospital*.[5] A 47-year-old AIDS patient was admitted to hospital in a stuporous condition. The patient, who was diagnosed as suffering from toxoplasmosis (based upon tests indicating multiple brain lesions), had signed a living will that stated:

> I direct that life-sustaining procedures should be withdrawn or withheld if I have an illness, disease, or experience mental deterioration such that there is no reasonable expectation of recovering or regaining a meaningful quality of life.

A conflict arose between the patient's physicians and his partner as to whether his condition was covered by the document, and the latter responded by petitioning the County Court for an order directing the hospital to discontinue treatment. According to the physicians, the patient was expected to recover from the toxoplasmosis within two weeks and to regain the ability to communicate during that time. However, his partner insisted that even if there were a reasonable hope of recovery, there was no possibility of his ever regaining "a meaningful quality of life."

In denying the petition, the Court ruled that because there was hope of recovery from "the clear and present threat" of toxoplasmosis, it was not prepared to conclude that the patient could not recover "a meaningful quality of life." Thus, although the patient had no doubt intended that his living will serve the purpose of directing the course of his medical treatment during a state of incompetency, the vagueness of its terms frustrated that objective. As the Court concluded its opinion: "It is our suggestion that great pains be taken by the drafters of living wills to dispel the ambiguities which necessitated this proceeding."

At the very least, however, the patient who signs a living will is providing tangible evidence that he rejects the notion that life should be maintained at all cost, however dismal and hopeless the prognosis. Whatever its deficiencies, the living will is a clear expression of the patient's awareness that there may come a time when death is preferable to life. If the patient (directly or through his family) has tendered a living will to his physician, he is conveying the message that he fears being kept alive by treatment that is more burdensome than beneficial. When the physician assesses the treatment in that light, she breaches no law when she complies with the patient's directive. The reason is that the living will directs the physician to do what she is already lawfully entitled to do — terminate life-prolonging treatment when it ceases to offer a reasonable hope of benefit for the mentally incompetent patient.

In addition, the living will assumes a valuable function when it affords an opportunity for the patient to discuss his medical future with his physician. The physician should regard that act as an invitation to open a dialogue with the patient about his medical management. In that event, the living will is the first step toward an agreement as to the circumstances under which the physician will step aside to enable her patient to die a natural death.

Still, physicians cannot not be faulted for regarding standard form living wills as too vague and imprecise to guide decision-making for incompetent patients. It was in light of the living will's deficiencies that the concept of the medical treatment proxy arose; and in 1979 an editorial in the New England Journal of Medicine proposed legislation enabling patients to appointment health care agents to make treatment decisions on their behalf in the event of mental incompetency.[6] The next response to the living will appeared in 1989 with the publication of a landmark article — "The Medical Directive: A Comprehensive Advance Care Document" — in the Journal of the American Medical Association.[7] Co-authored by physicians Linda and Ezekiel Emanuel, the article outlined a second generation living will, to which we now turn.

3. THE SECOND GENERATION DIRECTIVE: THE ADVANCE DIRECTIVE

The striking feature of the Emanuel/Emanuel second generation directive (hereinafter called the Medical Directive) is its scenario-and-treatment specificity. The directive's key feature is a 9x6 grid that allows one to decide upon nine medical interventions for each of six patient conditions: (A) permanent unconsciousness (coma or persistent vegetative state); (B) coma with likelihood of either death or permanent mental and physical disability; (C) mentally incompetent and terminally ill; (D) irreversible brain damage but not terminally ill; (E) a situation "that is important to you and/or your doctor believes you should consider in view of your current medical situation"; and (F) "in my current state of health" but then temporarily incompetent during life-threatening but reversible condition. The grid is set out in *Figure 1*.

Figure 1

MY MEDICAL DIRECTIVE

This Medical Directive shall stand as a guide to my wishes regarding medical treatments in the event that illness should make me unable to communicate them directly. I make this Directive, being 18 years or more of age, of sound mind, and appreciating the consequences of my decisions.

SITUATION A

If I am in a coma or a persistent vegetative state and, in the opinion of my physician and two consultants, have no known hope of regaining awareness and higher mental functions no matter what is done, then my goals and specific wishes — if medically reasonable — for this and any additional illness would be:

☐ prolong life; treat everything
☐ attempt to cure, but reevaluate often
☐ limit to less invasive and less burdensome interventions
☐ provide comfort care only
☐ other (*please specify*): _____

Please check appropriate boxes:

	I want	I want treatment tried. If no clear improvement, stop.	I am undecided	I do not want
1. Cardiopulmonary resuscitation (chest compressions, drugs, electric shocks, and artificial breathing aimed at reviving a person who is on the point of dying).		Not applicable		
2. Major surgery (for example, removing the gallbladder or part of the colon).		Not applicable		
3. Mechanical breathing (respiration by machine, through a tube in the throat).				
4. Dialysis (cleaning the blood by machine or by fluid passed through the belly).				
5. Blood transfusions or blood products.		Not applicable		
6. Artificial nutrition and hydration (given through a tube in a vein or in the stomach).				
7. Simple diagnostic tests (for example, blood tests or x-rays).		Not applicable		
8. Antibiotics (drugs to fight infection).		Not applicable		
9. Pain medications, even if they dull consciousness and indirectly shorten my life.		Not applicable		

SITUATION B

If I am near death and in a coma and, in the opinion of my physician and two consultants, have a small but uncertain chance of regaining higher mental functions, a somewhat greater chance of surviving with permanent mental and physical disability, and a much greater chance of not recovering at all, then my goals and specific wishes — if medically reasonable — for this and any additional illness would be:

☐ prolong life; treat everything
☐ attempt to cure, but reevaluate often
☐ limit to less invasive and less burdensome interventions
☐ provide comfort care only
☐ other (*please specify*): _____

Please check appropriate boxes:

	I want	I want treatment tried. If no clear improvement, stop.	I am undecided	I do not want
1. Cardiopulmonary resuscitation (chest compressions, drugs, electric shocks, and artificial breathing aimed at reviving a person who is on the point of dying).		Not applicable		
2. Major surgery (for example, removing the gallbladder or part of the colon).		Not applicable		
3. Mechanical breathing (respiration by machine, through a tube in the throat).				
4. Dialysis (cleaning the blood by machine or by fluid passed through the belly).				
5. Blood transfusions or blood products.		Not applicable		
6. Artificial nutrition and hydration (given through a tube in a vein or in the stomach).				
7. Simple diagnostic tests (for example, blood tests or x-rays).		Not applicable		
8. Antibiotics (drugs to fight infection).		Not applicable		
9. Pain medications, even if they dull consciousness and indirectly shorten my life.		Not applicable		

SITUATION C

If I have a terminal illness with weeks to live, and my mind is not working well enough to make decisions for myself, but I am sometimes awake and seem to have feelings, then my goals and specific wishes — if medically reasonable — for this and any additional illness would be:

☐ prolong life; treat everything
☐ attempt to cure, but reevaluate often
☐ limit to less invasive and less burdensome interventions
☐ provide comfort care only
☐ other (*please specify*): _____

Please check appropriate boxes:

	I want	I want treatment tried. If no clear improve- ment, stop.	I am undecided	I do not want
1. Cardiopulmonary resuscitation (chest compressions, drugs, electric shocks, and artificial breathing aimed at reviving a person who is on the point of dying).		Not applicable		
2. Major surgery (for example, removing the gallbladder or part of the colon).		Not applicable		
3. Mechanical breathing (respiration by machine, through a tube in the throat).				
4. Dialysis (cleaning the blood by machine or by fluid passed through the belly).				
5. Blood transfusions or blood products.		Not applicable		
6. Artificial nutrition and hydration (given through a tube in a vein or in the stomach).				
7. Simple diagnostic tests (for example, blood tests or x-rays).		Not applicable		
8. Antibiotics (drugs to fight infection).		Not applicable		
9. Pain medications, even if they dull con- sciousness and indirectly shorten my life.		Not applicable		

SITUATION D

If I have brain damage or some brain disease that in the opinon of my physician and two consultants cannot be reversed and that makes me unable to think or have feelings, *but I have no terminal illness*, then my goals and specific wishes — if medically reasonable — for this and any additional illness would be:

- ☐ prolong life; treat everything
- ☐ attempt to cure, but reevaluate often
- ☐ limit to less invasive and less burdensome interventions
- ☐ provide comfort care only
- ☐ other (*please specify*): _____

Please check appropriate boxes:

	I want	I want treatment tried. If no clear improvement, stop.	I am undecided	I do not want
1. Cardiopulmonary resuscitation (chest compressions, drugs, electric shocks, and artificial breathing aimed at reviving a person who is on the point of dying).		Not applicable		
2. Major surgery (for example, removing the gallbladder or part of the colon).		Not applicable		
3. Mechanical breathing (respiration by machine, through a tube in the throat).				
4. Dialysis (cleaning the blood by machine or by fluid passed through the belly).				
5. Blood transfusions or blood products.		Not applicable		
6. Artificial nutrition and hydration (given through a tube in a vein or in the stomach).				
7. Simple diagnostic tests (for example, blood tests or x-rays).		Not applicable		
8. Antibiotics (drugs to fight infection).		Not applicable		
9. Pain medications, even if they dull consciousness and indirectly shorten my life.		Not applicable		

SITUATION E

If I . . . (describe a situation that is important to you and/or your doctor believes you should consider in view of your current medical situation):

☐ prolong life; treat everything
☐ attempt to cure, but reevaluate often
☐ limit to less invasive and less burdensome interventions
☐ provide comfort care only
☐ other (*please specify*): _____

Please check appropriate boxes:	I want	I want treatment tried. If no clear improvement, stop.	I am undecided	I do not want
1. Cardiopulmonary resuscitation (chest compressions, drugs, electric shocks, and artificial breathing aimed at reviving a person who is on the point of dying).		Not applicable		
2. Major surgery (for example, removing the gallbladder or part of the colon).		Not applicable		
3. Mechanical breathing (respiration by machine, through a tube in the throat).				
4. Dialysis (cleaning the blood by machine or by fluid passed through the belly).				
5. Blood transfusions or blood products.		Not applicable		
6. Artificial nutrition and hydration (given through a tube in a vein or in the stomach).				
7. Simple diagnostic tests (for example, blood tests or x-rays).		Not applicable		
8. Antibiotics (drugs to fight infection).		Not applicable		
9. Pain medications, even if they dull consciousness and indirectly shorten my life.		Not applicable		

SITUATION F

If I am in my current state of health (describe briefly): _____

_____

and then have an illness that, in the opinion of my physician and two consultants, is life threatening but reversible, and I am temporarily unable to make decisions, then my goals and specific wishes — if medically reasonable — would be:

☐ prolong life; treat everything
☐ attempt to cure, but reevaluate often
☐ limit to less invasive and less burdensome interventions
☐ provide comfort care only
☐ other (*please specify*): _____

Please check appropriate boxes:

	I want	I want treatment tried. If no clear improvement, stop.	I am undecided	I do not want
1. Cardiopulmonary resuscitation (chest compressions, drugs, electric shocks, and artificial breathing aimed at reviving a person who is on the point of dying).		Not applicable		
2. Major surgery (for example, removing the gallbladder or part of the colon).		Not applicable		
3. Mechanical breathing (respiration by machine, through a tube in the throat).				
4. Dialysis (cleaning the blood by machine or by fluid passed through the belly).				
5. Blood transfusions or blood products.		Not applicable		
6. Artificial nutrition and hydration (given through a tube in a vein or in the stomach).				
7. Simple diagnostic tests (for example, blood tests or x-rays).		Not applicable		
8. Antibiotics (drugs to fight infection).		Not applicable		
9. Pain medications, even if they dull consciousness and indirectly shorten my life.		Not applicable		

As indicated by the grid, the directive presents four paradigmatic scenarios — A, B, C, and D — that describe a patient's condition with more precision than is encompassed by such terms as "incurable" or "extreme physical or mental disability." Furthermore, although the focus of standard form living wills is upon terminal illness, such is the specified case in only one of the patient conditions, (C). With reference to treatment options, the directive substitutes nine specific interventions for the vagueness of such terms as "artificial means" and "heroic measures." And regarding each intervention, the directive offers four treatment options to the patient — "want", "don't want", "undecided", or a "trial." The broad range of choice stands in stark contrast to the living will, which by definition is a document restricted to the refusal of treatment. This feature of the directive is implied in its introduction: "The Medical Directive allows you to record your wishes regarding various types of medical treatments in several representative situations so that your desires can be respected." Of course, if the whole point of a treatment directive is to maximize patient autonomy, then it is fitting that the patient be allowed to express his wishes for or against medical interventions. In that sense, the Medical Directive can be regarded as a progressive step beyond the treatment-refusal limitation of the living will. However, as will be noted, that step may in truth be a mixed blessing.

Aside from the treatment/scenario grid, the Medical Directive also provides for the appointment of a medical proxy under the heading, "Health Care Proxy."

> I direct my proxy to make health-care decisions based on his/her assessment of my personal wishes. If my personal desires are unknown, my proxy is to make health-care decisions based on his/her best guess as to my wishes. My proxy shall have the authority to make all health-care decisions for me, including decisions about life-sustaining treatment, if I am unable to make them myself.

One is also allowed to specify any limitations upon the proxy's authority. The proxy direction also asks the document's maker to resolve two potential conflicts: which proxy has final authority if more than one proxy is appointed and there is no consensus regarding treatment; and whose decision prevails if the proxy wishes to override a treatment direction specified by the patient in the interventions section of the document.

The directive also contains a provision for a personal statement with the following direction:

> Please mention anything that would be important for your physician and your proxy to know. In particular, try to answer the following questions: (1) What

medical conditions, if any, would make living so unpleasant that you would want life-sustaining treatment *withheld*? (Intractable pain? Irreversible mental damage? Inability to share love? Dependence on others? Another condition you would regard as intolerable?) 2) Under what medical circumstances would you want to *stop* interventions that might already have been started?

As explained by the authors:

> Since personal goals and values cannot be accurately translated into specific decisions by anyone as well as they can by the patient, these personal statements do not stand in isolation but with the specific selections in the scenarios.

In sum, the Medical Directive is the prototype of a more sophisticated approach to health care planning than is provided for in the living will. The second generation document is commonly referred to as an *advance directive*; and as illustrated by the Medical Directive, it contains two parts: the *instructional directive* (directions regarding treatment decisions for particular conditions) and the *proxy directive*. The theory is that by combining the two directives in the same document, the maker is able to maximize control over his medical care if and when he becomes mentally incompetent to make his own treatment choices.

The Centre for Bioethics at the University of Toronto has published an advance directive inspired by the Medical Directive.[8] Developed by the Centre's associate director, Dr. Peter Singer, it contains both proxy and detailed intervention-focused instructional directives. A definitions section explains the clinical scenario and interventions terminology. The instructional directive's 9x7 grid, which is set out in *Figure 2*, is prefaced as follows:

> For each of the health situations (found in the first column of the table), imagine that you are in the situation described, and then develop a further medical problem that requires some life-sustaining treatment (found in the top row of the table). If you do not receive this treatment, you would die. If you receive the treatment, the chance that you will live depends on the nature of the medical problem. Even if you recover fully from the medical problem, you would return to the health situation you were in before you developed the further medical problem.

> As an example, imagine that, at some future time, you suffer from a severe stroke. Then, you develop pneumonia requiring life-saving antibiotics. Without the antibiotics you would die. With the antibiotics, your chance of surviving depends on the nature and severity of the pneumonia. Of course, even if the antibiotics were successful in treating your pneumonia, you would still have severe stroke.

You should then decide whether or not you would want the particular treatment (antibiotics) if you were in this condition (severe stroke).

Write your treatment decision (*Yes, No, UNDECIDED, or TRIAL*) in the box for every combination of health situation and treatment....

In some cases, it may be unclear initially whether a given treatment will be beneficial or not. In these cases, you may want to try the treatment for an appropriate period, usually a few days to a couple of weeks. During this time your doctors would monitor and assess the effectiveness of the treatment and determine how beneficial it was for you. If the treatment proved to be beneficial, it could be continued. If not, it could be stopped. If you wish such a treatment trial, then write "TRIAL" in the box. For CPR and surgery, a treatment trial is not appropriate because these treatments are given all at once in a short time.

Then, the rest of the boxes may be filled in, by imagining yourself in each health situation and that you require each of the life-sustaining treatments listed.

Figure 2

	CPR	VENTILATOR	DIALYSIS	LIFE-SAVING SURGERY	BLOOD TRANSFUSION	LIFE-SAVING ANTIBIOTICS	TUBE FEEDING
CURRENT HEALTH							
MILD STROKE							
MODERATE STROKE							
SEVERE STROKE							
MILD DEMENTIA							
MODERATE DEMENTIA							
SEVERE DEMENTIA							
PERMANENT COMA							
TERMINAL ILLNESS							

There is another Canadian second generation directive, which differs from the Emanuel and Singer models because its focus is upon levels of care rather than upon specific medical conditions and treatment options. The directive is featured in a pamphlet titled, "Let Me Decide", written by Dr. William Molloy, an Ontario Geriatrician.[9] The directive enables the maker to specify a particular level of care (palliative, limited, surgical, intensive), level of feeding support (basic, supplemental, intravenous, tube), and CPR or no CPR in the event of a life-threatening illness. The level of care is to be assessed according to whether the patient classifies his underlying condition as either irreversible/intolerable or acceptable. (All terms are carefully defined.) Regarding the intolerable-versus-acceptable equation, the maker is advised:

> Since each person would accept different irreversible disabilities, it's important to know in advance what you would not be prepared to accept.... Diseases such as cancer, multiple sclerosis, stroke, Parkinson's or Alzheimer's may affect your ability to think and function independently. But don't think in terms of specific illnesses. Instead, consider how these illnesses could impair your independence and freedom or your ability to carry out everyday activities such as walking, dressing, eating and talking. Consider how that would affect your quality of life....

The section headed "Personal Statement" begins with the incomplete sentence, "I consider an irreversible/intolerable condition to be any condition...." The maker must define the circumstances considered irreversible/ intolerable and then — in the event of a life-threatening illness — specify what is to be done in terms of care, feeding support, and CPR. For example, if the patient's current condition is deemed "intolerable", then he might opt for the lowest levels of care and feeding support and for no CPR. Or if the patient's current condition is "acceptable", then he might opt for the highest levels of care and feeding support and for CPR. Yet, as Dr. Molloy is careful to point out, what is intolerable for one may be acceptable for another:

> People have different ideas about what disabilities and medical treatments they consider intolerable. Some would not want to be resuscitated if they were paralysed. Others fear losing bowel or bladder control. Some would not want to live in an institution, and others would not want to be tube fed. Others would not tolerate being washed and fed by others.

The accompanying commentary suggests that the maker carefully consider the circumstances that she "would and would not accept", and in particular that she consider the following situations: living in a nursing home or other institution; chronic incurable pain; permanent coma; inability to feed, wash, dress, walk or talk; blindness and deafness; inability to recognize family; inability to communicate; loss of bladder and/or bowel control; and paralysis from the neck down. The Molloy directive thus provides the maker with the opportunity to spell out her notions of what losses make life no longer worth living or still worth living. Examples of personal statements by persons filling out the Molloy directive are presented, including the following:

> I would consider an irreversible/intolerable condition to be any condition that left me totally bedridden and totally dependent on others for personal care such as washing, dressing or feeding.
>
> I would consider an irreversible/intolerable condition to be any condition that left me unable to wash or dress myself, or that left me unable to speak, or incontinent, or that left me quadriplegic.
>
> I would consider an irreversible/intolerable condition to be any condition that left me permanently confined to bed or that caused me to spend most of my time in hospital.

The key feature of the Molloy directive is called a "Personal Health Care Chart" and is reproduced in *Figure 3*.

Figure 3

2. PERSONAL CARE

I would consider an irreversible/intolerable condition to be any condition

_____

_____

_____

_____

_____

_____

_____

_____

_____

_____

I would agree to the following procedures: (write YES or NO)

Blood Transfusion _____   Post Mortem _____

Organ Donation _____   Cremation _____

3. THE HEALTH CARE CHART

If my condition is **Acceptable**			If my condition is **Irreversible/Intolerable**		
Life Threatening Illness	**Cardiac Arrest**	**Feeding**	**Life Threatening Illness**	**Cardiac Arrest**	**Feeding**
Palliative Limited Surgical Intensive	No CPR CPR	Basic Supplemental Intravenous Tube	Palliative Limited Surgical Intensive	No CPR CPR	Basic Supplemental Intravenous Tube
Date Signature		Power of Attorney Signature(s)		Physician Signature	
Date of next review should be once a year, after an illness, or if there is any change in health					
Date Signature		Power of Attorney Signature(s)		Physician Signature	
Date Signature		Power of Attorney Signature(s)		Physician Signature	

DEFINITIONS

Reversible/Acceptable condition: Condition where I have an acceptable quality of life

Irreversible Condition: Condition where I have intolerable or Unacceptable disability, e.g. multiple sclerosis, stroke, sever head injury, Alzheimer's disease

FEEDING

Basic Feeding: _Spoon feed with regular diet. Give all fluids by mouth that can be tolerated, but make no attmept to feed by special diets, intravenous fluids or tubes._

Supplemental: _Give supplements of special diets, for example, high calorie, fat or protein supplements._

Intravenous: Give nutrients (water, salt, carbohydrate, protein and fat) by intravenous infusions.

Tubes: Use tube feeing. There are two main types.

> Nasogastric Tube: a soft plastic tube passed through the nose or mouth into the stomach.

> Gastrostomy Tube: a soft plastic tube passed directly into the stomach through the skin over the abdomen.

CARDIAC ARREST (CPR)

No CPR: Make no attempt to resuscitate.

CPR: *Use cardiac massage with mouth-to-mouth breathing: may also include intravenous lines, electric shocks to the heart (defibrillators), tubes in throat to lungs (endotrachial tubes).*

Palliative Care

— keep me warm, dry, and pain free
— do not transfer to hospital unless absolutely necessary
— only give measures that enchance comfort or minimize pain; e.g. Morphine for pain
— intravenous line started only if it improves comfort; e.g. for dehydration
— no x-rays, blood tests or antibiotics unless they are given to improve comfort

Limited Care (includes Palliative)

— may or may not transfer to hospital
— intravenous therapy may be appropriate
— antibiotics should be used sparingly
— a trial of appropriate drugs may be used
— no invasive procedures; e.g. surgery
— do not transfer to Intensive Care Unit

Surgical Care (includes Limited)

— transfer to acute care hospital (where patient may be evaluated)
— emergency surgery if necessary
— do not admit to Intensive Care Unit
— do not ventilate (except during and after surgery); i.e. tube down throat and connected with machine

Intensive Care (includes Surgical)

— transfer to acute care hospital without hesitation
— admit to Intensive Care Unit if necessary
— ventilate patient if necessary
— insert central line; i.e. main arteries for fluids when other veins collapse
— provide surgery, biopsies, all life-support systems and transplant surgery
— do everything possible to maintain life

(a) Commentary on the Instructional Directive

The detailed intervention-focused directive is designed to enhance patient self-determination by reducing uncertainty in medical decision-making when the patient can no longer speak for herself. Of course, even the most detailed directive cannot guarantee coverage of every treatment contingency that may come to pass. As one commentator has observed:

> As doctors and lawyers have gained more experience with living wills, they have recognized several limitations inherent in such documents. First, no living will — no matter how broadly or how specifically worded — can possibly anticipate the full range of difficult decisions to be made. Inevitably, questions of interpretation arise concerning whether an incompetent patient's actual situation conforms to the situation described in the living will. A written instrument prepared before the onset of illness is generally more useful in excluding certain procedures that are totally unacceptable to a patient than in fine-tuning decision-making about a full range of possible health care choices.[10]

In a medical journal article, "Limitations of Listing Specific Medical Interventions in Advance Directives", Harvard physician Alan Brett argues along the same lines.[11] As he notes with particular reference to the Emanuels' Medical Directive, its primary focus is upon discrete interventions as means to a patient-specified end — "the use of mechanical ventilation, dialysis, or transfusions is appropriate or inappropriate with reference to objectives such as living longer, living more comfortably, or dying more peacefully." In questioning the efficacy of that very format, he states that

> the intervention-focused directive runs the risk of promoting the selection or rejection of interventions because of their inherent characteristics, rather than as appropriate means to the ends that the patient would have wanted.

To illustrate, he takes the example of a patient who, in filling out the Medical Directive, is asked to decide upon an intervention (e.g. antibiotics) in a specific clinical context (e.g. advanced irreversible dementia).

> But a problem quickly arises, because the person would be unable to choose or reject antibiotics categorically without knowing the reasons they were proposed and whether those reasons were consistent with his or her perspective. For example, assume the position of a person whose projected wish in such a context would not be longevity, but rather physical comfort until death ensues. This person might desire penicillin for a painful skin infection but not a relatively toxic antibiotic such as amphotericin B for a probably fatal systemic fungal infection. Or, the patient may not want an antibiotic for a virulent pneumonia that will lead to rapid death but would prefer an antibiotic

for an indolent pneumonia that is not expected to result in death but is causing an uncomfortable cough and chest pain.

As he adds, the checklist of interventions does not resolve the question: whatever the patient's views about medical care for advanced dementia, will antibiotics applied in the context of a specific infection produce a greater balance of benefits over burdens? (Note that the Singer directive addresses Dr. Brett's concern by referring to "life-saving antibiotics.") Consider then a patient who rejects all treatment options — including "life-saving antibiotics" — in the event of severe dementia because he does not regard that condition as compatible with a meaningful life. If the patient is afflicted with a urinary tract infection, then the directive would not preclude treatment with antibiotics. But if he had simply indicated a blanket rejection of antibiotics, he would continue to suffer from a condition that would cause discomfort but would be unlikely to cause his death.

Dr. Brett also suggests that when applied in a real-life context, "various combinations of preselected interventions...may contradict the patient's goals or suggest unusual patterns of medical practice." In that regard, he presents a case from his own practice in which the patient had completed the Medical Directive. In the event of advanced dementia the patient opted for blood transfusions but rejected diagnostic procedures. However, as Dr. Brett comments:

> If that patient developed upper gastrointestinal bleeding, we would be asked to administer transfusions, while avoiding an endoscopic procedure that might not only be diagnostic but also therapeutic (e.g. by coagulating the bleeding site). If the patient's goal in these situations was a speedy death, he would likely not want either transfusions or endoscopy. If he wanted to continue to live, he would likely want both. But it is absurd to dissociate the two inter-ventions by replacing blood losses but not performing a simple procedure to stop the bleeding.

(Or consider a patient who directs the rejection of surgery and radiation if afflicted with terminal cancer. Yet the spurned therapies can reduce the size of the tumour blocking his bowel or obstructing his windpipe, thus providing comfort measures that he surely would want.)

In short, it is Dr. Brett's contention that an intervention-focused checklist "may shift attention away from overall treatment goals or may prescribe inappropriate medical care." Although his critique is well taken, it simply highlights the fact that an instructional directive is by nature an imperfect decision-making instrument. The trademark of the instructional directive is that it anticipates contingencies, and as such it is second best to face-to-face discussion between physician and patient about treatment options.

In theory, the instructional directive broadens the scope of patient autonomy because it enables one, while competent, to project her preferences regarding treatment onto situations of future incompetency. But such an exercise is really tantamount to gazing into a crystal ball, particularly for one who is in general good health when filling out the directive. On the other hand, the future is more predictable for a patient in the early stages of a debilitating process (e.g. Alzheimer's disease, AIDS, or multiple sclerosis). When such a patient has been well informed by her physician of the natural course of the disease, she is well positioned to anticipate the specific treatment scenarios that likely lie in her future. But bear in mind that there are no guarantees that the patient's document will provide sufficient guidance for the physician when it comes time to apply the directive during a subsequent stage of incompetency. As Professor Meisel explains in his text, *The Right to Die*:[12]

> If advance directives are to be useful, it is necessary in their drafting to strike a balance between generality and specificity to avoid the dual risks of having the directive so precisely drafted that it fails to cover the contingency that has in fact arisen and having it so broadly drafted that it is unclear what decision the declarant would make if currently capable of doing so. In turn, the risks of the latter kind of situation are that a patient will receive treatment that he would have refused or will fail to receive treatment that he would have approved.

Moreover, as Dr. Brett correctly points out, it is not the inherent characteristics of particular interventions that should control their selection or rejection; what should count instead is whether they are appropriate means to serve the patient's ends. As Drs. Zweibel and Cassel indicate, it follows that before completing an instructional directive the patient should:[13]

> (1) clarify and priorize the qualities of life one values; (2) be able to think about and comprehend how those qualities of life may be threatened under various illness scenarios; (3) be able to understand in at least general terms what available treatment options there are likely to be; and (4) be able to comprehend the implications of choosing or refusing treatment options for each identified life value.

On the other hand, it is doubtful whether these objectives can be fully accomplished without a medical consultation; yet given how pressed for time physicians are in the course of daily practice, one wonders to what extent that goal can be achieved. (Perhaps there is a role here for nurses in helping patients plan their directives.)

Although the instructional directive is an imperfect mechanism for future decision-making, it is likely the best that one can do because, after all, decision-by-directive is an imperfect substitute for the mentally competent patient who can speak for himself in direct discussion with his caregivers. It is true that even with physician input, carefully drafted directives cannot guarantee clear-cut treatment answers in every case. Still, at the level of public policy, the question is whether the instructional directive counts as a step forward — whether it is more of a help than a hindrance to the physician who seeks guidance from a document that speaks for a patient who can no longer speak for himself. Perhaps the treatment dilemmas poised by Dr. Brett happen infrequently; and if in such a case the patient has also appointed a proxy as a back-up to deal with unanticipated events, the situation might well be resolved. (The nature of proxy decision-making will be considered shortly.)

Finally, we turn to the implications of the shift from the treatment-refusal focus of the living will to the second generation directive, which empowers its maker both to opt for and against particular treatments (or to vest that authority in a proxy). In contrast to the living will's exclusive focus upon the rejection of life-prolonging treatment, the expanded role of the advance directive as a mechanism for both treatment refusals and treatment demands has been heralded as a truer commitment than the former to the principle of patient autonomy. However, the provision of treatment for the various situation scenarios in the Emanuels' Medical Directive is conditioned upon their being "medically reasonable." In their view, that phrase obviates the duty to comply with a directive's demand for treatment that the physician deems to be futile. Unfortunately, the very notion of medical futility is not as clear-cut as the Medical Directive suggests.* Furthermore, as the Emanuels discovered when they conducted a survey in which 405 out-patients and 102 "members of the general public" in the Boston area completed their Directive, many individuals were inclined to opt for aggressive treatment regardless of prognosis. For the clinical scenario (persistent vegetative state), between 6 and 9% of respondents were "undecided" for each of the treatment interventions. However, the following percentages were recorded for the "want" option: 10% for CPR; 10% for blood transfusions, 8% for renal dialysis, 9% for major surgery, and 12% for minor surgery.[14]

---

* Medical futility is considered in Chapters 21 and 22.

With the exception of a sparsely worded decision by the Manitoba Court of Appeal,* Canadian law has yet to take a stand on the question whether a demand for treatment can be rejected because it is not considered — in the Emanuels' terminology — "medically reasonable." Still, if a patient cannot enforce a spoken demand for treatment deemed medically unreasonable (futile) by his caregivers, then surely his physician is not bound to that end when the demand appears in an instructional directive or when the patient's grieving or guilt-ridden proxy insists upon such treatment. Be that as it may, it remains to be seen whether a case will arise in which an instructional directive or a proxy's insistence upon treatment becomes a battleground in the debate over the meaning of medical futility.

(b) Commentary on the Proxy Directive

As noted in Chapters 21 and 22, the American and Canadian legal systems have no quarrel with the medical custom of relying upon family members for input in the decision-making process for mentally incompetent adult patients. Physicians do not hesitate to consult the family on the incompetent patient's behalf because they act on the reasonable assumption that it is the patient's family who knows him best and who has his best interests at heart. Moreover, it is the family who is most likely to know the patient's treatment preferences. According to a legal commentator:

> Family members have a unique knowledge of the patient. They will know (the patient's) life style, values, medical attitudes, and general world view.... Even if no prior specific statements were made, (it is) in the context of the individual's entire prior mental life, including his or her philosophical, religious, and moral views, life goals, values about the purpose of life and the way it should be lived, and attitudes toward sickness, medical procedures, suffering and death that the individual's likely treatment/non-treatment preferences can be discovered. Family members are most familiar with this entire life context.[15]

In contrast to the instructional directive, the proxy directive provides for the appointment of a representative/agent, whose role is to be on hand to engage in a continuing dialogue with the patient's caregivers and to make decisions based upon the patient's condition over time. When the patient appoints a surrogate to make health care decisions in the event of her mental incapacitation, she presumably is choosing someone whom she trusts to stand in her stead and to enforce treatment preferences that are consistent with her views or that otherwise promote her best interests. When

---

* See Chapter 22.

there is no proxy — which is far more often the case — one can only speculate as to whether the patient would approve of the role of particular family members who are consulted by her caregivers when she loses decisional capacity. In theory, a family member is more likely to express the patient's actual wishes or interests if the patient had gone out of her way to appoint that person as her medical proxy. (As will be shortly considered, the nature of proxy decision-making is more problematic than its advocates care to admit.)

Aside from the intervention-focused instructional directive, the proxy directive is another mechanism that can substitute for patients who can no longer speak for themselves. To begin with, one may fill out an instructional directive and still appoint a proxy as back-up with a direction along the following lines: "Here are my treatment preferences. Your role is to deal with any contingencies that I have not covered. In other words, you fill in the gaps." Aside from its role as a back-up, the proxy directive may stand on its own for those who do not choose to complete an instructional directive. There are, for example, persons (often elderly) who are averse to engaging in the kind of soul-searching necessary for an instructional directive but who simply say: "My children will know what to do when the time comes." On the other hand, an instructional directive would stand on its own for the person who lacks friends or family upon whom she can entrust the role of proxy. In short, one can complete both instructional and proxy directives, or one or the other.

As explained in Chapter 21, the bio-medical ethical principles of *autonomy* and *beneficence* are the appropriate guideposts for surrogate decision-makers; and the *substituted judgment* and *best interests* tests are the legal mechanisms that apply those principles on behalf of mentally incompetent patients. The substituted judgment test is satisfied when the proxy is confident that she can make the decision that the patient would make if able to speak for himself. Otherwise, the proxy is duty-bound to serve the patient's best interests.

In theory, then, the directive-appointed proxy will know the patient well enough to make the decision that the incompetent patient would make if he could speak for himself. What substituted judgment means is that the proxy stands in the patient's shoes and makes the same decision that the patient would make in the circumstances. (The best interests test only comes into play when the proxy cannot apply the substituted judgment test.) It is likely that patients would choose family members as proxies for the reasons noted by Newman, whose commentary extols the family's "unique knowledge" of the patient. Or the proxy might prefer to delegate that responsibility to someone other than a family member. However, the point is that, whoever is chosen as proxy, the patient presumably had sufficient confidence in that person's judgment to assign him that role. Moreover, in theory the proxy will have current information about the patient's condition, which may be a more certain guide to appropriate treatment than preferences expressed in an instructional directive that may have been written years before the patient lost decisional capacity.

Unfortunately, there is scant reason to believe that directive-appointed proxies can reliably determine the treatment preferences of close friends or family members. As the Emanuels have acknowledged:

> In the absence of specific directions, any proxy decision making is, as one (New Jersey Supreme Court) judge put it, "at best only an optimistic approximation." Proxy decision making requires synthesizing the patient's diverse values, beliefs, practices, and prior statements to reconstruct what the patient would want under the specific circumstances. Not only does this synthesis require a tremendous imaginative effort that may be beyond the capacities of most people, but it also is liable to the proxies' biases, prejudices, and psychological agendas.[16]

Empirical research on proxy decision-making suggests that the Emanuels' concerns are well taken. The theory of substituted judgment has been put to the test in a number of studies involving close family members of patients, who are asked to predict the latter's treatment preferences as expressed in hypothetical scenarios. The findings uniformly cast doubt on the overall ability of surrogate decision-makers to confirm the treatment wishes of their spouses, partners, and adult children. Summaries of three of the studies are as follows.

In a study by Ouslander et al., four clinical scenarios — two high risk procedures (aortic valve replacement and carotid endarterectomy) and two low risk procedures (flu vaccination and sleep medication) — were presented to 70 nursing home residents.[17] For each patient, the closest relative living outside the facility, primary nurse, physician, and social worker were selected as surrogates. The surrogates were instructed to make the treatment decision for each scenario that they believed the resident would make. Overall, there was "a striking rate of disagreement" across the four scenarios. For example, the percentages of agreement for the two high risk scenarios were as follows. For the aortic valve replacement: relative 61%, physician 53%, social worker 52%, and nurse 48%. For the carotid endarterectomy: relative 69%, social worker 53%, nurse 42%, and physician 38%. There was greater concurrence for the flu vaccination scenario but even less for the sleeping pill scenario. (Other studies have confirmed that although relatives often err when applying substituted judgment, they are still more accurate than physicians in predicting patients' treatment choices.)

In a study by Hare et al., case scenarios were presented to 50 patients (randomly recruited from a community family practice clinic) and their selected surrogates.[18] The scenarios involved: (1) ventilation, resuscitation, and tube feeding for a patient "unlikely to come out of a coma" and with uncertainty as to level of functioning if the unlikely result did occur; (2) amputation of the leg of a diabetic who would otherwise die; and (3) chemotherapy for a "type of cancer that cannot be cured." Within individual pairs, there was 70% agreement. There was thus an overall discrepancy rate of 30% — ranging from 40% for the chemotherapy scenario to 22% for the amputation scenario. Note, however, that roughly two-thirds of both patients and surrogates indicated "no treatment" for four of the five scenarios.

In a study by Suhl et al., 50 hospitalized patients and their chosen surrogates were questioned regarding various life-support measures — CPR, ventilation, tube feeding, and surgery — as options in four clinical scenarios: persisting coma, terminal cancer, severe emphysema, and progressive paralysis.[19] Of the 50 surrogates, 43 were family members, including 26 spouses, eight adult children, and five parents. Overall, the surrogates correctly indicated the patients' responses in 59.6% of the scenarios, which according to the authors "was not more accurate than random chance." In nearly two-thirds of the 40.4% of mixed responses, the surrogates favoured treatment that was rejected by the patient. Thus, from the patients' perspective, their surrogates were twice as likely to opt for overtreatment as undertreatment.

Notwithstanding these findings, the studies do not necessarily discredit the theory of substituted judgment. That is because they do not provide data regarding the extent to which the patients — none of whom had signed proxy directives — had previously discussed treatment preferences with their surrogates. (Although Suhl et al. did comment that: "We found that the amount of discussion between patient and surrogate regarding LS [decisions to forego life-support] was the only identified factor that correlated with accurate surrogate decision-making." But they presented no supportive data.) Presumably the results would be much improved upon if comparable studies were undertaken involving patients and their appointed proxies. It may be that a person who would go out of her way to appoint a proxy would take the time to discuss treatment preferences with the designee. Or perhaps not. Whether expressed or implied, the message conveyed to the proxy might be: "This is something I don't want to think about so, when the time comes, you make the decisions. You talk it over with my doctor and I know that you'll do what is best."

In the absence of substituted judgment, the proxy is directed to make treatment decisions that serve the patient's best interests. As discussed in

Chapter 21, there is an inherent vagueness and lack of concreteness to the best interests test. When the question is whether life-support measures should be terminated for a patient whose treatment preferences are unknown, the proxy in effect has to ponder whether the patient is better off dead. One suspects that in that situation the proxy's decision would be based upon her own value system — whether she would rather be dead or kept alive if she were in the patient's circumstances. Aside from the inherent subjectivity of the best interests test, its value as a tool of surrogate decision-making would appear to be compromised by several studies indicating that patients' family members cannot be relied upon to assess accurately their quality of life.[20] In fact, patients tend to provide higher ratings of their emotional health and satisfaction than do their spouses and children, who also tend to underestimate patients' functional status.[21] Thus, if a proxy cannot accurately assess a patient's quality of life, how can she determine wherein lies the best interests of the patient?

Furthermore, it goes without saying that making treatment decisions for others can be psychologically stressful. In fact, surveys indicate that people are more hesitant to terminate life-support measures for a relative than for themselves. It follows that even if a proxy has reason to believe that the patient would want life-prolonging treatment stopped, he might hesitate to so inform the caregivers because of an inability to bear the moral and psychological responsibility of directing that the patient be allowed to die. The burdensome nature of proxy decision-making for the gravely ill is well put by Dr. Linda Emanuel:[22]

> First, proxies are commonly deeply connected to the patient. Emotional ties of such depth may hinder as much as help, as the proxy struggles to act on behalf of the patient. Whether the proxy is unable to face the death of a loved one, or anxious to end the overwhelming financial burden of caring for the patient, or in moral disagreement with the patient's decisions, the considerations can be hard to disentangle. Second, even for a previously disinterested party, proxy decision-making regarding life-sustaining care is necessarily very burdensome. This, in and of itself, may become an impediment in making suitable judgments for the patient.

Still, it is premature to write off the proxy's efforts as mere groping in the dark; in that regard Dr. Emanuel suggests that health care providers have a role to play in uplifting proxy decision-making into the light of informed judgment:[23]

> Proxy decision-making that is informed by prior discussions is likely to be considerably more accurate, less burdensome, and less conflicted than proxy decision-making in the absence of prior discussion. Proxies need to be en-

couraged by physicians and others to become a member of the team ahead of time, to listen to the discussion as the patient completes an advisory document with the physician, and to be supported by the physician as the proxy disentangles the considerations of substituted judgment from less legitimate interests.

4. THE STATUS OF ADVANCE DIRECTIVES IN CANADA: AT COMMON LAW

We have elsewhere referred to the 1990 case of *Malette v. Shulman*, in which the Ontario Court of Appeal affirmed a trial court judgment awarding $20,000 damages for battery to a critically injured auto accident victim who had received life-saving blood transfusions from the defendant-physician.* The physician was held liable for battery because a nurse had called his attention to a Jehovah's Witness medical alert card that she had found in the patient's handbag. The signed document stated that the holder was a Jehovah's Witness and that "no blood or blood products be administered to me under any circumstances." Notwithstanding that information, the physician transfused the patient (undoubtedly saving her life in the process). In affirming the verdict the high court declared:

> The right to determine what shall be done with one's own body is a fundamental right in our society. The patient has the freedom to exercise her right to refuse treatment and to accept the consequences of her decision. To deny individuals freedom of choice with respect to their health care can only lessen, and not enhance, the value of life.

Given the no-treatment direction in the document, the Court concluded that its legal effect was that of an unqualified anticipatory refusal of that specific form of treatment (blood products). The decision in the *Shulman* case thus amounts to judicial recognition of an instructional directive, provided of course that the direction is treatment-specific. In that sense, a medical alert card refusing blood is really no different from an instructional directive refusing mechanical ventilation or tube-feeding if the person winds up in a persistent vegetative state, or a direction by a patient in a cardiac care unit that he is not to be resuscitated in the event of a cardiac arrest.

The *Shulman* case thus sets a binding legal precedent in Ontario that caregivers are legally bound to honour an advance directive that specifies the refusal of particular treatment options. In any event, the recent enactment of the Ontario *Substitute Decisions Act* has provided a statutory basis

---

* See Chapters 2, 19, and 20.

to that right of anticipatory treatment refusal. However, in provinces that have not yet enacted advance directive legislation, the *Shulman* case is what lawyers refer to as a persuasive legal precedent. In other words, although the ruling is not binding outside Ontario, there is every likelihood that it would be followed in a comparable case.

5. THE STATUS OF ADVANCE DIRECTIVES IN CANADA: LEGISLATION

In 1992 Manitoba became the first province to grant statutory recognition to both types of advance directive (instructional and proxy).[24] As the *Health Care Directives Act* provides:

A directive may express the maker's health care decisions, or the maker may appoint a proxy to make health care decisions on the maker's behalf, or both.

Regarding the maker:

A health care decision expressed in a directive is as effective as if made by the maker when the maker had capacity to make the decision.

Regarding the proxy:

A health care decision made by a proxy on behalf of a maker is as effective as if made by the maker when the maker had capacity to make the decision.

Who may make a directive?

Every person who has the capacity to make health care decisions may make a health care directive.

What does "capacity" mean?

A person has capacity to make health care decisions if he or she is able to understand the information that is relevant to making a decision and able to appreciate t reasonably foreseeable consequences of a decision or lack of decision.

When does the directive take effect?

A directive becomes effective when the maker ceases to have capacity respecting a proposed treatment; or is unable to communicate his or her wishes respecting a proposed treatment; and continues to be effective for the duration of the incapacity or the inability to communicate.

What about minors?

In the absence of evidence to the contrary, it shall be presumed that a person who is 16 years of age or more has the capacity to make health care decisions;

and that a person who is under 16 years of age does not have the capacity to make health care decisions.*

When does the directive come into effect?

When the maker ceases to have capacity respecting a proposed treatment, or is unable to communicate his or her wishes respecting a proposed treatment, and continues to be effective for the duration of the incapacity or the inability to communicate.

How is the proxy to decide? The Act provides that the Proxy — who "must be apparently mentally competent and at least 18 years old" — shall act in accordance with the following principles:

1. If the maker has spelled out the decision to be taken, then the proxy must follow suit.
2. If the maker has not spelled out the decision to be taken, then the proxy "shall act in accordance with any wishes that he or she (the maker) expressed when the maker had capacity, and believes the Maker would still act on if capable."
3. "If the proxy knows of wishes applicable to the circumstances that the maker expressed when the maker had capacity, and believes the maker would still act on them if capable, and if the wishes are more recent than the decisions expressed in a directive, the wishes must be followed."
4. If the proxy has no knowledge of the maker's wishes, then "the proxy shall act in what the proxy believes to be the maker's best interests."

Note that the first principle does not involve proxy-decision making, which after all means that it is the proxy who makes the decision. When the patient has already decided — either pursuant to an instructional directive or otherwise conveying specific treatment preferences to the proxy — the latter's role is simply to ensure that the patient's directions are carried out. In short, the proxy is not making the decision but is simply the messenger conveying the patient's decision. The second principle invokes the substituted judgment test (assuming that "wishes" means any evidence from which to infer the patient's treatment preferences). The third principle is a refinement on principles one and two. It recognizes that patients' wishes are not necessarily stable over time, and that the proxy should be guided by the most recent expression of opinion. If the patient has directly addressed the particular treatment decision at hand, then the proxy's duty is to see that it is carried out (first principle). If the later view is not treatment-

---

*   In other words, the Act does not foreclose the legal validity of a directive by a minor under the age of 16 if the person can show the requisite mental capacity to qualify as a mature minor. The mature minor rule is discussed in Chapters 3 and 20.

specific but does indicate the direction of the patient's treatment preferences, then the proxy must make the decision that the patient would make (principle two). At the end of the line is the best interests test, which applies only when the proxy cannot act in accordance with the previous three principles.

What if the physician believes that the proxy is not acting in "good faith" — breaching his trust by not acting in accordance with the statutory mandate? (Of course, simply because the physician disagrees with the proxy's decision does not in itself establish the latter's lack of good faith. Rather the question is whether the proxy is conscientiously carrying out his mandate. If the bone of contention is the matter of a judgment call that could go either way, then the proxy has the upper hand.) If the conflict cannot be resolved, the physician is authorized to seek judicial relief — which is, of course, an available option whenever an incompetent patient's family insists upon measures that the physician cannot in good conscience comply with. In particular, the Act states that when a court is satisfied that a proxy is not acting in good faith, it "may suspend or terminate the proxy's appointment and rescind any health care decision made by the proxy."

Bear in mind that the proxy cannot automatically discharge the physician from her duty of care to the patient as spelled out in section 215 of the *Criminal Code*: "Everyone is under a legal duty...to provide necessaries of life to a person under his charge if that person is unable, by reason of...illness...to withdraw himself from that charge...." Moreover, there is a comparable duty in tort law because of the fiduciary relationship between physician and patient. Thus, even though the proxy stands in the patient's shoes, the physician cannot legally comply with his direction if she has strong reason to believe that it does not accord with the wishes/values or best interests of the patient.* (It is of course a different matter when the patient is mentally competent and asks that life-prolonging treatment be halted. When that happens, the patient is in effect discharging the physician's duty to treat.) Hence, the statute's "good faith" requirement merely assures the physician that the law does not seek to interfere with her duty of care under both criminal and civil law.

What if a proxy who is clearly acting in good faith insists upon treatment that in the physician's considered opinion amounts to an exercise in medical futility? (Or, for that matter, there is the same objection to a treatment preference contained in an instructional directive.) This troublesome issue is not addressed by the Manitoba statute, although there is a provision that: "Nothing in this Act abrogates or derogates from any rights or responsibilities conferred by statute or common law." In other words, a

---

* See the section on The Role of the Family in Chapter 22 where this point is considered.

patient's right to self-determination pursuant to a directive is no greater than his right to self-determination as a mentally competent patient. If the law were to restrict the latter's right to insist upon "futile" treatment, then it would follow that the restriction would apply equally to an advance directive. (As we see in Chapter 22, with the exception of the Manitoba Court of Appeal courts elsewhere in Canada have yet to provide direction on the question whether a physician can take it upon herself to refuse a patient's demand for a treatment regimen that the physician regards as "futile." If, however, the patient cannot demand such treatment, then it follows that neither can his proxy.)

The Act also provides that there is no onus upon anyone (including caregivers) "to inquire into the existence of a directive." Thus, there is no liability for treating a patient in breach of a directive whose existence was not known. What if, however, a patient is knowingly treated in breach of a directive dictating a different course of action? Recall the provision that a "health care decision expressed in a directive is as effective as if made by the maker when the maker had capacity to make the decision." In that event, as in the *Shulman* case the caregiver commits a battery against the patient.

Aside from Manitoba, Alberta, Newfoundland, Ontario, Quebec, Prince Edward Island, and the Yukon have enacted legislation governing both proxy and instructional directives. In Nova Scotia, the applicable statute covers only proxy directives.[25] British Columbia has passed but not yet proclaimed legislation for both types of directive.[26] In Quebec, the law is briefly stated in the *Civil Code*:

> A person who gives his consent to or refuses care for another is bound to act in the sole interest of that person, taking into account, as far as possible, any wishes the latter may have expressed.[27]

In Ontario the applicable legislation is found in the *Substitute Decisions Act* (SDA)[28] and the *Health Care Consent Act* (HCA).[29] The former authorizes mentally capable persons over the age of 16 to grant a "power of attorney for personal care" (which includes decisions about health care). The maker of the document decides upon the extent of the proxy's role, which may include the authority to refuse treatment and also may include specific treatment instructions. The legislation thus provides for an instructional directive tacked on to a proxy directive.

What if one wishes the former but not the latter? In that regard, the *Health Care Consent Act* provides that one may record his treatment "wishes" either orally or in writing and that such direction is legally binding.

6. FINAL COMMENT

The health care directive is the wave of the future, even though it is by no means a magic wand that can facilitate the resolution of all treatment dilemmas for mentally incompetent patients (even assuming that all or most such patients had signed directives). In an article aptly titled "Advance directives: Are they an advance?", Dr. Peter Singer and colleagues weigh the arguments pro and con and suggest that: "In principle, advance directives are a valuable method for people to express their preferences about life-sustaining treatment."[30] The "in principle" caveat is in recognition of the kinds of limitations that we have considered, leading the authors to conclude that "although advance directives may be desirable in principle, if they are not carefully designed and implemented, they may have undesirable effects in practice."

Be that as it may, there is no guarantee that physicians will follow directives to the letter. In a prospective American study of nursing home patients with directives, researchers compared the treatment received in hospital with the treatment preferences expressed in the directives.[31] They found that in 25% of the cases the treatment given was in breach of the instructions; that was because the physicians exercised their judgment as to what was best for their patients, notwithstanding the patients' previously expressed wishes to the contrary. The study puts paid to the notion that legal paternalism is a relic of the past.

Medical researchers in the United States thus have reason to question the high hopes that health care directives would enhance patient autonomy. For one thing, a directive must find its way onto the patient's chart or otherwise be brought to the attention of the caregivers, and all too often this does not happen. For another, even when the directive is on site it may be ignored — either because its language is imprecise (as in the first generation living will that physicians still come across), or simply because the physician chooses not to follow it. In the case of a proxy directive, the surrogate may be unavailable or so overwhelmed by the situation that he cannot exercise his role. Or the physician may disregard his instructions because they conflict with her assessment of the right thing to do.[32]

In 1997 the so-called SUPPORT* study reported on end-of-life care for 4,800 ICU patients in the United States.[33] Only 12% (569) had any kind of health care directive; and only 16% of that cohort (90) provided specific instructions for medical care (the rest either named a proxy or signed a vaguely worded living will). In 22 of these 90 cases, the patient's condition

---

* The acronym stands for Study to Understand Prognoses and Preferences for Outcomes and Risks of Treatments.

was covered by a provision calling for the termination of life-prolonging treatment. Yet the direction was followed in only nine of the cases.

For all we know, the same disquieting picture might apply if we sought to measure the impact of health care directives on medical practice in Canada. There is certainly no reason to think otherwise. In any case, the fact is that only a minority of patients have taken the time and thought to make out health care directives, which means that in most cases incompetent patients will have left precious little guidance for their physicians as they struggle with end-of-life decision-making.

NOTES

1. D.J. Cook et al., Determinants in Canadian health care workers of the decision to withdraw life support from the critically ill. 273 **Journal of the American Medical Association** 703 (1995).

2. Toronto **Globe and Mail**, March 6, 1995, p. A3.

3. *Ibid.*

4. Law Reform Commission of Canada. Report 20: **Euthanasia, Aiding Suicide and Cessation of Treatment** (Minister of Supply and Services Canada 1983).

5. New York Law Journal, July 28, 1987, at 7.

6. A.S. Relman, Michigan's sensible "living will." 310 **New England Journal of Medicine** 1270 (1979).

7. L.L. Emanuel & E.J. Emanuel, The Medical Directive: a new comprehensive advance care document. 261 **Journal of the American Medical Association** 3288 (1989).

8. University of Toronto Centre for Bioethics, **Living Will** (1993). Note that the Centre uses the outdated term "living will" to describe the document.

9. W. Molloy, *Let Me Decide* (Newgrange Press, Toronto, 2000).

10. M. Fowler, Appointing an agent to make medical treatmentchoices. 84 **Columbia Law Review** 999 (1984).

11. A.S. Brett. Limitations of listing specific medicalinterventions in advance directives. 266 **Journal of the American Medical Association** 829 (1991).

12. A. Meisel, *The Right to Die*. John Wiley & Sons, New York, 1989), at 317.

13. N.R. Zwiebel & C.K. Cassel, Treatment choices at the end of life: a comparison of decisions by older patients and their physician-selected proxies. 29 **The Gerontologist** 615 (1989).

14. L.L. Emanuel et al., Advance directives for medical care — a case for greater use. 324 **New England journal of Medicine** 889 (1991).

15. S.A. Newman, Treatment refusals for the critically and terminally ill: proposed rules for the family, the physician, and the state. 3 **New York Law School Human Rights Annual** 35 (1985).

16. E.J. Emanuel & L.L. Emanuel, Proxy decision making for incompetent patients: an ethical and empirical analysis. 267 **Journal of the American Medical Association** 2067 (1992). Our critique of the proxy directive is indebted to this very informative article.

17. J.G. Ouslander et al., Health care decisions among elderly long-term care residents and their potential proxies. 149 **Archives of Internal Medicine** 1367 (1989).

18. J. Hare et al., Agreement between patients and their self-selected surrogates on difficult medical decisions. 152 **Archives of Internal Medicine** 1049 (1992).

19. J. Suhl et al., Myth of Substituted Judgment. 154 **Archives of Internal Medicine, 154**, 90 (1994).

20. One such study is A.M. Epstein et al., Using proxies to evaluate quality of life. 27 **Medical Care, 27**, S91 (1989).

21. One such study is J. Magaziner et al. (1988). Patient-poxy response comparability on measures of patient health and functional status. 33 **Journal of Clinical Epidemiology** 1065 (1988).

22. L.L. Emanuel, Advance directives: what have we learned so far? 4 **Journal of Clinical Ethics** 8 (1993).

23. *Ibid.*

24. R.S.M. 1993, c. 33, CCSM, c. H27.

25. R.S.N.S. 1989, c. 279.

26. S.B.C. 1993, c. 67.

27. *Civil Code*, Book 1, Title 2, Chapter 1, s. 12

28. S.O. 1992, c. 20.

29. S.O. 1992, c. 31 [now am. S.O. 1996, c. 2, Sched. A].

30. Advance Directives Seminar Group, Centre for Bioethics, University of Toronto, Advance directives: are they an advance? 145 **Canadian Medical Association Journal**, 127 (1992).

31. M. Danis et al., A prospective study of advance directives for life-sustaining care. 324 **New England Journal of Medicine** 882 (1991).

32. J.M. Tano et al., Role of written advance directives in decision making: insights from qualitative and quantitative data. 13 **Journal of General Internal Medicine** 439 (1998).

33. J.M. Teno et al., Do advance directives provide instructions that direct care. 45 **Journal of the American Geriatrics Society** 508 (1997).

25

MERCY-KILLING AND ASSISTED SUICIDE

SUMMARY

The term *mercy-killing* (sometimes called *active euthanasia*) refers to a *compassionate killing by a direct act of commission* — such as when a physician deliberately injects her patient with a lethal dose of morphine or potassium chloride (KCl). The criminal law regards the act as murder, even if the patient had repeatedly implored his physician to put him out of his misery. However, the legal system contains built-in escape hatches that can bend the letter of the law. They are: (1) the Crown's discretion to not proceed with the matter; (2) the Crown's discretion to reduce the charge from murder to a lesser offence (either manslaughter or the offence of "administering a noxious thing"); (3) the trial judge's authority to accept a guilty plea to a lesser offence; and (4) the jury's power to acquit on compassionate grounds, even if instructed that the accused has no defence in law. The result is that the mercy-killer, whether layperson or physician, is rarely convicted of murder. We canvas cases in common law jurisdictions in which physicians have been accused of mercy-killings (and the one Canadian case involving a nurse). The *Latimer* case (the Saskatchewan farmer who killed his disabled daughter) is also considered.

Under the *Criminal Code*, it is an offence for anyone to counsel or aid a person to commit suicide. We present three hypothetical cases in which a cancer patient commits suicide; the question in each case is whether the physician has committed the offence of counselling or aiding suicide. The 1993 Supreme Court decision in the *Rodriguez* case, in which an ALS patient challenged the constitutionality of the *Criminal Code* ban on aiding suicide, is summarized.

PART ONE — MERCY-KILLING

1. INTRODUCTION

As explained in Chapter 18, the term *euthanasia* has come to refer to a case in which someone prompted by compassion causes a suffering person's death by a direct act of commission: e.g. a physician or nurse deliberately injecting her dying patient with a lethal dose of morphine or potassium chloride (KCl). Although such a death may be called a mercy-killing or a compassionate homicide, the motive of the accused (the reason why he or she was prompted to kill) is legally irrelevant. In all common law jurisdictions, the criminal law defines the act as murder, even if the deceased had repeatedly implored the accused to put him out of his misery. This chapter opens with a view of the law in action, beginning with Canadian mercy-killing cases involving accused laypersons, and then turning to Canadian, English, and American cases involving accused physicians (a Canadian case where the accused was a nurse is also presented). As indicated by the title of this chapter, the euthanasia debate implicates both mercy-killings and assisted suicides. However, the two scenarios are considered separately because they fall under different legal headings: the former is the crime of murder and the latter is the crime of aiding suicide.

2. LAYPERSONS AND CANADIAN MERCY-KILLING CASES

We report here the legal outcomes of seven Canadian cases involving accused laypersons. We cannot guarantee that we have covered the field, as a case that is settled without media fanfare (the charge dropped or a guilty plea accepted) may not be easily traceable.

Canadian juries have rendered verdicts in mercy-killing trials on three occasions: the first two cases happened in the early 1940s and the third a half century later. In the 1941 *Ramberg* case, an Alberta couple faced a murder charge in connection with the death of their two-year-old son, who was asphyxiated when his father attached a rubber hose to the exhaust pipe of his automobile, ran the hose through a window into the child's room, and started the engine.[1] The parents had resolved to kill their son because he was in unremitting pain from terminal cancer. Although the prosecution proved a case of premeditated murder, the jury acquitted after deliberating for only 10 minutes. The junior defence counsel was Ronald Martland, who capped a distinguished legal career with an appointment to the Supreme Court. As he later said about the case: "Legally it was murder, but the jury wasn't prepared to convict them. I think the attitude of the jury was that it was a very decent young married pair who were doing their best."[2]

Within a year the *Davis* case was heard by a Winnipeg jury.[3] George Herbert Davis, a 68-year-old pensioner, was charged with the murder of his legless wife whom he killed with the blunt end of an axe. The accused was a retired Canadian Pacific railway baggage man and army veteran; the couple was childless. When arrested he admitted to the killing, telling detectives that: "She kept asking all the time for morphine, and I couldn't give her any more." Neighbours of the couple, many of whom had known them for over 25 years, were quick to extol the slayer's virtues. Four friends of the family who had helped look after Mrs. Davis stated that she had often expressed the wish to die, and they described her husband as "the kindest, most patient and the most devoted man they had ever known."

In his statement to the police, the accused never suggested that he killed his wife at her request. After committing the deed he telephoned her physician, Dr. Henry McFarlane, and asked him to come immediately to their home. When Dr. McFarlane arrived Davis met him at the door and said: "I have finished her. I couldn't bear to see her in distress any longer." Dr. McFarlane had been treating her since 1924; and he testified at the preliminary hearing that she was afflicted with asthma, a severe heart condition, and had had both legs amputated in 1937. He described her condition over the weeks before her death: "She was in a great deal of distress, moaning continually. I told Mr. Davis I didn't think she would live very long."

At the two-day trial, Dr. McFarlane testified that the accused was kind and attentive to his wife and that, in his opinion, he was doing her a favour by killing her! According to the pathologist, Mrs. Davis was at death's door from heart disease when her husband took her life. The friends and neighbours of the couple who appeared as witnesses for the Crown were in agreement that the accused was kind to his wife and that no one had ever heard them quarrel. The defence called no witnesses.

When the six-man jury returned with a not guilty verdict after deliberating less than 30 minutes, the judge expressed astonishment. After all, the accused had admitted to the murder and had no legal defence to the charge. Nonetheless, the jury had chosen to ignore the judge's instructions that it must convict if convinced beyond a reasonable doubt that the accused had killed his wife. The judge turned toward Mr. Davis and informed him that he was a free man. Perhaps he himself did not regret that result because he added: "I think your record of many years as a kindly, faithful husband has served you in good stead and brought about this reward at the hands of the jury."

In 1993 Robert Latimer, a 40-year-old Saskatchewan farmer, killed his 12-year-old daughter by venting fumes from his pick-up truck's tail pipe into the cab where he had placed her. Gravely affected at birth by cerebral palsy, Tracy Latimer was a totally body-involved spastic quadriplegic, whose constant muscle spasms and seizures had wrenched her body into a twisted frozen position. She weighed 38 pounds, was incontinent, had impaired vision, and could not sit up, talk, or feed herself. Although severely mentally handicapped, she enjoyed being with her parents and other children, as well as riding on the school bus and listening to music.

When questioned by the police a few days after Tracy's death, Latimer exclaimed: "My priority was to put her out of her pain. Each time you moved her, she was in pain. We just couldn't see another operation...so I thought the best thing for her was that she be out of pain."

It was uncontested that pain was a constant feature of Tracy's life; but it is also uncontestable that as the Crown prosecutor at the second trial told the jury, "Pain is a condition of life, not a reason for death." Still, it was his daughter's pain — past, present, and future — that drove him to the conviction that the only way to end her pain was to end her life. Tracy was not in pain all the time, but she was in pain much of the time; she had her good days and she had her bad days. And the bad days — year after year — drove Latimer (and his wife) to distraction.

My wife, a long-time paediatric and neonatal nurse, has quoted to me an old refrain: "A child's hurt is a parent's hurt. A child's pain is a parent's pain." It was Tracy's hurt and Tracy's pain that gnawed at the Latimers for years, and then her father reached the breaking point when hip surgery was scheduled by Dr. Anne Dzus, a paediatric orthopaedic surgeon. Tracy had a dislocated hip that was causing her considerable pain. Dr. Dzus proposed to remove the ball part of the ball-and-socket hip joint and the top of her femur, leaving her leg attached to her body only by muscle and tissue. (Since Tracy could not walk in any event, there would be no point to replacing the ball.) Yet from the Latimers' standpoint, the impending surgery was seen as the mutilation of their daughter's ravaged body. It meant that their daughter was going to be "cut up" and they were appalled at the prospect.[4] As Latimer later said: "How many medical intrusions which carry a cost of great pain can you inflict on someone?"

In 1994, a jury convicted Latimer of second-degree murder and he received the mandatory minimum sentence for that offence: life imprisonment with no parole eligibility for 10 years. But evidence of prosecutorial misconduct led to a retrial, and three years later he was again convicted of second-degree murder.

Before passing sentence, Justice Noble of the Court of Queen's Bench asked the jury to recommend the number of years along the range of 10-

25 that Latimer should spend in prison before parole eligibility.* Some of the jurors appeared distraught upon learning that there was a mandatory 10-year minimum, and when the jury returned from its deliberations it defiantly recommended that Latimer serve but one year before eligibility for parole. Surprisingly, the judge saw it the jury's way as he went on to rule that, given the facts of the case, the mandatory life sentence breached section 12 of the *Charter of Rights and Freedoms* (the prohibition against cruel and unusual punishment) and that a constitutional exemption from the mandatory penalty was thereby in order. In handing down a two-year sentence — the first year in custody and the second to be served on the Latimer farm — Justice Noble stressed that the evidence established that Latimer was

> a caring and responsible person and that his relationship with Tracy was that of a loving and protective parent...(and that he) was motivated solely by his love and compassion for Tracy and the need — at least in his mind — that she should not suffer any more pain....[5]

Justice Noble did not have the last word, because he was reversed by the Saskatchewan Court of Appeal, which imposed the mandatory minimum sentence. The Supreme Court in turn upheld the conviction and minimum 10-year sentence in January 2001.[6] The courts have spoken and Latimer's only recourse now is to petition the federal government either to release him or reduce his sentence by the exercise of the time-honoured Royal Prerogative of Mercy.

Aside from ruling that the minimum penalty was not cruel and unusual punishment because of the gravity of the offence, the Supreme Court also rejected the defence claim that the trial judge had erred in refusing to allow the jury to consider a defence of necessity. Necessity is a narrow based defence, which applies when an accused faces an emergency situation that compels him to commit a crime in order to prevent a greater evil. The claimed necessity defence was that killing Tracy was a lesser evil than the pain that marked her life and that would have followed her impending hip surgery.

In ruling that there was no credibility to a necessity defence, the Supreme Court deemed it self-evident that the harm avoided (pain present and future) was "completely disproportionate" to the harm caused (Tracy's death) — "particularly when better pain management was available." As the Court put it:

---

* Section 745.2 of the *Criminal Code* stipulates that when an accused is convicted of second-degree murder, the trial judge shall ask the jury for its recommendation on the appropriate sentence within the statutory range. The judge is not bound by the recommendation but must ask for it.

Killing a person — in order to relieve the suffering produced by a *medically manageable physical or mental condition* — is not a proportionate (reasonable) response to the harm represented by the non-life-threatening suffering resulting from that condition. (Emphasis added.)

Given that Latimer confessed to the police that he had killed Tracy to put her out of pain, it is surprising that the Supreme Court made no reference to the testimony of Dr. Dzus, who had scheduled the surgery on Tracy's dislocated hip that triggered Latimer's resolve to take her life. According to Dr. Dzus, Tracy had "severe pain" that could not be adequately controlled because "she already was on convulsant, anti-epileptic medications to control her seizures (and) combining drugs can have side effects...depressing the respiratory function." Noting that Tracy had a poor gag reflex and limited respiratory functioning, she explained that the resort to narcotics for pain control ran the considerable risk of causing her to stop breathing or choke to death. As far as the Latimers knew the strongest pain-killer that they could give Tracy was Tylenol. Furthermore, as Dr. Dzus testified, the post-operative pain could only be controlled in the short term by the insertion of an epidural catheter (freezing the bottom half of the body). But she went on to say that Tracy would likely suffer "incredible" pain because the catheter "is only good while they're in the hospital. The children still have to go somewhere, either home or to another institution to recover and that is not the end of the pain."

The anticipated recovery from the hip surgery was estimated at one year — with who knows how much untold pain during that projected time. As Dr. Dzus warned Mrs. Latimer, there was also the prospect of additional surgery because Tracy's other hip would inevitably dislocate.*

The Court's contrary assumption that "better pain management was available" is subject to qualification. An anesthetist, whom I consulted and who is a renowned expert on paediatric pain, expressed the view that Tracy's pain was manageable: that it could have been eased if not eliminated. However, he added that the level of expertise to accomplish this may not have existed in Saskatoon in 1993. On the other hand, a distinguished paediatric neurologist told me that he was uncertain whether the pain was in fact controllable. He explained that pain control is still an uncertain art at the dawn of the 21st century, and that he could not guarantee that even practitioners of the state of the art in 1993 would most probably have been able to keep Tracy relatively pain-free most if not all of the time. He summed it up by saying: "maybe yes, maybe no." However, both agreed

---

* The occasion was Tracy's last appointment with Dr. Dzus. Mrs. Latimer was there with Tracy but her husband was not.

that Tracy's anti-seizure medication was not incompatible with potent pain-killers. Be that as it may, even if Tracy's pain could have been better managed, one cannot blame the Latimers for the fact that it wasn't.

Dr. David Kemp, the Latimers' family physician, testified that Tylenol was "probably too mild to do any good", but that the problem with opiates was that "they could increase seizure activity and they could cause acute constipation, which would be difficult to manage." When asked on cross-examination whether, aside from the dislocated hip, Tracy's pain was increasing as she got older, he replied: "Yes, I'm sure it was."

As far as the Latimers knew, unrelenting pain was Tracy's inevitable lot in life. According to their perception of reality, there was nothing that could ease her pain. So what was Latimer supposed to do? Perhaps a more sophisticated person would have sought second opinions or canvassed the medical literature, but surely he cannot be faulted for accepting the reality that was presented to him and his wife — that as Dr. Dzus testified there were no effective pain-killing drugs that offered a long-term solution to Tracy's pain.

One can be critical of the Supreme Court's handling of the pain issue and yet reluctantly conclude that it was right in its result. My concern relates to the interface between proportionality and murder, about which the Court had this to say:

> It is difficult, at the conceptual level, to imagine a circumstance in which the proportionality requirement could be met for a homicide. We leave open, if and until it arises, question of whether the proportionality requirement could be met in a homicide situation. In England, the defence of necessity is probably not available for homicide.

Well, difficulty is not impossibility as was recognized in the recent English *conjoined twins* case (discussed in Chapter 23). The medical evidence was that one twin (Jodie) was salvageable whereas the other (Mary) was not because of severe brain, heart, and lung anomalies. The question was whether the surgeons could lawfully separate the twins, because a direct effect of the surgery would be to kill Mary by the severance of the aorta that she shared with her sister. Although such a direct killing would ordinarily constitute murder, the Court invoked the defence of medical necessity to allow it.

In the context of necessity it cannot be denied that the law must act with extreme caution before excusing one who acts upon the belief that someone who cannot speak for herself is better off dead or should be sacrificed to save another. It follows that there must be evidence of an extraordinary and compelling set of circumstances to provide substance to the defence. In that sense, the law sets no troublesome precedent by excusing those responsible for the death of a conjoined twin with no hope of survival.

Although the *conjoined twins* case can be seen to fall within the boundaries of the defence of necessity, the same cannot be said for the *Latimer* case. After all, the killing of one's disabled child is an act fraught with not only legal but also political implications; the recognition of the defence in the *Latimer* case would amount to a declaration that the killing of Tracy Latimer was a necessary act and — however necessary the act appeared to her father — this is not the message that should be delivered by this tragic case. In my view, the facts of the *Latimer* case do not meet the heavy burden that must be satisfied before an act that is otherwise defined as murder can be excused on the grounds of necessity. This conclusion is admittedly driven more by public policy than by law, keeping in mind the adage that hard cases make bad law.

Still, one can concede the crime but not the punishment. In other words, even if the facts could not sustain a defence of necessity, they were arguably compelling enough to warrant mitigation in sentencing. There is, however, a mandatory minimum sentencing scheme for murder in the *Criminal Code* and the Supreme Court was not prepared to bend the law for Latimer's sake.

Be that as it may, the sentiment expressed by disability organizations was that Latimer's punishment emphatically fit the crime. The two-year sentence handed down by Justice Noble was greeted by a storm of protest from that community. Typical was the comment of Pat Danforth of the Council of Canadians With Disabilities, who interpreted the sentence as "telling every senior citizen, every quadriplegic, anyone injured in a car accident that their life is of diminished value." As reported in the media: "Representatives of national disability groups decried the ruling as a travesty that amounts to 'open season' on vulnerable people."

Yet, in the Montreal case that we consider shortly, in which a distraught mother killed her disabled child, there were no protests from the disabled community when she received a suspended sentence. It may well be that what has fuelled the crusade against Latimer is not so much what he did but who he is — a blunt, defiant man who has exhibited no emotion but anger that anyone should question his judgment that killing his daughter was a "private matter" and therefore not the business of the courts or the disabled community. He has been called "his own worst enemy" by courtroom observers and perhaps this explains why there are so many voices clamouring that he not see freedom until January 2011.

Robert Latimer is the only Canadian ever sentenced to prison in a mercy-killing case. Aside from the jury acquittals in *Ramberg* and *Davis*, the handful of other such cases have been disposed of by verdicts that did not result in incarceration. We turn now to these cases.

Within weeks of Latimer's first conviction, a judge imposed sentences of probation and community service upon a Halifax couple, Cheryl Myers and Michael Power, who had pleaded guilty to manslaughter in connection with the death of Myers' 68-year-old father.[7] Layton Myers was a widower whose wife had died from cancer of the liver in 1991, which prompted him to tell his daughter that he would never want to suffer the indignities that she had experienced. He was diagnosed with lung cancer in December 1992 and was being cared for at home by his daughter and her partner. As his condition worsened, Myers repeatedly pleaded that they end his life, and in May 1993 they finally complied by smothering him with a pillow. An agreed statement of facts was later filed with the Court, and the following is our summary of the pertinent parts of that document:

> In April 1993 the patient's condition was "very bad." He was almost constantly confined to bed, and it had became necessary for him to use adult diapers, as he had lost control of his bodily functions. Power frequently helped to change the diapers. Myers was "very uncomfortable and embarrassed as the result of the loss of control of his bodily functions and the consequent loss of dignity." By May 14 his breathing was laboured and he was in great pain. He had not eaten since May 11. On May 15 his physician advised the couple that he would be dead within "one or two days at the most." He was receiving large doses of morphine, but it was apparent from his breathing (he had not been conscious since May 11) that he was in "considerable pain."

The physician returned later that day, at which time the patient's breathing was "very laboured and irregular." He advised the couple that Myers would not last the night, and when he left they discussed "their earlier decision not to allow him to continue to suffer." His daughter then cleaned, shaved, and dressed her father. She then lay on the bed and held him while Power suffocated him with a pillow. When the physician was summoned, he signed the death certificate as he had no reason to suspect foul play. There was consequently no autopsy.

The case came to light because the couple had been quite open in telling friends and family what they had done. In accepting a guilty plea to manslaughter, the judge commented that they had acted out of "compassion, mercy, and love." Myers and Power were each sentence to three years' probation and 150 hours of community service. In passing sentence, the judge opined that the crime did not warrant a lengthy prison sentence and that a short term would make a "mockery" of the principle of general deterrence.

Not long after the *Meyers and Power* case, 81-year-old Jean Brush was charged in Hamilton, Ontario, with the murder of her husband of 45 years, who was blind, hearing impaired, and afflicted with Alzheimer's disease.[8] He had repeatedly begged her to help him die, and a month before the killing the couple was rushed to hospital after overdosing on sleeping pills. Just before his death she had written in her diary: "He is a shell — dead but not buried because he still breathes." After stabbing him twice, she then attempted suicide by stabbing herself five times. Hours later their daughter found them clasped together on the dining room floor of their home. When pleading guilty to manslaughter, Mrs. Brush told the Court that she did not regret killing her husband and that "I was disappointed when they resuscitated me." In March 1995 — three months after the lenient sentence in the *Myers and Power* case — Jean Brush was likewise spared incarceration. In sentencing her to 18 months' probation, the judge described the killing as "a desperate attempt to end her husband's life with some dignity" and that "she has already suffered a harsher sentence than could ever be imposed on her life — the loss of her loving husband."

Another case is *R. v. Cashin* (Alberta, 1995),[9] in which the accused was charged with the attempted murder of his 68-year-old mother, who was in the throes of end-stage breast cancer. The accused had fed her painkillers in the attempt to end her life. The patient was bed-ridden, had wasted away to 65 pounds, was in constant pain from the cancer that had invaded her bones, and desperately wished to die. Although the pills did not kill her, she died three days later when life-support measures were withdrawn. Cashin was allowed to plead guilty to the *Criminal Code* offence of "administering a noxious thing."* He explained the crime to the Court: "She asked me not to let her suffer. I knew what she meant. It was clear between us. It was a very emotional day. I was telling her: 'You can go now, you can go to sleep now.' " In sentencing Cashin to two years on probation, the judge told him that: "Given the fact this was an act of love, it would be contrary to the whole philosophy of criminal law to incarcerate you."

Finally, there are two cases from Quebec that involved the killing of disabled children by parents. A guilty plea to manslaughter was the outcome of a 1996 case, *R. v. Blais*.[10] Daniele Blais drowned her six-year-old autistic child in the bathtub, and the defence contended that the stress and frustration of caring for the child had so depressed her that she was driven to take his life. She received a two-year suspended sentence.

Barely two months after the Supreme Court ruling in *Latimer*, another Montreal mother was charged with the murder of her child. Rachel Capra

---

* The offence is found in section 245.

Craig killed her 14-year-old daughter, who was afflicted with Rhett's Syndrome, a devastating neurological disease that by and large affects only females.[11] The girl had been fed a "potent poison cocktail" by her mother who then attempted suicide. (Whatever one can say about this tragic case, one thing is certain: the accused was not deterred by Latimer's minimum 10-year sentence.)

Media accounts were quite sympathetic to Mrs. Craig. Support groups were quoted as saying that the demands of caring for girls with Rhett's Syndrome "place a tremendous strain on families." The vice-president of the Quebec Rhett's Syndrome Association stated that: "Parents have to feed them, clothe them, toilet them, and bathe them. For these parents the stress is really great." According to a caption photo in the *Globe and Mail*, "Montreal police say she was severely depressed about her daughter's condition and the constant care she required." Friends and neighbours of Mrs. Craig were quick to proclaim that the accused was a devoted and protective parent who provided constant care for her daughter.

As it turned out, the accused was not a mercy-killer; what explained the act was not compassion but rather mental disorder. A psychiatrist called by the defence testified that the accused had resolved to kill herself because of depression compounded by the burden of caring for her daughter. But she also suffered from paranoid delusions that the girl's father was sexually abusing their daughter (the autopsy found no evidence of sexual abuse). Since her suicide would leave the child in her father's care, she decided to poison her and then herself.

The psychiatric evidence persuaded Crown counsel to concur with defence counsel that the case should be disposed of by a ruling that the accused was not criminally responsible on account of mental disorder (formerly called the insanity defence).* The judge accepted their joint recommendation, entered the verdict and ordered her committal to a psychiatric facility for an unspecified period.

Although this was not a case of compassionate homicide, it was treated as such by the media and the disabled community until the trial revealed otherwise. Until that happened there was not a whisper of public criticism of Mrs. Craig, and it is likely that the sympathy initially expressed for her would have persisted even if the evidence had shown that she had killed her daughter to end her suffering. It is true that the ordeal of tending to her severely disabled child had led her to consider suicide in the first place. But the point is that the stresses that fall upon the parents of children with Rhett's Syndrome, which support groups were so quick to explain to the media, apply no less to the parents of children with cerebral palsy of the

---

* The defence of mental disorder is found in section 16 of the *Criminal Code*.

magnitude afflicting Tracy Latimer. Yet there were no support groups on Latimer's side, and once again I suggest that the reason was not so much the crime itself but rather the abrasive personality of the defiant Saskatchewan farmer who was quick to show his contempt for anyone who did not see the case his way.

3. PHYSICIANS, A NURSE, AND THE MERCY-KILLING OF PATIENTS

We report here on 16 cases involving physicians in common law jurisdictions — four in Canada, four in England, and eight in the United States — which are summarized below. (A Canadian case involving a nurse is also considered.) In most of the cases, the accused did not contest the prosecution's claim of intent to kill the patient, although in some cases the defence was that the intent was to palliate — not kill — the patient. In some cases the accused made an incriminatory entry on the patient's chart, thus in effect inviting disclosure and prosecution. There were also cases in which the accused acted in the presence of other caregivers (usually nurses) who informed hospital personnel. The reader will note that only two of the cases resulted in conviction and a prison sentence: the American *Naramore* and *Kevorkian* cases. (In another American case (*Wood*), the physician served time in home detention with electronic monitoring before his manslaughter conviction was reversed.) To our knowledge, no other physician has ever been imprisoned in a common law jurisdiction for the mercy-killing of a patient. We do not include here about a dozen American and English cases where scant information is available, and in which either the jury acquitted or the accused was never charged.

(a) The Canadian Cases

(i) *Dr. N.G. (Alberta, 1982)*[12]

In 1982, a neonate died at an Edmonton hospital in circumstances that led to a charge of first-degree murder against one of her treating physicians. The infant was severely brain damaged and subjected to incessant convulsions. Sixteen hours after birth, she was injected with 15 mg of morphine and died within an hour. The physician admitted to a colleague that he had deliberately given the fatal dose because he was appalled at the infant's suffering. The physician was a foreign national and returned home upon learning that the matter was under investigation. A judicial inquiry was held, which concluded that the exact cause of death could not be determined. That was because the neonate was in any event dying from other causes and also because the autopsy had been incomplete. The physician was nonetheless indicted, although the matter lapsed because the Canadian government was unable to obtain his extradition.

(ii) *Nurse Scott Mataya (Ontario, 1992)*[13]

A Toronto nurse, Scott Mataya, 27, was charged with first-degree murder after informing hospital authorities that he had given a lethal dose of potassium chloride (KCl) to a dying 79-year-old patient. The comatose patient was suffering from kidney, liver, and lung failure. After consultation with his family, the attending physician disconnected his ventilator after injecting him with 40 mg of morphine and 30 mg of valium and leaving an order calling for repeated dosages in 30 minutes if needed. Mataya was then left alone with the patient, whose laboured breathing prompted the second infusion 30 minutes later. Mataya explained what then happened:

> And he still goes on breathing with 80 milligrams of morphine and 60 of valium — a massive dose. And then he started to twitch. He started to produce tons of mucous, which was frothing out of his tracheostomy. I was trying to suction this stuff up. He was coughing and hacking. The twitching was getting more and more severe. It was going against all the drugs we had given him. I didn't like the man's wife to come back and see him like this. I didn't want her to learn that he had choked and suffocated to death. I looked at the heart monitor and could see its strong, steady beat. It was a healthy, bloody heart and I thought this guy's heart has got to stop. I knew there was a drug right on my tray that would stop it. I drew up some potassium chloride; we use it all the time to balance electrolytes. I diluted it in an IV chamber because I didn't want it to burn going in. And I gave it to him.

The patient's heart stopped four minutes later, and when Mataya told a nurse what he had done she informed senior staff. When asked to explain his actions, he replied:

> I just thought a man shouldn't have to choke and suffocate to death. It wasn't as if he was going to recover. His fate was decided when the respirator was turned off. I thought he shouldn't suffer.

Although Mataya was charged with first-degree murder, the Crown accepted a guilty plea to the *Criminal Code* offence of "administering a noxious thing." Mataya was placed on probation for three years and banned for life from the practice of nursing. When the sentence was pronounced, the patient's family expressed gratification that Mataya was not imprisoned.

(iii) *Dr. X (Quebec, 1992)*[14]

In 1990 the Quebec Justice Ministry declined to lay a murder charge against a Montreal physician (called "Dr. X" in the media) who had administered a lethal dose of KCl to his dying AIDS patient. The 38-year-old patient was suffering from Kaposi's sarcoma. His body was covered with abscesses and massive doses of morphine were insufficient to relieve his agony. He had repeatedly begged for a lethal injection and Dr. X was prompted to act upon his plea after the nurse said to him in desperation: "If you don't end this, I will." The incident came to light after he entered the cause of death on the patient's chart.

Dr. X's conduct was presented in a sympathetic light by Dr. Augustin Roy, the head of the Quebec College of Physicians:

> It was intolerable to suffer that much pain, and the pain was not being relieved by narcotics. Even huge amounts of morphine weren't working any more. This was a real terminal case; he was probably hours away from dying. The doctor acted in the interests of his patient.

Dr. Roy also described the physician as a well respected colleague of many years standing. The decision by the Justice Ministry was likely the result of the recommendation by Dr. Roy and the College that "Dr. X" not be prosecuted because of the extraordinary circumstances of the case.

(iv) *Dr. Alberto De La Rocha (Ontario, 1993)*[15]

Dr. de la Rocha, a 48-year-old surgeon in Timmins, was charged with second-degree murder after giving an injection of 20 milliequivalents of KCl to a 68-year-old dying patient afflicted with cancer of the mouth, cheek, and lungs. The patient had asked him to disconnect the respirator to hasten her death; and immediately after doing so, Dr. de la Rocha administered 40 mg of morphine to prevent her from experiencing the terrors of suffocation. However, he then injected the KCl, which the Crown alleged was the direct cause of death. The patient's family refused to condemn the act of the accused, and her sons went so far as to state publicly that he had given their mother a "very peaceful, very dignified, and very humane death."

As in the *Mataya* case, the accused was permitted to plead guilty to the offence of administering a noxious thing, and he received a three-year suspended sentence. Two years later Dr. de la Rocha was called to account by a disciplinary panel of the Ontario College of Physicians and Surgeons. Although he admitted that he had acted wrongfully he nonetheless declined to testify, thus offering no explanation for what he had done. The panel's decision stands in stark contrast to the court-imposed lifetime ban imposed upon Mataya. Although Dr. de la Rocha was advised that he would be suspended from practice for 90 days, he was given the option of avoiding the suspension by developing a protocol on the withdrawal of life-support from terminally ill patients.

(v) Dr. Nancy Morrison (Nova Scotia, 1997)[16]

In the most recent Canadian case, Dr. Nancy Morrison, a 41-year-old respirologist working in the intensive care unit of a Halifax hospital, was charged with first-degree murder for giving an injection of KCl to a 65-year-old patient with terminal cancer of the esophagus. As in the *Mataya* case, the patient's life-support had been withdrawn with the expectation that death would quickly follow. He was extubated at 12:30pm but did not quickly die as anticipated. According to his primary nurse, his struggling for air was "a horrible and hideous scene." (At the preliminary inquiry she testified that in her eleven years of experience in intensive care nursing, she had never witnessed that much suffering in a patient.)

During this time the patient was getting incredibly high doses of narcotics and sedatives, but to no apparent effect. All told, between 6:50am and 2:30pm on his last day, the patient received intravenously four drugs to ease his dying: Ativan (generic name lorazepam), Versed (generic name midazolam), morphine, and Dilaudid (which is five-to-eight times more potent than morphine.) He received 10 mg of Ativan, which is not an unusual amount. However, the amount of Versed was in excess of 230 mg, whereas the recommended "common range" of Versed for the intractable distress of a dying patient is 30-60 mg/24 hours. Hence, the total given (mostly between 12:30pm and 2:30pm) was four times the highest daily dose recommended for such cases. The patient received 40 mg of morphine and in excess of 800 mg of Dilaudid. In effect, then, this was equivalent to 4,400-6,800 mg of morphine.

To place this drug history in context, consider a study appearing in the journal, *Palliative Medicine*,[17] which reviewed 30 cases in which morphine was administered to relieve the intractable distress of dying patients. The dose range over 24 hours was between 150-600 mg for 18 patients, 600-2,500 mg for nine patients, 2,500-5,000 mg for one patient, and in excess of 5,000 mg for two patients.

Bear in mind that Mr. Mills received somewhat in excess of 4,400-6,800 mg of morphine equivalents (i.e. morphine and Dilaudid) over seven hours and 40 minutes. In other words, he got more opiates than 90% of the patients in the study — and although he received comparable amounts to the other 10%, their time frame was 24 hours whereas his was slightly less than one-third as long.

A case reported in the journal *Clinical Pharmacy*[18] relates the drug history of a terminally ill cancer patient "who required exceptionally high doses of narcotic analgesics to control chronic, severe pain." Over the last few days of her life, her daily intravenous intake of morphine was in the range of 8,100-8,500 mg. Again, recall that in less than eight hours Mr. Mills received in excess of 4,400-6,800 mg of morphine equivalents. In sum, one can say that — putting it mildly — Mr. Mills was infused with an extraordinary (although not unheard of) amount of opiates.

Be that as it may, the nurse was appalled at what she perceived as a tortuous dying, and she did not hesitate to convey her feelings in that regard to Dr. Morrison. Shortly after expressing her frustration to Dr. Morrison that the sedatives and narcotics were not working, the latter appeared at the bedside at 2:52pm and proceeded to inject 10 cc of nitroglycerine into the patient's IV line, telling the nurse that it was to lower his blood pressure in order to end his suffering. His systolic blood pressure immediately dropped to 50 mm Hg, although it then increased to 55-60. At 2:59pm, Dr. Morrison returned to the bedside with a 10 cc syringe of clear liquid that she injected into the IV. When the nurse asked what it was, she answered: "It is KCl." Within a minute there was no electrical activity in the heart. Both the Nitroglycerin and the KCl were administered by IV push, which causes drugs to move more quickly into the bloodstream than when given by infusion.

Four days after the patient's death, the ICU nurse told the nurse manager what had happened, and the latter promptly confronted Dr. Morrison with this startling news. According to the nurse manager, Dr. Morrison responded that it was true and when asked why she had done it, she answered: "I, Oh, my God! I don't know why." When asked at the preliminary inquiry whether Dr. Morrison had told her that the patient "had been gasping for hours and was in the process of dying a horrible death", the nurse manager replied "Yes." When asked whether Dr. Morrison had told her that the nurse "was begging (her) to do something to relieve Mr. Mills' pain and suffering from his agonizing death", she again answered "Yes."

It was not the hospital that reported the incident to the police but rather a physician who had seen an internal review of the patient's death and concluded that Mr. Mills was a victim of "active euthanasia." Dr. Morrison was then charged with first-degree murder and a preliminary inquiry was called in Provincial Court. (Keep in mind that at the preliminary inquiry stage of criminal proceedings, the onus on the Crown is not to prove guilt beyond a reasonable doubt but simply to establish a "prima facie" case — that a reasonable jury properly instructed *might* return a guilty verdict.)

From the defence standpoint the charge hinged upon the issue of causation. Two days before the patient's death, his pain and discomfort during a procedure to drain pus had been relieved by 5 mg of Dilaudid and 2 mg of Versed. These were a mere fraction of the amounts administered two days later to no apparent effect (in excess of 800 mg of the former and 230 mg of the latter), and the groundwork for an argument on causation lay in explaining why such massive doses had failed to relieved Mr. Mills' distress. According to a defence witness, Dr. Geoffrey Barker, a specialist in intensive care, the amounts of Dilaudid and Versed given on November 10 were outside his range of experience. He agreed with defence counsel's suggestion that the levels of Dilaudid (up to 500 mg/hour) were "in the lethal range." He answered "Yes" to the question: "You would anticipate that this level of Dilaudid would have a profound depressant effect on respiration and blood pressure?" Dr. Barker stated that if he had been in attendance, the apparent ineffectiveness of such massive doses would have prompted him to check whether the IV line was intact. Given the small amounts of Dilaudid and Versed that had relieved the patient's distress two days earlier, Dr. Barker agreed with defence counsel that a possible explanation was that the tip of the IV line had migrated such that the drugs were only seeping into a body cavity. In that event, they would work far more slowly than if the IV line were functioning properly. Since the line was apparently working two days before, the theory of the defence was that it had somehow slipped out since that earlier procedure. (Presumably because the Crown attorney did not anticipate the migrating IV theory, he had not asked the nurse whether anyone had bothered to check the line.)

The pathologist who examined the body after it was exhumed testified that, although there should have been traces of Dilaudid and morphine in the liver, he could not find any. He agreed with defence counsel that the absence of these drugs in the liver was consistent with the theory that the drugs were not getting into the bloodstream. He could not find evidence of nitroglycerine or KCl simply because they dissipate in the body and cannot be detected.*

In sum, the defence was that if the IV line was not working and the drugs were therefore not getting through, then the same would apply to the KCl. Thus, "whatever the intention, the act didn't occur." Still, at the end of the day there was a *prima facie* case of murder because, as would be

---

* Because Mr. Mills had been embalmed, there is a counterargument that this process may have interfered with the drug assay. In fact, there is medical evidence that embalming can block the detection of these drugs. See W.W. Wanders & B.R. Keppler, The Effect of formaldehyde solution in the gas chromatographic determination of morphine, (1980) 51 *Aviation, Space, and Environmental Medicine* 993-5. For whatever reason (perhaps not doing its homework), the Crown did not challenge the pathologist's evidence.

expected, the patient's heart stopped within one minute of the injection of the KCl. Furthermore, the theory of the dislodged IV line was simply that — a theory — and there is another theory that could just as easily explain why the drugs did not work. The reference is to neurotoxicity (also called opioid hyperexcitability), a phenomenon whereby high doses of narcotics paradoxically aggravate instead of ease pain. Such cases have been reported in the medical literature; there is, however, no medical understanding of why this happens. In other words, there arguably was a *prima facie* case of murder to go to trial.

Moreover, even if not murder, it was evident that Dr. Morrison had attempted to commit murder. The mere fact that she injected the KCl (which she had readily admitted to the nurse and later to the nursing supervisor) proves beyond the shadow of a doubt that her intent was to kill. This is because there was simply no medical reason to explain the act — deliberately giving 10 cc of KCl to a dying patient is only explainable as an act intended to kill the patient. (And of course by her own admission she had committed the same offence — administering a noxious thing — to which both *Mataya* and *de la Rocha* had pleaded guilty.)

In the result, the judge accepted the defence causation theory and accordingly discharged Dr. Morrison, ruling that there was no case to go to the jury for murder or any included (lesser) offence. The Crown appealed, but Justice Hamilton of the Supreme Court* denied the appeal, notwithstanding that she agreed with the Crown that "at the very least the Preliminary Inquiry Judge should have committed Dr. Morrison to stand trial for (the) attempt to commit murder." Still, she refused to overturn the ruling on the grounds that the decision of a preliminary inquiry judge stands even if he errs with regard to the sufficiency of the evidence.

But in a sense all this is beside the point because the Crown has the inherent power to by-pass a preliminary inquiry and lay a direct indictment. Thus, the Crown could have responded to Justice Hamilton's ruling by charging Dr. Morrison with murder, or in the alternative, either manslaughter or administering a noxious thing. Or it could have appealed her ruling. But it did neither and that was the end of the case as far as the courts were concerned.

What remained was the judgment of her peers, and in 1999 Dr. Morrison was reprimanded by the provincial College of Physicians and Surgeons (the profession's disciplinary arm). The College ruled that her actions were inappropriate and "outside the bounds of currently acceptable medical practice." At the same time, the College commended Dr. Morrison for not

---

* In Nova Scotia, the Supreme Court is the highest level trial court and also hears appeals from Provincial Court rulings (as in this case).

abandoning her patient and acknowledged her belief that she was acting in his best interest. In accepting the reprimand, Dr. Morrison acknowledged wrongdoing; and on her behalf the defence counsel issued the following statement:

> She now realizes after much thought that there was a mistake made by herself. Sometimes when you have a person who is dying and going through an agonizing death, you have to make a snap call, and she made it and she made the wrong one. It was a mistake on her part.

There were, however, expressions of support for Dr. Morrison from her peers. The Medical Society of Nova Scotia responded to the reprimand by writing her that:

> It is our sincere desire that any further legal or regulatory actions will be considered unnecessary. As a practicing physician you have discharged your duty with diligence and compassion, and have acted in what you believed to be your patient's best interest.

(b) The English Cases

(i) *Dr. John Bodkin Adams (1957)*[19]

In 1957, a jury in England deliberated only 44 minutes before acquitting Dr. John Bodkin Adams, a 57-year-old general practitioner, who had been charged with the murder of his 81-year-old dying patient, Edith Morell. It was the Crown's contention that the accused had given her a deliberate lethal injection of morphine. The theory of the defence was that the accused had not intended to kill his patient, but that progressive increases in dosage were necessary to relieve pain. Furthermore, his concern to ease her dying took precedence over the foreseeable risk of death from morphine overdose. In his summation to the jury, the defence counsel argued: "There is a world of difference between giving drugs which shorten life, and giving merciful administration to ease the passing — not to hasten it — but to give quiet at the end." The trial judge (Patrick Devlin, one of Britain's most distinguished 20th century jurists) in effect endorsed that distinction. As he charged the jury:

> If the first purpose of medicine — the restoration of health — can no longer be achieved, there is still much for the doctor to do. He is entitled to do all that is proper and necessary to relieve pain and suffering, even if the measures he takes may incidentally shorten life. If the treatment that was given by the doctor was designed to promote comfort; and if it was the right and proper

treatment of the case, the fact that incidentally it shortened life does not give any grounds for convicting him of murder.

The law set forth by Lord Devlin in the *Adams* case enshrines the so-called *doctrine of double effect* in the criminal law. The doctrine will be considered shortly under a separate heading. (There is, by the way, more to the case of Dr. Adams than the precedent established by Lord Devlin. Shortly before her death, Mrs. Morell had changed her will in order to bequeath a prewar Rolls Royce and a silver plate collection to the good doctor. It later turned out that two other elderly patients of his had died not long after naming him as an heir of their estates, although autopsies performed on their exhumed remains failed to produce incriminating evidence. Following his acquittal on the murder charge, he pleaded guilty to 15 counts of forging medical prescriptions and was fined. The General Medical Council responded to the conviction by striking his name from the Register of Medical Practitioners.)

(ii) *Dr. Leonard Arthur (1981)*[20]

John Pearson was born on June 28, 1980, and the death of the Down syndrome infant three days later led to a charge of murder against Dr. Arthur. When informed of the diagnosis, the parents rejected the child and asked that he be allowed to die. They were then seen by Dr. Arthur, a 55-year-old senior consultant paediatrician at the hospital. When they refused to alter their position he complied by writing in the case notes: "Parents do not wish the baby to survive. Nursing care only." He entered a prescription for dyhydrochlorine on the treatment chart and directed that it be mixed with distilled water and given orally "as required" in doses of 5 milligrams at four-hourly intervals. After the infant died — of broncho-pneumonia according to the death certificate — the police received an anonymous tip that the infant had been killed, and the police investigation led to the charge of murder against Dr. Arthur.

It was the Crown's case that the cause of death was lung stasis produced by the dyhydrochlorine, and that it was prescribed by the accused for the express purpose of killing the infant. However, the defence countered the alleged cause of death by presenting the evidence of a paediatric pathologist, who had prepared slides indicating that the infant had been born with brain and lung damage. That evidence led the Crown's pathologist to concede that the prosecution's claim that the infant had been born healthy was both inaccurate and misleading. (For whatever unexplained reasons, Dr. Arthur was not aware of the brain and lung anomalies and thus had assumed that the infant's sole handicap was Down syndrome.) When the defence submitted that the evidentiary basis of the case for murder had collapsed, the trial judge agreed and substituted a charge of attempted murder.

A parade of paediatricians called by the defence testified that the accused had acted within the currently accepted norms of medical practice. As one such witness testified:

> Some children are born with such frightful handicaps that we think it is reasonable to accept the parents' decision that, in the interests of their own child, prolonging life is not in that interest. It is an extremely complex matter. No paediatrician takes life, but we accept that allowing babies to die — and I know the distinction is narrow and we all feel it tremendously profoundly — is in the baby's interest at times.

After two days of deliberation the jury returned with a not-guilty verdict. During the trial, a BBC documentary team mailed 600 question-naires to British consultant paediatricians and paediatric surgeons and re-ceived 280 fully completed replies. One of the questions was whether the respondent would provide "normal care" to an "otherwise healthy" Down syndrome baby who was rejected by his parents. If the answer was No, the respondent was asked to select one of three options: (1) feed and care but no active treatment in the event of a potentially fatal illness; (2) give drugs so that the infant was unlikely to demand food and consequently would die; (3) give it a quick and painless death. Some 90% indicated that they would provide normal care; all the others selected the first option. In short, not one of the 280 respondents indicated that he would have followed Dr. Arthur's choice of sedation and nursing case only.[21] Still, the professional ranks had closed around Dr. Arthur, and one can assume that the jury acquittal was influenced by the testimony of his peers that he had acted in accordance with medical norms.

(iii) *Dr. Nigel Cox (1992)*[22]

In 1992, Dr. Nigel Cox, a 48-year-old rheumatologist, was charged with attempted murder after he gave a lethal dose of KCl to a 70-year-old patient who had begged him to end her life. The patient was dying of rheumatoid arthritis, complicated by gastric ulcers, fractured vertebrae, internal bleeding, gangrene, and body sores. Massive doses of heroin were unable to relieve her agony because her ravaged body could not absorb them. A nurse recalled that "she howled and screamed like a dog" when anyone touched her, and a hospital chaplain said that he had never seen anyone else "so much eaten by pain." As Dr. Cox told it:

I seemed to have no more options left. She was going to die very soon in any case. I was faced with a choice of several evils. I chose what seemed to me the least evil with respect to (the patient) at that time.

In directing the jury, the judge explained the legal bounds of a physician's duty to relieve pain along the lines of Judge Devlin's direction in the *Adams* case:

> If a doctor genuinely believes that a certain course is beneficial to a patient, either therapeutically or analgesically, even though he recognizes that course carries with it a risk to life, he is fully entitled, nonetheless to pursue it. If sadly...the patient dies, nobody could possibly suggest that...the doctor was guilty of murder or attempted murder. There can be no doubt that the use of drugs to reduce pain and suffering will often be justified notwithstanding that it will, in fact, hasten the moment of death. What can never be lawful is the use of drugs with the primary purpose of hastening the end of life. Is it proved that in giving that injection in that form and in those amounts Dr. Cox's primary purpose was to bring the life of Lillian Boyes to an end? If it was, then he is guilty.

The judge went on to instruct the jury that it really had no option but to convict since there was overwhelming evidence that Dr. Cox's "primary purpose" was to kill the patient. The jury complied, although a number were in tears when the verdict was announced. Dr. Cox received a one-year suspended sentence, and although reprimanded by the General Medical Council he was not stricken from the medical rolls.

(The reason that Dr. Cox was not charged with murder was that, since the patient's body had been cremated, the Crown concluded that it could not prove the medical cause of death. But since KCl is naturally present in the body in any event, an autopsy cannot in itself produce the forensic evidence necessary to prove causation. As suggested in our brief review of the *Morrison* case, the Crown has a rough hurdle to prove causation when the alleged lethal drug is KCl. The best case scenario from a prosecution standpoint is when the patient's death is not relatively imminent, his heart stops within roughly one minute after the drug is given, and the pathologist can find no other apparent cause of death. In that regard, recall the *Mataya* and *de la Rocha* cases, which were resolved by guilty pleas to the "noxious thing" offence in the *Criminal Code*. In each case, the patient's death was imminent, and therefore the Crown would have been hard pressed to satisfy the jury beyond a reasonable doubt that the medical cause of death could be attributed to the KCl. Hence, this factor — and not compassion for the compassionate act of the accused — is what may explain the Crown's willingness to plea bargain in these two cases.)

(iv) *Dr. John Moor (1999)*[23]

Dr. John Moor, a 52-year-old general practitioner, was charged with a murder of George Liddell, an 85-year-old widower who was afflicted with cancer of the colon. He had also suffered a stroke and heart attack, was doubly incontinent, deaf, diabetic, anaemic, and in considerable pain. The patient was being treated at home by Dr. Moor and a team of experienced nurses. The events surrounding his death are detailed in the English journal, Criminal Law Review:

> A syringe driver set up by the district nursing sister on the instructions of Dr. Moor contained 120 mg of diamorphine (which breaks down into morphine but is more potent than oral morphine) to be infused subcutaneously at the rate of 30 mg every six hours for 24 hours. By the evening Mr. Liddell was sleeping peacefully. Dr. Moor thought he was near to death. The doctor rang next morning to be told that Mr. Liddell was alive, but making a loud retching noise in his throat. Dr. Moor administered largactyl and waited to see the effect.... He was Cheyne-Stoking, that is breathing in an irregular manner characteristic of a person close to death. (The nurse) left the house intending to return. Dr. Moor waited with the patient who made a further retching noise. The syringe driver had by now run out. Thinking that the patient was close to death Dr. Moor decided not to renew the diamorphine in the driver, but to give a further bolus injection of diamorphine (60 mg) and largactyl. According to him the purpose was to make sure that the patient suffered no break through pain. Within about 20 minutes Mr. Liddell died.

The Crown's position that the accused had given his patient a massive amount of diamorphine with the express purpose of ending his life. The defence attorney submitted to the jury that:

> [The patient] was a very sick man. There was a time he was screaming in agony. A doctor treating someone who is terminally ill is walking a tightrope. If he gives a high dose, there a possibility the patient could die, Dr. Moor did not set out deliberately to kill (the patient). He was at all times trying to do the best for his patient as he saw it. He was trying to ease the suffering of someone very close to death.

In the result, the jury deliberated for only an hour before returning a verdict of not guilty. What explains the murder charge is that shortly after Mr. Liddell's death, Dr. Moor had given an interview to the BBC in which he acknowledged that in his career he had given deliberate lethal injections to about 300 patients, and he specifically referred (although not by name) to Mr. Liddell's death. In that interview Dr. Moor acknowledged that although the law defined these 300 deaths as murder: "I am acting with care, compassion, and consideration on behalf of my patients, and I have no problem with that." However, at the trial he steadfastly denied that he had sought to kill his patient. A year after his acquittal Dr. Moor died of a heart attack.

(c) The American Cases

(i) *Dr. Hermann Sander (New Hampshire, 1950)*[24]

In December l949, Dr. Hermann Sander, a 40-year-old family physician, was charged with the murder of his 59-year-old cancer patient, Mrs. Abbie Borroto. (The *Sander* case marked the first time that a physician in the common law world stood trial before a judge and jury for the alleged mercy-killing of a patient.) The patient had been bedridden for weeks before her admission to hospital for "terminal care", by which time her weight had dropped from l40 to 80 pounds. She was admitted a few days before her death, which occurred on December 4. In the last 17 hours of her life, she received 700mg of Demerol and three grains of Pantapon (a purified opium alkaloid). The patient was examined by another physician just minutes before Dr. Sander injected air into her veins in the presence of a nurse. At the trial that physician testified that he had detected no heartbeat with his stethoscope and had found neither pulse nor pupillary reflex. Not surprisingly, he had concluded that she was already dead.

On December 5, Dr. Sander filled out Mrs. Borroto's death certificate, certifying the cause of death as cancer of the large bowel with metastasis to the liver. But seven days later, he dictated the following notation on her hospital chart: "Patient was given l0 cc. of air intravenously, repeated 4 times. Expired within l0 minutes after this was started." A few days later, the notation was discovered during a routine review of patients' records at a hospital staff meeting. The police were promptly informed, and in February Dr. Sander stood trial for murder.

The prosecution called five witnesses to testify that the accused admitted killing the patient with injections of air. One witness was the nurse who had watched as Dr. Sander injected the empty syringe. She testified that he had then turned to her and said: "Air in the veins acts like an embolus." Another witness was the arresting officer, who claimed that the accused told him that the patient's husband had begged him to relieve her pain, even if that meant killing her. According to the officer, the accused had expressed his concern that Mr. Borroto's "bad heart" would not survive the ordeal of his wife's terminal illness.

The deceased was exhumed seven weeks after death. The autopsy revealed evidence of bronchopneumonia and cancer of the large bowel, which had spread to the liver, kidneys, pancreas, thyroid glands, and lymph nodes. The search for evidence that death was caused by pulmonary air embolism was precluded because the deceased had been embalmed. Moreover, there was the evidence of a key defence witness, the acting head of the Department of Legal Medicine at the Harvard Medical School. He had attended the autopsy and testified that the veins in Mrs. Borroto's arms were "collapsed and plugged" and therefore incapable of carrying air to the heart.

When Dr. Sander took the stand, he swore that he had not admitted guilt to the five witnesses who had testified to that effect. In fact, he insisted that the patient was already dead when he injected her and further that he knew she was dead. But he admitted that he had no rational explanation for injecting air into the veins of a corpse.

When asked to explain why he had dictated the incriminating notation on her chart, he replied: "I think it is the duty of every doctor to put down on the charts what he has done for every patient, whether it has any effect or not." He laid stress upon his "upset mental state", which he attributed to several factors — the constant look of pain on his patient's face, the devastating impact of her terminal illness upon her ailing husband, and his exhaustion from overwork and insufficient sleep. Dr. Sander could offer no explanation for his actions, except that "something snapped in me." As he testified: "I felt impelled, possessed, or obsessed to do something that now doesn't make sense to me. I didn't know what I was doing at the time I did it. I was confused."

The trial lasted 17 days. In his closing argument to the jury, the defence counsel contended that the prosecution had failed to prove that the deceased was alive when the accused acted, and if alive that her death was caused by pulmonary air embolism. In his charge to the jury, the trial judge explained that the prosecution had to prove beyond a reasonable doubt that the accused had killed the deceased by lethal injection; and that if she were dead when the act was committed, the accused was not guilty because one cannot murder a corpse. For whatever reason — compassion for Dr. Sander or ignorance of the law — the judge failed to inform the jury of the common law principle that an accused is guilty of attempted murder if he mistakenly believed that his victim was alive when he struck. The jury was not so advised and was consequently left with only two options: to convict of murder or to acquit.

After only 70 minutes' deliberation, the jury returned with a not-guilty verdict. Throughout his ordeal, Dr. Sander had received overwhelming community support. When he and his wife emerged from the courthouse, they were engulfed by the cheers, applause, and blaring car horns of hundreds of well-wishers. Upon hearing the verdict, Mr. Borroto declared: "It is the most heartwarming news I have ever received." The acquittal not-withstanding, the New Hampshire State Board of Registration in Medicine promptly revoked Dr. Sander's licence. Its stated reason was that, even if he thought his patient dead before he acted, his conduct was nonetheless "morally reprehensible." Three months later it reversed its position. His licence restored, Dr. Sander continued to practice medicine until his retirement in 1981.

(ii)   *Dr. Vincent Montemarano (New York, 1974)*[25]

In 1974, Dr. Vincent Montemarano, 34, a Vietnam veteran and chief surgical resident at a Long Island hospital, was charged with the murder of a 59-year-old cancer patient. The prosecution alleged that the accused had killed his patient by injecting a lethal dose of KCl. The patient, who had recently undergone throat surgery by Dr. Montemarano, had been discharged but was readmitted to the hospital five days before his death. On his last day he lapsed into a coma. Although then given but two days to live, he was dead within a matter of hours.

The State's case hinged on the testimony of two witnesses. One was the patient's nurse, who swore that the accused had ordered her to fill a syringe with KCl, and that in her presence he had injected it into the patient's arm. The other key witness was the chairman of the hospital's surgery department. He testified: "Dr. Montemarano came into my office and said that he had a confession to make — that he had a patient with terminal cancer to whom he had given potassium chloride to stop his heart."

Aside from these two witnesses, the State had no case against the accused. Moreover the prosecution presented no evidence to support the theory that the patient was the victim of a mercy-killing, which was hardly surprising. Since the patient was comatose and beyond pain on the day of his death, it would have been hard pressed to prove that the accused had acted to put an end to his suffering. The deceased's remains were exhumed six months after death. Even if death had resulted from an injection of KCl, the autopsy could not have detected it because as noted earlier the drug is naturally present in the body. The autopsy revealed extensive cancer of the pharynx, advanced heart disease and pneumonia, and a blood clot in the lungs.

The case for the defence was that the accused did not commit the alleged act and that the patient had died from natural causes. Unlike Dr. Sander, Dr. Montemarano did not testify in his own defence. In the *Sander* case, the jury was out for 70 minutes. In the *Montemarano* case, it took the jury only 55 minutes to return its verdict of not guilty.

(iii)   Dr. John Kraii (New York, 1985)[26]

Dr. John Kraii was a 76-year-old small town family physician who was charged with the murder of an 81-year-old nursing home patient. The deceased, who was not only his patient but also long-time friend, suffered from Alzheimer's disease, ulcerous sores in his foot, and constant pain. Dr. Kraii injected three large doses of insulin into his chest cavity and the patient died hours later. After his arrest, the sheriff had only words of praise for the accused, stating in part: "Dr. Kraii was overwhelmed with emotion at the deteriorating condition of his patient. This is the saddest kind of thing."

The townspeople rallied to the support of Dr. Kraii, who had given 50 years of devoted service to his community. He was released on bond, and two weeks later committed suicide by injecting a lethal dose of Demerol in his leg. He was apparently despondent over "mounting pressures" and failing eyesight. In a letter published in the local press, his rabbi wrote:

> He made house calls and was not always particular about receiving payment. He carried food in his car to leave with the destitute hungry.... He rushed to relieve pain and was devastated by the suffering of others. He cared too much. He is a tragic figure like Prometheus. But like Prometheus he is also a giant.

(iv)   Dr. Donald Caraccio (Michigan, 1988)[27]

Dr. Donald Caraccio, a 33-year-old ICU resident, was charged with the murder of a 74-year-old dying patient to whom he gave "a massive" dose of KCl. The patient was suffering grievously but he did not act at her behest. He asked a nurse for the drug, and she and a medical student witnessed the injection. Within a minute a monitor sounded a loud alarm signalling that her heart had stopped. After an emotional appeal by the defence counsel, who argued that his client "took leave of his senses" because of the stress of his own father's terminal illness, the judge accepted a plea of guilty to manslaughter and sentenced Dr. Caraccio to five years' probation.

(v)   Dr. Ernesto Pinzon-Reyes (Florida, 1997)[28]

Dr. Pinzon-Reyes, a nephrologist in private practice, was charged with the murder of a 70-year-old patient with metastatic lung cancer. He was covering for his partner over a weekend; and the patient, whose life expectancy was "a few days", was scheduled to leave hospital on the Monday pursuant to a home hospice program. On Sunday, Dr. Pinzon-Reyes set up a morphine pump allowing the patient to give himself 2 mg doses of morphine every six hours. But the pain did not abate and when contacted by the nurse, he prescribed 10 mg of intravenous morphine. When the nurse protested that the dose was too high, he cancelled the order and returned to the hospital. He then administered a 20 mg dose of morphine, followed within the hour by six injections totalling 117 mg of morphine and 10 mg of Valium. The patient's widow testified at the trial that her husband was rendered unconscious after the first two of the six injections of morphine, although the accused insisted that he remained alert and in pain. According to the nurse who had refused to administer the 10 mg dose, Dr. Pinzon-Reyes then proceeded to inject between 10 to 20 mEq of KCl into the patient's IV port at the wrist. However, he wrote in the patient's chart that he had given 30 mEq of KCl diluted in saline solution through an IV infusion and that the slower delivery system would minimize the risk of cardiac arrest. The patient breathed for about 45 minutes after the KCl was administered.

The nurse reported the matter to the nurse-administrator; and according to the latter Dr. Pinzon-Reyes admitted that he had given the KCl to end the patient's life and had made a false entry on the patient's chart — that he had indeed injected the KCl into the intravenous port. The incident was reviewed by two oncologists who concluded that the use of KCl was inappropriate, and that its administration by way of an IV push indicated that its "intended effect was to hasten the death" of the patient. This damning review led to a charge of murder against Dr. Pinzon-Reyes.

At the trial the accused's admission to the nurse-administrator was not allowed into evidence because the defence attorney successfully argued that confidentiality applied to information obtained during a hospital's peer review process. There was testimony from defence medical witnesses that the 137 mg of morphine given the patient was well within the standard of care for patients in intense terminal pain. The witnesses also opined that the KCl was not the cause of death because the patient would have died quickly if the dose had been lethal. In the result, the jury acquitted and jurors polled afterwards stated that the 45-minute time lapse satisfied them that the KCl had not caused death. Further, as one juror said: "He was really trying to help his heart rate." (Even if not murder, had the jury been allowed to hear from the nurse-administrator it would have had grounds to convict the accused of attempted murder.) The Florida State Board of Medicine had suspended Dr. Pinzon-Reyes' medical licence two weeks after the patient's death but restored it after his acquittal.

(vi) *The Trial of Dr. I. Stan Naramore (Kansas, 1998)*[29]

Aside from Dr. Jack Kevorkian (whose case is discussed shortly), Dr. Naramore is the only other American physician convicted of murder for the mercy-killing of a patient. At his trial he was also convicted of the attempted murder of another patient. He had spent two years in custody between his arrest and trial and when convicted was handed a 5- to 20-year sentence. He was paroled six months later. His convictions were then overturned by a Kansas appellate court because the jury had ignored "strong evidence from an impressive array of...medical experts who found the defendant's actions to be not only noncriminal, but medically appropriate." Each of the charges will be considered in turn.

(A) The Charge of Attempted Murder of Patient Leach

Ruth Leach was a 78-year-old hospital patient dying of cancer. The accused (an osteopathic physician) consulted with her family after the nurse had advised him that the morphine patches were apparently ineffective (the patient was restless and said that she "felt terrible"). After he explained the risk that painkillers could stop respiration, the family told him to go ahead. He accordingly gave the patient a 4 mg dose of Versed and a 100 mcg dose of Fentanyl. According to her son, her respiration slowed to a very low level such that he thought death was imminent. The accused then prepared a syringe of morphine (the dosage not noted), and the son instructed him not to administer it because it would likely kill her. The son then told the accused that: "I'd rather my mother lay there and suffer for ten more days than that you do anything to speed up her death." The accused complied with the son's wishes to give her "minute amounts" of morphine by IV drip. Not surprisingly, the accused informed the son that he wanted no further involvement in the case and the patient was transferred to another hospital. She died a couple days later, "presumably from the course of the cancer."

(B) The Charge of Murder of Patient Wiltt

Chris Willt was an obese 81-year-old diabetic with a history of heart disease who collapsed a few days after he stopped taking his blood thinner medication. Dr. Naramore attended to him shortly after he arrived in hospital and quickly injected a paralysing agent (Norcuron) through his IV to facilitate intubation. The patient died three hours after admission. At some point Dr. Naramore told the hospital administrator that the patient had suffered a massive stroke and that treatment was "futile." When Dr. Naramore advised the patient's brother of the situation, the latter consulted with his niece and minister and advised that the patient would not want to be kept on life-support. When slight movement of the patient's arms and legs was noticed, Dr. Naramore opined that this was only seizure activity. Dr. Naramore asked a local physician to examine the patient, and the latter later testified that the patient had [no pulse, respiration, or reflexes." After examining him he turned to the accused and said, "He's gone." Referring to the ventilator, he added, "It's like beating a dead horse." Shortly thereafter, life-support was stopped and eight minutes later the patient was pronounced dead. When questioned by the police, Dr. Naramore stated that "it didn't make sense for him to do everything medically possible for three hours to save Mr. Willt's life just so he could kill him."

(C)   The Prosecution and Defence Arguments

Both the State and the defence grounded their arguments in the evidence of their respective medical witnesses. It was the State's case that in combination the doses of Versed and Fentanyl given to Mrs. Leach were excessive and life-threatening, and that the accused knew that the dose of morphine he intended to administer would prove fatal. Further, it was the State's case that paralysing Mr. Willt so that he could not breathe and then stopping artificial respiration constituted murder. The gist of the medical evidence for the defence was that the accused did not intend to kill Mrs. Leach; that the Versed and Fentanyl did not together constitute an overdose; and that Mr. Willt was already clinically dead when artificial respiration was stopped.

(D)   The Court's Ruling

In overturning the convictions the Court ruled that, given the impressive array of defence medical witnesses, there was no way that a rational jury could have convicted the accused of the two charges. The Court quoted at length from friend-of-the-court briefs filed by the Kansas Medical Society and the Kansas Association of Osteopathic Medicine. The briefs explained the use of drugs in the palliative care of terminally ill patients, and the Court quoted the following from the KAOM brief:

> The modern literature documents time and again that physicians significantly undertreat pain, including cancer-related pain.... Reasons cited for this phenomenon include a fear of discipline for use of opioids and a fear of malpractice claims. The modern consensus in medical thinking, however, is that pain must be controlled even if hastening death is a possible outcome.

The Court also noted that the medical profession has developed standards for terminating artificial respiration for patients like Mr. Wiltt and that the six defence witnesses did not fault the accused in that regard. Since the Court was more focused upon the treatment of Mrs. Leach than that of Mr. Willt, it did not ponder whether the latter was still alive when his artificial respiration was discontinued. If he were still living, then however much his breathing was compromised by his medical condition the paralysing agent would guarantee his death when the life-support was halted. And if alive at that point, is it murder? The law has yet to address the question, although it is arguable that it is not murder so long as the decision to discontinue treatment is medically reasonable. Be that as it may, in England the Royal College of Paediatrics and Child Health took the position in 1997 that "[w]hen the decision is made to withdraw treatment, it is not necessary to withdraw the paralysing agent before respiratory support is withdrawn."[30]

The legacy of the *Naramore* case is summed up by American law professor Alan Meisel:

> The case should prove somewhat helpful in further establishing the importance of the doctrine of double effect in end-of-life decision-making. Unfortunately, the lesson that physicians may take away from this case is that they risk criminal prosecution if they use large doses of pain relief medications, especially as there was not even an allegation that what Dr. Naramore did actually shortened the patient's life.[31]

(vii)   *The Trial of Dr. Jack Kevorkian (Michigan, 1999)*[32]

In the rogue's gallery of physicians accused of mercy-killing, the one name that the reader will no doubt recognize is that of Dr. Jack Kevorkian. In 1999 a Michigan jury convicted him of the murder of 52-year-old Tom Youk, who was afflicted with amyotrophic lateral sclerosis (ALS) and whose death had been seen a few months earlier by about 15 millions viewers of the CBS-television news programme, *60 Minutes.*

What the *60 Minutes* audience witnessed was a videotape supplied by Dr. Kevorkian, in which he provided a play-by-play account of the death of Thomas Youk, a haggard looking man slumped in a wheelchair. Dr. Kevorkian asks him if he wants to die, and he haltingly says "yes." The onetime pathologist — dubbed "Dr. Death" by the media — then proceeds to inject an anesthetic, and when Youk becomes unconscious follows with a dose of KCl. Dr. Kevorkian describes the effect of the KCl and within minutes of its administration he pronounces death. As he explained to newsman Mike Wallace, Youk was "terrified" of choking to death on his own saliva, and "if the man is terrified it's up to me to dispel that terror." (Yet that kind of death is preventable by proper medical management.) In the interview, he challenged the state to prosecute him for murder and the state was quick to oblige.

As outlined in the following chapter, Dr. Kevorkian had achieved notoriety by his involvement in about 130 assisted suicide cases, but this time he chose to administer the death-dealing agent by his own hand. For whatever reason, he chose to act as his own lawyer, which given his lack of legal training and strident personality was a guaranteed prescription for disaster. The trial judge refused his request to call the deceased's wife and brother to testify that Youk had sought him out to end his life. She ruled that their testimony would be legally irrelevant since the consent of the deceased is no defence to a charge of murder. At the trial he insisted that what the prosecution called murder, he preferred to define as a "medical service." In his closing remarks, he urged the jury to render an acquittal and thereby endorse euthanasia as "the final solution to incurable agony." (In his rebuttal the prosecutor told the jury that "final solution" was the Nazi euphemism for the Holocaust and that the dress rehearsal to the Holocaust was Hitler's so-called euthanasia programme, which involved the killing of approximately 100,000 physically and mentally disabled Germans.) In his courtroom display of arrogance and zealotry, Dr. Kevorkian gave the impression that he was indifferent to his fate, smiling when taken from the courtroom in handcuffs after being sentenced to prison for 10 to 25 years (with parole eligibility after six years). Perhaps the last word on Dr. Death belongs to Judge Jessica Cooper who told him as she passed sentence:

> This trial was not about the political or moral correctness of euthanasia. It was all about you. It was about lawlessness. No one, sir, is above the law, no one. And you had the audacity to go on national television, show the world what you did, and dare the legal system to stop you. Well, sir, consider yourself stopped.[33]

(viii)   *Dr. C. Douglas Wood (Oklahoma, 2000)*[34]

In 2000, a U.S. Circuit Court of Appeals overturned the involuntary manslaughter conviction of a physician at a Veterans Administration hospital who was prosecuted for the death of an 86-year-old patient.* The patient was admitted to hospital in February 1994 with severe abdominal pain, and Dr. Wood, the attending physician, diagnosed and then surgically repaired a perforation in the proximal duodenum which had caused diffuse peritonitis. (The patient was also afflicted with tuberculosis, emphysema,

---

* The case was heard in the federal court system because the death occurred at a Veterans Hospital, which is a federal, not state, facility.

and congestive heart failure.) Over the next eight days, the patient remained under Dr. Wood's care in the surgical intensive care unit. A blood test on the morning of the eighth day revealed that the patient had an extracellular potassium level of 3.2 milleqivalents (mEq) per litre, which was below the lower limit — 3.3 to 5.5 — of the normal range. At around 9am, a fifth-year resident ordered a 40 mEq dose of KCl to raise his potassium level, which was given in an elixir form through a nasogastric tube into the patient's stomach. Since the patient had excess lung fluid, the nurse was directed to administer a diuretic (Lasix), which has the side effect of reducing potassium levels. Soon afterwards the nurse determined that the patient was not absorbing the KCl.

Dr. Wood arrived at the hospital at 11am and, after reviewing the patient's chest x-rays from earlier that morning, concluded that he was drowning from pulmonary edema. He promptly ordered the nurse to prepare 40 mg of Lasix and an IV bag with 40 mEq of KCl in 100 cc of saline solution. When the nurse informed him that, according to hospital policy, the quickest rate at which she could administer that amount of KCl was over one hour, he ordered her to draw up a syringe of 40 mEq of KCl in 30-50 cc of saline. The nurse prepared the KCl solution in a 60 cc syringe but refused to give it, whereupon Dr. Wood took the syringe from her and administered the KCl himself. This happened in the presence of two nurses and a medical intern. (At the trial, the witnesses gave conflicting testimony with respect to how much was given and how quickly. The estimates ranged from 20-32 cc of fluid [13.3-21.3 mEq of KCl] over 15-40 seconds.) During the injection, the heart monitor flat-lined and the patient stopped breathing. Dr. Wood stopped the injection and made one or two precordial thumps in an effort to restart the heart. Chest compressions were applied to no avail, and within a few minutes Dr. Woods pronounced the patient dead.

After a four-year investigation, Dr. Woods was charged with first-degree murder and the case went to trial in the U.S. District Court. At the outset, the defence argued that an acquittal should be ordered on the grounds that there was no evidence to support a guilty verdict for murder, but the judge denied the motion. At the conclusion of the evidence the jury rejected the murder charge, but convicted the accused of the lesser offence of involuntary manslaughter. (Involuntary manslaughter is equivalent to the offence of causing death by criminal negligence in section 220 of the Canadian *Criminal Code*. In both U.S. and Canadian law, it is a killing marked by "reckless or wanton disregard" for the life of the victim.)

On the one hand, the Court of Appeal ruled that the defence motion for dismissal of the murder charge should have been granted because there was no evidence that Dr. Wood had the requisite intent for murder. However, it ruled that the evidence was sufficient to sustain conviction for involuntary manslaughter because the accused had failed to comply with medical guidelines for the administration of KCl. As the Court explained:

> When administered at a high concentration over a short period of time it (KCl) can be lethal; administering KCl by intravenous injection (rather than titration from an IV bag) into a central vein was appropriate only in extreme situations; and in general, a dosage of 40 mEq of KCl in an hour was appropriate, though one mEq per minute was acceptable in emergency situations. An FBI agent testified that Dr. Wood responded affirmatively when the agent asked whether 10 mEq in one minute would be too fast. As to the dosage administered in the instant case, the conflicting evidence taken in the light most favorable to the government indicates that Dr. Wood injected (the patient) with approximately 20 mEq of KCl over 30 seconds.

Although the evidence did not suggest the deliberate killing of the patient — the Court noting that he did after all attempt to resuscitate the patient — it concluded that "the manner in which Dr. Wood performed the injection was reckless enough to constitute a lack of due caution and circumspection" and thus sufficient to support the jury's verdict. But still, the Court went on to overturn the conviction and allow a new trial because of evidentiary errors committed by the trial judge. However, Dr. Wood's ordeal came to an end when the prosecution chose not to proceed in the matter. Twelve months after the Court of Appeal ruling, the state board of medical licensure reinstated the 64-year-old Dr. Wood's licence to practice medicine.

4. SURVEYS ON EUTHANASIA (MERCY-KILLING) AND ASSISTED SUICIDE COMMITTED BY PHYSICIANS AND NURSES

Surveys of physicians in Canada, Australia, England, and the United States report enough cases that the law defines as murder or assisted suicide to warrant the comment that the cases canvassed so far are but the tip of the proverbial iceberg.

In 1995, a survey was conducted by the Manitoba Association for Rights and Liberties on "physician assisted-suicide and euthanasia."[35] A 33-item questionnaire was mailed to a random sample of 400 Manitoba physicians (excluding paediatricians, dermatologists, ophthalmologists, and plastic surgeons), who were provided with the following definitions:

> "Assisted suicide" is when a physician, acting on a patient's request, helps a patient to end her or his life, by providing the patient with the means to commit suicide. "Euthanasia" is when a physician, acting on a patient's

request, administers a lethal injection to the patient, in order to end her or his life.

The physicians were asked whether a patient had ever requested euthanasia/assisted-suicide and whether the physician had ever complied with such a request. Although there was a guarantee of anonymity, the survey produced only 112 usable returns (28% of those canvassed). Still, the results were enough to attract nationwide media attention. Of the 111 who answered the statement — "A patient has asked me to shorten her or his life through assisted-suicide or euthanasia." — 18 (16%) answered Yes. Of the 109 who answered the statement — "I have facilitated a patient's request to shorten her or his life by way of assisted-suicide or euthanasia." — 15 (14%) answered Yes. Unfortunately, there were no questions on diagnoses, prognoses, and the particular manner of death. Thus, there was no data on how many were deliberate lethal injection cases and of that number how many involved drugs other than pain-killers (e.g. potassium chloride).

In 1988, the *Medical Journal of Australia* reported the results of a survey conducted the previous year in which questionnaires were sent to 2,000 physicians selected at random from the Victoria Medical Register; there were 869 completed returns.[36] Amongst the questions asked was:

> In the course of your medical practice, has a patient ever asked you to hasten his or her death (whether by withdrawing treatment or by taking active steps to hasten death)?

Of the 369 who had been asked to take "active steps", 107 (29%) admitted to carrying out the patient's request. Of that number, 70 (61%) had done so two or three times; 22 (19%) had done so "more frequently" than two or three times.

In 1993, a questionnaire modeled after that used in the 1987 survey was sent to a random sample of 1,667 physicians on the Medical Register of New South Wales; and the results were reported in 1994 in the *Medical Journal of Australia*.[37] Of 1,268 respondents, 46% had been asked to take "active steps to hasten death" (42% in the Victoria study), of whom 28% had complied (compared to 29% in the Victoria study).* Furthermore (as in the Victoria study), 80% of those who had performed euthanasia admitted to doing so more than once.

In 2001, the results of an anonymous poll of 683 surgeons in New South Wales was published in the *Medical Journal of Australia*.[38] It was found that 247 (36%) had administered high doses of painkillers with the intent to cause death, and half of these respondents stated that the patient

---

* Unlike the Victoria study, the 1993 New South Wales study reported only percentages and not absolute numbers.

had not asked for lethal drugs. According to the author of the study: "The vast majority of patients were only a few hours or days away from death."

The English survey was also conducted in 1993.[39] By means of a postal questionnaire ("with no possibility of follow-up") sent to "all 221 general practitioners and 203 hospital consultants in one area of England", the investigators sought to determine the proportion who had "taken active steps to hasten a (competent) patient's death." They received 312 completed returns. Since the respondents were also asked about hastening death by the withdrawal and withholding of life-prolonging treatment, the questionnaire thus distinguished between what the investigators referred to as "active and passive euthanasia." As reported in the *British Medical Journal*, 273 of the 312 respondents chose to answer the question whether they had ever been asked to hasten death by "active steps." Of the 273, 45% (124) answered Yes. Of that 124, 119 answered the next question, which was whether they had complied with the patient's request. And nearly one-third (32%) — 38 of the 119 — answered Yes. The results are thus remarkably consistent with those found in the Australian surveys.

There is also pertinent data from the United States. A study reported in the *New England Journal of Medicine* in 1997 involved 118 respondents to an anonymous self-administered questionnaire sent to physicians treating AIDS patients in the San Francisco Bay area.[40] A majority — 53% — indicated that they had assisted suicide at least once. The mean number of times was 4.2. A study published in the *New England Journal of Medicine* the following year detailed the results of a questionnaire answered by 1,902 (61% response rate) physicians in the 10 specialties "most likely to receive requests from patients for assistance with suicide or euthanasia."[41] Of that number, 320 (18.3%) were asked to write prescriptions for the purpose of aiding patients to commit suicide, and 196 (11.1%) were asked by patients for a lethal injection — 42 of the 320 and 59 of the 196 complied with the patient's request.

In 1996 the same journal had published an article, "The role of critical care nurses in euthanasia and assisted suicide", which reported the results of a questionnaire answered by 852 nurses practicing exclusively in ICUs in the United States (71% response rate).[42] The findings are summarized as follows: 141 nurses (16%) had received requests to engage in either euthanasia or assisted suicide and 129 (15%) had complied (how many in each category was not specified). Almost half (64) had done so within the year before the study; 65% had acted in three or fewer cases while 5% had acted more than 20 times. Sixty-two nurses reported at least one case without a request from the attending physician, although in some cases with the knowledge (tacit consent) of the physician. Forty nurses had acted 133 times at the behest of the patient, and 72 had acted 264 times at the request of the family (the latter were presumably euthanasia cases because assisted suicide requires the active involvement of the patient). Ten had acted 60 times at the urging of another nurse, and 108 had acted 517 times when asked by the physician. Approximately 58 nurses had on one or more occasions committed euthanasia without request from either the patient or the family (although the extent of physician request or tacit consent is not reported). What explains the willingness of so many nurses to flout the law? According to the authors:

> Recurring themes reported by the nurses include concern about the overuse of life-sustaining technology, a profound sense of responsibility for the patient's welfare, a desire to relieve suffering, and a desire to overcome the perceived unresponsiveness of physicians toward that suffering.

However, as the author added, another factor is the perception by nurses that physicians are not sufficiently responsive to the needs of their patients. Quoting two respondents:

> Doctors need more bedside training — especially with patients and their families in the critical care setting. They should step into our shoes for about one month to get a much better idea of how much patients and their families are allowed to suffer.

> I have experienced tremendous frustration and anger with physicians who either stress the possibility of a good prognosis, giving false hope — or place their belief system above that of their patients. The physician spends 5 to 10 minutes each day with the patient and then leaves me to carry out his orders and deal with the patient and his/her family for 8 to 12 hours. I'm left with the dilemma of carrying our orders that I believe — and sometimes know — are not in the patient's best interest or what the patient or family has expressed as their desires.

Note also that American bio-ethicists David Thomasma and Glenn Graber have acknowledged that:

> Physician friends confide in us that several times during their practice they have induced death through injections in order to bring the relief to patients that only death could provide. In this decision, the goal was to induce death in order to relieve pain, not the opposite...to relieve pain without directly intending the death accompanying the relief.[43]

Still, at the end of the day an act intended "to induce death in order to relieve pain" will not necessarily amount to murder even if the patient's death soon follows. At the very least, such intent amounts to attempted murder. But as we see shortly in a commentary on the doctrine of double effect, it is not easy to kill a patient with opiates when the patient has become habituated to the drug. (KCl is a different matter.) Particularly when death is imminent in any event, one cannot discount the possibility that it was the disease — not the lethally intended dosage of opiates — that in fact caused a patient to stop breathing. Be that as it may, the surveys do indicate a widespread readiness to seek an end that the law defines as murder.

5. THE LAW'S HARD LINE

In only three of the 14 canvassed cases of a deliberate lethal overdose — *Dr. X* (Quebec), *Dr. Cox* (England), and *Dr. Kevorkian* (Michigan) — was the act prompted by the plea of the patient. Yet, as we see in Chapter 18, whether the act was voluntary or non-voluntary on the patient's part is not the law's concern. In other words, the consent or non-consent of the deceased is deemed legally irrelevant. Rather it is the deed itself — the deliberate lethal overdose — that constitutes the crime of murder.

The net result is that the health caregiver who commits an act of voluntary or non-voluntary euthanasia theoretically stands defenceless before the bar of justice if the case comes to light. Under the *Criminal Code*, the factor that distinguishes mercy-killing from all other intentional killings — compassion for the victim — is legally irrelevant. According to the conventional wisdom, the criminal law has traditionally regarded an accused murderer's motive (the reason why he killed) as irrelevant. As explained by the Law Reform Commission of Canada (LRCC) in its 1982 working paper, *Euthanasia, Aiding Suicide and Cessation of Treatment*:

> Canadian criminal law does not take into account the motive of the person who commits homicide. Only the fact that he did or did not mean (intend) to cause death is considered relevant. The motive behind this intention is of little consequence from the legal point of view.[44]

If an accused has purposely killed his victim, the law is not concerned whether he acted out of greed, anger, jealousy, or revenge. Nor is it relevant if his deed was activated by compassion, empathy, or love. Nor does it matter that the accused acted at the behest of the deceased (recall that in the *Kevorkian* case, the trial judge refused to allow the wife and brother of the deceased to testify that he had consented to be euthanized because his consent was legally irrelevant). Motive aside, the stark fact that the killing was intentional is considered sufficient to support a murder conviction. With due deference to the LRCC, this unqualified assertion that Canadian homicide law ignores motive is misleading. Consider the defence of self-defence to a charge of murder. An accused who pleas self-defence does not deny that his act was intentional. After all, if he deliberately shot the deceased between the eyes, he could hardly deny his intent to kill. Although he admittedly intended his lethal act, his defence is that his reason — his motive — for killing was to defend his life against an unlawful aggressor. In other words, it is the motive of the accused that grounds his defence of self-defence.

Furthermore, self-defence is not the only motive-grounded defence. Another example is the plea of provocation, which if successful reduces murder to manslaughter (unlike self-defence which leads to an outright acquittal). The provocation defence is available to an accused who explodes in murderous rage in response to an assault or mere verbal insult by the victim.* That he kills in hot blood does not negate the fact that his is an intentional killing. His plea of provocation does not amount to a denial of his intent to kill. It rather addresses his motive — the reason why he intentionally killed. And if it is mercy and compassion that drive the mercy-killer, then anger and rage are what motivate the provoked killer to his deed.

But still, under the *Criminal Code*, the former is deemed more blame-worthy because his act is labelled as murder whereas the latter only commits manslaughter. The law that tempers justice with mercy for the provoked killer shows no mercy for the mercy-killer. In its aforementioned working paper, the LRCC refused to endorse a euthanasia defence to a charge of murder. (It reiterated that position in its 1983 report, published under the same title.) The LRCC justified its stance as an expression of society's commitment to the sanctity-of-human-life principle. Although adopting a hard line position, it took comfort in the fact that our legal system contains built-in escape hatches that can bend the letter of the law. As the LRCC explained, there are four internal regulating mechanisms that can temper justice with mercy for the accused mercy-killer:

> (1) the Crown's discretion either to stay the charge or not bring it at all (recall the Montreal case of Dr. X);
> (2) the Crown's discretion to reduce the charge from murder to manslaughter or even to the offence of "administering a noxious thing" (in either case there is no mandatory minimum prison sentence as there is for murder);
> (3) the trial judge's authority to accept a guilty plea to a lesser offence than that charged (recall that Mataya and de la Rocha both pleaded guilty to "administering a noxious thing");

---

* Killing in a rage is not enough to establish provocation. Section 232 of the *Criminal Code* requires additional evidence that an "ordinary person" would have lost self-control in the situation facing the accused.

(4) the jury's power to acquit on compassionate grounds, even if instructed that the accused has no defence in law (or to bring in an insanity verdict that is not supportable by the evidence).

In short, the mercy that the sanctimonious face of the law denies the mercy-killer remains an option that can be exercised in turn by the prosecutor, trial judge, or jury. A perusal of the literature on mercy-killing cases in common law jurisdictions (the cases are mostly American and British) indicates that the most frequent outcome is a guilty plea to manslaughter. The offender receives either a short prison term — one or two years — or more frequently is placed on probation or given a suspended sentence.

As noted, when the case goes to trial the accused is rarely convicted of murder when the evidence indicates that the killing was motivated by compassion. The reality is that mercy-killing trials are usually — but not always — resolved by a process called *jury nullification* (or *jury equity*). Trial by jury means that the jury, not the judge, is the ultimate arbiter of the accused's fate. The jury will be advised that it has a sworn duty to reach a verdict based upon the evidence; but it is still for the jury to deliberate and decide. Thus, no matter how persuasive the Crown's case, an acquittal is always open to a jury because, no matter how compelling the case against the accused, the trial judge cannot direct the jury to convict (although, as illustrated by the jury instructions in the *Cox* case, English judges sometimes come very close to directing juries to convict).* A Canadian jury can defy the law and get away with it because the Crown cannot appeal a so-called *perverse verdict* — one that flies in the face of the evidence — unless the trial judge incorrectly stated the law when charging the jury. If the jury instructions cannot be faulted, then the verdict stands.

Aside from outright acquittals in mercy-killing trials, a compassionate jury may accept a defence of legal insanity even if unsupported by medical evidence. That is what happened in *Zygmanik*, a New Jersey case in which the accused took a shotgun to the intensive care unit to kill his quadriplegic brother. The verdict was temporary insanity, even though there was no credible psychiatric evidence to support it.[45]

The escape hatch mechanisms notwithstanding, the principle holds firm in Canadian law: mercy-killing is murder, whether the compassionate act is committed by the victim's spouse, sibling, child, parent, or physician. Obviously, the source of society's long-time adherence to the principle that mercy-killing is murder is not grounded in notions about the relevance of

---

* However, a jury cannot be informed by the defence attorney or trial judge that it has the inherent power to acquit notwithstanding an open-and-shut case of guilt. It must figure that out for itself and then be prepared to return a perverse verdict by ignoring the law that it has sworn to uphold. The acquittals in the 1941 *Ramberg* and 1942 *Davis* cases illustrate the point.

motive in the law of homicide. An inquiry into the nature of that commitment is beyond the scope of this book. Suffice it to note that it found expression in the LRCC's curt response to proposals calling for the enactment of a *Criminal Code* amendment that would authorize a terminally ill person to request her physician to administer a quick and painless death by lethal injection. In the 1982 working paper, the LRCC responded with a categorical repudiation of proposals for voluntary euthanasia legislation as contrary to a "well established tradition based on time-honoured morality."

It is true that in the common law world, the historical record documents a "well established tradition" opposed to legally sanctioned mercy-killing. In 1906, a euthanasia bill was introduced in the Ohio legislature; it survived to a floor vote but was soundly defeated. Throughout the 20th century, legislative proponents of voluntary euthanasia introduced bills in a number of states but none came even close to enactment. In 1991, the voters of Washington State rejected a proposal (a so-called initiative) to legalize "physician aid-in-dying" (defined to encompass both lethal injection and aiding suicide scenarios). The margin of defeat was 54% to 46%. The following year a similar proposal appeared on the California ballot, and although defeated it likewise received 46% of the vote. However, in 1997 Oregon became the first state to allow physicians to assist the suicide of terminally ill patients.*

Widely publicized attempts to legalize voluntary euthanasia occurred in Great Britain in 1936 and 1969. In 1935 the Voluntary Euthanasia Legalization Society was formed under the chairmanship of Lord Moynihan, President of the Royal College of Physicians. Its lobbying efforts soon bore fruit in the Voluntary Euthanasia Bill, which was introduced the following year in the House of Lords. The bill provided that the patient must be over 21 years old and afflicted by a severely painful, incurable, and fatal disease. Amidst spirited debate the bill survived to a second reading whereupon it was rejected by a vote of 35-14. The Society persisted in its efforts, and in 1969 battle was again joined in the House of Lords. Like its predecessor, the proposal was defeated by a 21-vote margin on second reading, 61-40.[46]

In Canada, the decision by the Supreme Court in the *Rodriguez* case (shortly considered under the heading Physician-Assisted Suicide) prompted the striking of a Special Senate Committee on Euthanasia and Assisted Suicide. In its 1995 report, *Of Life and Death* a divided committee recommended against the legalization of either practice. However, the last decade has witnessed significant shifts in public opinion with increasing support for the legalization of EAS, which threaten the "well established tradition based on time-honoured morality" that undergirded the viewpoint

---

* The Oregon law is discussed in the next chapter.

of the L.R.C.C. in the early 1980s. All one can say with certainty is that the Senate Report is not the last word on the subject of euthanasia/assisted suicide and that proponents and opponents of legalization will continue to battle for their respective causes.

In the non-English speaking world, one finds a middle ground approach to the murderer who is prompted to her deed by compassion for the victim. Although mercy-killing is labelled as murder in all common law jurisdictions, Swiss and German criminal law classify the offence as manslaughter. Other European penal codes (e.g. Italy and Norway) define the act as murder but permit "compassionate motive" to reduce the penalty. Mercy-killing is murder under the penal code of Uruguay, except that: "The judges are authorized to forgo punishment of a person (when) he commits a homicide motivated by compassion, induced by repeated requests of the victim." (The situation of the Netherlands is considered in the next chapter.)

Finally, it should be noted that, in *Of Life and Death*, the Senate Committee endorsed such a middle ground approach to mercy-killing. Under the heading, "Nonvoluntary Euthanasia", the Committee recommended that:

> The Criminal Code be amended to provide for a less severe penalty in cases where there is the essential element of compassion or mercy. Parliament should consider the following options:
>
> A third category of murder could be created that would not carry a mandatory life sentence but rather would carry a less severe penalty; or
>
> A separate offence of compassionate homicide could be established that would carry a less severe penalty.[47]

The Committee's recommendation has been filed in the political deep freeze as our honourable members of Parliament have not shown the slightest inclination to deal with the contentious issues of euthanasia and assisted suicide.

6.   DOUBLE EFFECT AND TERMINAL SEDATION

(a)   Double Effect

As illustrated by the *Mataya*, *de la Rocha*, and *Morrison* cases, giving a large and/or rapid dose of KCl to a dying patient is only explainable as an act intending to stop the patient's heart. Notwithstanding the compassionate motive prompting the act, the law is clear that it amounts to murder or, at the very least, attempted murder (e.g. the English *Cox* case).

On the other hand, if the drug causing death is a narcotic, the intent to kill is not necessarily present. That is because of the doctrine of "double effect", which as noted was first recognized in the 1957 English case, *R. v. Adams*. (Double effect is a long-standing concept in Roman Catholic moral theology that in effect was borrowed by Justice Devlin for application to the medical management of pain.) The law set forth in the *Adams* case provides an avenue of defence to the physician or nurse charged with killing a patient with a deliberate overdose of narcotics. Even if the caregiver knows that sooner or later she might very well administer a lethal overdose, she acts within the law so long as: (1) the drug regimen is necessary to combat the patient's pain; (2) the caregiver regards the risk of respiratory arrest as acceptable because the patient's suffering cannot otherwise be relieved; and (3) the caregiver's intent is directed to that end — the drug is given for the express purpose of relieving pain, not for the express purpose of killing the patient.

Our analysis is more refined than that often found in medical journals, where the double effect doctrine is explained by calling on the difference between intention and foreseeability: that intending death is culpable whereas foreseeing death is not. This paints with too broad a brush because it fails to distinguish between degrees of foreseeability. In criminal law, what the double effect doctrine requires is that the caregiver does not deliberately administer a fatal dose, although it is foreseeable that this might happen. It is medically reasonable to run the risk of a fatal result because aggressive pain control measures are called for as the only way to relieve the patient's pain; the point is that in such circumstances the caregiver does not intend to kill. The crux of the matter is therefore the difference between running a risk that something might happen and acting deliberately to make it happen. As one commentator aptly put it:

> We run the administration of morphine to reduce suffering not really as killing but as an act of risking death to secure pain relief, analogous to risking death by submitting to a potentially life-saving operation.[48]

It is safe to conclude that in Canada as well as England, this manner of death would not be defined as an unlawful killing. For one thing, cases in which caregivers act in accordance with the double effect doctrine regularly occur in Canadian hospitals and the practice is not questioned by the justice system. For another, Justice Sopinka of the Supreme Court of Canada took the opportunity in the 1993 *Rodriguez* case to acknowledge that, in the provision of pain-killing drugs, there is in effect a legal distinction based upon the intent of the physician:

The administration of drugs designed for pain control in dosages which the physician knows will hasten death constitutes active contribution by any standard. However, the distinction drawn here is one based upon intention — in the case of palliative care the intention is to ease pain, which has the effect of hastening death, while in the case of assisted suicide, the intention is undeniably to cause death.... In my view, distinctions based upon intent are important, and in fact, form the basis of our criminal law. While factually the distinction may, at times, be difficult to draw, legally it is clear.[49]

In its 1995 report, *Of Life and Death*, the Canadian Special Senate Committee on Euthanasia and Assisted Suicide recommended that "the Criminal Code be amended to clarify the practice of providing treatment for the purpose of alleviating suffering that may shorten life."[50] While that has yet to happen, the medical practice of aggressive pain control continues without interference from the law.[51]

To reiterate, the double effect doctrine draws a crucial legal distinction between risking death (knowing that the drug *may* cause respiratory arrest) and intending death (knowing that the drug *is virtually certain* to cause respiratory arrest.) In the courtroom, it thus becomes a matter of interpreting the evidence to sort out whether the intent was to palliate or to kill. (From the law's standpoint, an accused would escape culpability unless the dosage were so out of line as to wave a red flag or he acknowledged the intention to kill.*) In any case, it is exceedingly rare for narcotics to cause respiratory depression in dying patients — unless the caregiver intends that result. As explained in an article on pain relief and the criminal law:

> Considerable evidence indicates that pain and other discomfort serves to counteract any depressive effects of the drug. Risk obviously is involved in suddenly and sharply elevating any patient's morphine dosage, just as it is risky to give large doses to an "opiate naïve" patient.[52]

Although the extent to which morphine unintentionally hastens death is unknown, experienced physicians have expressed the view that it rarely happens because patients quickly become more tolerant to increased dosages. According to Dr. Balfour Mount, the director of the division of palliative care at McGill University, it is "a common misunderstanding that patients die because of high doses of morphine needed to control pain."[53] Dr. Kathleen Foley, who is co-chief of the pain and palliative care service at the Memorial Sloan-Kettering Cancer Center in New York City, has described patients ingesting up to 2,000 mg of morphine per day without

---

* This is shortly subject to qualification in the concluding paragraphs of this commentary on double effect.

respiration being compromised.[54] There are also studies indicating that terminally ill cancer patients can tolerate enormous doses of opiates.

Be that as it may, there is anecdotal evidence of what is called "slow euthanasia" — caregivers administering increasing dosages of opiates past the point of pain relief in order to hasten death. According to an Oregon physician:

> Dying patients are given larger and larger doses of morphine. We talk about the "double effect" and know jolly well we are sedating them into oblivion, providing pain relief but also providing permanent relief....[55]

Needless to say, if the "permanent relief" of death is intended, then murder is no less murder even though the end result is not as quick and dramatic as that produced by a deliberate massive overdose of opiates. Still, as noted by an English physician who has acknowledged resort to slow euthanasia:

> For the legal authorities to be successful in convicting the doctor of wrong-doing, it must be proved that the intention was to end the patient's life rather than merely relieve specific symptoms. Therefore, a conviction is most un-likely if regular pain-relieving or sedative drugs are given, and those around the patient remain silent. And, in terminally ill situations, who can really be certain that death was due to these drugs rather than the fatal disease?[56]

In other words, if done discretely no one would question a death that was not unexpected in any event. But even if silence were broken, the Crown could not prove murder. The reason is that, although the levels of morphine in the blood are detectable at the postmortem, it cannot be clearly determined that it was the drug that killed. The caregiver may have intended to kill and may believe that he/she has killed, but the point is that there is no way of knowing whether it was the disease or the incremental doses of the drug that caused the patient to stop breathing. On the other hand, if the intent can be proven that is enough for the crime of attempted murder.

(It follows that the uncertainty whether death is directly attributable to the disease or the drug also applies in double effect scenarios. In other words, a caregiver may believe that her moribund patient stopped breathing because of the dosage lawfully administered under the double effect doctrine, but the point is that it is unknowable whether the drug or the disease was the direct cause of death.)

What about the massive overdose scenario? The total amount of the narcotic in the body can be measured at the postmortem, but what cannot be determined is whether there was a sudden massive increase in dosage. In short, from the postmortem alone, death by massive overdose cannot be established. But what cannot be proven by the medical evidence alone may be proven in a particular case by supportive evidence. A culprit could facilitate the Crown's case by entering his actions on the patient's chart, as happened in the Quebec *Dr. X* case. But what if the offender is not so accommodating? Consider a scenario involving a patient on 10 mg of morphine every four hours and whose death was not reasonably considered to be imminent. The evidence from a nurse is that the patient stopped breathing within minutes after a colleague gave an injection of 50 mg. And assume that the Crown can prove the intent to kill — even without an admission by the actor, the intent could likely be inferred from an act which would not appear subject to a different interpretation. Given then the act and the expected consequence, a jury could if so inclined consider the evidence sufficient to convict of murder.* (In other words, such evidence could lead to a cause-and-effect inference that cannot be drawn in a slow euthanasia scenario.)

Finally, an historical note. The death of Sigmund Freud in London in 1939 has been cited by medical historians as an instance of active voluntary euthanasia. Freud was 83 years old and sorely afflicted for years with a malignant oral epithelioma, no doubt caused by his incessant cigar smoking. The account of Freud's death was written by Max Schur, his physician and longtime friend, but not published until after Schur's death. As Schur reported, the time came when Freud grasped his hand and said:

> My dear Schur, you certainly remember our first talk. You promised me then not to forsake me when my time comes. Now it's nothing but torture and makes no sense anymore.

When Schur replied that he would keep his promise, Freud

> sighed with relief, held my hand for a moment longer, and said "I thank you." All this was said without a trace of emotionality or self-pity, and with full consciousness of reality.... When he was again in agony, I gave him a hypodermic of two centigrams of morphine.** He soon felt relief and fell into a deep sleep. The expression of pain and suffering was gone. I repeated this dose after about 12 hours. Freud was obviously so close to the end of his reserves that he lapsed into a coma and did not wake up again.[57]

Although Schur believed that he had euthanized his patient, it may well be that since Freud was near death in any event it was the cancer — not the 40 mg of morphine — that killed him. Given that Freud was already on morphine, it is only conjecture that it was the drug, and not the cancer,

---

* I say "if so inclined" because juries as often as not will acquit in mercy-killing cases even when the evidence clearly points to guilt.

** 20 milligrams.

that caused him to stop breathing. The point is made by an Australian palliative care physician:

> [P]ublished sources debate the actual dosage and frequency of morphine that Freud received. Regardless of whether Freud was given two cg of morphine and whether the dosage was repeated once (12 hours later), 36 hours unfolded before Freud subsequently died.

> This period strongly suggests that Freud died as a result of his disease process and not from receiving morphine. It is the size of the dose and the rate of the subsequent increase that determines whether the morphine causes or hastens death. In pain management, a gradual dosage escalation of 50% to 100% is the usual practice, although substantially higher increases may be well tolerated by patients who are not new to the drug. Freud received what was then the common dosage of morphine given to relieve the pain of acute myocardial infarction.[58]

(b) Terminal Sedation

Although the term "terminal sedation" was not coined until 1991, it now frequently appears in the palliative care literature. It has been defined as

> the intention of deliberately inducing and maintaining deep sleep, but not deliberately causing death, in specific circumstances for the relief of one or more intractable symptoms when all other possible interventions have failed and the patient is perceived to be close to death....[59]

In its 1995 report, *Of Life and Death*, the Canadian Senate's Special Committee on Euthanasia and Assisted Suicide recognized and endorsed the practice of total sedation for terminal patients. An illustration of the technique was provided to the Committee by Dr. Marcel Boisvert, a palliative care physician at the Royal Victoria Hospital in Montreal:

> What we are pushed to do occasionally — not often — in palliative care is that in some circumstances in the dying process where distress is so bad that the only way to relieve people is sedation. Shortness of breath is the best example. In the palliative care field it is very often the paradigm of a difficult death — running after and catching each breath, 40, 50 times per minute. We can administer drugs that will relieve this. We can very often relieve 100 per cent of the pain, but rarely can we relieve 100 per cent of severe shortness of breath except by severe sedation.[60]

Other symptoms that may be treated by total sedation for the dying include severe pain (e.g. from nerve and bone cancer), persistent vomiting, and agitated delirium. The drugs reported used in such cases are opiates, benzodiazepines, barbiturates, neuroleptics, and propofol. In 1997 the U.S. Supreme Court had occasion to endorse the practice of terminal sedation when it upheld the constitutionality of state laws prohibiting assisted suicide in the companion cases, *Washington v. Glucksberg* and *Vacco v. Quill.** The American Medical Association had submitted a friend-of-the-court brief in order to assure the Court that even the most intractable pain can be alleviated by total sedation (in response to the claim that assisted suicide is a reasonable option when pain cannot be controlled). According to the brief:

> The pain of most terminally ill patients can be controlled throughout the dying process without heavy sedation or anesthesia.... For a very few patients, however, sedation to a sleep-like state may be necessary in the last days or weeks of life to prevent the patient from experiencing severe pain.

This assurance from the AMA prompted three of the justices to conclude that if a right to assisted suicide turned on the need to relieve refractory pain, then resort to terminal sedation — not assisted suicide — was the answer. However, as the justices failed to acknowledge, there are two reasons why terminal sedation may not always be the answer: (1) data from the Netherlands indicate that most requests for euthanasia/assisted suicide are not prompted by pain but rather by a perceived loss of dignity and impatience with dragging out the dying process; and (2) not all patients can be sedated to deep unconsciousness — a survey of palliative care experts reported that the use of total sedation was unsuccessful in 10 out of 100 cases.[61]

In sum, the resort to terminal sedation is permissible provided that the dosage is intended to render the patient unconscious but not to kill him. If that inadvertently happens, then the doctrine of double effect insulates the physician from criminal responsibility for death directly caused when sedating the patient. Admittedly, since there is no point to tube-feed the patient, the resort to terminal sedation is certain to end in death. Yet this is not murder simply because it would be nonsensical for the law to require tube-feeding a patient who has been rendered permanently unconscious. A subsidiary reason is the absence of relative certainty that the combination — terminal sedation and no tube-feeding — will bring about death. Given the kinds of cases in which this scenario unfolds, it is just as likely that the patient will succumb from the underlying disease process before death would occur from the lack of nutrition/hydration.

---

* The cases are briefly summarized in the next chapter.

7. GUIDELINES

In September 2002, the Joint Centre for Bioethics at the University of Toronto released a study, "Consensus guidelines on analgesia and sedation in dying intensive care unit patients."[62] According to Dr. Peter Singer, the Centre's director: "Job number one in caring for patients and their families is to make sure they die with dignity, not in pain." The guidelines stress that the distinction between palliative care and "euthanasia" is found in the intent of the physician:

> The principle of double effect whereby analgesics and sedatives may be administered to alleviate distress even though death may be hastened by their administration (is) useful in allowing physicians to achieve an effective level of analgesia. The physician's intent when administering these drugs (is) the distinguishing factor between palliative care and euthanasia.... In order to avoid any misinterpretation, intensivists must clearly document, in the patient's chart, their intentions and justify their actions in the withholding/withdrawal process.

The guidelines are also at pains to define terminal sedation as palliative care, not euthanasia.

The case of Dr. Nancy Morrison prompted the Centre to commission the study because of its chilling effect on end-of-life care. In the view of Dr. Singer: "It certainly didn't improve the aggressiveness of pain and symptom control in intensive care units."[63] The expectation is that the guidelines will guide medical practice in the years to come:

> Our hope is that the guidelines will decrease the confusion and anxiety regarding the use of opiates and sedatives at the end of life and thereby improve the quality of care received by dying patients.

It is true that the guidelines simply restate the law as explained by Supreme Court Justice Sopinka in the *Rodriguez* case. Still, they may help reassure physicians and nurses — whether in the ICU or elsewhere — that there is no legal impediment to the aggressive pain management of their terminally ill patients.

8. THE CASE OF DR. ROBERT WEITZEL (UTAH, 2000-2)[64]

Finally, we note a recent Utah case that pitted a defence of comfort care against the accusation of death by deliberate morphine overdose. In 2000, Dr. Robert Weitzel, a 44-year-old psychiatrist, stood trial on five counts of murder with respect to the deaths within 16 days of five elderly

patients in a 10-bed geriatric/psychiatric unit that he directed. As the prosecutor put it, quoting one of the patient's daughter: "Five victims in just
over two weeks in a unit of only 10 patients that had only one death in the
previous two years screams of wrongdoing." (This case stands apart from
the cases previously considered because neither the prosecution nor the
defence raised the issue of mercy-killing. According to the prosecutor: "He
didn't like these people. They were old and of no more use to society.")

The patients ranged in age from 72 to 93 (average age was 86) and all
were afflicted with severe dementia and extensive co-morbidities. The
prosecution claimed that the accused systematically weakened them by
prescribing massive doses of sedatives, which slowed their breathing, and
then prescribed the morphine to end their lives. (The drugs were administered by the nurses.) According to the defence's medical witnesses, all five
patients were terminally ill and needed the morphine for pain control; the
state's medical witnesses were of the opposite view — that none was dying
nor in pain. The post-mortems were conducted after exhumation; the medical examiner reported that one death was caused by "morphine intoxication" but that morphine's role in the other deaths was "undetermined."

Although the jury did not find murder, it convicted Dr. Weitzel of
manslaughter for two deaths and negligent homicide* for the other three.
He was sentenced to 15 years' imprisonment but was released on bail after
serving six months when the trial judge reversed the convictions and ordered a new trial. The reason for the reversal was the failure of the prosecution to disclose to the defence that it had interviewed a medical expert
whose opinion was that Dr. Weitzel had not acted unlawfully.** In November 2002 Dr. Weitzel again stood trial, although the prosecution decided to proceed with charges of manslaughter and negligent homicide
instead of murder (presumably because it deemed it easier to persuade a
jury to convict of these charges than of murder).

At trial expert witnesses called by the prosecution testified that the
deaths were deliberately caused by morphine, whereas the expert witnesses
called by the defence said otherwise. Amongst the latter were: a geriatric
psychiatrist who testified that the drugs and dosages prescribed were entirely appropriate; a forensic pathologist who testified that the patients died
of natural causes associated with old age — weak hearts, clogged arteries,
and diseased lungs; and another forensic pathologist who testified that all
five patients "were close to death" when admitted to the unit and that

---

* Negligent homicide in the Utah Criminal Code, s. 76-5-206, is comparable to the crime of causing
death by criminal negligence in the Canadian *Criminal Code*, s. 220.

** In Canada as well, the Crown is under a duty to disclose any evidence it comes across that may
be helpful to the defence.

morphine was prescribed not to kill but for comfort relief. (The prosecution had claimed that aside from dementia they were all relatively healthy.) After deliberating for only 90 minutes the jury returned a verdict of not guilty on all charges.

Notwithstanding his acquittal, Dr. Weitzel was on his way to federal prison to serve a one-year sentence after pleading guilty to two counts of prescription fraud for keeping some of the morphine and Demerol that he had prescribed for two patients. Twenty other counts of prescription fraud were dropped in return for the guilty plea.

Months before the second trial, the Weitzel case was featured on the CBS news programme, *Sixty Minutes*. The segment, which aired on March 3, 2002, included interviews with Dr. Ira Byock, one-time president of the American Academy of Hospice and Palliative Medicine, and Dr. Perry Fine, a specialist in pain management and end-of-life care at the University of Utah Medical Center. (Dr. Fine was the medical expert whose views the prosecution had fatally failed to disclose.) Both were of the opinion that the morphine dosages given to the patients were warranted. Dr. Fine acknowledged that Dr. Weitzel was not well qualified to treat the terminally ill and that he would "send him for remedial training." But he added that Dr. Weitzel had treated the five patients "reasonably" and protested the laying of criminal charges against him.

CBS correspondent Ed Bradley had introduced the segment by observing:

> It's a sad fact of life, or perhaps death, that nearly half of all Americans spend their last days in severe pain. What's worse, some doctors say they don't want to treat them for fear they will be blamed for their deaths.

The fear that the prosecution of Dr. Weitzel could hamper aggressive pain management was voiced by Dr. Fine at the end of the segment:

> An individual has been charged with murder who, in his best estimation, was practicing a legitimate form of medicine. And if that can happen to him, then it can happen to any physician. This is absolutely the wrong message to give physicians. They will pull back, and who will suffer is you, me and anybody we care about.

Suffice it to express the hope that this dire prediction is not borne out.

PART TWO — PHYSICIAN-ASSISTED SUICIDE

9. THE MENTAL ELEMENT OF THE OFFENCE OF COUNSELLING AND AIDING SUICIDE

We have thus far considered cases involving physicians who give deliberate lethal injections to afflicted patients. What if the hand that brings about death is not the physician's but that of her patient? What does it mean to counsel and/or aid a patient to commit suicide? Consider the three hypothetical cases of *Dr. Compassionate and her Suicidal/Dying Patient.*

(a) Case 1

Dr. C's patient is a 40-year-old female. Her diagnosis is breast cancer, which is widely metastatic and unresponsive to chemotherapy and hormonal therapy. She suffers from severe bone pain and her condition is essentially untreatable. The prognosis is death in two months.

The patient informs Dr. C that it is her wish to die at home, and that after taking a few days to settle her affairs she intends to commit suicide. She asks Dr. C to discharge her from hospital with sufficient medication to end her life at the time of her choosing. After days of soul-searching, Dr. C agrees to honour her request. As the patient is being readied for discharge, Dr. C hands her a prescription for a 1,000 mg bottle of oral morphine solution and advises her:

> A 60 milligram dose should effectively control your pain. Take that amount as often as you think necessary, but only at three to four hour intervals. I would think that a lethal dose in your case is about 180 milligrams. When you decide that your time has come, gulp down about a quarter of a full bottle. That will do it.

The patient is discharged, and two days later she dies at home after ingesting roughly 200 mg at one sitting.

(b) Case 2

Dr. C has the same patient with the same diagnosis and prognosis. The patient informs her that she prefers to die at home and asks for sufficient medication to control her pain. As she is being readied for discharge, Dr. C hands her a prescription for a 1,000 mg bottle of oral morphine solution. The following conversation, marked by pregnant pauses on both sides, then transpires:

Dr. C - A 60 milligram dose should effectively control your pain. Take that amount as often as you think necessary, but only at three to four hour intervals. When it starts to run out, let me know and I'll order a refill.

Ms. P - What if I don't wait that long — three to four hours?

Dr. C - Well, you could overdose.

Ms. P - Tell me, what would it take to kill me — a fatal overdose?

Dr. C - I'm not about to tell you how to kill yourself.

Ms. P - That's not why I asked. Look, I know that if I drank half the bottle that would kill me, wouldn't it? (Dr. C nods.) I'm just curious how far 60 milligrams is from a fatal dose.

Dr. C - Well, I can tell you that if you drank half the bottle at one time, that would do it. Actually you wouldn't even need that much — 180 milligrams would probably be enough to push you over the edge. So be careful and don't do it.

Ms. P - Don't worry, I won't.

The patient is discharged, and two days later she dies at home after ingesting roughly 200 mg at one sitting.

(c) Commentary on Cases 1 and 2

In Case 1, Dr. C commits an offence under section 241 of the *Criminal Code*, which provides a maximum sentence of 14 years' imprisonment for anyone who "counsels, or aids or abets a person to commit suicide, whether suicide ensues or not...." Counselling — and its synonym, abetting — mean to encourage, advise, or recommend. Aiding means to assist intentionally — i.e. knowingly and deliberately. The crime is committed even if the person counselled or aided does not in fact kill herself as the offence is to counsel or aid, regardless of outcome.

In Case 1, Dr. C counsels/abets the offence by advising the patient how to commit suicide. She knows full well that the patient intends to take her life, and yet she provides information for the purpose of assisting her to that end. She also aids by providing the means for the patient to kill herself, knowing full well that she is helping the patient to that end.

In Case 2, Dr. C neither counsels/abets nor aids suicide. She does not counsel/abet because the *Criminal Code* requires that she inform with the express purpose that her advice will be acted upon. Even though she tells the patient that 250 mg is a fatal dose, that is not tantamount to advising or directing her to act upon that information. Dr. C has merely answered a question that the patient is surely entitled to ask. Even if she suspects that the patient is pondering suicide, her suspicion does not amount to counselling/abetting. In the same vein, she does not aid, even though she provides the means. That is because her purpose is not to enable the patient to commit suicide but to rather to manage her pain.

(d) Case 3

The same patient is going home to die with her prescription for a 1,000 mg bottle of oral morphine solution. As she is being readied for discharge, Dr. C says:

> Remember, 60 milligrams at a time, and a three to four hour interval between doses. Don't do anything foolhardy like taking a 200 milligram dose at one sitting because you would go to sleep and never wake up.

The patient has not broached the subject of suicide, but Dr. C suspects that it is on her mind. Her reason for telling her how to kill herself is that she believes that the patient is entitled to know. In Dr. C's view, she has pointed the way but it is for the patient to take that road if she so chooses. Two days later the patient dies at home after ingesting about 200 mg at one sitting. At her bedside is found this note addressed to Dr. C:

> Thanks for letting me know how I could control my fate and die in my own time. I admit that the thought of overdosing was never far from my mind. But I knew that what you were telling me was not simply how to do it but that it wouldn't be the wrong thing to do. You gave me the courage to act, and for that I bless you.

(e)   Commentary on Case 3

Has Dr. C counselled/abetted suicide? The answer is No. That the effect of her words was to encourage the patient to commit suicide is not enough to convict. What the Crown must prove is that it was Dr. C's intent to encourage or persuade the patient to commit suicide. But that was not her intent, which was rather to make the patient aware of an option that was hers to exercise if she so chose. All that she counselled was the exercise of the patient's free choice.

Nor did Dr. C aid the patient's suicide. Dr. C prescribed the medication for the legitimate purpose of pain relief. Even if she foresaw that she was providing the means for the patient to commit suicide, that is not sufficient to prove the charge. She did not aid because she did not provide the prescription for the express purpose of enabling the patient to commit suicide.

10. THE CASE OF SUE RODRIGUEZ (SUPREME COURT OF CANADA, 1993)[65]

On September 30, 1993, the Supreme Court of Canada upheld the constitutionality of section 241(b) of the *Criminal Code* in the case of *Rodriguez v. British Columbia (Attorney General)*. The law banning the act of assisted suicide was challenged by Sue Rodriguez, a 42-year-old victim of amyotrophic lateral sclerosis (ALS), who sought a court order allowing a physician to provide the means for her to commit suicide at the time of her choosing. Her claim was based upon sections 7 and 15 of the *Charter of Rights and Freedoms*. (According to section 7, "Everyone has the right to life, liberty and security of the person and the right not to be deprived thereof except in accordance with the principles of fundamental justice." According to section 15, "Every individual is equal before and under the law and has the right to the equal protection and equal benefit of the law without discrimination...based on...physical disability.")

Her petition was initially heard in the British Columbia Supreme Court* and the following exchange occurred during her direct examination by her lawyer (Q is question and A is answer):

Q Why do you want to have the option of committing suicide?

A I would like that option because I feel that I don't want to die a gruesome death of trying to get air or go into a choking spasm or starve. I want to be able to live as long as possible and have that option for the time when I feel that I don't want to experience any more discomfort.

Q Will you be able to commit suicide without assistance of a physician?

A No. I would never be able to swallow the number of pills that would be required to do that.

Q Why do you not wish to commit suicide while you are still able to swallow an overdose of medication, though I appreciate you've described today it's becoming very difficult for you to do that?

A I'm still enjoying life and my family, and I'd like to live longer while I'm still having a good time.

Q How do you think your family will react to seeing you choking, having difficulties breathing, suffocating, and pneumonia?

A I know it would be very difficult for them, very stressful, and I don't want to put them through that.

---

* The highest level trial court in the province.

Q Okay. You're asking for the assistance of a physician to help you commit suicide, such as perhaps making an I.V. drip available to you, which you would actually activate yourself, is that correct?

A Yes.

Q Why is it important to you that you be the person who actually activates the device and in effect commits suicide at that point?

A Because I want to be in charge of my life and my death. I feel it's a choice that I've made for myself, and I would like to be the one that does, you know, the final deed.

Her petition was denied and her appeal rejected by the B.C. Court of Appeal. She then appealed to the Supreme Court, which ruled against her by a narrow 5-4 margin. The majority held that even though section 241(b) violated the plaintiff's liberty and security interests, the deprivation was "in accordance with the principles of "fundamental justice." Justice Sopinka (speaking for the majority) held that the blanket prohibition on assisted suicide reflects "fundamental values at play in our society" as it serves "to protect the vulnerable who might be induced in moments of weakness to commit suicide." He added:

> The purpose is grounded in the state interest in protecting life and reflects the policy of the state that human life should not be depreciated by allowing life to be taken. This is part of our fundamental conception of the sanctity of human life.

Justice Sopinka further ruled that even though the ban on assisting suicide may well have violated section 15, it was clearly justified under section 1. (According to section 1: "The Canadian Charter of Rights and Freedoms guarantees the rights and freedoms set out in it subject only to such reasonable limits prescribed by law as can be demonstrably justified in a free and democratic society." What this in effect affords is the invocation of public policy to restrict rights and freedoms otherwise recognized in the *Charter*.) As he put it:

> The prohibition on assisted suicide without exception reflects a substantial consensus that it is the best approach to protecting life and those who are vulnerable. Attempts to fine tune that approach by creating exceptions have been unsatisfactory. The legislation was not overbroad as no halfway approach could fully achieve the legislation's purpose.

In their dissenting opinions, Justices McLachlin and Cory argued that the assisted suicide ban did breach section 7 of the *Charter* and could not be saved by section 1. According to the latter:

Section 7 emphasizes the innate dignity of human existence. Dying is an integral part of living and is entitled to the protection of section 7. The right to die with dignity should be as well protected as any other aspect of the right to life. State prohibitions that would force a dreadful, painful death on a rational but incapacitated terminally ill patient are an affront to human dignity.

Chief Justice Lamer based his dissenting opinion upon section 15, the *Charter's* equality provision:

> The effect of section 241(b) is to create an inequality since it prevents persons physically unable to end their lives unassisted from choosing suicide when that option is, in principle, available to other members of the public. This inequality is imposed solely because of a physical disability, a personal characteristic among the grounds of discrimination listed in section 15(1) of the Charter. The inequality...limits the ability of those subject to the inequality to take and act upon fundamental decisions regarding their lives and persons. For them the principle of self-determination has been limited.

He then concluded that the breach of section 15 could not be trumped by section 1:

> The fear of a "slippery slope" cannot justify the over-inclusive reach of the Criminal Code to encompass not only persons who may be vulnerable to the pressure of others but also persons with no evidence of vulnerability and, in the case of the appellant, persons where there is positive evidence of freely determined consent.

Thus, by a one-vote margin, Rodriguez lost her valiant battle for the legal right to assisted suicide. Four months later she killed herself, apparently with the help of a physician who was prepared to breach the law that she had strived to overcome. Although she lost her case, her plight not only focused attention upon the legal proscription against physician-assisted suicide but also stimulated a public debate on the legitimacy of the legal status quo.

11. COMMENTARY

By upholding the ban on physician-assisted suicide, the Supreme Court in effect tossed the ball into Parliament's lap. The response from Ottawa (as noted in Part One) was to appoint a Special Senate Subcommittee on Euthanasia and Assisted Suicide, which proceeded to hold year-long public hearings beginning in March 1994. By coupling euthanasia (the lethal injection scenario) with assisted suicide as its agenda, the Subcommittee recognized that both manners of death were implicated by the euthanasia debate. As it turns out, there is a compelling argument that one cannot be legalized without the other. If Parliament were to permit only physician-assisted suicide, then the law would not cover the patient who was so debilitated that she could not kill herself with the aid of another but would have to find someone to risk prosecution for murder by acting on her behalf (e.g. by administering a lethal injection). In our view, that result would amount to discrimination against the physically handicapped as prohibited by section 15 of the *Charter*, given that the more disabled the patient the less likely would she be able to perform the death-dealing act herself. Thus, if section 241(b) is amended to legalize physician-assisted suicide, then section 14 — which stipulates that "no person can consent to have death inflicted upon him" — must also be amended to provide a physician-based exception.

The countervailing argument is presented by Dr. Timothy Quill. (Dr. Quill achieved notoriety by publishing an article in The New England Journal of Medicine in 1991 in which he recounted a case in which he had assisted the suicide of his terminally ill leukemia-patient.[66] Although he publicly admitted to breaching the ban on aiding suicide in the New York Penal Code, a grand jury refused to indict him.) In a follow-up article advocating a change in the law, he argued that it is only physician-assisted suicide that warrants legalization because in that case there is a relative balance of power as between physician and patient:

> In assisted suicide, the final act solely is the patient's, thus greatly reducing the risk of subtle coercion from doctors, family members, institutions, or other social forces.... With voluntary euthanasia (lethal injection), the physician must provide both the means and the actual conduct of the final act, greatly amplifying the physician's power over the patient, and increasing the risk of error, coercion, or abuse.[67]

In the context of Canadian constitutional law, advocates of the Quill perspective would contend that, even if section 15 of the *Charter* is breached by the law that allows the physician to assist suicide but not to give a lethal injection, the distinction is justified under section 1 on public policy grounds — that the "risk of subtle coercion" and "other social forces" makes it too dangerous to permit the death-dealing act to be that of the physician. In response, one would assert that the highly speculative nature of Dr. Quill's concern is overcome by the forceful argument that section 15 precludes the differential treatment of assisting suicide and lethal injection cases, and that there are no countervailing public policy grounds sufficient to warrant the invocation of section 1.

In any event, the difference between these two means of physician-assisted death is without ethical significance. Assume that the law were to follow the Quill proposal. Consider that at the last minute an enfeebled patient loses the precious little strength required to raise the glass containing the lethal cocktail to his mouth and to swallow the contents. Would the physician walk away because otherwise she would have to empty the glass into the patient's mouth (which would be murder because the physician, not the patient, would be performing the act that directly causes death). Or would she help the patient to die by performing the death-dealing act herself, acting on the belief that she is crossing no ethical divide by stepping in to do for the patient what he cannot do for himself. Be that as it may, a mechanic of assisting-suicide technology, following in the footsteps of Dr. Jack Kevorkian, could likely construct a devise such that the feeblest breath from a totally paralysed patient would be sufficient to release the hair trigger mechanism that would enable the patient 'to kill herself''by a drug overdose.

In sum, it is submitted that there are no moral or legal distinctions that warrant the granting of lawful authority for the physician to assist the death-dealing act but not to perform it herself. This is not to suggest that both sections 241(b) and section 14 of the *Criminal Code* should be accordingly amended, but simply that the *Charter* cannot accommodate the legalization of one without the other.

In a 2001 case paralleling *Rodriguez*, the Judicial Committee of the House of Lords rejected a challenge to the English law against assisted suicide brought by a late-stage ALS patient. Diane Pretty wished to take her own life with assistance from her husband, but his part was prohibited by section 2(1) of the Suicide Act 1861 (the same law as in Canada). She asked the Divisional Court to rule that the prohibition was in breach of the European Convention on Human Rights, but the Court ruled against her and the decision was affirmed by the House of Lords. In language reminiscent of that of Justice Sopinka in *Rodriguez*, their Lordships ruled that the various rights guaranteed in the Convention were not breached by section 2(1) because of its overriding concern to protect the vulnerable.[68] Pretty then took her case to the European Court of Human Rights, but in April 2002 a seven-judge panel unanimously ruled against her. Although the Court stated that it 'could not but be sympathetic''to her wish to avoid 'a distressing death," it rejected her claim that section 2(1) infringed the provisions in the Convention that prohibit inhuman or degrading treatment and that protect respect for private life.[69] Two weeks after the ruling the media reported that Diane Pretty had died after 'experiencing breathing difficulties for several days."

Finally, there is the case of *R. v. Genereux* (Ontario, 1997).[70] Dr. Genereux has the dubious distinction of being the only Canadian physician convicted of the crime of aiding suicide. The facts of his sordid case explain not only why he was convicted but also why he was sentenced to a jail term of two years less a day. The 50-year-old physician pleaded guilty to the offence for prescribing barbiturates (Seconal) to two depressed men who were HIV-positive and who told him that they wanted drugs to commit suicide because they dreaded the onslaught of AIDS. One survived a suicide attempt but the other succeeded. (Recall that the offence of aiding suicide is committed even if the person aided fails in the attempt.) Evidence presented during the preliminary inquiry depicted the accused as a physician who dispensed narcotics and tranquillizers virtually on request. The suicide survivor testified that he told the accused that he had read that 40 Seconal tablets was a lethal dose and that the physician responded by writing a prescription for 50 tablets, telling him: 'I can't know what these are for." He had also prescribed 50 Seconal tablets for the deceased.

In a letter published in the *Globe and Mail* shortly after his conviction, a psychiatrist at a hospital HIV clinic referred to a 'deep therapeutic nihilism" that had prompted Dr. Genereux to respond to his patients' sense of hopelessness by prescribing lethal drugs. As he explained:

> In my and my colleague's experience, suicidal ideation in the presence of HIV infection is most often an expression of a desire for a sense of control in the face of an uncontrollable life circumstance.[71]

In his view, the appropriate response to a patient's plea for suicide pills is to acknowledge the patient's despair and assure him of support for his treatment choices, including the right to refuse life-prolonging treatment —that this is the prescription to restore his sense of control. In contrast, 'Dr. Genereux's practices are cowardly and speak to a lack of fortitude in the face of a horrible epidemic."[72]

Three months after his conviction, Dr. Genereux was stripped of his medical licence by a disciplinary committee of the Ontario College of Physicians and Surgeons. He pleaded guilty before the committee to four counts of unprofessional conduct, including improperly prescribing drugs and engaging in what the Committee described as actions 'that would reasonably be regarded by members as disgraceful, dishonourable, and unprofessional."

Although prosecutions under section 241(b) are extremely rare, there is evidence that desperate people have been helped by physicians to commit suicide. A criminologist has documented 37 cases of aiding suicide in the Vancouver AIDS community, in which some (number not specified) of the aiders were physicians.[73] A Vancouver AIDS support group was not surprised by his findings and suggested that in B.C. between 10% and 20% of the deaths of persons with AIDS are the result of assisted suicide. Moreover, there have been anecdotal reports of physicians in other parts of Canada likewise assisting persons with AIDS and other diseases to commit suicide.

(Also recall the San Francisco study in which 53% of 118 respondents acknowledged assisting the suicide of AIDS patients.)

NOTES

1. **Toronto Star**, November 18, 1994, at A5.
2. *Ibid.*
3. B. Sneiderman, Mercy killing an old debate. **Winnipeg Free Press**, January 31, 1998, at A13.
4. **The News Magazine**, October 19, 1998.
5. *R. v. Latimer* (1997), [1997] S.J. No. 701, 1997 CarswellSask 680 (Q.B.).
6. *R. v. Latimer* (2001), 39 C.R. (5th) 1 (S.C.C.). See B. Sneiderman, Latimer in the Supreme Court: Necessity, compassionate homicide, and mandatory sentencing. 62 **Saskatchewan Law Review** 511-44 (2001).
7. **Halifax Chronicle Herald**, Dec. 24, 1994, p. A1.
8. **Winnipeg Free Press**, March 3, 1995, p. A9.
9. **Toronto Star**, April 9, 1995, p. A3.
10. D. Paciocco, **Getting Away With Murder: The Canadian criminal Justice System** (Irwin Law, Toronto, 1999), at 55.
11. **Toronto Globe and Mail**, March 21, 2000, at A3; **Winnipeg Free Press**, February 21, 2002, at B4.
12. E.W. Keyserlingk, Nontreatment in the best interests of the child. 32 **McGill Law Journal** 416-7 (1989).
13. **Toronto Star**, October 15, 1994, at A1.
14. **Montreal Gazette**, June 19, 1992, at A3.
15. **Toronto Star**, April 3, 1993, at A3.
16. B. Sneiderman & R. Deutscher, Dr. Nancy Morrison and her dying patient: a case of medical necessity. 10 **Health Law Journal** 1 (2002).
17. S. Chater et al., Sedation for intractable distress in the dying — a survey of experts. 12 **Palliative Medicine** 255 (1998).
18. L. Lo & R.C. Coleman, Exceptionally high narcotic analgesic requirements in a terminally ill cancer patient. 5 **Clinical Pharmacy** 28 (1986).
19. S. Bedford, **The Trial of Dr. Adams**. (Simon & Shuster, New York,1958).
20. Legal Correspondent, Dr. Leonard Arthur: his trial and its implications. 283 **British Medical Journal** 1340 (1982).
21. I. Kennedy, Reflections on the Arthur trial. **New Society**, January 1982, at 14.
22. **London Sunday Telegraph**, September 20, 1992, at 1.
23. A. Arlidge, The trial of Dr. David Moor. [2000] **Criminal Law Review** 31. J. Gross, A postscript to the trial of Dr. David Moor. [2000] **Criminal Law Review** 568.
24. **New York Times**, December 29, 1949, at 1; January 2, 1950, at 25; February 24, 1950, at 1; March 2, 1950, at 5; March 7, 1950, at 1, March 8, 1950, at 1; March 10, 1950, at 1.
25. **New York Times**, June 29, 1973, at 1; February 6, 1974, at 1.

26. D. Humphrey & A. Wickett, **The Right to Die** (Harper & Row, New York, 1986), at 14O-2.

27. **Detroit Free Press**, November 10, 1988, at 4A; November 14, 1988, at 3A; November 22, 1988, at 3A; December 3, 1988, at 3A.

28. This case is not reported. Our summary is taken from a detailed account of the case by A Alpers, Criminal act or palliative care? Prosecutions involving the care of the dying. 26 **Journal of Law, Medicine & Ethics** 308 (1998).

29. *State v. Naramore*, 965 P.2d 211 (1998).

30. Royal College of Paediatrics and Child Health. **Withholding or withdrawing life saving treatment in children: a framework for practice**. (London: RCPCH, 1997). Also see, Ethical debate: the distinction between withdrawing life sustaining treatment under the influence of paralysing agents and euthanasia. 323 **British Medical Journal** 388 (2001).

31. A. Meisel & K.L. Cerminara, **The Right to Die** (Aspen Law & Business, New York, 2002 Cumulative Supplement), at 73.

32. **National Post**, April 14, 1999, at A1; Sneiderman B. The zealot who played God. **Winnipeg Free Press**, August 26, 1999, at A13.

33. *Ibid.* (National Post).

34. *U.S. v. Wood*, 207 F.3d 1222 (2000).

35. Manitoba Association of Rights and Liberties. (1995). **Silence doesn't obliterate the truth: a Manitoba survey on physician assisted-suicide and euthanasia**. (Unpublished.)

36. H. Kuhse & P. Singer, Doctors' practices and attitudes regarding voluntary euthanasia. 148 **Medical Journal of Australia** 623 (1988).

37. P. Baume & F. O'Malley, Euthanasia: attitudes and practices of medical practitioners. 181 **Medical Journal of Australia** 137 (1994).

38. C. Douglass, The intention to hasten death: a survey of attitudes and practices of surgeons in Australia. 175 **Medical Journal of Australia** 511-15 (2001).

39. H.J. Ward & P.A. Tate, Attitudes among NHS doctors to requests for euthanasia. 308 **British Medical Journal** 1332 (1994).

40. L.R. Slome, Physician-assisted suicide and patients with human immunodeficiency virus disease. 337 **The New England Journal of Medicine** 417 (1997).

41. D. Meier et al., A national survey of physician-assisted suicide and euthanasia in the United States. 338 **The New England Journal of Medicine** 1193 (1998).

42. D. Asch, The role of critical care nurses in euthanasia and assisted suicide. 334 **The New England Journal of Medicine** 1374 (1996).

43. D.C. Thomasma & G.C. Graber, **Euthanasia: Toward an Ethical Social Policy**. (Continuum Press, New York, 1990), at 147.

44. Law Reform Commission of Canada, Working Paper 28: **Euthanasia, Aiding**

Suicide and Cessation of Treatment (Minister of Supply and Services Canada 1982), at 4840

45. P. Mitchell, **Act of Love**. (Alfred A. Knopf, New York, 1976).

46. *Supra* note 26, at 13-15, 89.

47. Senate Special Committee on Euthanasia and Assisted Suicide **Of Life and Death**. (Minister of Supply and Services Canada, 1995), at 88.

48. R.N. Wennberg, **Terminal Choices: Euthanasia, Suicide and the Right to Die** (B. Eerdman, 1989), at 105.

49. In the *Glucksberg* and *Quill* cases (see Chapter 26), the U.S. Supreme Court likewise approved of the double effect doctrine in the context of pain management.

50. *Supra* note 47, at 32.

51. What about insufficiently aggressive pain control? In a 2001 California case, the family of an 86-year-old patient with chronic lung disease, whose last weeks were spent in acute pain, sued his physician for improper pain management. The jury awarded $1.5 million in damages, which was reduced on appeal to $250 thousand. See *Bergman v. Eden Medical Center* (August 20, 2001), Doc. H205732-1 (U.S. Cal. Super. Ct.).

52. P.S. Huagen, Pain relief for the dying: the unwelcome intervention of the criminal law. 23 **William Mitchell Law Review**, 325, 336 (1997).

53. G. Kolata, When morphine fails to kill. **New York Times**, July 23, 1997, at C7.

54. *Ibid.*

55. R.S. Magnusson. **Angels of Death: Exploring the Euthanasia Underground** (Melbourne University Press, 2002), at 60.

56. http://wwww.ves.org.uk/DpAperCmDE.html. The physician quoted is Dr. Michael Irwin, the chairman of the Voluntary Euthanasia Society in London.

57. M. Schur, **Freud: Living and Dying** (International University Press, New York, 1972). As recounted in: J.D. McCue & L.M. Cohen, Freud's physician-assisted death. 159 **Archives of Internal Medicine** 1521 (1999).

58. Dr. Michael Kissane, in a letter to the editor, 160 **Archives of Internal Medicine** 117 (2000), in response to the McCue & Cohen article. See also: M. Ashby, The fallacies of death causation in palliative care. 166 **Medical Journal of Australia** 176 (1997).

59. *Supra* note 17, at 257-8.

60. *Supra* note 47, at 33.

61. *Supra* note 17.

62. L.A. Hawryluck et al, Consensus guidelines on analgesia and sedation in dying intensive care unit patients. 3 **BMC Medical Ethics** 3 (2002). May be found at: http://www.biomedcentral.com/1472-6939/3/3 .

63. **The National Post**, Sept. 16, 2002, at A5. Aside from the *Morrison* case, a reason for focusing on the intensive care setting is provided by Dr. Mike

Harlos, director of palliative care for the Winnipeg Regional Health Authority: "In palliative care scenarios, end of life circumstances generally unfold more gradually, and there is time to titrate medications and to comfort and discuss with families. There is less risk than in the ICU of conveying the impression that you are somehow causing or hastening death." (Personal communication)

64. See the **Associated Press Newswires** for June 29, 2001, and the following dates in 2002: March 4, Nov. 3, Nov. 19, and Nov. 22.

65. *Rodriguez v. British Columbia (Attorney General)*, [1993] 3 S.C.R. 519.

66 T.E. Quill, Death and dignity: a case of individualized decision-making. 324 **New England Journal of Medicine** 691 (1991).

67. T.E. Quill, Care of the hopelessly ill: potential clinical criteria for physician-assisted suicide. 327 **New England Journal of Medicine** 1380 (1992).

68. *R. (on the application of Pretty) v. Director of Public Prosecutions*, November 2001.

69. Assisted suicide case rejected by European court. **Associated Press**, April 29, 2002.

70. **The Globe and Mail**, December 23, 1997, at A1.

71. *Ibid.*, December 31, 1997, at A22.

72. *Ibid.*

73. R. Ogden, **Euthanasia, Assisted Suicide & AIDS** (Peroglyphic Publishing, New Westminster, 1994).

26

EUTHANASIA/ASSISTED SUICIDE: AMERICAN AND DUTCH DEVELOPMENTS

SUMMARY

This chapter is for the reader whose interest in the subject of euthanasia/assisted suicide is not confined to a Canadian context. In any event, we think that a broader perspective is helpful to Canadians who ponder the issue of legalization because developments in other jurisdictions, particularly the Netherlands, are relevant to the formulation of Canadian public policy on these contentious issues. The career of "Dr. Death", Jack Kevorkian, is surveyed because the issue of physician-assisted suicide is invariably linked to the controversial Michigan pathologist who was involved in 130 such cases. In 1997 physician-assisted suicide was legalized in Oregon and we survey the data on its practice. That same year the United States Supreme Court ruled in two companion cases (decided at the same time) that it is not unconstitutional for a state to ban assisted suicide. The cases are summarized. Finally, the Dutch experience is examined in some detail.

1. DEVELOPMENTS IN THE UNITED STATES

(a) The Assisted Suicide Cases of Dr. Kevorkian

In 1990, Janet Adkins, a 54-year-old schoolteacher in the early stages of Alzheimer's disease, killed herself by activating a suicide contraption placed at her disposal in the Volkswagen van of a 62-year-old retired Michigan pathologist, Dr. Jack Kevorkian. The device — which he called a "mercitron" — consisted of a frame holding three chemical solutions feeding into a common intravenous line, which was controlled by a switch and a timer. After shaking the bottles to ensure a correct flow, he started an intravenous line of saline solution. At his direction, Adkins then switched the saline to an anaesthetic (thiopental), which activated the timer that released a lethal dose of potassium chloride.[1]

Dr. Kevorkian committed no crime, because then there was no law in Michigan prohibiting the act of assisted suicide. Although about a dozen other states have not defined the specific crime of aiding/abetting suicide, they deem the act subject to prosecution as either negligent homicide or manslaughter. However, the Michigan Supreme Court had ruled in a 1968 case that "the term suicide excludes by definition a homicide."[2] In other words, there now was a gap in the law and into that gap strode Dr. Kevorkian. In August 1993 he recorded his 20th case of assisted suicide when Thomas Hyde, a 30-year-old landscaper in the advanced stages of amyotrophic lateral sclerosis (ALS), ended his life in Kevorkian's van. Kevorkian strapped a mask over his nose and mouth that connected to a tank of carbon monoxide, whereupon Hyde switched on a mechanism that started the gas flowing. Kevorkian's technique had changed not only because a court injunction had prohibited the use of his "suicide machine" but also because the removal of his medical licence in 1991 had deprived him of access to prescription drugs.

By the time of Hyde's death, Kevorkian's notoriety had prompted the state legislature to criminalize the act of assisted suicide, and he was accordingly charged with the offence. Although it was an open-and-shut case, the jury acquitted Kevorkian, whose most effective witness was Thomas Hyde. Several jurors were moved to tears as they watched a videotape in which Hyde, barely able to swallow, spent agonizing minutes choking out the words: "I want to end it. I want to die."[3] (Following the advice of his lawyer, Kevorkian videotaped the interviews in all his assisted suicide cases.)

Kevorkian was prosecuted twice more but acquitted both times, at which point the state threw in the towel in the belief that no jury would convict him. All told, he assisted about 130 desperate persons who flocked to his door to commit suicide under his guiding hand; but his bizarre career came to a dramatic end with the Youk case, which resulted in his conviction for murder and imprisonment.*

It must be stressed that there is a sense in which the cases of Dr. Kevorkian do not fall under the heading of physician-assisted suicide. For one thing, Kevorkian — who as a pathologist never dealt with live patients — retired in 1982 and as noted was stripped of his state medical licence in 1991. Furthermore, those who sought out his services were never his patients. After contacting him, they showed up at his doorstep with medical

---

* The *Youk* case is discussed in Chapter 25.

records in hand; and after reviewing the records he chatted with them over coffee, had them declare their intentions on videotape, and then made arrangements for rendezvous in his dilapidated Volkswagen van. Although Kevorkian's notoriety helped fuel the debate on physician-assisted suicide, those who lobby for legalization came to regard the acid-tongued "Dr. Death" as a hindrance to their cause. As Dr. Timothy Quill, an ardent proponent of legalization, pointed out when Kevorkian's crusade was in midstream: "Suicide is the sole basis of the relationship he has with his patients [*sic*], and that is frightening."[4] That it true enough, but around that time Quill also condemned his all too quick rush to judgment that he had the only answer for those who sought him out:

> He is a retired pathologist and not a clinician. He therefore does not have the knowledge and experience to ensure that all alternative medical approaches to achieving patient comfort have been exhausted, or that the patient's request for death is not distorted by depression.... He has shown little interest in working with or learning from dying patients who are finding alternatives to suicide. He has not thoroughly reviewed all available information about the irreversibility of each patient's illness, not the extent to which comfort measures had been tried and failed. He has assisted patients whose medical conditions have potential for considerable ambiguity and uncertainty, even for experts.[5]

(b) Physician-Assisted Suicide and the U.S. Supreme Court

Four years after the Supreme Court of Canada decided the case of *Rodriguez v. British Columbia (Attorney General)*, it was the turn of the Supreme Court of the United States to consider whether there was a constitutional right to physician-assisted suicide.* In the 1997 companion cases of *Washington v. Glucksberg* and *Vacco v. Quill* (the same Dr. Quill),[6] the Court dealt with challenges to the prohibition against assisted suicide in the Washington and New York penal codes. Whereas the Canadian justices upheld the law by the narrowest of margins, 5-4, all nine of their American counterparts did so.

In *Glucksberg*, the Court proclaimed that there was no fundamental right or liberty interest in physician-assisted suicide based upon the due process clause in the 14th Amendment — that no state shall "deprive any

---

* *Rodriguez* is discussed in the previous chapter.

person of...liberty...without due process of law."* There is of course no absolute right to liberty, and the issue in both *Rodriguez* and *Glucksberg* was whether the state could deny a person's liberty interest in seeking help to commit suicide. Like Justice Sopinka in *Rodriquez*, Chief Justice Rhenquist in *Glucksberg* stressed that the legalization of assisted suicide would place vulnerable groups (the elderly, poor, and disabled) at risk of being pressured to opt for a quicker and less expensive alternative to continued medical and comfort care.

In *Quill*, the Court ruled that the New York ban did not breach the 14th Amendment's equal protection clause — that no state shall "deny to any person...the equal protection of the laws."** The Court rejected the argument that because a patient on life-support had the right to demand its cessation, a patient not on life-support was deprived of equal protection because the law prohibited the acceleration of death by way of lethal drugs furnished by a physician. In so ruling, the Court affirmed the distinction between active and passive means of death has long been recognized in both law and medicine. And it went out of its way to endorse the double effect doctrine:

> It is widely recognized that the provision of pain medication is ethically and professionally acceptable even when the treatment may hasten the patient's death, if the medication is intended to alleviate pain and severe discomfort, not to cause death.

In the result, the Court was at pains to explain that it was only deciding that it was constitutionally permissible for a state to ban physician-assisted suicide; and therefore that individual states were at liberty to legalize the practice, so long as accompanied by safeguards strict enough to withstand constitutional scrutiny. Four months after the *Glucksberg* and *Vacco* rulings physician-assisted suicide was legalized by the voters of Oregon, and we turn now to the workings of a law that is found nowhere else in the common law world. (It is true that in 1996 the parliament of the Northern Territory of Australia, the country's most sparsely populated region, legalized assisted suicide/euthanasia by a 15-10 vote. The law permitted mentally competent terminally ill adults to make written application for physician-assisted death — either by lethal injection or aided suicide. However, nine months after its enactment, the law was repealed by Australia's national

---

*   The Canadian parallel is found in section 7 of the *Charter*: "Everyone has the right to...liberty...and the right not to be deprived thereof except in accordance with the principles of fundamental justice".

**   The Canadian parallel is found in section 15 of the *Charter*: "Every individual is equal before and under the law and has the right to the equal protection and equal benefit of the law...."

parliament. During its brief life, four people who were terminally ill with cancer committed suicide with medical help.[7])

(c) Physician-Assisted Suicide in Oregon

Since October 1997, the Oregon Death With Dignity Act has allowed physicians to give prescriptions for self-administered lethal drugs to terminally ill adult residents of the state.[8] Terminal illness is defined as "an incurable and irreversible disease that has been medically confirmed and will, within reasonable medical judgment, produce death within six months." However, physicians are prohibited from directly administering the drugs. In short, the Act legalizes physician-assisted suicide but euthanasia — mercy-killing whether by physician or layperson — is still murder.

To qualify for "medication for the purpose of ending his or her life", the patient must sign a request that "shall be in substantially the following form":

I, _____, am an adult of sound mind.

I am suffering from _____, which my attending physician has determined is a terminal disease and which has been medically confirmed by a consulting physician.

I have been fully informed of my diagnosis, prognosis, the nature of medication to be prescribed and potential associated risks, the expected result, and the feasible alternatives, including comfort care, hospice care and pain control.

I request that my attending physician prescribe medication that will end my life in a humane and dignified manner.

I understand that I have the right to rescind this request at any time.

I understand the full import of this request and I expect to die when I take the medication to be prescribed.

I make this request voluntarily and without reservation, and I accept the full moral responsibility for my actions.

If the patient has family, the form must indicate whether the family has been informed of the decision. The form must be signed by two witnesses who attest that the patient "appears to be of sound mind and not under duress, fraud or undue influence." At least one witness cannot be a relative (by blood, marriage or adoption) of the patient nor a beneficiary of the patient's estate.

The form must be proceeded by two oral requests, and the patient cannot obtain the prescription until at least 15 days after the initial oral request. The form must be submitted 48 hours before the prescription is written.

No physician is obliged to honour a request for assisted suicide (a so-called conscience clause), but in that event there is a duty to transfer the patient's medical records to another physician at the patient's request. It is for the physician to decide whether to be present when the patient commits suicide. The physician is immune from criminal/civil liability and professional disciplinary action so long as the law's provisions are scrupulously adhered to. The responsibilities of the physician prepared to comply are as follows:

1. Determine whether the patient is terminally ill, whether the patient is "capable" (defined as "the ability to make and communicate health care decisions"), and whether the request is voluntary.
2. Inform the patient of the diagnosis, the prognosis, and "feasible alternatives", including comfort and hospice care and pain control.
3. Refer the patient to a medical consultant for confirmation of the diagnosis and that the patient is "capable" and acting voluntarily.
4. Ask the patient to notify next-of-kin, although the request cannot be denied solely because the patient refuses to comply.
5. Advise the patient that the request can be rescinded at any time.
6. A patient must be referred for counselling if the attending or consulting physician has reason to suspect that the patient "may be suffering from a psychiatric or psychological disorder, or depression causing impaired judgment." The lethal medication cannot be provided until the "person performing the counselling" determines that the patient is not suffering from these conditions.
7. Immediately before writing the prescription verify that the patient is making an informed decision.

There is a notification procedure requiring physicians to forward detailed documentation of each such case to the state health department, which is directed to release annual statistical reports of assisted-suicide cases.

In 1998 the statute was supplemented by a guidebook for physicians prepared by the Task Force to Improve the Care of Terminally Ill Oregonians.[9] A brief summary of the guidebook (usually referred to as the Guidelines) is as follows:

It is not for the physician but rather for the patient to initiate a discussion about assisted suicide (albeit the Act does not prohibit a health caregiver from doing so). Once there is a request, the physician must engage in a thorough discussion with the patient and seek to determine whether the patient is motivated by fear of pain or fear of becoming a burden to family. In either case, the physician must see whether the pain can be managed or the burden eased. The physician should also try to learn whether financial factors explain the request. The physician should encourage the patient to involve family members in the discussion but must respect the patient's refusal to do so. The physician should arrange for a clinical psychologist or psychiatrist to determine the capacity of the patient to decide upon assisted suicide. (Although the Act does not mandate a mental health consult, the Guidelines recognize that attending physicians are often unable to assess competency.) It is suggested that the consultant come from outside the physician's "practice community" in order to guard against conflict of interest. And the consultant must review the medical record and examine the patient. The authors of a critique of the Guidelines have observed:

> Because these are voluntary Guidelines, there is no specific penalty for doctors who cannot afford their patients this kind of intimate discussion. Nevertheless, the Guidelines spell out an ethical responsibility that seems to expand a doctor's traditional role in care of the dying. To the extent that this guideline raises the awareness of doctors about the importance of open communication, it may add to the impact of the Act on the overall quality of care for terminally ill patients.[10]

In February 1999 a special report, "Legalized physician-assisted suicide in Oregon: the first year's experience", appeared in the New England Journal of Medicine (NEJM).[11] In the calendar year 1998, the Oregon Health Division was notified that 23 persons had received prescriptions for lethal drugs. By year's end, 15 had died from ingesting the drugs; six had succumbed to their underlying diseases; and two were still alive. Thirteen of the 15 had terminal cancer (lung, ovarian, and breast cancer accounted for nine of the cases). Their median age was 69 years; eight were male and all were white. The first to die was an 84-year-old woman with breast cancer whose life expectancy was estimated at two months. She ingested a lethal doses of barbiturates mixed with syrup and washed it down with brandy. She lost consciousness after five minutes and "died a half hour later, very peacefully."[12]

The patients were no different from controls with respect to sex, race, urban or rural residence, level of education, health insurance coverage, and hospice enrolment. However, they were more likely than the controls to express concern about loss of autonomy and control of bodily functions. As the report notes:

> Many physicians reported that their patients had been decisive and independent throughout their lives or that the decision to request a lethal prescription was consistent with a long-standing belief about the importance of controlling the manner in which they died. Thus, the decision to request and use a

prescription for lethal medications...was associated with views on autonomy and control, not with fear of intractable pain or concern about financial loss.

Some of the physicians who assisted suicide were emotionally drained by the experience, reporting such remarks as: "It was an excruciating thing to do...it made me rethink life's priorities." "This was really hard on me, especially being there when he took the pills."

In February 2000 the NEJM issued a report on the second year of the Oregon experience with assisted suicide.[13] The data for 1999 were substantially similar to 1998. Of the 33 with prescriptions, 26 died from ingesting the drugs, five died from their underlying diseases, and two were alive at year's end. All but one of the 26 was white and 10 were male. One other patient died by lethal drugs in 1999 who had gotten his prescription the previous year. The median age of the 27 patients was 71 years — 17 had cancer, four had amyotrophic lateral sclerosis (ALS), and four had chronic obstructive pulmonary disease (COPD). They were similar to the patients dying the previous year in terms of demographic characteristics, underlying diseases, use of hospice care, and health insurance coverage. (All had health insurance and 21 were receiving hospice care.) According to their physicians and families, the requests for assisted suicide were prompted by such factors as: loss of autonomy, loss of control of bodily functions, and a determination to control the manner and timing of death. Of the 26 patients for whom data was available, only 8 received the prescription from the first physician asked. Of the remaining 18, 10 had to ask a second physician and the other eight had to ask two or three.

The data for 2000 closely parallel the 1999 data.[14] There were 27 deaths by assisted suicide (the same number as the previous year). The median age was 69, all but one were white, 12 were male, and 18 were married. Twenty-one had cancer and two had ALS.

The data for 2001 show only 21 patient deaths.[15] The median age was 68, all but one were white, eight were male, and 18 had cancer.

In sum, from 1998 through 2001 physicians reported assisting 90 patients to commit suicide.* The most frequent underlying disease was lung cancer, which accounted for 17 of the cases. There were also five or more cases of the following cancers: breast (nine), pancreas (seven), prostate (six), ovarian (six) and colon (five). In most cases the death-dealing drug was secobarbital, while in others it was pentobarbital (each accompanied by an antiemetic agent).

---

* Although the NEJM has reported 91 deaths from 1998-2001, I calculate the number as 90. It seems that the patient who got the prescription in 1998 but didn't take it until 1999 was counted for both years.

Recall that pain was not amongst the factors mentioned by physicians and families as prompting pleas for assisted suicide. That may be because pain control is a top priority item in the state; per capita consumption of morphine is higher in Oregon than in any other state. Physicians in Oregon are improving their knowledge of palliative care and referring more patients for hospice care. Hospice deaths as a percentage of total deaths increased from 21% in 1993 to 36% in 2000, whereas the figure for the entire United States in 2000 was only 25%. As noted in a health policy report published in the NEJM in 2002:

> In Oregon, substantive palliative interventions, such as control of pain and other symptoms, referral to a hospice program, consultation with another physician, or a trial of antidepressant medication, led about half the patients who were considering assisted suicide to change their minds.[16]

In addition, studies by the Oregon Health Department (OHD) suggest that fears that poverty and the lack of health insurance would fuel requests for assisted suicide are unfounded. As one commentator has written:

> Although these results are based on a relatively small number of patients, and ongoing supervision is needed, these findings suggest the conclusion that PAS (physician-assisted suicide) will not be disproportionately chosen by or forced on unwilling, uneducated, and/or socially and economically disadvantaged individuals. Judging from the reported motivations of the patients...PAS seems to be associated more with the desire for autonomy and control than with fear of intolerable suffering or devastating financial consequences.[17]

A study of Oregon nurses and social workers involved with hospice patients confirms that autonomy and control are indeed the primary factors prompting requests for assisted suicide.[18] Researchers mailed a survey to 545 eligible nurses and social workers, of whom 397 (73%) responded. The survey was prompted by the fact that hospice patients constituted 78% of assisted suicide deaths from 1998-2001. The respondents reported that the primary reasons of their patients' decisions were a desire to control the circumstances of one's death, a readiness for death, and the wish to die at home. According to Dr. Linda Ganzini, the study's lead author:

> Patients make the choice to request assisted suicide because they want to control the timing and manner of their death. It's surprising how we found so little variation with regard to this characteristic, almost as if the nurses and social workers were all seeing the same patient.

Still, aside from philosophical opponents of physician-assisted suicide, there are critics who question the workings of the law. The most prominent critics are Dr. Herbert Hendin, the director of the American

Foundation for Suicide Prevention, and Dr. Kathleen Foley, a neurologist and palliative care specialist at the Memorial Sloan-Kettering Cancer Center in New York City. Amongst their concerns are the following. Training in palliative care is not required of physicians who assist suicide. And without such training they cannot offer effective alternatives to suicide. Nor are they required to find a consultant knowledgable about palliative care options. Furthermore, most lack the expertise to assess mental competency and need only seek a mental health consultant when they deem it necessary (and without the expertise they will only know when to consult in the obvious cases). Although required to report their cases to the OHD, they need not explain how they made the diagnosis or prognosis. The last noted deficiency in the law prompted them to comment:

> The missing information is particularly essential since under the Oregon statute a diagnosis of a terminal illness and a prognosis of six months to live are the sine qua non of assisted suicide. A monitoring process that does not inquire how they are determined is no monitoring process at all.[19]

Some of the most impassioned opponents of physician-assisted suicide are members of the U.S. Congress, and they have sought to render the Act a nullity. Their goal is a statute that would provide that any physician who prescribes controlled substances for the purpose of hastening death — with the proviso that this does not apply to so-called double effect cases — commits a federal offence. (Note that the U.S. Controlled Substances Act controls the authorized distribution of barbiturates and narcotics.) Bills to that effect have been introduced but have not become law. But then the executive branch of government stepped in. In November 1991 U.S. Attorney General John Ashcroft authorized the Drug Enforcement Administration to take action against Oregon physicians prescribing lethal drugs for a terminally ill patient.[20] Even if the physician were acting under Oregon law, his license to prescribe controlled substances could thereby be revoked. In his view the Oregon law violated the Controlled Substances Act because assisting suicide was not reasonable medical practice. Yet Ashcroft was quick to reassure physicians that his ruling would not interfere with palliative care management because, as he saw it, a clear distinction could be drawn between controlling pain and assisted suicide. Yet many physicians thought otherwise, and the following concern was voiced in the NEJM:

> If his ruling is upheld, physicians will have to decide whether they should alter their prescribing practices. Some may believe that no clear distinction can be made between good practice and potentially illegal prescribing, or that

even if the distinction could be made, federal drug agents might not make it.[21]

Two weeks after Ashcroft's order, a federal judge issued a temporary restraining order at the behest of the Oregon attorney general. On April 17, 2002, a judge of the U.S. District Court in Portland ruled that Ashcroft had no legal authority for his directive. Judge Jones scolded Ashcroft for attempting "to stifle an ongoing, earnest and profound debate in the various states concerning physician-assisted suicide", and that "with no advance warning...he fired the first shot in the battle between the state of Oregon and the federal government."[22] The battle continues because Ashcroft promptly announced his intention to appeal the District Court ruling.*

2. EUTHANASIA/ASSISTED SUICIDE IN THE NETHERLANDS

(a) The Law

When the parliament of the Netherlands legalized "euthanasia" in 2001, the media made much of the event. Yet this was not a signal that the country was embarking upon a radically new policy. That was because the judiciary had already given Dutch physicians the green light to perform euthanasia as far back as 1984. Furthermore, the Dutch approach links both lethal injection and assisted suicide cases, which explains why Dutch commentators have taken to use the acronym *EAS* — euthanasia and assisted suicide — as a shorthand description of the policy in their English language publications. In that regard, any reference to euthanasia in the Dutch literature (and in the following commentary) should be taken to encompass physician-assisted suicide as well. We begin with a review of the history of judicially-sanctioned *EAS* in the Netherlands.

As in Canada, the *Dutch Penal Code* contains provisions that prohibit the act of aiding suicide (*article 293*) and that disallow the consent of the deceased as a defence to a homicide charge (*article 294*). However, in the 1984 *Schoonheim* case the Supreme Court of the Netherlands (hereinafter called the *High Court***) carved out an exception for physicians acting pursuant to prescribed guidelines. In crafting its ruling in that case, the High Court was in effect acting in concert with the Royal Dutch Medical Association (KNMG). Earlier that year the KNMG's Executive Committee had issued a position paper titled "Vision on Euthanasia," which called for the legal recognition of circumstances under which physicians would be

---

* As of this writing (February 2003), the appeal has yet to be heard.
** We use the term High Court because that is its official name.

allowed to circumvent these Penal Code provisions. As it happened, the guidelines stipulated by the High Court in *Schoonheim* are modeled along the lines of the KNMG's proposal."[23] The current Dutch policy is thus the result of a collaborative effort by the legal and medical establishments to empower physicians to engage in EAS.

In its position paper, the KNMG had expressed the view that in terms of public policy "it makes no difference whether the lethal medicine is administered directly by the physician or that a physician assists the patient in administering it himself." If the former is acceptable then so is the latter, since there is no moral distinction between these two means whereby the physician responds to the mentally competent patient's plea for a drug-induced death. According to the position paper, the resort to euthanasia does not breach the code of medical ethics provided that the following conditions are satisfied:

1. It must be the voluntary choice of a mentally competent patient whose desire for death is "consistent, durable and well considered." The caveat is that the patient have "a clear picture of his medical situation and the appropriate prognosis."
2. The patient's request cannot be granted unless he is experiencing "unacceptable and hopeless suffering that cannot be rendered bearable." By unbearable suffering, the report means either "unbearable physical pain" or "unbearable mental suffering as a result of a physical disorder."
3. Since the focus is upon a compassionate response to unbearable and irremediable suffering that causes the patient to prefer death to life, it is unduly restrictive to insist that the patient be terminally ill.
4. The physician cannot act on his own but must consult with an experienced and independent colleague, who must confirm his judgment that the euthanasia criteria have been fulfilled in the particular case.

As noted, within the year the High Court followed suit with its landmark *Schoonheim* decision.[24] The case had arisen in 1982 when the accused-physician had complied with the repeated plea of his 95-year-old nursing home patient for a lethal injection. The patient had experienced a steady physical deterioration such that she was bedridden (unable even to sit up), incontinent, progressively losing vision and hearing, and finding it "difficult to drink and impossible to eat." She was, however, "fully alert and completely lucid." She repeatedly begged Dr. Schoonheim to end her life, which he agreed to do but only after lengthy discussion with the patient, her son, and another physician. In bidding farewell to her son and daughter-in-law, the patient expressed her gratitude to Dr. Schoonheim and urged them to "always honour this doctor." He then injected diazepam and thiopental, followed minutes later by an injection of curare — a muscle relaxant that caused her to stop breathing.

Dr. Schoonheim was acquitted, but the ruling was overturned by the Amsterdam Court of Appeal. The High Court in turn reversed that decision for its failure to consider whether the accused had acted in circumstances sufficient to establish a defence under article 40 of the Dutch Penal Code, which states that: It is a defence to a criminal charge if the accused was forced by *overmacht* to commit an offence. (The term *overmacht* translates literally as overpowering force.)

According to Dutch case law, the defence envisions a situation of urgency in which the accused is driven by her conscience to commit an offence which amounts to a lesser evil than would have ensued had she permitted events to run their course. It is in effect "a back to the wall" defence; the accused makes the deliberate moral choice to break the law because the force of circumstances precludes delaying action. However, the defence is not allowable if there was a reasonably available option whereby the accused could have avoided the commission of the offence. Overmacht is, therefore, the Dutch analogue to the common law defence of necessity, which likewise requires that the accused be driven by desperation to commit an offence as the only way to prevent a greater harm. The Dutch courts also use the term *force majeure*, which conveys the same meaning as overmacht.

In *Schoonheim*, the High Court ruled that the accused's duty to comply with the law could be overborne by his conflicting duty to end the life of a consenting patient whose unbearable suffering could not otherwise be alleviated. The issue was whether Dr. Schoonheim had been confronted with an emergency situation "according to responsible medical judgment, tested by norms of medical ethics." It was therefore necessary to consider: (1) whether, according to professional medical judgment, it was likely that his patient would experience increasing disfigurement of her personality and/or a worsening of her already unendurable suffering; (2) whether the spectre of further deterioration made it necessary for Dr. Schoonheim to act when he did in order to enable the patient to "die with dignity"; and (3) whether there were less drastic means to ease her suffering.

The High Court accordingly sent the case back for reconsideration. In subsequent proceedings all the medical witnesses supported Dr. Schoonheim's action and the charge was consequently dismissed by the Public Prosecutor. Furthermore, by omitting to stipulate that the euthanasia candidate must be in the so-called "terminal phase," the Court was in effect endorsing the KNMG's position that euthanasia not be restricted to the terminally ill. In any event, in 1986 the High Court specifically ruled that euthanasia was permissible to relieve the "dire distress" of a non-terminal 73-year-old patient severely incapacitated by multiple sclerosis.[25]

The decision in the 1986 case was in accord with the definition of "unbearable suffering" (as a criterion for euthanasia) as provided in the KNMG's 1984 position paper — as either "unbearable physical pain" or "unbearable mental suffering as a result of a physical disorder." On the other hand, in 1993 a committee of the KNMG released a position paper on "assisted suicide of psychiatric patients", in which it gave cautious endorsement to helping such patients die even when the mental suffering was not linked to physical disorder. According to the position paper, the crux of the matter is the state of mind of the patient. The issue is particularly complex in psychiatric cases, as the wish may stem from a disorder (e.g. depression or psychosis) that is treatable in the individual case. If, however, the patient's psychiatric disorder is not amenable to treatment, the physician must then determine whether the patient is mentally competent and whether the wish to die is persistent, voluntary, and well-considered. Of course, the physician must understand the source of the patient's suffering because otherwise he/she cannot consider alternative measures.

Still, with regard to the criterion of unbearable suffering, the paper stressed that what counted was the suffering itself, not whether it stemmed from a somatic or psychological condition. In short, the issue was whether the patient's affliction — whatever its source — could be alleviated. (It should be noted that a position paper expressing the same view had been released the previous year by the Netherlands Association of Psychiatry.)

Once again the law responded in kind to the public policy of the medical establishment, when in 1994 the High Court ruled in the *Chabot* case that a physician could assist the suicide of a mentally competent patient whose irremediable suffering was not grounded in a physical disease process.[26] Although the Court ruled in principle that physician-assisted suicide was allowable in non-somatic cases, it concluded that Dr. Chabot was guilty of the Penal Code offence of assisted suicide because he had failed to ensure that his patient was seen personally by at least one of his consultants. He was not sentenced to prison, however, as the Court exercised its discretion to impose no punishment at all. Still, in *Chabot* the High Court established the precedent that a patient who was not physically diseased could qualify for physician-assisted suicide.

The pertinent facts of the *Chabot* case are as follows. Hilly Bosscher was a divorced 50-year-old social worker whose two sons were the pride of her life. The elder went into the army, and at the age of 20 committed suicide after a broken love affair. She was devastated by his death, but managed to get on with her life, drawing comfort from her relationship with her second son. About four years later, he was stricken with cancer. She quit work to devote herself to his care, and on the day he died (also at the age of 20) she attempted suicide.

After a second attempt to take her life, she wound up entering into a contract with Dr. Boudewijn Chabot, a psychiatrist with extensive experience in treating suicidal patients. He would attempt to persuade her to alter her bleak outlook, and if he could not he would take her request for suicide under advisement. After 30 sessions over a seven-week period, she informed him that he had failed to change her mind and that the time had come for him to fulfil his part of the bargain. He responded by sending detailed notes of all their sessions to seven experienced colleagues, all of whom agreed that it was a hopeless case. One did suggest that Dr. Chabot urge her to continue their dialogue, although he could offer no grounds to think that anything he said could persuade her to change her mind. They all agreed with his assessment that, although she was profoundly unhappy she was not clinically depressed, but none of the seven thought it necessary to interview the patient. Soon thereafter, Hilly Bosscher died at home after ingesting lethal drugs provided by the psychiatrist. Dr. Chabot was emphatic that in his 25 years of practice, he had never come across a patient with such a fixed determination to die. Her day-to-day existence had become a living hell, and he never saw even a glimmer of hope that she could turn her life around. Her plight was, he said, a case of "existential suffering."

The *Chabot* ruling prompted critics of the Dutch euthanasia policy to invoke the spectre of the slippery slope: that a precedent involving a dying 95-year-old patient was inevitably bound to lead to a physically healthy patient who wished to die simply because of profound unhappiness. On the other hand, there are those who respond that the ruling is the logical outcome of a policy grounded in patient autonomy and beneficence — that it is illogical to restrict unbearable/irremediable suffering to that which is traceable to a physiological disease process.

But still, since suffering — like beauty — is in the eye of the beholder, there is no end point to this brand of logic. If unrelieved sorrow over personal tragedy is sufficient warrant for a prescription for death-dealing drugs, then what of the "existential suffering" that can accompany old age even when not linked to ill health? In 2000, six years after the *Chabot* case, a family physician, Dr. Philip Sutorius, assisted the suicide of his 86-year-old patient who was obsessed with his "physical decline" and was experiencing a profound sense of loneliness and emptiness. The patient was aging but was otherwise healthy and had no mental disorder. He had begged Dr. Sutorius to help him die on at least eight occasions before the latter complied. According to the physician:

He longed for the end with all his heart. He experienced life as futile, was unhappy and lonely. There was only emptiness. He no longer wanted it and knew that it would only get worse.[27]

Dr. Sutorius was charged with assisted suicide on the grounds that "tiredness of life" did not fall within the "suffering" component of the mandated EAS guidelines. Although the trial court acquitted, the Amsterdam Appeal Court entered a conviction — but only because the physician should have explored alternative measures to help a patient whose major complaint was simply that he was "tired of life." (What he had done was not considered adequate; he had consulted two physicians, one of whom was a psychiatrist, but neither had anything to offer.) However, the Court imposed no punishment because Dr. Sutorius had acted in "good faith."[28] In essence, then, the Court ruled that in the absence of alternative measures to relieve a patient's distress, assisted suicide is allowable for "life fatigue" that amounts to "unbearable suffering." It is hardly an understatement that this de-medicalization of EAS has profound implications for society generally and particularly for the medical profession. It is noteworthy that when Dr. Sutorius was acquitted the KNMG expressed its disapproval of the result, and it was certainly not pacified by the decision of the Amsterdam Appeal Court. In any event, Dr. Sutorius appealed his conviction to the High Court. The Dutch solicitor general welcomed the appeal, stating that — since the case was tried before the Dutch parliament legalized EAS in 2001 — the High Court should consider whether the law now encompassed cases of "existential suffering."[29]

In December 2002 the High Court released its judgment, not only affirming the conviction and but also in effect discarding the option of alternative measures. (However, the Court left untouched the suspension of punishment.) As it emphatically ruled:

> Medical expertise, by its nature, does not extend to questions and complaints that do not have a sickness — mental or physical — as their source. The law does not state that in the absence of medically classified physical or mental diseases and afflictions — such as being wary of life — euthanasia (or assisted suicide) is permitted.[30]

Given the KNMG's impassioned stance against Dr. Sutorius, it is hardly surprising that the High Court followed suit. As we have seen, since the Schoonheim case in 1984 the High Court has been guided by the KNMG in setting the boundaries of the Dutch EAS policy.

Finally, it must be understood that in a sense nothing substantial has changed with the legalization of EAS by the Dutch parliament. It is still only physicians who can so act, and the guidelines announced by parliament

— that the patient has made a voluntary and carefully considered request, that the patient understand her diagnosis and prognosis, that the physician be satisfied that the patient's suffering is unbearable and without prospect of improvement, that the physician and patient agree that there is no reasonable alternative to EAS, and that a consulting physician must see the patient and confirm these requirements — are in essence simply a reiteration of the judicial safeguards already in place.

(b) The Data — The 1990 Remmelink Commission Study[31]

In 1990 the Dutch government established a committee charged with the task of organizing a comprehensive study of "medical decisions concerning the end of life" (for which the Dutch use the acronym, *MDEL*). The focus was thus not restricted to euthanasia but rather upon decision-making generally in end of life cases. The study followed three avenues of data collection: (1) detailed interviews with 405 physicians — 152 general practitioners, 5 nursing home physicians, and 203 specialists; (2) an analysis of 5,200 completed questionnaires by physicians signing death certificates (from an original stratified sample of 7,000 deaths); and (3) a prospective study in which 80% of the 405 physicians (322) were interviewed on the cause of death of all patients within a six-month period. Physicians were guaranteed immunity from prosecution in order to secure their participation in the study. The results from the three substudies have been combined where possible, weighting the results of the separate substudies. Because the data are from 1990, we learn about MDEL only over the course of that one year; however, a second Remmelink study was conducted five years later (its findings are summarized below).

The study examined three categories of MDEL: non-treatment decisions (NTD); alleviation of pain and symptoms by opioids (APS); and euthanasia and related MDEL – "the prescription, supply or administration of drugs with the explicit intention of shortening life, to include euthanasia at the patient's request, assisted suicide, and life-terminating acts without explicit and persistent request." In short, "related MDEL" refers to cases in which physicians performed euthanasia without strict adherence to the medico-legal criteria.

Of the 128,000 deaths reported in the Netherlands in 1990, about 30% were acute and unexpected. "In the remaining 70% there was enough time to take medical decisions, and in more than half of these cases (54%), a MDEL was taken." Therefore, 38% of all deaths resulted from a medical decision at the end of life (MDEL). The respective shares of that 38% are presented in Table 1.

Table 1: Estimated incidence of medical decisions at the end of life, as percentage of all deaths, per year.

Type of Decision	Best Estimate
Euthanasia	1.8%
Assisted suicide	0.3%
Life-terminating acts with-out explicit request	0.8%
Alleviation of pain and symptoms	17.5%
Non-treatment decisions	17.5%
Total	38.0% (deviation due to rounding)

(i) *Euthanasia/Assisted Suicide*

Of the 2,700 EAS deaths, about 2,300 were by lethal injection and the remainder by assisted suicide. About 70% were performed by the patient's family physician. The study found that there were about 9,000 explicit requests for euthanasia throughout 1990, of which about 30% were granted. "In most cases alternatives are found that make life bearable again, and in some instances the patient dies before any action can be taken."

If there is a typical euthanasia patient profile, it is that of a male patient afflicted with cancer, who resides in the urbanized western part of the country and who dies at a relatively younger age than those whose deaths are not caused by euthanasia. Males account for 52% of all deaths, whereas they constitute 61% of the euthanasia cases. Although only 8% of all deaths happen to those under the age of 50, that age category accounts for 14% of euthanasia deaths. Those between 50-64 account for 13% of all deaths and 24% of euthanasia deaths. And while 42% of all deaths occur to those over 80, they constitute only 25% of the euthanasia deaths. The fact that 68% of euthanasia deaths were cancer-related would help to explain the age differentials. Aside from cancer, major euthanasia disease categories were: cardiovascular disease 9%, pulmonary disease 6%, diseases of the nervous system 2%, and infectious diseases (mostly AIDS) 2%.

What prompts EAS patients to conclude that life is intolerable and that they are better off dead? Physicians who took part in the Remmelink study reported the reasons of 187 patients, of whom 57% mentioned "loss of dignity." "Unworthy dying" and pain were both mentioned in 46% of the cases, but in only 6% was pain the sole reason.

These findings confirm observations by Dutch physicians that what fuels most euthanasia requests is not intractable physical pain but rather "unbearable or senseless suffering." Examples provided by physicians include: shortness of breath caused by tumour in the lung or mouth that leads to slow suffocation, nausea and vomiting that for some cancer patients cannot be alleviated, and the total paralysis experienced by patients afflicted with ALS and multiple sclerosis.

Dutch physicians often comment that patients asking for euthanasia have lost the will to live; and a phrase that crops up in the literature is "the disintegration of personality and the wish to die with no further loss of dignity." Dr. Borst-Eilers, vice-president of the Health Council of The Netherlands, has provided the following euthanasia patient profile:

> The total decay and disintegration of the bodily functions and the certain knowledge that it will become worse cause a sense of slowly losing all dignity and cause the wish to die as soon as possible. Many patients at this stage feel completely prepared for death, and already begin to feel detached from life and from their environment. They have said goodbye to it all and they only long for the end. Every extra day alive means an extra day of unbearable suffering.[32]

(ii) *Life-Terminating Acts Without Explicit Request (LAWER)**

It is this category of about 1,000 cases that has fuelled the controversy on the Dutch euthanasia policy, as well it should since they involved the deliberate administration of lethal drugs in direct breach of the voluntary choice/informed consent guidelines. In Dutch law, these cases — which the Dutch refer to by the acronym *LAWER*, would all fall under the Penal Code heading of murder.

The LAWER cases break down into two categories. In 59%, the patient had at some time during his illness uttered a plea for life-ending measures in the event of unbearable/irremediable suffering, such as by saying: "Doctor, don't let me suffer; you'll know what to do when the time comes." Still, at the time that the physician acted there was no explicit request from the patient, and the physician had taken it upon herself to act because in her judgment the patient was suffering grievously (and usually lapsing in and out of consciousness). In the remaining 41% of LAWER cases, the patient had never spoken to the matter. This latter figure translates into

---

* Under the now dated terminology discussed in Chapter 18, the LAWER cases would fall under the heading, *active Non-voluntary euthanasia.*

about eight cases per week in which a physician had deliberately given drugs to end the life of a patient who had never indicated that he would want his life ended in that fashion.

In most of the LAWER cases, the physician acted only after consulting others: medical colleagues in 66% of cases, nursing staff in 66%, and relatives in 83%. In only 2% did the physician act solely of her own accord. In 86% of the cases, the patient's life was considered to have been shortened by a few hours or days at the most. Most of the patients were mentally incompetent at the time of death; and the one-third who were not incompetent were all suffering grievously and were incapable of verbal communication.

According to an oncologist at the Netherlands Cancer Institute, the provision of narcotics for dying patients may work only at the cost of keeping the patient unconscious (and some patients ask to be kept that way).* From her experience what then happens is the decision to shorten the coma by lethal injection. In her view, a patient-centred reason for LAWER cases is that it is pointless and inhumane to continue the sedation-induced drugs because "the patient will die very slowly with a number of complications unworthy of men." Another reason is to relieve the "heavy burden for the family members who have already had a very hard and exhausting time." As the oncologist admitted: "According to the rules this procedure is not pure euthanasia because the patient did not ask for it, and it is not purely for the relief of pain."[33]

In an article on LAWER cases published in 1993 in the British medical journal, *Lancet*, the Remmelink researchers illustrate the spectrum of such cases with three illustrations, which we summarize as follows.[34] (The second and third cases fall under the 41% category — no indication that the patient had ever discussed the subject of euthanasia.)

(1) The patient, 81, was terminally ill with breast cancer and widespread bone metastases and was being cared for at home, where she wished to remain. Her pain was becoming progressively more difficult to alleviate with opioids, and she had repeatedly told her family physician that "everything should be finished" when her suffering became unbearable. However, she lapsed into unconsciousness before making an explicit request for euthanasia. After discussion with a medical colleague, the home care nurse, and the patient's son, the physician ended her life with a very high dose of morphine. In his estimation, her life was shortened by a week at most.

(2) The patient, 75, had suffered a stroke three years earlier and was admitted to hospital with a basilar artery thrombosis. She was totally par-

---

* See the section on terminal sedation in Chapter 25.

alysed and suffering from bronchitis, which antibiotics failed to relieve. Her consciousness deteriorated rapidly and asphyxia seemed imminent. There were no treatment alternatives nor prospects for improvement. The treating physician discussed the situation with a medical colleague, nurses, and the patient's husband, after which he ended her life with high dosage opiates. In his estimation, her life was shortened by less than 24 hours.

(3) The patient, 64, was permanently unconscious and frequent seizures caused by a brain tumour could not be controlled. There were no treatment alternatives nor prospects for improvement. After discussing the case with a medical colleague, the nurses, and the patient's wife, the treating physician gave the patient an intravenous drip of potassium chloride that ended his life within three minutes. In his estimation, the patient's life was shortened by one to six months.

So what do we make of these cases? Legally they are inexcusable, as they fall outside the prescribed medico-legal criteria. Are they equally deserving of moral condemnation? Do they prove that the spectre of the slippery slope has come to pass: that when euthanasia is legally permitted for the patient who asks for it, then it will inevitably happen that physicians will take it upon themselves to act in cases in which there is no explicit patient request?

It is arguable that there is no clear answer to the first question — that it simply depends upon one's philosophical perspective whether the scenarios illustrated by these LAWER cases are morally justifiable. On the other hand, it seems beyond argument that physicians teeter on a moral tightrope when they act in concert with others to give lethal injections to non-consenting patients on what they regard as humanitarian grounds.

Regarding the second question, it is submitted that the data do not prove that Dutch physicians have interpreted their unique legal privilege as a licence to run amok and to kill non-consenting patients who they believe are better off dead. That is, of course, the contention of proponents of the so-called "slippery slope" — that but for the Dutch euthanasia policy, the LAWER cases would not be happening. Still, the 1,000 cases in which the guidelines were not followed are not necessarily the inevitable spin-off from the policy permitting the 2,700 cases that fall within the guidelines. It may be that the LAWER cases would occur even if euthanasia were not legally tolerated; and it may be that such cases were happening in the era before the Dutch moved to their current policy on euthanasia. Furthermore, there is anecdotal evidence that in jurisdictions where euthanasia is prohibited, LAWER cases also occur. In sum, the case for a cause-and-effect relationship between the Dutch euthanasia and LAWER cases has not been proven.

As noted in the previous chapter, physician surveys in Canada, Australia, England, and the United States indicate that what happens in the Netherlands is happening elsewhere. The surveys lend credence to the sentiment often expressed by Dutch physicians who practice euthanasia that the major difference between them and medical colleagues outside the Netherlands is that they are doing openly what the latter are doing secretly. And if physicians outside the Netherlands are taking "active steps" to end the lives of consenting patients, who can say that they are not taking "active steps" to end the lives of non-consenting patients? There is in fact confirmation of this supposition from a recent Australian study that the authors summarize as follows:

> The proportion of all Australian deaths that involved a medical-end-of-life decision were: euthanasia, 1.8% (including physician-assisted suicide, 0.1%; ending of patient's life without patient's concurrent explicit request, 3.5%.... Overall, Australia had a higher rate of intentional ending of life without the patient's request than the Netherlands.[35]

(iii) *Alleviating Pain and Symptoms (APS)*

As a general rule, APS cases encompass scenarios that trigger the application of the so-called *double effect doctrine*. As explained in the previous chapter, these are cases in which the physician's considered judgment is that the relief of pain necessitates an increase in the dosage of opiates. The physician thereby assumes the risk of shortening life by respiratory arrest. Although death directly attributable to the pain relief is a foreseeable — albeit not relatively certain — outcome, the physician has not acted with the intent to end the patient's life. Her intent is rather to relieve pain, and the foreseeable death of the patient by respiratory arrest is deemed the unintended byproduct of necessary pain control measures. In such cases the physician has acted lawfully. On the other hand, if the physician deliberately injects a lethal dosage then she has crossed the line from APS to euthanasia. In that event, her intent is to kill the patient, and in all common law jurisdictions that intent is defined as the mental state of murder. Her reason for killing — her motive — is to end the patient's pain, but the reason why she killed is legally irrelevant.*

It was found that in 6% of the Dutch APS cases, the physician administered opiates with the express purpose of shortening the patient's life. The Remmelink Commission came up with that figure because, in one of

---

* See Chapter 25. The crucial legal distinction under the double effect doctrine is between the foreseeability that death *might* happen and the foreseeability that death *will* happen. In the former scenario the caregiver acts lawfully; in the latter he commits murder.

its three sub-studies (the physician interviews), 16 respondents indicated that they had acted with such intent; from a statistical standpoint that relatively small number indicates that this finding is not necessarily a reliable estimate of such practice.

Still, the Remmelink researchers were prepared to describe these cases as falling within a "boundary area" overlapping euthanasia and LAWER cases. In other words, these roughly 1,300 cases — 6% of 17.5% of 128,000 cases — should fall under the heading of "euthanasia and related MDEL" because they involved physicians who deliberately gave lethal dosages.* Since the drugs were given at the patient's explicit request in only 15% of the cases, the remaining 85% would fall under the LAWER heading. When one adds these cases to the euthanasia/MDEL category, it means that roughly 5,000 deaths could be attributed to the decision to use drugs to end the patient's life, which amounts to about one in every 25 deaths all told.

The figure of 17.5% APS deaths means that there were roughly 22,000 reputed opiate-related deaths in 1990 (leaving aside an unknown number of the LAWER deaths that were also caused by opiates, as in two of the three *Lancet* case examples). Is that figure abnormally high? One has no way of knowing simply because there are no comparable data elsewhere.

On the other hand, the view has been expressed by both Dutch and Canadian caregivers that there is no way of knowing in any particular APS case that the patient died from an opiate overdose. These were very debilitated patients who may well have died from the disease process, albeit their physicians simply assumed that the dosage was the immediate cause of death. In other words, the patient is near death; the physician/nurse increases the dosage; and the patient soon stops breathing. But the point is that this time sequence does not necessarily prove cause and effect. As noted in the discussion in the previous chapter on double effect and slow euthanasia, it cannot be proven at the postmortem in such cases that it was the drug that caused the death.

Yet, as the data reveal, Dutch physicians have admitted to crossing the dividing line by acting with the "primary intent" to end the lives of grievously suffering patients who were not then asking for euthanasia. The likely reason for their frankness is that the Dutch government guaranteed immunity from prosecution to physicians taking part in the Remmelink study.

---

* The acronym DLD (deliberate lethal dosages) is used for these 1,300 "boundary area" cases.

(c) The Data — The 1995 Remmelink Commission Study[36]

This second investigation was structured the same as the 1990 study and the new findings were not startlingly different. Although euthanasia cases increased, LAWER cases slightly decreased. (The 1995 figures are in each case an average of the results from two separate studies, one involving interviews and the other mailed questionnaires.) The comparable figures are as follows:

Euthanasia:	2.3% (1.8% in 1990)
Assisted Suicide:	0.3% (0.3% in 1990)
APS	16.9% (17.5% in 1990)
LAWER	0.7% (0.8% in 1990)

Once again, cancer was the predominant disease in the sample population. And once again, about two out of three requests for EAS were turned down.

Recall that the 1990 study reported about 1,300 cases involving deliberate lethal dosages [DLD] that were not included in the euthanasia/LAWER statistics, and that 85% would fall in the LAWER category. The 1995 study reported 1,900 such cases, with about 80% falling in the LAWER category. In sum, then, there were about 5,000 deaths reported in 1990 from EAS, the LAWER cases, and the DLD. The comparable figures from 1995 total about 6,350 — 3,500 EAS, 950 LAWER, and 1,900 DLD. This represents a 27% increase in such cases from 1990 to 1995. Furthermore, the cases in which there was no explicit patient request have also increased: in 1990 it was 2,100 — 1,000 LAWER cases and about 1,100 DLD cases; and in 1995 it was about 2,400 — 950 LAWER and about 1,500 DLD cases. This is nearly a 15% increase. These figures are certainly cause for concern, although who can say that the cold hard data give us a balanced picture of these thousands of physician-patient encounters.

(d) Palliative Care and Pain Control

In theory, the Dutch policy regards euthanasia as the measure of last resort when the patient's pain and/or suffering is not only unbearable but also cannot be alleviated. Yet as we have seen, the 1990 Remmelink study reported that pain was often mentioned as a factor by patients requesting euthanasia, although it was the sole reason in only 5% of cases. Was pain in fact uncontrollable for these patients, or were they suffering needlessly because of deficiencies in pain control measures? Did EAS offer the only way out of an intolerable existence, particularly in the few cases in which pain was the sole reason for the request? One cannot say because these questions were not explored by the Remmelink study.

The state of palliative care and pain control in the Netherlands is a much debated issue. Critics of the Dutch euthanasia policy have pointed to studies critical of the state of palliative care training for Dutch physicians. Be that as it may, a concerted effort is currently being made to improve pain control techniques. Pain teams have been established in every regional hospital and cancer centre; pain research receives designated funding in the health budget; and a 64-page brochure on pain management is sent to every Dutch physician.[37]

The Netherlands is often criticized for an alleged lack of commitment to the concept of palliative care, particularly because of the relative absence of free-standing hospices and independent hospice care units in hospitals. It is true that, particularly compared to the English-speaking countries, the Dutch do not traditionally institutionalize the dying. In fact, double their number die at home compared to their English-speaking counterparts, which reflects the direction of the health care system toward home care for the dying. As one of the Remmelink researchers expressed it, the Dutch policy is summed up by the phrase: "Bring the care where it is needed, instead of bring the needy to the care."[38] Still, the Dutch are slowly beginning to turn to the hospice model as well, although the policy is keep the dying at home if possible. A commitment to palliative care (including state-of-the-art pain control) is a necessary moral underpinning to an EAS policy, and a question for the next few years is the extent to which the Dutch meet that commitment.

(e) Reporting and Consultation Requirements

A persistent concern has been the under-reporting of EAS cases. A simplified notification procedure was set up after the 1990 study indicated that only about 18% of cases were reported as required by the guidelines. The rate more than doubled by 1995, climbing to 41%. But still roughly three out of five cases were not reported that year. Critics of the Dutch policy interpret the data to indicate widespread noncompliance with the guidelines. As one critic has claimed, the reason that prosecutions hardly ever occur is that:

> physicians, having been informed about the requirements for prudent care, only report those cases of which they are almost certain that they will not be prosecuted; and if they report them, they tend to present the cases in such a way that it will fit better into the requirements.[39]

Yet it does not necessarily follow that cases are not reported only because the guidelines are not followed, and there are many known cases of physicians who follow the guidelines scrupulously but still omit public notification (in the process committing an offence under the Burial Act by signing a death certificate falsely reporting a natural death). In any event, the EAS policy of the Netherlands has placed tremendous power in the hands of physicians, and it hardly needs to be said that there must be constant and diligent oversight of the exercise of that power. That over 40% of the Dutch die at home is a commendable feature of their health care system, but the downside is that the physician who performs euthanasia in the home can choose to insulate the act from public scrutiny. It is a dilemma that is apparently unresolvable, although the KNMG is doing its best to encourage its members to comply with the reporting requirements.

(In 1998 the system of reporting cases to a local magistrate was changed by the setting up of five regional euthanasia assessment committees — each composed of a physician, lawyer, and ethicist — to receive the reports. A recent decline in reported cases has been noted: 2,054 cases reported in 2001 compared to 2,216 in 1999. In only one of the 2,054 cases was the physician faulted for not following the EAS guidelines, although others were asked for more information.[40] It is not known why the numbers have been dropping, although the chairwoman of the assessment committees suggests that there is more resort to palliative care and therefore fewer cases to report. However, a physician opposed to EAS is of the view that the decline reflects a reluctance to report cases to the regional committees because their review procedures are more stringent than under the previous system. The explanation for the decline awaits the results of a current study.)

According to the KNMG guidelines, the physician cannot resort to euthanasia based on her own solitary judgment, but rather must consult with an experienced and independent colleague. It is beyond dispute that a peer review process is essential. Hospitals that permit euthanasia (and some religious-based hospitals do not) have set up protocols to monitor the process. But most cases occur in the patient's home where there is no oversight mechanism in place to ensure that the physician has complied with the KNMG's consultation requirement; and there is evidence of widespread failure to follow the mandate. It is true that consultation occurred in about 80% of the reported cases, but data from 1995 indicate that there was consultation in only 11% of the unreported cases.[41] In sum, there was no consultation in roughly 60% of the total cases.

The concern expressed by Drs. Hendin and Foley about assisted suicide in Oregon — that most physicians lack the expertise to assess mental competency and will only consult a psychiatrist in obvious cases — is also applicable to the Netherlands. Even though requests for euthanasia may be prompted by treatable depression, family and nursing home physicians do not generally have the expertise to determine whether a patient's judgment is compromised by psychiatric disorder. A particularly disturbing finding is that only 3% of patients asking for EAS were referred for psychiatric consultation. Furthermore, all too many of the consulting physicians are not experts in palliative care and consequently are unable to steer patients in that direction.

In formulating a euthanasia policy, the Dutch medico-legal establishments have bestowed not only enormous responsibility but also enormous power upon physicians. In a sense, then, this grant is a testament of faith in the integrity and professional judgment of Dutch physicians. Still, so long as there are physicians who refuse to report and consult, how can we be assured that they are truly promoting the autonomy and best interests of their patients?

(f) The Dutch Health Care System

The Dutch euthanasia policy is integrated into a health care system that has two features that are especially relevant in the euthanasia context. The first is the extended coverage offered under the national health insurance scheme. Whatever the setting in which care is provided — hospital, nursing home, or home — all health care costs are borne by the state. The system thus factors out economic incentives for euthanasia, whereas for a country such as the United States the fear has been expressed that euthanasia would come to be regarded as an enticing option by patients (or their families) haunted by the spectre of bankrupting health care costs. (Although as noted, there is no evidence that requests for assisted suicide in Oregon are motivated by financial concerns.)

There is also the pivotal role of the family physician in Dutch medical practice, who typically resides in the same neighbourhood as her patients, has her office in her home, and makes house calls. Most euthanasia cases occur in the patient's home and at the hand of the family physician, who usually is the long-term primary caregiver for the patient and family. Given a health care system that features such a high degree of personal contact, proponents of the Dutch euthanasia policy claim that family physicians are well positioned to assess mental competency and to determine whether a plea for euthanasia truly expresses a firm and durable belief that life is no longer bearable. Not surprisingly, critics of the policy see it otherwise.

(g) Final Comment

In this brief survey, one cannot do justice to the myriad of issues fostered by the medical practice of euthanasia in the Netherlands. Although there is an enormous amount of data, the facts and figures have not diminished the intensity of the debate on whether Dutch patients are well or ill served by access to euthanasia. How one interprets the data is truly in the eye of the beholder; proponents are convinced that the data prove that the policy is working reasonably well, whereas opponents are equally convinced that the data portray a precipitous slide down the proverbial slippery slope.

I leave the reader with the admonition often heard in the Netherlands that the Dutch euthanasia policy is not for export. What the message means is that the policy is explainable in terms of the nature of Dutch culture and society, and that other places must make their own way on the question of whether to legalize these contentious forms of physician-assisted death. Still, the physician surveys summarized in the previous chapter indicate that what the Dutch are doing openly is elsewhere being done covertly.

3. RECENT DEVELOPMENTS

As noted, in 1996 the Rights of the Terminally Ill Act was enacted in the Northern Territory of Australia; it authorized physicians to euthanize consenting terminally ill patients experiencing unacceptable pain/suffering. A second physician had to confirm the diagnosis and prognosis, and the request could not be approved unless a psychiatrist determined that the patient did not have a treatable clinical depression. In addition, the patient had to be advised of the option of palliative care. Nine months after its passage, the Act was repealed by the federal parliament (which is empowered to overrule territorial legislation). During the Act's short life four patients died, all of whom were assisted by one physician, Philip Nitschke, a euthanasia advocate whose fervour for the cause reminds one of Jack Kevorkian.[42]

In 1997, the Constitutional Court of Colombia ruled by a 6-3 margin that a physician cannot be held criminally responsible for ending the life of a terminally ill patient "who exercises free will to concur in his own death." Ironically, the case arose when an anti-euthanasia attorney challenged the constitutionality of article 326 of the Code of Criminal Law, which provides, under the heading of "Mercy Killing", that anyone who kills "to end the acute suffering caused by a bodily injury or serious or incurable disease, will be sentenced to imprisonment between six months and three years." The attorney argued that the penalty should be increased to deter the killing of the elderly and infirm, but surprisingly the Court ruled that even a relatively light sentence was not in accord with "elemental considerations of humanity." Bear in mind, however, that rulings by the Constitutional Court do not become the law of the land until approved by the Colombian Senate, which rejected the Court's euthanasia decision in 1999. Needless to say, the Church in this overwhelmingly Roman Catholic country expressed bitter opposition to the Court's ruling.[43]

In May 2002 Belgium legalized "euthanasia" — which in effect includes physician-assisted suicide — by an act of parliament. As defined: "the act of euthanasia, practiced by a physician intentionally ends the life of a person upon their request." The patient need not be terminally ill but must be afflicted with "constant and unbearable physical or psychological pain" from an accident or incurable illness. The law allows for an "anticipated declaration" requesting euthanasia if the person winds up in a state of irreversible unconsciousness.[44] However, in contrast to the Netherlands the patient must be an adult. (The Dutch legislation allows EAS for a minor between 16 and 18 without parental consent, and furthermore a minor as young as 12 may qualify with parental consent.) In a sense, the new law is simply catching up with medical practice, as evidenced by the results of recent research that replicated the Remmelink study in Flanders (an area in western Belgium). Based upon a random sample of deaths in 1998, the study reported that 1.3% of deaths were attributed to euthanasia and assisted suicide (compared to 2.6% from the 1995 Dutch data). However, what is startling is that the LAWER deaths were calculated at 3.2%, whereas the comparable 1995 Dutch figure was 0.7%. In other words, the EAS deaths in Belgium were only half as much as in the Netherlands but the LAWER deaths were more than four times as much.[45]

4. THE SPECTRE OF THE NAZI EUTHANASIA PROGRAM

The subject matter of this chapter is haunted by the historical spectre of Nazi Germany's so-called Euthanasia Program. In 1939 Adolf Hitler issued a decree which he titled, "Order for the Destruction of Lives Which are Unworthy of Being Lived." Its implementation resulted in the extermination of some 200,000 German citizens — handicapped children, institutionalized mental patients, and nursing home residents. According to Dr. Robert Lifton, author of *The Nazi Doctors*,[46] the disease categories for children were idiocy and mongolism (especially when associated with blindness and deafness); microcephaly; hydrocephaly; malformations of all kinds, especially of limbs, head, and spinal column; and paralysis, including spastic conditions.

Whereas for adults, the disease categories were

schizophrenia, epilepsy, senile diseases, therapy-resistant paralysis and other syphilitic sequelae, feeblemindedness from any cause, encephalitis, Huntington's chorea, and other neurological conditions of a terminal nature.

The victims — most were gassed with carbon monoxide, although others were killed by injections of phenol, morphine, morphine and scopolamine, or by forced ingestion of veronal or luminal tablets — had been written off by Hitler as "useless eaters", a phrase that captures the essence of this exercise in medicalized mass murder. The Nazi Euthanasia Program served as Hitler's dress rehearsal for the extermination of six million Jews and countless other "useless eaters." The Nazis excelled in the use of euphemisms (e.g. the Final Solution of the Jewish Question), and in consequence the very word "euthanasia" has been irrevocably tainted because of its appropriation by the Nazis.

The proponent of legalized euthanasia is inevitably confronted with the historical record on the fiendish outcome of Hitler's 1939 decree. That history lesson is also bound to be accompanied by invocation of the so-called slippery slope argument: that we dare not bend the law today because the likely, if not certain, result somewhere down the road is the proverbial Orwellian nightmare. In other words, state sanctioned mercy-killing today means state sanctioned genocide tomorrow of the less than perfect. In response, it is said that the debate is being sidetracked by reference to a policy that had absolutely nothing to do with mercy and compassion and everything to do with the diabolical ideology of the Fuhrer and his Third Reich.

Be that as it may, health care professionals in particular should take notice of the central feature of Hitler's euthanasia policy — that the killing centres were mental hospitals and nursing homes, and that the killing process was directed with remorseless efficiency and fanatic zeal by a staff of physicians, many of whom were German psychiatrists of international reputation. As historian Robert Proctor informs us in his book, *Racial Hygiene: Medicine Under the Nazis:*

Doctors were never *ordered* to murder psychiatric patients and handicapped children. They were *empowered* to do so, and fulfilled that task without protest, often on their own initiative.[47]

Even before Hitler assumed power in 1933, hordes of physicians had flocked to the Nazi Party; membership records for the Nazi Physicians' League indicated an enrolment of 46,000 by 1943, roughly half the profession. What explains the fatal attraction? For one thing, the job opportunities in a "Juden-frei" (Jew-free) profession. Although Jews were less than 1% of the population, they totalled 13% of practising physicians; in Berlin alone the figure was more than 60%. For another, Hitler often spoke of National Socialism (the Nazi ideology) as the political expression of racial biology. In that sense, there was the pull of his metaphor of the "volk"* and its desperate need to be purged of the alien elements — Jews and other non-Aryans — who were sapping its health and vitality. Beyond the traditional patient-physician relationship, many physicians thus came to envision a role as healer of the ailing body politic. In December 1933 the Deutsches Arzteblatt, Germany's leading medical journal, described the profession's future under the Nazis in glowing terms: "Never before has the German medical community stood before such important tasks as that which the National Socialist ideal envisions for it."[48]

Indeed, large numbers of physicians were actively involved in designing and administering key elements of Nazi racial policy. Aside from the victims of sterilization** and euthanasia, there were the unfortunates subjected to unspeakable medical experiments. There was Dr. Joseph Mengele, Auschwitz's "Angel of Death", who subjected 3,000 twins and dwarfs to his spurious and barbaric experiments (barely a hundred survived). And there were the physicians, including Mengele, who met the trains bringing Jews to Auschwitz and with a bare glance determined who would be gassed and who would be allowed to live until worked to death. As detailed by Dr. Lifton in *The Nazi Doctors*:

> In Auschwitz, Nazi doctors presided over the murder of most of the one million victims of that camp. Doctors performed selections — both on the ramp among arriving transports of prisoners and later in the camps and on the medical blocks. Doctors supervised the killing in the gas chambers and decided when the victims were dead. Doctors conducted a murderous epidemiology, sending to the gas chambers groups of people with contagious diseases and sometimes everyone else who might be on the medical block. Doctors ordered and supervised, and at times carried out, direct killing of debilitated patients on the medical block by means of phenol injections into the bloodstream or the heart.... Doctors consulted actively on how best to

---

* Literally meaning "people", the term "volk" had mystical overtones denoting a racially and culturally pure race of true Germans. Only so-called Aryans (an anthropological fiction) were members of the volk.

** See Chapter 15.

keep selections running smoothly; on how many people to permit to remain alive to fill the slave labor requirements of the I.G. Farben enterprise at Auschwitz; and how to burn the enormous numbers of bodies that strained the facilities of the crematoria.[49]

The abhorrent record of Nazi physicians is without doubt the blackest chapter in the history of medicine. Finally, one should note the invaluable assistance rendered in the euthanasia program by nurses, whose loyalty to the Nazi state was no less than that of their medical superiors.

5. THE LEGALIZATION OF EAS ISSUE

The issue of legalization has produced an enormous literature, marked by reasoned and persuasive advocacy of both proponents and opponents (and unfortunately much of the opposite by both sides as well). Suffice it to say that one can hardly do justice in a brief comment to the question whether the law should keep to the policy that letting die is lawful whereas killing/assisted suicide is not. That said, a word is in order about the central moral claim of the proponents: the packaging of EAS as the measure of last resort, as the option for the patient whose intolerable pain/suffering cannot otherwise be relieved. However, as argued by a medical witness before the Special Senate Committee on Euthanasia and Assisted Suicide:

> One cannot in a moral society consider terminating a fellow citizen's life, if that citizen is suffering because of a lack of access to good palliative care. Regardless of one's views on euthanasia (and physician-assisted suicide), one must consider that, as a first principle, impeccable care for dying citizens must be ensured.[50]

The distress that prompts calls for EAS is a core concern of Dr. Harvey Max Chochinov, a professor in the University of Manitoba Departments of Psychiatry and Family Medicine (Division of Palliative Care). Dr. Chochinov has made significant contributions to the literature on psychiatry and the terminally ill, and I cite here but one of his many publications. This study, published in 1995 in the *American Journal of Psychiatry*, investigated the prevalence of the desire for death in terminally ill patients.[51] Of 200 such patients recruited from two Winnipeg hospital-based palliative care units, only 17 (8.5%) acknowledged a serious and pervasive desire to die. Ten of the 17 (58%) were diagnosed with clinical depression, as compared to only 7% of the other patients. Thirteen of the 17 (76%) also reported moderate or higher pain severity compared to 46% of the other patients. (However, three of the 17 reported no pain at all.) Those wishing to die also reported significantly lower ratings on the family support scale than the other patients. In sum, "three main variables emerged as significant correlates of the desire for death: depression, pain, and low level of family support."

Follow-up interviews were conducted with six (the others had died or become too ill to participate), and over time the desire for death diminished in four of them. But still two persisted. A 72-year-old patient experiencing severe pain from prostate cancer continued to pray for death but lived 40 days after the second interview. A 61-year-old patient with lung cancer had no pain, was not depressed, but wished to die while still retaining "her mental competence, reasonable bodily self-control, and what she perceived as an acceptable level of dignity." She lived nine days after the second interview.

One can draw three general conclusions from this study. First, that a patient's expressed wish to die may be ephemeral (which explains why in Oregon and the Netherlands the patient's request must persist over time). Second, when a patient pleads for a hastened death — whether by the termination of life-prolonging treatment or EAS — the appropriate response is to probe the cause of the patient's distress and seek to overcome it. Third, as Dr. Chochinov acknowledges:

> On the basis of the experience in the Netherlands, it is probably inevitable that even with good palliative care, there will still be psychologically stable patients who are determined to end their struggle with terminal illness through euthanasia.

Of particular concern is that very few dying Canadians in need of palliative care actually receive it. This deplorable state of affairs prompts the assertion that a society not prepared to ease the dying process has no business even debating the legalization issue. The warning has been voiced by disability rights advocates that a state policy allowing EAS is at risk to slide into a cost-saving vehicle for our beleaguered health care system — and consequently that we cannot even begin talking about EAS until we act out a true commitment to "impeccable care for dying citizens." Still, notice must be taken of the countervailing view that the grievously afflicted who seek EAS should not have to wait for that time of "impeccable care" — a time that for all we know may never come to pass.

Be that as it may, I comment here on but two of the issues that mark the legalization debate: (1) whether legalization should be confined to assisted suicide; and (2) whether eligibility in the event of legalization should be restricted to the terminally ill. (Yes on both counts is of course the Oregon way, in stark contrast to the Netherlands which allows both euthanasia and assisted suicide for patients who need not be terminally ill.)

To begin with, consider a two-patient scenario in which one of the two can move her little finger, which is sufficient to set in motion a Kevorkian-inspired suicide device, whereas the second cannot move a muscle. Or what if the former is allowed an assisted suicide but then quickly becomes so debilitated that she cannot perform the act herself? Do we then withdraw the Yes and say No? Needless to say, how we resolve the two questions depends upon whether we follow the Oregon or Dutch model.

My position is that euthanasia and assisted suicide must stand or fall together — that both should either be kept unlawful or legalized. I say this partly from a moral stance; that to my mind these two means of physician-facilitated death are not distinguishable on moral grounds. On the other hand, what is clearly contentious is the issue at the very core of the legalization debate: whether the legal distinction between letting die (lawful) and killing/assisted suicide (unlawful) is morally grounded as well. But if the letting die barrier is breached — if the law allows a physician to enable a patient to die by her own hand — then I see no moral impediment to allowing the patient to die at the physician's hand when the patient cannot do it herself. In that sense I believe that the Oregon model only goes halfway — that the moral choice is between two options: no way (no EAS) or all the way (EAS). There is the argument that assisted suicide gives more control to the patient than euthanasia because the patient, not the physician, has to perform the act that directly causes death. I am, however, not so persuaded. On that note, the prominent medical ethicist Dr. Timothy Quill (the lead plaintiff in the *Vacco v. Quill* case) was a leading proponent of this position but subsequently decided that the two must be bracketed together.

Furthermore, there is the equality provision in the *Charter* (section 15), which prohibits discrimination against the physically handicapped. In my view, the restriction of the law's ambit to assisted suicide is discriminatory because it denies the legal option of euthanasia for patients who are physically incapable of committing suicide. In his dissenting opinion in the *Rodriguez* case, Chief Justice Lamer* held that section 241(b) of the *Criminal Code* (the crime of aiding suicide) infringed section 15 of the *Charter*:

> In my view, persons with disabilities who are or will become unable to end their lives without assistance are discriminated against by that provision since, unlike persons capable of choosing their own deaths, they are deprived of the option of choosing suicide.

---

* Chief Justice Lamer has since retired from the Supreme Court. The *Rodriguez* case is discussed in Chapter 25.

What if Canada were to follow the Oregon model, granting an exemption under section 241(b) for physicians but leaving section 14 intact? (As explained in Chapter 18, consented-to mercy killing [so-called active voluntary euthanasia] is prohibited by section 14: "No person is entitled to consent to have death inflicted upon him, and such consent does not affect the criminal responsibility of any person by whom death may be inflicted on the person by whom consent is given.") As a justice agreeing with the Lamer approach might put it:

> In my view, persons with disabilities who are unable to end their lives except by lethal injection are discriminated against by section since, unlike persons capable of committing suicide, they are deprived of the lawful option to end their lives.

Moreover, I see no public policy grounds sufficient to trump section 15 by invoking the overriding provision of section 1 of the *Charter* — that the rights guaranteed are "subject only to such reasonable limits prescribed by law as can be demonstrably justified in a free and democratic society."

And what of the question of eligibility? Although the Oregon model hardly seems fair to those who find their lives intolerable though they are not terminally ill, the terminally-ill qualification is arguably a reasonable public policy position. However, although in law the restriction is clear-cut, its implementation is not. After all, estimating life expectancy is far from an exact science, and in any event a sympathetic physician might well fudge the prognosis to qualify a patient. Nonetheless, it does set a standard, however imperfect its application in practice. As we have seen, the Netherlands model has its internal logic: that the litmus test is not the nature of the patient's condition but rather the presence of intolerable and unrelievable pain/suffering. In other words, why should the patient's longing for death only count if traceable to a terminal disease? Yet it seems a long road from the precedent-setting case of Dr. Schoonheim — whose 95-year-old patient was afflicted with multi-organ failure — to the cases of Drs. Chabot and Sutorius, whose patients' afflictions were of the soul and not the body.

If I had to choose, I would opt for the Oregon model as a more reasoned policy, although one could make a case for a modified version to include non-dying patients with degenerative diseases such as multiple sclerosis, amyotrophic lateral sclerosis (ALS), and AIDS. If I had to stray from the Oregon model (only the terminally ill qualify), I would draw the line at physiological disease. I say that out of concern for the long-term effects on the medical profession if it were to become the vehicle for ending the lives of the physically intact, who for whatever reason find life not worth living. Although we rightly value the core principles of autonomy and beneficence, I believe that they must yield to another valued principle: the integrity of the medical profession. Surely the profession would be sorely undermined if allowed to dispense suicide pills as the cure-all for an ailing spirit trapped in a relatively healthy body. Note well that legalization of EAS means giving to physicians, as was given to James Bond of 007 fame, a licence to kill — and that is to endow the holder with an awesome and frightening power. So, if it does happen, at least the licence should not be open-ended as it has in effect become in the Netherlands.

At the end of the day, whatever one's views on the legalization question,* all of us as mortal beings have a stake in improving the care of our suffering and dying brethren. If there comes a time when physicians are legally allowed to assist suicide and give lethal injections, pray that it be a time when that option is a true choice for patients and not one driven by financial constraints and/or societal indifference to their plight.

6. POSTSCRIPT

On March 6, 2003, the data on physician-assisted suicide in Oregon in 2002 were reported in the *New England Journal of Medicine*.[52] The number of prescriptions written for lethal drugs has increased each year since the law came into effect: 24 in 1998, 33 in 1999, 39 in 2000, 44 in 2001, and 58 in 2002. And 38 patients died in 2002 from ingesting the drugs (eight were still alive at year's end; the other 12 died of natural causes). This compares to 16 deaths in 1998, 27 in 1999, 27 in 2000, and 21 in 2001. In short, there were more prescriptions and more deaths in 2002 than in any of the previous four years. Since the law's inception, the likely profile of an assisted suicide patient was someone of either sex and beyond middle age, well educated, and afflicted with cancer. Data regarding the 129 patients who have died since the law's inception include the following:

> 89% were over the age of 55, and the median year at death was 69 (the comparable figures for all deaths in Oregon from 1998-2002 were 92% and 76 years).

> 22% were widowed and 25% were divorced (the comparable figures for all deaths were 33% and 14%).

> 49% had at least one university degree (the comparable figure for all deaths was 13%).

> Underlying illnesses included: cancer 79%, ALS 8%, and COPD 6% (the comparable figures for all deaths were 40%, 1%, and 18%).

---

* I personally am uncomfortable with both the pro and con camps because, after decades of interest in the subject, I am still torn both ways.

Of the 129 assisted suicide cases, 94% died at home, Secobarbital was prescribed for 66% and Phenobarbital for 32%, and 60% ingested the drugs in the presence of the prescribing physician. The median number of days between initial request and death was 43; the median interval between ingestion and unconsciousness was 5 minutes (the longest was 38 minutes); and the median interval between ingestion and death was 30 minutes (the longest was 37 hours).

As the report concludes: "Despite increases, the number of terminally ill Oregon residents using physician-assisted suicide remains small relative to the overall number of deaths." (Assisted suicides accounted for 0.1% of deaths.)

NOTES

1. S. Woodman. **Last Rights**. (Plenum Press, New York, 1998), at 106-7.
2. *People v. Campbell*, 335 N.W.2d 27 (1983).
3. **New York Times**, May 6, 1994, at 7A.
4. **Newsweek Magazine**, March 8, 1993, at 48.
5. T. Quill. **Death and Dignity** (W.W. Norton, New York, 1993), at 124.
6. *Washington v. Gluckberg*, 117 S.Ct. 2258 (1997); *Vacco v. Quill*, 117 S.Ct. 2293 (1997).
7. H. Kuhsc et al., End-of-life decisions in Australian medical practice. 166 **Medical Journal of Australia** 191 (1997).
8. OR. REV. STAT. 127.805. (It is available on line at: http://www.rights.org/deathnet/ergo orlaw.html)
9. K. Haley & M. Lee, **The Oregon Death With Dignity Act: A Guidebook For Healthcare Providers.** (Center for Ethics in Healthcare, Portland, 1998).
10. C.N. O'Brien et al., Oregon's guidelines for physician-assisted suicide: a legal and ethical analysis. 61 **University of Pittsburgh Law Review, 61**, 329, 339 (2000).
11. A.E. Chin et al., Legalized physician-assisted suicide in Oregon — the first year's experience. 340 **New England Journal of Medicine** 577 (1999).
12. **Toronto Globe and Mail**, March 26, 1998, at A5.
13. A.D. Sullivan et al., Legalized physician-assisted suicide in Oregon — the second year. 342 **New England Journal of Medicine** 598 (2000).
14. A.D. Sullivan et al., Legalized physician-assisted suicide in Oregon, 1998-2000. 344 **New England Journal of Medicine** 605 (2001).
15. K. Hedberg et al., Legalized physician-assisted suicide in Oregon, 2001. 346 **New England Journal of Medicine** 450 (2002).
16. B. Steinbrook, Physician-assisted suicide in Oregon. 346 **New England Journal of Medicine** 461 (2002).
17. R. Cohen-Almagor, **The Right to Die With Dignity** (Rutgers University Press, New Brunswick NJ, 2001), at 178.
18. L. Ganzini et al., Experiences of Oregon nurses and social workers with hospice patients who requested assistance with suicide. 347 **New England Journal of Medicine** 582 (2002).
19. H. Hendin & K. Foley, Letter to the editor, 30 **Hastings Center Report** 5 (2000).
20. **Washington Post**, November 7, 2001, at A10.
21. *Supra* note 16, at 463.
22. **Washington Post**, April 18, 2002, at A1.
23. Central Committee of the Royal Dutch Medical Association. Vision on Euthanasia. 39 **Medical Contact** 990 (1984).
24. The High Court of the Hague, N.J. 1985, No. 106.

25. The High Court of the Hague, N.J. 1986. A summary of the case is found in: 3 **Issues in Law and Medicine** 445 (1988).

26. Supreme Court, N.J. 1994, No. 320. For a detailed account of the **Chabot** case see: B. Sneiderman & M. Verhoef, Autonomy and the defence of medical necessity: Five Dutch euthanasia cases. 34 **Alberta Law Review** 374 (1996).

27. M. Moller & R. Huxtable, Euthanasia in the Netherlands: the case of "life fatigue." **New Law Journal**, November 2, 2001, at 1600.

28. T. Sheldon, Existential suffering not a justification for euthanasia. 323 **British Medical Journal** 1384 (2001).

29. T. Sheldon, Doctor convicted of helping patient to commit suicide may be retried. 325 **British Medical Journal** 924 (2002).

30. TCM Breaking News, Dec. 24, 2002. http://archives.tcm.ie/breakingnews/2002/12/24/story81954.asp

31. P.J. Van der Maas et al., Euthanasia and other medical decisions concerning the end of life. 338 **Lancet** 669 (1991). The entire report is available in English as Volume 22 of the journal, **Health Policy** (1992).

32. Unpublished Dutch euthanasia conference proceedings.

33. Unpublished Dutch euthanasia conference proceedings.

34. The LAWER findings are summarized in L. Pijnenborg et al. Life terminating acts without explicit request of the patient. 341 **Lancet** 1196 (1993).

35. C. Douglass, The intention to hasten death: a survey of attitudes and practices of surgeons in Australia. 175 **Medical Journal of Australia** 511 (2001).

36. P.J. Van der Maas et al., Euthanasia, physician-assisted suicide, and other medical practices involving the end of life in the Netherlands, 1990-1995. 335 **New England Journal of Medicine**, 1699 (1996).

37. K.L. Dorrepaal et al., Pain experience and pain management among hospitalized cancer patients. 63 **Cancer** 593 (1989).

38. J.M. Van Delden, Euthanasia in the Netherlands: the medical scene. In B. Sneiderman & J.M. Kaufert (eds.), **Euthanasia in the Netherlands: A Model for Canada?** (University of Manitoba: Legal Research Institute, 1994), at 20.

39. G. Van der Wal, **Euthanasia en hulp by zelfdoding door huisartsen (Euthanasia and Assisted Suicide By Family Physicians)**. Rotterdam: WYT Uitgeefgroep, 1992, at 12.

40. T. Sheldon, Reported euthanasia cases in Holland fall for second year. 324 **British Medical Journal** 1354 (2002).

41. G. van der Wal et al., Evaluation of the notification procedure for physician-assisted death in the Netherlands. 335 **New England Journal of Medicine** 1706 (1996).

42. D. Kissane, Deadly days in Darwin. In K. Foley & H. Hendin (eds.), **The Case Against Assisted Suicide**, at 192-209 (The Johns Hopkins University Press, Baltimore, 2002).

43. Agence-France-Presse, Colombia allows euthanasia for terminally ill patients,

AFP, June 5. 1997. See also Euthanasia in Colombia, http://www.nrlc.org/news/2001/NRL06/rai.html .

44. Chamber of the Representatives of Belgium, November 5, 2001. Doc 501488/001. See CNN.com—Belgium passes right-to-die bill — May 16, 2002.

45. L. Deliens et al., End-of-life decisions in medical practice in Flanders, Belgium: A nationwide survey. 356 **Lancet** 1806 (2000).

46. R.J. Lifton, **The Nazi Doctors**, (Basic Books, New York, 1986), at 52, 65.

47. R.N. Proctor, **Racial Hygiene: Medicine Under the Nazis**. (Harvard University Press, Cambridge, 1988), at 193.

48. *Ibid.,* at 70.

49. *Supra* note 45, at 18.

50. Senate Special Committee on Euthanasia and Assisted Suicide **Of Life and Death**. (Minister of Supply and Services Canada, 1995), at 17. The Committee is discussed in Chapter 25.

51. H.M. Chochinov et al., Desire for death in the terminally ill. 152 **American Journal of Psychiatry** 152 (1995).

52. K. Hedberg et al., Five years of legal physician-assisted suicide in Oregon. 348 **New England Journal of Medicine** 961 (2003).

INDEX

[References are to page-number]